Dear

G000255097

A HISTORY OF
NORFOLK

Dear Granny

Enjoy your holiday

lots of love xxx

A history of
NORFOLK

CHRIS BARRINGER

To Helen and Robert, with great affection

A History of Norfolk

Copyright © Estate of Chris Barringer, 2017

Photos and captions © Alan G. Crosby unless otherwise stated

First edition

Published by
Carnegie Publishing Ltd
Chatsworth Road,
Lancaster LA1 4SL
www.carnegiepublishing.com

All rights reserved
Unauthorised duplication contravenes existing laws

British Library Cataloguing-in-Publication data
A catalogue record for this book is available from the British Library

ISBN 978–1–85936-233-4

Designed, typeset and originated by Carnegie Publishing
Printed and bound by Cambrian Printers

Contents

Foreword ix

Preface xi

Introduction 1
    The setting 2
    The human story 6

The early settlement of Norfolk 11
    The Palaeolithic (Old Stone Age) 12
    The Mesolithic (Middle Stone Age) 15
    The Neolithic (New Stone Age) 16

The Bronze and Iron Ages in Norfolk 23
    The Iron Age 26

Roman Norfolk 35
    The Roman conquest and its background 35
    Material evidence of the Roman presence in Norfolk 37
    The road network and the countryside 39
    Caistor by Norwich and other towns 43
    Forts 47

Norfolk under the Anglo Saxons and Vikings 51
    Place-names as a guide to settlement 59
    The local Church, 500 to 1066 60
    The Viking period 64
    Towns in Norfolk 65
    A summary of Dark Age Norfolk 69

The Norman Conquest and its aftermath 70
    Norwich: the new capital of East Anglia 77
    The other towns of post-Conquest Norfolk 85
    The Norman Church in Norfolk 97

Early medieval Norfolk 105
    Breckland 111
    The Fens 114
    The Broads 116

Woodland 117
The Black Death (1349) 118
The towns between 1150 and 1350 120

Wool, sheep and textiles 133
The evolution of Norwich stuffs 141

Churches and parishes 145

From Black Death to Reformation 165
The land, 1330 to 1550 166
The Rising of 1381 in Norfolk 168
Monastic houses as landowners 170
Some major families 172
Boroughs, markets and guilds 178
The lives of the 'middling sort' 182
The Dissolution 184
Kett's Rebellion of 1549 187

The Fens 191
The new farming 201

Norfolk from 1550 to 1750 205
Faith and belief 207
The impact of the Dissolution 212
The views of visitors 216
The social structure of the county 219
The land 222
New estates and new farming 223
The yeomen 228
Matters of faith: challenge and dissent 229
The Civil Wars and Commonwealth 231
The Nonconformist churches 234
The survival of Catholicism 236
Schools 238
The poor 240
Architecture and buildings 244
Francis Blomefield (1705–1752) 248

Norfolk from 1750 to 1830 249
Parliamentary enclosure 254
Church and chapel 260
Social issues and rural discontent 264
Rivers and roads 267
Changing towns 272

The Broads   289
    The impact of man in Broadland   291
    Early tourism   294
    The grazing marshes and coastal protection   296
    Conservation and management   298
    Commerce and tourism   301

Vernacular architecture in Norfolk   303
    Stylistic changes   317
    Estate maps   318
    Farm buildings   318
    The towns   321
    Three case studies   325
    Conclusion   327

Norfolk from 1830 to 1914   329
    Churches, chapels and schools   330
    The New Poor Law   336
    Social change   340
    The towns   344
    'Poppyland' and the Railway Coast   363
    The great estates   371
    The nineteenth century in Norfolk: a summary   375

Norfolk from 1914 to 1945   377
    The First World War   378
    The county between the wars   380
    Norwich and the towns   385
    The Second World War   391

After the Two Wars   397
    Movement   399
    Social provision   403
    Changing agriculture   405
    Building conservation   408
    Nature conservation   412
    The towns   414
    Conclusion   430

Conclusion   433

Agricultural terms used in Norfolk   435

References   436

Index   445

Chris Barringer

VIII

Foreword

THIS BOOK IS THE LAST AND GREATEST WORK of Chris Barringer, who died in the summer of 2013. John Christopher Barringer was born in Croydon, but soon afterwards his father, a Yorkshireman, changed jobs and the family moved back to Yorkshire, settling in Ilkley. Chris went to Ilkley Grammar School, where he was head boy and was actively involved in sport, especially cricket and rugby. There his love of walking and the countryside introduced him not only to geography but also to local history, showing him the patchwork of distinctive landscapes and localities which make up England. His uncle Harry Scott was editor-proprietor of *The Dalesman*, Yorkshire's celebrated county magazine founded in 1939. Chris told me that its strong emphasis on landscape, people and history was a formative influence.

After national service he was awarded a scholarship to St John's College, Cambridge, where he read geography and decided to become a teacher. He qualified and gained the remarkable distinction of being appointed head of geography in his first position, at the Royal Grammar School in Lancaster. In 1965 his career changed course, when he became resident tutor in Norfolk for the Cambridge University Board of Extra-Mural Studies. He and his family moved to Hethersett, and he quickly started local history groups across the county, at Blakeney, Downham Market, King's Lynn, Mattishall, North Walsham, Norwich and Reepham. He began researching aspects of archaeology and local and regional history, and in 1984 his first two books appeared, volumes on the Yorkshire Dales and the Lake District published for the National Trust.

Chris was a wonderful teacher, practical and down to earth yet inspirational, blessed with the ability to challenge and stimulate and his students so that they began to pursue their own researches and investigations. He had the gift of reading landscape, instinctively questioning it—why was there a sharp bend in that road, what were those hummocks in a field, when was that house altered? David Dymond, his colleague and friend for very many years, said that 'He was never happier than when organising and leading open-air excursions'.

He was involved in a tremendous range of county and local organisations. At the time of his death he was president of the Norfolk Archaeological and Historical Research Group and vice-president of the Norfolk and Norwich Archaeological Society. From 1987 to 2002 he was chairman of the Norfolk and Norwich Heritage Trust. One of his finest achievements during this period was working tirelessly to raise money for the restoration and conservation of Dragon Hall in King Street, securing the future of a medieval merchant's house which is among the greatest architectural and historical treasures of the fine city of Norwich.

In 1991 responsibility for the county's adult continuing education was transferred to the University of East Anglia, and Chris became Director of Extra-Mural Studies. This involved him in a lot more administrative work, which he confessed he did not always relish—he liked being out and about—but it strengthened his links with Norfolk's history. When he retired in August 1995 many of his friends and colleagues gathered at the Sainsbury Centre to celebrate his achievements and to present him with *East Anglian Studies*, a book of 37 papers written in his honour.

Chris had lost his heart to Norfolk when he moved there back in 1965 and had become passionate about his adopted county, its landscapes and its extraordinarily rich history. In his last years he wrote this book, which brings together half a lifetime's experience of walking the fields, exploring the towns and villages, researching a treasury of archives, discussing and debating with colleagues, friends and students, and absorbing the unique magic of this wonderful county. *A History of Norfolk* is a monument to Chris, his contribution to the heritage of the county, and to all the joy, intellectual excitement and infectious enthusiasm which he brought to so very many people over so many years.

Alan Crosby

Preface

IN 1966, when I was appointed to teach in Norfolk for the University of Cambridge Board of Extra-Mural Studies, I could scarcely have foreseen being invited, in the distant future, to write this study. It has been an ambitious and a challenging task, but a fascinating and rewarding one, and has been undertaken with the great support of Dr Alan Crosby and Carnegie Publishing, with their acceptance that the result is a personal slant on this long and always interesting story. My personal bias was that I began my career as a landscape historian, via a geography degree, but with a great family interest in history which was inherited from my father and my uncle Harry Scott, the founder of the *Dalesman*. I had enjoyed these subjects with several of my close school friends, with whom I explored the Yorkshire Dales.

I came to Norfolk in 1966 and have stayed there ever since. The demand for extra-mural and WEA teaching showed what a great interest there was in studying Norfolk's history and landscape, and over the years, in every type of course from day schools in the field, tutorial courses for one year and certificate courses for three years, we looked at more aspects of the county's history than I could ever have imagined possible. From the tip of Blakeney Point via the meres of Breckland, across moated sites to ruined great houses and derelict union workhouses, the picture widened. From the Baptist hamlet near Worsted and the infilled estuary of the Glaven Ports, to such additions as the wildfowl-filled waters of Pensthorpe and the 'restored barns' that are bringing new life back to many of the small villages in the county, we visited, researched and analysed. All of this it has been my good fortune to call 'work'. The groups that I have led, such as those at Blakeney, Aylsham, Mattishall, North Walsham, East Dereham and at Wensum Lodge and Dragon Hall in Norwich have been a delight and privilege to work with, as have those in the certificate classes doing fieldwork and documentary research.

I have had the good fortune to be a member of the Council of the Norfolk and Norwich Archaeological Society and served for many years on the Scole Committee for Archaeology in East Anglia. The Centre of East Anglian Studies at the University of East Anglia took me under their wing. I have benefited for almost half a century from the wonderful resources of the Norfolk Record Office and its ever-helpful staff, and more recently the Norfolk Heritage Centre, and I have been fortunate to meet so many people working in both who are steeped in their interests in the story of the county. Three close friends with whom I have shared many interests and from whom I have learnt so much have been Dr David Dymond, the late Alan Davison, and David Yaxley and their contributions to the history of the county show in the many sources referred to in this text. Two others, the late Tony Gregory and the late Alan Carter, both of whom made huge contributions to the study of Norfolk's history, spent much time with my students on memorable field outings.

The production of this volume owes a great deal to my wife Charlotte who has word-processed the whole text and has made many most helpful suggestions. Dr Alan Crosby has also given much assistance resulting from his great experience in the writing of regional and county histories and his personal knowledge of Norfolk. Finally, a small group of friends kindly proof-read various sections – but of course any errors are entirely my responsibility. Exploring the county's history in its broadest sense has been a delight to me during my time in Norfolk. I can only hope that some of my enjoyment shows through in this study.

The great market place which lies at the very heart of Norwich was laid out in the late eleventh and early twelfth centuries as the focal point of the new French or Norman borough, the rival to the major Anglo-Saxon settlement which had its market place in Tombland. The new market place swiftly became the commercial and social focus of the city. Since Norwich was the second or third largest provincial city in medieval England, this market was among the most dynamic in the country. Today, despite the many changes to the adjacent area (from the building of the medieval Guildhall and St Peter Mancroft church, via the redevelopment of Gentleman's Walk in the eighteenth century, to the redesign of the civic area in the mid-1930s) the market continues to flourish. Brightly painted wooden roofs have replaced the old (and equally bright) awnings, and City Hall towers proudly over the scene.

Introduction

W HEN WE LOOK at the map of Great Britain, the notably distinctive shape of our island includes not only the pointed and jagged peninsulas of the west, but also the long smooth rounded curve of East Anglia, stretching from the Wash towards the Thames and for long miles scarcely broken by estuaries or islands. Norfolk and Suffolk push out into the North Sea, which has been responsible for that remarkably uninterrupted coastline, for millennia smoothing and grading the soft and easily eroded clays, sands and gravels. Throughout recorded history, and far beyond that into the distant past, the sea has been an ever-present element in the life of the two counties. Bounded by the sea to the north and east and by the Fens to the west, East Anglia proper has always been to some extent isolated from the rest of England. Far to the east of the Great North Road, it lay away from the north–south axis that linked London with Edinburgh via York and Newcastle. Although for centuries Norwich was the second city of the realm, it was always somehow away from the mainstream, a feeling that can still be discerned even today.

But Celts, Romans, Saxons and Normans all found it a far more accessible and much more amenable area in which to settle than the wilds of the west, or the moors and mountains of the Pennines and Northumbria. We can see this very easily: the Normans built many dozens of castles in Northumberland, but in Norfolk they built only a handful. Here, instead, they chose to build country houses. Norfolk was and still is perhaps the most fertile of England's arable farming regions, and its small ports were for many centuries the outlets for cereals and other agricultural produce. Thornham at the north end of the Peddars Way was the port from which Fenland corn could be sent to the Roman legions guarding Hadrian's Wall. King's Lynn exported malt to the Baltic in return for timber and pitch, and for a thousand years Great Yarmouth sent fish to everyone. In return iron, spices, fabrics, pottery and wine flowed the other way, through Yarmouth to Norwich.

The sheer wealth of archaeological finds in Norfolk reminds us how long this area has been settled. This in turn underlines how long its soil has been worked. The nature of Norfolk's surface geology and the resultant soils has an impact on how the land is used and on the appearance of its landscapes. Several major sub-divisions can be recognised, their limits determined in part by the underlying physical geography. The coast is a recurrent theme in this study and it in turn has its sub-divisions of creeks and salt marshes and cliffs of chalk or of glacial, easily eroded materials. The south-west of the county, the Breckland, has poor sandy soils, long exploited for sheep-grazing but in the twentieth century transformed by new forests and a huge military training area. Broadland, with its shallow lakes and wide marshes, is another distinctive area, the part of Norfolk best known to outsiders.

The core of the county, an area of gentle upland and plateau, itself changes character as one moves across it. In the north-west there are lighter, more easily worked soils, where a sheep-corn economy evolved early. In contrast, the heavier boulder clays of central and south Norfolk were difficult to drain and remained well wooded; these were often referred to as wood pasture land. The drainage from the chalk ridge that lies to the west is mainly eastward, and a series of river valleys – those of the Ant, Bure, Wensum and Yare – is incised into this plateau. They are modest by the standards of, say, Yorkshire, but their wide marshy floors and gentle slopes provide sites for many of the county's villages. A series of faster flowing streams (all things are relative) runs west to the Great Ouse; these include the Little Ouse, Wissey and Nar. This edge of Norfolk focuses on King's Lynn rather than Norwich. Away to the west across the Great Ouse is the distinctive area of the Fens, one that has undergone the greatest changes of all the county's regions, as man has gradually drained it, first for grazing and later for highly productive cropland. The phases of the evolution of the face of Norfolk owe much to these regional characteristics, to the many links with Europe and, of course, to the major themes of English history and the various revolutions and wars that have contributed to its present appearance.

Norfolk, lying relatively near to London and with rich and fertile land, was attractive to successful merchants. As the authority of the Crown became stronger many of those families, such as the Howards and the Pastons, bought or were rewarded with estates in Norfolk. Successful soldiers such as Sir John Fastolf and Sir Simon Felbrigg built up major landholdings, and later generations of successful politicians such as the Townshends, Walpoles and Cokes continued the process. Norfolk still has a landscape dotted with the great houses in their parks. To some extent the charm of the county is that it has changed less than its Midland and northern counterparts; it had no coal. Instead, the county had wool and the skills of spinning and weaving, so that the first industrial revolution led to the prosperity of Norwich and of many small market towns and villages surrounding it.

The setting

The natural background

On first examination, Norfolk's landscape is undramatic. There are no sharp ridges, the valley sides are almost always gentle, the valley floors wide and easily flooded, and the highest point in the county (Beacon Hill near West Runton) is only 343 feet above sea level. On closer examination, though, there are more distinctive features: stand in front of Downham Market church tower and look over the flat fens to the west, or drive to King's Lynn from Norwich on the A47 and a comparable vista opens to the east of Middleton from the crest of the East Anglian heights. Cliffs revealing Norfolk's earlier geology at Hunstanton and its late glacial geology at Happisburgh contrast with the salt marshes of the southern fringe of the Wash, the shingle spits and marshes of the north coast and the sand dunes protecting the Broads from the invasions of the sea. There is variety but it is subtle – the changes in soil types, the various vegetational regions and the many different wildlife habitats such as the ternery on Blakeney Point, the heaths where stone curlew breed, and rivers and broads where grebes and bitterns flourish.

The basic geology of the county is that of a raft of chalk several hundred feet thick, gently tilted from west to east, which provided the material which the glaciers scoured and then redeposited as the chalk-rich glacial deposits that now cover the chalk. Below the chalk is a zone of greensand which includes the carstone, an attractive, rather crumbly building stone which is orange or orange-brown as a result of its high iron content. The chalk has some harder layers which have been used in west Norfolk for building, where it is termed 'clunch'. Buildings in Old Hunstanton and villages such as Flitcham have attractive compound walls in which carstone, clunch and brick have all been used. Brick has been made since Roman times from the Jurassic clays that underlie the carstone. Hunstanton's dramatically coloured cliffs provide an excellent starting place from which to understand Norfolk's geological foundations, over which a thick layer of various glacial materials were spread during the three ice ages.

These foundations have had a major influence on the ways in which man has been able to use the surface of the county. The chalk itself forms only a narrow belt of downland on the crest of a ridge in the west and north, which is followed by the Peddars Way. Warham Camp, at the end of this ridge, is a splendid site where the chalk flora flourish. To the east of this belt lies a much more mixed range of soils derived from the immense erosive power of the icesheets that covered the area during the ice ages. The boulder clays of the central and southern plateau are rich in chalk fragments derived from the platform as the ice ground over it. On the north-west and north-east areas, south of the glacial end moraine known as the Cromer Ridge, lie the lighter, better drained soils often referred to as the 'good soils' or loams. The boulder clays vary in depth and consistency but they did not drain easily and they tended to be less densely settled than the areas to the north, east and west. 'Cold', heavy, and wet, they were shunned by early man.

To the south-west the glacial deposits were much thinner and more sandy. Over the centuries these easily worked sandy soils were intensively used for agriculture, but that took much of the goodness out of them, so that by the time of the Norman Conquest much of this Breckland area had reverted to heath and scrub and even, from time to time, blowing sand. It was a landscape of sheep runs and rabbit warrens. Further west still lie the Norfolk Fens stretching to the estuary of the river Nene. The much altered channel of the Great Ouse collects the rivers of west Norfolk and the pumped drainage of large areas of land below sea level which, were it not for embanking and pumping, would be flooded by sea or land water depending upon the balance between the two.

The cliffs at Happisburgh are characteristic of those on long stretches of the Norfolk coast. Low, and composed of soft sands and clays, they offer no resistance to the fierce onslaught of the North Sea and for thousands of years have been steadily retreating. Many coastal communities have been lost to the waves over the centuries, and the process now seems to be accelerating. In an effort to stem the erosion the authorities have many times tried to construct coastal defences of shingle, brick, concrete and rock, but eventually the sea works its way behind these, undermining them and resuming its attack. Here we see the lines of huge boulders dumped at low water mark in the aftermath of the great gales and storms of December 2013.

In south-west Norfolk the brecks were, historically, a bleak area of windswept sandy heaths, known for the poverty of their agriculture and their people and extending west to the edge of the Fens, north toward Swaffham and Watton, and south to the Suffolk border. In the later medieval period and through to the nineteenth century rabbits were a major commercial commodity here. But in the 1920s the newly created Forestry Commission, looking round for cheap poor-quality land to grow timber, discovered the Breckland (as it has fairly recently been christened), bought up huge swathes, and planted England's largest forest. This view is from the Mundford to Thetford road north of the A11, looking south-west across the corner of Norfolk. A century ago, almost no trees would have been visible here.

To the east of the clay plateau lie the Broads. The shallow river valleys of the Ant, Bure, Yare and Waveney were much deeper at the end of the Devensian glaciation. Since then, over many thousands of years, they have filled up, mainly with marine sediments, creating flat semi-tidal saltmarshes and, further inland, riverside wetlands that were quickly covered with alder carr. Man has influenced the area greatly, by cutting immense quantities of peat between 1100 and 1400. These medieval peat cuttings flooded as sea levels rose to produce the distinctive Broads that give the area its particular attraction.

The upper valleys of the Ant, Bure, Wensum, Yare, Tas and Waveney are set into the clay plateau. Their flat valley floors are still easily flooded and provide excellent grazing marshes. Villages lie on the valley sides where crops could grow on the slopes and on the plateau where cattle grazed on the

Morston marshes, seen from the seabank just north of the village: here, as with almost the entire stretch of the north Norfolk coast from Kelling Head in the east to Holme next the Sea in the west, the ancient cliff line is fronted by an expanse of saltmarsh, itself edged at the shore by a shingle and pebble bank. These saltmarshes, which are broken by the mouths of small rivers such as the Burn and the Stiffkey, are very vulnerable to flooding by unusually high tides or surges. The marshes developed particularly in the period since the fifteenth century, and attempts in the eighteenth and nineteenth centuries to drain them met with only partial success. They are now of international significance for their natural history, especially their bird life.

One of the highest parts of the Norfolk coast is between Weybourne and Sheringham, where the northern edge of the Cromer ridge meets the sea. The long smooth curve of the cliff line is constantly being reshaped by the erosive action of the waves as they chew and nibble at the base of the cliffs. The longshore drift carries the debris westward, forming the long spit of Blakeney Point, but the steady retreat of the coast itself is inexorable. Here, in April 2014, the recent cliff falls resulting from the storms of December 2013 can be seen from Weybourne, looking east towards Sheringham.

The saltmarshes which developed along much of the north Norfolk coast spelled the slow decline and eventual extinction of the once-thriving commercial ports of Blakeney, Wiveton, Cley and elsewhere. During the seventeenth and eighteenth centuries the marshes became increasingly important for grazing, and eventually were considered to have potential for reclamation and drainage. The earliest major activity was in the 1650s, but the most important phase followed the building of a new sea bank in 1851–52 and the enclosure of the marshes in 1853. The long straight drainage channels, such as this, were constructed in the mid-1850s.

pastures among the woodland. The plateau, drier in the north and west, has been termed sheep-corn country and the heavier clays of the southern plateau provided a wood-pasture economy.

Wrapped around the northern and eastern edges of Norfolk lie narrow but contrasting coastal zones. To the north-west silts accumulate at the southern end of the Wash, but the north-western point of the county is bounded by the Hunstanton cliffs. The north coast – perhaps Norfolk's most attractive area for holidaymakers – has a mix of sandbanks, saltmarshes and creeks beloved of sailors, seabirds and seals. The north-east corner is subject to particularly severe marine erosion and that affecting the soft glacial deposits in places such as Happisburgh causes constant concern. The debris from the cliffs is swept westwards by the sea into the Wash and southwards down the coast to form the sandspits and dunes at Yarmouth and further south. Norfolk, although a county of gentle relief, therefore has several distinctive areas which, to a greater or lesser extent, influenced the ways in which man was able to make use of them through time.

The human story

The physical face of Norfolk is only about 10,000 years old – its topography is largely as the last phase of the Ice Ages left it. But in places, especially on the coast as at Happisburgh, it is apparent that the glaciations obscured the evidence of *homo erectus* and *homo neanderthalensis*, our unimaginably distant human forebears. The evidence of their existence, in the form of tools, is among the first record of a human presence anywhere in Europe. Countless generations later, *homo sapiens* had evolved by the time the ice melted and many

The cliffs at Happisburgh are subject to exceptionally rapid erosion, as the slumping and lines of protective boulders in this view indicate. This continuing problem has had unexpected archaeological benefits, by exposing strata of sands and clays that are rich in prehistoric remains. In 2010 archaeologists from University College London found flint implements which have been provisionally dated to *circa* 900,000 years ago, by far the earliest evidence of human activity in what is now the British Isles. In 2013 erosion on the beach revealed human footprints in mudstones exposed at low tide. These have been dated to at least 800,000 years ago and are the earliest known from outside Africa. Together, the items found at Happisburgh represent the oldest known evidence of human occupation in Western Europe.

hundreds of his flint tools have been found across the county. As technology developed Mesolithic peoples learned how to use bone and wood to create a more sophisticated culture including fishing, the use of dug-out canoes and the hunting of deer, wild cattle and sheep. The Neolithic period witnessed the building of monuments, some of which still survive, such as long barrows and the Arminghall Henge. In the Bronze Age, with the help of improved tools, the people of what became Norfolk constructed hundreds of burial mounds, many of which remain to this day, while a great number of their bronze implements have been found in the county. The Iron Age sees the first evidence of organised settlements with roundhouses and field systems and in its later stages the use of coinage and of gold jewellery. The first 'towns' or exchange points began to appear, and we have the first names of people who lived in Norfolk – the royal clan of the Iceni, their king, Prasutagus, and one of the most famous characters in the history of these islands, his wife Boudica.

The impact of four centuries of Roman colonisation and development is clear. Road systems, villas, temples and farms spread over much of the county and, in particular, the development of *Venta Icenorum*, the regional capital at Caistor St Edmund, was of major significance. Their pottery survives well, their coinage was sophisticated, and Norfolk had nearly 400 years of Romano-Celtic rule, as long as the period from the reign of Elizabeth I to our own time. As the Romans departed others arrived. Anglo-Saxon and Scandinavian peoples flowed into south-east England from the middle of the fifth century to the middle of the eleventh. Nearly every surviving settlement in Norfolk already existed by late Saxon times, a record enshrined in Little Domesday Book of 1086. Yet apart from Roman walls at Burgh Castle and Caistor St Edmund, and a scatter of Anglo-Saxon church towers, the built environment has little to show of these earlier periods. The Saxons bequeathed the boundaries of the county and its administrative sub-divisions, the hundreds, as well as the vills which emerged as the Norman parishes – of which Norfolk has more than any English county.

After the Norman Conquest in 1066 this was the most prosperous, economically advanced and densely populated part of England. The great Norman castles of Norwich, Castle Rising and Castle Acre, the abbeys of Norwich, Thetford and Castle Acre, and parish churches such as Hales, demonstrate the power and might, and architectural and technological skills, of the new regime and its local representatives. Agriculture, the source of wealth, developed further: sheep were important in the Fens and north-west of the county and cattle in the boulder clay centre. The ancient woodland (of which little now survives) was being steadily cleared by the early medieval period.

It is dangerous to summarise the history of an area in a few sentences, but this perhaps can be justified in an introductory section. During the period from the Norman Conquest to the Black Death the density of population in Norfolk rose sharply, putting increasing pressure on the resources of the county and on its farming land. At the same time, the manorial system was imposed, and numerous lesser lords and their tenants encouraged the sub-division of holdings in response to the demand for land to accommodate the growing population. Wool production, followed by the emergence of the cloth industry, became a major part of the economy. Norwich became the key town, Yarmouth flourished on fishing, and Thetford slowly declined. The Black Death reduced the population of Norfolk by between 30 and 50 per cent. After the Black Death the feudal system declined as surviving tenants bargained for larger holdings and landowners increased their sheep flocks in response to the demands of the cloth industry. Norwich claimed the title of the second city of England. The Church, in terms of its monastic houses, tithes and glebe holdings, became a major landholder in the county until the Dissolution of the Monasteries radically changed the patterns of land ownership. Bishop's (later King's) Lynn emerged as a key outlet for north-west Norfolk and the whole of the Fenland drainage basin.

The Dissolution of the Monasteries led to the creation of much new wealth in Norfolk and families such as the Howards, le Stranges, Bacons, Cokes and many others benefited. The top men of Norfolk had considerable influence at court, and this was a county of major political significance. In 1549 the rebellion in Norfolk was one of the most serious popular uprisings in the whole Tudor period, while four years later Norfolk was the springboard from which Mary Tudor fought for and gained her throne. The county later became dominated by many large estates such as Holkham and Raynham. The towns grew steadily but not as rapidly as the coalfield towns of the Midlands and the North. Norwich 'stuffs' (high-quality worsteds) took the city to an even greater dominance of its region, which in the eighteenth century included much of north Suffolk.

From 1750, although Norfolk lost its industrial importance to the new textile centres of the north of England, the work of Townshend, Coke and many others ensured that its agriculture became famous and highly influential. Many thousands of acres of common land were enclosed and passed into private ownership, especially during the Napoleonic wars. After 1830 the county saw less change than many other parts of Britain. The growth of a railway system helped Norwich, East Dereham and Great Yarmouth but much of it came quite late, after 1850, and most of it lasted less than a century, with wholesale closures taking place in 1964–68 following the Beeching Report. The railways created new holiday resorts at New Hunstanton, Sheringham, Cromer, Mundesley and Great Yarmouth, and in the county tourism emerged as a significant new element of the economy in the later nineteenth century. In Norwich the industrial base changed from cloth to shoes, light engineering and insurance. But Norfolk's population was increasing only slowly, and over much of the rural county population loss became a characteristic of small remote parishes.

Norfolk's geographical position led to its being a key strategic area in World War I and, more especially, for aerial warfare in the Second World War. The sandy heaths north of Thetford became important military training areas. After 1945 both Thetford and King's Lynn took part of the overspill population from London. New industries came at the same time, helping to rejuvenate the economy of stagnant and declining towns. Agricultural processing industries grew rapidly, as agriculture itself changed, and mechanisation and farm

The row of brightly coloured beach huts at Mundesley seems to defy the waves. This is perhaps the most exposed of the Norfolk resorts, and currently in the Mundesley area the cliffs are retreating at an average of 0.3–0.5 metres per year. The policies which have been formulated by local and national government agencies suggest that in the medium term places such as Mundesley will be defended from erosion, but that the coast between the defences will erode rapidly, so that eventually Mundesley may be on a promontory. But they also pessimistically imply that in the long term – perhaps before the 22nd century – there is no real hope of preventing coastal retreat from affecting the town itself.

reorganisation transformed the visual appearance, as well as the society and economy, of swathes of rural Norfolk.

In the 1970s and 1980s rapid population growth – a phenomenon not hitherto experienced – began to affect the county. The influx continues and a major debate centres on the key question of where development and expansion should be permitted – might it be in eco-towns, or new towns, or dispersed rural communities, or new villages and suburbs attached to existing urban areas? The impact of the North Sea oil, gas and wind turbine industries is a new development. Battles between conservation and landscape management on the one hand, and the pressures for growth, development and urban expansion have become a central feature of Norfolk's twenty-first-century life.

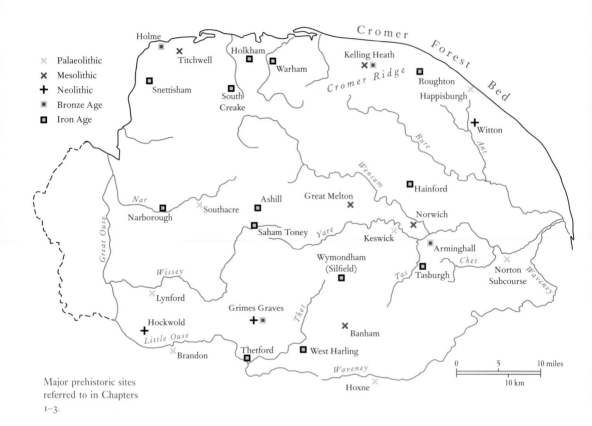

Major prehistoric sites
referred to in Chapters
1–3.

Palaeolithic
Mesolithic
Neolithic
Bronze Age
Iron Age

Holme
Titchwell
Holkham
Warham
Kelling Heath
Cromer Forest Bed
Cromer Ridge
Roughton
Happisburgh
Snettisham
South Creake
Witton
Bure
Ant
Nar
Wensum
Hainford
Narborough
Southacre
Ashill
Great Melton
Norwich
Saham Toney
Yare
Keswick
Great Ouse
Wissey
Wymondham (Silfield)
Tas
Arminghall
Chet
Tasburgh
Norton Subcourse
Waveney
Lynford
Grimes Graves
Hockwold
Thet
Banham
Little Ouse
Thetford
West Harling
Brandon
Waveney
Hoxne

0   5   10 miles
10 km

1

The early settlement of Norfolk

THE subject of this first chapter goes back an unimaginably long way, almost a million years to the earliest evidence we have of human settlement in what eventually became Norfolk. It is a theme of continuing major importance in the archaeology of early man itself, for in Norfolk we have some of the most important evidence for the beginnings of human settlement in Europe, and knowledge has increased dramatically over the past fifty years – and continues to grow with new discoveries, some of them of international significance. It is essential to recognise that although we are referring to 'Norfolk', the landscape a million years ago bore no resemblance to that of recent times: indeed, Norfolk itself was not a coastal area at all for much of the period until 5,000 years ago, and so the context of human occupation and settlement was radically different.

Approximate dates	geological stage	cultural stage	key sites
c.900,000 BC	Cromer Forest Bed; Crag series	Palaeolithic	Happisburgh; Pakefield (Suff.)
c.472,000 BC		Lower Palaeolithic	
c.470,000–400,000 BC	*Anglian glaciation* Lowestoft till/Norwich brickearth	Clactonian	Clacton on Sea
c.400,000–367,000 BC	Hoxnian inter-glacial	Acheulian hand axes	Hoxne lake bed
c.367,000–130,000 BC	*Wolstonian glaciation* chalky boulder clay		
c.130,000–75,000 BC	Ipswichian inter-glacial		Ipswich/Stoke Tunnel/ Bobbit's Hole
		Upper Palaeolithic	Keswick river gravels
75,000–10,000 BC	*Devensian glaciation* Hunstanton esker + outwash gravels	Mesolithic	Kelling Heath; Carrow Road
8500–7500 BC	Pre-Boreal		
7000–5500 BC	Boreal		
5000 BC		Neolithic	Grimes Graves
5500–3200 BC	Atlantic	Beaker phase	Hockwold
2000 BC		Bronze Age	Arminghall
3200–600 BC	Sub-Boreal		
500 BC	Sub-Atlantic	Iron Age	Warham Hillfort; West Harling
50 BC–AD 64		The Iceni (Boudica)	Gallows Hill
AD 64		Roman	Caistor St Edmund

J. Wymer, *Palaeolithic Sites of East Anglia*, table 15 (Geo Books, 1985) has been used as a major source for this table.

The Palaeolithic (Old Stone Age)

Although there are immense gaps in our knowledge, with periods of many thousands of years for which little or nothing is known, pieces of the great jigsaw continue to be found and put in place and context. In recent years, for example, there have been two exciting discoveries. The first is the earliest man-made tool to be found in western Europe, the Happisburgh hand axe which is dated to c.900,000 BC and was located within the geological stratum known as the Cromer Forest Bed. It opens up a massive new timespan for human activity in Norfolk.[1] A comparable coastal site at Pakefield in Suffolk, just south of the county boundary near Lowestoft, has produced similar evidence. The Cromer Forest Bed, which was laid down between about c.900,000 BC and 500,000 BC, lies immediately below the deposits of the first or Anglian glaciation, and on top of the shelly estuarine crag series which has fine, horizontal layers of sands, clays and

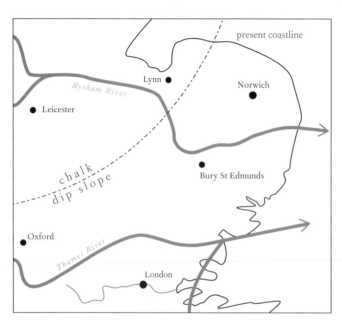

The pattern of major drainage in East Anglia before it was obliterated by the advance of the ice sheets during the glaciation rather less than half a million years ago. During this period estuarine sands and gravels were spread over the region; they are known as Crag deposits.

darker organic zones. McWilliams, in his 1967 account of the Cromer Forest Bed, wrote that 'despite diligent searches by many people no evidence has been found to indicate the presence of early man in the Cromer Forest Bed series'.[2] This picture has now been extensively modified by the findings referred to above, which since the year 2000 have greatly extended our understanding of this distant period.

The Cromer Forest Bed contains a wide range of present-day plant species, and pollen analysis suggests that this was a period of mixed oak forest, but in the lower (and therefore earlier) geological layers were species more typical of colder climates. The mammals, however, included some from warmer climates than Norfolk currently enjoys. Their remains were washed down into the estuarine beds, and some bones, and especially teeth, have survived, including those of the southern elephant and straight-tusked elephant, and teeth and bones from many species of deer, some now extinct. Remains of modern and extinct species of elk, bison, musk ox and wild horses add to the picture, as well as those of hippopotamus, rhinoceros, bear and lion. Closer to the land surface the strata change their fossil characteristics, so that the uppermost layers of the 'Arctic Freshwater Bed' give a forewarning of the Anglian glaciation.

As the map above shows, the physical geography of East Anglia was very different before the onset of the three glaciations shown in the chronological table above. The pre-glacial Bytham River, flowing eastwards from what is now the Midlands, reached the present coast roughly on the line of the Norfolk/ Suffolk boundary. The great river-cut terraces on the sides of its broad valley, and on one of these terraces, at High Lodge just over the Suffolk border near Brandon, an important archaeological site has revealed remains dating from before 400,000 BC. Thus, by then man had reached the area and this, with the key discoveries at Pakefield and Happisburgh, indicates that the free movement of nomadic folk from west Europe to eastern England was possible (and was taking place) before the flooding of the North Sea basin, which had been completed by about 6500 BC.

The gravels of river terraces – for example, at Keswick near Norwich – have been highly productive of Palaeolithic tools. These could have been washed downstream from elsewhere, but collections of worked materials suggest that more probably they were left by hunting groups. South Acre on the river Nar in west Norfolk is another area where many implements have been found, at the Bartholomew Hills and nearby sites. Hand axes come in different forms, but the commonest is the small, pointed 'F type', shown in the drawing (*right*). The map on page 14 summarises the information to date on the distribution of Palaeolithic hand axes. The Broads and the boulder-clay plateau are least productive, but it was suggested to me by Charles Green in 1970 that this was simply because many sites were buried under later sediment. However, it seems equally plausible that the heavily wooded claylands offered little attraction to groups of hunter-gatherers. The cliffs at Happisburgh have produced numbers of these axes, exposed by coastal erosion, while the glacial gravels of the Wensum and Yare valleys in the east and the Nar and Wissey valleys in the west produced good source materials in the form of extensive quantities of loose flint nodules. The gravels of the Cromer Ridge also provided a large supply of flints.

A sketch of a Type F hand axe of the Palaeolithic period (the tip is missing), from Southacre (from J. Wymer, 1985).

The Hoxnian interglacial is named from the famous interglacial lakebed at Hoxne in Suffolk, in what is now the Waveney valley. There a sequence of *in situ* almond-shaped hand axes and their associated worked flints provided evidence of a hunting community living in part from fishing on the lake shores. Archaeologists have ascribed these Hoxnian people to the Acheulian (Lower Palaeolithic) culture. Deposits of the Hoxnian interglacial vary in character and suggest that an area which was originally forested later acquired a more open grassland-type vegetation. These deposits were themselves later covered by the chalky boulder clay of the Wolstonian glaciation, a complex series of advances and retreats of the ice between 367,000 BC and 129,000 BC.

The earliest people were of the type known as *homo erectus*, but by 60,000 BC Neanderthal man had arrived in the area. A crucial discovery, described as 'the best Neanderthal site ever found in Britain', is dated to *c.*65,000 BC and

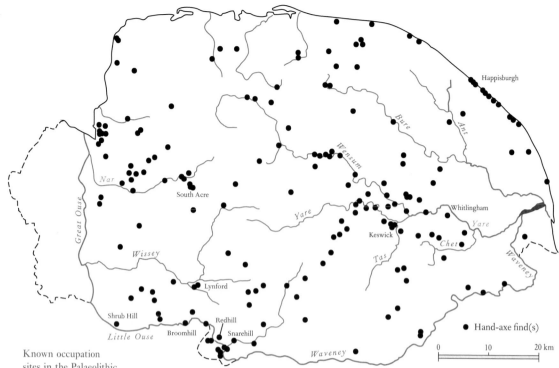

Known occupation sites in the Palaeolithic period (prior to 75,000 BC), based upon discoveries of hand axes (after J. Wymer, 2005).

resulted from excavations carried out by the Norfolk Archaeological Unit at Lynford in West Norfolk. Not only do the archaeological maps of Norfolk have to be redrawn regularly, to keep pace with the flow of new discoveries, but the interpretation of these discoveries allows us continuously to rewrite the story itself. The very important site at Lynford was discovered in 2002, and John Wymer gives a vivid picture of a location on the banks of the river Wissey, where 'mammoths were trapped in the soft peaty mud, either accidentally or after chasing by Middle Palaeolithic hunters'. The site has been dated by optical stimulated luminescence (OSL) to 64,000–67,000 years ago, 30,000 years before the appearance of 'modern' man. It was then a bleak riverside site in a region occupied by woolly rhinoceros, brown bear and spotted hyena. There were no trees, and the climate was significantly colder than today. There were remains of nine woolly mammoths, which showed signs of butchery, the only such site known in the British Isles. A large quantity of flint tools which had been made on the spot were recovered, 'as fresh as the day they were made'. Among them were 45 hand axes, one of which is a particularly fine example of a 'bout-coupé' axe (one which is triangular in shape and rounded at the head).[3] The site is the most significant from the Middle Palaeolithic period in Norfolk, but it is also of national importance. No human remains were found here, but it can be assumed that these people were of Neanderthal type.[4]

The Mesolithic (Middle Stone Age)

As sea levels rose because of the melting of the ice sheets the marine inundation was steady and inexorable. Areas such as the Leman and Ower Banks, now far offshore but rich in archaeological finds, were submerged by about 10,000 BC. Post-glacial changes in sea levels are a complex subject, but raised beaches and former wave-cut platforms on the western side of Great Britain suggest that the land was rising there because of the reduction of the thick ice sheets lying on top of it. However, sea levels were rising as the ice caps melted, while Great Britain in effect tilted slightly towards the North Sea, so that on the eastern side of the island a rise in sea level and fall in land level led to flooding of the North Sea Basin, the Low Countries and the West European plain.

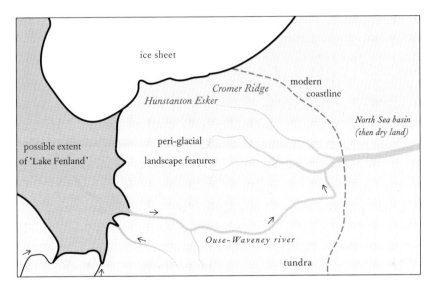

A possible reconstruction of the landscape of northern East Anglia during the last Ice Age (the Devensian period: 75,000–10,000 BC) (after J. Wymer, 1985).

After the final melting of the Devensian ice sheet, the development of a sequence of innovative techniques for working flint gave advantages to new groups of people. Animals such as deer, elk and wolves moved north as the ice receded and the permafrost melted, keeping to the colder areas, and at the same time, as the temperatures warmed, the limits of vegetation shifted northwards. There were no more ice ages to lay down new deposits or destroy earlier evidence of previous glaciations and inter-glacials. This means that the archaeological record becomes potentially more complete, even though frequent fluctuations in land and sea levels led to the infilling of estuaries and the accumulations of layers of silts and peats which can conceal earlier deposits. At Carrow Road Football Ground, Norwich, excavation revealed how an area of sandy mounds which had been settled and occupied in the Mesolithic period was later covered by thick peats and silts, highlighting the extent to which land and sea levels influenced conditions for human occupation.

Jacobi, quoting Graham Clarke, shows how the Mesolithic (or Middle Stone Age) of Norfolk and Suffolk can be subdivided into three phases, roughly from 10,000 to 9000 BC, 9000 to 7000 BC, and 7000 to 4500 BC, by which date the so-called Neolithic revolution had begun.[5] The evidence of the new techniques of working flints, combined with that pointing to fishing and hunting, has been used to define the Mesolithic in the region. The Wensum Valley gravels again show up as areas of major flint-working – for example at Lyng, and under the most recent stand at Carrow Road, a site which provides what is currently the earliest evidence of human occupation in the heart of Norwich.[6] But evidence of human activity extends well beyond the river valleys: two very productive areas of archaeological finds have been found on the plateau at Great Melton and Banham, the latter through the intensive field-walking carried out over many years by Charles Clarke. These two sites were perhaps those of temporary hunting camps – indeed, that may be true of most Mesolithic sites. Other sites on Kelling Heath and at Titchwell RSPB Reserve have also produced masses of worked flints.[7]

Although it means 'Middle Stone Age', Davies also describes the Mesolithic as the 'age of wood', as exemplified by discoveries of log boats, fishnets and traps. Although none of these has yet been found in Norfolk, they are known from Lincolnshire and the Fens, and it is likely that in due course evidence will be found from this county. This period is primarily evidenced in the form of worked flint, with only occasional finds made from other materials. A superb barbed spearhead was dredged up from the North Sea floor on the Dogger Bank (an area now often called 'Doggerland') and this has been dated to 9800 BC, immediately after the retreat of the ice but before the rising waters of the North Sea had flooded the area. The separation of Norfolk from the Continent took place around 6500 BC, and after that the Mesolithic hunters were cut off from their European origins. The major distinguishing feature of their culture was the *microlith* ('tiny stone'), and many generations left these miniature flint points, which were used for spears and arrows; they have been found, for example, in large quantities on Kelling Heath in north Norfolk. Typical Mesolithic sites usually contain axeheads, flint blades, scrapers, 'burins' (flint chisels used for engraving soft stone, bone and wood) and the associated waste flint that went with this work. But the most important technological change, one which was simple but of fundamental importance, was the perfection of the hafted flint axe, in which the stone head was mounted on a handle of wood or antler. That allowed these people to begin to clear woodland, so for the first time man was able to change his habitat and begin to alter the landscape.

The Neolithic (New Stone Age)

The Neolithic phase of cultural development saw two further great changes in human activity – man learned to grow crops, and to control the rearing of stock. From this time onwards human activity had a significant and growing impact upon the landscape of Norfolk. Crop-growing and stock-rearing led to boundaries and enclosures being constructed, and the need for permanent settlement sites as opposed to the shifting patterns of the Mesolithic. The 'shadows' of these activities can at times be picked up by aerial photographs, even in the soft soils of Norfolk. The chronological extent of the Neolithic period in East Anglia is the subject of debate. Rainbird Clarke suggested that it began around 2500 BC, while Frances Healy argued for a date nearer 5000 BC, which would imply some 2,000 years between the earliest Neolithic people and the first emergence of the Bronze Age.[8] She argued that archaeologists can recognise and identify a significant change, from 'Mesolithic microlithic projectile points' to 'single-piece leaf-shaped arrow heads and axes, many of which were polished', from c.5000 BC, and pointed out that Neolithic people were settling in increasing numbers on the lighter soils of the loam region and of the central and northern river valleys during the thousand years between 4350 BC to 3300 BC.

During this period, for the first time, we have substantial evidence of the building of structures, traces of which survive in the present landscape, sometimes in impressive form. The importance of this is very clear – large and long-lasting structures, such as burial mounds, imply a permanent, settled population. Two distinctive features of the Neolithic landscape of Norfolk are the causewayed enclosure and the long barrow. For example, a causewayed enclosure has been identified at Hainford, four kilometres miles north of Norwich, while at Roughton near Cromer a ploughed-out long barrow was set among a number of other Neolithic features, including a near-circular enclosure of 1.22 hectares: jet beads dating from the Neolithic period were found in a barrow at this site. Other long barrows have been found at Harpley and West Rudham in north-west Norfolk, and at Broome Heath in the Waveney Valley, where there was also another monumental complex in the form of a C-shaped enclosure with two banks and ditches and evidence of stake holes.

The custom of building round barrows carried on from the Neolithic period into the Bronze Age. Aerial photography has revealed some 1,200 examples in

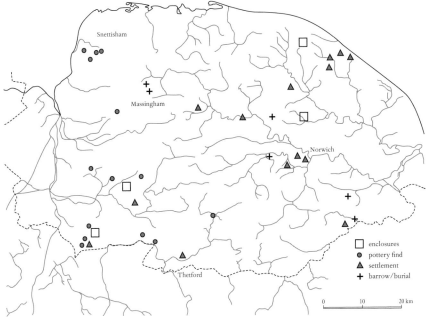

The early Neolithic period in Norfolk: settlement sites, pottery finds and key monuments (after F. Healey, 1984).

_____

17

Norfolk, some of them in major 'cemetery' groups, as at Little Cressingham, Salthouse and Weasenham All Saints. These groups of barrows occur especially in the Breckland and north-west Norfolk, although one group was excavated in advance of the Norwich southern bypass and was dated to 2880 BC to 2490 BC. It is rare for objects to be associated with the barrows, but at Little Cressingham an amber necklace, a gold plate, three small gold boxes and two daggers were found.[9]

Just south of Norwich is an enclosure known as the Arminghall Henge, a circle that was built of wood (probably because of the lack of stone locally).[10] This is one of the earliest henge sites in Britain, and a radiocarbon date of 3250 BC was given for charcoal from the base of one of its central postholes. We can place the chronology of its construction in a national context. Stonehenge, which like Arminghall originally had 56 postholes inside its great ditch, has been dated to c.2900 BC, while the famous blue stones and sarsen stones that survive there were set out c.2500 to 1650 BC. At Avebury the great 'circle', which is over a quarter of a mile in diameter, has similarly been dated to c.2900 to 2600 BC. Arminghall was therefore rather earlier than either of these celebrated sites. The whole monument, with its external ditch, a large bank and a 90-foot central enclosure, was 270 feet across. In the central area was a horseshoe of eight massive oak posts which were up to 3 feet in diameter and sunk into the ground to a depth of 7½ feet. Fragments of two types of beaker wares were found in the main ditch. Nearby, on a promontory at the confluence of the rivers Tas and Yare, there is a D-shaped crop-mark enclosure next to a double ring ditch where many circular flint scrapers were found. This group of monuments has been described as 'part of an extensive ritual-funerary monumental complex'.[11]

Neolithic people, like their forebears for thousands of years, relied on flint for their supply of tools. The outstanding Norfolk site for making axe heads and other flint tools was at Grimes Graves, just north of Thetford, which is internationally renowned.[12] The thick chalk 'raft' which underlies Norfolk is tilted from west to east, so the chalk and associated beds are closest to the surface in the west of the county, on the eastern margins of the Fens. The lowest levels of the chalk carry little flint but the 'middle chalk' (which underlies Grimes Graves) and the upper chalk contain many layers of discontinuous flint (silica) nodules. The thin, light sandy soils of the Breck could be quite easily removed to reach the flint-rich layers below.[13] That easy access, and the excellent quality of the flint itself, produced an intensive and extensive industry four and a half thousand years ago. Neolithic workers sank over 400 shafts in the famous 'hills and holes' area, which stretches over 37 hectares. There were two main phases of working: an earlier period, from roughly 2675 to 2200 BC, and a later one involving shallow pits dug c.1975 BC (that is, extending into the Bronze Age). The shafts are up to 15 metres deep and from these tunnels were dug out laterally to access the dark black flints of the Brandon Flint Series. Grimes Graves is now an English Heritage site and many excavations have taken place as new shafts have been explored. The flints were worked mainly with tools made of red deer antler, the very large quantities used suggesting that the deer were deliberately herded (rather than randomly hunted) in order to provide a

The prehistoric flint mines at Grimes Graves, north-west of Thetford, were first investigated by amateur archaeologists in the late 1860s and early 1870s but they had been known for many centuries – the name was given to this strange landscape by the Anglo Saxons, who called it after the god Grim (or Woden). More than 430 shafts have been identified within an area of about 100 acres, the largest of them over 40 feet deep and 30 feet wide at the surface. Recent estimates suggest that in total some 16,000–18,000 tons of flint may have been excavated, using picks made of deer antlers, many of which have been found. Today one shaft is open to visitors, but the entire area is pockmarked with the pits and hollows of infilled workings.

good supply. Small chalk figures have been found, interpreted as evidence of religious belief. Despite its scale and longevity, Grimes Graves seems to have been a purely 'industrial' site and so far no settlement related to this complex has been found, although clearly the miners and their families must have lived within relatively easy reach.

Though by far the most famous and best researched, it was not the only area of flint working on this western outcrop of the chalk. Other quarry sites have been found at, for example, Lynford and Great Massingham. The Peddars Way, a Neolithic routeway that follows the chalk scarp, links many of these sites and it is probable that large quantities of roughed-out Grimes Graves flint moved along this route. In east Norfolk the flint-rich layers of the Upper Chalk are exposed in the river valleys cut by the Wensum, Yare and Tas. At Whitlingham, just east of Norwich, there was a major axe-producing site. However, very hard stone axes from, among other places, Langdale in the Lake

District, and from Cornwall, have also been found in Norfolk, showing that trade took place in these valuable and highly prized items across the length and breadth of England.

The last stage of the Neolithic overlapped into the Bronze Age and is recognised by its distinctive type of beaker pottery.[14] The key site, for which excavation results were published in 1982, was at Hockwold on the Fen edge where 60 pots were found, 32 of them 'rusticated' (that is, pinched with fingernails to provide a simple form of decoration). None of the beakers was complete. Several hearths were identified, which contained much charcoal, animal bone, flints, and bone implements, and there were the imprinted marks of barley grains on some of the Beaker pottery. There were also traces of an arc of holes for birch stakes, which perhaps supported a screen to shelter the outdoor open-air workplace. The site, near Black Dyke Farm, also yielded large quantities of flints, sherds of Early Neolithic pottery, food vessels, Bronze Age wares and Romano-British pottery. It thus demonstrates, like so many Fen edge sites, a remarkable continuity of settlement. In the Neolithic period the area was on the eastern margins of extensive tracts of freshwater marshes and meres, with small sandhills and gradually rising ground to the east and beyond that open woodland. Bamford suggests that with its rich diversity of habitats this was an area well suited to hunting, fishing and wildfowling, and pasturing of stock, rather than to settled arable agriculture, but she does note that the bones of oxen, sheep and goats were numerous, and that deer-hunting was important. However, the impression of grain on the pots surely indicates some form of cultivation.[15] She suggests, too, that 'the composite picture which is emerging of the life of people in the later Beaker culture in Britain suggests fairly small communities practising agriculture and animal husbandry, supplemented by hunting and food gathering', and that they 'may have inhabited, loosely organised, though perhaps not absolutely static farmsteads and villages of a kind which might underlie the development of more obviously structured settlements such as are known in Bronze Age Britain'. Healy's map of beaker finds in Norfolk shows the importance of the Hockwold area, but also reveals how widespread finds have been, especially those dating from the 'late' Beaker phase or Neolithic/Bronze Age overlap. The repeat of other distribution patterns in which the Fen edge and the river valleys are prominent is also noticeable: it seems certain that, even allowing for less systematic research and the loss of evidence during later agricultural activity, the clay plateaux were still little settled four thousand years ago.

The Neolithic economy of Norfolk seems, therefore, to have been focused

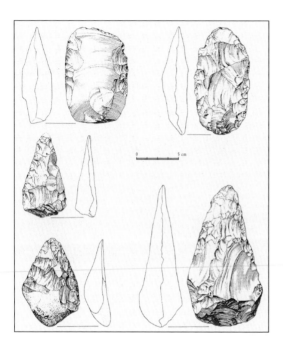

Examples of flint axes of the later Neolithic period, produced at the important site at Whitlingham, just east of Norwich (from J. Wymer, 1985).

especially on the grazing of stock, which led to the gradual clearance of woodland. At Grimes Graves, as well as red deer, evidence of domestic pig, roe deer and horse was found. Analysis of the funnel-shaped entrance to a site close to Hunstanton has suggested that it was a corral for cattle, and the remains of cattle, sheep and pigs were found there. Not surprisingly, given its location, mussels and oysters were collected and eaten in large quantities, and the site also produced evidence of cereal-growing, revealed by the existence of querns for grinding grain. Our present knowledge of Neolithic settlement from modern Norfolk is derived mainly from their stone tools and distinctive pottery types, as well as the numerous long barrows, causewayed enclosures and cursuses (parallel banks with outside ditches, running across the country for long distances). Ashwin sums up their way of life: 'perhaps they shifted through a tract of landscape in a cyclical movement, visiting favoured locations repeatedly over a space of centuries. These dynamics may have been influenced by an agricultural regime involving repeated temporary clearance of woodland for cultivation and grazing, but might equally reflect ritual, religious or commemorative needs.'[16] We can be sure that there is more to discover, and that the story of the Neolithic, like that of the Mesolithic and Palaeolithic, will be not only revised but also become clearer as further archaeological investigation is undertaken.

The 'Beaker' period in Norfolk (5500–3200 BC): known settlement and burial sites (after F. Healey, 1984).

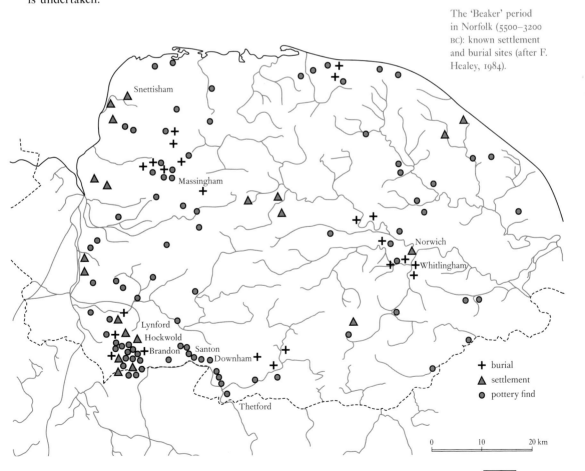

Snettisham

Massingham

Norwich

Whitlingham

Lynford
Hockwold
Brandon   Santon
Downham

Thetford

+ burial
▲ settlement
● pottery find

0   10   20 km

The group of Bronze Age tumuli at Harpley Common in north-west Norfolk are among the finest (and most easily visited) in the county. They were probably constructed in the period from about 2000 to 1500 BC, and more than ten can be identified here and in the adjacent parish of Anmer. Until the eighteenth century they stood on the empty common but since then enclosure, ploughing and plantation woodlands have greatly altered their setting. The traces of a ring ditch and outer bank can still be identified. They stand on the edge of the summit plateau of the main north–south ridge, the dominant topographical feature of the western half of the county, very close to the Peddars Way, suggesting that their siting was of significance in terms of territorial boundaries.

2

The Bronze and Iron Ages in Norfolk

THE table below helps to place what happened in Norfolk into a wider context. It also shows how archaeologists have developed a chronology for the Bronze Age, based upon the evolution of pottery making and metal working as parallel developments, and on the discovery of key sites which have given their names to specific types of pottery or metal. Recognising that over a period of 1,500 years many changes of course took place, researchers now usually divide the period into three main phases: the Early Bronze Age (2000 to 1550 BC), the Middle Bronze Age (1550 to 1100 BC) and the Late Bronze Age (1100 to 500 BC). There is no sharp division between them; nor is there a sudden break from the Neolithic at the beginning of the Bronze Age, or between the Bronze and Iron Ages at the end.

Date	Location	Culture	Norfolk activity
4000 BC	first evidence of bronze production (Northern Thailand)	Neolithic period	increasing Neolithic settlement in Norfolk river valleys
3500 BC	first Sumerian cities at Uruk and Ur		
3100 BC	Kingdom of Egypt established		
3000 BC	Stonehenge and round barrows		Arminghall Henge 2900 BC
2240 BC	Stonehenge abandoned		main period of activity at Grimes
2000 BC	Minoan palaces in Crete	Early Bronze Age	Graves; numerous Neolithic barrows;
1700 BC		(pottery of Bell beaker folk from Rhineland)	Sea Henge (2000 BC)
	New Stonehenge built		
1550 BC		Middle Bronze Age	exceptional output of bronze weapons and decorative objects
1150 BC	Trojan Wars		spectacular bronze hoards and water burial of ritual objects
1050 BC	first use of iron in Greece	Late Bronze Age	
753 BC	founding of Rome		
500 BC		Early Iron Age	

Bronze is an alloy of copper and tin, the ores of which are found only in specific and limited areas, and its production and use therefore spread gradually as traders and migrants carried the materials and technologies ever further afield. Initially tools and ornaments were made of pure copper, which is comparatively soft and easily worked, but correspondingly subject to rapid wear and easy damage. It was soon discovered that when copper and tin were mixed a harder metal can be produced, much more suitable for weapons and ploughshares. Neither copper nor tin occurs in East Anglia (the nearest sources of copper are two hundred miles away, in Cheshire and Devonshire, and of tin 300 miles in Cornwall), and the limited evidence we have suggests that the main source for the bronze used in Norfolk was possibly Ireland, where copper was abundant in County Wicklow. Half a century ago Rainbird Clarke wrote that

> Native smiths in East Anglia during 800 to 600 BC were producing socketed axe heads in large quantities, making two-edged socketed knives and slashing swords with straight shoulders, and hammering out sheet metal to make magnificent circular shields of the type recovered from Sutton in Norfolk. The smiths made socketed bronze sickles for the farmer, saws, chisels and gouges for the carpenter, who in his turn constructed wooden containers and dug-out boats for river transport.[1]

Bronze does not oxidise, and therefore material from that metal, and that period, survives far better than objects made of iron, which of course rust all too easily. A magnificent hoard of Bronze Age items has been found on the edge of Norwich containing six socketed axeheads, four spearheads and two halves of a bronze mould.[2] Recently a second hoard has been found on the same site. Such hoards may have been buried for safety, and perhaps represent the working capital of an itinerant smith. The dominant metal forms that survive include swords and daggers, which were beaten from metal rods or bars. As yet the only Norfolk hoard to have included a mould for casting solid objects was found in Unthank Road in Norwich. The axes and spears might have had a military purpose but they more likely represent the tools needed for woodland clearance and hunting, both of great importance to newly arriving folk. The best-known pot form of the late Neolithic/Early Bronze Age is that of the urn dating from c.1400 BC which was found in the Witton barrow. These 'ill fired, handmade urns of coarse clay' were used primarily as cremation urns.[3]

Davies comments that Norfolk was an 'empty land from 1700 to 700 BC', drawing attention to the surprising lack of evidence for actual settlements, yet he goes on to observe that 'the quantity, quality and variety of Bronze Age metal objects from Norfolk is unsurpassed elsewhere in Britain'. This apparent contradiction is especially apparent along the fen edge of the county. At Methwold, for example, no evidence of buildings has been discovered, but finds of metalwork, dating from 1500 BC to 1300 BC, include a bronze rapier, and bracelets and dress pins with amber centres to the heads. These are of the 'Picardy' type, produced in France, emphasising the importance of long-distance trade 3,500 years ago. Organic remains included human bones, as well as those of red and roe deer, beaver, cow, sheep and horses. In Norfolk, as at the famous site of Flag Fen near Peterborough, there is much evidence for ritual 'water burial', with large quantities of broken swords and hoards of sword fragments having been found at Weston Longville and South Creake, where the distinctive design of a massive flanged axe suggests trading links with the Rhineland. At least fifty mid- to late Bronze Age hoards have been

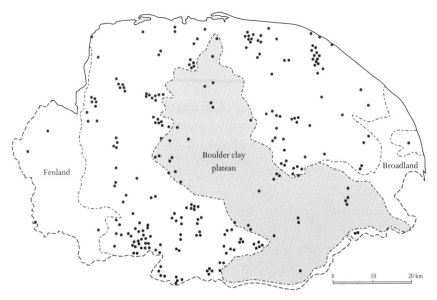

Fenland

Boulder clay
plateau

Broadland

0   10   20 km

The distribution of
Bronze Age round
barrows in Norfolk
(after T. Ashwin, 2005)

found across the county. At Waterden some 180 items were found, among them leaf-shaped swords and socketed spearheads, while at Eaton, on the western edge of Norwich, three hoards were revealed within one mile, and in 2005 some 150 pieces of bronze were found buried in a pit just above the floodplain of the river Yare. Little gold has been found in the hoards, although seven Late Bronze Age gold bracelets were found at Foxley in 2006. Before the Roman period the only major source of gold in the British Isles was Ireland, and it is likely that this gold was of Irish origin. Such items could only have belonged to the very wealthy, underlining the fact that Norfolk was a prosperous region by the Late Bronze Age.[4]

The major surviving evidence of the Bronze Age in our present-day landscape is that of the numerous barrows, or burial mounds, and the ring ditches which are their ploughed-out remains. Bronze Age barrows continued a burial tradition from the Neolithic period, and normally contain a skeleton or an urn of cremated ashes. The associated finds of flint knives, jet and amber beads, bone necklaces, some gold objects, and even blue beads of faience from Egypt, suggest that only the more important members of the community were buried beneath these structures. There has been a suggestion, based on the distribution of known examples, that the mounds were constructed on the boundaries of Bronze Age village communities, but Lawson – who noted in 1981 that there were 625 recorded barrows and 549 ring ditches in Norfolk – has shown that many in fact lay on the common wastes which survived until the last years of the eighteenth century.[5] Perhaps, therefore, there were once many more such burials on the claylands, where cultivation over 3,000 years has destroyed the evidence. As the map above shows, there is a county-wide spread, but with an emphasis along the Fen edge and the north coast. In Flegg, north of Great Yarmouth, ring ditches have shown up on aerial photographs, but this area contains some of the best soils in the county, and their sites have been worked over by the plough for thirty centuries. It is thus not surprising that nothing can be seen on the surface.

Some of the most dramatic and fascinating Bronze Age sites in Norfolk are the wooden henges. Near Norwich is Arminghall henge, discussed in the previous chapter, where none of the great timbers survives although their sites are marked by concrete posts. This important ceremonial focal point, perhaps comparable with Stonehenge or Avebury, dates from 2000–3000 BC, but remained in use well into the Bronze Age. Far more extraordinary is the site now known as Sea Henge, discovered in 1998. This elliptical pattern of 55 close-set oak timbers was found at low tide off the shore at Holme-next-the-Sea. After much debate, the timbers were lifted for preservation, including the massive central feature which is the inverted base of an oak tree. The remains of honeysuckle 'ropes' around the central timber have survived and may have been used for haulage. This unique monument was not a true henge, there being no surrounding ditch or bank; nor is it thought to be the remains of the interior of a barrow. It has been suggested that it belongs to 'a distinct class – a free-standing circle – that may either have been used for the commemoration and veneration of the dead, or for offerings and celebrations'.[6] Radiocarbon dating places the circle at about 2000 BC, in the Early Bronze Age, when it was well away from the sea in oak woodland. After careful preservation of the timbers, part of the circle is displayed in the museum at King's Lynn.

A crucial question now is whether the late Bronze Age people of Norfolk were organised into tribes, or even kingdoms. During the Iron Age Norfolk was within the kingdom of the Iceni, and it has been tentatively suggested that before then west Norfolk may have been one focal area, and east Suffolk, around the estuary of the river Deben, another. However, no evidence of Bronze Age territorial boundaries comparable with those of Wessex has yet come to light. Nevertheless, the peoples capable of organising the construction of sites such as Arminghall and Sea Henge must surely have had some form of coherent territorial divisions, and effective forms of administration. A sweeping summary of the Bronze Age in Norfolk would be that the earlier pastoral and partly nomadic economy was replaced in the later Bronze Age by the development of mixed farming and a more settled lifestyle. The greatest tangible impact of these peoples on our present landscape is the barrows they left behind. Perhaps more importantly, however, they greatly accelerated the clearance of woodland on the sandier soils and helped to shape and mould the county's appearance for many centuries. What we do not have, as yet, is the evidence of their settlement sites.

The Iron Age

The transition from the Bronze Age to the Iron Age was gradual, not marked by any dramatic or sudden changes. As Barry Cunliffe observes, the period from 1400 BC to 700 BC was a time of 'massive continuity'.[7] But changes were happening inexorably, not just in Britain but across Europe as a whole. By 800 BC trade between Brittany and Britain was increasing significantly; more

Approximate dates	Stage	Culture	Key sites
800 BC	Late Bronze Age		
700 BC–400 BC	Early Iron Age	various pottery types + round houses	West Harling near Thetford
400 BC–200 BC	Middle Iron Age	La Tene culture; decorated ironwork; Marnian settlers	Snettisham area; north-west Norfolk; Fen edge; Caistor St Edmund; site of settlement near Wymondham
100 BC–50 BC	Late Iron Age	gold and silver coins; horses and chariots; Belgic invasions (Iceni)	hillforts at Warham and Narborough
AD 43	Iceni organised in 'kingdoms'	coin hoards	Caistor by Norwich area and north-west Norfolk
AD 60	Roman military control	military roads and staging camps	*Venta Icenorum* and smaller towns; villas along Icknield Way.

bronze goods were being produced by native craftsmen; and technological innovation was being pursued. Many historians and archaeologists accept that the Iron Age had its beginnings in this period, and perceptions of the Iron Age itself have changed radically as archaeological investigation reveals more of the period. Once seen in terms of its rather uninteresting, crumbly pottery, and oxidised remains of iron goods, the sophistication of the period is now assessed in the context of superb gold coins and jewellery, decorative horse harnesses, hillforts and exciting politics – culminating in Boudica's famous rebellion, one of the greatest events in the long history of the Roman Empire. The later Iron Age has another distinction, for we move from purely artefact-based archaeological analysis to the earliest written evidence: this is the first period referred to in literary sources, such as those of Julius Caesar and Tacitus.

Celtic-speaking peoples had reached the southern and south-western shores of the North Sea by 500 BC, with many distinct tribes linked by a common language and a shared druidical religion. The Belgae had settled north-east France and the Low Countries by about 300 BC and were particularly important because groups of them subsequently colonised parts of south-east England. Gaul, a territory occupied by a number of Celtic tribes and roughly equivalent to modern France, was conquered by Julius Caesar in 58 to 55 BC. Among the Celts of Gaul there were strong connections with tribes in Britain, and much cross-fertilisation of culture, trade and kinship. Gallo-Belgic coinage from the first century BC has been found over much of south-east Britain, implying that trade was taking place. Amphorae (large wine jars) from Brittany were reaching Britain by 100 BC, and tin, salt, wool and leather were being exported to Gaul. Iron Age Britain was already tied, culturally and economically, to mainland Europe.

The Iron Age time-chart above gives some approximate dating. The period is generally regarded as lasting from c.700 BC until AD 43, ending with the invasion of Britain by Roman forces under the leadership of the emperor Claudius – although there was no sudden or abrupt change in culture, society or economic circumstances as a result, for it took some decades for the impact of Rome to deepen and to extend to all corners of what is now England and Wales. As with the Bronze Age, archaeologists have developed a threefold division of the Iron Age in Norfolk: first, from *c.*600 to 400 BC, the continuation of the Late Bronze Age, in which pottery rather than iron provides the main source of evidence; second, the Middle Iron Age, when a major invasion of Marnian people swept in from northern France; and finally, from *c.*50 BC to AD 43, the Belgic invasion. This provided a new ruling class in Norfolk for the people who had become known as the Iceni, and whose final suppression came with the crushing of the rebellion of Boudica in AD 60.

In the past thirty years archaeological methods have changed greatly, and are now far removed from the early days when pottery collecting was supplemented by the discovery of random pieces of Iron Age material which had survived natural oxidation as ploughs continually turned over arable land. Techniques of metal-detecting, systematic field-walking and analysis of aerial photography have advanced to a remarkable extent, so that although Norfolk has been farmed since the Neolithic period, and pottery has been continually broken up by ploughing, much is still being found, while modern scientific analysis gives abundant additional information. The art of coin recognition has also advanced hugely, and the analysis of the silver and gold in coins and in jewellery such as torcs (solid gold necklaces) has progressed greatly. All these developments add much to our knowledge of this crucial period in the history of Norfolk. Furthermore, better reconnaissance and large-scale excavation have revealed major new sites. Thus, at Shropham in 2001 the Norfolk Archaeological Unit investigated 'the most extensive area of Iron Age domestic occupation uncovered in the county to date'.[8]

The use of iron further increased the advantages that bronze had already given. Iron weapons, ploughshares and axes enhanced the power of those who had them, including their capacity to fell woodland and to cultivate more difficult land. Although some of the county's glacial gravels and the lower greensands were quite rich in iron ores, there is little evidence that ore from Norfolk sources was smelted before the arrival of the Romans. Like bronze,

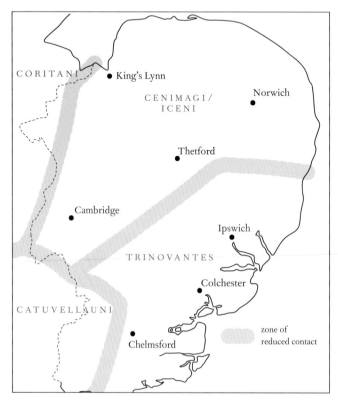

The late Bronze Age and Iron Age cultural and political geography of East Anglia: the 'zones of reduced contact' are generalised, since we do not know exact boundaries and indeed they may not have existed (after A. Lawson, 1984).

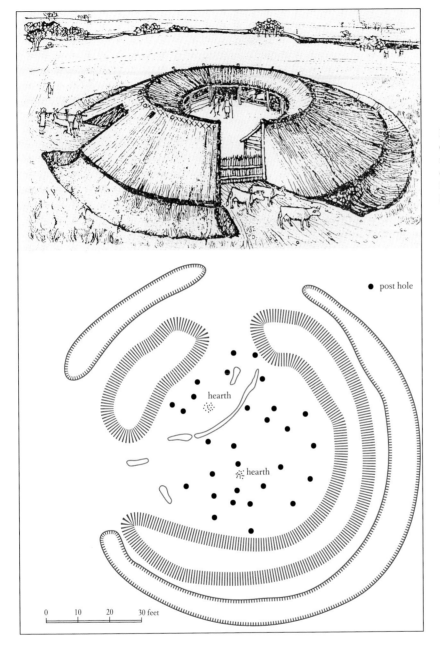

Plan and reconstruction
of the Iron Age
round house that was
excavated at West
Harling (after R.
Rainbird Clarke, 1960).

• post hole

hearth

hearth

0   10   20   30 feet

iron must have been brought in, possibly from the Jurassic iron ore beds in Northamptonshire, by travelling smiths and at the request of high-status landowners.

What is the evidence for the lifestyles of the Iron Age people of Norfolk? At West Harling, six miles east of Thetford, a site called Micklemoor Hill was excavated in 1960. This revealed the full plan of a farmstead of the Early Iron Age, with three enclosures and, in the eastern one, the postholes of the oak framework of a round house. This was penannular in plan – that is, almost a full circle, with a circular courtyard. Two other buildings, one smaller and circular and the other rectangular, were found in the other enclosures. The Harling farmers kept oxen and sheep and cultivated wheat; they had saddle querns for grinding the grain. Bones of wild boar, red deer, crane and beaver reveal evidence of hunting, and the remains of a dog suggested that it might have been used for that purpose. Pieces of no fewer than 530 pots were found in the ditch, flint tools were knapped on the site, and spindle whorls and loom weights provided evidence that cloth was made. Large pottery jars may have been used for grain storage. No iron goods and very few ornaments were found on this site, which may have served one or two families over several generations.[9]

In the Middle Iron Age, 300 BC to 100 BC, a very distinctive culture had developed in north-west Norfolk. A series of hoards revealed by ploughing at Ken Hill, Snettisham, between 1948 and 1950, was then considered by Rainbird Clarke as 'the largest accumulation of precious metal so far recorded from Iron Age Britain … testimony to the power and wealth of a local dynasty'. Coins from Snettisham made from speculum, an alloy of copper and tin, were dated from c.100 BC and indicate that a money economy was gradually developing. In 1990 at Harford Farm, a mile north of Caistor St Edmund, excavations of Neolithic and Bronze Age ring ditches exposed an important Middle Iron Age site. This included four round houses and several pit groups, emphasising the significance of the promontory between the Tas and Yare valleys for settlement since Neolithic times. In 1989–1991 other evidence of Iron Age settlement was found in Trowse, on the slope facing County Hall. Although there were no round houses, scattered across the site was a series of ditched enclosures with pits, one of which contained 4.5 kg of pottery and loom weights. Both Harford and Trowse contained many 'four poster sites', structures 2–3m square which it has been suggested may have been granaries. All this came to light because of the construction of the Norwich southern bypass – how much more evidence of the Neolithic, Bronze Age and Iron Age is still concealed in this area?[10]

Intensive field-walking in various parts of Norfolk has revealed great variations in the distribution of Iron Age activity, and emphasises that a great deal of additional evidence will be found after more detailed investigation. For example, field-walking carried out by Andrew Rogerson in two sample parishes, Barton Bendish and Fransham,[11] revealed far more pottery concentrations than in adjacent parishes which have been less intensively studied. At Barton Bendish, on thin soils over chalk, 21 'sites' were found. Outside these was a sparse 'aura' of sherds paralleling Roman and medieval scatters, suggesting that they had also originated in farm muck carried out from middens and spread over arable land. The fact that the Iron Age pottery was in very small abraded fragments (and thus heavily damaged in the Iron Age itself) supports this view, while the discovery of first-century brooches on five sites, and two Icenian coins, argues for some continuity of activity from the Iron Age into the Roman period. Fransham lies on the boulder-clay watershed, and only six sites were found, although field-walking was more intensive than at Barton Bendish. After an initial find of four pieces of Iron Age pottery at one 'site', more intensive re-walking subsequently revealed 250 pieces.

The contrast between the density of sites on the chalk uplands and that on the wet boulder clay is significant, suggesting that Fransham was an area of wood pasture with stock rearing and timber production, whereas Barton Bendish was an arable area with manure used as fertiliser, taken out to the fields from scattered settlements. The interdisciplinary nature of modern archaeological work is illustrated elsewhere by the use of pollen analysis and radiocarbon dating.[12] While many sites, such as Diss Mere, show evidence of a reduction in woodland in the Iron Age, two Breck-edge meres at Hockham and Stow Bedon show that this area was heavily wooded between c.900 and c.500 BC. Some of the dating on such sites makes exact distinctions between the Bronze Age and Iron Age difficult, but a broad picture of woodland reduction in this period suggests an increase in population and in arable farming. But the process was not spread evenly across the county – in some areas extensive woodland remained into the Roman period, while elsewhere it was fast declining half a millennium before.

Another aspect of the Iron Age economy, the production of salt, is related to the character of the East Anglian coastline, with its many shallow tidal inlets. Salt production is now thought to have begun in the Bronze Age. Briquetage, the burnt waste and residue resulting from salt making, has been found on the fen edge at Fengate near Peterborough and at Mucking in Essex, and it is probable that it was widespread in coastal Norfolk. On the fen edges there was tidal saline water, and the peat and timber which were needed to fuel evaporation pans. Small islands rising above the peat, and natural river levees, provided settlement sites. It is probable that during the Iron Age and into the Roman period salt making was a seasonal activity, taking place on favoured sites during the summer months.

Hillforts and linear earthworks are two types of feature which have left a strong visual impact on the Norfolk landscape. Clearly, given Norfolk's relatively low topography, these differ markedly from those of, for example, Wiltshire or Dorset, but they share many characteristic features with the hillforts of Wessex. As the map on page 32 shows, a series of such forts lay from north to south on the western edge of the county, along the coastal ridge and the chalk hills. That at Warham, a superb defensive location, is the best preserved and is accessible to the public. Its western edge is clipped by the river Stiffkey, and the river may have been navigable as far as the fort. There is much debate about the role of these forts. The earthworks at Warham are impressive, but there has only been limited excavation and that has so far revealed little clear evidence as to its use. Were they bolt-holes in times of trouble, or centres for communal meetings, rather like the meeting places for the Saxon hundreds, or even sites with a religious function?

Whatever their function, it is clear that the Iron Age people of Norfolk were capable of the high degree of social organisation that would have been required to construct the great double-ditch ramparts. Linear earthworks are also found mainly in the western part of the county. The Bitcham Ditch ends at the Narborough hillfort, at a crossing point on the river Nar: this would seem to be no accident, though whether the Nar was navigable as far as Narborough is an open question. These dykes may represent some sort of territorial boundary.

The Iron Age hillfort at Warham Camp is the best preserved in East Anglia. It was built on a low hill in a curve of the river Stiffkey, probably in the second century BC. Three other hillforts are known nearby, at South Creake, Narborough and Holkham. Their precise role is unclear – suggestions include a religious function, a high-class residential location, a military defence or a trading centre (or any combination of these). This circular fort covers an area of over two acres. Excavation has shown that the ditches were more than six feet deeper than today, making them a formidable barrier, and on the top of the inner bank was a wooden palisade. The fort remained in use during the early Roman period.

Further south, the Devil's Dyke on Newmarket Heath in Suffolk was a major earthwork which may have marked the western limit of the Icenian territory, and the Norfolk examples perhaps served the same role. Medium-sized and rectangular enclosures survive mainly in the wealthy north-western part of the Icenian kingdom and are shown on the location map below. Some have recently been discovered as a result of aerial photography, such as that at South Creake which is now levelled and cannot be seen on the ground. Two important sites

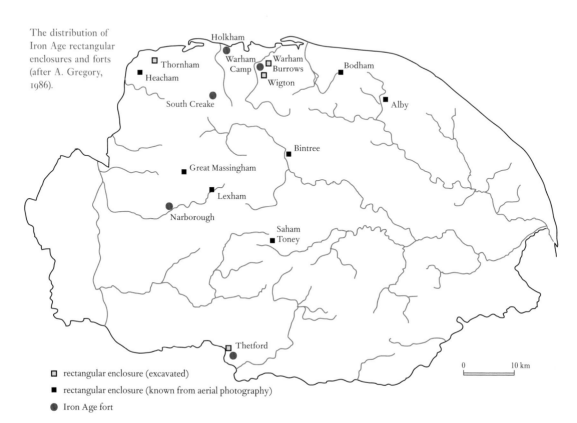

The distribution of Iron Age rectangular enclosures and forts (after A. Gregory, 1986).

Holkham

Thornham
Heacham

Warham Camp

Warham Burrows

Wigton

Bodham

South Creake

Alby

Bintree

Great Massingham

Lexham

Narborough

Saham Toney

Thetford

0   10 km

□ rectangular enclosure (excavated)

■ rectangular enclosure (known from aerial photography)

● Iron Age fort

at Thetford emphasise the key importance of that location, where the Icknield Way crossed the Thet and the Little Ouse. The double-ditched oval castle site was reused over a thousand years later by the Normans for their great motte and bailey, while the site at Fisons Way, on the north side of the town, has proved to be of exceptional interest and is now interpreted as a major religious centre.

Apart from the hillforts, evidence of Iron Age settlement is limited in Norfolk, and there is a marked scarcity of information about the domestic circumstances and lifestyles of people in this period. The house at West Harling has already been discussed on pages 29-30 and further round houses were found just to the south of Norwich, on the line of the southern by-pass. The construction of the Wymondham bypass led to the discovery of another Iron Age site at Silfield, south of the town of Wymondham.[13] It lies on a gentle south-facing slope on the boulder-clay plateau, near a source of water but with no evidence of either pre- or post-Iron Age activity. This was an 'open settlement', unplanned and at a low density (only the threatened part was excavated). No round houses were found, but a great deal of evidence of 'a versatile and craft-based economy' appeared and there were many 'working hollows' which in some cases showed evidence of iron working. They may originally have been quarried for flint, but as yet there is no full explanation of their purpose. Substantial quantities of sherds of coarse coiled pots of gritty ware were found and were dated to the Middle Iron Age, c.300–100 BC. Red-deer antlers had been used to make handles, toggles and bone combs. It has been suggested that such a site may represent a period of Middle Iron Age expansion onto the boulder clays.

The Iceni first used coins from about 55 BC,[14] by which date tribes such as the Trinovantes to the south of Norfolk were already familiar with them. The earliest coins were of gold, indicating that this was initially perhaps as much a way of storing wealth as commercial currency, but silver was soon used as well. All the Icenian examples have a lively horse on the reverse. Two of the greatest collections of Icenian coins from Norfolk were found at Honingham and Western Longville.[15] Iron Age Norfolk is also justly famed for the large number of gold and silver torcs found in the west of the county, especially in the Snettisham area – some of these are now among the most important exhibits of pre-Roman Britain in the British Museum and other national collections. They are huge, often richly ornate with twisted 'rope-like' forms, and because of their immense weight would clearly have been almost impossible to wear except for brief periods. As Robinson and Gregory say, these torcs have been found in discrete 'nests' and were evidently buried with great care, possibly as a treasury for a tribe or for religious reasons. The latter is now regarded as the most likely explanation, given the caution with which they were concealed, the fact that they were usually arranged in sequence, and the apparently ceremonial designs. Even in this period, though, bronze was still much used for sword scabbards, helmets and shields as well as for women's brooches and horse and chariot harness. It is immediately apparent, as their coinage designs further indicate, that horses, chariots and their decoration were of great importance to the Iceni.

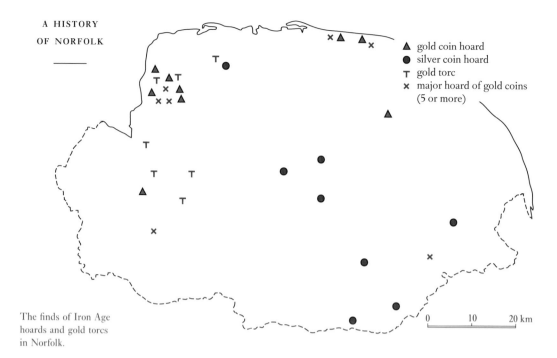

▲ gold coin hoard
● silver coin hoard
T gold torc
✗ major hoard of gold coins
   (5 or more)

The finds of Iron Age
hoards and gold torcs
in Norfolk.

At Norfolk's major Roman site, Caistor St Edmund (*Venta Icenorum*), the area within the walls had not been archaeologically investigated in detail since Atkinson's excavations between 1929 and 1935, until recent work in 2010–11 by the Archaeology Department of Nottingham University. Even now, little is known of what lies beneath the deep Roman levels. However, many La Tene-style brooches, terrets (horse harness) and gold and silver coins have been found, as a result of metal detecting, on or near the site. It lies within a rich Iron Age landscape close to the important Harford Farm site (discovered in 1990) and is central to a cluster of Iron Age hoards. An early Roman military presence may have followed the Boudican revolt, but Davies comments that 'accumulating evidence may suggest that the Roman town was a direct successor to an earlier Iron Age site of regional significance'.[16] In the site at Caistor we may have the Icenian equivalent to the *oppida*, the quasi-urban settlements of Iron Age Britain which are better known from examples further south, at places such as Winchester, St Albans and Canterbury.

Peter Salway suggests that the Roman occupation of Norfolk had less influence on the existing way of life than the changes that were already taking place in the Late Iron Age. He argues that a pattern of small fields, settled farmsteads and extensive corn growing had already replaced a more pastoral economy, and that it was not until *c.* AD 100 that Roman influence became more pervasive. Indeed, archaeological evidence hints that in some cases Roman villas superseded existing Iron Age farmsteads, and that in the pre-Roman period hand-made pottery had already given way to wheel-made ware. Evidence of slavery, and of the beginnings of towns, shows that an aristocracy was also evolving.[17] In other words, pronounced and accelerating economic and social change was already becoming apparent in the area *before* the Roman occupation.

3

Roman Norfolk

AD 43	Invasion by Claudius
47	Military presence on border of Icenian territories but kingdom remains semi-independent
50	Roman political and cultural influence begins to penetrate Norfolk
60	Brampton pottery kilns operating (until AD 400)
	Death of Prasutagus, the Icenian king
61	Boudica's rebellion
61–70	Fenland occupied for military settlement
125	First masonry buildings at Caistor by Norwich
125	Caister by Yarmouth founded as a port
150	Flint walls built round Caister by Yarmouth
180	Caistor by Norwich walled
200–220	Two Romano-Celtic temples at Caistor
250	Masonry and timber replacing wattle and daub houses
	Saxon shore forts constructed at Brancaster and Burgh Castle
300 onwards	Most villas derelict by 330
330	Saxon Shore forts becoming derelict for military purposes
360	Caistor by Norwich in decline
367	Attacks by the Saxons and the Picts
400	Many Fenland farms still working; Feltwell villa still functioning
410	The Romans leave Britain
450	Civilian occupation of Burgh Castle continues

The Roman conquest and its background

During the later Iron Age southern England was divided into several kingdoms, among them that of the Iceni which included Norfolk, north-west Suffolk and Cambridgeshire. Although most authorities accept that this was the extent of Icenian territory, its precise boundaries are far from certain; nor is it clear how long this kingdom had been in existence. The earliest Icenian gold coins are dated to about 100 BC, the earliest coins of silver to c.35 BC, but it is unknown how long before this the Celtic-speaking Belgic-descended people of Norfolk had become unified as a coherent political group. Current academic opinion, based primarily on archaeological evidence supplemented by the very limited (and often frustratingly ambiguous) written references, suggests that the Icenian kingdom was established about a century and a half before the Roman conquest, fifty years or so before Julius Caesar's abortive invasion. That would coincide roughly with the minting of the earliest coins. Caesar himself referred to a group living north of the Thames as the *Cenimagni* (which perhaps is a version of a word *Icenimagni*, meaning 'the great Iceni'), and there is at least a possibility that the Icenian name was used by the historian Tacitus, writing between AD 75 and 120, as a term to cover a group of smaller tribes which had developed a sense of unity, perhaps against external threats, even before Caesar's first invasions of 55–54 BC.

Davies argued that the Iceni lived mainly in unenclosed settlements, although we know that they also had hillfort-type enclosures. They produced a wide range of metalwork which reflected their horse-focused society – items such as terret rings for chariots, and various harness fittings, have been found, for example, in large quantities at Saham Toney and Ashill. The Iceni used the symbols of sun, stars and moons on the reverse of their famous horse coins. As already indicated, a key question concerns whether an Icenian *oppidum* (a defended town or capital) existed on the site of the later Roman town at Caistor by Norwich. Despite many Iron Age finds in the area, the existence of an *oppidum* has never been confirmed, but Davies concludes that 'evidence for important late Iron Age occupation predating the Roman town has been steadily accumulating'.[1] Suggestions are now being advanced that towns of some sort may have existed elsewhere in the Icenian kingdom, particularly at Thetford and Saham Toney/Ashill.

Caesar appears to have claimed that the conquest of Britain was necessary in order to protect Gaul, which he had recently 'pacified'. There were already many contacts between the Roman Empire and Britain – tin from Cornwall, lead from Wales, corn, cattle, gold, silver, iron, hides, hounds and even slaves were being exported from Britain to the Empire, and in return came imported Roman luxuries such as ivory, amber, glass and metalwares. Caesar's invasion was brief because he was called back to Gaul, but it introduced the Roman world to the Iron Age tribes. The practicality of a serious invasion was in doubt, because the small Roman army lacked its cavalry – storms had forced some of the ships back to Gaul – and they experienced very difficult landing conditions. The British tribes of southern England sued for peace, but no political arrangements came out of this preliminary attack. In Rome, Caesar's venture was regarded, perhaps correctly, as a successful reconnaissance which allowed better understanding of the challenges which would eventually face a full-scale invasion.

Almost ninety years later, in AD 43, the emperor Claudius, perhaps fearing a unification of British tribes, who could in turn become a threat to Rome, assembled an army of 40,000 men under the command of Aulus Plautius. This consisted of four legions of 5,000 men, each divided into ten cohorts of 480, together with many specialist technicians, auxiliaries, and some cavalry. Claudius landed his forces at Richborough in Kent, Chichester, and a third harbour which is as yet unidentified. Richborough was the main starting point for the Roman conquest of south-east Britain. The territories of the Cantiaci (Kent), Catuvellauni (Essex), Trinovantes (East Suffolk) and the Iceni were quickly overrun. The Celtic tribes of the South East had a tradition of friendship with Rome which predated the time of Julius Caesar and meant that initially they could, like the Brigantes in northern England, be regarded as client kingdoms. For the Iceni, under their king Prasutagus, this arrangement worked well during the first decade and a half of the Roman presence in Britain. There was some initial trouble: after a rebellion in AD 47 by part of the Iceni the IX Roman Legion, having conquered Colchester, skirted the Fens and reached the Humber avoiding the Icenian heartland. Prasutagus then opened the Icenian territory to trade with Rome and remained in power, though unlike some others in his position he left no great buildings as evidence of his status and authority.

However, the death of Prasutagus in AD 60 was followed by greedy Roman demands to acquire part of his wealth. The cruel and humiliating treatment meted out by the governor Suetonius Paulinus to the king's widow, Boudica, and her daughters led to the celebrated rebellion. The Iceni rose up against the Romans, and the Trinovantes to the south, also disillusioned by Roman rule, joined the rebel army. Four great towns – Colchester, London, St Albans and Silchester – were burned and ransacked. However, at a battle which was almost certainly near Mancetter, south-east of Atherstone on the borders of Warwickshire and Leicestershire, the disciplined Roman forces of the XIV and XX legions defeated the Iceni and their allies. After this, in order to maintain control over the erstwhile rebels, forts were built on the line of two new roads (Pye Road and Peddars Way) which led from the south into the heart of East Anglia. Military sites of this period are known at Great Chesterford, Chelmsford, Coddenham, Ixworth and probably Saham Toney. The land of the Iceni came under temporary military government but, remarkably, it was soon freed from army control, and after about AD 70 was once more under civilian rule.

Material evidence of the Roman presence in Norfolk

Important evidence for the Roman presence in Norfolk comes, of course, from archaeological investigation. Apart from the forts and the roads, there are three key sources: coins, pottery and metalware. In this context the results of metal-detecting have been striking. Coins, sometimes found singly, sometimes in hoards, provide key dating evidence in excavations and invaluable clues when gathered by field-walking. The Mattishall and Scole hoards are typical. The former comprised 1,080 silver *denarii* and *antoniani* dating from between 154 and 260, while that from Scole was deposited in the late third century.[2] Roman coins have been found in virtually every parish in the county. Green has shown that metalware forms another source of information – thus, the 25 brooches discovered at Hockwold in 1957 are made of copper alloy, providing evidence of sophisticated and skilful craftsmanship, but the outstanding finds from this site were the unique crown and diadems which, he suggests, may have been worn by priests at a temple or some other sort of religious centre.

Two further important sites have been found at Great Walsingham and Hockwold. The former is very extensive, and seven scatters of building material and remains of masonry suggest that there was probably a bath-house or temple. Metal detectorists found 200 Romano-British brooches, 7,000 coins and several religious objects including three statuettes of Mercury, two figurines of goats,

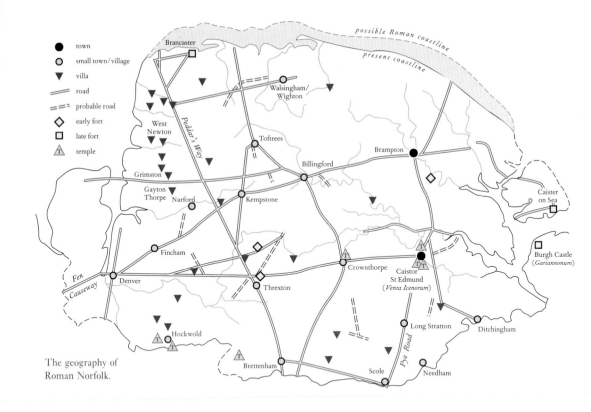

Legend (top map)

- ● town
- ○ small town/village
- ▼ villa
- ═══ road
- ═ ═ probable road
- ◇ early fort
- ☐ late fort
- 🔺 temple

Brancaster

possible Roman coastline

present coastline

Walsingham/
Wighton

West
Newton

Peddar's Way

Toftrees

Brampton

Billingford

Caister
on Sea

Grimston

Gayton
Thorpe

Narford

Kempstone

Burgh Castle
(*Gariannonum*)

Fincham

Denver

Fen
Causeway

Threxton

Crownthorpe

Caistor
St Edmund
(*Venta Icenorum*)

Long Stratton

Ditchingham

Hockwold

Brettenham

Scole

Pye Road

Needham

The geography of
Roman Norfolk.

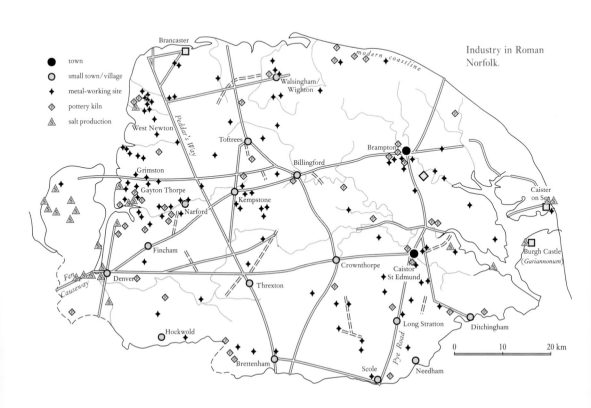

Legend (bottom map)

- ● town
- ○ small town/village
- ✦ metal-working site
- ◈ pottery kiln
- 🔺 salt production

Industry in Roman
Norfolk.

Brancaster

modern coastline

Walsingham/
Wighton

West Newton

Peddar's Way

Toftrees

Brampton

Grimston

Billingford

Gayton Thorpe

Kempstone

Caister
on Sea

Narford

Fincham

Crownthorpe

Caistor
St Edmund

Burgh Castle
(*Gariannonum*)

Fen
Causeway

Denver

Threxton

Long Stratton

Ditchingham

Hockwold

Pye Road

Brettenham

Scole

Needham

0   10   20 km

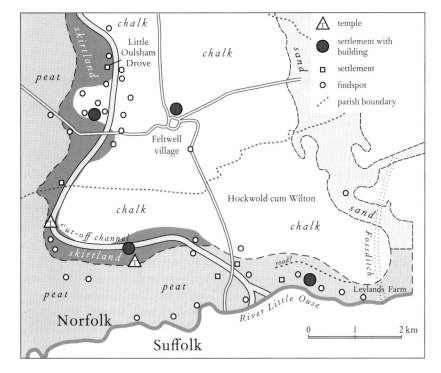

Romano-British sites in Feltwell and Hockwold cum Wilton, showing the relationship with the physical geography and geology.

and three of cockerels. At Hockwold there are the remains of two temples, with collections of religious material and many coins. It is suggested that these were centres for fairs and festivals and served as regional markets – the discovery of large numbers of small late-Roman bronze coins of low value are interpreted as evidence of commercial trading.[3] In 1985 the stock of an itinerant jeweller was found at Snettisham. A nearly complete greyware vessel was excavated containing 356 items including bronze and silver coins, gemstones, finger rings and bracelets, dated to the second century AD.[4]

Pottery making was concentrated on sites where clays such as the Norwich Brick Earths and the Kimmeridge beds were readily accessible. Brampton, the point where the west–east Roman road through Norfolk crossed the river Bure, had many kilns and was clearly an important commercial centre whose significance is only now being fully understood. The standard product was Norfolk greyware, but the potteries manufactured a very wide range of other goods and more specialised items, including great *amphorae* for carrying wines and olive oil. Greyware formed a major part of the pottery found in those three excavations. However, it is known that, because they lay on the Fen edge, wares from other Fenland kilns in the Nene and Nar valleys were also brought in.[5]

The road network and the countryside

The impact of the Roman road system of Norfolk on the present highway network is considerable. The major strategic route was the Peddars Way, short sections of which survive in use along the crest of the chalk scarp. The alignment of the road is also marked by hedgelines and field tracks, and in its northern section it forms the boundaries of several Anglo-Saxon parishes. Many settlements lay west of this military road, which ran northwards from Chelmsford and Great Chesterford and then partly superseded the roughly parallel Icknield Way before reaching the coast at Holme-next-the-Sea. The main road from Colchester, known as the Pye Road in its Norfolk stretch, is followed closely by the present Ipswich to Norwich road, the A140. Long Stratton ('settlement on the street', or Roman road) lies on it, as does the little-known and largely unexcavated Roman port of Scole on the Waveney. A fine view of Caistor is provided from the A140 as it crests the hill to the north of Dunston, whence it dropped down to the west gate of the Roman town.

The northward route of this road beyond Caistor, through what later became Norwich, is the subject of continuing debate, but it has been suggested that it crossed the Wensum in the parish of St Lawrence to head northwards through Stratton Strawless to Brampton, the great Roman pottery centre, and perhaps on to a putative lost port in the Bacton area, between Caister and Happisburgh, where the incessant coastal erosion over two thousand years may have removed evidence of a site. The place-name Eccles, where the remains of a church tower still lie on the beach and are visible at low tide, suggests an early Christian site which may have been part of a Roman settlement now washed away. It has also been suggested that a possible Roman port at Brundall was connected to Holm Street in Norwich, which crossed the south–north road just west of Tombland, the future Saxon marketplace.[6] The major west–east route is known as the Fen Causeway, running from Water Newton on Ermine Street near Peterborough, across the Fens to Denver, and thence via Fincham and Kempstone to Billingford and Brampton. Its alignment fades out east of Brampton but it may have made for Caister-by-Yarmouth.

Peddars Way was originally a prehistoric trackway running across the whole of Norfolk, from the Suffolk border at Knettishall, between Thetford and Diss, north-west to the coast at Holme-next-the-Sea, where in 1998 the extraordinary Bronze Age 'Seahenge' timber circles were discovered. There were several versions of the route, including a trackway that ran roughly parallel and a few miles to the east from the Icknield Way at Thetford to Hunstanton and Holme. The photograph shows a section of the main route at Anmer, near Docking, where it runs immediately adjacent to a series of fine Bronze Age burial mounds. The Peddars Way remained in use during the Roman period and into the Middle Ages (the name is derived from a Middle English word for a track or footpath).

The Roman occupation lasted for 400 years, during which there were many changes. During that long period, how did the population of Norfolk feed itself and provide the very wide range of domestic and industrial goods that have come down to us as archaeological finds? The basic economy was rural, in many ways a continuation of that found in the Late Iron Age. Small patterns of enclosures around clusters of buildings were linked by the new Roman system of roads and waterways, and a complex secondary network of smaller Roman roads spread out into the countryside, connecting small villages, villas and single farmsteads over much of the county.

During the third century the production of grain in Britain was certainly enough to feed the population, and East Anglia has usually been thought of as a cereal-growing region. However, the traditional view that the Fens exported large amounts of grain northwards to Hadrian's Wall has more recently been modified. The corn which was exported across Fenland waterways was grown on the villa estates of the East Anglian upland. In some senses the landscape which they imply at, for example, Gaytonthorpe must have had similarities with the great corn farms that evolved on the Holkham Estate and elsewhere in the eighteenth century. Excavations carried out ahead of residential development in Hethersett, 8 km south-west of Norwich, have revealed the very well preserved base of a Roman drying kiln for corn, some 4 metres square. This emphasises not only that the Romans were growing corn in the area but also that drying the grain, a problem with which present-day farmers are familiar, was also a challenge for their Romano-British predecessors. But it is also known that there were large open grassland areas in Norfolk, which implies that stock rearing remained important. The Roman army needed huge supplies of leather and it is now thought that there were many sheep, providing wool for the making of the *byrrus Britannicus* (duffle coats) and *tapete Britannicum* (woollen rugs), as well as cattle kept for their meat and hides.[7]

On the coast and especially in the shallow tidal lagoons and inlets there were also fisheries, while another important element in the economy of the Great Estuary of east Norfolk, and especially of the Wash, was salt making. The Romans succeeded the Iceni as salt makers along the many estuaries of the Norfolk coast, carrying on the Iron Age enterprises already mentioned, while the Domesday Survey reveals that the industry was also flourishing in the eleventh century, suggesting continuity in economic activity spanning 1,500 years.[8] The only Norfolk salterns so far investigated are an example by the Fen Causeway in West Downham and a late Roman site at Middleton in the Nar Valley. In the latter case a splendid suggested reconstruction shows a sophisticated saltern oven. Crowson comments that 'the saltern has an overwhelming air of discipline about it as though its running was formally governed … evaporation techniques and equipment were the most sophisticated so far recorded in the Fenland', and it is clear that it produced large quantities of refined salt. The site, on the north bank of the tidal Nar and slightly raised above flood levels, was apparently fuelled by cut roundwood rather than by peat. Nearby was a deposit of gault clay, which was used both for constructing the oven bricks and also for pottery making. The oven has been dated from *c.*270 to *c.*330–55, the latter on coin evidence. By this date lead pans might have been used for evaporation. Perhaps the demand for fuel, and the consequent felling of woodland, led to the area becoming heathland by the middle of the fourth century, when the saltern ceased production. There were many other salterns in Lincolnshire around the fen edge, the best place for the supply of fuel and where there were many tidal channels. The Norfolk section of the Fen Causeway, from Upwell through Nordelph and Downham to Denver, has also been examined and out of 31 sites some 21 have been found to have burnt brick remains (briquetage). Silvester considers that all the sites may have been salterns. It is clear that salt making was an important element in the Roman economy of the Norfolk fens.

In the popular view a typical element of the Roman countryside was the villa, a term which has acquired an increasingly general meaning. To date sixteen such sites – large groups of sizeable buildings – have been discovered in Norfolk, mainly by means of aerial photography, and they are recognised as having been centres of farming estates. Gurney describes them as well-appointed farmhouses which showed aspirations to a Roman lifestyle, with such 'civilised' features as mosaics, wall plaster and hypocausts (underfloor heating systems). Associated with them were smaller dwellings and arable field systems. The map of Roman Norfolk on page 38 shows a line of villas running north to south, west of the Peddars Way and closer to the Icknield Way. The villas were built of chalk, flint and carstone as, for example, at Gaytonthorpe,[9] where there were two very similar buildings side by side. Lack of suitable building stone elsewhere in Norfolk meant that timber and wattle and plaster were used, perhaps on a plinth of flint which helped to prevent damp and guarded against the rotting of structural timbers. Great spreads of *teguli* (clay tiles) and sometimes *tesserae* from mosaic floors may be the only visible remains of buildings on these sites. Typical villas were colonnaded in the front with a line of rooms behind, a large dining room, or triclinium being in the centre of that range. A hypocaust provided warm air and also hot water for the bath house.

In the 1960s a new cut-off channel was constructed to skirt the Norfolk fen edge and stop floodwater from the west-flowing Norfolk rivers reaching the Great Ouse. At this time a rescue excavation near Feltwell revealed an important villa site beside the proposed channel, after a bath house had been excavated on its actual line.[10] A corridor, facing east, gave access to a sequence of rooms running north to south. The walls, unusually for Norfolk, were built of chalk blocks with brick bonding courses at intervals. The villa had floors of wood rather than tiles. A great many postholes were found, and these were thought to have been used for scaffolding rather than being part of the main structure. Greenfield interpreted the site as a fourth-century estate but also pointed out that villas such as this 'are only a small part of the Romano–British landscape and they should be seen in the context of the broader landscape which surrounds them'. This line of settlement reflects the junction between fen and upland, providing different types of agricultural land for sheep (reared primarily for their wool), cattle and a few pigs and horses, with the cereals grown on the drier uplands where small buildings or enclosures were scattered.

Compared with some other parts of southern and eastern England the villas of Norfolk were – as far as our present knowledge extends – relatively few in number and lacking the sometimes spectacular features found elsewhere, such as large and elaborate mosaics and complex and sophisticated landscaping. Here, as in other aspects of archaeological research, more may yet be revealed, but it is likely that Norfolk had a comparatively modest complement of villa sites. It was not yet, as it was to be in the medieval period, the richest part of England.

Caistor by Norwich and other towns

During the Roman period Caistor St Edmund or Caistor-by-Norwich, known to the Romans as *Venta Icenorum* ('the market town of the Iceni') was the most important town in Norfolk. A beautiful aerial photograph of the site taken in 1928 was a key moment in revealing the value of this new technology in archaeological research, but its local significance was the revelation of the grid plan of Roman Caistor, which was shown with extraordinary clarity. The site, with its abutting meadows and the surviving walls of flint and brick, is now in the hands of the Norfolk Archaeological Trust and provides a most evocative place in which to contemplate the Roman history of the county. As the recent work carried out by the Caistor Research Project, under the direction of Professor William Bowden, is beginning to show, much more detail is still to be revealed. His latest plan of Caistor is given here (page 44), incorporating the fascinating geophysical results of work carried out by David Bescoby. This, and a recent aerial photograph by Derek Edwards, show how much more information modern methods of investigation can reveal.[11]

Venta Icenorum, at Caistor by Norwich or Caistor St Edmund, was the most important Roman town in East Anglia, and served as the 'capital' of the former Icenian territories. Nothing now remains in the interior of the site, although aerial photography and excavation have revealed the full detail of its plan (since there was almost no post-Roman occupation), but the huge perimeter ramparts and short stretches of masonry walling remain. The impressive scale and height of the ramparts is shown in this view of the eastern side, taken from the deep wide ditch which runs on the outside of the bank on which the wall stood.

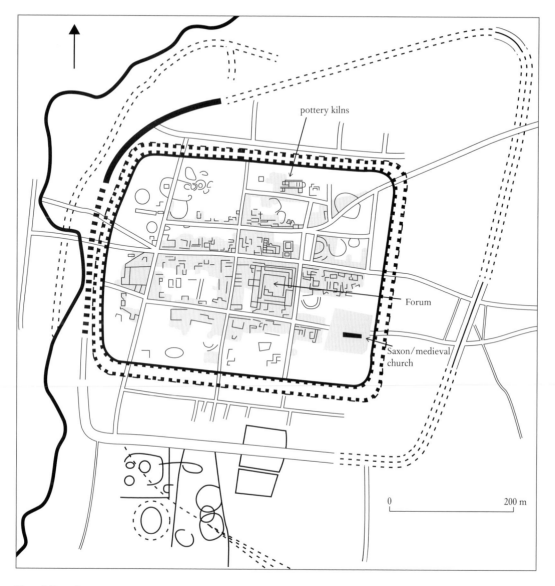

pottery kilns

Forum

Saxon/medieval church

0   200 m

Plan of *Venta Icenorum*, based upon information available in 2013 (after Bowden, 2010).

The main elements of this key Roman site must be stressed. The walled and ditched town lies three miles south of Norwich, on the east bank of the little River Tas, a tributary of the Yare. It has been suggested that, despite its small size today, in Roman times the river may have been navigable, at least for barges, as far as the town. In the first stage of its development, by *c.* AD 70, Caistor seems to have been a 'small cantonal capital and market town'.[12] By *c.*125 it had become both larger and more sophisticated, with a forum (market place) and basilica (town hall) in a central area, surrounded by a colonnaded façade. There were also public baths and pottery kilns, but apart from these buildings the rest were still of wattle and daub. The walls were rebuilt in about 190, but this was followed by a period of decay, lasting until a revival in about 280. During this later period glass making and metal working took place. The town had a water supply, drainage and sewerage systems, utilising springs and small streams on the eastern slope of the valley, flowing from the chalk at its junction with the Norwich Crag beds.

At Caistor there were two temples within the walls, together with one outside the walls to the south, and another to the north-east. Their layout was similar to that of another important temple at Crownthorpe near Wymondham.[13] A series of excavations around the site of the temple north-east of the walled town has revealed a *temenos* (holy area) of 2.5 hectares within which was a cobbled ambulatory, within which in turn was a *cella* (core area) with a tessellated floor containing a central series of altars. As yet there is no clear evidence as to which god or gods this cella was dedicated. Of the *temenos* Gurney concludes that 'this wall, with the monumental gateway located on a slope overlooking the Tas Valley and visible for a considerable distance, must have been an impressive and imposing sight when viewed from the northern approaches to the Roman town'. As the map of Roman Norfolk (page 38) shows, there were several other excavated temple sites and possible additional sites in the county, the valley of the Little Ouse being an especially important area, with Gallows Hill on the northern edge of Thetford of particular significance.

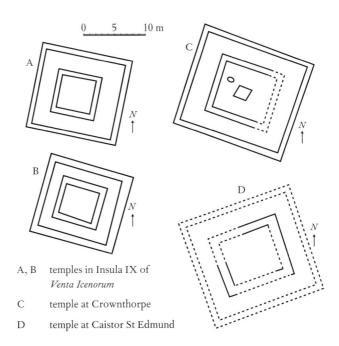

A, B   temples in Insula IX of *Venta Icenorum*

C   temple at Crownthorpe

D   temple at Caistor St Edmund

Plans of the Roman temples at *Venta Icenorum* and Crownthorpe.

It is not surprising that evidence of further important buildings is still coming to light in the region around Caistor. In 2005–07 what William Bowden describes as 'an intriguing site' was discovered 1.5 km south-east of the Roman town. It was 'an unusual winged building intersected by an aisled building'. The foundations were of rammed clay and chalk, suggesting that it had timber and clay-lump walls, with a thatched roof, and a date of the second to fourth centuries is suggested. A long line of twin postholes crosses the west wing, extending from about 20 to 40 metres to the west. There is also evidence of a 'corridor villa' to the north, and an aisled building to the north-east. The whole complex must have been a major rural establishment, similar to other sites such as Winterton and Mansfield Woodhouse in Nottinghamshire. The hilltop location suggests that it could have been a shrine or temple visible from some distance. Bowden concludes that the structure is a singular discovery in a region of England not known for architectural innovation during the Roman period.[14]

Caistor declined rapidly during the fourth century, and by 360 early Saxon cemeteries were located near to its walls. There is still much to find out about the period from 360 to 500, and the exciting new Caistor Research Project under the auspices of the University of Nottingham Archaeology Department aims to investigate both the Iron Age origins and the post-Roman use of the site of the town, as well as its successor village of Caistor St Edmund. An obvious question to ask of Caistor is why its site has remained largely undeveloped ever since the end of the Roman period, when nearly all the other major cantonal capitals, such as York, Winchester and Chester, lie underneath later county towns. The answer is surely that Norwich, which evolved in late Saxon times from a cluster of early settlements along the steep sides of the Wensum valley, stood on a fully navigable river, making it more accessible to trade than Caistor. In short, although Caistor had a good site, Norwich had an even better one, with conspicuous natural advantages. Perhaps one might turn the question round, to ask why the Romans did not make use of the site at Norwich? The answer to that may lie in the existence of a pre-Roman Icenian 'capital' at Caistor, which was adopted naturally as the focus of Roman administration.

The next most important urban site was Caister-by-Yarmouth, the port for east Norfolk and the probable terminus of the west–east road from the Fen Causeway via Billingford and Brampton. The only other walled town was at Brampton, south of Aylsham. It stood on the Norwich brick earth and was the site of at least 132 pottery kilns which produced large quantities of a grey sandy ware. Timber-lined wells and evidence of iron and bronze working have been found, together with the remains of wooden buildings and a bath house. The existence of this town, though long suspected, has only been confirmed and to some extent clarified by archaeological work in recent decades. Other small towns were situated along the main roads. Key sites included Scole, a forerunner of modern Diss, where only the edges of the settlement have been excavated: there were no ditches or walls but evidence of smelting, malting and tanning has been found. Another small town was Denver, where the Fen

The Roman fort at Caister-by-Yarmouth or Caister-on-Sea was built in about AD 200, on what was then a small island on the edge of the great estuary. It had been abandoned by about 380. Although not designed as such, it eventually played a part in the defensive system of 'Saxon Shore' forts which is best exemplified by Burgh Castle on the south side of Breydon Water. Only a small part of Caister's fort has been excavated, and much lies under the adjacent housing estates, but the foundations of barrack blocks and other buildings in the interior have been exposed.

Causeway met drier corn-growing country. At Billingford, a crossing point on the Wensum, no buildings have been found but evidence of iron-smelting, and 1,500 coins covering the whole of the Roman period, underline its importance.

Forts

Although not a heavily militarised area, Norfolk had several Roman forts, most of them clearly intended to serve in coastal defence. Burgh Castle was a major site, overlooking what was then a wider tidal estuary: the spit on which Yarmouth later developed had not yet grown across its entrance. The western wall of the fort has gone completely but the other three sides of the rectangle, built of flint and layers of tile, have survived to a remarkable degree. Indeed, this is one of the finest examples of a standing Roman structure anywhere in Britain. There is still much to find out about it, but between 1958 and 1961 three seasons of work directed by Charles Green revealed something of its Roman and Saxon history.[15] This fort appears to have been built on a greenfield site during the Constantinian period (AD 306–60). It has been claimed that it was constructed to house a garrison of *equites stablesiani* (cavalry), which would have been mobile enough to deal with the Saxon attacks which are thought to have prompted the establishment of the fort. A fine hoard of glassware dated to *c*.450 supports the idea that civilian and domestic occupation of the site continued long after the formal end of the Roman presence, which took place in 410.

It has been claimed that Burgh was *Gariannonum*, a site mentioned in the *Notitia Dignitatum*, a list of Roman official posts compiled in about 395. It is also thought to have been an early Christian monastic site, called *Cnobheresburg*. Green uncovered a mid-Saxon cemetery in the south-west corner of the fort, containing 164 inhumations. The burials lay west to east (the Christian orientation) and it was suggested that they related to the monastic site which is known from documentary evidence. However, more recent reinterpretations suggest that, given the range of people buried there (including women and children) it was in reality a community cemetery, rather than one belonging solely to a monastery. The argument that a Saxon church lay to the south of the cemetery has so far not been confirmed. The final stage in the life of the fort was the construction of a Norman motte in the south-west corner and this, according to Domesday Book, was in 1086 the manorial site of Ralph Ballistarius. So Burgh is a site that was in use, and subject to adaptation and building, from the late Roman period through the Saxon and into Norman times before its final abandonment in the twelfth century, a remarkable example of continuity over perhaps 700 years.

Opposite Burgh Castle lay the fort of Caister-on-Sea, on the northern side of the great estuary. Only a small part of the south-east corner has been excavated, but this demonstrated that it was an almost square, walled and ditched site, with buildings constructed of flints from up river and flint cobbles from the beaches further north. The fort at Caister existed before Burgh Castle, being built in the early third century if not before, and it was abandoned in about 370. Brancaster (*Branodunum*) was a Roman fort on the north coast. The

The Roman fort at Burgh Castle, just south-west of Great Yarmouth, is unusually well preserved. Along three sides the outer walling remains almost to its full height, although nothing is visible of the buildings which occupied the interior. The fort stands on a low cliff above the marshes of the Waveney and Yare where they combine to form Breydon Water, but when it was built in the early years of the fourth century it overlooked the broad estuary, up to six miles wide, which extended inland almost to the later site of Norwich. Burgh Castle (or *Gariannonum*) was a 'Saxon Shore' fort, part of a coastal defence system designed to deal with potential incursions from the other side of the North Sea.

At Burgh Castle, because so much of the Roman walling survives, it is particularly easy to see the construction methods. The walls consisted of massive quantities of raw unshaped flint nodules, held in place with thick mortar. At regular intervals a horizontal layer of thick poor-quality red tiling was placed, partly to give strength to the wall and partly to create an impressive appearance, for the flint layers were covered with a 'skin' of dressed and shaped flints within which the red tiles would have shown as dramatic brightly coloured horizontal bands.

Burgh Castle had a simple rectangular plan – though one side of the rectangle has fallen victim to coastal erosion – and its walls were reinforced at regular intervals by massive drum-like bastions. They were not part of the original design but were added halfway through construction – the awkward join between bastion and main wall is clearly seen in this view. Although the walls are almost full-height, they lack the parapet and wall-walk that once ran along the top, and much of the dressed flint and tile facing has long since been robbed.

seventeenth-century antiquarian Henry Spelman recorded that in about 1600 the stone walls were still standing, but now none survives. Sandstone facings from the fort are to be found in local buildings, especially in the churches. The fort is dated from c.225 to c.380. Outside the walls there is evidence for a *vicus*, or native settlement, and many animal bones have been found on the site.[16]

The line of what are usually known as the 'forts of the Saxon Shore' runs from Burgh Castle to Caister-by-Sea and on to Brancaster. The forts themselves were only one element in a more complex system of coastal defences. There is, for example, evidence of Roman signal stations on the key hilltop sites at

Iron Age and Romano-British sites in north-central Norfolk (after A. Gregory, 1986).

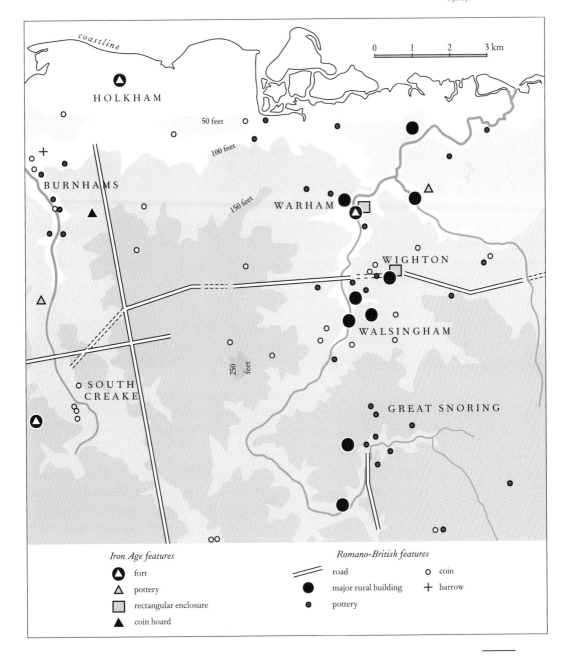

Warborough Hill, Stiffkey, Gramborough Hill, Salthouse, Muckleborough Hill and Kelling. At Reedham, situated at the entrance to the Chet, Yare and Waveney valleys, there is evidence of Roman blocks of the same sandstone reused in the church, suggesting that there may have been a fourth fort which would have guarded the upper estuary of the Yare.[17] These forts were manned by cavalry units for defence against attacks by Jutes, Frisians, Angles and Saxons, which were growing in frequency and intensity from the middle of the third century onwards. Davies also suggests that with their excellent accessibility for sea-going boats they were trading centres, from which goods could be transferred to small vessels and taken up river.

Such patterns of trade would foreshadow those between the great estuaries and the Rhine delta which were to be so important in the medieval period. In 1993 a major find of 27 late Roman gold *solidi* at Deopham near Wymondham emphasised the wealth of the region and, since the coins were struck in Trier in Germany, Sirmium on the Danube, and Milan, the find also demonstrates the considerable complexity of fourth-century trading patterns. Twenty-five of the known fourth-century coin hoards in Norfolk were buried in the area of the Waveney river system, on the eastern estuary, and on the western fen edge: did these reflect local wealth, buried for safety, or did incomers bury them?[18] We do not yet know for certain.

In AD 410 the Emperor Honorius withdrew the last Roman troops from England, but it is unclear whether by that time any military presence was left in Norfolk. This marked the formal end of any Roman jurisdiction in Great Britain, and from the early fifth century onwards Anglo–Saxon cemeteries appear in the archaeological record – for example, three have been found near *Venta Icenorum*. In his book *East Anglia*, written in 1960, Rainbird Clarke summarised the then prevailing view of the end of the Roman period:

> By 425 the grass was growing over the ruins of towns, forts and country mansions; Fenland farms, once the granary of Roman Britain, were abandoned because of flooding; elsewhere the peasantry were scratching a living from the soil side by side with barbarians who were constantly reinforced by compatriots from across the North Sea. This obvious collapse of the high culture of Roman Britain and return to conditions as primitive as any since Neolithic days heralded the period long known as 'The Dark Ages'.

Certainly, the volume and range of written historical evidence decline markedly in this period. However, as the next chapter explains, the traditional view of the Dark Ages has been modified substantially in the past half-century. Current interpretations, based on a wealth of new archaeological and historical research, suggest that the immediate post-Roman period was not as 'dark' as was once thought.

4

Norfolk under the
Anglo Saxons and Vikings

B Y virtue of its location – facing across the North Sea to the shores of
Denmark and north Germany – Norfolk experienced the influence of the
Anglo-Saxon world earlier than almost any other part of the British Isles. As
Roman power started to wane, during the third and fourth centuries AD, some
Angles and Saxons began to arrive on British shores. East Anglia was a natural
destination for such migration, which though as yet small was clearly of the most
profound significance. We have evidence that from about AD 350 Saxons were

Date	Kings of East Anglia/England	Key events
410–650		end of Roman influence; early Saxon colonisation; cremation burials (e.g. Spong Hill); 'ham' place-names
590–625	Raedwald	Sutton Hoo burials (Suffolk)
630–670	Sigbehrt	Christian conversion: bishopric of East Anglia (based at Dunwich)
638	Anna	one of Anna's daughters is Etheldreda, foundress of Ely Abbey
673–680		Bishops of East Anglia have their seat at Elmham
749	Hun, Beonna and Alberht	division of the kingdom of east Anglia
mid-8th century		Ipswich Ware the dominant form of pottery; 'ton' place-names
850 – 1100		Thetford Ware produced
855–869	Edmund	killed by the Danes in 869
871–896		first main phase of Viking invasions; collapse of diocese
880–890	Guthram	first Danish king of East Anglia
890–902	Eric (Eohric)	
917		West Saxons conquer East Anglia and take it from Danish rule
899–925	Edward the Elder	first Norwich mint
955		re-establishment of diocese, based at North Elmham
980		first documentary reference to Norwich
1004		the Danes sack Norwich and Thetford
1013–1014	Swein Forkbeard	de facto, first Danish king of England
1016–1935	Cnut	king of England, Norway and Denmark; 'by' place-names; Cnut refounds St Benet's Abbey
c.1040		first documentary reference to Norfolk
1042	Edward the Confessor	
1066		Thetford the fifth or sixth largest town in England
1071–1085		Bishop Herfast moves diocesan seat from Elmham to Thetford
1091–1119		Herbert de Losinga, Bishop of Thetford (to 1094) and then of Norwich

coming to Norfolk, some of them to be employed in the Roman army. After the beginning of the fifth century, when the Roman Empire finally relinquished its already limited control and influence in Britain, the peoples of northern Europe came in increasing numbers – there was a political and economic vacuum to be filled. As the great historian Bede described three centuries later, drawing upon oral history which was only ten generations old, the colonisers were from three related but distinct groups of people: the Jutes, whose name survives in modern Jutland; the Angles (who, we now know, came from the areas on the margins of Denmark and Germany, and south-westwards towards the Dutch border); and the Saxons, from the lands between the Elbe and the Ems known ever after as Saxony. The Angles, organised into what contemporary chroniclers term (using the Latin word) *comitates*, or 'bands of followers', soon came not in small groups but as a large-scale colonising movement, sending ships to Britain and landing at Ebbesfleet near Sandwich in Kent in 449.[1] Before very long an Anglo-Saxon ruling order may have controlled the existing Romano-Celtic population, at least in the south and east of what was fast becoming England (*Angle-land*), and early Anglo-Saxon place-names reflect the influence of this ruling group as earlier communities were absorbed between perhaps 400 and 550.

The major source of evidence for the study of the Anglo Saxons in the period immediately after 410 is their cemeteries, and the associated burial practices and grave goods. Cemeteries of the pagan period (that is, before the conversion to Christianity which took place in the years after 597) are mainly found in lowland Britain – especially south-east England and East Anglia – and,

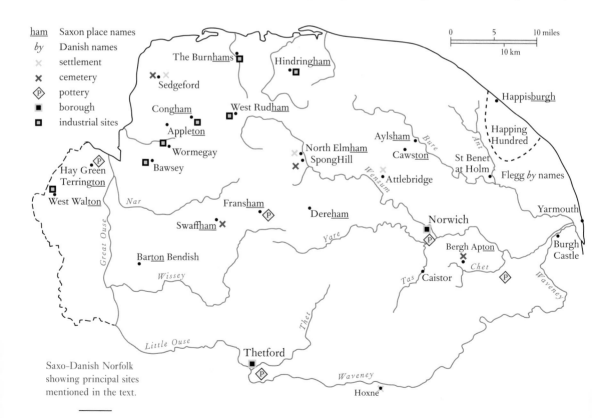

Saxo-Danish Norfolk
showing principal sites
mentioned in the text.

_____

as the map on page 52 shows, significant numbers of such sites have been located in Norfolk.[2] Their distribution suggests a continuous line of settlement down the Fen edge and in the valleys of the northward-flowing rivers, but they also occur on the boulder-clay plateau at sites such as Bergh Apton south of Norwich and, outstandingly, at Spong Hill in North Elmham parish. Over 2,000 burial urns for cremated ashes and 58 inhumations (burials of the uncremated body in graves, as at Sutton Hoo) were excavated from Spong Hill between 1972 and 1976.[3] The complex patterns on the exteriors of the urns have provoked much discussion, with questions that cannot as yet be answered with confidence. Were these the distinctive and distinguishing marks of communities or families? For how long were cremation burials typical of this site? And how large was the early Saxon population? One Saxon settlement lay a little farther up the valley of the Blackwater River, and many Roman sites, including the town of Billingford, lay to the east, so there is considerable debate about the geographical extent of the area served by the great Spong Hill cemetery. It seems clear that its siting was not accidental, but was governed at least in part by the existing importance of this area. The early Christian cathedral at North Elmham, founded c.670, lies in the same parish just to the north of Spong Hill – and the immediate vicinity has evidence of earlier Neolithic and Bronze Age settlement, prior to the Iron Age and Roman periods. This hillside was an area of human activity from 6000 BC to AD 700.

At Bergh Apton, six miles south of Norwich, a different sort of cemetery was excavated on a site which had already been damaged by quarrying and ahead of further quarrying.[4] In this case 63 inhumations were uncovered, from which large quantities of grave goods were retrieved. These included domestic as well as ornamental items: thus, Grave 6 had a fine collection of metal brooches as well as 13 amber beads and surviving evidence of 'tabby fabric', in which the oxide replacement of fibres had preserved the form of the fabric, 'leaving a cast in which spinning and weaving details can be seen'.[5] Tabby fabrics were made on a warp-weighted loom requiring a single heddle rod.[6]

From the contents of the urns at Spong Hill and the inhumations at Bergh Apton some idea of the crafts and skills of the Anglo Saxons – their material culture and technological development – can be realised. At Spong Hill some categories of grave goods were burned at the time of cremation, while others appear to have been placed in the urns later. The range of goods found is remarkable and includes, among others, cruciform brooches; toilet sets containing tweezers; iron shears, full size and miniature; many bronze objects; iron tools and arrow heads; crystal beads, glass beads, and glass vessels; bone playing pieces; and spindle whorls. The excavators analysed the pattern of the urn pot markings and the contents of the vast number of urns and concluded that the variety of metals used, the crystal beads, glass objects, and complex uses of iron all betoken a society within which many skilled crafts existed: 'It is at least clear from the high proportion of early material that the cemetery came into use near the beginning of the Anglo Saxon settlement and that a substantial population existed to continue to use it throughout most of the pagan and Saxon period.'[7]

The best-excavated Saxon settlement (rather than cemetery) in Norfolk is also at North Elmham. This site is exceptional in that during six years of excavation led by Dr Peter Wade-Martins a cluster of high-status buildings was found to the south-west of the Anglo-Saxon 'cathedral',[8] only a few hundred yards north of the Spong Hill cemetery. The special interest of this location is that it is generally believed to have been the seat of the bishopric of East Anglia from c.680. The origins of the so-called 'cathedral', a striking building constructed of flint and large quantities of iron conglomerate, have been much debated – it is now known to be the chapel of Bishop Herbert de Losinga, c.1091–1119, and that an earlier timber cathedral lay beneath it. Why this site was chosen as the centre of the East Anglian diocese is not certain, but it has been suggested that its proximity to the important Spong Hill cemetery site may be relevant and that it involved the continued use of a revered pagan site through into the Christian period. There is no Early Saxon evidence beneath or near the present building, but the major excavations at North Elmham aimed to clarify the history of the structure which has for over 200 years been called the 'cathedral'. They revealed a remarkable sequence of important buildings, and the reconstruction by David Yaxley, below, shows one which could well be the first timber cathedral.

The size and number of related buildings emphasised the significance of the site and suggests that this was perhaps a royal settlement. Wall-posts were set in foundation trenches in these buildings, which appear to have been timber-framed in oak with hipped roofs. Hazel wattles and daub or Roman

Plans of excavated buildings at North Elmham (after P. Wade Martins).

Reconstruction of building Z2 at North Elmham (by D. Yaxley).

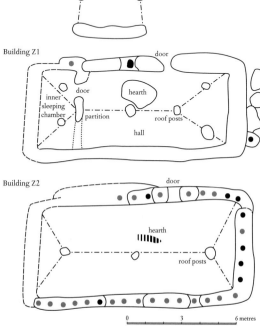

The ruins at North Elmham were long thought to be those of the Anglo-Saxon cathedral, but it is now known that although the cathedral was on this site it was of timber and was demolished in about 1100, thirty years after the diocesan seat moved to Thetford and six years after it had then shifted to Norwich. The site was then redeveloped, in the first decade of the twelfth century, with a large and architecturally ambitious stone chapel which served Bishop Herbert de Losinga's nearby palace. This is the building whose ruins survive today, although in the late fourteenth century there were considerable alterations when the chapel was converted into a small stone castle.

tile fragments were used to fill in between the posts; the exteriors were coated with clay daub, and the roofs were thatched; and there is evidence of internal sub-divisions. Of the buildings excavated by Wade-Martins, and shown on the plan on page 54, that labelled A dated from the late seventh century and the two buildings labelled Z were of the eighth century; there were also later eighth- and early ninth-century buildings. There was relatively limited dating evidence other than the buildings themselves, but the pottery found was primarily Ipswich ware (that is, of mid-Saxon date, c.600–800). The area was ravaged by the Danish invasions, but during the subsequent period of recovery a new cathedral was established and the bulk of the excavated area became the Christian cemetery serving an extensive religious site. The history of the diocese itself is considered in more detail later in this chapter.

A much smaller site at Attlebridge was excavated in 1989.[9] It comprised a Romano-British ring ditch which lay just to the north of late Anglo-Saxon buildings. One of these, designated no.3, was 7.75 metres by 4.75 metres with posts set in foundation trenches. The other three had paired posts but no corner posts. Some 28 sherds of Thetford ware (which was produced from about 850 to the end of the eleventh century) were recovered. These buildings are interpreted as a rural domestic settlement, exactly the sort of grouping we should regard as typical of much of the county by c.800.

The cemetery evidence for the Middle Saxon period (c.650–850) is notably different from that of the Early Saxon. The earlier practice of disposing of the dead by cremation gave way to Christian burials, in which the body was placed intact in a grave. That was not unknown before the Christian period, but was very much more unusual. Now it became the standard practice. Furthermore, whereas pre-Christian interments often include substantial quantities of grave goods, in the Christian period this became ever less common. Three late Roman sites – Caistor St Edmund, Caister-by-Yarmouth and Burgh Castle – and, of increasing importance, Sedgeford in north-west Norfolk all have closely associated Anglo-Saxon cemeteries (in the case of Burgh Castle, within the Roman fort). Rogerson suggests that by the eighth and ninth centuries nearly every Norfolk parish shows evidence of Saxon activity.[10]

Recent archaeological work in the county has revealed a group of what are referred to as 'productive sites' or industrial locations.[11] These sites have yielded many coins and much metalwork and, although their nature and origins are still debated, they seem to have been meeting places or to have functioned as informal markets. Although it is clear from the map that the seven such sites in north-west Norfolk did not progress to become even small market towns in the medieval period, it is essential to recognise that any of the present market towns – places such as East Dereham, Fakenham, or North Walsham – may have had such origins, all trace of which has been concealed from our gaze because of their later intensive development. The urban hierarchy was not fixed, and some places may have flourished for several centuries before being superseded by later locations. In that context Bawsey is a particularly fascinating case, with its ruined Norman church standing upon a promontory of higher ground east of King's Lynn. Iron Age torcs, Roman material, more than 50 Anglo-Saxon coins dating from the seventh to the mid-ninth centuries, many metal finds, and quantities of eighth- and ninth-century Ipswich ware all point to intensive use of the site in that period and for many centuries before. Of course, Lynn did not then exist, so perhaps Bawsey was its predecessor as a trading place, eventually eclipsed by the growth of the medieval new town to the west.

The evidence of pottery can often be invaluable in helping to date sites. In the Mid Saxon phase a type of pottery known as Ipswich ware – so called because the only known kilns for this ware were in Ipswich – became widespread. Dating from c.725 to c.850, pieces were made on a turntable and fired in a kiln at a high temperature to produce ware that is usually mid to dark grey in colour.[12] Large concentrations of this pottery have been found at Hay Green in Terrington St Clement, Fransham in central Norfolk, and the Chet Valley from Loddon downstream. These three areas have been intensively field-walked, and the quantity of finds reflects the more detailed investigation. Finds have come from other parts of the county, although overall the central boulder-clay plateau and the Broads show the lowest density. Further field-walking in other areas may yet change this general picture. The Hay Green site in the Fens revealed clear evidence of pastoralism, the growing of wheat and barley, and the production of salt in the many tidal creeks on the southern edge of the Wash. The Late Saxon phase (c.850–1066) saw the introduction of Thetford ware, a well-fired, wheel-thrown, hard sandy grey pottery which was quite widely produced. Thetford was the main site for its manufacture, but it was also made in Norwich, Ipswich and many rural sites. It was the standard type of pottery in Norfolk from c.900 to 1100.

By 750 there were settlements of some kind in virtually every one of the county's future parishes. In many instances these settlements took the form of clusters of rectangular huts round a large hall, together with one or two farmsteads; many also had a watermill. On the boulder-clay plateau the woodland was much thicker and more extensive than it is today, but small clearings were being carved out of it, sometimes recalled by modern place-names, as at Wood Dalling and Wood Norton. Although every place was different in detail, common characteristics are apparent from the archaeological, documentary and physical record. The farmsteads, often sited just above the flood level of the flat valley floors, had field systems which stretched up the valley slopes behind and were ploughed by teams of oxen (perhaps shared between several farms). Common grazings shared the wet riverside meadows, and there were cleared woodlands and heaths where bees were kept. The extent to which common fields, with their complex sub-divisions of furlongs and strips, already existed, is a major subject of debate. Cattle, sheep and goats grazed the pastures and provided skins, wool and meat. Sheep flocks were largest on the chalklands of west Norfolk and in those Fenland parishes which had dried out sufficiently – a pattern well revealed by the map of Freebridge Hundred, which plots the distribution of sheep and woodland as recorded in the Domesday Book of the late eleventh century. Wheat, barley, oats and rye were grown, and local trade patterns were developing, between rural areas and emergent market centres, and also between the market places themselves. Trade in specialised produce such as pottery, leather or metalwork, increasingly involved the use of coinage for payment.

From about 700 documentary evidence begins to supplement the picture derived from archaeological investigation. Bede (who was born in about 671

Freebridge Hundred in 1086, showing churches, sheep and woodland mentioned in the Domesday Book.

and died in 735) produced one of the greatest studies of our early history –
the *Ecclesiastical History of the English Nation* – a few years before his death.
The *Anglo-Saxon Chronicles* provide a later, longer and more detailed account,
running from about 871 to 1154. This source tells us, for example, of the
destruction of Norwich by the Danish king Swein (father of the more famous
Cnut) in 1004. Another local source, the *Book of Ely*, noted in about 980 that
Norwich was a civilised town.[13]

The political origins of East Anglia, and of Norfolk and Suffolk, are
shrouded in a good deal of mystery, but the growing quantity of written sources
allows at least some of the story to be sketched. The first ruler of the East
Anglian kingdom was, as far as can be ascertained, Raedwald (up to about 620),
a member of the Wuffing dynasty. The first bishop of East Anglia, close in time
to Raedwald's reign, was St Felix, who founded the diocese in about 630, at a
place called *Dommoc*, which is most probably Dunwich, with land provided by
king Sigbehrt. By 680, though, East Anglia had been split into two dioceses,
probably based at Dunwich and at North Elmham. This may have been the
point at which the northern half of the kingdom became known as Norfolk ('the
[land of] the North Folk') and the southern as Suffolk – though, as Williamson
points out, the first surviving written reference to Norfolk does not appear until
the 1040s, when 'one Thurstan bequeathed all his possessions in Norfolke'.

During the Danish Wars of the ninth century the twin bishoprics of
East Anglia disintegrated, the focus of ecclesiastical power having shifted
from place to place in the preceding decades as administration became ever
more problematic. Bishops were probably based, for periods, at *Dommoc*
(Dunwich), Hoxne, South Elmham and North Elmham, but eventually all
Church organisation collapsed. When the wars abated, administrative and
spiritual authority could be re-established. The first bishop of the revived
see of East Anglia, covering both Norfolk and Suffolk, was Athulf, whose
diocesan seat from about 955 was North Elmham. In 1071 the first Norman
bishop, Herfast, moved the see to Thetford and in 1094 Herbert de Losinga
transferred it once again, this time to Norwich, where it has remained for more
than a thousand years.

Under the late Saxon kings most individual counties had a sheriff (the title
is a corruption of 'shire reeve') whose main task was to collect taxes due to
the Crown, and to be responsible for key aspects of law and order. However,
Norfolk and Suffolk, just as they had a joint diocese, also shared a sheriff.
This probably reflects the aftermath of the Danish Wars, when the whole of
the administrative structure had disintegrated and had to be reconstructed as
quickly as possible. Even so, it is clear that by the end of the tenth century
Norfolk was becoming officially recognised as a distinct and separate political
unit, with a formal identity of its own.

Beneath the level of county government, as it emerged in the decades
before the Norman Conquest, were administrative and political sub-divisions
whose origins can be traced to two separate processes. As royal authority was
established after about 700 some areas of land were allocated to key followers
of the king or to important institutions, so that a series of large estates was

created. In some cases, as with Mitford (which was given to the abbey of Ely), a separate hundred then evolved from that estate. The tax known as geld, collected under Danish rule, established a fiscal and administrative system which the later Anglo-Saxon and Norman kings continued and maintained. Roughly comparable areas were established from which this tax could be collected. These may have been former royal estates, or alternatively were the territorial districts of former 'folk' or sub-tribes: for example, the territory of a 'folk' called the Happingas, in East Norfolk and with its centre at Happisburgh, became the later hundred of Happing. Erpingham seems to have had a similar origin and a comparable unity, though it was eventually split into two hundreds, north and south. Some have suggested, from the name of the administrative unit, that hundreds may have represented areas capable of producing 100 fighting men, while others have argued that they consisted of one hundred hides of ploughland (a hide equals 120 acres). Land quality must have affected this process of division because the small, densely populated hundreds in East Norfolk contrast with the larger ones in the west, where population density was lower. Whatever the origins of particular units, the structure of hundreds meant that after 1066 the Normans had a ready-made taxation structure of 36 hundreds for their use, and the Domesday Book of 1086 was based on this framework (see map on page 61).

Place-names as a guide to settlement

The evidence of the Domesday Book shows that most of Norfolk's place-names were in existence in 1086, the majority being of Anglo-Saxon origin and the bulk of the remainder from the Danish period of occupation and settlement between 870 and 1035. Of approximately 700 named settlements, 110 have since disappeared or were absorbed into larger units by 1316,[14] but Hallam calculated that only 17 new settlements were named after 1086.[15]

It is now accepted that the place-name element 'ham' very often relates to places which had an early importance. It is often taken to mean simply a village or settlement, Williamson pointing out that *hams* can be long (Langham) or broad (Bradenham) but that they are rarely related by direction to another place. But the fact that these places were often of more than purely local significance is now generally agreed: North Walsham, for example, was the focus of twelve vills and was perhaps an early royal estate given by Cnut to the Church when founding St Benet's Abbey. Six of these subordinate vills have 'ton' names, which suggests that they were subsidiary settlements within one great estate. Another, Westwick ('the western dairy farm'), may have been subsidiary to either Walsham or its neighbouring vill of Worstead. Sometimes the same name was used for several settlements in the same district, and a means of distinguishing them had to be found: thus, the second part of the name Swanton Abbot distinguishes it from three other Norfolk Swantons, as it belonged to the abbey of St Benet. The name Swafield implies open land (*feld*), and this settlement perhaps originated as a cleared area north of Walsham.

The element 'ton', meaning a small settlement or farm, often occurs and sometimes includes a point of the compass – for example, Norton Subcourse,

Easton, Weston Longville and Sutton. These 'tons' appear to be secondary settlements, defined in relation to more important places. Many other place-names refer to economic specialisation: for example, Horsey means the horse island, and Winterton and Somerton provide evidence of seasonal occupation. Mulbarton means 'an outlying milk farm' (*meolc beretuna*); Roughton was a 'rye growing settlement', and Bickerston a bee-keeping settlement. The type of stock kept may also be revealed, as in Keswick (the cheese farm), Oxwick, and Guestwick (the 'goat farm'). 'Wicks' in this sense are very small and late settlements, probably Danish in origin.

Under the Danish administration that functioned from about 870 to 1035 the east Norfolk hundreds were probably reorganised, and during that period of nearly 200 years there was considerable Danish settlement in the eastern part of the county. The remarkable density of 'by' place-names (the Danish element meaning 'village' or 'settlement') in the two hundreds of the Fleggs has no parallel elsewhere in the county: there are 21 of them in that limited area. Many of these were very small settlements and a number have subsequently disappeared. In nearly every case a small church, perhaps initially built of timber, remains or has been revealed by aerial photography, as at Ormesby St Peter. The settlements may have carried the names of individuals, the founders of these communities. The name element 'thorpe', also of Danish origin, occurs 41 times in Norfolk, often as a subsidiary to a bigger settlement such as Burnham Thorpe or Honingham Thorpe. 'Kirk', the word for 'church' (as in Kirby Cane) also gives a clue to Scandinavian origins. The Danish origins of Norwich itself are considered in more detail later in this chapter.

The names of Norfolk's hundreds pose interesting problems of derivation. Although 'ham' names are thought to be of early importance, only the hundreds of Holt and Diss carry the name of their central place, and neither is of course a 'ham'. Wymondham counted as a half hundred, part of the whole hundred of Forehoe. But the names of several hundreds point not to settlements but to key meeting points at ancient sites: for example, Forehoe means the four burial mounds, and Grimshoe and Greenhoe also imply burial mounds as focal points. The hundred of Guiltcross was so named because its meeting place was at the site of an early preaching cross. Mitford, Eynsford and Depwade were key river-crossing points within their hundreds – but exactly why Humbleyard, the place where bees gathered, was chosen as a meeting place remains a mystery!

The local Church, 500 to 1066

Two strands of Christianity spread through western Europe from Rome in the early seventh century. One was the structured form of Church administration and organisation, based on bishoprics, beneath which were parishes which evolved from the network of preaching priests. The other, which had only a limited impact in East Anglia, was the monastic form where visionary monks established self-contained and usually isolated monastic communities. These were numerous on the west coast of the British Isles, a good example being the famous site on Iona, while on the east coast Lindisfarne was a focus of

Christianity for many generations. In Norfolk, at Burgh Castle, the Irish monk St Fursey founded the monastic site of *Cnobheresburg* in the bounds of the old Roman fort, and there were other monasteries at Blythburgh and Iken in Suffolk.

In 597 Augustine was sent to Britain by Pope Gregory to convert the English, and – having successfully persuaded the royal family of Kent to change faith – became the first archbishop of Canterbury. In due course Felix came from Burgundy to become the first bishop of East Anglia, the unity of that kingdom having been established under Raedwald. The archaeological evidence which was revealed at the celebrated ship mound at Sutton Hoo, in which Raedwald was buried, demonstrated that his beliefs were part-pagan and part-Christian. He, or a successor, established Felix at *Dommoc* (probably Dunwich), and from there priests began to spread out and convert the kingdom; Felixstowe and Flixton in Suffolk carry the name of the founder of East Anglian Christianity. The history of the East Anglian diocese has been outlined above, but we can now turn to the local churches, of which Norfolk has a quite exceptional number and variety.

Outside the focus of the bishop's church and palace the Church spread its influence under the protection of the local lords who adopted Christianity. Minster churches were founded, the focal points from which the word was spread in each locality. They were subsidiary to the cathedral and its bishop, but had a major significance as the places from which further expansion of the Church took place – perhaps initially by the placing of a preaching cross in a settlement, which served until a local lord, or maybe the community, built the

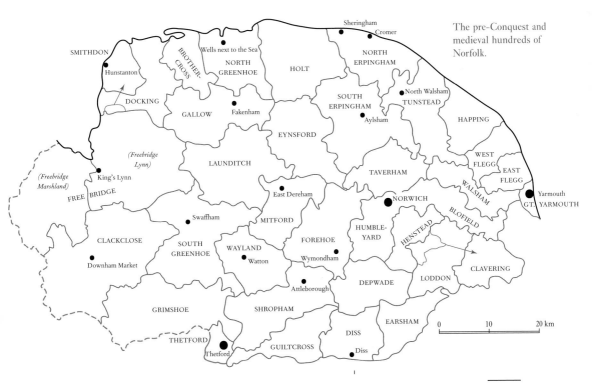

The pre-Conquest and medieval hundreds of Norfolk.

church. These minsters, which were endowed with their 'parishes', derived an income from the glebe, the land allotted to provide for the priest, and tithes (one-tenth of the annual gain from the agricultural land). Gradually, as the Christian message spread to smaller lordships, new parishes were founded as sub-divisions of the minster's territory. In Norwich, for example, several churches founded after 1066 still paid some of their tithes to St Clement and to St Lawrence until the end of the Middle Ages, because their small parishes had been carved out of these earlier large parishes. By the early ninth century most settlements in Norfolk probably had a church made of wood, in appearance much like the hall of a principal landowner. Some churches in Denmark give a good idea of those which must have existed in pre-Conquest Norfolk, as does that at Greensted in Essex, with its timber frame and weatherboard exterior.

The typical Anglo-Saxon church plan had a west tower, a nave and an apsidal chancel. There are examples of this form at Hales and Heckingham,

Hales church, near Loddon, is early Norman but with some traces of Anglo-Saxon work – in practice the difference between the two is minimal. It stands in a delightfully grass-grown churchyard in glorious isolation, almost a mile from the village, and half a century ago was described by Pevsner as 'a perfect Norman village church'. The round tower may be partly Anglo-Saxon but there is no doubt about the rest – built around 1100 and with a sequence of round-arched windows and arcades wrapping round the east end. In the thirteenth century some pointed windows were punched through some of the early Norman work, an early instance of architectural vandalism. Inside there are medieval wall paintings, and the thatched roof adds to the sense of antiquity.

Given the generally modest and homely quality of Hales church it comes as a surprise to find that the early Norman south door is a superlative piece of sophisticated design and craftsmanship, with its riot of zigzags and other decorative motifs, a beautiful frieze (or 'hood mould') of spoked wheels over the arch, and capitals and decorated surfaces framing the doorway. It is hard to avoid the feeling that the craftsman-designer allowed his fertile imagination free rein when working on this masterpiece nine hundred years ago.

Heckingham church is almost the twin of that at Hales, and it seems certain that the same master mason worked on both churches. Unlike Hales it has lost all but one of its early Norman windows and arcading at the east end, and its tower is only partly Norman as the upper octagonal section is a much later rebuilding.

The south doorway at Heckingham is, like that at Hales, a masterpiece of inventiveness. In this close-up view of the capitals of the stone doorframe we see the extraordinary intricacy of the detail, including the peppering of tiny holes in geometric patterns, and the bands of deeply incised zigzags along the outer edges of the capitals themselves.

although both of these probably just post-date the Conquest. Some, perhaps early minsters, have a central tower (as at Newton by Castle Acre, Fundenhall and South Lopham). The double-splayed windows and the circular windows often show evidence of having been built around a wickerwork frame. But dating remains difficult because it is now apparent that the arrival of the Normans did not immediately change the way in which masons carried out their commissions. Only slowly did single-splay windows, decorated Norman doorways, flat pilasters and zig-zag string courses became *de trop*. Relatively few Norfolk parish churches have surviving pre-Norman fabric. It has long been suggested that round towers, that distinctive form so typical of rural Norfolk, are pre-Norman, but this is now regarded as questionable. Other supporting evidence, such as triangular bell openings and 'long and short work' (the alternating stone quoins of windows and walls) are now demanded as proof for such antiquity. Pevsner and Wilson suggest that there are 22 examples of pre-Conquest churches in the county, from over 700 parishes existing at the time of the Norman Conquest. This is much more than in most other English counties, but it is still a small minority. They note that 'at Forncett St Peter is a complete pre-Conquest tower with rings of circular windows and other features', and suggest that Breccles and Witton churches may also be late-Saxon.

As archaeological work on church sites is undertaken it becomes apparent not only that most existing churches stand on pre-Norman remains and were initially of timber, but also that from the early eleventh century these were being rebuilt in flint, sometimes also with the use of imported stone. The church of St Martin at Palace in Norwich has been fully excavated, and its first timber framework was dated to the late Saxon period. Two stages of timber building were identified and one burial, assumed to have been in the church, was dated to the middle Saxon period (550–770). This argues for an early church on this site close to the river Wensum,[16] perhaps founded not long after the conversion of the East Angles which took place from the 620s onwards.

After the Viking destruction of the early monasteries at Ely, Peterborough, Bury St Edmunds and St Benet at Holm, there was a revival at all those places. The rebuilding of St Benet's was undertaken around 1019 with the patronage of King Cnut (1016–35). On an island at the edge of what later became the Broads, this ancient site, with its surviving gatehouse (with a later mill inserted) and a spread of walls and earthworks, is still wonderfully evocative of its origins a thousand years ago. At the Dissolution of the Monasteries in the late 1530s the lands of the abbot of St Benet were exchanged with those of the bishops of Norwich, so by a technical oversight the monastery remained in the hands of the bishop and has never been dissolved; the bishop of Norwich still holds an annual service on the site of the abbey. Cnut endowed the abbey with many neighbouring churches, thus confirming that they already existed by the beginning of the eleventh century – examples include the churches of North Walsham, Swanton Abbot and Hoveton.

The Viking period

The terms 'Viking', 'Scandinavian', 'Norwegian' and 'Dane' are all used fairly loosely, both by historians and in popular literature. The peoples involved in this period of our history came from Norway, southern Sweden and Denmark, but the Vikings have, for many centuries, been regarded as invaders who simply went plundering, pillaging, burning and raping. That view has, for several decades, been challenged by historians and archaeologists, but it remains an abiding image. The Vikings might have been either of Norwegian or Danish origin, but it was essentially the latter who bore down upon eastern and south-eastern England: initially they destroyed and subsequently they settled, but in their attacks after 850 they put an end to the period of early Christian culture.

There were two main phases of 'Viking' settlement in Britain. The first began with an attack on Portland in Dorset in about 789 and reached its peak with the killing of King Edmund of East Anglia in 869. During this period

East Anglia, including Norfolk, gradually came under Danish rule (known to posterity as the Danelaw). Early Benedictine monasteries such as those at Ely and St Benet's were destroyed, and the structures of Christian belief were swept aside, to be replaced by pagan gods. Yet Stenton wrote that the great host which invaded England in 865 turned, at the very beginning of their settlement, from war to agriculture and that the chief concern of its people was to live in accordance with their own customs on the lands which they had won.[17] The size of 'the great host' must always be a matter of debate; current views reduce the picture and suggest it was not a massive fleet, a 'D-Day invasion'. The Danes were superb sailors and built great longboats. These skills allowed them to settle the coast and penetrate the river systems of Norfolk, Suffolk and Essex. As already noted, place-name evidence suggests that the greatest area of Danish settlement was the two hundreds of Flegg and elsewhere in East Norfolk where the -by component is commonly found. Further north and west in Norfolk there are many names where a Scandinavian first name (that is, the name of a Scandinavian landowner) has been linked to the Saxon '-ton'. These are known, from the classic example, as 'Grimston hybrids' and seem to indicate that a Danish occupier took over an existing estate, renamed it for himself, but left the basic structure of the settlement undisturbed.

A second phase of Viking invasions came in the late tenth century, during the long and troubled reign of Aethelred II (better known as Ethelred the Unready), from 978 to 1016. The *Anglo-Saxon Chronicle* reports that 'in 1004 Swein came with his fleet to Norwich, ravaged all the borough and burned it down … the force came to Thetford within three weeks of ravaging Norwich and were there for one night, ravaged the borough and burned it down.'[18] These invasions and their reported ferocity are only one aspect of the Viking arrival. The Danes extracted huge tributes from the Anglo Saxons in 994, 1002, 1007 and 1012, and then in 1018 Cnut raised a further amount to pay off his army, and finally in 1040 Cnut's son, Harthacnut, imposed the last such exaction. It is estimated that £250,000 (many billions of pounds in modern terms) was paid by the English to the Vikings. The widespread distribution of Scandinavian place-names and the large number of what are known as 'sokemen' (privileged tax-paying residents) recorded in east Norfolk suggest a later settlement phase following the early raids. It has been suggested that sokemen status resulted 'from Danish settlement and as descendants of the demobbed Danish army'.[19]

Towns in Norfolk

The Anglo-Saxon/Viking period saw the emergence of towns as focal points where an aristocratic class could control the trade in prestige goods. In different parts of southern England entrepots (known as *wics*) emerged: in the West Saxon kingdom there was *Hamwic*, the forerunner of Southampton; *Eoferwic* (York) served the Northumbrians; and from the beginning of the seventh century *Gippeswic* (Ipswich), on the north bank of the Orwell, served East Anglia. By about 750 craft and trading areas spread to the north of the Ipswich quays; evidence for weaving, metal and leather work has been found in excavations. It may well be that Norwich (the *north-wic*) became the entrepot for the northern part of East Anglia, complementing the role of Ipswich for the South Folk. Excavations in Fishergate in Norwich, on the north bank of the Wensum, have shown large quantities of Ipswich ware, but it is clear that initially Ipswich was the more important of the two centres.

If we move forward two centuries, the existence or otherwise of market towns in the middle of the eleventh century is an important historical issue. Apart from Norwich, Thetford and Yarmouth, only one other market is mentioned in the Domesday Book – at the royal manor of Holt – but two other enigmatic entries, for half a market in Great Dunham and a quarter of a market in Litcham, suggest that others may have existed but remained unrecorded.[20] Where might they have been? It is possible that West Walton, a manor held by Ely Abbey, was one such, originating as a trading point at the mouth of the river Nene opposite Wisbech (which was also a major Ely manor after 1000).[21] Pestell argues that sites at Hindringham and Wormegay may have been centres of early large estates, and by implication market centres, though neither 'succeeded' later. Very often the growth of new and important market towns was bound up with questions of ownership – Aylsham, for example, was an important royal estate. The origins of Swaffham are interesting: a major Anglo-Saxon cemetery was nearby, and it was a royal manor given by King Edward to Earl Ralph and then by William I to Count Alan. Nevertheless, it was in the shadow of Castle Acre, and its Domesday entry is much less impressive than that for Litcham, with its one quarter market. Swaffham's emergence as a major sub-regional centre was delayed until the thirteenth century. For many Norfolk markets, whether successful or failures, there is a paucity of documentary evidence: significant numbers must already have existed before the charter dates which represent the earliest written record.[22]

As noted in the previous chapter, the great surprise in the history of Norwich is that it does not overlie Caistor St Edmund, the site of the Roman town of *Venta Icenorum*. Many other English county towns evolved on Roman sites even if there was not a continuous record of settlement. Colchester and Cambridge are much more typical from that point of view. As already explained, there were early Saxon cemeteries near to Caistor, and a Roman road ran north from Caistor into Norwich along the line of modern Ber Street and across the river to Oak Street, but there is remarkably little evidence of early settlement in the vicinity of the modern city centre. Brian Ayers observed that, 'it is not until the eighth century that it becomes possible to suggest that proto-urbanised settlements were beginning to appear in the Wensum Valley',[23] but looking at the settlement of Norwich, with its hilltop castle dominating the valley and river, it is very surprising that neither the Iceni nor the Romans used the site.

There was an important settlement on the north side of the Wensum by about 830, known as *Northwic* to differentiate it from nearby Westwick, which was a settlement later absorbed within Norwich but recalled by the name Westwick Street. Even earlier, from the early eighth century, there had been a scatter of smaller Saxon settlements on both banks of the Wensum. This means that there was a break of 300 years from the last days of Roman Caistor

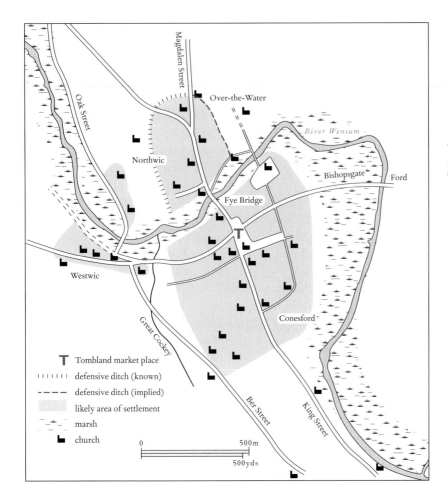

The topography of
pre-Conquest Norwich
(after B. Ayers, 1994).

Map labels: Magdalen Street · Oak Street · Over-the-Water · River Wensum · Northwic · Bishopsgate · Ford · Fye Bridge · T · Westwic · Great Cockey · Conesford · Ber Street · King Street

Legend:
T — Tombland market place
‖‖‖‖‖ — defensive ditch (known)
- - - - defensive ditch (implied)
⬛ likely area of settlement
⌁ marsh
⌐ church

0   500m
     500yds

to the emergence of these new settlements five miles distant. The settlements gradually coalesced below the head of navigation which is at New Mills, and in the ninth century a coherent community began to develop. By the year 930 Norwich had a mint, which certainly implies that in the reign of Aethelstan (924–39) it was a borough and had been fortified in some way, but although it can be identified from coinage, the first documentary reference comes as late as 980.[24]

As the map above shows, by the beginning of the tenth century there was a separate Danish community on the left bank of the river, the area still known as 'Over-the-Water', centred on the junction of Magdalen Street and Colegate.[25] South of the river the fast-growing town spread southwards along King Street and Ber Street. It was defined by river marsh to the east and the Great Cockey, a small stream, to the west. Tombland was the focal market centre, where the major north–south and west–east routes into Norwich met. The north and south parts of the borough were linked by Fye Bridge across the Wensum. Throughout the half-century from 870 Norwich was in the front line of Danish invasions: in 917 the town was occupied by the Danes, and defences were erected on the north bank of the Wensum. Edward the Elder (reigned

899–924) retook the town, but three-quarters of a century later, in 1004, it was sacked by Swein. Though it was an emergent centre of national importance, life for Norwich people in the ninth and tenth centuries was far from secure.

As Norwich grew it rivalled, and ultimately eclipsed, the fortunes of the most important town in Anglo-Saxon Norfolk. In 1066 Thetford was the fifth or sixth largest town in England, with an estimated population of 4,750. This was about the same as that of Norwich, Oxford and Lincoln, and slightly less than that of York. In that year it had 944 burgesses (male heads of households who enjoyed full citizen status), but by 1086, when the Domesday survey was compiled, this had fallen sharply, to 720. Domesday records that the town had 224 vacant properties, implying a very serious decline in its prosperity and fortunes. Thetford evolved round three fords on the rivers Little Ouse and Thet, and Penn suggests that the town developed from about 870 when the Viking army wintered there.[26] The river crossings, Gallows Hill (the Icenian religious centre), the line of the Icknield Way and an Iron Age fort all show the importance of the location of Thetford long before the arrival of the Vikings, while Anglo-Saxon defences to the south of the river and later ones to the north and west of the castle demonstrate the great extent of the town in its heyday. The Vikings remained in control of the site until 917.

After the Danes sacked Thetford in 1010, followed by their victory at nearby Ringmere, the town became in effect the capital of East Anglia under the rule of Swein (1013–14). It had a mint before 959 and six moneyers were recorded in 1040–42. Cnut's reign, from 1016 to 1035, appears to mark the peak of Thetford's prosperity. It flourished as a trading and manufacturing centre – archaeological excavation has shown that the area south of the river was once covered with timber-framed huts and pottery kilns.[27] The making of Thetford ware was a crucial local industry, and the rapid reduction in output from the mid-eleventh century onwards was therefore a key factor in the swift decline of the town. Having become the seat of the bishop in 1070, it quickly lost this asset to Norwich in 1094, underlining the way in which the latter was rising dramatically in the urban hierarchy. With Norwich having both the royal castle and the cathedral, Ely and Bishop's Lynn developing as important ports on the Great Ouse, and Bury St Edmunds gaining rapidly in wealth and territory, Thetford quickly began to lose its strategic position.

Great Yarmouth was the third borough of Norfolk at the time of Domesday Book. It was much smaller than Norwich and Thetford, having only 70 burgesses, and its Domesday population was no greater than that of many of the manors of the county – Aylsham, for example, had 76 villagers and smallholders but was not a borough. Yarmouth, like Norwich, was a newer arrival in the urban system. The sandbank on which it lies only became habitable in the late ninth or early tenth century, initially as a site for fishermen to camp during the herring-fishing season. As the sandbank grew larger and drier, permanent occupation became feasible and a port began to grow, soon gaining borough status under royal control. At this stage the town was still very vulnerable, not only to incursions of the sea but also because of its absolute dependence on the sea: it had no arable land to support a larger population.

A summary of Dark Age Norfolk

In 1066, at the time of the Norman Conquest, Norfolk was the most densely populated county in England. Its people were a mixed community of Danes and Anglo-Saxons, spiced with a still considerable element of Romano-British blood. Its bishop, with his cathedral at Thetford, oversaw the operation of a diocese which had over 700 parishes in Norfolk alone, far more than any other English county. It had 36 hundreds and a sheriff, who provided their link with the Crown and collected the geld, the national taxations first imposed by the Vikings.

The population of Norfolk was distributed relatively evenly across the county, with the exception of the largely uninhabited wetlands north-west of Yarmouth (the area later known as the Broads) and the comparable wetlands in parts of the Fens. There were greater estates, held by thanes and worked by villagers and smallholders tied by forms of service to their lords. There were also smaller settlements of freemen and sokemen, subject to fewer ties and restrictions. Arable lands lay around most settlements with a mixture of common heaths, pastures and marshes and significantly more woodland than in later centuries. Sheep, cattle and goats were reared not only on the lord's lands but on those of the villagers, though there were more sheep on the Fens and the chalklands and more cattle on the boulder clays.

Norwich was growing fast, Thetford was shrinking, and Yarmouth was becoming established on its sandbank. King's Lynn did not yet exist. We know that at least two other market towns, Dereham under the abbey of Ely and North Walsham under that of St Benet's, were already established, but Holt, Litcham and Great Dunham were the only smaller centres to have a market recorded in 1066. In 1086, though, the Normans would replace the former landowners and establish a much more formalised manorial administrative and military structure over the county. A revolution was about to take place.

5

The Norman Conquest
and its aftermath

T HE Norman Conquest was effected with surprising speed, in the southern half of England at least. On 14 October 1066 William, having sailed from the mouth of the Seine and landed at Pevensey, won the Battle of Hastings. King Harold, his brother Gyrth and many other Saxons including those holding great estates in Norfolk were killed. William was crowned king of England at the newly consecrated Westminster Abbey on 25 December 1066. In just over two months, a kingdom had been won. Although the process of pacifying the northern counties took another four years, and in the Fens the rebellion of the semi-legendary Hereward the Wake kept alive for some time hopes of an English resistance, the speed of the conquest itself was remarkable. But the new king was fully aware that he had to consolidate his hold on power, and understood very well the importance of establishing firm military and political control as quickly as possible. William immediately implemented a strategy of castle building and the creation of heavily fortified bases in each county. By 1070 a castle had been built in Norwich. It was a motte and bailey, a great earth mound topped by a wooden tower and surrounded by palisaded enclosures, and is assumed to have been built on the same site as the new stone keep which replaced it in the mid-1090s. The additional significance of its construction is

1066	TRE (*in Tempore Regis Edwardi*: in the time of King Edward) William's victory at Hastings and control of England
1067–70	construction of the first castle at Norwich, and of Thetford Castle
1070	manor house built at Castle Acre by William de Warenne II
1070–86	almost all Saxon-held manors taken over by Norman lords; Roger Bigod the greatest of the new owners
1086	Little Domesday (survey) giving additional detailed information for Norfolk, Suffolk and Essex
1094	Herbert de Losinga transfers the diocesan seat from Thetford to Norwich; first Norwich Cathedral begun
mid-1090s	great stone castle built to dominate Norwich
1096–1100	consolidation of monastic interests: Ely gains lordship of East Dereham, St Benet's of North Walsham; foundation of Carrow Abbey and St Leonard's Priory in Norwich
1100	Bishop de Losinga's charter for the creation of Bishop's (later King's) Lynn
1107	Roger Bigod founds Thetford Priory
1121	Henry I spends Christmas in his newly finished castle at Norwich
1138	William d'Albini II begins construction of castle at Castle Rising
1208	Great Yarmouth receives its first borough charter

clear: for, although other castles were built, including that at Thetford, this was the first and the largest, confirming that Norwich was now the county town of Norfolk.

William I's political strategy, a vital complement to the military planning, involved the redistribution of Saxon estates to his Norman supporters, a process made easier by the fact that so many of the previous owners had been killed at Hastings. By confiscating Saxon lands and handing them to his followers he sought to establish a power base, and also to ensure tight Norman control in the provinces, giving the new owners a vested interest in remaining loyal. Thus, William de Warenne, a distant relative of the new king, was made earl of Surrey and given Castle Acre as the centre for his Norfolk estates, having also been given the Rape of Lewes in Sussex, Reigate in Surrey and Conisbrough in Yorkshire. The fascinating site at Castle Acre has been the subject of very extensive archaeological excavations, which revealed – to the surprise of all concerned – that the castle was not the original structure. Jonathan Coad concluded that the first major building on the site was William de Warenne's large manor house, built in about 1070 and therefore constructed immediately upon the takeover. Only later was this converted into a substantial fortified castle.[1]

The Domesday Book (1086) is the first national record to list the vills of England with details of their ownership and other fiscal matters. Domesday was primarily a record of taxes paid by the vills, and a comparison was always

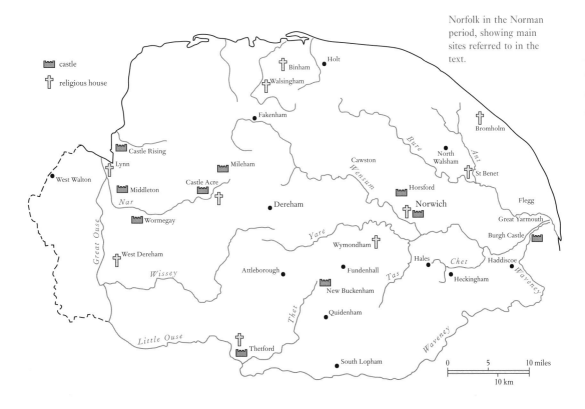

Norfolk in the Norman period, showing main sites referred to in the text.

castle

religious house

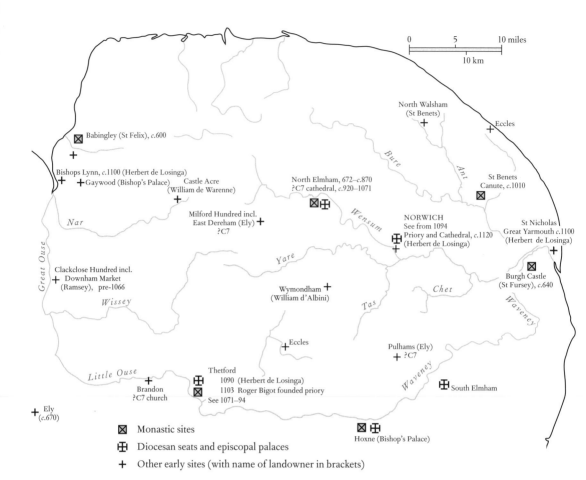

Some pre- and
post-Conquest religious
sites.

given between 1066 and 1086 to show what changes had taken place since the
Conquest. A separate volume, the Little Domesday Book, was compiled for
Norfolk, Suffolk and Essex, providing fascinating, though abbreviated, details
on the nature of the holdings. One example is that of the manor of Pulham,
which was held by the abbey of St Etheldreda at Ely:[2]

> HENSTEAD Half Hundred
> St. E[theldreda] held PULHAM before 1066, as 15 c[arucates] of land.
>   Always 60 villagers; 25 smallholders; 7 slaves.
>   3 ploughs in lordship. Then 20 men's ploughs, now 16. Meadow,
>   16 acres. Woodland, then 600 pigs, now 300. 1 Mill. 3 cobs;
>   11 head of cattle; 40 pigs; 50 sheep; 40 goats; 4 beehives.

> Value then £8; now £15.
> It has 2 leagues in length and 1 league in width, tax of 30d.

The lands of principal landowners were described under the heading of the
relevant hundred: the Ely lands are therefore listed in several different hundreds
in Norfolk, and Pulham lay in the half-hundred of Henstead. This entire manor
belonged to Ely, and there was no other manor in Pulham, but in many instances

a vill had more than one manor, so its description might be divided and given under three or four separate headings. We are told that the abbey of Ely already held Pulham before 1066 and that it was valued on the assumption that its arable land consisted of 15 carucates (each carucate of 120 acres, so a total of roughly 1,800 acres is implied). Assuming that the number of carucates is correct, and that they did indeed measure 120 acres, the villagers in Pulham must have held an average of about 25 acres each (amounting together to some 1,500 acres) and smallholders perhaps ten acres apiece (another 250 acres in total).

In these Domesday entries a 'plough' means a plough team of six or eight horses or oxen. The home farm had three teams and the villagers sixteen in 1086. The entry then describes the different categories of land, with 16 acres of meadow (a very small amount, showing how dominant arable farming had become) and a sizeable area of woodland – though as that was able to feed only half the number of pigs in 1086 compared with 1066 there may well have been substantial woodland clearance in 20 years on this part of the boulder-clay plateau of south Norfolk. Mixed stock were kept on the lord's farm, but we do not know what stock the villagers held. The geld paid was 30 pence and the annual value of the manor had risen from £8 to £15 between 1066 and 1086. So we are given a good deal of information about Pulham, albeit no church is mentioned, and it is not possible to say how the village was laid out.

The Norman Conquest had a great impact on the county. Castles were built by several tenants-in-chief (those who held their lands directly from the Crown), and abbeys, priories, hospitals and colleges were founded by some of those major landowners. The *Victoria County History* lists 124 religious foundations that were dissolved in the 1530s, and most of these had been established under the auspices of the new land-owning class which took control from 1066 onwards.[3] In 1086 the chief landowners in Norfolk were, in order:

Roger Bigod with 187 manors (mainly in south-east Norfolk)
William de Warenne with 139 manors (mainly in west Norfolk)
King William with 95 manors (widely spread across the county)
William, Bishop of Thetford, 80 manors (mainly in north Norfolk)
The Abbey of St Benet at Holm 77 manors (mainly in east Norfolk)

A further 11 tenants-in-chief had 20 manors or more each, and Munford lists an overall total of 64 tenants-in-chief in the county.[4]

Roger Bigod, the greatest of all Norfolk landowners in the last two decades of the eleventh century, was another trusted supporter of King William. He became sheriff of Norfolk and then a royal councillor, and accumulated sufficient wealth to build Framlingham Castle in Suffolk and to found Thetford Priory in 1107; he established the Bigods as a family of the first rank.[5] Roger Bigod IV, the last of the line which he founded, died in 1306 without a male heir, and the Bigod lands then reverted to the Crown. The huge estates which had by then been built up suffered on his death, but they subsequently provided the core of the Mowbray family's landholdings as dukes of Norfolk in the late fourteenth and early fifteenth centuries, and thus passed in due course to the Howard family when they acquired the dukedom. The emergence of

The castle at Castle Acre is now a sequence of impressive earthworks, together with the now-exposed remains of the great stone keep and the hummocky foundations of buildings in the interior ward. The castle has an extraordinary history. It was founded by William de Warenne, a right-hand man of William the Conqueror, in the 1070s as a stone-built house – a country mansion. Some time after 1135, during the civil war between Stephen and Matilda, William's grandson, also William, began to convert the house into a much larger and heavily fortified castle, raising the existing ramparts, building a stone perimeter wall, and turning the house itself into a taller powerful keep (as seen in this view). Despite this huge expenditure and effort, the castle seems to have been derelict and abandoned by the end of the fourteenth century.

Roger Bigod as the dominant figure in the county in the two decades after the Conquest thus helped to shape the fortunes of the greatest lords in Norfolk for many generations after, and indeed of the county itself. Bigod's rival as Norfolk's leading landowner, William de Warenne, was a favourite of William I who rewarded him with 296 manors, of which 139 lay in Norfolk, especially in the west of the county. At Castle Acre he built his manor house and founded the priory, although his principal base was Lewes in Sussex.

Domesday Book provides us with invaluable detail about individual communities as well as the great landowners and monastic houses. Thus, we learn that in the time of King Edward the Confessor (1042–66), Aylsham, with 16 carucates of land (1,920 acres) was held by Gyrth, brother of King Harold II, while neighbouring Cawston had belonged to Harold himself. Gyrth, like his brother, died at Hastings and all their lands, here and elsewhere in Norfolk and beyond, were taken over by William. The new king also acquired the lands of Stigand, the archbishop of Canterbury at the time of the Conquest. The bishop of Thetford held the lands of the former bishops of East Anglia, which were mainly in north Norfolk, but after 1096, when the diocesan seat had been moved to Norwich, these were split between Norwich Cathedral Priory and the bishop. The abbot of St Benet at Holm held lands mainly in the north-east of the county, within reasonable distance of the abbey and formed of the endowment given by King Cnut for its support.

The economic system by which food and other specialised products such as salt were produced depended on the relationship of the lords to their tenants. On Norfolk estates the main categories of tenants at the time of Domesday were villagers, smallholders and slaves.[6] As noted for Pulham, the typical holding of a villager might be about 25 acres and that of a smallholder rather less; slaves of course held no land. There were also freemen and sokemen, who usually held between 10 and 50 acres. The villagers and smallholders were tied to their lord by their feudal tenure: in return for their land they performed a range of services for the lord during the year, from ditching and ploughing to haymaking and harvesting. In return they could pass their land on to their descendants, male or female. Freemen and sokemen had greater freedom, and could buy and sell land, but all came under the protection of their lord and they could be called upon for military service by and for him.

We can gain some idea of how the land was managed, and regional variations within the county, from the Domesday accounts of demesne estates, those held directly by the lord rather than being let to tenants. For example, the large royal manor of Cawston, in South Erpingham Hundred, had an exceptional area of woodland, described in 1086 as capable of feeding 1,000 pigs (see maps on pages 76 and 77). There were two mills, presumably for grinding the corn from the 1,360 acres of arable land. On the lord's own farm (the demesne) were 20 acres of meadow, 20 cows, four horses, 40 pigs, 60 sheep, 50 goats and five hives of bees. The demesne carried four plough teams and the villagers 16. This gives a total of 93 households, and if we use the commonly accepted multiplier of 4.5 people per household, implies that the settlement had a population of about 450. Cawston is a well-documented village, and it is clear from post-Domesday written sources that it had a classic medieval field system around the centre. The stock kept by the villagers must have been many times more than that kept on the king's demesne. Large areas of heath and common provided grazing for these animals in summer.

In west Norfolk a very different balance appears at West Walton, on the edge of the Fens. There William de Warenne's manor and demesne had been granted to his newly founded abbey of St Peter at Lewes. It included 100 acres of meadow and the stock consisted of eight horses, 23 cattle, 114 pigs and 800 sheep. The special importance of the latter is immediately apparent, for this was a very great flock by medieval standards – indeed, it would be regarded as large even today. Sheep provided both wool and meat, but the demesne also included seven salthouses, some of the produce of which was probably used for salting fish. There were seventeen smallholders who between them had another seven salthouses. The amount of salt produced would have been sufficient to supply not only local needs but also those of the abbey of St Peter. This first Domesday Book entry for West Walton is significant enough, but the abbey of St Etheldreda at Ely had an even greater manor there. On its West Walton estate there were 100 acres of meadow, 24 salthouses and a huge flock of 1,300 sheep. The two manors, both of which extended into nearby vills, thus had the remarkable total of 2,100 sheep and 38 salthouses, which as well as supplying the abbeys provided an important cash income.

On the other side of the county lay the two small hundreds of East and West Flegg.[7] They, like West Walton, had much marshland but here several of the manors were populated by sokemen or freemen. In Martham in West Flegg, for example, there were 43½ freemen and 33 sokemen. These accounted for 76½ of the 86½ individuals. The careful noting of a half-freeman means that two different lords must have shared him or more probably his holding. Caister in East Flegg has an unusual entry, recording that there were 80 freemen before

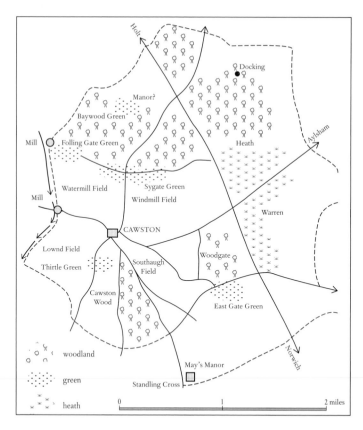

The medieval landscape
and geography of
Cawston.

Holt

Docking

Manor?

Baywood Green

Mill · Folling Gate Green

Heath

Aylsham

Watermill Field

Sygate Green

Mill

Windmill Field

Warren

CAWSTON

Lownd Field

Woodgate

Thirtle Green

Southaugh
Field

Cawston
Wood

East Gate Green

○ ○ ☆ ⌐
○   ⌐   woodland

green

May's Manor

heath

Standling Cross

Norwich

0   1   2 miles

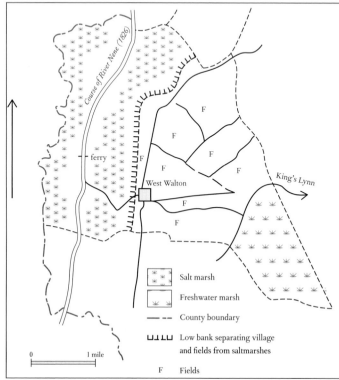

The medieval landscape
and geography of West
Walton.

Course of River Nene (1826)

F

F

F

ferry

F

F

F

F

King's Lynn

West Walton

F

F

Salt marsh

Freshwater marsh

County boundary

Low bank separating village
and fields from saltmarshes

0   1 mile

F   Fields

South Erpingham Hundred in 1086, showing economic resources mentioned in the Domesday Book.

woodland sufficient to support *x* pigs

number of sheep

number of beehives

number of goats

1066 with the note that 'Earl Ralph made a manor of all this'. Perhaps the fact that it had 39 salthouses and 500 sheep reflects a group of 'salt entrepreneurs' with their smallholdings, who had to be fitted into the new Norman manorial system. This gathering of freemen contrasts with the manors belonging to Lewes and Ely on the Fen edge, with their villagers and smallholders of the two great abbeys.

Norwich: the new capital of East Anglia

Saxon–Danish Norwich was already an important borough, but the Norman takeover had a profound and lasting impact on the layout and development of the city. In 1067 William's army began work on his great castle on the hill overlooking the Wensum and shortly afterwards a new 'French borough', occupied by Norman colonisers, was laid out west of the castle. These developments confirmed that Norwich, which was now the largest town in Norfolk, would be the headquarters of royal power and in effect they mark its

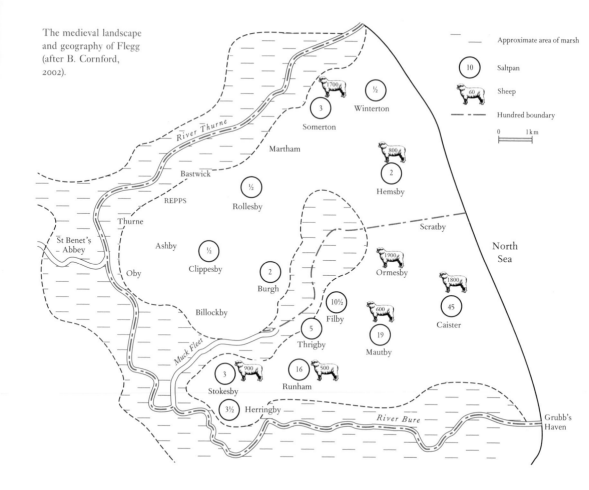

The medieval landscape and geography of Flegg (after B. Cornford, 2002).

Approximate area of marsh

10 Saltpan

60 Sheep

Hundred boundary

0 ___ 1 km

River Thurne

St Benet's – Abbey

Thurne

Oby

Ashby

REPPS

Bastwick

Rollesby

Martham

Somerton

Winterton

Hemsby

Scratby

North Sea

Clippesby

Burgh

Ormesby

Billockby

Filby

Caister

Thrigby

Mautby

Stokesby

Runham

Herringby

River Bure

Grubb's Haven

Muck Fleet

emergence as county town. The founding of the castle and the creation of its 'precinct' took a great western wedge out of the earlier tenth-century borough, involving the clearing of houses and the annexation of their sites. The process was repeated after 1094, when Bishop de Losinga moved the seat of the East Anglian see from Thetford to Norwich, founding the cathedral and priory. The site for the new cathedral was immediately adjacent to the market place of the Saxon borough, and its precincts were laid out on the site of houses and streets. The main west–east road into the town was cut off by the new cathedral and its precinct, and the route was therefore diverted round its northern edge to reach Bishop's Bridge. Partly because of the drastic reduction in the size of the Saxon town (the 'English borough' as it was known) and partly because of the creation of its new twin, the 'French borough' to the west at the foot of the castle hill, the focus of market trading soon shifted westwards to the new borough, where the great market place was laid out. Tombland, its ancient predecessor, became a quieter backwater.

Monasteries of the eleventh and twelfth centuries followed the rule of St Benedict (480–543). He established the famous house at Monte Casino in Italy, and half a century after his death his rule was brought to England

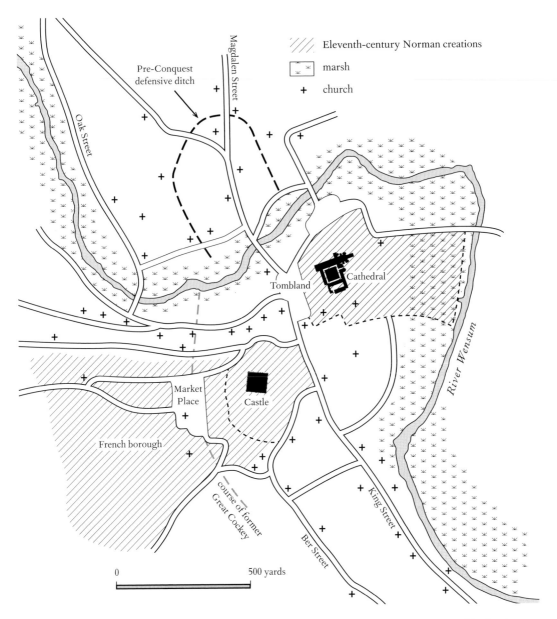

Magdalen Street

Pre-Conquest
defensive ditch

Oak Street

Tombland

Cathedral

River Wensum

Market
Place

Castle

French borough

*course of former
Great Cockey*

King Street

Ber Street

0   500 yards

Norwich after the
Norman Conquest,
showing the newly
created castle precinct,
'French borough', and
cathedral precinct (after
B. Ayers, 1994).

by St Augustine. It set out the pattern of religious life that was to be led in monasteries, and almost 1,500 years later remains the underlying guide for monastic existence. As the plan on page 82 shows, Norwich Cathedral was both a monastic and an episcopal building. Herbert de Losinga's new religious complex, purpose-designed as the base for the Church in East Anglia, had a monastic area south of the great cathedral and the bishop's area to the north. Both were within a great encircling precinct wall, between Tombland on the west and the river on the east, Palace Plain to the north and St Faith's Lane to the south. A formidable gate, later to become the Erpingham Gate, was the only link between the precinct and the city. A canal from Pull's Ferry on the

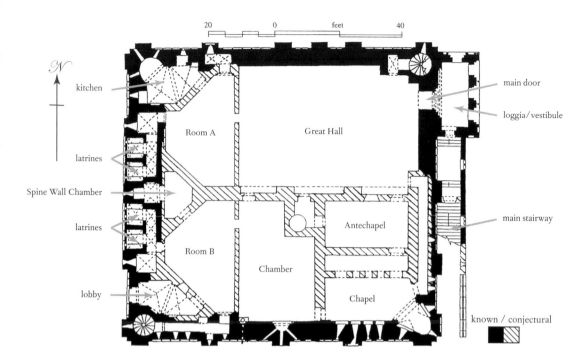

kitchen

latrines

Spine Wall Chamber

latrines

lobby

Room A

Great Hall

main door

loggia/vestibule

Room B

Spine Wall Chamber

Antechapel

main stairway

Chamber

Chapel

known / conjectural

20 0 feet 40

N

Plan of the great
Norman keep of
Norwich Castle (after
T.A. Heslop, 1994).

The huge bulk of the
great keep of Norwich
Castle is accentuated by
its hilltop location and
by the massive artificial
mound upon which it
stands. It was designed
to dominate both the
Anglo Saxon borough
to the north-east,
around Tombland, and
the market place of the
new French borough to
the west. Today, almost
a thousand years later,
its looming presence is
still a crucial element
in the dramatic
townscapes of the city
centre.

The river Wensum at Riverside Road, Norwich, is now an attractive and tranquil scene, contrasting sharply with the incessant traffic along the road and especially at Foundry Bridge. Historically this was a commercial waterway, with small vessels coming up to the edge of the medieval city, and this stretch of the river also acted as the main defensive 'moat' along the eastern side of Norwich.

The soaring and beautiful spire of Norwich Cathedral has been the city's most prominent landmark for centuries. It is 315 feet high, the second tallest in England after Salisbury Cathedral. The building of the cathedral began in 1096 and the main phase of the work was completed in 1145. It was a cathedral priory, served by a Benedictine community, and the cloister and some other monastic buildings survive, though many disappeared after the priory was dissolved in 1539. The present spire was added in 1480 to replace a smaller twelfth-century predecessor which blew down in 1362. Much of the magnificent Norman interior remains unchanged, including the superb nave.

Wensum led into the heart of the precinct, allowing the Caen and Barnack stone to be brought up to the building site of the new cathedral and monastery.

Much of the Norman plan still survives, as does a remarkable amount of the Norman structure itself. The immense nave of the cathedral church, with its massive circular columns, is topped by two tiers of Norman arcading, the lower one dark and the upper lightened by the clerestory. The original plan of the east end has been lost, because a Gothic lady chapel replaced the earlier Romanesque apse, but the transepts and the other apsidal chapels have survived – although the south transept was remodelled by Salvin in the 1830s. The cloister is on the Norman plan but the arcading, through which sublime views of tower and spire are visible, is all Gothic. At the Dissolution the chapter house, a focal point of monastic life, was demolished leaving only its three great Early English doorways on the east side of the cloister. As the plan shows, there were many other monastic buildings, some of which survive. On the north side of the cathedral was the Bishop's Palace, linked by a covered

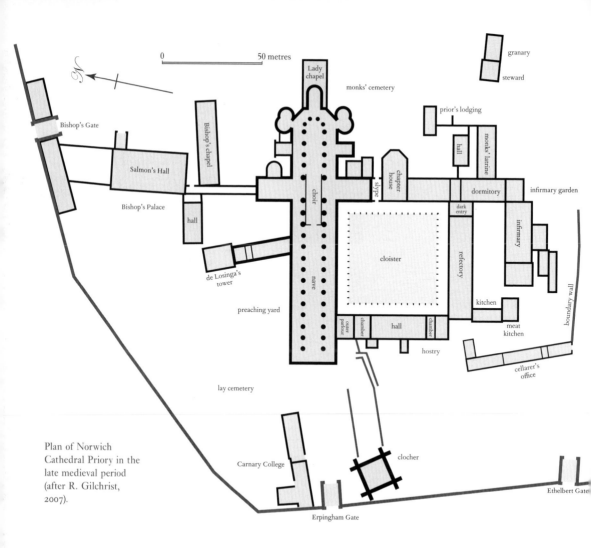

Plan of Norwich
Cathedral Priory in the
late medieval period
(after R. Gilchrist,
2007).

walkway to the church. A mini-keep provided accommodation, and the bishop
had a separate chapel of St Mary, to the east of his living quarters. He also
had his own gatehouse, which led out onto Palace Plain on the north side of
the precinct, where it can still be admired. There can be no doubt that, from
the outset, Herbert de Losinga intended to impress by the magnificence of the
new church and its complex of attendant buildings and residences, and in doing
so reflected the ambition of what was destined to become one of the wealthiest
dioceses in medieval England.

Norwich had two other Norman monastic houses: St Leonard's Priory,
overlooking the precinct from Mousehold Heath, was also built by Losinga,
but nothing of it survives, while outside the south gate of the city lay Carrow
Abbey, a Benedictine nunnery of considerable importance. Although fragments
of its buildings remain, they are hidden from view, deep within the Colman
factory site.

The second great Norman building which dominates Norwich is the castle.
As we have seen, the first castle, built in 1067, was probably on the same site
but comprised timber buildings on a large motte. As was usual with castles

Pull's Ferry is one of the most famous of Norwich landmarks, beloved of postcard producers and calendar photographers. The little foot-ferry over the Wensum has long since ceased to operate but the medieval buildings, the embowering trees and the little 'quay' create an unforgettable picture. In fact, this had workaday origins, for the inlet is the mouth of a canal which was built in the late 1090s to carry stone for the construction of the great cathedral itself. The stone was brought by sea from France then up the Yare, the Wensum and the canal to the building site. The canal was later used for the shipment of general provisions and doubtless served as a drain. It remained open until the late eighteenth century, and was finally filled in in about 1780.

The great keep of Norwich Castle ranks with those of Dover, Rochester and the Tower of London, all of them built immediately after the Norman Conquest as practical centres for military control and administrative organisation, but also as towering and formidable symbols of the might and power of the new regime. The uncompromising bulk and solid symmetry of the keep are relieved by the decorative arcading and tremendous buttresses that break up the flatness of the walling. The castle has lost almost all of its ancillary buildings, and its setting is altered almost beyond recognition, but the Norman keep reminds us of the impact of conquest in the late 1060s and early 1070s.

built in county towns, Norwich Castle was later reconstructed in stone and greatly enlarged, in this instance on the instructions of William II (1087–1100) to create a vast keep equalled in size only by the Tower of London. To support this huge building, a massive earth mound was raised, itself a great feat of engineering. As well as the great Caen-stone keep, a complex of earthworks surrounded it. The central keep was approached by a bridge across the inner moat, beyond which a large bailey stretched south and west towards the new market place of the French borough, while on the north-east side the outer bailey almost touched the wall of the cathedral precinct. In 1121 King Henry I spent Christmas at the castle, perhaps to mark its completion.

As with the cathedral, the building of the castle destroyed large numbers of houses. Domesday Book recorded that 'on that land over which Harold had jurisdiction there are 15 burgesses and 17 vacant houses which are in the occupation of the castle. And in the borough are 190 empty houses there which were in the jurisdiction of the king and the earl and 81 in the occupation of the castle.' Such destruction of property for the needs of Church or State was certainly not unusual – other places where the same happened include Oxford, Chester and Wallingford – but in few towns was the impact so extensive as in Norwich. Heslop suggests that the castle and cathedral were conceived as a 'pair', as Norwich was established as the new capital for Norfolk and Suffolk. The Caen stone which was used for the keep and the cathedral not only came from the same quarries in Normandy, but has masons' marks which show that the same masons worked on both great buildings, as though they were a joint project. Of the castle, Heslop concluded that, 'it was architecturally the most ambitious secular building in western Europe, a tribute alike to the almost godlike vision of kingship of its patron and to the potential which he saw in the new administrative centre of East Anglia in Norwich'.[8] In its scale and splendour, and imposing appearance, it was truly a match for the cathedral – yet despite the huge amount of time and vast financial resources lavished on the castle, in 1371 Edmund Thorpe, sheriff of Norfolk and Suffolk, complained of its poor state, lamenting that 'no man can dwell in it'.[9]

The evolving plan and form of Wensum Lodge (after R. Smith in J.I. Dent and J.S. Livock, 1990).

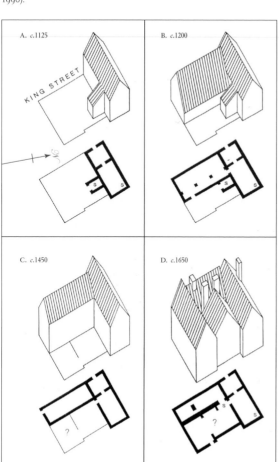

There were already some 30 churches in the pre-Norman city, more than in all but a handful of English towns, but during the next two centuries, as Norwich grew rapidly in population and prosperity, an extraordinary number of new churches were founded, perhaps in some cases beginning as private chapels. By 1300 a total of at least 60 churches could be counted, and there were some areas (such as the streets around St Gregory's Alley) where the churches stood almost side by side. As archaeological excavation has taken place, for example in the preparation for the Anglia Television building in Rose Lane, evidence of churches which were hitherto completely unknown has been revealed, suggesting that in fact the late medieval city may have had substantially more than sixty. This number is exceeded only by London among the cities of medieval England, though close to the figure for York, the other great provincial capital.

It is no longer easy to recognise Norman (Romanesque) elements in the surviving churches. A few, such as St Etheldreda in King Street, still have Norman doorways, zig-zag string courses and flat pilasters, and a

Norman doorway from St Michael-at-Thorne has been moved to the entrance of the shrine of St Julian. Yet further along King Street the church of St Peter Parmentergate was completely rebuilt at the end of the fifteenth century and has not a trace of Norman work; nor do St Peter Mancroft or St Stephen in the city centre. A great fifteenth-century wave of rebuilding replaced the churches that were Norman or Early English in origin, and likewise the early medieval houses were, with few exceptions, swept away by later reconstruction. One almost miraculous survivor is Wensum Lodge in King Street, now part of an adult education centre, which incorporates the fabric of the Jew's House, the oldest residential building in the city and one of the very earliest in the British Isles. It was built by a wealthy owner in about 1125 and became the home of the Jurnets, a very rich Jewish family. Later it was owned by a string of major Norfolk families with evocative names, including the Felbriggs, the Pastons, and the Cokes. It stood at right angles to the street, with a massive Norman undercroft below an open hall. An aisled range had been added to it by the beginning of the thirteenth century, and there were other later additions. Its position by the river was ideal for trade, and it was built of humble Norfolk flint but also, impressively, with expensive and prestigious imported Caen stone.

The other towns of post-Conquest Norfolk

We have already seen how Thetford, which in the years around the turn of the first millennium was one of England's largest towns and was the *de facto* capital of East Anglia, was heading into depression and decline half a century later. It could potentially have derived much benefit from the transfer of the bishop's see from North Elmham, and in 1067–68 a huge motte and bailey castle had been constructed within, and using the ramparts of, a major Iron Age fort on the north bank of the Little Ouse. The river was certainly navigable as far upstream as Brandon, but possibly also to Thetford for flat-bottomed boats of shallow draught. But though all of this held promise, the reality was starkly different. By 1120 the diocesan seat had been moved again, to Norwich; the royal power-base had been established at Norwich Castle; and the river and sea port of Lynn had started to grow and draw trade away from Thetford. Henceforth, the town would never again recapture its prominence or significance.

The motte and bailey of Thetford Castle, where the central mound is one of the two highest in Britain, was built in 1067–69 within the encircling ramparts of a very large Iron Age hillfort. The mound has suffered some erosion over the centuries, and was damaged by tree planting on the summit in the 1820s, while in 1908 the entire area became a public park with the consequent landscaping and construction of paths, but the immense earthworks, some of them 2,500 years old, remain extremely impressive.

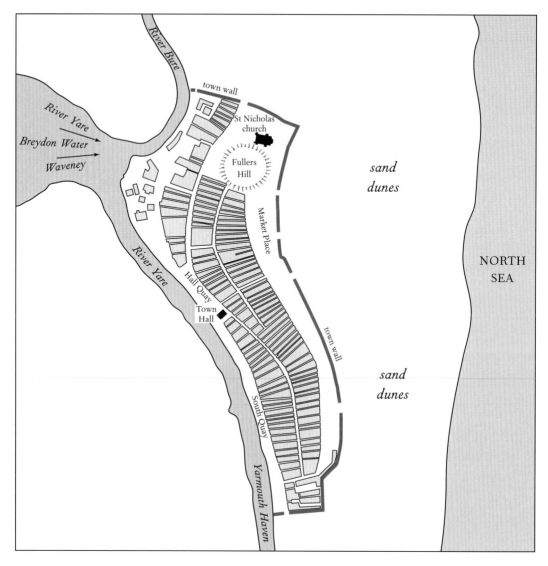

The topography of medieval Great Yarmouth (after D. Dymond, 1987).

In contrast, the growing dominance of Norwich helped the emergent town of Yarmouth, for although the Wensum was navigable up to Norwich the new town on the sandbank in its estuary was destined to become the major seaport for east Norfolk and, for larger vessels, the nearest commercial port to the great fast-growing city upriver. On his move to Norwich, Bishop de Losinga became closely involved in the affairs of Yarmouth, extending his influence by building the great parish church of St Nicholas and founding a priory. By now Great Yarmouth had superseded Caister-by-Yarmouth as a port, greatly helped by the physical changes to the outlet of the east-flowing rivers. As already noted, settlement of the sandbanks began in about 900, when fishermen began to live there seasonally and to establish a fish market. By 1008 the Fullers Hill area had permanent houses, and in 1086 there were 70 burgesses and 24 fishermen, all part of the manor of Gorleston. The next step was independence, as in

Great Yarmouth St Nicholas is the largest parish church in England, its cathedral-like proportions being emphasised by the extraordinary width of the aisles, said to be the widest in the world. Founded in 1110 by Bishop Herbert de Losinga, as the church for the newly developing borough, it remained the only church until the early eighteenth century and thus received all the patronage of wealthy burgesses – by the 1530s there were no fewer than eighteen side chapels and chantries. As the commercial focus of the town shifted southwards St Nicholas was increasingly peripheral. The church was very extensively restored in the Victorian period, after a prolonged phase of neglect. That work was completed in 1905 but in 1942 St Nicholas was gutted by fire during a German air raid, with only the tower and outer walls left standing. Demolition was considered but rejected, and rebuilding took until 1961.

1208 King John granted a borough charter in return for an annual rent of £55 (Norwich had to pay £100). The late Norman borough included only St Nicholas church, Fullers Hill and the market. The area was greatly extended after 1284, when the town wall and exterior moat were constructed.[10] The walls, 23 feet high and 2,200 yards long (1½ miles), enclosed 133 acres.

In 1086 Lynn was a very small place, with nine freemen, three smallholders, nine salterns, only a little land, and no recorded livestock. It is not clear whether the population was scattered about on the banks of the creeks and on the salt mounds, or whether there was a more coherent community in the area of the salterns between the Purfleet and the Millfleet. Richards argues that in 1101, when Bishop Losinga's charter to found St Margaret's church and priory was drawn up, there was already an emergent town in the area.[11] The 'sand market', now the Saturday Market Place, was already there, and by 1130 the main axis of settlement ran eastwards to the chapel-of-ease of St James. In about 1140 Losinga's successor, Bishop Turbe, granted a charter which established the Tuesday Market Place on the Newland north of the Purfleet, together with the chapel of St Nicholas as a chapel-of-ease to St Margaret. One factor explaining the development of this second market was a grant by Henry I to William d'Albini, allowing him to take 50 per cent of the market tolls of the port of Lynn from the Newland. By 1200 merchant houses stretched along the eastern side of King Street.[12] The emergence of this successful new town resulted from a complex interplay between, on the one hand, merchants who recognised the advantages of its geographical situation, and on the other two bishops who established religious institutions which drew income from the success of the two markets.

In scale and ambition the castle at Castle Rising, now in the custodianship of English Heritage, is second in Norfolk only to that of Norwich. Its splendid keep still stands high and proud at the centre of a massive system of earthworks,[13]

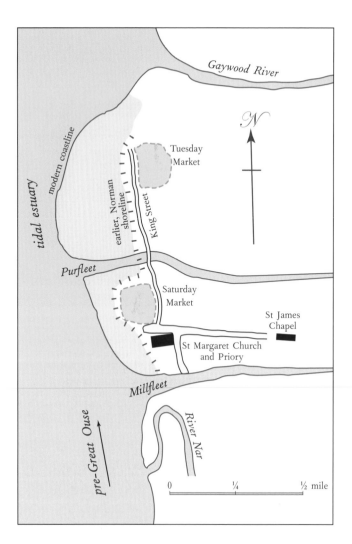

Lynn in the Norman period: the key elements of the emergent town.

Lynn grew rapidly in the eleventh century on a challenging site, already occupied by a pre-Conquest salt-making community. Low-lying, and with a combination of marshy fen and sandbanks and the waste mounds of the salt industry, it was intersected by channels – to the north was the Gaywood river, to the south the river Nar, while two watercourses, the Purfleet and the Millfleet, flowed west into the Great Ouse. In the rectangle of land between them the core of the town developed. In the first half of the twelfth century a second phase of development saw the laying out of an urban extension on Newland, north of the Purfleet. This photograph shows Millfleet, which still marks the southern boundary of the town proper and of the quays on the riverside.

on the south bank of what was once the open estuary of the Babingley river, opposite the deserted church of Babingley on the north bank. In 1086 Rising was an outlier of Snettisham, and had 13 salt pans, four mills and a fishery. All of Rising and Snettisham, a very large holding, was in the hands of Archbishop Stigand in 1066 and those of Odo, Bishop of Bayeux, half brother to King William, in 1086. Its real development came after 1138 when William d'Albini II, inheriting the vill from his father, a major supporter of William I, chose it as the site for a castle. William d'Albini II was a great builder and planner: he had already built a castle at Old Buckenham and a planned new town at New Buckenham, and had founded Wymondham Abbey. His castle at Rising was much more impressive, but why he chose this site is not clear – perhaps he saw it as a future seaport of importance. This was before the bishops of Norwich had given their powerful support to the growth of Lynn, which had much greater advantages as the outlet of the Fenland river system.

William d'Albini II built the massive keep using some local stone but larger quantities of ashlar from Spilsby and Barnack – the high quality of the stonework on the great staircase helped to provide an entry to the castle that

The great keep at Castle Rising was built at the end of the 1130s by William d'Albini II, the son of a leading knight of the reigns of William I and William II. In 1138 d'Albini married Queen Adeliza de Louvain, the second wife (and widow) of King Henry I. This extraordinary and brilliant marriage brought d'Albini into the highest social and political circles, and it seems possible that this rapid elevation both encouraged, and helped to finance, the tremendous project for the castle at Castle Rising. The keep, shown here, is at once a massive military fortress and a sophisticated residence, as suggested by the elaborate decoration of the exterior and especially of the forebuilding on the right hand side of the picture. The keep measures 78½ feet by 68½ feet, but only 50 feet high.

Outside the castle and inner bailey at Castle Rising is a series of massive earthworks which form a roughly rectangular banked and ditch enclosure to the east, and a similar, though slightly smaller, enclosure to the west. These outworks were contemporary with the castle and its oval bailey, and so must have served as additional barbicans defending the main entrance to the castle, and creating two outer baileys or level spaces bounded by high ramparts. Archaeological investigation has shown that major alterations were made to these earthworks in the late twelfth century, probably in response to heightened tension and the threat of civil war. This view shows the northern side of the eastern rectangular bailey, with the huge ditch to the north and the ramparts of the inner bailey in the foreground.

The great stairway of the forebuilding, on the east side of the keep at Castle Rising – the forebuilding itself is perhaps the finest and best preserved in England. It was built in about 1140 and was the main entrance to the keep and provided a ceremonial approach and also extra protection for the main structure. The stairway, which is still so impressive with its solid grandeur, has two long flights, eight feet wide, separated by a handsome columned doorway halfway up. The top flight leads to the first floor, and a vestibule at the principal entrance to the keep giving access to the state apartments and main public reception rooms including the great hall.

A sketch of a 1588 map of Castle Rising, showing the small planned town set in its agricultural landscape of marshland, woods, commons and fields.

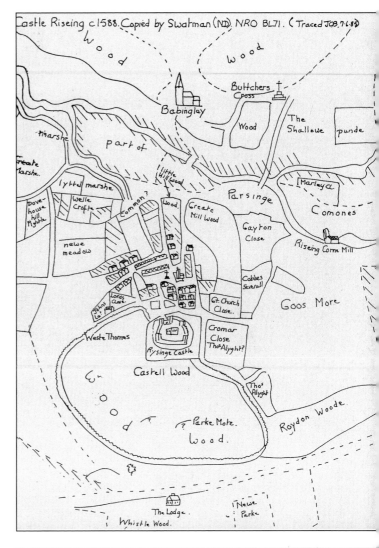

The forebuilding at Castle Rising is richly decorated with interlaced blank arcading, an elaborate and unusual feature (though comparable decoration once existed at, for example, the great keep of Norwich Castle). The masonry is of exceptional quality and, particularly when the full scheme of the decorative work was complete, the building must have presented a remarkable image of political and military power mixed with elegance and sophistication.

The late Norman church of St Lawrence at Castle Rising matches the nearby castle for richness of decoration. Much of it dates from the second half of the twelfth century, and is thus contemporary with the castle. However, the church was heavily restored in the nineteenth century, by Anthony Salvin in the 1840s and George Street in the 1850s – both architects later became leading figures in ecclesiastical restoration. They were responsible for the distinctive top of the prominent central tower, the south porch and most of the doorways.

could not fail to impress contemporaries, and it still impresses visitors today. Outside the keep is a great earthen bank enclosing 12 acres, with an outer ditch and a main entrance to the castle through an east-facing gateway. In the northern section of the embankment archaeological excavation has revealed an apsidal Norman church, which had been the original parish church and in about 1140 was replaced by a new and very impressive church outside the earthworks, with a 'swagger' west front and central tower.[14] To the north of the castle, as at New Buckenham, a grid-plan settlement was laid out, below which were the quays on the edge of the flood plain. To the south of the castle lay a hunting chase.

The d'Albini line failed in 1243, and Cecily d'Albini, one of four co-heiresses, succeeded to the Rising estate. Eventually, in 1329, it was acquired by the Crown, and Isabella – wife of the deposed and murdered King Edward II – was

The west front of Castle Rising church was described by the architectural historian Nikolaus Pevsner as 'a swagger piece of Norman decoration'. Above the very fine doorway is a double arcade, in two layers: at the back there are narrow and relatively plain arches, but in front of them superb interlaced arches with complex diamond or chevron designs, deeply incised so that they stand out crisp and sharp even after more than eight and a half centuries. The window has diamonds, chevrons and zigzags, the tightly twisted columns to left and right being topped by tiny crouched figures and the frame of the window including grotesque faces reminiscent of the 'Green Man' device so common in medieval churches.

The castle at New Buckenham was built in 1146–71 by William d'Albini, who was lord of (Old) Buckenham and developed the new castle as an integral part of a wider scheme that included a planned new town. The castle has a massive circular mound, now heavily overgrown, and water-filled moat, with an outer bailey and the substantial remains of a circular two-storey keep built of flint. At the approach to the castle stands this, the late Norman chapel of St Mary, likely to have been the original place of worship for the new town which was developed from the middle of the twelfth century, continuing as such for perhaps a hundred years until the building of the church of St Martin in the town. The chapel eventually became a barn and is now converted to residential use, but the blocked-up early medieval windows are still clearly seen.

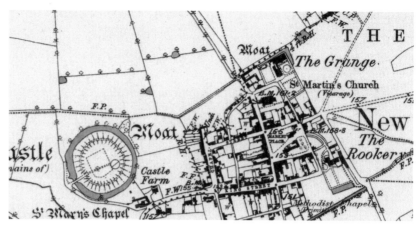

New Buckenham is Norfolk's best example of a planned Norman town – indeed, one of the finest in England. It consists of a grid pattern of streets with a huge central market place (now the green), and closely resembles the rather later 'bastides' of south-west France. Behind the main streets are narrower back lanes, such as Rosemary Lane shown here, which give access to the rear of properties. As with Castle Acre, New Buckenham's layout has been preserved almost intact because the miniature town stagnated throughout the eighteenth and nineteenth centuries, and indeed until recent decades experienced very little change or development.

The first edition of the six-inch Ordnance Survey map (1882) clearly shows the rudimentary grid pattern of the planned town and the great market place, slightly off centre, placed so that the traffic on the Norwich to Kenninghall and Bury St Edmunds road passed through, bringing (it was hoped) additional trade. A main cross of roads, and parallel back lanes, can be identified, as can the lines of the burgage plots which were the building blocks of the town. The dotted line is the parish boundary – a new parish was created but its boundaries were so tightly drawn that the castle lay outside, in the mother parish of Old Buckenham.

imprisoned there under house arrest until her death in 1356. It was thus a royal residence, albeit also a comfortable prison, for almost thirty years. The Crown held the castle until Henry VIII gave it to the duke of Norfolk, and it remained in the hands of various branches of the Howard family until transferred to state ownership in 1958. In 1616 Henry Howard, earl of Northampton, had founded the Trinity Almshouses which have a beautiful brick courtyard and still provide housing for nine women pensioners. But the town of Castle Rising never flourished, for the estuary silted and the rise of Lynn put paid to any real chance of commercial success. Though sending two MPs to parliament until 1832, Castle Rising was for centuries a classic example of a failed borough.

As we have seen, in the years after the Norman Conquest the second greatest landowner in Norfolk was William de Warenne, whose local base was at Castle Acre. From there he or his stewards administered his estates, which mostly lay in the north-west of the county. The great country house which he built there immediately after the Conquest was gradually extended and then converted into a classic Norman keep, standing inside a great earthwork which faced south across the valley of the river Nar. Like so many leading Norman lords the de Warennes were enthusiastic patrons of religious houses. Having founded a priory at Lewes, they then established another at Castle Acre. There the Norman architecture has survived far better than at the nearby castle – indeed, the west front of Castle Acre Priory is one of the acknowledged gems of the Norman style of architecture in England. Between the castle and the

The planned borough of Castle Acre was laid out on a basic grid pattern in the twelfth century immediately adjacent to the Norman manor house, which had been converted into a sizeable castle. The main street of the town, Bailey Street, runs roughly north-east to south-west, a few yards south-west of the alignment of the Peddars Way as it heads for the crossing of the river Nar. The surviving back lanes can readily be traced, and (as in this example which runs between Bailey Street and the great outer ditch of the castle) are delightful corners of a fascinating small town, though others have been absorbed into gardens and backyards.

Castle Acre has a remarkable medieval landscape, with its great castle earthworks and stone fortifications, splendid priory ruins, and the well-preserved layout of a Norman planned town and borough. The latter was itself defended by large ramparts and substantial gateways. The north gate of the town survives, still spanning Bailey Street at the top of a steep hill. The more recent centre of the village lies to the north of the north gate, outside the perimeter of the medieval borough and occupying the site of the outer ditch, so that the gateway is now well within the built-up area.

The present centre of Castle Acre is High Street, which forms a long rectangular green that once served as a market place. This unusually wide street lies on the alignment of the outer ditch of the Norman planned town, and therefore outside the original defences. The planned town itself does not appear to have had a market place, which probably explains the migration of the urban focus to the area outside the north gate.

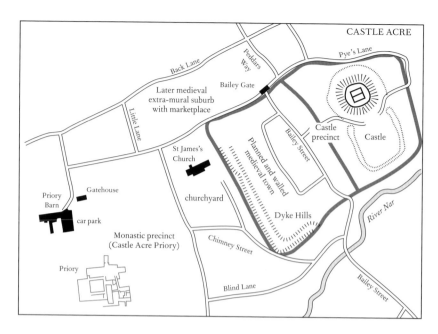

Elements in the plan of
medieval Castle Acre
(after J. Coad and G.
Coppack, 1998).

priory lay the town of Castle Acre and the parish church of St James. Like
Castle Rising this is a failed town. The castle appears to have been derelict
from the 1330s, the priory was dissolved in 1537, and the market dwindled and
died. The whole town, including the castle and priory, came into the hands
of Sir John Coke in 1615, and this single unified ownership explains how the
entire site has kept its character. The town lay in the outer bailey of the castle,
bounded by a deep ditch and bank and leaving no space for the church, which
stood outside it to the west. Castle Acre, one of Norfolk's most attractive and
fascinating places, is a town to explore with Pevsner and Wilson and the English
Heritage guidebook in hand.

The previous chapter showed how a number of other market towns were
already developing by the time of the Conquest. Two great monastic houses,
Ely and St Benet at Holme, had been endowed with big estates, and these
institutions encouraged commercial and urban development. Ely held the
hundred of Mitford and the large manor of East Dereham where a fine collegiate
church and perhaps a priory were built. Dereham lay almost at the centre of the
county and flourished under the wing of its monastic lords. Similarly, North
Walsham became the market town for the estates of St Benet. At Fakenham,
which was a royal manor, the small priory of Hempton stood close by, while
at Harleston, originally part of Redenhall, there was Mendham Priory. In
1086 one of the largest Norfolk towns, apart from Norwich and Thetford, was
Wymondham, on the great main road down to London. There William d'Albini
II created a separate manor to provide an estate for his new abbey which would
supply its demands for corn and livestock.

The market at Holt is mentioned in the Domesday Book and, like Fakenham,
the town had a number of outlying subsidiary settlements which emphasised
its wider administrative role. In the case of Holt one of the outliers was Cley,

In 1240 the bishop of Norwich issued an instruction that a market was no longer to be held in the churchyard at Reepham because it was consecrated ground – a rare glimpse into the informal and unregulated trading which often preceded the grant of a market charter. Thirty-three years later, in 1277, John de Vallibus, the lord of Reepham, was granted the right to hold a (legal) market, and it is probable that at this point the square market place was laid out west of the churchyard at the top of the low hill. It was often known as Hackford market, because of the highly complicated parish and manorial geography of the community. The buildings around are all sixteenth-century or later, because in 1542 a great fire destroyed most of the town centre. Many of the smaller markets have long since disappeared but in Reepham a weekly market is still held every Wednesday.

which gave it a valuable maritime trading place – though ultimately Cley, as a flourishing medieval port, became more important than Holt itself, a status which it only lost when the shipping trade dwindled and the market role of Holt was rejuvenated. Some of the future market towns were small in 1086, and some villages that never had a market, such as Hethersett and Mattishall, were already larger than many that did. By 1334 the relative importance of many settlements had changed. Thus, Harleston, later to evolve as a market town, was merely part of the large parish of Redenhall, while only in the late eighteenth century did Reepham become the name for what was once Hackford market.

The Norman Church in Norfolk

The Normans brought to England an established tradition of the founding of religious houses by aristocratic and land-owning patrons. The belief that one's progression from deathbed to heaven via purgatory was guaranteed by leaving gifts to the fabric of a church 'for tithes forgotten', and to various altars and guilds, was found much more widely in society, but for the wealthy the founding of a monastic house was almost routine. There were some 127 religious houses in Norfolk at the time of the Dissolution in the late 1530s.[15] Many were founded soon after the Conquest, but the four orders of friars, which emerged on a wave of renewed spirituality and reform in the early thirteenth century, did not become established – and then mainly in the larger towns – until the years after 1230.

The monasteries ranged from major institutions, such as Norwich and Castle Acre, both of which had perhaps 30 monks, to the very small foundations with just a few canons. The origins of the abbey of St Benet at Holme and the cathedral priory of Norwich have already been discussed, but

in the decades after the Conquest other important Benedictine houses were founded at Lynn, Great Yarmouth, Binham and Wymondham – at the latter two, the splendid naves of the churches survive. Three Benedictine nunneries were also founded, but their structural remains are negligible. Revision of the Benedictine rule led to the development of the Cluniac order, focused on the strict and unvarying routine of daily worship to an even greater degree than the Benedictines: Castle Acre Priory and Thetford Priory were their two main houses, both with extensive surviving remains (though in the case of Thetford robbed of the dressed stone and now appearing as almost abstract shapes of flint and rubble).

There were 18 houses of Augustinian (or Austin) canons in Norfolk, most of which were mainly post-Norman in origin, but at Westacre there are surviving remnants of the Norman structure, built in about 1100, in parts of the south-west tower, the cloister and the chapter house. The Austin canons followed the rule of St Augustine and were less tied to their monasteries than the Benedictines and Cluniacs. They frequently served nearby churches as parish priests, especially if their houses were patrons of the living and held the rectory. Two Norfolk monasteries became major shrines and the focus of important national and even international pilgrimage routes. Bromholm in the parish of Bacton, three miles east of North Walsham, was a Cluniac house. It was founded in 1113 as a daughter house of Castle Acre, and its evocative ruins retain some Norman work. In 1195 it became independent of its mother and then developed as a shrine in the thirteenth century when it acquired a precious relic of the True Cross. The celebrated house at Walsingham was an Augustinian foundation of about 1153, originating as a chapel built by Richelde of Fervaques after she had received a vision. Like Bromholm its great days as a shrine were in the later thirteenth century, when it was visited by Henry III and Edward I. Henry III gave it valuable oak timber for the church and guest hall in 1232 and 1234.[16] But Walsingham retained its power for another three centuries, being visited by, for example, Queen Margaret of Anjou, the wife of Henry VI – she came in April 1453 to give thanks at the shrine of the Virgin Mary for her pregnancy after nine barren years of marriage. The devout Queen Katherine of Aragon was a regular visitor until her husband, Henry VIII, first divorced her and then destroyed the monastery at the Dissolution.

The influence of religious houses extended widely. Apart from the friaries, which in principle at least derived their income mainly from charitable almsgiving or bequests, the monasteries were endowed with income from parish churches or from lands which were given to them by the founders and

The nave of Wymondham Abbey is a perfect and unaltered example of Norman architecture, of top quality and dramatic in scale. The abbey was founded in 1107 by William d'Albini, a prominent landowner with extensive Norfolk estates whose son was made 1st earl of Arundel. The nave survives because this was always the part of the church used by the townspeople as their parish church. In the centre of the picture is Sir Ninian Comper's magnificent gilded reredos, which was dedicated in 1921 as a war memorial (though not finished until 1934). It fills the east end, behind the altar, where there would otherwise be the blank wall which was built after 1539 to fill the gap where the crossing and the east end once stood.

Castle Acre priory was founded in about 1090 by William de Warenne, and was a daughter house of the great Cluniac priory at Lewes in Sussex. The priory housed between 26 and 30 monks and at the Dissolution was said to be worth £306 11s. 4¾d., placing it in the 'upper middle' rank by national standards. The priory church was built between the 1090s and 1140s, and although much of the building has gone the magnificent west front survives almost intact as one of the greatest examples of Norman architecture in Britain. It is particularly notable for the sumptuous and complex decoration, with the elaborate and beautiful interlaced blank arcading, the principal doorway with its richly decorative mouldings, and the exceptional sophistication of the four-decker structure – damaged only by the insertion of the huge west window, punched through the upper levels of the Norman work in the fifteenth century.

Detail of the decorative work on the west front of the priory: interlaced blank arcading, grotesque corbels supporting the stringcourse, geometric patterns in the intervening spaces, and the dancing line of chevrons above the arches of the upper arcading – almost no surface was left undecorated, and the artistic imagination of the designers and masons was given free rein.

At Castle Acre the buildings around the southern and eastern sides of the cloister, and the great priory church, are largely ruinous. In a region with little good building stone the dressed stone was too valuable and useful to be left, so it was quickly robbed and taken for re-use locally. This left the flint rubble cores of the walling, which were vulnerable to weathering and decay. Here, as at Thetford Priory, the appearance of the ruins, with the strangely amorphous quality of the flint walling, has been likened to melting candle wax.

other pious folk. When a church was given to a religious house the latter held the rectory and established a vicarage to oversee the parish church. In this way the monastery received the tithe income from the parish, and from that allocated the small tithes to maintain the vicar. At the height of the monastic system, in the fourteenth and fifteenth centuries, as much as one-third of the profit from the agricultural land of Norfolk went to religious houses. Monastic houses were landowners of major importance and large employers of labour, controlled extensive estates including urban properties and market rights, engaged in industrial production and long-distance trading, and provided work for craftsmen such as masons, glaziers, skilled wood-carvers and paviors whenever new building or extensive repair work was undertaken. Places such as Thetford, which had five major and several minor religious houses in or immediately outside the town, were heavily dependent on them for their economic well-being.

When it came, in the late 1530s, the Dissolution of the Monasteries – in Norfolk as in the rest of England and Wales – put an abrupt and sometimes violent end to more than four centuries of monastic life. Across the county, churches and domestic buildings were torn down or converted to other uses though some managed to survive. At Wymondham Abbey, which was partly destroyed, the choir and chapels disappeared but the Norman nave was retained because it also served as the parish church for the town. The abbey had had two western towers, but before the Dissolution these had already been replaced by the present single great west tower, paid for by benefactors and parishioners. The cloister and other monastic buildings survive only as earthworks to the south of the abbey. Fortunately the immediate surroundings to the south remained open and provide a beautiful setting, edged by the river Tiffey.

Bromholm (or Broomholm) Priory was a Cluniac house, founded in 1113 by William de Glanville. It stood on a windswept site which is now only a few hundred yards from the cliffs between Bacton and Walcott (though in the twelfth century it was much further inland). Always poor and often troubled by maladministration, its great claim to fame was that it possessed a cross, brought to England in 1223, which comprised fragments of the True Cross. The cross of Bromholm was an object of pilgrimage – for example, King Edward II came in 1313 on account of his special devotion to the relic – and it is mentioned in 'The Vision of Piers Plowman' and Chaucer's 'The Reeve's Tale'. The priory was dissolved in 1536 and some of the buildings were converted into a farm. It stands on private land and today the most impressive remnant is the gatehouse spanning the lane leading from the village.

The fifteenth-century gatehouse of Walsingham Priory (*circa* 1440) faces immediately on to High Street in the centre of the little town. It is built of flint with stone quoins and facings, and above the entrance arch are statue niches and panels carved with heraldic shields. The Augustinian priory (now often but wrongly called an abbey) was founded in the middle of the twelfth century and became a celebrated place of pilgrimage, of international significance. In the eleventh century the Virgin Mary had appeared there in a vision to the noblewoman Richeldis de Faverches and there she built a 'Holy House' which replicated the house of the Holy Family as seen in her vision.

Of course, monasticism was only one element in the life of the Norman and medieval Church. Many new parish churches were founded by the Norman tenants-in-chief, though it is often difficult to establish who paid for them. In fact, the origins of churches are frequently undocumented, and even the Domesday Book only records 317 churches in Norfolk, though other evidence (such as architecture, other written sources, and archaeological excavation) demonstrate that there were at least twice that number by 1086.[17] Many churches in the county show at least some Norman or Romanesque architectural elements (round towers, rounded heads to single windows, flat buttresses, zig-zag string courses and highly ornamental south and north doorways, together with apsidal chancels), especially in the south-east, where Hales, Heckingham and Haddiscoe provide especially good examples. Although few churches have their complete Saxo-Norman or Norman fabric, many others have obvious Norman elements which survive surrounded by later structures. Thus, Thorpe-next-Haddiscoe has a Saxon tower with a Norman bellstage. The Saxon work includes blank arcading and small windows in alternating

Creake Abbey is one of the lesser known religious houses of Norfolk, tucked away down a narrow lane beside the tiny river Burn between North Creake and Burnham Thorpe. It was founded, as a simple chapel, in 1206 by Sir Robert and Lady Alice de Narford, was extended in 1217 with the establishment of a hospital, and shortly afterwards became an Augustinian priory, elevated to abbey status in 1226. In 1484 the abbey was devastated by fire and on restoration was drastically reduced in size, the nave and part of the transepts being demolished – which explains why in this view the eastern end retains substantial ruins but the nave (foreground) has almost entirely vanished. The troubles did not end there – at the beginning of the sixteenth century plague ravaged the little community and when on 12 December 1506 the abbot died, all alone, the house ceased to exist.

Wymondham Abbey remains a very impressive building even though substantial parts of it became ruinous after the dissolution of the monasteries. This view shows the mighty three-stage central tower, built in the later fourteenth century and with its two upper stages being octagonal, which is now a dramatic empty shell rearing above the huge space that was formerly the crossing and, beyond it, the foundations of the chancel. Even mightier is the huge west tower of the second half of the fifteenth century, six massive storeys and uncompromisingly solid. It was begun in 1448 and building carried on into the mid-1470s. Together they give the abbey its unmistakeable appearance, unique in this country.

At the charming small church of St Andrew, West Dereham (near Downham Market) the lower stages of the Anglo-Saxon tower are made up of massive irregular blocks of dark brown puddingstone, an iron-rich conglomerate found in association with carstone in a band running south from Hunstanton via Denver to the edge of the Fens. Other than flint, this is Norfolk's only indigenous building stone. The tower at West Dereham is claimed to be the fattest round tower on any Norfolk church, with an internal diameter of 17 feet 6 inches, perhaps a consequence of the greater suitability of puddingstone for more ambitious structures than were possible with flint. The top of the tower is an octagonal brick structure, added at the beginning of the sixteenth century, and an unusual feature is the charming cream-painted south porch built in the early seventeenth century.

positions while the upper bellstage has two rounded Norman windows with a central shaft. The nave is also Norman.[18] At the opposite end of the county West Dereham tower is made of distinctive carstone blocks; it is exceptionally wide, with an inside diameter of 17 feet 6 inches: the much later bellstage is of attractive brickwork.[19] South Lopham 'has the most powerful Norman tower of any Norfolk parish church', centrally positioned and built in about 1120.[20] There is evidence of an even earlier Saxon nave, but the placing of the tower has led to suggestions that this is an example of a 'mother' or collegiate church. St Nicholas, Fundenhall, is another example of a strong Norman central tower, but one of the great curiosities is Attleborough St Mary, which originally had a central tower supported on massive arches. At the Dissolution the chancel (or east end) of this great collegiate church was demolished, leaving the once-central tower incongruously placed at the east end of the nave.

6

Early medieval Norfolk

1200–1350	intensive exploitation of peat in Broadland
1200–1350	population growth, pressure on the land and extension of cultivated area
1249	foundation of the Great Hospital in Norwich
1250	foundation of St Mary in the Field in Norwich
1250–1350	rapid increase in importance of rabbit farming in Breckland
1270	Forncett was manorial and administrative centre for the earls of Norfolk
1275–1300	assarting of woodland in, for example, Cawston
1275 onwards	expanding trade between King's Lynn and the Baltic
1287–1307	many commissions for Fenland drainage set up
1290–1310	evidence of extensive sub-division of agricultural holdings
1297–1334	construction of Norwich city walls and Great Yarmouth town walls
1300	by this date, four friaries in Norwich, three each in Thetford and Great Yarmouth
1334	Fenland has the wealthiest parishes in England
1338	very severe flooding in the Fens
1349–1350	The Black Death, with mortality of at least 40 per cent

THE previous chapter considered the impact of the Norman Conquest upon Norfolk, especially from the perspective of power: the new Norman lords, the building of castles, and the monastic system all represent the establishment – albeit with an almost completely new structure of authority, as Norman replaced Saxon. But we also need to consider the lives and lifestyles of ordinary people and to explore what can be revealed about their houses, economic activity and social organisation. In this pursuit, an archaeological approach to reconstructing the development of settlement and agriculture can be very helpful in giving us some idea of the form and character of the post-Domesday settlements in Norfolk. Aerial photography of the earthworks of Rougham, a shrunken village some ten miles south of Swaffham, shows clearly the line of the village road with its arrangement of tofts (plots containing a dwelling and an attached paddock). Such evidence can only be gleaned from deserted or shrunken sites because in the great majority of settlements the continued occupation and frequent change over the centuries has modified the original layout that lies beneath. At Rougham mapping of the abandoned parts of the village emphasises the layout of the area west of the early hall (see page 107). A similar layout appears at Kilverstone, a shrunken village which shows the layout of the tofts and the village street. There, fieldwork by Alan Davison showed how the finds of pottery, mainly of the thirteenth and fourteenth centuries, tied up with the earthwork evidence.[1]

The deserted medieval villages of Norfolk (after J. Coad and G. Coppack, 1998).

Pudding Norton near Fakenham has been described as 'probably the best example of a nucleated deserted medieval village to be seen in Norfolk, associated with a well-known family of flockmasters [the Fermors]'.[2] Within a south–north line of tofts there were a church and hall on the west side and two small moats on the east. The population remained relatively constant between 1334 and 1449, and some of the inhabitants were still making bequests to the church guilds in the early sixteenth century. The settlement probably survived into the 1550s, but by the seventeenth century documentary evidence of a village peters out; Blomefield, writing in 1746, said it was a depopulated place, where only a hall and manor house with a farmhouse remained. The Fermors, who acquired the manor at the Dissolution, were great sheep farmers, and the first stages of the decline may reflect the process whereby arable land was put down to grass for grazing.

Many deserted village sites include a moat, and these features probably represent the remnants of a manorial site, as at Forncett. The moats may have been defensive but were more probably designed at least in part as drainage systems for raised house platforms, and as fishponds. They were also a status symbol: any self-respecting gentleman needed a moat. The site at Park Farm in Wymondham was a manor of the abbot of Wymondham which later came into the hands of the Hobart family. It was central in a splendid medieval park. The moat at Kerdeston lies in a village recorded as deserted by Faden on his map of 1797. It was then considered to be a rectory moat but almost certainly

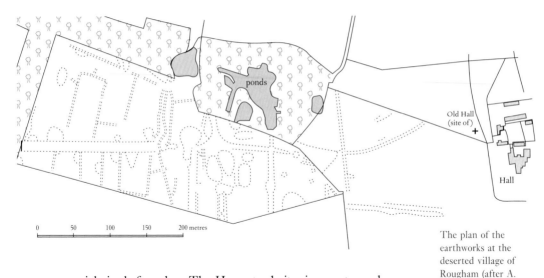

ponds

Old Hall
(site of)
+

Hall

The plan of the
earthworks at the
deserted village of
Rougham (after A.
Davison, 1991).

0   50   100   150   200 metres

was a manorial site before that. The Hempstead site, in a wet meadow, was discovered by a farmer when draining the field. He sensibly reported the floor of thirteenth-century patterned tiles to the Norfolk Archaeological Unit and these were saved by excavation. No moat now survives at the site but its shadow can still be seen in the same wet meadow.

Rogerson notes approximately 800 moated sites in Norfolk, of which 700 were on the wet boulder clays, clearly the most suitable terrain for their construction. Many are in the river valleys, but there are others, such as Kerdeston, which are up on the plateau.[3] Very few moated sites have been excavated in the county, but Rogerson suggests that the majority of them date from between 1200 and 1350, the period when the Broads were flooding and the climate became perceptibly wetter in a relatively short period of time. Climatic deterioration was particularly apparent in the context of coastal flooding, which affected the Broads, and in the very wet conditions on the boulder clays, where manorial sites needed to be raised and drained by the surrounding moats. Most moats are rectangular, as at Park Farm and Kerdeston, and the great majority, including both of those, have at least some evidence of a variety of buildings on the interior platform (as in the account of Forncett which follows). A few of the great houses, notably Mannington, Oxburgh and Blickling, are set in moats which must have been primarily status features, because there was little obvious practical need for them. Their moats are later in origin than those already discussed and, just as parks and avenues became the status features of the later estates, the moat, gatehouse, bridge and formal entrance to the buildings smacked of wealth and power.

While archaeology can help us in many ways, giving some idea of the layout of settlements before the Black Death of the mid-fourteenth century, documentary sources allow us to build up a fuller and more rounded picture. Norfolk lacks the early charters, dating from between 800 and the 1060s, that are so helpful in elucidating the early history of the counties of Wessex: during most of that period the county was under the Danelaw. However, after the Norman Conquest the deficit was soon made up. The founding of so many

At Mileham the extensive motte and bailey castle is one of the most impressive in the county, although surprisingly little known. It retains its complete and largely water-filled moat, with two baileys, and the substantial, though tumbled and overgrown, remains of the stone buildings on the summit of the motte. The castle was built in about 1100, probably by Hugh Bigod, Earl of Norfolk, and then passed by inheritance first to William d'Albini, lord of Castle Acre, and then to the FitzAlan family, earls of Arundel. It seems to have been abandoned by the end of the fourteenth century.

Weeting Castle, in the far south-west of the county, is a very rare example of a twelfth-century manor house. It was built in about 1180 by Hugh de Plais and remained the family home until the middle of the fourteenth century. Hugh's superior lord was William de Warenne, earl of Surrey, who had built a stone manor house at Castle Acre, and the resemblance between the two sites suggests that Hugh copied the idea. A stone house with a great hall was surrounded, at a later date (probably in the thirteenth century) by a rectangular moat, probably as a status symbol rather than for defence. The house remained occupied by other inferior families, into the early eighteenth century.

religious houses by the Norman lords is of particular importance, because careful registers were kept by the monasteries of the endowments made to them. Furthermore, the major families – the Albinis, Warennes and Bigods – developed their own sophisticated record keeping, as in the example of Forncett discussed below. Finally, the development of the manorial system required the keeping of court rolls, large numbers of which have survived to give a picture of land transactions and the names of the tenants. The Church also kept a careful record of its holdings and, as has been seen, many landowners gave property to the church, often for specific purposes. The bishops of Norwich and their archdeacons made regular 'visitations' to the parishes, and the visitation books give a good account of the state of repair of the churches. Finally, the wills and inventories of many thousands of the population survive from the early fourteenth century onwards, and give us much detail not only of families and possessions but also of landholdings, bequests and endowments to or for religious houses.

Davenport's 1967 study gives a masterly impression of the manorial complex at Forncett after the Conquest.[4] Forncett is set along the meadows of the small River Tas, in a valley cut into the boulder-clay plateau. In the medieval period clay was used for the buildings, or at least for their external coating (known as 'daubing'), and straw for the roofs, but the hall was thatched with reed. Clay walls, topped with thatch, surrounded the outer and inner courts. In 1270 the manor of Forncett was in the hands of Earl Bigod, and was a large and important holding with many freemen scattered across the hundred of Depwade. The manorial hall had a dozen chambers and outbuildings as well as barns and stables. In addition to the earl's chamber there were others for knights and the bailiff (the man who ran the manor and kept the crucial accounts from which historians can glean so much). There was housing for the ploughman and carter as well as a kitchen, salser (for making sauces), buttery, larder, bakehouse, dairy, granary and housing for geese and chickens. Because Forncett was such an important holding, with a major collection of buildings, it can be regarded as the chief or capital manor of the earl's holdings in Norfolk.

Remarkable sets of accounts for Forncett have survived for the late thirteenth century. These show that the main source of income for the manor was grain (both wheat and barley), which provided £52 6s. 8d. of the total income of £109 5s. 2d. in 1277/78. Stock sales raised £5, produce from the dairy £3 13s. 6d., and various feudal rents amounted to £45. The expenses of the same year amounted to £13 9s. 1d., of which the bailiff received £3 12s. and the steward £1 13s. 7d., while £3 15s. 6d. was spent on the maintenance of the buildings. The year 1277/78 would seem to have been good for the demesne farm, not least because this was a favourable period in terms of climate, the last time of optimism before conditions deteriorated in the early fourteenth century.

The detailed nature of these accounts gives impressive evidence of the level of organisation and efficient administration of the earl's lands. The home farm belonging to the lord, the demesne, covered about 300 acres or one-ninth of the total area of the manor. The cropping was on average 80 acres of barley, 50 of wheat, 40 of oats and 40 of peas, oats being used to feed the stock on the manor and the peas for human consumption. The bulk of the demesne lay on the edge of the settlement and may well have been in the form of assarts, or small enclosures, which had recently been taken in from the woodland as the population grew. This was typical of developments on the boulder-clay plateau; we know that the nearby manor of Wacton was also clearing woodland in this period.

The tenants of the Forncett manor were the labour force for the demesne as well as having their own holdings. Analysing the accounts for 1272, Davenport divided them into four groups. A few were favoured tenants who paid small rents (sometimes in the form of hens and eggs) and did not have to do agricultural labour or work on the demesne. A second group was required to do particular tasks for the lord, such as 'autumn works' on his land, carting, and some 'week works' of directed labour. A third group owed two days' work in winter, summer and spring, and each held a five-acre tenement. They had to perform three cartings of manure, make a quarter of malt, pay 12 bushels of oats, a hen and five eggs, 1¾d. as a 'salt penny', and a money rent of 6½d. A final group had one day of work each week and tenancies of 24 acres. It is noticeable that these tenancies were smaller than the full holdings of 30 acres which were known as *virgates* (that is, the land needed to support a villager) like those in Pulham mentioned in the previous chapter.

That the tenants owned stock is confirmed by the fact that the sokemen had to pay a penny for any cow and for every five sheep not sent to lie in the lord's fold. This complex balance between the lord and the tenants was the feudal contract for this manor on the wet clay plateau. As time progressed the 'real' labour portions of payment gradually declined and the cash rent increased. Quit rents, paid by tenants to the lord in lieu of the complex services, survived as very small manorial 'rents'. Commercial rents gradually replaced these in real terms, but as token financial contributions they continued to be paid on most manors until 1925.

During this period population was growing and monastic records, because they tend to be more continuous and more carefully kept than many others, have been the most valuable source in studying these changes. Hallam used those of St Benet at Holme to give an idea of the increasing population of the eastern part of Norfolk between 1086 and 1250.[5]

Number of plough-teams in Norfolk		
	1086	*thirteenth century*
Horning	6	25
Neatishead	14	51
Hoveton	14	40
Ludham	14½	75
Potter Heigham		35
Paston	½	3
North Walsham	17½	45
Witton	½	3½
Felmingham	1½	5
Smallburgh	5½	13
Honing	5	15
Stalham	3	7
Waxham	3½	8½
Worstead	5	30
Beeston St Lawrence		9½
Total	90½	365½

The fourfold increase is striking. Hallam argues that although population was increasing in this period, farming was improving and more land was perhaps being put down to the plough. In the St Benet area marsh reclamation may have taken place as well as assarting, or clearance, of woodland.

A second detailed study of this period, paralleling Davenport's account of the wood pasture on the clay-plateau area, is Bruce Campbell's discussion of the common fields of East Norfolk,[6] an area of very fertile brickearth soils. He discussed the pattern of agricultural events in a series of east Norfolk parishes, concluding that the increase in population from about 1200 led to considerable pressure on the land, so that holdings were steadily reduced in size until the early fourteenth century. Partible inheritance led to a steady reduction, as holdings were split between all the children rather than going only to the eldest son. As elsewhere, the population grew and holdings were sub-divided. Campbell estimated that the population of Martham increased by 250 per cent in the thirteenth century.

There, for example, Syware Blakeman's toft, probably taken in from the waste, was initially a single unit of six acres, but by 1292 it had been divided into ten separate pieces. This 'parcelisation' reached its maximum in about 1290, when the common fields attained their greatest size and most complex sub-division. In Martham in 1292 there were 2,122 parcels in the common fields, with a mean size of half an acre, and they were held by 376 people with a mean holding of 2.8 acres in six parcels. Robert Gerven, for example, held 2 acres 1 rood in Estfeld, 1 acre 1 rood in Westfeld, 1 acre 30 perches in Southfeld, 1 rood in Tomers, 20 perches in Clovenhove and 1 acre 2 roods as a toft with a messuage. This was a total holding of 6 acres 2 roods and 10 perches, but scattered in six different parts of the parish. The point must have been reached when such tiny and scattered holdings were uneconomic, whereupon living standards would have begun to fall.

In several of these east Norfolk parishes the common fields abutted those of neighbouring parishes and there was little waste or common land left, and even if some did remain in the thirteenth century it was fast being taken into agricultural use. Cawston, the westernmost of the parishes in Campbell's study, had huge wooded areas in 1086 but by 1290–91 a survey recorded 109 acres of assarts, and few other parishes still had such areas of woodland left. During the period of Martham's increase in population there was very little increase in the total farmed area, simply because almost no 'spare' land was available, and this inevitably led to much greater pressure on the existing farmed land. Furthermore, that land was already intensively exploited. Evidence from St Benet's lands in the mid-thirteenth century shows that a sophisticated level of agriculture already existed in which bare fallow – land on which weeds grew for a year – was minimal, and one-tenth of all arable land was down to legumes which provided nitrogen: 750 years ago, though the scientific reason for that benefit was unknown, the practical value of such cropping was well understood. There, barley was the major cereal crop grown.

Breckland

The sandy, dry soils of the Breckland define a distinctive sub-region, or *pays*, within the Norfolk landscape.[7] These soils retained only limited surface water, apart from that of the rivers Little Ouse, Thet, Wissey and Nar and their flood plains, and that in turn restricted settlement to these valleys except along the Fen edge where, as we have already seen, there was continuity of settlement from the Bronze Age onwards.

Bailey's detailed study of many Breckland records, especially those of manors belonging to the abbeys of Ely and Bury St Edmunds, emphasised the importance of the 'fold-course' system of farming. This was based on the grazing of sheep, which ate the often sparse vegetation but, when pastured on heaths or arable land after harvesting, manured the thin soils with their droppings and thereby helped to maintain fertility. Before the Black Death, as Bailey's research revealed, the lords of manors were not able to dominate the fold-coursing system. Many freemen and even some villeins had fold-courses as part of their holdings, and in 1367 the Duchy of Lancaster granted a fold to a tenant in Methwold on condition that it 'did not prejudice the lord's fold'. So a freeman might have a fold-course for 200 sheep which he could graze on his field land and on specific heaths. This, in turn, required the production of large numbers of hurdles to create temporary enclosures within which to fold the sheep at night. The system must have been one of great complexity, and Bailey suggests that a 'lord' of a parish could have had ruling powers in such cases – exercising arbitrary powers to allocate fold-course boundaries and the size of the flocks to graze them. Sometimes tenants could rent a fold-course, and they could also place some of their own sheep, known as cullet sheep, with the lord's flock. In other cases, as at West Harling, they had to make a payment of a penny for every ten sheep which they placed in the lord's flock.

Comparatively little of the 'natural' Breckland landscape now remains. Enclosure and agricultural improvements in the eighteenth and nineteenth centuries, and the massive afforestation programmes of the early twentieth century, eliminated vast swathes of the dry sandy heath which characterises much of south-west Norfolk. Some areas remain within the Battle Area, inaccessible to the public, but the haunting, lonely and empty landscapes of the area north of Thetford and south of Swaffham, unique in England, are now almost vanished. This view shows an area of cleared forest, close to Thetford Warren Lodge, where on a few acres of land something of the old character has re-emerged, with coarse grassland, scrub and heather growing on a sandy stony soil, dusty and flinty.

Thetford Warren Lodge was built in the late thirteenth century by Thetford Priory as the headquarters of its extensive rabbit warrens which stretched across the empty heaths of Breckland, north-west of the town. The head warrener lived there with his family, and the building was fortified to protect them from poachers. It was used as a store for the equipment – traps and nets – used to catch the rabbits, and rabbit skins would also be held there before they were taken for curing and use in the fur trade. The lodge was once larger – wings on either side were demolished after a fire in 1935, when the building fell into disuse.

The crucial value of sheep in maintaining soil fertility was obvious, but there were other options. Chalk (or marl) pits might be dug, in order to dress land with lime: sandy soils are easily leached by rainwater, because they are so porous, and liming or marling redressed the chemical balance. We know that in West Harling rye, barley, peas and small oats were grown between 1328 and 1336, the peas helping to replenish the mineral content. Relatively small areas of 'infield' arable lay immediately adjacent to the settlements on the edge of the valley floors, beyond which were large areas of heath into which irregularly cropped land was opened up from time to time: because of its poverty it could only be cropped sporadically. Areas which were 'broken up' in this way were termed *brecks*.

A second vital element of the Breckland economy was the rabbit. Although unknown in 1086, rabbits were well established in Breckland parishes by the

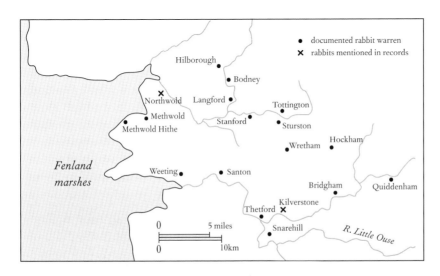

Known rabbit warrens in the Breckland of Norfolk (after M. Bailey, 1989).

middle of the thirteenth century.[8] The dry, easily burrowed soils provided good conditions for the animals, and warrens were established with artificially constructed pillow mounds, raised mounds of sand several feet high into which rabbits could easily burrow and set up their colonies. Many of these mounds, arranged in clusters, were provided by monastic lords who were keen to produce valuable yields of meat and fur. At Hilborough in 1370–79, for example, the warren produced 348 rabbits of which one-quarter went to the lord and nearly two-thirds were sold: so important was this trade that in 1376–77 six acres of oats were sown solely to feed the rabbits. The combination of intensive grazing by sheep and rabbits reduced the vegetation cover to a minimum, and was instrumental in creating the heaths which were so typical of much of the Breckland landscape, with its wide vistas of open treeless country. This produced serious over-grazing which, when combined with strong winds, allowed sand dunes to develop – locally, a man-made ecological disaster, as at the famous site of Santon Downham on the Suffolk side of the Little Ouse, where the church was half-submerged in blown sand.

The Fens

West of the Brecks lay the Fens, where an entirely different economy existed. Life there was a gamble, a constant battle with sea floods, freshwater floods and shifting river channels. Owen notes that the first time the Crown intervened in Fenland drainage was after the great storms of 1253–54. Specific reference was made to the inundations of the sea and of fresh waters. In 1287–88 the first Commission of Sewers (that is, drains) was established, for the Wiggenhalls in Marshland. The severity of the problems of bank maintenance is shown by the appointment of no fewer than 17 commissions for this area in the last twenty years of Edward I's reign (1287–1307). After the flood of 1338 a jury at Wiggenhall reviewed the disasters that had overtaken the town since Edward III had come to the throne in 1327:

> On the morrow after Epiphany, in the third year of the then King a certain bank on the west part of the said river by means of the raging of the sea broke; so that the tides entered and overflowed 1000 acres of land, sowed with corn, to the great damage of the same town. And that on the west part of the said river by reason of the like tempests, happening on the eve of St Hillarie next before, the before specified bank was broken and torn so that the tides entered, bore down a house and overflowed 200 acres of land sown with corn. And that on the eve of St Andrew, in the 8th year of the same King, the said bank was by the said mishap, broken again, for the length of three furlongs in a certain place called Burtyshithe, insomuch as the tides flowing in overwhelmed 1000 acres of land sowed with corn.[9]

But while the sea and the great rivers of Fenland constantly sought to inundate the flat lands, local landowners and farmers no less assiduously attempted to reclaim and exploit the fertile soils of the area. Extensive drainage and reclamation works were already under way by the fourteenth century. Evidence for this comes, for example, from an account written some time between 1380 and 1420 of the lands around Crabhouse Nunnery, which was founded in 1181:

> There was neither any habitation, nor ground that yielded profit, within that part of Wigenhale from Bustardesdole unto the south side of the same town, except the monastery of Crabhous with some lands belonging thereto; all being then waste and in the nature of a fen: but afterwards the inhabitants of that place and of diverse others, came; and, with draining and banking, won as much thereof, by their industry, as they could: and that they might the more securely enjoy the same were contented to be tenants for it unto such great men of whom they held their other lands; and upon this occasion, by a common consent amongst them, was the Old Podike first raised about the year 1223.[10]

Much of the fenland grazing was non-parochial: that is, it was created from the sea or sodden wetlands after the system of parishes had been established, so that it belonged to none of them. In the spring great flocks of sheep and head of cattle were taken down the droveways from the silt fen and out on to the great expanse of the new grasslands, known as the Smeeth (a term used to describe the smooth stretch of grazing marsh). Darby distinguished two sorts of arrangement: the *intrinsec*, in which any number of stock could graze without payment at any time, and *forinsec* by which the rights of the lord developed to the detriment of commoners, either because he demanded rent for the grazing or because he restricted the number of stock. Peat, locally referred to as turf, was the essential fuel for the fen villages, and in order to avoid conflicts over turf-cutting the boundaries between parishes had to be carefully defined.

Although much of this was new land, lying beyond the old-established boundaries, and despite the continuous uneasy relationship between land, seawater and freshwater, this was a remarkably prosperous area, as its superb medieval churches demonstrate. In the 1334 subsidy of tenths and fifteenths a group of north Fenland parishes was assessed as being wealthier than many important Norfolk parishes to the east; Terrington, for example, paid £40 whereas North Walsham paid a mere £15, the Wiggenhalls £37 while Swaffham only paid £20. This reflects the wealth from wool and hides that was coming from the fen. The wet wastes of three hundred years before had become, in large measure through human endeavour, very valuable land.

The process carried on into the sixteenth century. In 1584 Richard Cooper of Terrington St John made his will.[11] Although he described himself as a husbandman (which elsewhere would mean merely a smallholder) his possessions were worth the substantial sum of £126 5s. 4d. He left his wife '20 wethers [sheep] of the best, 20 ewes with their lambs of the best, 20 hog sheep, 6 milch neat [cows] and the best young mare'; to one daughter he bequeathed 'two bullocks of the best and one other of the worst'; three other three daughters received two bullocks each; a nephew was left 20 ewes and 20 lambs; each daughter received one-fourth of the rest of the flock of ewes and lambs, apart from a servant who had a ewe and one lamb, and his maid who was bequeathed a ewe hog. This will emphasises the absolute dominance of stock in the possessions of a Fenland farmer: animals constituted perhaps 75 per cent of Richard's wealth. Terrington St John, a southern extension of Terrington St Clement, was probably not taken in from the Smeeth until about 1200, when the construction of new drains allowed new enclosures to be taken in from the seasonally flooded grazings.

The Broads

The mouths of the east-flowing rivers of Norfolk, and the Waveney system of Suffolk, join to form Breydon Water to the west of the Great Yarmouth spit. Before the development of the spit this was a more open estuary, far wider and with tidal marshes and shifting channels over what is now reclaimed land. The slow infilling of these channels had a complex history, but when vegetation grew in fresh water layers of peat formed, while marine silts were laid down nearer to the sea. In post-Norman times these marshes, and the peat which underlay them, became more accessible to man. The peat itself was soon recognised as a particularly valuable resource.

Peat working is recorded from the twelfth century until the end of the fourteenth, when it began to lose significance because extensive extraction gave rise to major flooding of the workings themselves. Peat cuttings (known as turbaries) were rented from the manors by their tenants. The 1337–38 account for the priory estate in Ormesby, for example, refers to turbaries in the area where Ormesby Broad now lies. Ten thousand turves, $3\frac{1}{2}$ inches square and 2–3 feet long, made one measure, which was known as a 'last'. In 1338 two lasts were used on the manor, five lasts (that is, 50,000 turves) were sold, and the remainder sent to the priory by water from Yarmouth, having been carted there by eight men over two days.[12] It was clearly a massive undertaking.

The removal of huge volumes of peat from the cuttings on the marshes near the rivers left the wide pits which rapidly filled with water to become the Broads, a change particularly apparent during the fourteenth-century storm surges in a period of deteriorating weather and rising sea levels. The consequences can be traced in the written record: for example, by 1380 Norwich Cathedral Priory had to begin to use wood for its kitchens instead of peat because the deeper peat cuttings had been drowned by encroaching water.[13] The marsh-covered, peat-rich valley floors lay close to the river channels which were also parish boundaries, but those boundaries which ran at right angles to the rivers were cut across by the peat diggers. Thus, Hickling Broad, as it filled up, stretched from Hickling across Catfield parish to Potter Heigham and encompassed, by drowning, the turbaries of all three parishes.

It was only in the 1950s that the origins of the Broads were revealed. It had always been presumed that these were natural lakes, but a careful study of the surviving maps and the medieval accounts of the abbey of St Benet's and Norwich Cathedral Priory, together with painstaking fieldwork, showed the value of interdisciplinary work by historians, archaeologists and botanists in attempting to understand one facet of our landscape more clearly.[14] The research produced much new evidence, including meticulous surveys of the edges of the Broads, which showed incontrovertibly that they were man-made. Further detailed analysis of the monastery documents revealed how much peat had been dug out from the Broads to serve those two houses. These fascinating explorations are discussed in more detail in chapter 13.

Woodland

Oliver Rackham's map of woodland in medieval Norfolk shows that only 12 per cent of the county was wooded in 1086 and that this had been reduced to a mere 6 per cent by 1350.[15] The great historical geographer H.E. Darby shows in his map of the Domesday woodland of the eastern counties that Norfolk was better wooded than Lincolnshire, had about the same percentage as Suffolk, and was far less densely wooded than Essex or the Weald of Kent.[16] In the early medieval period the damp boulder-clay plateau had the greatest extent of woodland, while the Broads and the Fens had the least. The demand for timber for building was very considerable, and Rackham suggests that much of the timber used in Norwich came from the Continent, but this question is much debated. There is no doubt that the impact of building in Norwich must have diminished the extent of nearby woodlands, such as those at Mousehold, on the eastern edge of the city, which were important to both the priory and the bishop for their timber, and where the tree cover was gradually reduced until it became heathland grazing for sheep. On the other hand, King's Lynn certainly imported large quantities of Scandinavian softwoods, and even in Norwich imports of oak boards and wainscot were significant in the mid-fifteenth century. The manorial, or vill, wood was a vital part of the economy of most

Foxley Wood, near Foulsham, is the largest surviving area of ancient woodland in the county, covering some 300 acres. Now managed by the Norfolk Wildlife Trust as a nature reserve, it has a rich and diverse ecology, with over 350 species of flowering plants recorded. In late spring bluebells carpet the woodland floor, especially in areas where more light is available as a result of clearance or coppicing, or along the edges of paths and rides.

Coppicing is an ancient method of woodland management involves felling species such as hazel on a regular cycle (usually every ten years or so). The new growth which shoots from the base produces long straight poles which were used for tool handles, fencing, charcoal production and other agricultural and domestic needs. Coppicing helps to maintain the ecological balance in the woodland and, by creating temporary glades and areas of open ground, encourages species diversity. It is also deeply embedded in local history – woodlands such as this have been coppiced for many centuries.

parishes, and rights of felling of timber and brushwood were strictly protected. Most Norfolk tenants had rights to take timber for repairing their houses as well as the right to cut reed and sedge for thatching, and turf. As already noted, Cawston's huge area of woodland was reduced heavily between 1066 and 1086, and this process continued as the population increased.

Woodland was managed carefully to provide a range of timber products. Foxley Wood, a surviving ancient wood, is gradually being brought back into its medieval management system by the Norfolk Wildlife Trust. Woods such as this provided cut timber (from the felling of mature trees, especially oaks) for major buildings, for which good single trees (standards) were left to mature, as in another ancient wood at Ashwellthorpe. When cattle had grazed within a wood, keeping down the undergrowth and saplings, a distinctive landscape emerged – pollard oaks were scattered across the stretches of grassland, to give what is usually known as 'wood pasture'. Without great care this would become full grassland, as the older trees died off and were not replaced because new seedlings and saplings were eaten by grazing livestock. Some patches of true wood pasture survive, as at Wattlefield, just south of Wymondham. From the beginning of the sixteenth century the demand for large timbers began to decline, as brick making on suitable areas of boulder clay (and especially on the brick earths of east Norfolk) began to provide an alternative construction material.

In these woods the adoption of a system of coppicing, as shown at Foxley and Ashwellthorpe, produced a range of wattles (hazel rods) and posts, their size depending on the cycle of cutting. The lesser growths of various species, especially hazel which was coppiced at intervals for use as hazel rods which were the 'wattles' in wattle and daub, were used for many other purposes such as hurdles for enclosing stock. Ash and elm were also important for farm tools: a typical cartwheel had an oak hub, ash spokes and an elm rim. All of this meant that woodlands had to be managed both efficiently and over a long period. The Domesday Book recording of woodland makes clear that it had a grazing value in its acorn crop for swine, and in the medieval period these woods were part of the demesne: in a properly managed piece of woodland the pigs were allowed to graze, but cattle and deer had to be kept out, so a deep ditch (with a thorn hedge on top of its inner edge) would be dug around the wood, a feature which can still be seen at Ashwellthorpe.

The Black Death (1349)

The evidence of the records of St Benet's Abbey indicates that in Norfolk, as elsewhere in England, population increased rapidly until the early fourteenth century, at which point climatic deterioration and then the Black Death had a devastating effect on numbers. The generally accepted view is that by the 1310s the stability of England's population was weakened by deteriorating weather, including greater storminess and higher rainfall. The flooding of the peat cuttings in east Norfolk was one result. Thus, even before the Black Death, the increase in population had ended or even been reversed. The Black Death, which raged from 1348 to 1351, took those who were sick but also ravaged the rest of the population, while further epidemics took a heavy toll in 1361–62, 1369 and 1375. Some of these may have been age-specific (picking out particular age groups) and Miller comments that 'population declined everywhere, or almost everywhere (and not merely in places suffering exceptional adversity or poorly endowed by nature) for two or three generations and had still shown little significant recovery by the time of the first Tudor ruler [i.e. 1485]'.[17]

It seems that roughly 40 per cent of the population was wiped out. It is impossible to be sure of actual numbers, but a register kept during the incumbency of William Bateman, bishop of Norwich from 1344 to 1355 covers the period of the Black Death and gives valuable evidence for the diocese of Norwich (including Suffolk).[18] It lists the institutions of clergy and vividly demonstrates that the impact of the pestilence was devastating. Whereas in non-plague times the number of clergy appointed in the diocese averaged a dozen in a month, in 1349–1350 the figures were:

April 1349	19	August 1349	145
May 1349	73	September 1349	71
June 1349	120	October 1349	75
July 1349	222	January 1350	17

The extraordinary figure for July 1349, twenty times the usual rate of appointment, implies that over 200 clergy had died in the diocese in the previous month. In that same month of July 1349 alone, new superiors were appointed for the Norfolk monasteries at Carrow, Holy Sepulchre of Thetford, Mountjoy, Wormegay, Hickling, Westacre, Crabhouse and Walsingham. At Hickling, Brother John Grys, priest and canon, 'was provided by the Bishop by his special grace to the priorate of that house, now vacant … no election was held because of the lack of canons there.' At Mountjoy, near Cawston, Brother Simon de Fleg, priest and canon of Wormegay Priory, was provided by the bishop to the priorate of St Lawrence 'now vacant because of the death of the Prior and all the canons of Mountjoy'.[19] These were small religious houses, and here the impact of the Black Death was catastrophic. As Ormrod and Lindley summarise in their study of the Black Death in England:

Plague led to social and economic mobility, to a break in the family–land relationship at all levels, peasantry and gentry. That brought land on to the market which in its turn opened the way for those with enterprise to engross and reorganise their holdings and to experiment with new methods of farming – and thus to the emergence of capitalist attitudes. The change in the nature of the family, from functionally extended to nuclear, the stress on individualism perhaps caused by the sense of the impermanence of life, also helped to promote structural change which offered the opportunities for those who were fortunate enough to survive and to have heirs, and who also had the necessary drive, to prosper. Plague is not seen as a dead hand but as a positive force for the social

and economic change which laid the foundations of early modern England.
... The Black Death must also be seen as the essential precursor of the
enclosure movement of the sixteenth and seventeenth centuries.[20]

The desertion of villages has often been linked to the Black Death, and
in some counties there may well be a direct relationship. However, Davison
maintained that in Norfolk no single village desertion can be related directly
to the pestilence.[21] In many cases the subsidy, or tax, records of 1334 showed
that villages were already declining when compared with their Domesday
Book population, or that the decline came later. At Mannington, for example,
the 1449 subsidy showed a 40 per cent population reduction compared with
1334, suggesting that the Black Death was a factor in, but not the sole cause
of, decline. There the hall was built in about 1360 and a map of 1565 shows no
village at all.[22] At Pensthorpe, where the remains of the church form the café of
the Wildlife Centre, there was a market in 1257 yet by 1332–34, over a decade
before the Black Death, the community was already very small. By 1603 the
church had only ten communicants, and Davison suggests that the village had
effectively disappeared by the sixteenth century. His research highlighted the
large number of deserted sites in the Breckland and on the boulder-clay divide
through the west-centre of the county, and a small cluster in the north-east is
probably related to the development of estates such as Mannington.

The towns between 1150 and 1350

The outstanding development in the shaping of Norwich in this period was
the massive project to build the city wall between 1297 and 1344. This highly
ambitious scheme involved the construction of 40 towers and 12 gates, with
boom towers erected beside the Wensum by the south gate to allow a chain to
be thrown across the river as a defence. A bank and ditch had already been
dug around the city by 1253, but the stone walls were not begun until 1294
and the city was given a murage grant (special funding for wall building) from
the Crown for five years from 1337. The area enclosed by the walls was larger
than that of London and Southwark combined, stretching 1½ miles from south
to north and one mile from east to west. It was initially a simple flint wall but
in 1344 Richard Spynk, a wealthy citizen, added the towers and engines of
war, and paid for the Bishop's Bridge gate. The motive for all this work was
to provide 'for the profit and defence of the city and adjacent country and
for the honour of the king'. Profit, in a literal sense, was clearly important:
the complete wall with its gates gave the city control over goods entering and
leaving and enabled it to make a surplus from tolls and customs.[23] Norwich
straddles the river Wensum, and the northern defences therefore encompassed
'Over-the-Water', while the southern two-thirds of the wall took in the New
Borough and then swept down a steep cliff at the south gate to end in a boom
tower, which was matched by another on the marshy land on the north bank.
The Cow Tower was paid for by the city in 1398–99 as an artillery tower
to protect its eastern edge. In the area of the city itself the Wensum cuts

through flint and chalk, which were thus easily accessible and used as the main building materials, though there was also some brick. Unfortunately (at least for historical and architectural posterity) the gates were demolished between 1791 and 1810 because they constricted traffic.

The religious geography of the city also changed in this period. During the thirteenth century several orders of preaching friars were established in western Europe. They 'were a revolutionary force in the thirteenth-century church, the front line of a "counter reformation" directed against heresy'.[24] The Dominicans (Blackfriars) and Franciscans (Greyfriars) both came to Norwich in 1224, the Whitefriars (Carmelites) in 1256, and in 1288–89 the Augustine (Austin) Friars arrived. All four were 'begging' orders and, unlike the monastic orders, could own property only on their own site – in other words, they could not build up portfolios of property as a commercial asset. They were preachers and teachers and went out to the churches in Norwich and beyond the city. Gradually, by receiving gifts of abutting properties they built up four important precincts on formerly under-occupied sites on the fringes of the city: 'They came as poverty stricken radicals, settled on the margins. … Yet, within a century their convents were dominated by magnificent churches frequented and patronised by the most prominent figures of city and county society.'[25] It was the custom of many of the wealthy to make bequests and to be buried in their precincts. Two of the finest medieval buildings surviving in Norwich, Blackfriars and St Andrew's Hall, together form the only complete example of an English friary.

The arrival of the four orders of friars by 1300 meant that a very active religious life was added to the city's role as capital of the county. There were about 190 friars based in Norwich, compared with 60 monks in the cathedral priory, and the friars moved and taught freely among the citizens whereas the 'enclosed' monks were not always on the happiest terms with those outside the precinct. Two other important religious foundations were the Great Hospital – the Hospital of St Giles founded in 1249 by Walter Suffield, bishop of Norwich, for poor clergy and other poor people – and the College of St Mary in the

The medieval city of Norwich was ringed by a two-thirds circuit of walls, including Over the Water, but with no wall on the eastern side because there the Wensum, from Ber Lane to the boom towers close to the later site of Carrow Bridge provided at least some protection. Twelve fortified gateways gave access to the city within the walls. The walls were constructed between the mid-1290s and 1340, mostly of flint and at least partly on the line of an existing bank and ditch rampart, but within a few decades there were complaints about their deterioration and decay. In 1791–1810 all the gates were demolished, as obstacles to traffic. Few substantial stretches of the walls remain: the most visible are those along the inner road at Chapelfield, seen here.

Field which was established for a community of priests in 1250. The remains of the college survive in and under the modern Assembly House.

Norwich became increasingly important as a trading city and as a market which had many sub-divisions. It was, and would continue to be, the market centre for a large region, selling grain, meat, wool and, later, cloth. The enrolled deeds of the city, from the period 1285–1311, reveal that dyers, fullers and shearmen were numerous in the Westwick Street area along the river Wensum. Leather workers formed the biggest craft group, organised in a whole series of sub-divisions such as skinners, tanners, tawyers, shoemakers, saddlers and parchment makers. By 1345 there were 68 trades and services listed in these deeds, among them goldsmiths, masons, bellfounders and clothing crafts.[26]

Medieval Norwich on the eve of the Black Death (after B. Ayers, 1994).

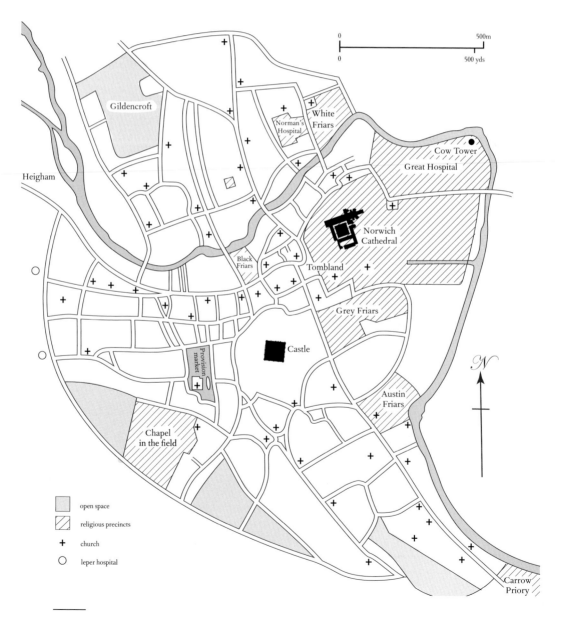

Bishop Bridge is the only surviving medieval bridge in Norwich, all the others having been rebuilt since the eighteenth century to cater for heavy road traffic. It survives because Bishopgate, once the main road into the city from the east, is now a quiet backwater (in marked contrast to the traffic congestion of Foundry Bridge half a mile downstream). Bishop Bridge was built in 1345, on the site of an ancient ford and at the point where a possible Roman road from Brundall into central Norfolk would have crossed the Wensum. It was originally defended with a fortified gatehouse, which was demolished in 1791.

Cow Tower, in the bend of the River Wensum north-east of Norwich city centre, was built in 1398-99. Almost fifty feet high, it was one of the earliest purpose-built artillery blockhouses in England, designed to accommodate cannon, as well as archers with longbows or crossbows. The river below was navigable, and this improvement to the city defences was intended to counter the threat of attack by water. The timing is no accident, as it coincided with heightened security concerns as the Hundred Years War with France entered a new phase.

The Great Hospital in Norwich was founded in 1249 by Bishop Walter de Suffield, for the benefit of aged priests, poor scholars and the sick poor. It was not a medical hospital in the modern sense – rather, as with other medieval hospitals, it provided residential care for the needy. Its buildings were arranged around a tiny cloister and the hospital annexed the existing parish church of St Helen. It has been providing care for the elderly ever since, and is probably the oldest continuously functioning elderly persons' home in Britain, working without a break for almost 800 years. Its medieval archive survives intact, and has now been included in the UK section of the UNESCO 'Memory of the World' listing.

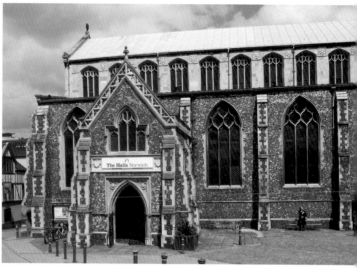

The interior of St Andrew's Hall, the intact nave of the Dominican friary church. Such buildings were designed primarily for preaching, with high open roof spaces for good acoustics, and the body of the church wide and uncluttered in order to accommodate large numbers of people. With such characteristics the hall is still a notably effective and popular venue for arts and cultural events, meetings, exhibitions and shows.

The Dominican friars (or Black Friars) came to Norwich in 1226 and in 1307 moved to the abandoned buildings of the Sack Friars. They began building the great friary church in 1326, although it was not finished until 1470. At the Dissolution the city of Norwich petitioned the king asking to purchase the friary and to 'make the churche a fayer and large halle, well pathed, for the mayor and his brethren ... for their common assemblyes'. The king accepted and in July 1540 the city paid £81 and £152 for the lead on the roof. Today, thanks to the city's foresight in the late 1530s, the St Andrew's and Blackfriars Halls (the former the nave of the friary church, the latter its choir) form the most complete medieval friary church surviving in the British Isles, and are a fine example of flint construction and decorative flushwork.

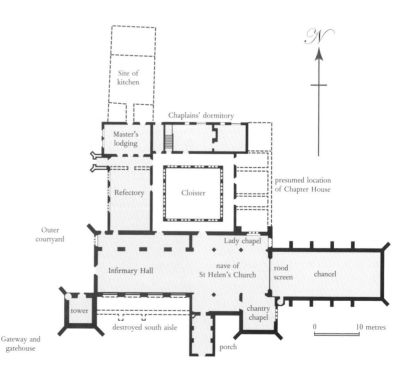

The inner precinct of St Giles Hospital and St Helen's church, Norwich (after Rawcliffe)

124

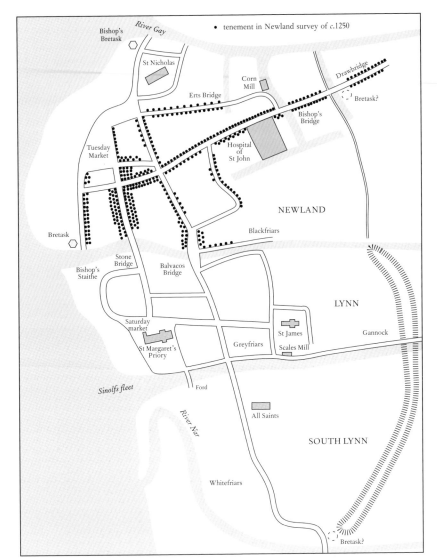

Lynn in the thirteenth
century (after V. Parker,
1971).

The need for more bridges, of which there were five after Bishop Bridge was
built in 1345, underlines the growth of the city. By 1333 it had a population of
perhaps 25,000 and may well have been second in size only to London – it was
certainly at least comparable with the other great provincial capitals, Bristol,
Lincoln and York.[27]

As in Norwich, the building of a wall in Lynn in the mid-thirteenth century
was a response in part to the civil wars of the period, but here the walls only
provided protection from the north, east and south, the wide estuary of the
Ouse forming the western boundary. Of the four gates of Lynn, only the South
Gate of 1350, rebuilt in 1450, still survives.[28] Again like Norwich, the four orders
of friars were established between 1220 and 1300. The tower of the Greyfriars,
recently restored, is the only one of their buildings to have survived, in part
because it was regarded as a useful marker for shipping. Lynn's trade with the

Thoresby College in King's Lynn, was founded at the beginning of the sixteenth century by Thomas Thoresby, a merchant who served as mayor of the borough on three occasions. When he died in 1510 the project was incomplete, but his executors saw that his intentions were fulfilled – a college of 13 priests, kept by the Holy Trinity Guild, should serve in the churches of St Margaret, St Nicholas and St James, and pray for the well-being and the souls of the king, the kingdom, and the mayor, aldermen and brethren of the Guild. Less than forty years later the Reformation swept away such institutions. The College was divided and altered and had many incongruous uses until in 1963–68 it was restored by the King's Lynn Preservation Trust. This view shows the north wing, remodelled in the early eighteenth century by the local architect Henry Bell.

The Tolhouse at Great Yarmouth dates from the early thirteenth century and was originally the residence of a wealthy merchant of the fast-growing town, although some architectural interpretations suggest that it originated in about 1150 and was subsequently altered and extended. From the fourteenth century onwards it was first leased and then bought by the borough, and from 1261 until the early twentieth century was variously used as a prison, courthouse, town hall, tollhouse for the port, library, and museum. Following an air raid in 1941 the building was gutted by fire but in 1960 it was restored and is now used as a museum. The Tolhouse is a remarkable survival – one of the earliest domestic properties remaining in any English town, and Britain's oldest civic building still in use.

Great Yarmouth was a walled town and, despite decay and redevelopment, the medieval town walls survive astonishingly well – indeed, those of Yarmouth rank with York and Chester as the most complete in England. The building of the walls did not begin until the mid-1280s, following the granting of a licence by Henry III in 1261, and they were completed by the end of the fourteenth century. Extending for just over a mile, and almost 25 feet high, they protected three sides of town (the fourth being the river Yare) and there were eighteen towers, of which eleven survive – but the ten fortified gateways were all demolished in the eighteenth and nineteenth centuries. The picture shows the tower on the east side which stands behind the Park Surgery in Alexandra Road.

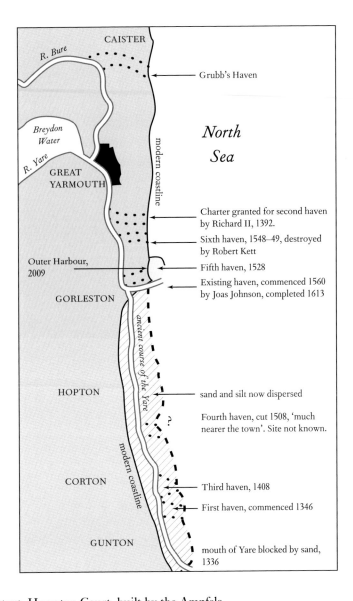

The 'Seven Havens' of Great Yarmouth and the new outer harbour (after Hedges, 1959).

CAISTER

R. Bure

Grubb's Haven

Breydon Water

R. Yare

GREAT YARMOUTH

modern coastline

North Sea

Charter granted for second haven by Richard II, 1392.

Sixth haven, 1548–49, destroyed by Robert Kett

Outer Harbour, 2009

Fifth haven, 1528

Existing haven, commenced 1560 by Joas Johnson, completed 1613

GORLESTON

ancient course of the Yare

HOPTON

sand and silt now dispersed

Fourth haven, cut 1508, 'much nearer the town'. Site not known.

modern coastline

CORTON

Third haven, 1408

First haven, commenced 1346

GUNTON

mouth of Yare blocked by sand, 1336

Baltic and Iceland was vitally important. Hampton Court, built by the Ampfels family in the fourteenth century, and the Hanseatic warehouses of 1480, reflect this growth. The fifteenth century also saw the building of the Trinity Guildhall in the Saturday Market Place and the nearby Thoresby College was constructed in the early sixteenth century as a merchant's foundation for a college of priests. In Queen Street the St George's Guildhall still stands between the street and the quay. By the end of the fifteenth century, though, Lynn was losing ground. Its population declined, in part because of outbreaks of the plague in 1518–19, and by the 1520s there were many vacant plots. By the late sixteenth century the Dissolution, the associated loss of pilgrims on their way to Walsingham, and the collapse of cloth making (which switched to rural areas) had all contributed to an atmosphere of decay.

During the later Middle Ages Yarmouth had national strategic importance

Market Row, Great Yarmouth, was among the widest of the ancient rows which formed such a distinctive street pattern in the town – indeed, in the eighteenth century it was just about wide enough for wheeled vehicles and in 1784 the inhabitants successfully petitioned the Corporation to have it pedestrianised, as the row was frequently blocked by carts taking a short-cut from the market place at the east end. This is likely to have been one of the oldest of the rows, since it is in the northern part of the long peninsula or sandspit upon which the town stands – it is believed that building gradually extended southward as the spit dried out in the thirteenth and fourteenth centuries.

The Bell Inn at Thetford is a long timber-framed building with a jettied upper storey. It was first mentioned in 1493, and the architectural evidence suggests that most of the range along King Street (shown here) and on the corner of Bridge Street dates from the 1490s. Interior details are puzzling: Chris Barringer suggested that the ground floor was originally divided into a series of stall-like units which were perhaps shops, before being converted in to a single inn building.

stemming from its geographical position, because it was regarded as a key defensive site during the French wars of the 1380s.[29] In 1287 it had suffered severe sea flooding, and in 1297 there were battles with the ships of the Cinque Ports (though both were on the English side!). It was an important ship-building centre by the 1290s, but only in 1427 was a bridge built between Great and Little Yarmouth. However, in terms of its changing economic base and its long-term significance, the crucial development was that it became the major English port for the herring fisheries. The fish were off Yarmouth from September to December, and the fishing, as well as the associated salting, smoking and drying industries, became central to the economy of the town.

Nuns' Bridges at Thetford, where three narrow hump-backed bridges cross channels of the Thet and the Little Ouse, was the fording point where the Icknield Way crossed into Norfolk. It was a main access route from the south into the market place of the medieval town and retained some importance until the sixteenth century, when the Town Bridge half a mile downstream became pre-eminent. Until 1538 the town paid for the upkeep of the northern arch and the priory for the others, but it derives its name from the Benedictine nunnery of St George, about a quarter of mile south of the bridge.

Within the borough, enclosed by a massive brick and flint wall built between 1284 and 1396, there were developments similar to those in Lynn and Norwich. The four orders of friars established their churches and precincts, and the Tolhouse (Court House) was established in 1261. The unique system of narrow 'rows' developed between the main north–south roads, along strips of land that were gradually infilled with tiny properties. In 1273 the Benedictine priory had been founded and in the later thirteenth century the great market place evolved as the centre of the borough. The constant fluidity of Yarmouth's site was emphasised by continuous change in the shape of the shoreline. The drift of shingle and sand from the north meant that it was always a problem to keep the harbour open, and the present harbour mouth represents the sixth

Elements in the medieval town plan of Thetford. The town became focused on the north bank of the Little Ouse and the extensive Saxon town to the south had shrunk. St Mary's Priory, the Priory of the Holy Sepulchre and the Dominican friary bordered the town on its west, and the castle, the market place and its bailey to the east. (After A. Crosby, 1986.)

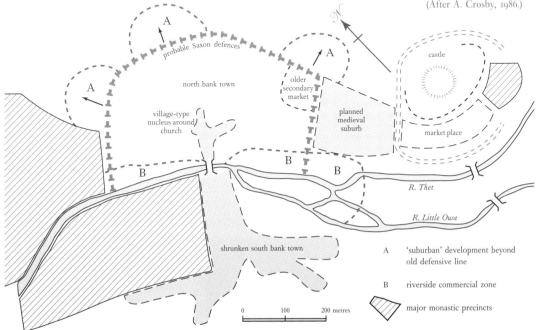

attempt to do this. At its longest the spit stretched to Gunton, where the first haven was begun in 1346.[30] The construction of a new outer harbour, completed as this book was being shaped, underlines the changing nature of Yarmouth – now desperate to be a new outlet for trade with Europe, but with evocative echoes of the medieval period.

Despite its decline in the period of the Norman Conquest, Thetford retained considerable importance until the Dissolution. It lay at the head of navigation on the Little Ouse and was on the main road to London from Norwich, which gave it the benefit of passing trade. The impact of the monastic system, with the numerous religious houses in and around the town, and the later development of the friaries, had a great and beneficial impact.[31] The important Norman Cluniac priory of St Mary possessed a miraculous statue of the Virgin and thereby became a place of pilgrimage, bringing financial benefits so that in the thirteenth century it was able to add a lady chapel to its church. Its patrons, the dukes of Norfolk, made it the burial place of their family, and in 1536, Henry Fitzroy, the illegitimate son of Henry VIII and son-in-law of the duke, was buried there. The priory had extensive properties in Norfolk and Suffolk, and its flocks of sheep grazing on the Breckland heaths were a key source of its wealth. A second priory, that of the Holy Sepulchre, lay on the south bank of the river but never achieved the prosperity of St Mary. There were three other religious houses: in 1335 the Dominican friars founded a house supported by Henry, Duke of Lancaster; in 1387 John of Gaunt founded an Augustinian house at the east end of the market place; and none of these was as important as that of the Blackfriars. Crosby notes that, 'by the middle of the fifteenth century the religious houses dominated Thetford physically and economically'. Despite the existence of 14 pre-Conquest churches and five post-Conquest churches the 1291 taxation of Pope Nicholas listed only five churches as being sufficiently prosperous to pay the tax, which is surely indicative of the early-medieval decline of the town. As several parish churches were subsequently absorbed into religious foundations which disappeared at the Dissolution, no fewer than 16 of the 19 had vanished by 1550.[32] No other Norfolk town, and few elsewhere in Britain, can show such a dramatic decline in fortune.

The evolution of the smaller market towns such as Wymondham, East Dereham and Swaffham depended on a range of controlling influences. Wymondham, like Thetford, was on the main London route and also had a

The village of Salthouse, between Sheringham and Cley, is dominated by its church. The settlement used to stand on the shore, and was a minor medieval port, but in the past three hundred years, as at Cley and Blakeney, the growth of Blakeney Point as a seven-mile long sandspit has encouraged the silting of the area behind and the development of saltmarshes. The old cliff-line can still easily be seen as a low but steep bank running parallel with, and immediately south of, the A149 and is easily visible in this photograph.

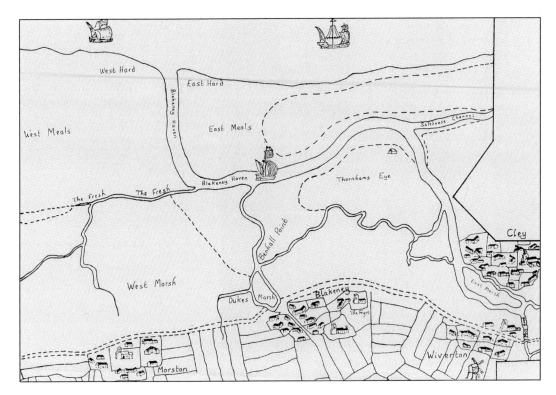

The following labels appear on the map:

West Hard

East Hard

Blakeney Haven

West Meals

East Meals

Salthouse Channel

Blakeney Haven

Thornhams Eye

The Fresh   The Fresh

The Fresh

Cley

Benhall Point

East Marsh

West Marsh

Dukes   Marsh   Blakeney

The Frys

Wiverton

Morston

The Glaven ports of
Blakeney and Cley,
a map redrawn and
simplified from that
published in 1586 and
used in the 2nd report
of the Tidal Harbours
Commission in 1846.

great monastic house as a key point in the fabric of the town and its economy. Dereham was at a distance from its controlling landowner, the abbey of Ely, but nevertheless benefited from its patronage. It was on the main Norwich to Lynn road, as was Swaffham. Dereham stood on the boulder-clay plateau in a mixed farming area but Swaffham, on the edge of sandy Breckland, was surrounded by heaths and fold-courses and was a centre for sheep and wool. On the north coast were the Glaven ports – Blakeney, Cley and Wiveton – and further west was the port of Wells. By the middle of the thirteenth century Cley and Blakeney were well established, with fish as the main component of their trade, and they provided ships for the navy. The Glaven ports had no river link to their hinterland, but they were an outlet for exports of barley and malt, salt, timber and canvas, a pattern found at Wells further west along the coast.[33] In the fourteenth century the fisheries to Iceland (which was ruled by Norway until 1397, and then by Denmark) dominated trade from the Glaven and Wells. The Glaven fishermen took salt with them on their voyages to the North Atlantic, and salted their catch between September and March before returning to Norfolk. At Shipden, the market town and port about a mile north of Cromer, long since washed into the sea, imported items included herring, salt, Riga boards (soft wood), wainscot (soft wood), *tunholt* (probably barrel staves), pitch, barrels of oil, fir spars, iron, corn, malt, sea coal, fish called *orgoys* (large ling), lob, ling and cod.[34] In 1417 several Cromer ships were pressed into service in France when Henry V retook Normandy. Many other north-coast havens, such as Stiffkey and Thornham, functioned as small ports.

The splendid tower of the church of St Peter and St Paul, Cromer, is the highest in East Anglia (160 feet), rising dramatically above the tiny narrow streets of the old town and acting as a landmark from the sea. It was built in the second half of the fourteenth century at the time when the ancient market town of Shipden was being washed into the sea, and the small village of Cromer, half a mile inland, was emerging as its successor and becoming an increasingly prosperous port.

Place-names in the county indicate that fords were once quite numerous, many of the shallow and slow-flowing rivers and streams being relatively easy to cross. They are not found in the wetland areas of east Norfolk or the Fens, because there fording rivers or streams was well-nigh impossible. Where parish names include this element, as at Thetford, Mundford, Billingford, Sedgeford and Tatterford, the implication is that the ford was of some importance, often on an ancient road or track. One of the few surviving examples is at Glandford, near Cley, whose name is a truncation of 'Glaven-ford' (it is on the river Glaven). Although now on a minor lane, this route was once the main road from Cromer and Weybourne, over Salthouse Heath to Blakeney and Wells.

The ferocity of the attacks of the sea upon the north coast of Norfolk is borne out by a grant given in 1291 by Edward I to the men of Shipden. It allowed them to charge duties for five years on goods coming into the port, in order to maintain their pier, but this financial gesture was to no avail. Shipden gradually disappeared beneath the waves as the always serious problem of coastal erosion accelerated. As it was lost, its commercial role shifted to the once-inland village of Cromer, which in compensation emerged as a new market town. The uncertainties of medieval life affected not just the individual and the family, but also society itself, and even the topography of land and sea.

7

Wool, sheep and textiles

T HIS chapter departs from the chronological approach, and instead gives a long overview of the history of an industry which for more than nine centuries was central to Norfolk's prosperity and well-being. Cloth production in the county was already established, with a high reputation, by the beginning of the fourteenth century; for the next 350 years it was the dominant industry in Norfolk, with a national significance which is demonstrated by the fact that a Norfolk village, Worstead, gave its name to a type of cloth for which England was famed throughout Europe.

The earliest references to the types of cloth produced in Norfolk relate to those known as 'aylshams' and 'worsteds', the former (first mentioned in 1301) being made of flax and hemp, and thus resembling a linen cloth. They were regarded as being of high quality and records show that in that year aylshams were bought in Oxford, indicating a market for Norfolk cloth that extended into areas, such as the Cotswold fringes, that were themselves important cloth producers. This would suggest that Norfolk cloths had a competitive edge of quality, a view reinforced by the fact that in 1302 the royal household itself bought aylshams at high prices. In 1332 the inventory of Richard Elsing (who was presumably from the village of Elsing, two miles east of Dereham) included 72 entries for linen goods, of which 13 were 'aylshams', five were 'coverchiefs' (probably made at Salle), one of 'Elmham', and one red *carda* (muslin) of Norfolk. By 1345 an ulnager – an official in charge of quality control – had been appointed for these Norfolk textiles. However, in the late fourteenth century imports of high-quality linen and specialist fabrics from Flanders and elsewhere in the Low Countries undermined the wider markets for linen cloths from Norfolk. The industry survived only in south Norfolk, producing merely for the local market and in a small-scale domestic setting, although it did carry on until the mid-nineteenth century.

Worsted cloth was made from fine, long-fibre wool which could be spun into a fine yarn to produce a lighter cloth than that which was made from short-fibre wools. The long-wool Lincoln and Fenland sheep were the best sources of this wool in Norfolk. The village of Worstead, after which worsted cloth was named, is a mile south of North Walsham and was an important weaving community for centuries, but other cloths were also named after villages in East Norfolk: thus a *say* (a type of serge) called 'dilhamsay' was produced in Dilham.

By the end of the thirteenth century worsted was competing with aylshams: in 1297 Norwich Cathedral Priory bought it for tunics, including purchases of cloths 12 yards in length. Especially famous was the 'magnificent bed of black

1086	Domesday Book lists large flocks of sheep in north-west Norfolk and Marshland
1200–1535	monastic production of wool, with Norwich and Thetford of great importance
c.1275–1325	heyday of production of Aylsham cloth (linen) and worsteds in north Norfolk
c.1300	mercers and linen drapers in Norwich market and Norfolk men trading in London
1329	argument about cloth sizes leads to standardisation of measurements
1338	Edward III allows immigration of alien cloth-manufacturers from Low Countries
1349	The Black Death: the shops and stalls of Norwich in decay
1378	'Aliens' (the Dutch and Flemings) in Norwich
1400–1550	the great Norfolk wool families: le Strange, Fermor, Heydon, Howard, Paston
c.1400	Norwich Guildhall, Common Inn and Worsted Seld (hall for sale of cloth)
1405–67	Robert Toppes and other wealthy Norwich cloth merchants
1440–80	St Peter Mancroft and many other Norwich churches rebuilt
1550–1600	the Mattishall 'broggers' or wool dealers
late 1550s	decline of worsted production
1565	royal licence to bring 'strangers' to Norwich
c.1680	calico imported to Norwich from India
1740–1760	Norwich 'stuffs' at their peak; trade with East India Company (Stannard & Co.)
1792	P.J. Knight, 'shawl man to Her Majesty'
1808	Weaver's portrait of T.W. Coke with his Southdown sheep
1822	Grouts establish the first steam-powered mills in Norwich; Norwich crepe
1835–60	peak period of shawl making in Norwich (Towler, Campin & Co.)

Chronology of the Norfolk wool, cloth and textile industries.

worsted made for Edward III worked with clouds of white worsted and angels of red worsted embroidered with gold and silk and playing diverse instruments of minstrels with six tapets ensuite'.[1] Sutton attributed the growth of this industry in part to the high density of population, which had created a need for alternative incomes because of the tiny holdings that were all that many families had, but she also argued that a lack of strong manorial control in this part of the county allowed a diversification away from traditional agriculture. In a very interesting exercise, she mapped the places in Norfolk from which the London mercers derived their surnames, showing that strong links between the county and the capital had already become established by the late thirteenth century.

The marketing of wool and cloth was well established in Norwich by about 1300, when drapers and linen drapers had stalls to the north of St Peter Mancroft church (then still a Norman building).[2] In 1397 an extent (or survey) of the city's property described the wool market and gave a detailed description of the Common Inn which lay on its northern edge, and of the worsted *seld* which was where all cloths brought in by foreigners (that is, those who were not freemen of Norwich) had to be sold and sealed with a lead seal, attached as a guarantee of the quality of the cloth being sold for export. The *seld* was a big building with many small rooms or chests which were hired by merchants, presumably for cloth storage. However, by 1414 there were complaints that many were avoiding this procedure, and were selling cloth from their own homes, thereby reducing the city's income and avoiding the sealing as a guarantee of quality.[3]

Many references to cloth are found in the records of disputes and

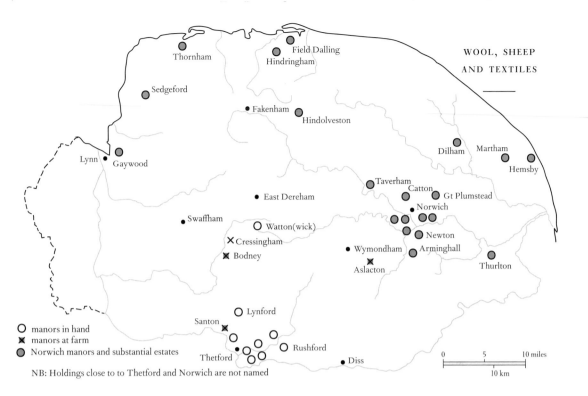

O manors in hand
✖ manors at farm
◉ Norwich manors and substantial estates

NB: Holdings close to to Thetford and Norwich are not named

0   5   10 miles

10 km

The landholdings of
Norwich and Thetford
priories in the early
sixteenth century

prosecutions. For example, as early as 1329 weavers in north-east Norfolk were condemned for failing to produce worsteds of the correct lengths. At this time the government of Edward III was encouraging the first wave of 'aliens', the skilled clothworkers who came to Norwich from the Low Countries. The fact that in 1410 the two water-powered fulling mills in the city were disused suggests that during the second half of the fourteenth century the production of woollen cloth (which has to be fulled to remove the dirt and grease in the wool, and to compress or 'felt' them) came second to that of worsteds, which were not fulled.

As the map of the land holdings of Norwich and Thetford priories shows, the monastic houses held a considerable proportion of all the land in the county. If we were to repeat this mapping for the other 65 houses, it would be clear that great swathes of Norfolk, perhaps as much as a quarter, were under ecclesiastical control. Norwich Cathedral Priory had 50 appropriated churches and 26 manors in the county, as well as a couple beyond its borders. A large monastic house made great demands on the surrounding area – it needed corn, fuel, meat, dairy produce and building materials. Some of the Norwich manors had specific functions, such as the Flegg manors on the Grade 1 arable land of the brickearth, which were the breadbasket for the priory. Hindringham and Hindolveston had large woods to supply timber and, as already noted, peat was cut in the Broads as an important source of fuel. But sheep farming represented a hugely important element of the commercial agricultural economy of these ecclesiastical manors. Sheep were farmed on the dry chalklands at Sedgeford and surrounding parishes, and Bailey, in his study of the sheep accounts for Norwich Priory, quotes the remarkable figures which are included in the account for 29 September 1517. It recorded the total of 8,335 sheep in the priory flocks (consisting of 82 rams, 64 riggs, 28 hoggs, 2,487 wethers, 3,987 ewes and 1,687 lambs). The manors of Gnatingdon and Sedgeford North both had flocks of over 1,000 sheep, though the composition of the flocks varied: for example, Gnatingdon had 1,363 ewes and 15 lambs whereas Robert Papere at Sedgeford had 824 lambs, 20 rams, 80 wethers and 103 ewes. It would seem that there were specialised roles for the different flocks.[4]

Sheep management could occupy a great deal of time for the steward of a lord's estate. In the early sixteenth century John Skayman kept careful records for his lord, Roger Townshend of East Raynham.[5] He recorded washing time in 1516: 'On Tuesday I was with Wolffe washing raggenelles [partly castrated sheep] at Helhoughton Mill. On Wednesday at Robin Hood's clipping the said sheep. On Thursday I was washing the Stibbard and Guist flocks. On Friday I was at Stibbard clipping these two flocks.' These notes are followed by references to another 13 flocks with which he was working. By Michaelmas 1516 Townshend, one of the greatest sheep farmers of early Tudor Norfolk, had over 18,000 sheep in 26 flocks spread out over the north-west of the county.[6]

Profits from these flocks were very considerable, providing there were no outbreaks of 'murrain' (an all-purpose term for a wide range of sheep diseases). To those lords who possessed fold-courses there was a great temptation to overstock, and to let flocks stray, which was not only environmentally damaging but also led to acrimonious disputes with neighbouring landowners. For example, a dispute which arose in 1450 in Swaffham is noted in volume II of the famous Paston letters.[7] Sir Thomas Tuddenham was the 'farmer' of the manor of Swaffham (that is, he held the lease of the manor). A letter sent on 20 December 1450 from Sir John Fastolf to Sir Thomas Howys (the Paston servant) referred to a letter from the rector of Swaffham, complaining that 'Grete extorcion have been done by the offices of the Duchy in taking away 90 acres of pasture at Swaffham which is of the King's demesnes and of hys enheritaunce as of the Duchee of Lancaster for which pastures ... it will be of the final destruction of the tenaunts there.' As Sir Thomas was the acting lord of the manor he would have been in a good position to overstock the commons with his sheep – and it was said that he had been doing this for 16 years.

Inevitably there were the arguments with other flock owners. For example, in the 1520s Richard Southwell, who already had the right to put 720 sheep on West Raynham common, added a further 480. This was potentially to the serious disadvantage of Roger Townshend and his tenants. In north-west and west Norfolk folding arrangements were firmly controlled by the manorial lords. Sheep manured the fallow arable land, but night folding (*tathing*) was a right of the lord, 'which tenants could only enjoy in return for a cash payment'. The shepherds ran communal flocks but gradually the fold area became a way of keeping large commercial flocks from which the lord, or his farmer, excluded the sheep of the tenants.[8]

The export of wool to the Continent was stopped by Edward III, who brought in Flemish weavers in 1328. The aim of these moves was to encourage

English weavers to produce more cloths, especially the worsteds of Norfolk and the broadcloths of Suffolk and Wiltshire. The cloth merchants (those who traded abroad) became an important new element in the county's social fabric. They provided a market for the wool-producing lords, such as the le Stranges, Sothertons and Heydons, some of whom (such as the le Stranges) were of long-established county families; others, such as the Heydons of Baconsthorpe, were new entrepreneurs. The cloth merchants, managing the marketing of cloth and its export, could become very wealthy in a relatively short period. Robert Toppes of Norwich (1405–67) is a fine example of a successful fifteenth-century merchant. Several times mayor and MP for Norwich, and a major figure in the city between 1427 and his death, he made sufficient money to build a large timber-framed hall by the river in King Street. This splendid hall, now known as Dragon Hall, had spandrels decorated with dragons and crown posts over seven great tie beams. It had been added to and built over properties held by earlier wealthy families such as the Cleres and the Meddays.

No documentation of Toppes' trade exists other than records of the customs accounts,[9] although it is clear that he and his merchant colleagues were sending undyed cloth to Flanders. However, his will gives a useful picture of his links to the worsted area of the county, the distribution of his bequests in north-east Norfolk underlining links with the well-known worsted centres of Cawston, Aylsham and Worstead. A remarkable list of his debtors has also survived. Those whose place of residence is given also show an emphasis on the north-east of the county. A list of occupations was also given, which indicates, perhaps

Dragon Hall in King Street, Norwich, is a unique medieval trading hall dating from around 1430. It stands just above the river Wensum, in the area which was the city's port from Anglo-Saxon times until the early twentieth century, and its gardens and yards once sloped down to the water's edge. Renowned for its spectacular timber crown-post roof, and the intricately carved and painted dragon from which it took its name, it was built by Robert Toppes, one of the wealthiest of Norwich merchants, who traded in wool, cloth, timber, spices, pottery and other imported items. Concealed for centuries within an unremarkable terrace of houses and shops, the hall was rediscovered in the late 1970s, restored and conserved, and is now one of the most significant heritage buildings in the city.

unexpectedly, that only a small number of those listed were connected with the textile trades. This raises the question of what the debts owed to Toppes were for, and suggests that he was in fact acting, at least in part, as a banker, making loans to a wide range of craftsmen. As Toppes was just one of a sizeable group of wealthy Norwich merchants, a picture of complex interaction between Norwich and its region begins to emerge. Perhaps it was already in an unofficial sense the banking centre of Norfolk, as it emerged more publicly in the eighteenth century?

Thus, the fourteenth and fifteenth centuries saw Norfolk prosper from the cloth trade. Worsted cloth production became important in the century and a half from the 1290s, faltered in the mid-fifteenth century, and then in the mid-sixteenth was revived under Elizabeth I with the help of the duke of Norfolk, who brought in Flemish weavers with their new types of textiles. These, the so-called Norwich stuffs, reached their peak importance in Norwich in the eighteenth century. During the sixteenth century documentary evidence for the cloth and wool trades becomes more abundant and helps to illuminate local circumstances. For example, Mattishall, like East Dereham, was close to the geographical centre of the county. The Norwich city records for 1562 state that Richard Baldewyn of Mattishall, together with a number of other men from the parish, was charged with having 'sold 300 stone of woll to men of Suffolk'. He and several others were accused of buying 'woll and bring none to Norwich Mechett but lode it and sell yt to the clothers of Suffolk'.[10] The purchasers there were men such as the Springs of Lavenham, who were famous for the production of broadcloth, which was made from shorter-fibre wool and was fulled to produce a heavier, more felted fabric than worsted. Richard and the other Mattishall 'broggers' (dealers) were buying wool from the great flockmasters such as the Townshends, Fermors and Heydons and diverting much of it to Suffolk, so avoiding the Norwich wool market which they were supposed to supply and thereby evading market charges.

These broggers were yeomen, in some cases prosperous enough to send their sons to Gonville and Caius College in Cambridge, which had strong Norfolk links. Richard Baldewyn of Mattishall had married a girl from the Fens, and they had a large family. In his will he left to her their property in West Walton, as well as five cows and four horses, while two of his four sons received lands in Terrington St John and West Walton, both marshland sheep-grazing areas. It is likely that they had flocks of Lincoln sheep for the worsted trade. The eldest son was left lands in Mattishall and the fourth son was given property at nearby Welbourne. The daughters were not left land, but specific instructions were tied to the lands which their brothers received, to ensure that the girls were provided for. No inventory survives for Richard, but the will makes it clear that his house had a hall, hall chamber, kitchen, kitchen chamber and a slaughter house.[11] One of the brothers, Henry, had already been a student at Gonville and Caius, and in 1590 his younger brother Thomas was admitted to the college.[12] Both were ordained, and their father's will instructed that if there was not enough from their inheritance their elder brother Richard was to help them. Although described in his will as a yeoman, Richard senior was able to provide all four of his sons with substantial farms and to see two of them become clerics. This placed him on the boundary between the status of yeoman, into which he had been born, and gentleman, which he almost became.

In his thesis on the Norfolk wool supply, Allison listed 33 Mattishall dealers.[13] The activities of Norwich and Thetford priories before the Dissolution have already been noted, and it appears that the Mattishall men, and other mid-Norfolk dealers, probably benefited from the closure of the monastic houses. The monasteries had previously marketed their own commercially produced wool direct to the clothiers of Suffolk and merchants of Norwich, but now local men, upwardly mobile individuals such as Richard Baldewyn, could fill the gap created by the loss of the monastic houses. Capitalising on a growing market and an expanding economy, and using their entrepreneurial talents, they grew in wealth and social status. A number of fine sixteenth-century farmhouses survive in Mattishall and Mattishall Burgh to remind us of this period of prosperity.

The central importance of sheep led to clashes over land use in the second half of the sixteenth century. In about 1598 a long petition was sent to Lord Burghley 'from the poor subjects of the Queen in the county of Norfolk',[14] complaining of how the sheep of the manorial lords encroached on common lands in and out of season:

> Gentlemen have enlarged their parks and made inclosures not only of their own land [thereby reducing shack, or stubble and stalks] but also of the commons where the Orators were wont to feed sheep and cattle. Thus the shakes [shacks] of many towns are straightened and taken away and the tenants not able to live.

This long complaint echoed those voiced half a century before by the rebels who rose with William Kett in 1549. The lords were accused of buying properties and allowing them to decay (so driving people off the land and reducing the housing stock) and of allowing their animals to graze on growing crops or on the shack after crops were cut. This went against the custom whereby the cattle of tenants were allowed to feed on the shack first. All of this underlines the fine balance between population growth, the prices of wool and cloth, and competition for land between stock (especially sheep) and arable crops. Not only did sheep provide the wool for the cloth and meat for the increasing urban markets, but their manure was, by careful control of the flocks in fenced areas at night, crucial to maintaining the fertility of the arable land. The management of flocks varied according to the region of the county in which they were reared. In the Breckland flocks ranged over heathland, only occasionally being enclosed on the infields near to settlements. Similarly, in the Fens large flocks grazed freely on the tidal salt marshes and the Smeeth when it had dried out in the summer. But in the sheep-corn country, where flocks had to co-exist with intensive arable farming, very complex arrangements of fold-courses and grazing rights existed.

The complexity of the system of commons was illustrated by Blomefield in 1746. In his study of Bressingham,[15] he noted them as 'very large' and listed them: Boyland Green, 35 acres; Whitehorse Green, 20 acres; Piddocks Green, 20 acres; the Great Common, 500 acres with Aldwood Green and Jays Green joined thereto; Roydon Green, the Fen Common, Derby's Green, Winley Green and Thwayt Green. With so much common land, arguments with adjacent parishes or manors, reflecting the complexities of the manorial structure and the practice of intercommoning, were inevitable. At Bressingham it was eventually established that only tenants from that manor had the rights to the Great Common and that people from Shelfanger had to pay as trespassers if they grazed their flocks there. Freehold and copyhold tenancies gave rights for all types of cattle (that is, sheep and cows) at all times of the year. Before the Dissolution the abbot of Sibton, the monastic lord, had rights for a flock of 200 sheep on the Great Common in return for paying 12*d.* to the lord of the manor and alms for the poor of the parish. In 1736 the duke of Norfolk, whose family had acquired the manor at the Dissolution, held this right. The interlocking boundaries of such a range of commons, and the complex rights attached to them, created many occasions for disagreements between parishes, especially if, as happened later, the population began to grow. The consequent increase in the number of beasts meant that the commons easily became over-grazed. In a dairying area, where butter and cheese production were important and linen weaving widespread, the survival of commons may not have been a crucial issue, but in any part of Norfolk where there was good arable land the commons were at a premium for grazing.

Simpson presents us with a remarkably detailed table of the income and expenditure of Sir Roger Townsend on his flocks of 450 sheep at Stiffkey on the north Norfolk coast.[16]

Stiffkey Flocks, 1625–26

Receipts		£	s.	d.
58 'morte' skins		1	11	2
208 'slaughte' skins		11	10	2
141 wethers sold		88	2	6
30 crone ewes sold		6	0	0
44 lambs sold at Rudham		7	6	0
100 lambs sold at Rainham		16	13	4
76 stones of wether wool		47	17	6
90 stones of ewes' wool		51	14	3
10 stones of locks		2	4	0
	Total	232	18	11
Expenses				
50 lambs bought		8	6	8
3 shepherds' wages	@ £4 each + liveries	13	8	0
Hired help at lambing time		10	0	0
10 dozen hurdles and carriage		2	0	0
2 stones of pitch for clipping			4	0
One barrel of tar			18	0
24 pints of oil			6	0

For greasing 528 hoggs	@ 1s. 6d. a score	1	19	6
For washing 1,748 sheep	@ 1s. a long 100		14	6
For throwing sheep into the pit			1	0
For clipping 1,147 ewes and hoggs @ 3s. a long hundred and 601 wethers for 3s. 4d. a long hundred		2	5	2
[Various small items omitted]				
4 stones of cheese for the clippers			9	4
For driving lambs to market			3	0
17 lbs of redding		2	10	0
	Total	32	7	8
Profit		200	11	3

The yield of wool from the wethers (castrated male sheep) was only just over 2 lbs per sheep: this compares with modern Dalesbred sheep yielding 4 lbs or a Suffolk sheep, about 7 lbs.

Norfolk Sheep – a short glossary

Ewes – **female sheep**
Ewe hogg – female sheep 6–12 months
Hogg – a ewe up to one year
Ewe gimmer – more than 18 months old
Crone – an old ewe to be sold for slaughter
Locks – loose clippings

Rams – **male sheep**
Ram – a male breeding sheep
Wether – a castrated male sheep
Rigg – an immature ram
Redding – the red colour used to mark sheep, especially rams before breeding
The pit – wash pit or pond for the sheep after clipping

The evolution of Norwich stuffs

In the 1560s and 1570s a flood of Dutch and Walloon immigrants arrived in several English cities, among them Norwich. It is estimated that by 1582 there were over 4,500 'strangers' in the city, amounting to about one-third of its population. They brought with them the skills of producing the 'new draperies', which were lighter and more varied fabrics than the traditional Norfolk worsteds. The Walloons in particular used dyed yarns and included various threads of cotton, linen and especially silk that led to 'Norwich stuffs' becoming known for their variety and high quality.

By the early seventeenth century the Norwich cloth industry was flourishing again, quality control was improved, and the fast-expanding home market began to buy new fabrics. The export trade developed and Norwich cloths went via the great market at Blackwell Hall in London, the bulk of them being sent by road to London rather than by boat from Yarmouth. As the industry developed, the demand for fine wool and yarns increased and wool was bought in from the long-woolled sheep of Lincolnshire and the East Midlands. As Richard Wilson says, 'by the last thirty years of the seventeenth century the city became famed in Britain and Europe for the novelty, variety and quality of its worsteds. It was an ascendancy which was to endure for a further century.'[17] In 1857 John James, in his title *History of the Worsted Manufacture in England*, compared Norwich at its peak with Manchester in the 1850s.

The middle decades of the eighteenth century, especially from about 1740 to 1760, were the great period of the revived Norwich textile industry. A wide variety of new fabrics had been created, developing from the basic worsted with the addition of cottons and silks, and giving many varied finishes. The new fabrics included bombazines, calimancoes and camelets. By this time the trade with the East India Company was the key element for the Norwich exports, and the outbreak of the Napoleonic wars in 1792 was a disaster for the industry. The market was badly disrupted, and the lost ground was never recaptured: East India Company orders from Norwich declined from 22,000 pieces in 1812 to 13,000 by 1826 – but none in 1831.[18]

The later days of the Norwich textile industry are well illustrated in the letters of Philip Stannard,[19] who, born in Bury St Edmunds, was apprenticed to a Norwich worsted weaver and then set up his own business. He established himself in a large house in St Giles, north of the market place, with a workroom and bought various other properties which he let to his workers. In the 1740s and 1750s he did what so many prosperous Norwich men did, and purchased a large country house – in his case, at Mulbarton, five miles south-west of the city. He married Priscilla Crowe, a member of a Norwich mayoral family. Hitherto, as noted above, Norwich manufacturers had sent their goods to London merchants, only about 15 per cent being exported from Yarmouth, and they relied on the expertise of the London men. By the 1770s, however, more goods went to Yarmouth for export and the Norwich manufacturers needed to establish their own agents in Europe. Stannard's training as a master weaver, rather than his experience as a merchant, led to his success in a volatile, fashion-conscious trade: 'Much of the Norwich output for Europe was in fancy fabrics.' The skills required to produce these fabrics helped to keep Norwich

A reconstruction of the layout of Norwich market, c.1300. (After U. Priestley, 1987.)

afloat when the new worsted manufacture of the Yorkshire mills began to develop. By 1755 Stannard had 300 looms at work – he had no weaving shop and employed journeymen at piece rates. New patterns were being asked for all the time. Yarn came in from Bury St Edmunds and Ireland, especially for calimancoes. Norwich dyers produced the colours demanded, and woven fabrics were frequently hot-pressed to finish them.

The complexities of marketing led Stannard to take on John Thaxter as a marketing partner and, through him, to gain contact with new markets. A list of Stannard's stock in 1758, and some of the items in the press shop, give an idea of the range of their fabrics, which included brocade, calimancoes, scarlet and white flowered satins, half engrained satins, tapizonnes, scarlet and white striped satins, scarlet and half engrained, and many others. An appendix for 1751 to 1755 'lists foreigners who have been at my [Stannard's] house'. They came from Cadiz, Venice, Leipzig, Copenhagen, Lubeck, Amsterdam, Zurich, Frankfurt, Cologne, Stockholm, Wermar, Bremen, Christiana, Basle, Lisbon, and Drammen in Norway. All had been recommended by various London agents. The letters record great success from 1751, but in 1769 Stannard went bankrupt. The new markets had failed him, for debts owed to the firm grew in Spain, South America and Mexico and finally it could only pay 10s. in the pound on what it owed.

By the late 1830s one-fifth of the Norwich handlooms were idle, but mechanisation had begun to influence the textile industry in the city. The first machine spinning factories were built in 1837 at Albion Mill in King Street and St James' Mill in 1840,[20] and within a few years there were two silk mills, three worsted mills, two woollen and one cotton mill (that in the parish of St James is now a listed building).[21] For a period the production of shawls (the name both of a fabric and an item of dress) became important, but that trade had almost ceased by the 1860s. Bayne noted in 1869 that, 'we are sorry to state that the manufacture of textile fabrics in Norwich has for sometime past been declining'.[22] He attributed this to the progress of mechanisation being far slower than in the north of England, suggesting that much East Anglian wool was being spun in Yorkshire and that 'Norwich weavers have not the energy of those in Bradford'. As the textile industry declined merchants began to diversify into banking and brewing, families such as the Gurneys, Pattesons, Morses in Norwich and the Oakes family in Bury St Edmunds becoming well known for these other businesses. The making of bombazines and crepe, both used in mourning dress, continued through the nineteenth century, and Grout's modern Norwich crepe remained successful until the eve of the First World War, but with the demise of these trades, just over a hundred years ago, nine centuries of Norfolk cloth and textile production came to an end.

Morningthorpe church seems a perfect example of the 'typical' Norfolk village church, with its lovely round tower, short nave and chancel all in flint. It was extensively restored in the Victorian period, but the tower was built in the twelfth century (and its battlemented top two hundred years later) and the large windows in the church date from the fifteenth century.

8

Churches and parishes

E ARLIER CHAPTERS have shown how Christianity came to East Anglia, and developed over the centuries with the emergence of a complex pattern of parishes, paralleled by the rise of the powerful monastic system, a process given a major boost by the Norman Conquest. Historians calculate that by the end of the thirteenth century Norfolk had 921 parishes, each with its church. This was by far the largest number of parishes in any county in the British Isles, and of these 610 are still in use – again, by a very large margin the greatest number in any county. For comparison, Lincolnshire had about 600 medieval churches and Suffolk 580, and in both counties a significant proportion have disappeared; most counties had far smaller numbers.[1] The existence of such an exceptional number of parishes, and parish churches, was a defining characteristic of medieval Norfolk, and remains an essential element in the landscape of the county, whether rural or urban. It is an architectural legacy of priceless quality, and Norfolk's churches remain one of the greatest treasuries of medieval art, sculpture and decoration in Europe. What is more, this remarkable inheritance is retained despite the loss of many churches because of population decline and village abandonment, the rationalisation of parishes, the impact of the Reformation and the Dissolution and even, in a few cases, destruction in wartime. Norfolk has lost more medieval churches

1000	Saxon: towers at Great Dunham, Colney and Kirkby Cane; excavations at Palace Plain
1066	new borough of Norwich: St Peter Mancroft, St Giles and St Stephen's churches
1070–1200	Norman: complete examples at Hales, Heckingham; towers at South Lopham, Attleborough
1100	approximately 300 parish churches in Norfolk
1100–1250	proliferation of new churches and parishes, especially in Norwich
1240	Early English: west front of Binham Priory, West Walton, Merton, Burgh-next-Aylsham
1290–1350	Decorated: Snettisham, Attleborough, Great Ellingham; Norwich Cathedral cloisters
1300	an estimated 921 parish churches in Norfolk (more than any other county)
1350–1450	Perpendicular: St Peter Mancroft, Terrington St Clement, Loddon, Cawston and Salle
late 14th century	the Felbrigg tombs
1530–1800	The decoration of church interiors with major family monuments (e.g. Paston tombs)
1535–1550	Almost 100 churches closed because of the Reformation and its aftermath
1600–1800	abandonment of numerous surplus churches or those in shrunken/depopulated communities
19th century	many churches 'restored', rebuilt (e.g. Booton) and newly built (e.g. Norwich St Mark)
2012	610 churches in use in the diocese of Norwich; 59 redundant; 252 ruined or vanished

New Buckenham St Martin was a relative latecomer among Norfolk churches, having been founded in the middle of the thirteenth century as the place of worship for the new town planned and developed from the 1140s. The church was very extensively rebuilt in the fifteenth and early sixteenth centuries, and this view shows the north and south arcades of the nave, built in the late 1470s and restored in 1879. The scale of the building is impressive – it was conceived as a town church, even though the town is scarcely urban today.

than Lancashire ever possessed, yet many hundreds still remain, their round towers and grey flintwork presiding over tiny villages or, as at Cley or Blakeney, churches which are mini-cathedrals dominate the adjacent settlement.

Batcock estimated that 330 of Norfolk's churches existed in 1086. The basic structure of parishes was then already in existence, but more were created after 1086, particularly in areas such as the Fens, where new land was being created and population was growing, and in Norwich, where tiny urban parishes proliferated. But in the context of the fourteenth century, a time of economic downturn and the serious population losses occasioned by the Black Death, the sheer numbers of Norfolk parishes and churches represented over-provision. As early as the 1380s some of the smallest or least populous parishes were being dissolved, combining with neighbours to form more viable units, but much greater losses came in the sixteenth century. As a result of the Dissolution, for example, some 98 churches were closed following the destruction of the monastic houses which had acted as patrons and protectors. In 2005 Batcock listed 610 Norfolk churches in regular use, 59 standing but redundant, 100 in ruins, and 152 with no visible remains above ground. The last three categories tell particularly of village desertion and the landscape and economic policies of landowners and manorial lords several centuries ago, as much as of the decline in churchgoing and other changes of modern society.

To those familiar with the huge ancient parishes of the north of England, such as Halifax or Kendal, which cover many dozens of square miles and embrace numerous separate communities, the multitude of tiny Norfolk

The partly ruined church of Barningham Winter, which stands in the grounds of Barningham Hall near Matlaske, was – like so many in Norfolk – a complete ruin by the middle of the seventeenth century. It never served more than a handful of villagers, and by 1700 the parish had largely been subsumed by the extension of the park. In this instance, though, the chancel was restored in the nineteenth century and thus appears as a small detached chapel, separated from the gaunt ruin of the medieval tower by a small courtyard which was once the western end of the nave. The adjacent parkland was landscaped by Humphrey Repton in 1805–15.

The chancel was filled with an eclectic collection of much older stained glass from Britain and the Continent. This is the royal arms or achievement of Charles I, brought from an unknown location. The restoration scheme was initiated by the Mott family of Barningham Hall.

The noble four-decker tower of Happisburgh church has been a landmark for mariners ever since it was erected in the fifteenth century. The church is another of those, so typical of Norfolk, which seems far too large for the small village at its feet – though in earlier centuries Happisburgh was a prosperous fishing and farming community. Now the sea is gradually destroying the village – over the centuries several nearby parishes and their churches, such as Eccles and Whimpwell, have been completely lost to the waves. South of the village the cliff retreated by 105 metres between 1992 and 2004 alone, and Happisburgh church itself is now only one small field away from the edge.

The church of St Andrew, Little Snoring (which is a larger village than Great Snoring) has a fine round tower built of flint, topped with an eighteenth-century cap. If one looks closely it becomes evident that the tower is in the wrong place – it is not at the west end but is in fact detached from the body of the church with gaps of a few feet between tower and porch and tower and nave. The reason is unclear – one theory is that there were two churches in one churchyard (certainly a familiar feature in Norfolk) and that the one which 'owned' the tower was demolished. More plausible is that there were structural problems with the original church and it was rebuilt, apart from the tower, a little way up the slope.

parishes seems surprising. The reasons for the difference can be sought in the much longer history of prosperous rural settlement in Norfolk, and the very much higher density of population in the pre-Conquest and medieval county. There were also many more 'lords' in Norfolk, who founded churches as personal acts of piety and patronage as the influence of Christianity spread, while many communities founded their own churches as well. The remarkable number of surviving medieval churches in Norfolk is now a major problem for the diocese of Norwich, particularly as the population of many of these parishes has continued to shrink. This unparalleled legacy of historic and architecturally important buildings is a continuing financial burden.

Beachamwell provides an excellent example of complex parochial structures within one settlement. In 1845 the parish had 4,000 acres and a population of 246, but it had three churches, St Mary (which survives) and All Saints and St John which are in ruins. Since its eastern half was mainly heath and warren the three parishes shared a maximum of some 2,000 acres of worthwhile land, the opposite end of the spectrum from those great northern parishes. All Saints appears to have been a Norman building, while St John was fourteenth-century, and St Mary was late-Saxon in origin. The papal taxation of 1254 merely lists Beachamwell, and does not distinguish any dedications at all, but it is known that St John was last mentioned in a document of 1541, suggesting early abandonment, and All Saints was described as 'virtually empty' in 1721. The population of the area seems to have declined from the late fifteenth century onwards, and it is evident that three churches for one small community was already regarded as unviable by the beginning of the sixteenth century.[2]

Beachamwell was a village with three churches, but there are several examples in Norfolk of two, or even three, churches in a single shared churchyard, an extraordinary circumstance. The market town of Reepham is perhaps the best example, where three churches share one churchyard at the

At Reepham the celebrated superabundance of churches in Norfolk reached perhaps its most extreme form. Here, within one churchyard, were three full-sized medieval churches, not just close together but actually in physical contact. There were three separate parishes (Reepham, Whitwell and Hackford) and for reasons that are not really clear they shared a single large churchyard which was therefore divided into portions in terms of ecclesiastical jurisdiction (the northern one-third being a detached portion of Whitwell which was embedded in Reepham parish). Two of the three churches survive, the third (All Saints, Hackford) having been destroyed by fire in 1542. In this view we see, in the foreground, the nave of the church of St Michael, Whitwell, and beyond, joined on to it, the nave and tower of St Mary, Reepham.

In Reepham churchyard stands a new memorial, erected in June 2010, to 'unknown local friends'. This followed the discovery in 2007, during drainage work, of 63 skeletons in a mass grave in Church Street, where the road had long ago encroached upon a former graveyard. The skeletons were reburied in the churchyard, but analysis showed that many were adults aged between 35 and 50 (and very few were older) and that a high proportion suffered from conditions such as spinal deformities and osteoarthritis, indicative of a life of hard manual labour. At the commemorative service an ancient prayer was read which serves perhaps as an epitaph for many medieval Norfolk people: 'Almightie God, we geve thee hertie thankes for these thy servauntes, whom thou haste delyvered from the miseries of this wretched world'.

south end of the market place. St Michael, Whitwell, is the nearest to the market: it is now redundant and used for parish purposes. St Mary was the parish church of the combined medieval parish of Reepham and Kerdeston (a parish which now includes Whitwell), while on the west side of the churchyard are the fragments of Hackford's church of All Saints. These four parishes were closely related, but why their churches were all built within one churchyard is very difficult to explain. It may be that Whitwell and Kerdeston both had earlier 'chapels', more centrally placed in their parishes, but if that were indeed the arrangement it is not clear why it was superseded. In the taxation of 1254 the three churches are all listed under Reepham, which means that as early as the mid-thirteenth century they were all there, almost touching each other.

Another example of a compound churchyard can be found at Antingham, on the northern edge of North Walsham. There the ruined St Margaret's church contains large blocks of conglomerate and may be Norman, while St Mary, the surviving church, appears to be largely mid-fourteenth century in date. St Margaret, which is not mentioned in the Domesday Book, was

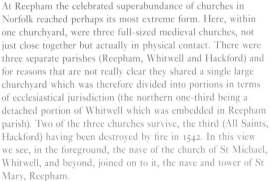

The screen at St Helen, Ranworth, is one of two great treasures in the church, the other being a beautifully illuminated fifteenth-century antiphoner (or singing book) which was produced at nearby Langley Abbey and used at Ranworth before the Reformation. The screen dates from the middle decades of the fifteenth century and is generally considered to be the finest in East Anglia and therefore among the best to survive anywhere in Europe. It stretches across the full width of the church, including projecting sections which form reredoses or screens (with delicate wooden tracery) behind the side chapel altars. This means that there are twenty panels, all painted with superb skill and remaining in outstanding condition. This is among the finest galleries of medieval art in the British Isles. In this view we see (left to right) St Philip, St James the Less, St Jude and St Matthew, with St Thomas a Becket carrying a red book.

This detail of the Ranworth screen, one of the side panels on the south side of the nave, shows a magnificent St Michael the Archangel killing a fearsome dragon on which he is standing in bare feet.

one of the many churches belonging to St Benet's Abbey, and was therefore transferred at the Dissolution to the bishops of Norwich. It was still in use in 1746, according to Blomefield, but it seems that subsequently the diocese was happy to lose one of its many churches whereas the parish church of St Mary, the patronage of which descended through a series of major Norfolk families, was more carefully guarded.

Despite the pattern of tiny parishes, though, it is striking that several of the market towns, such as East Dereham, Swaffham and Fakenham, have only one church serving a comparatively large area; another example is Wymondham, one of the largest historic parishes in Norfolk. This single-church characteristic seems to have depended on ownership; Ely Abbey controlled Dereham and the Duchy of Lancaster had Fakenham, and these powerful lords did not want competition from churches founded by actual or would-be rivals. At King's Lynn and Great Yarmouth the towns were new foundations, established by Bishop Herbert de Losinga to strengthen his control over Norfolk, and both were given a large church and an attached monastery. Norwich has already

Binham Priory is a particularly interesting monastic site. A Benedictine house, it was founded in the 1090s by Pierre de Valognes and Albreda his wife. At the Dissolution in 1539 most of the nave was retained as the parish church. This ensured the preservation of the magnificent Norman arcade, built between 1100 and the 1180s, its walls having a flint rubble core faced with golden limestone that was brought (mostly by water) from Caen in Normandy and Barnack near Peterborough. The westernmost of the seven bays of the nave was finished just as Gothic, rather than Romanesque, arches were becoming fashionable. It therefore has a pointed arch.

The nave at Binham was completed by the beginning of the thirteenth century, but the west front (shown here) was not constructed until 1220–45, under the auspices of Prior Richard de Parco. By this time Romanesque styles were being superseded by Gothic, and the great west window at Binham was among the earliest examples of Gothic tracery in the British Isles – of major churches, only Westminster Abbey was earlier. The window itself, and the interlaced arcading below, were exceptionally radical and modern by the standards of the second quarter of the thirteenth century. The monastic buildings at Binham are ruinous but extensive, and the high medieval precinct wall still surrounds much of the site, with its gatehouse largely intact.

been discussed; apart from the new cathedral of the 1090s it already had many 'chapels', private churches which evolved into the sixty or so medieval parishes. The New Borough of 1066 spread on open land and the large parishes of St Peter Mancroft, St Stephen and St Giles were laid out with much bigger parishes than any of the earlier ones.

Stylistic changes in church building provide a fascinating reflection of the prosperity of a parish, and its increase or decline. The Norman churches were discussed in chapter 6, but the arrival of the gothic styles – Early English, Decorated and Perpendicular – tell us much about the history of the parishes in which they were employed. The first appearance of the Early English style in Norfolk was the west front of Binham Priory, constructed *circa* 1240. Outstanding examples of Early English churches are relatively infrequent in Norfolk, but West Walton in Marshland was described by Pevsner and Wilson as 'one of the glories of Early English architecture and may be by masons trained at Lincoln'.[3] Smaller but equally delightful examples are at Merton, a mile and a half south-west of Watton, and at Burgh-next-Aylsham which has a beautifully arcaded chancel built in the 1220s, and where the church sits attractively above the lush meadows that edge the river Bure. The east window of St Andrew, Trowse, is an early example of the Decorated style. Master Nicholas, the master mason at the cathedral, was paid £2 15s. 6¼d. for the window in 1282–83.[4] Attleborough Church has a fine Decorated west window, while Great Ellingham also has much Decorated work in its east window.

The church of St Giles in Norwich is a fine example of a town church, with its 120 foot tower (the tallest in the city) being accentuated by the hilltop site on which it stands. Dedications to St Giles are invariably post-Conquest, as this was not a saint favoured by the Anglo-Saxons. St Giles was one of the three parishes in the French borough, laid out in the late eleventh century and centred on the market place which lies a quarter of a mile away. This was among the most prosperous of the city's parishes, reflected not only in the many monuments to doctors and other leading citizens but also in the high quality architecture of their houses in nearby streets, still evident despite the busy traffic.

The detached bell tower at West Walton, just north of Wisbech, was built in about 1240 of Barnack stone, brought by water from the quarries near Stamford. It is lavishly decorated, and stylistic analysis suggests that it was constructed by master masons who had worked on the great west front of Lincoln Cathedral. The upper part of the tower still contains its medieval timber bellframe. The ground floor is very obviously pierced by huge openings, so that the tower appears to stand on four legs – and to bear the tremendous weight of the upper storeys the four angles are strengthened by great buttresses, without which it would have collapsed. But why a separate belltower was built in this way remains unclear.

St Mary, West Walton, was described by Nikolaus Pevsner as 'one of the most sumptuous Early English churches – not only of Norfolk'. It dates from the 1220s to the 1250s. This is one of those churches where, entering for the first time, the visitor is likely to gasp in amazement. The remarkable lightness of the nave, with its tall arcades and slender pillars, highlights the most exquisite feature. Each pier of the arcades has a carved capital of foliage (technically, 'stiff leaf') and is framed by four slender detached shafts of Purbeck marble, linked to it only by a semi-circle of stone halfway up. There is a very fine fifteenth-century roof, with carved angels, and a simple, almost crude, octagonal font of the early fifteenth century.

In the middle of the fourteenth century the Decorated style gave way to the Perpendicular, distinguished particularly by its use of vertical mullions supporting even wider window arches. This style, with variations, remained in fashion until the Reformation, and during this period the majority of Norfolk churches were either added to or completely rebuilt. This – which was especially the case in Norwich – explains why there are so few which are recognisably Norman: the upgrading and improvement of the later Middle Ages swept away much older work. Nave arcades were often retained, but high clerestories, which poured light into the church, and new porches, which gave a grander sense of arrival, were added. Nave roofs were decorated with hammer beams, and flights of angels decorated these and the wall plates as at Cawston and Upwell.

	Contributors to the new tower of Redenhall church	£	s.	d.
1469	William Cowper	1	0	0
1469	Joan Bunting	3	6	8
1470	John Mayhell	0	6	8
1470	Richard Hawk	0	13	4
1470	Thomas Bacon	2	0	0
1471	John Poyntras	0	6	8
1473	William Payn	0	3	4
1473	John Wytham	3	6	8
1473	Thomas Tyte	6	13	4
1476	Katharine Newton	3	6	8
1484/85	Robert Honeypott	3	6	8
1487	Agnes Alderych	Bequest		
1487	William Totyll	Bequest		
1492	Thomas Bacon	0	13	4
1496	Margaret Roche (repair of steeple)	0	3	4
1498	Robert Drury	0	6	8[5]

A special feature is that towers were often rebuilt, in many instances by the collective efforts of the parishioners, as in the case of Redenhall. There are close similarities between this tower and that of St Peter Mancroft in Norwich: did the contributors ask for a tower in the style of St Peter, to show their awareness of fashionable taste, and were the same masons perhaps employed? As with any such building project, the contributions by the people of Redenhall and Harleston to the new church stemmed from the belief that one's time in purgatory could be reduced if one contributed to the welfare of the church. Particular items, such as rood lofts, were incised with the names of benefactors together with their coats of arms, giving a different sort of immortality. At Cawston in 1490, for example, William Atelreth paid for the painting of the eight panels on the north side of the screen.

The Perpendicular style achieved its apogee in Norfolk in three great churches: Terrington St Clement, St Peter Mancroft in Norwich, and Holy

With over 700 medieval churches, more than any other county in England, the Norfolk landscape is punctuated by towers and (much more rarely) spires. From some vantage points it is possible to see a dozen or more churches and frequently the towers act almost as guideposts, pinpointing the position of a town or village when one approaches across flat fields and along country lanes – which is surely how they must have seemed to travellers in the past. Here, the tall tower of the church of St Agnes at Cawston, built in the early fifteenth century, dominates the skyline of the little town, looking from the east.

In the second half of the Middle Ages the Fenland parishes were famous for their agricultural wealth, a prosperity achieved despite the seemingly disadvantageous location and the many challenges of a hostile environment. Their wealth is reflected in a succession of magnificent churches which, in this land of pancake-flatness, tower above the levels and formed prominent landmarks. At Terrington St Clement the church is vast – 168 feet long – and with a very sophisticated and complex plan, cathedral-like to serve what was always a fairly small and straggling Fenland village. Externally the most impressive feature is the large extent of the glazing, with spectacular fifteenth-century windows (dating from an almost complete rebuilding) in the nave and chancel, and a magnificent tall clerestory stretching the whole length of the church. A unique feature is the triple-decker design of the windows in the south (but not the north) transept.

Trinity in Loddon. Terrington St Clement was rebuilt in the fifteenth century on the foundations of an Early English church of the same size. Although it was originally intended to have a central tower, eventually (as in several other Fen churches) the tower was built to the side of the great church because its weight would otherwise have been too much for the soft and potentially unstable foundations. The Fens had no building stone, but beautiful limestone from Barnack near Stamford could readily be brought by water and this was used for facing the church. Just as the merchants of Norwich were paying for the rebuilding of many of the city churches so Fenland sheep farmers, making money from their flocks, were contributing (rather earlier) to comparable projects in their part of the county. Several bequests from 1426 for a new window, and a series from 1499 to 1527 for the 'newe stepull', show that at least the tower of Terrington St Clement was the result of collective endeavour.[6]

St Peter Mancroft is 'a Norfolk parish church par excellence'[7]. Although there has been a church on the site since at least the eleventh century, the present magnificent building was consecrated in 1455. Many of the great Norwich merchant families were major contributors to its reconstruction, making this a civic church, contrasting with the cathedral whose hierarchy were so often at loggerheads with the citizens. David King's brilliant study of the medieval glass includes a full list of bequests for the building and furnishing

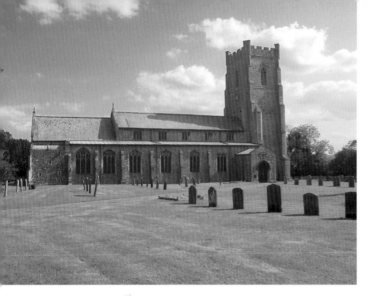

The church of St James, Castle Acre, was sandwiched between the priory precinct and the outer bailey of the Norman planned town. It is a large 'town' church, perhaps disproportionately so since the community it served remained relatively small. Most of the fabric dates from a great rebuilding in the fifteenth century, including the powerful and imposing tower in the Perpendicular style, but the chancel (left) survives from the older building and the difference in styles is very obvious. During the fifteenth century many Norfolk churches in larger villages and small towns underwent extensive change, a sign of the revival and reinvigoration of the Catholic church which many historians now recognise.

of the new church: thus in 1445 Robert Pert left £20 'for the making of the new end gable', stipulating that the sum be paid in three stages as the building progressed.[8] Churches and their related charities are expressions of the religious belief of their builders, whether they were the de la Poles building the tower of Cawston church or the most modest peasants giving a few pence to the poor box in the same building. Loddon church contrasts with Terrington and St Peter Mancroft in that it results from a single bequest made in 1485 by Sir James Hobart, who paid for almost the entire building. It was built with brick from the same brickyards that provided the materials for Hales Hall, but is faced with flint which gives a lightness to the exterior. Its clerestory has 15 windows, and there is no break between nave and chancel. It has an outstanding porch, on which the Hobart shields and initials remind us who built it. The tower was that of an earlier church, but later work was done on it between 1461 and 1504.

Two other fine churches are those at Cawston and Salle. The grey stone-faced tower of Cawston is attributed to Michael de la Pole, who died in 1414, and replaced one that fell in 1412. Many of the yeomen of that flourishing market

Cawston church is known for the richness of its decoration, all of it dating from the complete rebuilding at the beginning of the fifteenth century. The exterior of the great west door is surmounted by a long rectangular heraldic frieze, and master masons filled the triangular spaces formed between the arch of the door and the bottom of the frieze with wonderful carving – here, on the right hand side of the arch, a dragon tangled in a vine laden with grapes.

The early fifteenth-century hammerbeam roof at St Agnes, Cawston, is an outstanding example of late medieval craftsmanship. As was the case with many of the larger churches of East Anglia, the roof was decorated with angels. The form and construction of a hammerbeam roof allowed great height while offering opportunities for decoration. In this view the uprights (the wall posts) can be seen to be supported on decorative stone corbels built into the wall. The hammerbeams are the main horizontals, resting on the top of the wall and on the wall posts, and reinforced with the curving brace timbers. These in turn support a higher set of uprights (the struts) and a second set of braces. This produced a structure of tremendous strength despite the massive weight of the timbers and the roof above.

The roof at Cawston was decorated with a frieze of angels, wings outstretched and almost touching, and some carrying shields. At each of the hammerbeams is a freestanding angel, poised as though to take flight. These angels are feathered and have double sets of wings, originally painted in bright reds and greens and gilded: traces of paint and gilding are still visible.

The interior of Cawston St Agnes, entirely rebuilt in the early fifteenth century by the wealthy and upwardly mobile de la Pole family, earls of Suffolk. The interior is full of light, from the large windows in the aisles and the high clerestory, emphasising the graceful slender columns of the nave arcade. Above the screen – one of the finest in East Anglia – are the evocative remains of the medieval painting of the Rood, while above is the magnificent fifteenth-century roof, with its carved angels. Everything speaks of the late medieval wealth of the patrons and of the community in this small market town.

The early fifteenth-century screen at Cawston is one of the most complete surviving anywhere in England. With its exquisite and miraculously preserved paintings of saints in twenty separate panels (including two on each of the gates which open into the chancel), it forms a precious gallery of late medieval art. Analysis has shown that the painting is the work of three masters. Two of the paintings have been defaced and damaged – St Gregory, because he was shown wearing his papal tiara or crown; and the only non-saint depicted, Sir John Schorne (rector of North Marston, Bucks) who was said to be so holy that he once trapped the devil in a boot! His cult was favoured at nearby Binham and seems to have been popular elsewhere in mid-Norfolk, but after the Reformation was the subject of special condemnation – hence the damage to his image.

Detail of the screen at Cawston: this panel shows (left) St Thomas and (right) St John the Evangelist. The rich use of colour, and the sense that the delicate wooden tracery and the vivid paintings were designed as a single entity, are very clear.

The set of three misericords in the chancel at Cawston has apparently been moved from elsewhere in the church, and is rather awkwardly squeezed into the space where the sedilia (the seats for priests) were once situated – note how the right-hand seat has had to be supported on a stone plinth and clearly does not 'belong' there.

and cloth town contributed to the magnificent nave roof, though the chancel and the south transept have Decorated work of about 1300. Salle was described by Cautley as 'the finest church in Norfolk'. Pevsner and Wilson consider it to be entirely Perpendicular, indicating that it was more completely rebuilt than Cawston church. Unlike Cawston it lies, magically, in an isolated position remote from any sizeable place – there is little evidence that there was ever a village nearby.[9] Several leading families contributed to its building, including the Boleyns, Briggs and Roses. These families occupied, or built, some of the magnificent houses that are set in the otherwise open landscape around the church. For church enthusiasts Norfolk is a paradise: the two volumes on the county's architecture by Pevsner and Wilson, and the four by Mortlock and Roberts, are essential books to accompany anyone with this passion.

Most churches were endowed from their foundation with land known as the glebe, which was intended to provide an income to support the incumbent. The typical Norfolk glebe was about 30 acres, equivalent in size to an early-medieval villein's holding. At Weston Longville the celebrated Parson Woodforde farmed his glebe at the end of the eighteenth century, partly to provide barley for his own beer, but most clergy chose to let out the land to tenants and thus draw rent from their glebe. The glebe was in any case not necessarily conveniently arranged for farming as a unit: the 1614 terrier (land survey) of Saxlingham shows that there the glebe consisted of 57 scattered pieces of land, many of them very small. The process of rationalising land ownership was well advanced on Norfolk's bigger estates by this date, but the cost and complication of sorting out so many fragments meant that church glebelands were often fossilised strips surviving from the medieval field system (furlongs were the bundles of strips that ran in specific directions within the open fields). The extract below, transcribed in modern spelling, gives a flavour of the document:

> The terrier of the glebelands and parsonage
>   houses in … of Saxlingham
>   Nethergate and Saxlingham

For some, Salle is the finest of all Norfolk's hundreds of medieval churches. Its cathedral-like proportions, wonderful lightness because of the huge windows, and powerful atmosphere of antiquity combine with beautiful detail and a magical setting among the fields and woods far from a village to create an unforgettable sense of wonder. It owes its scale to the patronage of wealthy and influential families, including the Boleyns, the Morleys and the Kerdistons. It was entirely rebuilt, to the highest quality, in the middle decades of the fifteenth century, giving it a unity of style which is particularly appealing. The nave is grand in proportions, a vast space that leads almost without a break into the chancel. And yet who were its congregations, for there has never been a significant community around?

The octagonal font at Salle dates from the same period as the church, and shows the crucifixion and the seven sacraments (baptism, the mass, ordination, confirmation, penance, matrimony and the last rites) but it is completely eclipsed by the remarkable font cover, delicately carved to form slender wooden buttresses that meet, spire-like, in a soaring pinnacle.

Over the great west door at Salle are carvings which (as at Cawston) fill the triangular spaces between stone frame and arch. On both sides an angel with a feathered body and feathered legs swings, with great vigour, a censer for incense.

The north porch at Salle is a two-storey building accessed by a spiral stair from the north-west corner of the church. The upper chamber, which served as a schoolroom, has fifteenth-century vaulting with traces of richly painted decoration. Its bosses, recently repainted in their original colours, are jewel-like: they include green men, and angels playing musical instruments. The central boss is a representation of the Coronation of the Virgin.

Thorp made in the twentieth
day of May Anno Domini 1614[10]

1. Imprimis: the situation of the Parsonage of Saxlingham
    Nethergate containing by estimation one acre and a half
    … with a dwelling house with hall, parlour, kitchen,
    back-house, barns and stable with other houses of office.

2   The second piece was the situation of the rectory of Saxlingham
    Thorpe containing by estimation three roods … lying between the
    way leading to diverse men's land east and diverse men
    west and buts upon the churchyard north and
    the land of diverse men south.

A further 55 pieces of glebeland for the two parishes were listed: they totalled
approximately 42 acres. No piece totalled more than four acres, and many were
half an acre or less. However, in the nineteenth century glebelands were often
rationalised. At Booton near Reepham, for example, the church modified its
holdings so that by 1850 the glebe had been amalgamated or exchanged and a new
unified farm with a continuous ring-fenced boundary had been created, appro-
priately called Glebe Farm. As time went by the vicarages and rectories of earlier
times were also rebuilt or replaced. At Redenhall the early rectory in Wortwell,
built of clay and thatch, was replaced in 1804 by a newer house near the church.[11]

For many incumbents the tithes – the one-tenth collected by the church
from the annual gain on the land – provided the major source of income. When
lands were given by benefactors to monastic houses the pattern developed
whereby the great tithes, of wheat, barley, oats and rye, went to the monastery
and the small tithes of hay, wood, wool, milk, butter and cheese went to the
vicars, the clerics appointed by the monastery to run the parish. After the
Dissolution many lay owners, having bought monastic lands and rights from
the Crown, became rectors and collected the great tithes. This became a major
issue as lay rectors treated this income as their own, rather than considering
that it belonged to the Church. Nobody did more to establish the potential
value of his tithes than the Reverend John Smith, vicar of Mattishall from 1781
to 1801. He leased the tithes of Mattishall from Gonville and Caius College,
Cambridge,[12] then mapped the parish, recorded the land use of every field, and
calculated the value of the crop from each plot in order to produce his table,
shown below (the column of figures on the right represents one-tenth of the
value of agricultural produce shown in the calculations):

Valuation of the Rectory Tithes

	£	s.	d.
Barley 230 acres @ 700 comb @ 8s. a comb £644	64	8	0
Oats 70 acres £196	19	12	0
Peas, clover and nonesuch 225 acres @ £3 per acre	67	10	0
Wheat 240 acres @ 500 combs @ 18s. per comb £1,080	108	0	0
Hay 75 acres @ 30 cwt per acre 2s. per cwt £225	22	10	0
Total	282	0	0

Valuation of the Vicarage Tithes

Turnips 260 acres @ £2 10s. per acre £650	65	0	0
Cows 160 @ £6 each £960	96	0	0
Sheep 800 @ 1s. 6d. each for wool £60	6	0	0
Ewes 200 @ 6s. each for lambs £60	6	0	0
Young stock 150 @ £1 each £150	15	0	0
Young geese 500 @ 1s. each £25	2	10	0
ditto shacked 500 @1s. each £25	2	10	0
Pigs 300 @ 2s. 6d. each £37 10s.	3	15	0
Orchards and gardens 70 @ £1 each £70	7	0	0
Honey £40	4	0	0
Total	207	15	0

All this must have taken him a great deal of time and one can imagine that as he calculated the tithes due to him he created hostility, as he peered over garden walls and counted every goose and piglet. In doing this painstaking work he not only improved his income but left a fascinating record of later eighteenth-century agriculture in Mattishall. He concluded:

> Thus should it please God to grant me a few years of continuance of life and health, I hope to be able to leave to my successors a tolerably clear and satisfactory account of the value of this living; and to prove that tho' it formerly was for a long time despised, and more than once, I believe, refused by all the Foundation Fellows of Caius College, it is but little if at all, inferior to the best Preferment in the Patronage of that Society.

Ownership of a church is a key element to understanding its external and especially its internal history. Many in Norfolk are mausoleums of the family in whose gift they lay. Oxnead church, on the southern edge of Aylsham, stood by Oxnead Hall, home of the Paston family from 1580 to 1757. In it are the splendid monuments of Sir Clement Paston (1597) and Lady Katherine (1637). The small parish church of Stow Bardolph has a remarkable run of Hare family tombs including the bizarre half-figure wax effigy of Sarah Hare who died in 1744.

Norfolk is therefore, par excellence, a county of churches. The line of settlement along the Fen edge, which has been discussed in nearly every chapter, is reflected in many small churches between Downham Market and King's Lynn. The chalk ridge and the Breckland show up with fewer churches. The good soils and loams from Fakenham to the east coast, and particularly the zone of small parishes from Wymondham around the southern edge of Norwich to the great estuary, are notable for their many early churches. Surviving ruins and still-standing churches provide attractive and fascinating elements in the county's landscape.

At Carleton Forehoe, two miles north of Wymondham, the surviving small church stands lonely in a field with its brick tower of 1713. The tower of Godwick church, surrounded by the earthworks of a deserted village, make it easy to visualise, as you walk the public footpath, how Sir Edward Coke redesigned the landscape in front of his sixteenth-century hall, changing it from a scattered village to a vista planted with Spanish chestnuts and unspoilt by workers' dwellings.

The vast church of St Margaret at Cley-next-the-Sea is the finest on the north Norfolk coast. Here the prosperity of the late medieval port (now long since silted and hardly traceable) is reflected in a wonderful building that was never completed. Rebuilding began in the 1320s and the great nave was completed by the middle of the century. The chancel survives from the older building; it would presumably have been rebuilt on a much grander scale since it is now disproportionately small. The transepts were rebuilt but probably not fully finished – the north transept is now completely ruinous, the southern one (seen here) roofless and glassless. The architectural ambition of the patrons of the project, the de Vaux family, and the master mason, William Ramsay, is best revealed by the extraordinary clerestory of the nave, with its modest arched windows alternating with huge circular or rose windows.

A recent research project, the Norfolk Medieval Graffiti Survey, has revealed that at Cley, and many other Norfolk churches, walls and pillars were covered in graffiti. The designs are extremely varied, from simple crosses and hearts, initials, geometric devices, 'mystical' symbols, and crude portraits, to fish, animals and ships. Here at Cley a ship was scratched roughly into the face of a pillar on the north arcade of the nave. Ship graffiti are, not unexpectedly, common along the Norfolk coast – churches such as Wiveton, across the silted estuary of the Glaven from Cley, have other very good examples. They depict the typical small single-masted sailing vessels which in the later medieval period plied these creeks and estuaries, trading with other coastal ports along both sides of the North Sea.

The sites of many of the county's churches are memorable. Standing in Wiveton churchyard one looks across the Glaven estuary, as it once was, to Cley church which faces across the earlier harbour and is sheltered from the northerly gales by a ridge. At Cley the distinctive Decorated clerestory of alternating cusped circles and two-light windows, added to by the ruined south transept and magnificent Perpendicular porch which conceals the 'sumptuous' Decorated doorway, is one of Norfolk's gems in terms both of setting and of architecture. In the Fens the ruined church of Wiggenhall St Peter clinging to the raised bank of the Great Ouse, and the shell of Islington church just south of Tilney All Saints, contrast with the impressive churches of West Walton and of Terrington St Clement, the 'Cathedral of the Fens'. Nowhere in Norfolk is far from a parish church – and just about every parish church carries a vivid and important historical message. For many centuries they have been an integral and important part of the spirit and character of the county.

9

From Black Death to Reformation

T HE effects of the Black Death of 1348–50 were shattering. A slow recovery did take place, during which the established feudal system, with a rough balance between lords and tenants, collapsed. This led to a restructuring of the system of labour, and of agricultural landholdings, out of which in the fifteenth century emerged new social classes in the countryside – increasingly prosperous yeomen farmers, and growing numbers of poor and landless labourers. The national chaos of the Wars of the Roses of 1455 to 1487 had little direct impact on Norfolk – no major battles were fought in the county – but it led to a great deal of local politicking, and some families, such as the Pastons and Heydons, did very well. During the fifteenth century there was growing disenchantment with the monastic system, and religious houses and their inhabitants alike were seen by many as greedy and self-indulgent. The beginnings of protestantism can be traced back to the years after 1400, and by the early sixteenth century new ideas of religious reform began to come from the Continent.

Eventually, in the later 1530s, came the dissolution of the monasteries, which had a dramatic effect in Norfolk, for the county had 100 major monastic sites, and over a quarter of all land had been in monastic ownership. Many villages lost population – in part before, in part because of, and in part after the Black Death. The larger towns, with the exception of Thetford, began to expand further as trade (and especially the textile industry) developed, a trend which also affected the rising cloth-making villages such as Cawston and Worstead. As noted in the previous chapter, many Norfolk churches were rebuilt grandly, in the Perpendicular style, and embellished with increasing numbers of chapels and elaborate tombs. In the countryside weavers and woolmen began to rebuild or replace earlier timber-framed halls with more sophisticated two-storeyed and chimneyed dwellings. The impact of change was perhaps greater during this period in the history of Norfolk than in any other. In a space of two

The Erpingham Gate was built in 1420–35 as a fortified gatehouse between Tombland and the cathedral close in Norwich, and as the main approach to the west front of the cathedral itself. Notable for its splendid tall archway, it is embellished with the coat of arms (recently restored) of Sir Thomas Erpingham, an influential benefactor of the city and its religious institutions, and a hero of the battle of Agincourt. Sir Thomas provided the funds for the building, but his precise motive is unclear – though it was probably intended as a memorial to the man himself, it may also have been a way of further reinforcing his already close relationship with the key people in Norwich politics, religion and society.

1350	End of major phase of Black Death
1378	William Paston I born
1381	Peasants' Revolt
1404	Henry IV grants a new charter to Norwich, allowing a mayor and two sheriffs
1407–1414	Building of Norwich Guildhall
1422–1428	Building of King's Lynn's Guildhall
1436	William Paston II born
1437	King's Lynn's South Gate built
1440	John Paston I marries Margaret Mautby
1450	Baconsthorpe Castle begun by John Heydon
1455–1485	Wars of the Roses
1459	Death of Sir John Fastolf
1460–1500	Many Norfolk churches rebuilt in Perpendicular style
1460s	Mannington Hall built
1468	The Paston family claim Caister Castle
1469	Edward IV visits Norwich
1480s	Building of Hunstanton Hall by the le Strange family
1484	Death of Margaret Paston
1485	Battle of Bosworth, in which the duke of Norfolk was killed
1486–1500	Bishop Morton's Register: key source for pre-Reformation Norfolk wills
1504	Death of John Paston III
1534–1535	Break with Rome and creation of Church of England
1536–1540	Dissolution of the Monasteries
1548–1549	Dissolution of chantries
1549	Kett's Rebellion

centuries came a succession of calamitous and traumatic events, accompanied by profound and far-reaching reshaping of social, economic and political life. Much of what is familiar in Norfolk today originated in this period.

The land, 1330 to 1550

The Black Death is often seen as a turning point in the evolution of the agricultural economy. A chronic shortage of labour was one immediate effect of the calamitous loss of population, and it increased the bargaining power of the surviving workforce: workers were in high demand, and could expect considerably higher wages than before 1348. Indeed, some historians have suggested that agricultural labourers were better off in relative terms in the period from 1355 to 1415 than at any time before or since. Furthermore, those who emerged from the horrors of the Black Death were well placed to take up more land from the remaining lords – many tenancies were vacant, because of the death of the families which had farmed them, so landowners were willing to let holdings to anyone who could pay rent, or even to sell at reduced prices. Thus, some labourers and peasants began to build up property holdings, and a new class of yeomen started to emerge. The best documentary records of this period are those of the monastic estates or the largest secular landholders, both of which employed stewards to administer their properties and professional clerks to look after their estate accounts.

Large and standing on a low hillock, Morston church is a particularly imposing sight when approached from the east along the coast road from Blakeney. The church is sprawling and architecturally complicated, much less celebrated than its famous neighbours at Cley and Blakeney but with a superb fifteenth-century screen, a remarkable clerestory that is partly early medieval and partly sixteenth-century, and a tower which was struck by lightning in the eighteenth century and patched up with brickwork in a distinctly bodged way.

The Black Death, which killed perhaps 40 per cent of the entire population, gave rise to other fundamental changes. Particularly obvious in farming was the fact that the need for arable land decreased, simply because there were far fewer mouths to feed. This meant that poorer-quality land, including some that had been pressed into service during population growth a century earlier, was now less likely to be carefully managed and much of it was swiftly abandoned, soon reverting to heath, scrub or even woodland. The lack of tenants meant that in some areas lords were able to increase the size of their flocks: few labourers were needed to tend them (in contrast to labour-intensive arable farming) and this, combined with the increased demand for wool, meant that many sheep runs and fold-courses were extended. By the fifteenth century there was a widespread sense that sheep had replaced people in many parts of England, and this became a particular grievance, a cause for popular protest.

At Martham, an important corn-producing manor held by Norwich Cathedral Priory, the court rolls reveal how the Black Death threw the inheritance system into confusion. Between 1350 and 1357 only 15 out of 47 deaths resulted in direct inheritance of land, implying that whole families were wiped out. But some survivors benefited from the disarray: thus, a poor man, Nicholas, son of William Christmas, inherited in only a few years two acres from his father, 3½ acres from his uncle, two acres from his sister, and also two cottages and ten messuages, so that his outlook and prospects changed very considerably indeed. Many tenants in Martham refused to continue manorial services, and in 1354 seven men were presented at the manor court for not carrying meat and malt to Norwich 'as custom required'.[1] Another vivid quotation comes from the 1355 bailiff's account. To avoid weed infestation manorial leases were insisting on keeping land clean, but weeds also grew on the lord's own land. In 1355 the bailiff stated that 'I never hired to mow the thistles before ploughing – 4*d.*'. What this tells us is that in the past the weeding of thistles had been done for nothing by the tenants as part of their feudal contract: now, with so few tenants left, he had to pay cash for the work. Everything was in confusion – previously, tenants had given free labour for the harvest: now the bailiff had to hire 84 extra workers to do this essential task. As a result of these trends, some aspects of agricultural life were never the same again. The money economy of hired labour replaced much customary labour, units of holding increased, and some land remained derelict.

Davenport noted that on the earl of Norfolk's estate at Forncett many bondmen had disappeared after the Black Death: most of them probably died during the plague, but others may have moved to Norwich. Those who stayed behind were sometimes able, like Nicholas Christmas in Martham, to increase the size of their holdings. At Forncett the Bolytoute family accumulated four and a half messuages, one pightle (a tiny odd-shaped corner of land), 32 acres and nine other pieces of land. This substantial amount of property represented the beginning of a yeoman's holding.[2] The lord himself might also benefit, by being able to extend and reorder his own demesne lands. The lack of tenants made emparking easier, allowing abandoned holdings to be brought within the park and the demesne estate. At Winfarthing, for example, 15 acres of arable land were added to the park. Winfarthing was a Howard estate, and well managed, and there new woodland was also created, a valuable asset for the future. Britnell also notes that in much of Norfolk barley increased as a proportion of the cereal crops, because grain for flour was in less demand.

The Rising of 1381 in Norfolk

The social and economic instability that followed the Black Death was accompanied during the later fourteenth century by sporadic political turmoil. Nationally, the most serious episode was the Peasants' Revolt of 1381, which was triggered by the imposition of a series of heavy poll taxes. An army of rebels marched from Kent and Essex to London, led by John Ball, a chaplain who was 'the ideologist of the revolt' and was reported as 'the most famous preacher to the laity'. Watt Tyler led the Kent protestors to Blackheath, where they attacked John of Gaunt's palace, and then on to the Tower of London, which they seized. Tyler was killed at Smithfield on 15 June, and Ball executed on 15 July, and the short-lived revolt was over.

However, although the attention of popular histories has focused almost exclusively on events in and around London, the rising was actually more widespread. In East Anglia a mob seized and murdered the lord chief justice Sir John Cavendish, and the prior of Bury St Edmunds,[3] and then, led by John Littister, advanced on Norwich which they entered on 17 June. There they killed the governor, Sir Robert Salle. Froissart, the medieval chronicler, alleges somewhat implausibly that upwards of 40,000 people were involved in this attack. Thomas de Walsingham recounts how Henry le Spencer, bishop of Norwich, took military command, assembled Norfolk's gentry, and defeated Littister and his men on the heath just south of North Walsham on 26 June 1381. A commemorative cross stands there today.

There were attacks on 'establishment' properties across the county, though many of these seem to have been localised incidents rather than part of a greater undertaking. In the case of St Benet's Abbey the attack by the rioters has been described as a 'bitter war against parchment'. The main objective of the peasants was to destroy records of their tenancies, and in 20 June 1381 a 'company' obtained the surrender of charters and court rolls in order to burn them. This was an anti-manorial attack, rather than anti-monastic. The same happened at Carrow Abbey, which was unsuccessfully besieged by some 400 people on 23–24 June; at Binham Priory; and at the Duchy of Lancaster manor of Aylsham and other duchy manors. At Thurne and Thurgarton the first court records after 'the riot' were for 10 August, when the names of each tenant, the extent of their land, and a fine for re-entry were recorded – normal service was being resumed.

On 17 June rebels took Yarmouth, tearing up its charters and attacking the house of Hugh Fastolf and two others, all influential local gentry. There was unrest in the Fleggs – the court rolls of Ashby and Thurne reveal that there the corn was not cut, nor the hay made – but the unrest was patchy. The nearby manor of Martham, which belonged to Norwich Cathedral Priory, does not seem to have suffered. Barbara Cornford suggests that the manorial yoke bore more heavily on the peasantry at Ashby and Thurne, which were manors of St Benet's, rather than at Martham. It is likely that the policies and attitudes of individual manorial lords – albeit many of them institutions rather than individuals – were a determining factor. Cornford notes that rebel activity in Flegg seems to have been spasmodic and uncoordinated.[4]

John of Gaunt, the uncle of the young king Richard II and the most powerful man in the realm, was lord of the Soke of Gimingham. His deep unpopularity led to the destruction of many of the court rolls of that area. Gimingham Hall, the main manor house, was broken into and much was taken from it.[5] The king's commissioners, not entirely unbiased, subsequently reported on the following damage, claiming that the rebels

> have entered the free warren of the same King [Gaunt was, by right of his wife, titular King of Castile] at *Gymyngham*, *Methewold*, *Tonstede* and *Crabbegate*, with force and arms and have broken his closes, houses and park there, and have hunted in the same warren and park, without licence or leave and have dug in his soil there, and have thrown down the earth thereof, and have carried away the timber from the houses and also other his goods and chattels found there, to the value of £2,000, and have taken hares, rabbits, pheasants and partridges from the warren aforesaid and wild creatures from the park aforesaid, and have taken and led away 20 [of] his horses, 20 oxen, 50 cows and 1000 sheep, found there to the value of 200 marks and have burnt his charters, deeds, rolls and other muniments found there, and have made assaults upon his men and servants there and have beaten, wounded and ill-treated them; by all which the same king has lost the service of the same men and servants for a long time and suffered other grievances.[6]

Despite the widespread rioting and many incidents of destruction and attacks on property, the reaction of local lords was subdued, and most emerged unscathed. Elizabeth Rutledge has suggested that the absence of any strong response by the manorial lords was because the real discontent was with the agents of local government – the JPs, subsidy commissioners and any officers of, or property of, the hated duke of Lancaster.

Monastic houses as landowners

The local impact of the Peasants' Revolt highlights the significance of religious houses as landowners and manorial lords. Abbeys and priories functioned as the centres of landed estates as well as being religious houses, and their commercial and business dealings were of major importance, both to their own operation and also in the wider community. One example can be used to illustrate this role. As we saw in chapter 5, Bromholm Priory, on the coast three miles south-east of Mundesley, was founded in 1113 as a daughter house of the Cluniac priory of Castle Acre. It soon achieved independence, and by 1195 the connection with Castle Acre had ceased. Free to develop its own business and trading activities, the priory began to expand its commercial operations. In 1227 Henry III granted it the right to hold a fair and a market, both potentially lucrative privileges, and by 1291 it was valued at £109 15s. 11d., had property in 56 Norfolk and 16 Suffolk parishes, and housed 25 brethren.

Another source of wealth and status was income from pilgrims. The priory became a great centre of pilgrimage because it held a miraculous cross, made from fragments of the True Cross, which gave it national fame and brought the devout from far and wide. Chaucer, in 'The Reeve's Tale', mentions the 'holy Cross of Bromeholme', and in 1313 Edward II visited the priory to worship at the relic. Centuries later the priory has also become famous because of its close links with the Paston family, including the magnificent funeral there of John Paston in 1466. But all was not well, for the location close to the sea was perilous: in 1385 the priory was in 'much distress' because the sea had eroded its lands and in 1390 there were only eighteen brethren.

The officer who looked after the financial and commercial business of a monastic house was usually known as the *cellarer*. For Bromholm the cellarer's accounts for 1415–16 have been published,[7] and reveal much about the operation of a medium-sized monastic house in the later medieval period. From the produce of the monastic estate the cellarer had oats, barley, peas and malt to sell, but he often had to buy in corn. He purchased bullocks from Rudham, Bacton and Horsham St Faith (where there was a celebrated fair), as well as capons, chicken and geese. Fish, usually herring but with an occasional salmon or sturgeon, came mainly from Cromer, as did large amounts of imported timber. In return, Cromer folk bought malt from the priory. Salt came from Yarmouth via Horning fair (where cheeses were also bought) and eels, geese, rushes and thatch from Hickling. Spices were purchased at St Faith's and Yarmouth, and the cellarer bought green ginger on his visits to London. By this date, the early decades of the fifteenth century, monastic clergy enjoyed a lifestyle of which the peasantry could only dream, and which became an increasingly controversial matter later in the century.

The cellarer bought large quantities of peat as fuel, and paid for the labour of cutting wood and brushwood. Bacton Wood, like those at Foxley and Ashwellthorpe, was an ancient managed wood and was owned by the priory:

> In the wage of John Mayhew cutting brushwood in Baketon Wood for four days 8*d.*
> And in the wage of Thomas Besby cutting brushwood for four days 8*d.*
> And paid to Clement Atte Newhous for making 3,700 peats by the task there in the past year 3*s.* 1*d.* taking 10*d.* the thousand.[8]

Very detailed kitchen accounts, covering two full sides of the document, record an expenditure of £62 4*s.* 3*d.* The names of some local dealers were given: Sir John Paston sold mustard seed to the priory, for eightpence; peas came from Norwich; and Isabel Deye supplied diverse dairy produce. William Albon of Swathfield sold them saffron, onions, coarse salt, figs, mustard seed and garlic, all of which suggests that he was perhaps a merchant bringing these items back from Flanders. In the year 1415–16 the total expenses for the cellarer were £318 15*s.* 2½*d.*, and he calculated that he had a surplus balance of 33*s.* 4¼*d.* and 'half a farthing' (i.e. ⅛*d.*): with precision such as this, he must have been a valuable asset to the priory!

The *Valor Ecclesiasticus* of 1535, the last valuation of monastic property before the Dissolution, records that Bromholm Priory held seven Norfolk and two Suffolk churches, and had lands in 58 parishes. At the Dissolution it was valued at £109 0*s.* 8*d.*, was stated to be in good repair, and had a wood of 100 acres. The whole property was acquired by one of Norfolk's most prominent new gentry, Robert Southwell, solicitor to the Court of Augmentation.[9] The

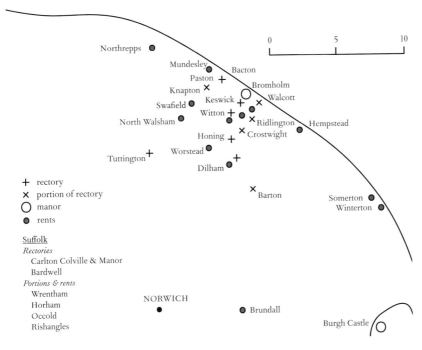

The lands of Bromholm Priory, as listed in the 1535 *Valor Ecclesiasticus.*

ruins of the priory now stand high on the cliff near the sea, much of its surviving stone bearing witness to salt spray weathering on the east side.

On the Duchy of Lancaster estate at Gimingham a rental of 1485 shows how the original holdings had been subdivided.[10] One example, 'The House of Gothemund', comprised a core property of 30 acres, held by Edmund Pounder, but the rest was fragmented: 14 tenants held 9½ acres in 18 separate pieces or 'furlongs', such as Bastbony's Hill, and 1 rood 20 perches was said to be 'in the sea'. The bond services relating to this holding were also detailed, split among the tenants of no fewer than 37 pieces of land which only totalled about 23 acres (indicating that tenants farmed well under an acre each). The services, which included carrying goods to Norwich, Horning or Blakeney, all had money values attached to them. This meant that those holding land which had been part of the original holding of Gothemund had to pay small proportions of those cash sums, to avoid having to plough, harrow, hoe, reap and carry corn on the lord's demesne. Presumably some of these same tenants were then employed by the farmer of the manor to carry out those activities as wage labourers. The pre-Black Death system was well on the way to extinction.

Some major families

There are many ways of looking at a county, and they overlap and interlock. Examination of Norfolk society between the 1350s and the Dissolution shows how various elements depended on or clashed with one another. Three great families provide examples: the Howards (dukes of Norfolk), the Pastons (because of the family letters that have survived) and the Heydons, who built up a sheep-farming and wool-producing empire around their castle at Baconsthorpe. Below them, the merchants, linked by marriage and business, formed an increasingly important group. Less tightly bound to the manorial lords were the increasing numbers of yeomen, and finally there were the agricultural labourers, by the fifteenth century bound to their lords more by economic rents than by feudal ties. Also very important until the 1530s were the many monastic houses, the hundreds of parish churches with their clergy, and the benefactors who were rebuilding a great number of the churches.

The original home of the Howards was East Winch, five miles south-east of King's Lynn, but as their importance increased and they progressed to the dukedom of Norfolk via a marriage to Margaret Mowbray in 1421, the palace at Kenninghall, midway between Attleborough and Diss, became their major Norfolk base. In Suffolk they owned the great castle at Framlingham. As well as holding estates in north-west Norfolk, which were gradually extended to include Castle Rising, the Howards acquired many manors in south Norfolk, inheriting the Bigod estates such as Forncett and a swathe of land from there south-eastwards to include Earsham, Harleston and, across the county boundary, Bungay with its castle. The Howard liberty included the hundreds of Laundon, South Greenhoe, Earsham and Guiltcross and 14 other manors. In 1540 they built a palace in Norwich, between St Andrew's church and the river, but at this time – despite their title – they shifted their main base to

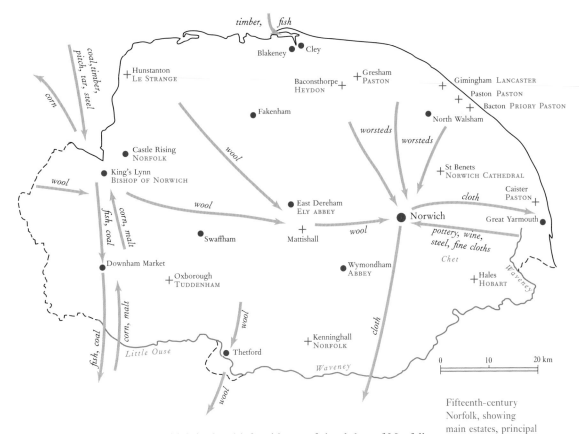

timber, fish

coal, timber,
pitch, tar, steel

corn

Blakeney • • Cley

Hunstanton
+ LE STRANGE

Gresham
+ PASTON

Baconsthorpe +
HEYDON

Gimingham LANCASTER
Paston PASTON
+ Bacton PRIORY PASTON

Fakenham

worsteds

North Walsham

Castle Rising
NORFOLK

worsteds

King's Lynn
BISHOP OF NORWICH

St Benets
+ NORWICH CATHEDRAL

wool

wool

East Dereham
ELY ABBEY

cloth

Caister
PASTON +

wool

Norwich

Great Yarmouth

corn, malt

fish, coal

Swaffham

Mattishall

wool

pottery, wine,
steel, fine cloths

Downham Market

Wymondham
ABBEY

Chet

Hales
+ HOBART

Oxborough
+ TUDDENHAM

corn, malt

wool

cloth

fish, coal

Little Ouse

Thetford

Kenninghall
+ NORFOLK

Waveney

0   10   20 km

wool

Waveney

Fifteenth-century
Norfolk, showing
main estates, principal
landholders and
selected trading routes.

Arundel Castle in Sussex, which is the chief residence of the dukes of Norfolk to this day. Nevertheless, the Norfolk estates were retained, and the dissolution of the monasteries further increased their influence: for example, in Norwich they acquired the sites of the Greyfriars and the Austin Friars. During the greater part of the Tudor period they were major players on the national scene, especially in the time of the third duke from the 1520s to the 1540s: his nieces, Anne Boleyn and Catherine Howard, were queens of Henry VIII.

The Paston family are best known for the remarkable collection of their surviving letters, which give a priceless and incomparable picture of national, local and domestic life in the fifteenth century.[11] Compared with the Howards they operated on a more limited stage: their estates were largely within east Norfolk and north Suffolk, but nonetheless were very extensive. John Paston II (1442–79) was at the king's court and was knighted in 1463, but maintained his Norfolk links as MP for the county in 1467 and 1470. His brother, John Paston III, had strong links with the 4th duke of Norfolk and after 1485 was a leading figure in Norfolk social and political life. By 1503, when John Paston III died, the family had huge landholdings in the east of the county, including Caister Castle, Gresham Castle, Drayton Castle and many manors, and a firm property base in Norwich, with houses in Elm Hill and Paston House by the river in King Street.

The Heydons of the village of Heydon, five miles west of Aylsham, were another important family of this period, and might be considered to some extent the 'baddies' of the upper level of county society.[12] Their rise began in 1221 when Thomas Heydon was a 'justice itinerant' for Norfolk, and steady progress in the family fortunes led to William Heydon I buying the manor of Baconsthorpe in about 1400. By 1479 John Heydon I, an eminent lawyer, had built the gatehouse at Baconsthorpe Castle, and in 1504 Sir Henry, the first of the family to be knighted, extended the impressive complex of buildings. Wealth derived from legal practice allowed them to purchase many other manors, upon which sheep-runs were established, so in due course wool became an important element in their income. Sir Henry, who died in 1504, left money to the poor folk 'being in my towns and dwellings in my possession'; these totalled 24, mainly in north-central Norfolk. Sir Christopher I was lord lieutenant in 1560 and in 1579 was licensed to crenellate (or castellate with battlements) at Baconsthorpe and to empark the surroundings. He was known especially

Caister Castle was built between 1432 and 1446 by Sir John Fastolf (the original of Shakespeare's Falstaff) as a house which would also become a collegiate foundation where priests would pray for the founder's soul. Rectangular and moated, and with three separate wards, it was one of the earliest major buildings in England to make extensive use of brick. This was in one sense a comfortable country house, but it also had a serious defensive purpose – in 1469 it was badly damaged after being besieged and captured by the duke of Norfolk with 3,000 men. When Fastolf died childless in 1457 the castle was inherited by his protégé, John Paston, but his ownership was contested by Norfolk. After the latter's death in 1476 Paston regained possession. These events are vividly described in the 'Paston Letters', the most important set of correspondence to survive from medieval England.

The gatehouse at Baconsthorpe Castle near Holt: the castle, with its characteristic high-quality flintwork and decorative use of stone for window mullions, doorways and quoins, was built in 1460-86 by John Heydon, whose upwardly mobile family had made a fortune in the law and the wool trade. Despite its name it was a fortified manor house rather than a serious castle – the gatehouse clearly could not have withstood anything but the most timid attack! The moat is particularly well preserved and widens out to form a small lake which served as a manorial fishpond.

as a wool magnate, and the imposing additions to the property reflect the tremendous wealth which could be gained from efficient large-scale commercial farming. The family line continued here until 1680 when the estates were sold. Today the ruins of Baconsthorpe, set in its tranquil moat, provide one of Norfolk's most evocative historic sights.

A partner of John Heydon I was Sir Thomas Tuddenham of Oxborough. Both were strong supporters of William de la Pole, earl of Suffolk. The de la Pole family originated as merchants in Hull, but built up extensive estates in East Anglia as they rose very rapidly through the ranks of English society between 1400 and 1480. This meteoric ascent provoked fierce antagonism: as Roger Virgoe says, in East Anglia the control exercised by William and his followers, of whom Heydon and Tuddenham were leaders, was bitterly resented by the members of older-established county families, including Sir John Fastolf and John Paston.[13] The fifteenth century was a time of greatly increased social mobility, producing tensions and hostilities which exacerbated the bitter conflict of the Wars of the Roses. While those civil wars produced no major fighting in Norfolk, there was intense local rivalry between old and new families.

By the fifteenth century merchants were playing an increasingly important part in the life of Norwich, Yarmouth and Lynn. These towns became centres for trade with Europe after the Black Death, although several smaller ports on the north coast, such as Wells and the Glaven ports of Blakeney, Wiveton and Cley, were also important in this period. Far up river from Yarmouth, Norwich was mainly accessible by keels, which were shallow-draft single-sail boats. At Yarmouth goods were craned from the seagoing 'carracks', the three-masted boats which can be seen in prints of Antwerp and other Low Countries ports and were in effect 'the tramp steamers' of the North Sea.[14] In Norwich, Robert Toppes was an example of an upwardly mobile merchant. He and other leading

Norwich citizens, such as Ralph Segrym, traded in undyed worsted cloth with Bruges, Ghent and Bergen op Zoom. From these Lower Rhine ports they imported German pottery, Swedish steel, quality fabrics and vegetable produce which were brought back to Norwich.

The social mobility of this period is shown by Robert Toppes' son, another Robert, for whom his father bought a manor outside Norwich. Robert junior married Margaret Lovell, the daughter of a major gentry family of Barton Bendish and East Harling. Having no heir, he left his Great Melton manor of Hacons to his nephew, Sir Gregory Lovell. Agnes, the daughter of Robert senior, married into the Fenn family of wealthy Yarmouth merchants. In his own second marriage Robert senior took as a wife Joan Knyvett of Buckenham Castle, a member of one of Norfolk's leading county families. It is clear just from this small period in the life of one family that the alliance of landed gentry status with mercantile wealth was much sought after. Ralph Segrym, who was mayor of Norwich in 1451, was extremely wealthy – he left money to divide the city's debtors' prison into sections for men and women, and also bequeathed £200 (about £150,000 in today's values) to repair the city walls.

The church of St Margaret in King's Lynn is of cathedral proportions, as befitted a notably prosperous medieval borough, and its twin west towers set it quite out of the ordinary in terms of parish churches. They were begun in the middle years of the twelfth century, the priory church itself having been founded in 1101. This view shows detail on the south face of the south-west tower, with superb late Norman interlace work and arcading.

The church of St Nicholas, King's Lynn, was founded as a chapel of ease to the church of St Margaret in 1146, but it is of the scale and grandeur of a major parish church, most of its fabric dating from the beginning of the fifteenth century. The splendid two-storey south porch has a lovely frieze of shallow niches, intended for statuary, with three larger niches in the gable (one for the Virgin Mary) divided by embroidery-like panels of decoration.
PHOTOGRAPH: SUSAN MADDOCK

The shallow waters of Blakeney Creek, almost four miles from the open sea via the Blakeney Channel, now provide a safe and sheltered haven for yachts and pleasure craft. Historically, though, this was (with Wells) the most important harbour between King's Lynn and Yarmouth, and medieval Blakeney was a flourishing port which traded with the Baltic, Iceland and the Low Countries as well as having an extensive coastal trade from north-east Scotland to the Channel ports of Kent and Sussex. The maritime trade gradually dwindled as the creek silted and vessels grew larger, but it continued on a small scale into the late nineteenth century, helped by the fact that the railway came late to north Norfolk and, indeed, never reached Blakeney itself, despite several proposals.

Other towns had merchants of wealth and status, though none as wealthy as the leading citizens of Norwich. At Lynn, William Norman had important trading links by river with Thetford Priory. The goods he supplied included tar, pitch, iron, millstones, wainscots, coals, salt, hops, blubber, three kinds of wine and a wide range of fish, and he traded at Thetford and Broomhill markets.[15] Even in Thetford, a town which because of its position deep inland lacked the commercial and trading dynamism of Norwich, Lynn or Yarmouth, there were specialist mercers such as Thomas Roberdes and smiths such as Thomas Pollet who were given regular orders by the priory.

Boroughs, markets and guilds

A medieval town became a borough by the grant of a charter, either from the Crown or from a manorial or baronial lord. By 1300 there were many hundreds of boroughs up and down the country, but remarkably few in Norfolk: only six places in the county had a borough charter (Norwich, Great Yarmouth, Thetford, Lynn, Castle Rising, and New Buckenham). This can be compared with, say, 27 places in medieval Lancashire for which a borough charter was issued. Why there were so very few in Norfolk is hard to ascertain, though the county had, in contrast, a prodigious number of places for which a market charter was granted (the current calculation is that no fewer than 174 places were granted a market between 1200 and 1516, although a very large number of these markets were either stillborn or short-lived).[16]

In the later medieval period major boroughs in England began to aspire to greater self-government, by means of a charter of incorporation (which gave significantly more powers and liberties than an 'ordinary' borough charter). It would create a formal and legally constituted corporation with a mayor, aldermen and councillors, their powers derived from a full royal charter. Charters of incorporation have been described as 'tools of an irresistible tendency towards exclusiveness. They were the treaties of alliance between a Crown which wished to see power in the hands of a group small and rich enough to be answerable to it, and urban elites determined enough to be answerable to it.'[17] Like many other cities, Norwich was eager to increase its authority *vis à vis* the Crown and London. This was a two-way bargain: a new charter cost the town a large sum of money (which Norwich duly paid in 1404), and the Crown felt it had some hold after making such a grant. In 1404 the city therefore received an important charter from Henry IV, allowing it to elect a

The delightful market house at New Buckenham was originally built in 1559, and served as a covered area for trading, with a court room or meeting chamber above. The timber-framed structure is supported on 'Tuscan' timber columns, inserted during major alterations in the mid-1750s – a little touch of the Renaissance in this remote location. The large square green was the market place of the planned medieval town.

The Guildhall in Norwich served as the centre of the city's government from the early fifteenth century until the opening of the present City Hall in 1938. It has been described as 'England's largest and most elaborate provincial medieval city hall', and its complex design and elaborate decoration in stone carving and flint flushwork were intended to emphasise the wealth, power and status of England's second city. The magnificent west front, with its seven-bay porch crowned with a three-storey battlemented gatehouse, faces on to the market place and looks over to the civic church of St Peter Mancroft, symbolising perfectly the three fundamentals of a successful medieval city – political power and good administration; thriving commerce; and the faith and dignity of the Church.

mayor in the place of the former bailiffs. An immediate response to the city's desire to be second only to London was to build its Guildhall (a misnomer, in that it was really a town hall). Like the old and rebuilt churches of the city, it was of flint, and its chequered west side, overlooking the market place, is still a distinctive piece of architecture. It is a complex building with court rooms for the City Assembly and the Mayor's Court, and an undercroft which was originally a gaol for the city. This was a civic building and carries no element of fortification.

A very important feature of urban society and government was the guild, although these varied greatly in character between different towns. Membership of guilds was a sign of having arrived in town society. Some guilds were exclusive and elite organisations while others were more broadly based. Many people who could afford the entrance fee were members of a religious guild, named after the patron saint or saints of their parish church, or the saints to whom a guild altar was dedicated within the church. Such guilds also existed in many rural communities, and were essentially religious – almost, perhaps, social – clubs rather than occupational. They provided support for their sick members, funding for their funerals and money towards the upkeep and beautification of the church fabric. Some owned property such as a guildhall and derived income from renting it out, and they held guild 'ales', which could be lively social events.

When such guilds kept accounts (as in the case of a number of Swaffham and Wymondham guilds) we learn a lot about medieval community life.[18] Swaffham is an example of a smaller market town from which the records build up a picture of guild activity. A return of 1389 records the five guilds that served the parish church:[19] the Fraternity of the Invention of the Holy Cross (the oldest, founded in 1322), All Saints (1333), The Ascension (1341), St Guthlac (1364) and St Peter (1384). Two more, the guilds of Corpus Christi and The Nativity of Our

The Ethelbert Gate stands at the south-west corner of Norwich cathedral close. It incorporates elements of an older structure but most of it was built in 1316–20 with a serious defensive purpose: in 1272, enraged by an incident at the fair in Tombland which got out of control, the citizens of Norwich had invaded the cathedral and monastic precinct, destroying the ancient church of St Ethelbert which stood immediately adjacent to the gate and wreaking havoc in the cathedral and monastery. The new gate was intended to defend the close against future outrages. Architecturally it is of outstanding importance, as it has what is believed to be the earliest surviving example of flushwork, the use of knapped flints to create intricate and decorative geometric patterns set within panels edged by the scarce and expensive freestone.

The Ethelbert Gate is also memorable for its fine medieval carvings, partly renewed and heavily restored in the Victorian period, which occupy the triangular spaces to the right and left of the arch. Here a very lively dragon and a pelican are intertwined with vines and bunches of grapes.

Lord, had been added by 1404, and the guilds of St George and St John the Baptist were established around the same time. By 1500 four more fraternities were meeting: the Holy Trinity, Our Lady, St Thomas and St Helen. Thus, in this comparatively small market town, no fewer than thirteen guilds can be traced in the fourteenth and fifteenth centuries. All the guilds gathered on the vigil of their patronal feast, offered alms at masses and burial ceremonies, said exequies at a member's death, and paid for candles for feast days. No reference to a guildhall appears at Swaffham, whereas at Wymondham there were several. The mixture of religious devotion and service to the fraternity is clear, though no single Swaffham guild seems to have become dominant (unlike the position in some larger towns).

In Norwich the Guild of St George was founded in 1385 and in 1420 received a charter from Henry V. This was not a craft or overtly religious guild but rather one of elite status: its membership was mainly confined to

The Trinity Guildhall at King's Lynn was completed in 1423 for the Guild of the Holy Trinity, to replace an earlier building which was badly damaged by fire in 1421. The great window of the guildhall is from the early fifteenth century, with smaller windows beneath to light a vaulted undercroft. Since the 1540s it has been in civic use and ownership, parts of it being converted in the 1570s to serve as a prison and in 1618 the eastern part (right) becoming the House of Correction. The porch to the left, with its intriguing venture into Classical or Renaissance styles, dates from 1624, though it carries the coat of arms of Queen Elizabeth, taken from another building and placed over the great 12-light window. Above are the arms of Charles II, placed there in 1664 in honour of the Restoration.

ex-mayors, aldermen and councillors. It was therefore a civic body, although knights and esquires of the county were also eligible for election, underlining the link between city and county which was always important. At Lynn the Trinity Guild, or Great Guild, was extant in the early thirteenth century.[20] Owen refers to it as a *Guilda Mercantoria* (or Guild Merchant) and records how its members met, for example, to decide on the toll to be levied on bringing timber into the town. The Guild contributed to many Lynn projects and in 1446 gave a loan to cover the cost of a visit by Henry VI. It took the profits of the Staithe and also had a monopoly on millstones and marble. The Trinity Guild and those of Corpus Christi and St George had lands in Boston, Louth and Wisbech, a reflection of the wide hinterland of Lynn. In 1377, 59 trade or craft guilds in Lynn returned certificates to the Crown. They acquired their own catering equipment, dined their members, buried them and helped charities such as an almshouse supported by Guilds of St Giles and St Julian. Lynn followed the example of Norwich and in 1420 built the Guildhall of the Holy Trinity, with its south side facing the Saturday Market Place. Like the Norwich Guildhall, this was built of chequered flint and stone, with a great hall raised above stone undercrofts.

In Thetford the Chapel of the Blessed Virgin Mary was founded in the thirteenth century next to the old market place. It was run by the Guild of St Mary the Blessed Virgin, 'the preserve of the elite of Thetford society', and owned properties in the Grassmarket and Nethergate and 1,000 acres of land at Barnham in Suffolk. The Guild of St Mary, which also built a guildhall, became known as the College, in the sense of 'a body of men'. Membership of it was '*de rigueur* for those who wished to succeed in Thetford social and business circles', such as the mayor and burgesses. Such guilds were 'bodies in which social, political, economic and religious powers were concentrated'.[21]

The lives of the 'middling sort'

In 1499 there was a vacancy in the bishopric of Norwich, and Archbishop John Morton of Canterbury (1486–1500) took the diocese under his wing.[22] A gathering of Norwich wills proved during Morton's period of authority has been edited by Christopher Harper Bill and these provide a fascinating snapshot of life in Norfolk towards the end of the medieval period. At the time wills were often very detailed, and the minutiae of possessions and domestic arrangements can frequently be reconstructed from their evidence. It must be accepted that they tell us nothing about the lives of the poor – the great majority of the population – but they can give us a revealing picture of the better-off families.

For example, William Laade of Terrington St Clement possessed extensive lands, and in his will he left 22 acres to his wife, and smaller areas to two daughters and a godson: in total, he left at least 75 acres. Most of his estates were freehold, and he was clearly a very careful manager of his property, for the will describes areas measured by the perch, or 16 feet. William also had grazing rights for stock on the salt marshes and on the smeeth, and gave four of his best cows (indicating that he had others), 15 adult sheep and 17 lambs to his family and godsons. The complexity of the parish geography is revealed by the named pieces of land. For example, his daughter Margaret was given land in Halsted field at Wynford, but holdings overlapped into neighbouring parishes and some of William's land was in Tilney.

The will of Joan Spenser (1499), 'lately servant' to Lady Anne Skrope of Harling, gives rich evidence of clothing and fabrics. Joan perhaps acquired her very impressive collection of clothing while in service. The materials listed are:

A tawny gown furred with black
Four quarters of a tawny gown to make a kirtle
A violet gown furred with white
A pair of sheets of 2½ breadths
A broadcloth of draper's work 5 yards long
A violet gown decorated with a border
4 quarters of a gown of blue cloth and 3 yards of blanket
A tawny gown lined with woollen cloth
A pair of sheets
An old tawny gown
A dark red gown furred with mink
A tawny gown with fur
A gown of mustard velour and an old tawny kirtle

Despite its name, the Guildhall at Blakeney is in fact the undercroft of a merchant's house dating from the early fifteenth century. It was built, facing the creek, at the time when the port was particularly prosperous as a result of the expansion of the fishing trade toward Iceland and the North Atlantic. The beautifully built brick-vaulted undercroft, supported on a row of three central columns, was used for storage, with the domestic accommodation for the merchant and his family above. Since at least the early seventeenth century it has been owned by the parish of Blakeney, managed by trustees and let out for rent, and in the years around 1900 served as a temporary mortuary for drowned bodies washed up on the shore. In the 1950s it was restored and taken into the care of the state.

A reminder of maritime Norfolk, meanwhile, is given in the will of Robert Strange of Cromer, whose house was to be sold for 25 marks. William Rugge was to have first offer of his ship, the *Mary*, for £15 'if he wants it'. His brother and his nephew were to have the *Fortune* and his little boat, the *George*, was to be sold. His wife Beatrice was to have one *manfare* (a pair of nets) of 12 score (about 20 feet deep), a *halferis* (half net) and a piece of *flue* (drift) net. His lad was to have a *manfare* of 12 score, four *halferises*, a hook, line and one hawser.

A final example illustrates something of the domestic contents of a dwelling. Robert Trewe, a burgess and draper of Bishop's Lynn, bequeathed various properties, and gave the usual gifts to local religious houses. To Symond, his son, he left a *maser* (silver bowl) of 8 ounces with a print of Jesus in the base, a little salt cellar with a cover of eight ounces, a little 'flat piece' of 6½ ounces, six silver spoons weighing 6 ounces, three brass pots, a pan weighing 40 lbs of which 20 lbs were latten (an alloy of copper and tin), a long candlestick for seven candles which hung in the hall, a complete harness with a harness barrel, and in ready money 10 marks. He also gave similar bequests of silver to his other son and two daughters. A later reference is to a 'standing piece' of 47 ounces part gilt, a pair of salt cellars of 40 ounces part gilt and a gilt cup of 27 ounces which, with other silverware, were to be sold by his executors. The residue of his jewels was to go to his wife. This very considerable collection of silver reflects the wealth which could be built up by a prosperous town merchant. Norwich, Lynn and Yarmouth had many such families, and the material comfort and conspicuous luxury of their lifestyles is testimony to the strength and vigour of the urban economy in these late-medieval international trading centres.

The Dissolution

'In no county can the universal confiscation and plunder have carried more terror and dismay than in Norfolk. The very number of foundations by which the spiritual and bodily needs of the people were looked after made their abolition the more universally felt.'[23] As the *Victoria County History* records, a total of 124 religious houses were dissolved, some as early as 1518, most by Henry's Act of 1538 or by the Act of 1547 dissolving the chantries. Arnold Baker estimated that the monasteries of England and Wales garnered 35 per cent of church income and owned between 35 and 38 per cent of the cultivable land; perhaps 25 per cent of the land in Norfolk was owned by religious houses.[24] This analysis makes it clear that the influence of monastic houses in medieval Norfolk was exceptionally important. As employers, landowners and traders they exerted a powerful economic impact, and in some places they were visually dominant as well. A tiny number of particularly small houses had been dissolved before the 1530s, but most remained, a powerful reminder of the huge role played by the medieval catholic Church. Yet within a space of only four years, from 1536 to 1540, the government of Henry VIII destroyed the monastic system in England and Wales, and in Norfolk as in every other county, centuries of history, and buildings which were architectural wonders, were wrecked and swept away before the eyes of local people.

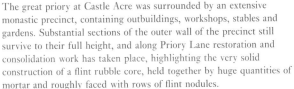

The great priory at Castle Acre was surrounded by an extensive monastic precinct, containing outbuildings, workshops, stables and gardens. Substantial sections of the outer wall of the precinct still survive to their full height, and along Priory Lane restoration and consolidation work has taken place, highlighting the very solid construction of a flint rubble core, held together by huge quantities of mortar and roughly faced with rows of flint nodules.

The gatehouse of Castle Acre priory is decorated with heraldry, dating from about half a century before the Dissolution and some of it commemorating the noble and gentry families who had given their patronage to the monastery. Here are shown (top) the royal arms of England and (below) the arms of the priory itself.

Among the many outstanding features of Castle Acre priory is the fine gatehouse, built of flint and brick in the years around 1500. It has a large central arch for the roadway, sufficient to take the largest wheeled vehicles, and separate smaller arch for the footway. On the east side is a porter's lodge and on the west side a waiting place where visitors were held before being admitted to the monastery. The upper storey formed a single large chamber, which served as the apartment for the porter/keeper of the gatehouse.

The prior's lodgings at Castle Acre was constructed during the last phase of the development of the site. By 1400 the entire west range of the cloister had been taken over for the use of the prior and his guests, and extensive improvements were made during the fifteenth century to create a spacious and comfortable lodging for the prior. In effect, a small country house – a 'secular mansion' – was fashioned out of the existing buildings, extending them to provide large first-floor bedchambers and guestrooms, a study and chapel, a great hall, and a new great kitchen. The ambitious architecture (including an oriel window in the study) and imposing entrance porch are well seen in this view. This side of the cloister survives in an almost perfect state of preservation because after the Dissolution it was used for three hundred years as a farmhouse.

The impact of the Dissolution was huge and traumatic. The gaunt remains of monastic houses both large (such as St Benet's) and small (such as Coxford) still provide us with vivid and evocative reminders of what once was. Around them the related secondary buildings and inner earthworks occupy considerable areas, as at Castle Acre or Bromholm, while in some places the barns and domestic buildings of the landed gentry who acquired the properties continue to occupy parts of the old sites (as at Old Buckenham or Thetford). In Wymondham the abbey buildings command one end of the town but the inner yards and gardens, bounded by the river Tiffey, have remained open, to provide a stunning setting for the monastic ruins when viewed from the west. In the cases of both Wymondham and Binham, as well as Norwich, the naves of the great churches have survived to the present as focal points of the sites. But in so many places, almost everything went. Norfolk has little good building stone, so the fine-quality masonry of the monastic buildings was swiftly carted away for use elsewhere – at Thetford Priory, for example, all that was left was the flint and rubble core of the walls, now a bewildering complex of shapeless ruins.

The fate of the Benedictine houses of Norfolk illustrates how the Dissolution benefited a few families, who acquired the valuable properties and in some instances became major landowners as a result:

Benedictine Houses

	Dissolved	To
Norwich	1538	The Dean and Chapter
Cells of Norwich		
Aldeby		
Lynn	1538	Thomas, third Duke of Norfolk
St Leonard		
Yarmouth		Dean and Chapter – leased in 1551 for 80 years to Robert Sowel
St Benet at Holm	1538	Bishop of Norwich
Wymondham Abbey	1538	The Crown
Binham	1539	Thomas Paxton, gentleman of the king's privy chamber
Horsham St Faith	1537	Richard Southwell (king's commissioner)
Molycourt	1449	Made a cell of Ely
Nunneries		
Blackborough	1537	Lease to James Joskyns for 21 years
Carrow	1538	Sir John Shelton
St George, Thetford	1536	Lease to Richard Fulmerstone of Ipswich

While the third Duke of Norfolk also acquired the estates of many other Norfolk monasteries, the Howard family was already a dominant element in the county's society. More striking, therefore, was the rise of new families, who gained much from the opportunities presented by the Dissolution. Thus, Richard Southwell and Sir John Shelton were classic examples of the new gentry, able to benefit from these changes in part because they were in the inner circles of power in government: close to the centre of decision making, they were well placed to use their connections. In Norfolk, as in many other counties, the long-term impact of the Dissolution was not just the loss of the monasteries and their immense significance in terms of economic activity and landholding – as well as their spiritual and religious role – but also the extensive reshaping of the social structure. Some of those who acquired monastic lands, including Robert Sowel, Thomas Paxton and James Joskyns, had no Norfolk connections – their families cannot be identified in the pre-Dissolution period and they were not known to Blomefield, Norfolk's great eighteenth-century historian. Instead, they regarded the newly acquired properties primarily as an investment, a means to extend their land portfolios which also included much property in other counties.

This, too, had an inevitable impact upon local communities, since absentee owners with commercial approaches to land management had very different perspectives from resident lords with a personal connection with the community. To what extent the middling people benefited or suffered therefore depended on how the new lords operated their estates. New buildings, the conversion of monastic buildings into private houses, emparking of land, and the enclosure of former medieval strip systems all followed this massive reorganisation of property ownership. The medieval rural landscape began to disappear rapidly as new methods and strategies of management were introduced, and swiftly changed the visual and physical geography of the rural communities.

In towns, too, the impact was extensive: not least, the demolition of monastic buildings created spaces in the urban fabric. In some cases these were soon swallowed up with other forms of development, but in others the sites of monastic houses remained as open land for centuries. In Thetford and other towns the fine-quality stone of the churches and monastic ranges was a readily accessible quarry for local people. A walk along King Street in Thetford soon reveals that embedded in the walls of post-1550 buildings, especially those constructed in the period between then and 1650, are countless fragments of dressed and carved stone, all that remains of parish churches and monastic properties that were swept away in the 1530s and 1540s.

Kett's Rebellion of 1549

The fifteenth century and the first half of the sixteenth was also a period of conflict. Perhaps the most significant instance, one which has a special place in the history of English popular protest, was Kett's Rebellion, in which Norfolk was the focus of one of the most serious threats to the regime of any Tudor monarch. Land, in his study of the rebellion, argues that Henry VIII's execution of the Earl of Surrey, the heir to the dukedom of Norfolk, at the beginning of 1547, followed by the imprisonment of his father, the Duke of Norfolk, by Edward VI, and the forfeiture of their estates, left the county leaderless in the late 1540s. But there were other sources of simmering discontent. The major changes in land ownership that resulted from the Dissolution, and the evident desire of the new landowners to put more land down to sheep, more sheep onto the commons, and more enclosure from the commons with enclosures, produced a growing antagonism in the county.[25] This can be traced back into the early sixteenth century, suggesting that the rebellion was not simply sparked by immediate events but was the culmination of a long-drawn-out social tension within Norfolk. Thus, in 1520 Sir Henry Fermor had created sheep walks with the consequent loss of grazing available to the commoners of Fakenham. This is known to have been opposed by local people. In 1539 there were riots at Hingham against Sir Henry Parker, and between then and 1549 sporadic outbreaks of rioting and unrest occurred elsewhere in the county.

In 1549 a group of villagers living south-west of Wymondham combined to throw down the fences of John Green, the lord of Wilby. On the feast of St Thomas the Apostle (3 July), there were various disturbances at Morley and Hethersett on the land of John Flowerdew. Out of these, under the leadership of Robert Kett, a prosperous local landowner, grew a rebel army which established a camp on Mousehold Heath to the east of, and overlooking, Norwich. The full story has been told by several writers ranging from a contemporary account by Nicholas Sotherton of 'The Commoyson [commotion]' in Norfolk to that of Stephen Land who argued, in rather Marxist terms, that the rebellion was 'a war between peasant farmers and small tradesmen on the one hand and

The Norfolk estates belonging to the Great Hospital, Norwich, in about 1500

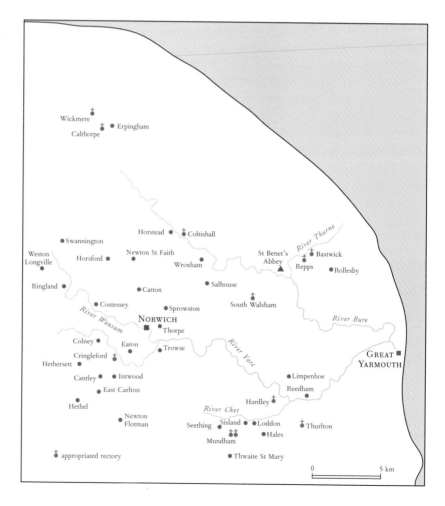

Thetford was the largest town in pre-Conquest Norfolk and was a place of continuing importance in the medieval period. It had five major monastic houses, six religious hospitals and colleges, and no fewer than twenty churches in 1200. By 1500 only nine of the latter remained, and after the Reformation all but three disappeared. The gaunt ruins of the church of St Giles in King Street (closed in 1540) remained and were sketched by the vicar of St Mary's, but shortly afterwards they were demolished. Pieces of dressed and carved stone from the church can be spotted in walls and buildings in the vicinity.

landowners, lawyers and merchants on the other, a war between classes'.[26] Kett's force produced a list of demands, their famous 29 articles. These represented the concerns of the middling folk, relating to the price of land, the right to graze herds and flocks on the commons, and the right to farm one's land without fear of eviction. They were not demands which were aimed at meeting the needs of paupers.[27]

On 13 July 1549 Matthew Parker, master of Corpus Christi College, Cambridge, and a future archbishop of Canterbury, preached a sermon to try to persuade Kett's army to disperse. This attempt failed and he had to withdraw quickly. Events thereafter became more serious, and the rebels attacked Norwich, breaking through Bishopgate Bridge. York Herald, representing the Crown, ordered that the participants should disperse, but his remonstrations were rejected, and the assembled throng was declared to be in rebellion.

Catherine Parr's brother, the Marquis of Northampton, was appointed to lead a force of Italian mercenaries, with support from the Norfolk gentry who were beginning to realise the seriousness of the rebellion. Northampton and his troops were beaten in a battle on St Martin Palace Plain, in which Lord Sheffield, one of his officers, was killed. Kett then set up his 'court' in the grounds of the cathedral. The final stage was marked by Kett's failure to widen the rebellion outside Norwich, largely because of the decisive actions of local gentry. A force led by the John Dudley, Earl of Warwick, and including many German mercenaries, cleared the city and, after heavy fighting at Dussindale, east of Mousehold, defeated the rebels. Robert Kett and his brother William were hanged with nine other rebel leaders.

The discontent expressed in the 29 demands, and these sporadic and flickering outbursts of real violence, were among the factors which led to the gradual creation of a new militia system, under the control of the local gentry.

More indirectly, later Tudor governments began to recognise that the pressing problems faced by ordinary people, in terms of poverty, loss of traditional rights, and the vicissitudes of economic downturns, represented a potential cause of ever-greater popular discontent. The answer was sought less in overt repression, and more in means of ameliorating the worst problems of poverty: the result was the creation of a national Poor Law system at the end of the sixteenth century, and in local efforts, as in the city of Norwich, to assess and take action on poverty and the poor. And for others, the loss of the Howard dominance in the county, which was never re-established, allowed the new gentry to take responsibility for peace in the county. Able to assert themselves more effectively and to fill the power vacuum which the crisis in the Howard family had created, these men and their descendants emerged as the new force in Norfolk. Some of the great names of the seventeenth and eighteenth centuries first gain prominence in the decades after 1550.

10

The Fens

T HE Fens extend over a large part of west Norfolk, a smaller tract of north-west Suffolk, much of Cambridgeshire and the Isle of Ely, and extensive areas of southern Lincolnshire. Their origins and physical development have been the subject of intensive research and investigation over many decades, and analysis in the past fifty years has emphasised the crucial importance of human activity in moulding and shaping the physical interface between land and water, the rivers and the coastline, and the low islands of drier land that were so vital to settlement.

Intensive pre- and post-glacial erosion opened up a gap between the chalk escarpment of the Lincoln Wolds to the west and the East Anglian Heights to the east. This meant that after the last Ice Age the drainage of the vast area which is now the catchments of the rivers Welland, Nene and Great Ouse, and their numerous tributaries, flowed out in shifting channels to the Wash. Previously rivers had flowed eastwards from the Midlands towards the North Sea, but now they ultimately flowed northwards to reach the sea between Boston and Lynn. The lime-rich waters of the river systems meet the huge expanses of marine silts, deposited from the erosion of the Lincolnshire and Norfolk coasts, which accumulate at the southern end of the Wash. The boundary of that wide zone of river and sea deposits was a variable one, constantly fluctuating, until at the beginning of the fourteenth century local landowners and residents began to construct banks to constrain the river channels, and to enclose and reclaim areas of marsh for arable and stock farming. Before then, as sea levels rose and the whole area was subject to saturation, the accumulation of peat became a dominant feature of the ecology and of the landscape itself, while marine silts also accumulated to create habitable areas seaward of the peat fen. The landscape and environment were unstable, and the main aim of human intervention was to consolidate and fix the shifting lines of rivers, watercourses, shorelines and boundaries of settlement.

Within the Norfolk part of the Fens, the Great Ouse river system changed its course several times after the Roman period. Until the thirteenth century the main channel flowed between the Isle of Ely and the modest uplands of west Norfolk to meet the Nene outfall at Wisbech. Thus, the geography of drainage was radically different from how it is today. Lynn, which today is at the mouth of the Great Ouse, then lay at the outfall only of the small west-flowing River Nar, while a major estuary extended northwards to the sea in the vicinity of Sutton Bridge. But in the years around 1300 a new channel for the Great Ouse was either cut deliberately, or was formed by natural processes (or possibly a

*c.*1300	The Great Ouse diverted to enter sea below King's Lynn rather than Wisbech
early 14th century	Major monastic involvement in drainage and reclamation works
1300–1500	Progressive draining of areas towards the sea – the 'siltlands'
1636	Vermuyden cuts Sam's Cut from Feltwell to the Great Ouse
1637	Vermuyden cuts the New Drain or Old Bedford Level
1651	The Hundred Foot Drain and New Bedford Level, with floodwater to Ouse Washes
1713	Denver Sluice 'blew up', and start of windmill drainage pumps
1720s and 1730s	Beginning of major shrinkage of the peat and pumping takes effect
1745	Downham butter market established, and beginning of major London trade
1790s	Reclamation in Terringtons and adjacent siltland parishes
1797	Faden's map of Norfolk
1804	Arthur Young describes in detail the Fenland sheep and their management
1821–1851	Steam pumping installed in Fenland mills
1826	Bryant's map of Norfolk
1830	The butter market moved from Downham to Swaffham
1840s	Corn, wool and beef replace dairying as mainstay of Fenland agriculture
1848	Holme Fen Pillar erected and subsequently marks the shrinkage of the fen
1851	Eau Brink Cut; Middle Level Drain to Wiggenhall
1865	New Cut from King's Lynn to the sea
1865–1939	Wash Land enclosures, north and west of King's Lynn
1889	County Smallholdings Committee formed: 1,300 tenants in Fenland smallholdings by 1914
1913	Diesel-powered pumping for drainage begins
1936 and 1947	Major flooding; work on raising the riverbanks follows
1948	Beginning of large-scale electric pumping
1953	Catastrophic flooding in Fenland and coastal areas
1964	Cut-off channel from Mildenhall to Denver; relief channel Denver to King's Lynn
21st century	Rising sea levels present growing challenge and threat to Fenland

combination of the two) from its confluence with the Wissey to Lynn. This was fundamental to the future history of the area, for it made Lynn the focal point – the key – to the trade of the large basin of the Great Ouse river system, extending inland to Cambridge and towards Bedford.

The unity of the Fens therefore cuts across the dividing lines of county boundaries: not only west Norfolk but also south Lincolnshire,

There were few triangulation points at a lower altitude than that which stands on the embankment of the Well Creek near Nordelph, between Downham Market and Outwell, at 5 feet above sea level. The river, which is partly natural and partly a man-made medieval channel, now links the old course of the Nene with the Great Ouse near Downham Market, though originally it flowed in the opposite direction, towards Wisbech. Because the level of the surrounding peat has shrunk, through centuries of drainage, the Well Creek is now significantly higher than the surrounding land.

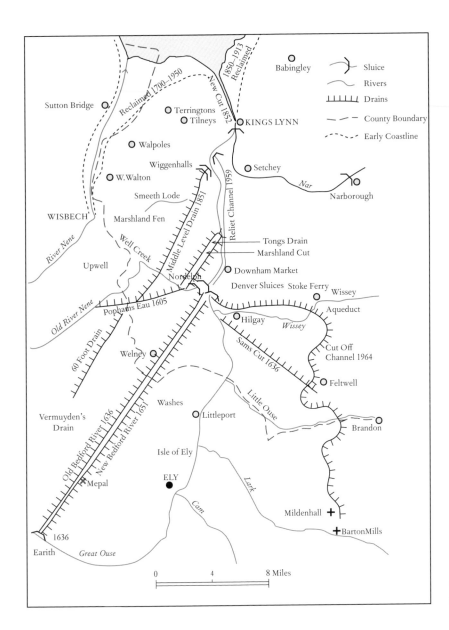

Sluice
Rivers
Drains
County Boundary
Early Coastline

Babingley
Sutton Bridge
Reclaimed 1700–1950
Reclaimed 1850–1913
New Cut 1852
Terringtons
Tilneys
KINGS LYNN
Walpoles
Wiggenhalls
W. Walton
Setchey
Smeeth Lode
Nar
Narborough
WISBECH
Marshland Fen
Reliet Channel 1959
River Nene
Well Creek
Middle Level Drain 1851
Upwell
Nordelph
Tongs Drain
Marshland Cut
Downham Market
Old River Nene
Pophams Eau 1605
Denver Sluices
Stoke Ferry
Wissey
Aqueduct
60 Foot Drain
Hilgay
Wissey
Welney
Sams Cut 1636
Cut Off
Channel 1964
Washes
Feltwell
Vermuyden's
Drain
Old Bedford River 1636
New Bedford River 1651
Littleport
Little Ouse
Brandon
Isle of Ely
Mepal
ELY
Lark
1636
Earith
Great Ouse
Cam
Mildenhall
Barton Mills

0   4   8 Miles

The drainage and
reclamation of Fenland

north Cambridgeshire, the Isle of Ely and the easternmost part of east
Northamptonshire are all parts of this region. The geography of river channels
was only part of the story, however. The greatest change in the Fens, that
immense expanse spanning those county boundaries, came with the emergence
of permanent drainage systems to replace the irregular and unpredictable
flooding by sea and inland waters. The changing pattern of channels had little
impact upon the wetlands all around, but the decisions to drain those wetlands,
to create new farmland from the sodden peaty wastes, was what really shaped
the geography and landscape of Fenland as we see it today. At the beginning
of the 1630s Cornelius Vermuyden, a highly experienced Dutch drainage
engineer, was appointed by King Charles I to drain the fens. The Crown, the

duke of Bedford (the main local landowner, after whom the Bedford Levels are named) and other 'adventurers' (that is, entrepreneurs) paid the costs of the drainage schemes and, in return, 95,000 acres of reclaimed land were shared out among them.

In 1636 Cornelius Vermuyden cut Sam's Drain from Feltwell to the Great Ouse and a year later a completely new drain (the Fenland term for an artificial channel) from Earith in Cambridgeshire to Salter's Lode in Norfolk – this became known later as the Old Bedford Level. Its straight course allowed flood waters from the Great Ouse basin to reach the sea more quickly than before, so reducing the risk of long-term flooding and allowing serious reclamation to begin. Vermuyden's work outlived the king who was his initial patron and sponsor – after all, many of the leading parliamentarians, including Oliver Cromwell himself, were local men, and they appreciated the potential of what had been set in train. In 1651 Vermuyden cut the Hundred Foot Drain or New Bedford River, from Earith to Denver, where it reached the tidal Great Ouse. It was cleverly conceived, so that high tides could flood back up it, heading inland, in order to reduce their impact on the older channel between Denver and Lynn. Between the two Levels he created the Wash Land, or 'The Washes', an elongated rectangle of land which was specifically available to fill with flood water, diverting it from the newly drained arable land on either side. It is fascinating to see that in the twenty-first century, faced with a heightened flood risk on Midland rivers, progressive hydrological engineers now favour exactly the same system of storing overflow and surplus waters.

The improved channel of the Great Ouse, just upstream from the main sluice at Denver, looking south. This is the point where the widened and upgraded original channel (in this view) broadens to meet the wide bypass channel which parallels the original river north to King's Lynn and was constructed in the 1950s. The river here is a key section in the complex network of Fenland waterways, now so intensively used for pleasure boating.

None of this would have functioned effectively without other controls, and in order to reduce flooding dangers from unusually high tides and to allow river water to escape at low tides, the all-important sluice at Denver, one of the most impressive man-made features of the Norfolk landscape, was built at the outlet of the Great Ouse. Additional drainage schemes transformed the marshes west of Downham: the St John's Eau was cut between the dry land and the Ouse, slicing the land between Downham and the river into two strips. A second pair of drains running north-east from Nordelph to join the Ouse west of Wimbotsham provided the western boundary to the parish of Downham; in 1797 Faden's map named them as Tong's Drain and Marshland Cut.

Thus, Vermuyden's work opened up the whole of the Ouse river system to trade into and out of Lynn from as far as Huntingdon and Cambridge and worked also to the advantage of Downham Market. Downham is a classic 'market site', lying between the uplands to the east and the lowlands of the Fens to the west. Traders bringing barley from the uplands met those driving cattle and sheep from the Fens, and exchanges between them took place at the market which grew up below the edge of the carstone cliff, upon which the church was so well placed as a dominant feature in the landscape, clearly visible to those who were crossing the Fen marshes to the west. Downham's growing importance as a market appears to have been especially for the summer trade in butter. The firkins (barrels) were gathered in from the summer grazings on the fens and moved by boat to Cambridge and then by cart to London (where it became known as Cambridge butter). A market seems to have operated at Denver in the medieval period, but it may have dwindled away more or less to nothing. However, the collapse of the sluice in 1713 was used to explain the need for a new market, and a series of papers in the Hare collection at the Norfolk Record Office throws some light on this.[1] An enquiry was held as to whether a market could be sited on Sir Thomas Hare's land at the Mash which was described as follows:

> Situated between the River Great Ouse on the west and ... St John's Eau on the east beginning at a house now inhabited by Richard Cook waterman and proceeding southward to Denver Gool ... for buying and selling of butter and also two fairs to be held every year to be kept at or upon a piece of waste ground belonging to Sir Thomas Hare called the Howdale [a piece of common land adjoining Downham Market church].

This all took a long time, but in the 1740s a petition from Sir Thomas to the King pointed out that:

> large quantities of butter are sent every year from Norfolk to London in firkins for the great benefit of landowners and farmers ... who make the chief part of their rents by butter and to the great convenience of the cities of London and Westminster who are plentifully supplied with it.

In 1745 a grant, with a beautiful royal seal, gave the market official status but stated that cattle fairs were also to be held 'on the Match [sic]'. The *Universal British Directory* of 1793 commented that firkins of butter contained 56 lbs

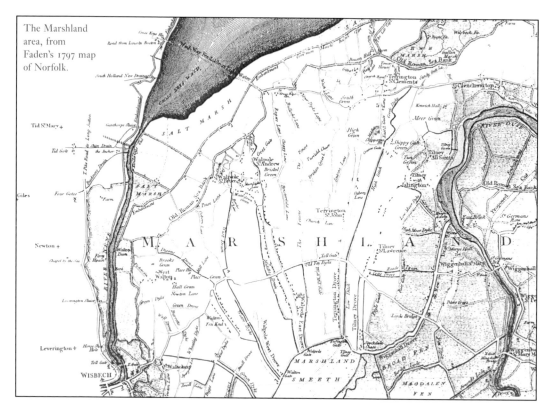

The Marshland area, from Faden's 1797 map of Norfolk.

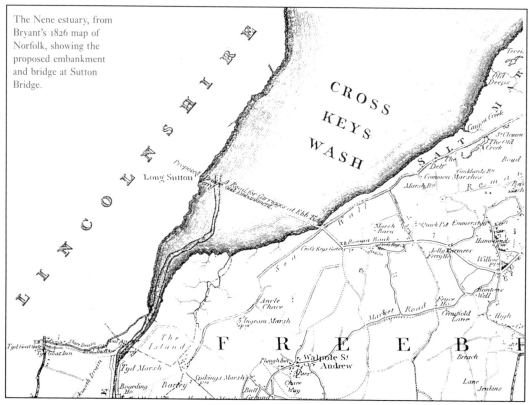

The Nene estuary, from Bryant's 1826 map of Norfolk, showing the proposed embankment and bridge at Sutton Bridge.

and that formerly 2,000 firkins a week came to the market, but that by the 1790s this had declined to 500. It stated that Burleigh's boats left the market at 11 a.m. on Monday to reach Cambridge on Tuesday, there linking up with the wagons. Many wagons were noted as leaving the Butter Market daily, and Hunt's Upwell boats were also listed. The importance of river traffic for this trade is notable. However, by the 1830s *Pigot's Commercial Directory* noted that the once celebrated Butter Market had moved to Swaffham, and in 1845 *White's Directory* recorded that the growing of corn, keeping of sheep for wool, and the feeding of cattle had replaced the previous emphasis on butter production. This reflects the continuing effects of draining the former grazing land.

The dependence of the Fen farmers on their sheep has already been mentioned in the chapter on wool and cloth. The trackways from the silt settlements of the North Fens to the great common grazings to the south, known as the Smeeth, allowed the movement of cattle and sheep to the rich grass of the summer grazings. The traditional Lincoln sheep of the Fens had the long fleeces of fine wool that was regarded as the best source for worsted cloth. Arthur Young, writing in 1804 about Mr Denis of Wiggenhall St Mary, noted that he only grazed the best Lincoln wethers and that by buying them in May and keeping them over a year he got two clips giving 18 lbs per sheep.

The villages of Outwell and Upwell have an extraordinary position, perched on the winding embankments of the Well Creek and the old river Nene, close to the county boundary with what used to be the Isle of Ely. On either side the land falls away to the flat fens, so the rivers, like the villages, are raised above the low-lying ground. Nevertheless, despite the physical challenges of the location, this was an area of very great prosperity in the later medieval period. That wealth is demonstrated by, for example, the great church of St Clement at Outwell, which stands at the confluence of the old Nene and the Well Creek (foreground), and by the unexpectedly large number of surviving substantial houses dating from the seventeenth and eighteenth centuries which line the waterside.

The first edition six-inch map of 1882 reveals vividly the remarkable topography of the twin villages of Outwell and Upwell. The sinuous and elongated form of the villages is shown to be because they stand on the dry embankments of the Nene and the Well Creek, producing a one-deep line of houses, shops and other buildings which cling to the edge of the short steep drop above the wet fenland. Behind them stretch exceptionally long narrow plots of land, like crofts, reaching out in finger fashion towards what was once wet peat bog. The Wisbech and Upwell Tramway, which for most of its length ran along the roadside and through village streets, opened in 1883 to Outwell and a year later to Upwell, linking the Great Eastern Railway with a string of communities and farms. Used mainly for bringing in coal and carrying out agricultural produce, it also carried passengers until 1927 and, rather surprisingly, was busy with freight traffic until closure in 1966.

On his good land six sheep grazed per acre in summer and in winter three and, drawing attention to the need to maintain the purity of the breed, he commented that 'even a stain of the New Leicester is hurtful'. On the other hand, he noted that Mr Swayne of Walpole preferred a Lincoln Leicester cross, some of which gave 17 or 18 lbs of wool.[2] In his Lincolnshire volume Young, who was secretary to the Board of Agriculture and produced a valuable series of county reports including those for Lincolnshire, Norfolk and Suffolk, gave a detailed picture of the state of agriculture in 1813. He gave some more details of the Lincoln breed, contrasting their high wool yield with the mere 2 to 4 lbs obtainable from the Norfolk breed – although he observed that the latter gave excellent mutton. Mr Coke's New Leicesters were giving 8 lbs of wool. In an admittedly exceptional case he quotes a Mr Graves in Lincolnshire, with a true Lincoln sheep, 'that clip the first year 23 lbs of wool and the second at

22½'. He also reported that Leicester rams crossed with Lincoln ewes would give 10 lbs of wool and he noted that the rich grazings near Boston carried two sheep an acre in winter and three or four sheep plus bullocks in summer.[3] All these comments were made at a time when the selected breeding of sheep by Coke and many others was an important theme in agricultural improvement. Sheep rearing and fattening in particular, but also bullock-fattening, were the major farming activities of the Norfolk fens. But, as is shown later, stock had virtually disappeared from this region by the 1930s and had been replaced by a wide range of ready-for-market crops.

The effect of Vermuyden's and later drainage schemes was that, once drained, the peat-rich soils began to shrink. The famous cast-iron pillar at Holme Fen in Huntingdonshire shows a shrinkage of 13 feet since 1848. While other areas have not shrunk as fast as this, the river system is now divorced from the field drainage system because of the increasing difference in vertical levels, so that first windmills, then steam mills and now an electric pumping system have been needed to lift field water into the rivers to be carried out to the sea. Godwin lists this sequence of drainage technology for the Fens.[4]

Until 1820, windmill and scoop wheel
Then, windmills in series
From 1821 to 1851, steam engines and scoop wheel
From 1851 to 1947, steam engines and centrifugal pumps
From 1913 onwards, diesel engines and centrifugal pumps
From 1948 onwards, electric motors and mixed flow or axial flow pumps
automatically operated

The Streatham steam pump in Cambridgeshire on the bank of the old West River is still in working order; the great sequence of pumps at Denver is the most impressive; and new pumps have recently been installed at Wiggenhall to carry water from the Middle Level Drain into the Great Ouse. But despite this concerted and continuous application of technology over four centuries, the battle to prevent renewed flooding and to avert the inundation of the Fens continues. A catastrophic Fenland flood forms part of the denouement of *Nine Tailors*, the famous detective story published in 1934 by Dorothy L. Sayers, while the serious floods experienced in 1936 and 1947 gave warning of worse to come. In 1953 the banks of the Ouse between Lynn and Denver were breached in 13 places. After the tremendous 1953 floods (which were particularly disastrous in the Fens, though the coastal flooding of east Norfolk is more familiar in popular remembrance), a key decision was made whereby in future flood water from the east-bank Norfolk tributaries of the Great Ouse would be transferred into a cut-off channel from Mildenhall to Denver. This would divert floodwaters away from the lowlands. The channel, a massive engineering project, was completed in 1964 and skirted the fen edge, taking the water to a new sluice at Denver. It was possible to use the spoil from the excavation of the channel to raise the riverbanks 2 to 3 feet above the level of the 1953 surge. From Denver a relief channel 11 miles long was cut to King's Lynn so that tides could be held back and flood water released. A third improvement was to the channel of the old Great Ouse, the Ely Ouse and the Ten Mile River over 19 miles. The combination of these additions to Vermuyden's work has so far been a great success.

A second element of change in the Fens has been the reclamation of land from the sea. The erosion of the east Yorkshire and Lincolnshire coasts, combined with that from north Norfolk, means that vast quantities of silt are brought by longshore drift into the southern end of the Wash. The siltland parishes had a medieval sea wall, known erroneously as 'the Roman Wall'. Gradual intakes of salt marsh beyond that medieval frontier have taken place in the last three centuries. As the map on page 196 shows, the parish of Terrington St Clement, for example, has seen several stages of reclamation from 1775 up to 1974; of which the last by the Crown Commissioners has provided a footpath on the sea bank between Sutton Bridge and King's Lynn known as Peter Scott Way. This, too, has had repercussions farther afield. The accretion of silt close to the shore has meant that the rivers have had to be embanked, to raise their level upstream in order to provide a gradient from the peat fen and to prevent fresh water flooding on the drained, reclaimed land.

In 1936, 1937, 1939 and 1947 the Fens were devastated by flooding, the last occasion being exceptionally severe. A 1940 proposal to building a flood relief channel was therefore implemented, and between 1954 and 1964 an artificial waterway 35 miles long was constructed from Barton Mills to Downham Market, meandering along the edge of the fen and crossing (or being crossed by) the rivers Lark, Little Ouse and Wissey. The cut-off channel, seen here near Wereham, is designed to capture the floodwaters coming down these rivers and divert them into the relief channel of the Great Ouse below Denver Sluice down to King's Lynn. Remarkably, in 1971 a second scheme was completed whereby in times of drought the flow can be reversed and the waters in the channel head south, supplying an underground channel at Blackdyke near Feltwell which links with a pumping station at Kennett, east of Newmarket, whence the water is fed into pipelines supplying Essex.

Draining the Fens has been achieved by the construction of many hundreds of miles of ditches and dykes and by the very careful control of the natural watercourses which thread the low-lying lands. As the peat shrank and much of the area is now at sea-level the risk of flooding has grown, so seabanks, embankments and sluices are essential elements in protecting the lands behind. Here at West Lynn the West Lynn Drain, which flows from Tilney All Saints and marks the line of the medieval seabank, reaches the tidal estuary of the Great Ouse, protected by two sets of strong sluicegates.

To the north-east of King's Lynn a second area of reclamation took place been 1865 and 1936 as was shown on Gore's map, published by the Land Use Survey of Norfolk in 1936.[5] These enclosures were made by the Norfolk Estuary Company which was founded in 1837. The first to be reclaimed is now part of the urban area of King's Lynn. The reclamation of marshland also continued in the Nene Estuary. On his map of 1826 (page 196) Bryant showed the projected line of the new causeway and bridge between Cross Keys Gate and Sutton Bridge, which revolutionised communications, and also the new embankments which led to the reclamation of marshes upstream to Wisbech and seaward from Walsoken to West Walton.

An even greater engineering project was the realignment of the Great Ouse in two stages. The first was the Eau Brink Cut of 1851, between the Wiggenhalls and Lynn. This straightened the course of the river and aimed to reduce silting at Lynn. The second alteration was the 'canalisation' of the river channel from Lynn to the open sea in 1865. This was known as the New Cut and it was this defined channel that allowed the marshes to its east to be enclosed. In 1851 the Middle Level Drain was cut from Three Holes in Upwell to Wiggenhall St Mary and this improved the drainage of Marshland Fen. These improvements led to the creation of a new Marshland civil parish over the area of the former Smeeth (see page 193).

The new farming

Gradually most of the former silt and peat land pastures became sufficiently well drained for arable farming to become the main basis of the economy. In 1889 the new county council in Norfolk set up a county smallholding committee. Partly because of the fertility of the soil, which could support a family on a relatively limited holding, many of the farms in the Fens were small. The county council bought or leased a large number, letting them to tenants. In 1904 the first estate was bought at Nordelph. Although this was a nationwide policy, Norfolk became the leading county in this process, and by 1914 had 1,300 tenants on 13,000 acres. A major concentration of holdings was bought from the Hare estate at Stow Bardolph, but many more were scattered across the Norfolk Fens. Housing was not always available and so new farmhouses and buildings often had to be erected.[6] The Norfolk Land Use Survey of 1936 gives good examples of farm types in the Fens by the 1930s. A farm at Terrington St Clement of 220 acres in 1936 grew:

potatoes	90 acres
wheat	25
sugar beet	15
green peas	25
strawberries	25
apples	10
spring cabbages	10
bulbs	40
glasshouses	2
clover	10
permanent pasture	20

Mosby stressed that there was a great variety of cropping patterns on the different farms. The great contrast with pre-drainage times is that sheep virtually disappeared, some bullocks were kept on marshland, and pigs and chickens became increasingly important. He noted that glasshouse production grew rapidly in the 1930s, a process which has continued to the present day.

Norfolk's encroachment on the Wash as shown by the date of each reclaimed parcel.

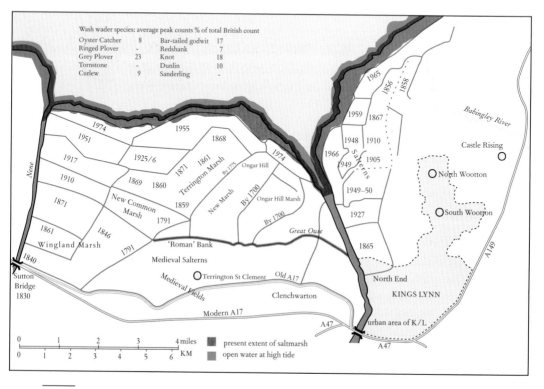

The thick peat soils of the Fens represent the largest area of top-grade agricultural land in Britain. For many centuries this has been a prosperous area, despite its marginal and sometimes hazardous environment, as the great churches of so many Fen communities testify. But it has also been, and remains, an area where many live in considerable poverty, and where the strange topography and huge empty spaces produce a powerful sense of remoteness. The characteristic landscapes are those of long straight lines, drainage dykes and embankments, isolated bungalows, and occasional rows of trees. Market gardening has been a major feature of agriculture in the Fens for over a century, ever since improved transport links gave easier access to urban markets. This view is from the back road from Methwold to Southery, on the reclaimed fen called Methwold Severals.

Kemp, writing on Norfolk agriculture in 1961, noted that Terrington St Clement had concentrations of mobile glasshouses growing tomatoes, cucumbers and flowers. On the peat fen celery, carrots and onions were important.[7]

The Norfolk Fens is a region at present under control, protected by engineering and technology from the terrifying reality of sea or river floods. On the northern silts greenhouses and intensive smallholdings have replaced both the earlier pattern of small cereal fields around the villages and stock grazing over many thousands of acres.

Denver Sluice is the point at which a series of man-made and semi-natural waterways meet –
the original course of the Great Ouse, the 1950s cut-off channel and Great Ouse relief channel,
the New Bedford River or Hundred Foot Drain and, a quarter of a mile downstream, the Old
Bedford River and the Well Creek. This is the crucial nodal point on the Fenland waterway
system, the key to water flow, drainage and flood control. In the 1950s, with the building of the
cut-off and relief channels, the entire area was extensively remodelled and huge concrete sluices
were constructed for flood control. This view shows the A.G. Wright Sluice (1964), named after
the chairman of the Flood Protection Scheme Committee, where the channels meet.

Yet the long-term future for the Fens must always remain questionable.
Having watched the effects of the 1953 floods breaching the banks of the Great
Ouse in the Wiggenhalls, I am only too well aware of the power of flood waters.
Although many miles of river banks were raised by several feet after the 1953
flood, as can be seen downstream of Denver Sluice, the marine silts accumulate
faster than the river deposits. This has meant that river banks have had to be
raised several times since 1953 to allow land water to flow out into the Wash at
low tides. At high tides the sluices have to hold the sea-water back, resisting the
immense pressure of the salt waters. In the effort to get land-water away once
the washes of the Bedford Levels are full, any increase in sea levels will put
an even greater strain on these vital structures, Victory in the battle between
land and sea may be temporarily ours, but we can never be sure that one day
the tide will not turn again.

11

Norfolk from 1550 to 1750

F OR historians of Norfolk the sixteenth century is a crucial and fascinating period. As well as seeing the involvement of the county in the great events and processes which transformed key aspects of national life – the Reformation, the Dissolution of the monasteries, and the rapid changes in economic and social activity – we have a much larger quantity of rich and diverse documentary material to support our researches and to inform our analyses and conclusions. For example, the extraordinarily wide-ranging and informative papers of Nathaniel Bacon of Stiffkey, a man who was of considerable national importance because of illustrious connections yet also deeply rooted in his estates and community interests in North Norfolk, provide us with a detailed picture of the inter-relationship between national events, those in the county, and those at the most local level in his part of Norfolk.[1] Nowhere could possibly be unaffected by the 'big issues' of the day: throughout the period from 1550 until the end of the seventeenth century, the fundamental question of religious alignments and differences, and the profound political divisions that they engendered, constantly come to the fore, reminding us that East Anglia, and Norfolk in particular, was at the heart of key developments in English history. With Norwich as the second city of the realm, it could hardly have been otherwise.

The growth of the boroughs is therefore a key element in this story. The significance of large urban centres is clearly demonstrated at Lynn, with its crucial international trading links with northern Europe; at Yarmouth with its ever more important fishing and North Sea trade; and at Norwich with its nationally significant textile industry, dominant place as one of the provincial capitals of England, and vital role as the main market centre for much of East Anglia. But as a primarily rural county, and a county of great estates, the aspirations and actions of the landowners in Norfolk were also fundamental. The new post-Dissolution gentry played Monopoly with the former monastic lands and some, such as the Pastons, Heydons, Hares, Southwells and Fermors, benefited hugely from the wholesale redistribution of property that the Dissolution set in train. There was palpable sense of dynamism and entrepreneurial spirit in the boroughs, where the trading and textile families begin to expand into early forms of banking. Helped by the survival of superb family and estate archives, and by the labours of pioneering historians such as Robert Ketton Cremer (1906–69) we can trace the evolution of the great estates at Felbrigg, Blickling, Holkham, Hunstanton and others in rich detail, charting the sweeping changes that were made to landscapes,

1549	Kett's Rebellion; population of Norwich about 15,000
1553	Princess Mary marches on London from Kenninghall to claim her throne
1557	William Fermor, who died this year, had 17,000 sheep
1558	Heretics burned in the Lollards Pit in Norwich
1560–1607	Nathaniel Bacon a key figure in Norfolk society, government and politics
1570	Census of the poor in Norwich; city population about 20,000
1572	Execution of Thomas Howard, 4th Duke of Norfolk; founding of Castle Rising Hospital
1575–84	Bishop Freke of Norwich
1578	Visit of Queen Elizabeth I to Norwich
1579	Plague in Norwich and Great Yarmouth
1580s–90s	Dutch and Walloon immigrants bring new fabrics and technologies
1590s	Early phase of enclosure (as at Horstead)
1603	Major outbreak of plague in Norwich
1621	Blickling Hall and Felbrigg Hall begun
1630	Hobart family acquires Blickling and manor of Aylsham from the Crown
1635–38	Matthew Wren, Bishop of Norwich
1637–38	Charles Townshend develops the Raynham estate
1641–46	Bishop Hall of Norwich, eyewitness to civil unrest during the Civil War
1642	Lynn briefly captured by Royalists during the Civil War
1643–60	36 Congregational churches in Norwich
1648	The 'Great Blow' (a massive ammunition explosion) in Norwich, and executions
1662–65	Robert Doughty, justice of the peace, keeps a diary of his magistrates's duties
1665	Plague in Great Yarmouth
1672	The Quaker Henry Fell is expelled from Thetford
1673–1685	William Windham's Green Book focuses on deer parks, gardens and woodlands
1690	Population of Norwich approximately 30,000
1697–1759	Thomas Coke has farming estate of 60,000 acres based on Holkham
1698	Celia Feinnes visits Norfolk: she notes production of crepes, callimancos and damasks
1702–34	Humphrey Prideaux, Dean of Norwich
1705–52	Francis Blomefield, the greatest Norfolk county historian
1708–1790s	Robert Marsham plants extensive new woodlands north of Norwich and records growth
1720s	Townshend reorganises the Raynham estate with large tenanted farms on long leases
1722–35	rebuilding of Houghton Hall by Robert Walpole
1722	Daniel Defoe visits Norfolk: very impressed with Great Yarmouth
1720s–1730s	Expansion of weaving brings prosperity to yeomen families; rebuilding of farmhouses

farming systems and houses. A rung or two down the social ladder, we may observe how the more prosperous tenant farmers were upwardly mobile, becoming steadily more gentrified and with high aspirations to emulate the 'true' gentry in lifestyles and farming methods.

And there is more, for the growing number of maps and prints provide us, for the first time, with a clear visual picture of the county. For example, Cunningham's map of Norwich of 1558 gives a bird's-eye view of the walled city, one of the first to survive for any community in England, while those who mapped the county, from Saxton in the 1570s, and John Speed in the reign of James I, to Corbridge in 1722, show the houses of importance and a wealth of other detail which helps us to understand the geography of Norfolk in the early-modern period. Social change was no less important. Grammar schools and charities began to replace the community provision of the monasteries, while at parish level the Poor Law legislation of 1598 and 1601 operated under the authority of the justices of the peace, the county gentry such as Nathaniel Bacon himself. These were indeed interesting times, which helped to shape the modern world.

Faith and belief

In the summer of 1553 there were many in Norfolk who, with enthusiasm or pragmatism, favoured Lady Jane Grey, granddaughter of Henry VIII's sister Mary and a devout Protestant, to succeed the young Edward VI, who had died on 6 July. She was declared queen by her father-in-law, the duke of Northumberland, former chief minister to Edward. The dying king had named her as his successor in his will, setting aside the much more powerful claims of Princess Mary, his own eldest sister, because he could not bear to contemplate a Catholic restoration. A hundred Norfolk gentry declared in favour of Jane, and at Bishops Lynn she was proclaimed queen to conspicuous silence from the

The font at the church of St Martin, New Buckenham, is a fascinating hybrid. The stem is medieval (albeit probably spruced up in the Victorian period) and is carved with wonderful lions and hairy wild men carrying clubs. But perched a trifle uncomfortably upon it is a Jacobean basin, which proudly names those responsible for its erection – the churchwardens Thomas Colman and Christopher Sudbury – and the date when it was finished, 1 February 1619. The basin is octagonal and has similarities with the fourteenth-century example at nearby Old Buckenham.

people. Meanwhile, Mary was staying at her country residence, Kenninghall in south Norfolk, which was owned by the Catholic duke of Norfolk. She cleverly avoided Northumberland's attempts to lure her to London – and inevitable imprisonment or death – and at Kenninghall swiftly established her position. As Helen Castor writes, 'with the able support of her household officers, she sent letters and messengers flying along the roads of Norfolk and Suffolk and westwards into the midlands and the Thames Valley to summon her subjects to their queen's defence'.[2] Jane reigned for only thirteen days from the king's death (just nine from the date of her official proclamation) before Mary was declared queen. From Kenninghall, Mary's spirited campaign to gain the throne which was rightfully hers began, and from there she began the week-long march on London which would lead to her triumphal entry into the capital. The importance of Norfolk, the wealthiest and among the most populous of English counties, was clear.

Kett's Rebellion of 1549, discussed in the previous chapter, and the events which followed the death of Edward VI in 1553, thus demonstrated that Norfolk could and often would play a prominent part in national events. During the reigns of Mary (1553–58) and Elizabeth (1558–1603) that was highlighted by the growing efficiency with which the county was organised and administered – the danger of rebellion had been revealed by the rising of 1549, showing that there was a need to provide for the poor after the loss of social provision previously given by the monasteries and, faced with concerns about military security, both national and local government became more effective. The appointment of lords lieutenant and the increased number of justices of the peace were matched by a series of commissions of enquiry, while the emergence of state policy making and new demands for taxation led to a great increase in the volume of information available about the state of the county and country. As with so much else, the papers of Nathaniel Bacon of Stiffkey provide many illustrations of these themes.

In 1549 Archbishop Cranmer forbade the saying of masses for the souls of the dead, or the giving of money for that purpose. He instead ordered that an existing 'voluntary' procedure whereby parishioners collected alms for the poor should become compulsory. Every church was to have a 'poor box' in which such donations could be deposited. At St Agnes, Cawston, the sixteenth-century poor box survives. It is made of a single hollowed-out block of wood, reinforced with metal plating and secured by three locks – one key to be held by the rector and one by each of the churchwardens. The box is on a pedestal which is embedded in an octagonal block of stone, reputed to be the base of a medieval cross.

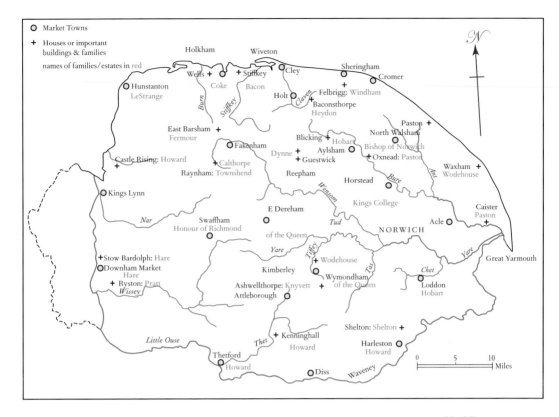

The map shows:

Market Towns (O)
Houses or important buildings & families (+)
names of families/estates in red

Holkham, Wiveton, Wells +, Stiffkey +, Cley, Sheringham, Cromer, Hunstanton, LeStrange, Coke, Bacon, Holt, Claven, Felbrigg: Windham, Baconsthorpe, Heydon, Burn, Stiffkey, East Barsham +, Fermour, Blicking +, Hobart, North Walsham, Paston +, Fakenham, Dynne +, Aylsham, Bishop of Norwich, Castle Rising: Howard, Calthorpe, Guestwick, Oxnead: Paston, Waxham +, Wodehouse, Raynham: Townshend, Reepham, Horstead, Bure, Ari, Kings Lynn, E Dereham, Wensom, Kings College, Caister, Paston, Nar, Swaffham, Honour of Richmond, Tud, Acle, NORWICH, of the Queen, Yare, Stow Bardolph: Hare, Yare, Great Yarmouth, Downham Market, Hare, Kimberley, Wodehouse, Ryston: Pratt, Wissey, Ashwellthorpe: Knyvett, Wymondham, of the Queen, Chet, Loddon, Hobart, Attleborough, Tse, Shelton: Shelton +, Little Ouse, Thet, Kenninghall, Howard, Harleston, Howard, Thetford, Howard, Diss, Waveney, Miles, 0 5 10

Norfolk 1550–1750: key towns, houses and landowners.

The accession of a Catholic queen in the summer of 1553, following more than a decade of steady – and sometimes rapid – adoption of Protestant beliefs, was of very great concern in East Anglia. The paradox was that although Norfolk was Mary's base – the springboard from which she claimed her inheritance – the county was not notably sympathetic to her religious views, and many of its people were positively hostile. As one of the most prosperous and literate parts of the country, and with its vital trading links with Europe, Norfolk was fertile ground for the new faith. Ideas about Protestantism came from the Low Countries and Germany, and also from Cambridge, one of the focal points of radical religious thought. Beginning in the mid-1520s, the new beliefs spread quickly and by the beginning of Mary's reign they had become adopted enthusiastically by many in the county – not just among the intellectual elite, but also increasingly within the lower levels of society, the urban craftsmen and village yeomen.

It was therefore perhaps inevitable that the diocese of Norwich saw extremes of religious intolerance during Mary's attempt to return England to the Catholic fold. More Protestant heretics were burned alive here than in any other English diocese apart from London and Canterbury. The majority met their fates in Norwich, though others did the same at, for example, Ipswich and Thetford. John Hopton, Mary's chaplain from her long days in semi-imprisonment at Kenninghall, was made bishop of Norwich. Of him, and his chancellor Michael Dunning, Bishop Burnet in his *Sufferings of the English Martyrs* said that 'among all the inhuman wretches not one could be compared for cruelty with these two tyrants'. Blomefield noted, for example, that Simon Miller of Lynn, Elizabeth Cooper and Richard Crashfield of Wymondham, Thomas Carman, Cicily Ormes, William Seaman and Thomas Hudson were all burned at one time in the Lollards Pit in Norwich in 1558.[3] He also listed several others and noted that the vicar of Aylsham, Commissary Berry, 'a most bloody persecutor … made 200 of [his parishioners] creep on their knees to the Cross on Whit Sunday'. There can be little doubt, therefore, that the accession of Elizabeth in November 1558 was warmly welcomed by the great majority of Norfolk people as a deliverance from the now-hated Catholic queen and her religious policies.

Although the majority of Norfolk's population were surely Protestant by 1558, nevertheless a significant minority remained steadfast in their loyalty to the 'old faith'. The problem of religious adherence split the country and the county, and in Norfolk twenty years into Elizabeth's reign four leading members of the county gentry were accused, as Catholic recusants, of failing to attend their local churches. Humphrey Bedingfield of Quidenham, Robert de Grey of Merton, John Downes of Boughton and John Drury of Godwick were all brought before the privy council in 1578 and had to pay £200 each, and to lodge with trusted citizens of Norwich so that their religious and political behaviour could be carefully watched in case they should stir up further Catholic support. The date is significant, for 1578 was the occasion of the queen's triumphantly successful visit to Norwich: the authorities were taking no chances.

For the people of Norfolk, and Norwich in particular, Elizabeth had a special significance. The most celebrated of all her famous royal progresses, the summer holiday tours of her realm, was her visit to Norfolk in the summer of 1578, by which date she had been on the throne for twenty years and was at the height of her power and magic. She came to Norfolk from Bury St Edmunds on 11 August in that year, visiting first the palace at Kenninghall.[4] This was the main Norfolk residence of the dukes of Norfolk: in 1578 it was owned by Philip, Earl of Surrey, whose father, the fourth duke, had been executed in 1572 having supported the claim to the throne of Mary Queen of Scots. When Norfolk had been imprisoned on charges of treason, an inventory was made of the contents of Kenninghall, demonstrating the luxury and wealth with which the Howards were surrounded. Thus, the great chamber had seven tapestries showing the history of Hercules, and two extremely expensive Turkey carpets. Following the execution of the duke, the palace had been closed, and therefore it was specially refurbished and reopened for the queen's visit. It was estimated that her visit (accompanied by almost the entire court) to Kenninghall, and then to Surrey House, the earl's residence in Norwich, cost him £10,000. In modern terms this would be several million pounds, but it was money well spent, because it marked the return of the Howard family to royal favour.

In her fascinating study of the royal progress, Zillah Dovey suggests that the queen's route after Kenninghall included Thomas Townsend's house at Bracon Ash, and Mergate Hall owned by the Appleyard family. The queen's favourite, Robert Dudley, Earl of Leicester, stayed at nearby Stanfield Hall, and many others of the retinue were accommodated in the nearest great houses to Bracon

Ash – though such were the numbers that some may have pitched tents! From the moment Elizabeth entered the city of Norwich at Harford Bridge, until she left it at St Giles Gate, she was presented with entertainments, speeches and decorations as well as bowls of gold coin. Richard Topclyffe reported to his patron, the earl of Shrewsbury, that, 'I never did see her Majesty better received by two countries in our journey than Suffolk and Norfolk, Suffolk of gentlemen and Norfolk of the meaner sort with exceeding joye to themselves and well-liking to her Majesty'. Why Norfolk men were of the meaner sort was not explained!

On the last day of her visit the queen knighted five of the Norfolk gentry in the great hall of the Bishop's Palace, where she had been staying. Foremost among them was her second cousin, Edward Clere of Blickling (they were both great-grandchildren of Sir William Boleyn), followed by Thomas Knyvett of Ashwellthorpe, a great landowner and philanthropist; Raphe Shelton of Shelton, also distantly related to the queen via the Boleyn line; William Paston of Paston; and Nicholas Bacon of Redgrave, son of Lord Keeper Bacon. On her departure she was addressed (albeit only briefly as she was late) at Earlham Bridge, the city's western boundary, by Mayor Robert Wood, and he too was knighted. Elizabeth departed saying, 'I have laid up in my breast such goodwill as I shall never forget Norwich'. She is also reported to have described Norwich, with tears in her eyes, as a 'fair city', a phrase still much loved, almost four and a half centuries later, by the city's publicity department. But some of its fairness was the result of hard work: Norwich, like any place which is the recipient of a royal visit, underwent a huge clean-up to give the royal route an attractive appearance. Privies along the riverside had been cleared, and the great muck hill at the Brazen Gates had been carted away.

A contrasting picture of Norwich comes from John Pound's examination of the state of the city's poor in 1570.[5] His analysis drew upon the remarkable 'Survey of the Poor' which was commissioned by the city council and is without parallel in any English city of that period. It was a careful census which recorded those needing help from the city and also those who were in danger of becoming poor – the latter being an exceptionally sophisticated concept at a time when social inquiry was scarcely considered. Given the Kett Rebellion

King's Lynn
St Nicholas, a
medieval chapel
converted to a
consistory court.

of 1549, the religious divisions between Catholics and Protestants, and the fact that some Norfolk gentry had sympathised with the 1569 rebellion of the Catholic earls in northern England, any group of malleable discontented poor could easily, and perhaps reasonably, be perceived as a danger to security. The result of this survey was 'one of the best conceived and best executed Poor Law schemes of the country'.[6] Pound calculated, from the contemporary evidence, that about one-third of the population living in the wards of Conesford and Over-the-Water could be classed as 'poor'. There were 459 dwellings inhabited by the poor, of which 159 were owned by aldermen and councillors. In addition, church houses, hospitals and almshouses numbered 63 and had an average of almost five people per house. As might be expected, most of the poor who were in work were textile workers, while of those not in work most were described as labourers. In many families the women were spinning white warp, the yarn for the long threads in undyed cloth, or knitting – as were many of the children. A typical entry, for a house in South Conesford owned by Widow Damme, reads: 'Anthoni Smythe, mason lieth myserablye of the goute of 50 years and Elizabeth his wife of 50 yearis, that spyn white warpe and their daughter of eleven yearis that knytt hose, that dwelt here 40 yearis.'

This degree of detail was given for every property with poor living in it. It was an exceptionally ambitious undertaking, and its records have proved immensely valuable to historians locally and nationally. The sequel to this investigation was also revealing of contemporary attitudes: as a result of this very detailed census the work-shy were sent to the bridewell to do compulsory labour, for which stocks of materials were provided, while in contrast money was given to those unable to work. The Poor Rate had to be trebled to meet the greatly increased costs, but the Norwich experiment of the 1570s was one of the pioneering projects which inspired the great Poor Law of 1598 and 1601, which shaped English social policy for 230 years.

The impact of the Dissolution

The Dissolution of the monasteries had a great impact on the fabric of the towns – their plan, appearance and built environment. In Norwich the loss of the Cathedral Priory, the College in the Fields, Carrow Abbey, St Leonard's Priory on Mousehold Heath, and the four friaries, led to great changes in the city. The beneficiaries of the priory site were the dean and chapter of the cathedral, who took over the monastic buildings within the cathedral precinct, in the Upper and Lower Closes. As a result the former monastic precinct survived largely intact, and is now one of the largest and most impressive complexes of medieval buildings in Britain. Henry Howard, the third Duke of Norfolk, acquired the Greyfriars and the Austin Friars sites, but the city managed to secure the Blackfriars, keeping – and almost miraculously retaining throughout the ensuing 450 years – the only full friary remains to survive in England. The Austin Friars site, in contrast, remained as 'my lord's garden' until the mid-nineteenth century when it became the site of Morgans Brewery which in turn has been demolished. Part of the site is still (2012) derelict, and

Norwich, as England's greatest provincial city in the medieval period, had a multitude of churches. The exact figure is uncertain, not least because hitherto unknown churches have occasionally been discovered during archaeological excavations, but the best estimate is that there were 57 within the walls, of which 31 survive – the largest concentration of medieval churches in Europe and an unequalled architectural inheritance. The city's population in 1300 may have been as many as 25,000, so there was an average of one church for every 400 or so people – which in fact equates well with provision in rural Norfolk. About 30 churches disappeared in the late medieval period or, especially, after the Reformation. One which remained was St George Tombland, whose fine tower is seen here above the delightful medieval and Georgian houses in Princes Street. The church is approximately 250 yards from the church of St Peter Hungate.

part has been rebuilt with private housing. The Hobarts secured the Chapel in the Field, but the city managed to keep the Hospital of St Giles and to transform it into a house for the poor freemen of Norwich, known as the Great Hospital. Today it is another remarkable treasure, not only because it is an intact medieval structure of national architectural importance, but also because as an almshouse it still serves the same purpose as it did in the late Middle Ages, six hundred years ago.

Many of the parish churches in Norwich that had previously been under the wing of monastic houses came under the ownership of the city, and significant numbers of them disappeared in this period – for example, St Clement-at-Well in Conesford. Very small urban parishes, some covering only a few acres, can never really have been viable, and a major rationalisation took place in the second half of the sixteenth century. Similar patterns of change, involving the amalgamation of parishes and the closure of small churches, took place in Thetford (where there were once 21 churches, but by 1700 only three remained), Great Yarmouth and Lynn, where monastic houses and friaries were dissolved. In Lynn, only the tower of the Greyfriars survived because of its value as a shipping beacon.

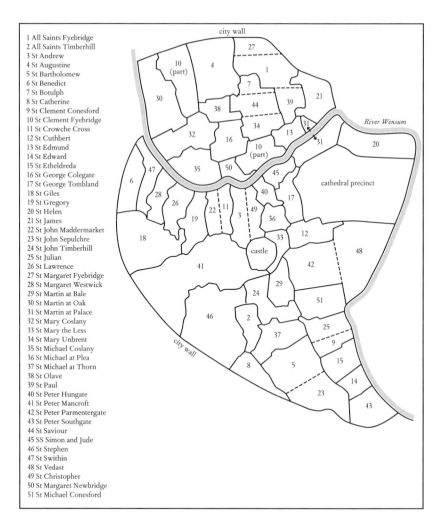

1 All Saints Fyebridge
2 All Saints Timberhill
3 St Andrew
4 St Augustine
5 St Bartholomew
6 St Benedict
7 St Botulph
8 St Catherine
9 St Clement Conesford
10 St Clement Fyebridge
11 St Crowche Cross
12 St Cuthbert
13 St Edmund
14 St Edward
15 St Etheldreda
16 St George Colegate
17 St George Tombland
18 St Giles
19 St Gregory
20 St Helen
21 St James
22 St John Maddermarket
23 St John Sepulchre
24 St John Timberhill
25 St Julian
26 St Lawrence
27 St Margaret Fyebridge
28 St Margaret Westwick
29 St Martin at Bale
30 St Martin at Oak
31 St Martin at Palace
32 St Mary Coslany
33 St Mary the Less
34 St Mary Unbrent
35 St Michael Coslany
36 St Michael at Plea
37 St Michael at Thorn
38 St Olave
39 St Paul
40 St Peter Hungate
41 St Peter Mancroft
42 St Peter Parmentergate
43 St Peter Southgate
44 St Saviour
45 SS Simon and Jude
46 St Stephen
47 St Swithin
48 St Vedast
49 St Christopher
50 St Margaret Newbridge
51 St Michael Conesford

The parishes of
Norwich at the time
of the Reformation
based on Rawcliffe and
Wilson (eds), *Norwich
since 1550* (Hambledon
and London, 2004).

From Norman times onwards Norwich had developed into a new commercial centre, and the focus of the fast-growing city had been established around the market place of the French Borough. This was, naturally, the location for some of the most impressive civic buildings and largest churches. In the fifteenth century the Guildhall, St Peter Mancroft and St Stephen's churches were rebuilt. Elsewhere, the city's churches could be divided between, on the one hand, those which were similarly rebuilt in the fifteenth century and, on the other, those (often in the poorer outer parts of the city) which were left largely unchanged – for example, St Julian, St Etheldred and St Peter Southgate in King Street by the river. As the civic responsibility for, or involvement with, key churches developed, the city fathers gave many gifts to the major churches and also erected impressive monuments. A good example was Robert Jannys, mayor in 1517 and 1524, whose fine terracotta tomb is in St George Colegate. He was the wealthiest citizen of his period, but also had important property interests and family connections elsewhere in Norfolk. Thus, he also endowed Aylsham Grammar School with the income from the water mill there. Another example is the impressive monument to Robert Suckling, mayor in 1572 and 1582, which was erected by his son Sir John Suckling in St Andrew's church, while the imposing tomb of Richard Berney and Elizabeth née Hobart of 1623 is in the now redundant church of St Peter Parmentergate.

For some, therefore, the wealth of the city and its trading role meant that personal fortunes could be made and sustained. For others, as the evidence of the 1570 census of the poor vividly reveals, life could be a great deal more harsh, and the city as a whole was not immune from economic and social malaise and decline. After 1549 Norwich experienced a long period of depression, which seriously affected the livelihoods of its population of 11,000: two severe outbreaks of plague, in 1579 and 1603, contributed substantially to this. It is significant that in the years after 1565, when many Dutch and Walloon immigrants came to Norwich, it was described as a 'great and empty city'. Thereafter the population rose sharply and by 1690 had topped 30,000. In the longer term the arrival of these skilled and entrepreneurial migrants from the Low Countries had a profound, and beneficial, effect: their industrial know-how, as highly regarded weavers, led to the development of the new draperies, fabrics made of a mixture of wool, linen and silk. Demographically, too, the impact was far-reaching: not only did the population grow substantially, but by the 1690s foreign-born immigrants and their families totalled 40 per cent of the population.

Dereham and North Walsham were towns which had a strong monastic presence in terms of ownership and control, while at Wymondham the abbey itself dominated the market town at its feet. Inevitably the Dissolution had a profound impact in all three places. The monastic manors of Wymondham and Dereham passed to the Crown and eventually to Queen Elizabeth, being

Wymondham received its market charter in 1204, granted by King John to the lord of the manor, William d'Albini. The market cross was rebuilt, like so much in the centre of this delightful town, after the Great Fire of 1615. Finished in 1617 at a cost of £25 7s., it was restored in 1863 and again in 1989 (when the present wooden staircase was constructed). It had the traditional form, with a chamber above for use as a meeting room and for strong storage, and an open arcaded trading area beneath – proverbially, favoured traders stood under the shelter, lesser ones took their chance in the market place outside.

The collegiate chapel of St John the Evangelist stands between the west end of Norwich Cathedral and the Erpingham Gate. It was founded in 1316 by Bishop Salmon and from 1322 onwards was served by six priests. Its undercroft was used as a charnel house or ossuary in which the bones of the dead were stored – the round windows close to ground level allowed people to peer through to view the collections of bones, and the building was known as Carnary College (a corruption of 'charnel'). On the dissolution of chantry chapels in 1547 it was closed and in 1553 Norwich School, founded by King Edward VI in 1547, moved here from its temporary home at Blackfriars, and it now serves as the school chapel.

specifically put aside to provide her with a sizeable and separate private income (that is, outside the Crown revenues which were in effect government income). Hence, 'Wymondham of the Queen' and 'Dereham of the Queen' functioned as important and lucrative royal manors until they were sold off to private owners in the nineteenth century. At North Walsham, because of the curious continuity whereby St Benet's lands passed to the bishop of Norwich, the town and manor remained firmly under the control of the bishops until the mid-nineteenth century. Other royal manors were gradually sold off as the Crown liquidated its assets to provide much-needed cash: thus, Aylsham came to the Hobarts in the 1630s and Fakenham first to the Fermors in 1546, then to the Calthorpes and Le Stranges.[7] In West Norfolk the Wimbotsham estate of Ramsay Abbey, which included Downham Market, went to the Hare family of Stow Bardolph. The Wodehouses of Kimberley also benefited, receiving Hickling and Ingham priories. Thus a new group of upwardly mobile land-owning gentry families was added to the smaller number of older landed families such as the Howards and the Pastons.

The views of visitors

In 1698 the intrepid lady traveller Celia Fiennes arrived in Norwich. Her journals are an essential source of evidence for England in the reign of William III, and her comments on towns and cities, landscapes and buildings

The church of St George Colegate, Norwich, was built between 1459 and 1513, replacing an earlier structure. The most striking feature is the very high clerestory of the nave, built of stone (in contrast to the top-quality flintwork of the rest of the church). This ambitious element of the design, which floods the interior with light, highlights the late-medieval prosperity of this parish of cloth merchants and businessmen, many of whom are buried and commemorated in the church. On the right, at the junction of Colegate and St George's Street, is Bacon House, built in the late fifteenth century as a courtyard house with a great hall. In the 1540s it was owned by Henry Bacon, a wealthy grocer (lord mayor, 1557 and 1566) but in the nineteenth and early twentieth centuries was divided up and neglected. Restoration in the 1970s revealed its impressive timber-framed south and east ranges with flint and stone dressings.

The abbey at Walsingham was a pilgrimage destination of international importance during the later Middle Ages. The original village was dominated – perhaps even overwhelmed – by the religious house in its midst, and because of the later revival of the pilgrim tradition the little town retains a unique atmosphere. The long range on the south side of Common Place, the sloping former market place in the town centre, includes (left) the Shire Hall, a partly fifteenth-century building where the quarter sessions were held from the sixteenth century until 1861, giving Walsingham a more than local importance. In the foreground is the octagonal medieval conduit house which supplied the town's water until the nineteenth century.

are frequently and justifiably quoted. Of Norwich she noted that none of the houses was 'of brick except some few beyond the river which are built of some of the rich factors like the London buildings'. In the middle of the city, she commented, was 'the Duke of Norfolk's house of brick and stone with several towers and turrets and balls that looks well with large gardens but the inside is all demolished. The whole city looks like what it is; a rich thriving industrious place.' She also noted that 'they have beside the Town Hall a hall distinct which is the Sealing Hall where their stuffs are all measured and if they hold their breadths and lengths they are sealed'. She refers to 'everyone spinning yarn for the Crepes, Callimancos and Damaskes which is the whole business of the place ... they are arrived to a great perfection of their work so fine and thin and glossy and their pieces are 27 yards in length ... they are all employed in spinning, knitting, weaving, dyeing, scarring [scouring], fulling or bleaching their stuffs.'[8]

A quarter of a century later, in 1722, Daniel Defoe visited Norfolk. He commented that 'when we come into Norfolk we see a face of diligence spread over the whole country'. He noted the number and size of the villages as well as of the market towns, and he claimed (with pardonable exaggeration) that 120,000 worked in woollen, silk and wool manufacture in and around Norwich. Acts of Parliament passed in 1720 and 1721 forbade the import of painted calicoes and thereby helped the Norwich stuff trade by protecting it from foreign competition. Defoe remarked that Norwich on a weekday was a town without inhabitants because the people were invisible, in their garrets at their looms, in their combing shops, twistering mills and other workhouses. He also commented on the number of Dissenters' meeting houses, though he is not always reliable – for example, he wrongly stated that the river Yare ran through the city. Defoe was also very impressed with Yarmouth, to which (he said) 1,123 ships belonged and noted that cured herring was going to many Mediterranean towns, and stuffs to Holland and the Baltic. He observed that the fish fair took place during October on the Denes and that only the bigger barks went up the river. His final comment was that some merchant houses looked like little palaces.[9]

A detailed picture of the trade of King's Lynn for five years between 1610 and 1614 has been drawn by Metters, based on the rich evidence of the town's Port Books.[10] The trade focused especially on the North German and South Baltic ports, with an important Scottish component as well. The export of corn, especially of barley, was its main item, but Thomas Snelling, for example, exported many sorts of hides and skins. The prosperity of the port of Lynn in the seventeenth century is reflected in surviving buildings. Henry Bell (1647–1711) had a powerful impact on the appearance of the town in the later part of the century. He was a member of an important Lynn family, had studied at Gonville and Caius College, and became mayor in 1692. In 1683 he designed the Exchange (more generally known today as the Customs House), which has become the symbol of Lynn's waterfront, and he was almost certainly responsible for the *Duke's Head* (1683–85), the inn much used by merchants conducting business at the Exchange.[11]

The social structure of the county[12]

The diagram shows not only how royal control extended down to the parishes, where people paid their many and varied taxes, but also how the parishes were woven into local structures at the level of manor, hundred and county. The justices of the peace were crucial figures, with their personal and community responsibilities, as well as their role as representatives of the Crown on the many commissions that were set up for specific purposes, as illustrated by the examples of Nathaniel Bacon (1560–1603) in the reign of Elizabeth, and Robert Doughty (1662–65) in the period immediately after the Civil War.

Over, above and interwoven in this fabric were key figures of national importance. In the reign of Henry VIII the third duke of Norfolk had consolidated the Howard estates in Norfolk and Suffolk, controlling a liberty which included the hundreds of Launditch, South Greenhoe, Earsham and

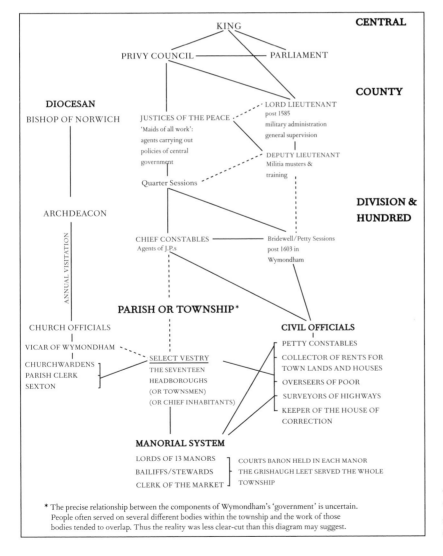

CENTRAL

KING

PRIVY COUNCIL ———— PARLIAMENT

COUNTY

DIOCESAN

BISHOP OF NORWICH

LORD LIEUTENANT
post 1585
military administration
general supervision

JUSTICES OF THE PEACE
'Maids of all work':
agents carrying out
policies of central
government

DEPUTY LIEUTENANT
Militia musters &
training

Quarter Sessions

DIVISION &
HUNDRED

ARCHDEACON

ANNUAL VISITATION

CHIEF CONSTABLES
Agents of J.P.s

Bridewell / Petty Sessions
post 1603 in
Wymondham

PARISH OR TOWNSHIP*

CHURCH OFFICIALS

VICAR OF WYMONDHAM

CHURCHWARDENS
PARISH CLERK
SEXTON

SELECT VESTRY
THE SEVENTEEN
HEADBOROUGHS
(OR TOWNSMEN)
(OR CHIEF INHABITANTS)

CIVIL OFFICIALS

PETTY CONSTABLES

COLLECTOR OF RENTS FOR
TOWN LANDS AND HOUSES

OVERSEERS OF POOR

SURVEYORS OF HIGHWAYS

KEEPER OF THE HOUSE OF
CORRECTION

MANORIAL SYSTEM

LORDS OF 13 MANORS

BAILIFFS/STEWARDS

CLERK OF THE MARKET

COURTS BARON HELD IN EACH MANOR
THE GRISHAUGH LEET SERVED THE WHOLE
TOWNSHIP

* The precise relationship between the components of Wymondham's 'government' is uncertain.
People often served on several different bodies within the township and the work of those
bodies tended to overlap. Thus the reality was less clear-cut than this diagram may suggest.

The government of
Wymondham in the
seventeenth century
(after Wilson, 2006).

The Custom House at King's Lynn was designed by Henry Bell (1647–1711), born in the town and the son of Henry Bell, a prosperous merchant who was mayor of the borough in 1658 and 1670. The younger Henry was an architect of very considerable distinction, although because he worked mainly in west Norfolk he was comparatively little recognised by the wider world. The Custom House was built in 1683 (paid for by Sir John Turner, MP for the town) primarily as a merchant exchange close to the riverside – the ground floor had open arcades as in a market house. In 1717 the Crown bought the property, the arcades were filled in, and it was then used by the Customs and Excise continuously until 1989. It now houses the tourist information centre. The architectural balance of the composition, its scale and its setting led the architectural historian Nikolaus Pevsner to describe it as 'one of the best public buildings of its date in England … one of the most perfect Classical buildings in provincial England'.

Guiltcross, as well as fourteen other manors. The third duke acquired several monastic sites at the Dissolution, owned the great palace at Kenninghall, had castles at Framlingham and Bungay and his own gaol at Lopham, and kept all the fines imposed on any of his tenants in any court in the country. He also made use of patronage in national politics, because in effect he appointed one of the two MPs in each of the four Norfolk boroughs. Hassell Smith suggests that 'benevolent estate management tied in the loyalty of his tenants' and comments that 'certainly the Duke ruled in his country'.[13] In 1558, when JPs sympathetic to the Catholic cause were removed from office, he exerted great influence in the appointment of the next generation of justices and sheriffs. His own son, the earl of Surrey, was executed in 1546 for alleged plotting against Henry VIII, and Norfolk himself was only saved from the same fate by Henry's timely demise. The vast Norfolk inheritance therefore passed to his grandson. In the Elizabethan period Thomas Howard, fourth Duke of Norfolk, was among the most powerful men in the realm and the dominant figure in Norfolk. As Hassell Smith says, Thomas Howard might well qualify for the description 'the last of the great overmighty subjects'.[14] Yet, as we have seen, in 1572 he was beheaded for plotting with the exiled and imprisoned Mary Queen of Scots, who, according to some sources, he himself planned to marry.

Among the gentry, one of the most vital social or community roles was that of magistrate or justice of the peace. The extraordinary complexity of the life of a leading Norfolk JP is revealed in the published volumes which summarise the huge quantity of papers kept by Nathaniel Bacon from 1556 to 1602. A superb indexing system makes it possible to follow the story of a place or of certain people over this period. A selection of items relating to the Glaven port of Wiveton illustrates this.[15] At the parochial level in 1602 there was a dispute as to whether a charity endowed by Ralph Greenaway was being misused. Sir John Popham, Lord Chief Justice, asked Nathaniel Bacon and his colleague 'to take some course that the poor maie have that that is their dewe'. This dispute ran on and it was declared that 40s. from Wiveton stock (the parish money) was to be spent to buy three stone of wool and to comb it 'to sett the pore a work therewith'. In April 1602 a stock of £3 was levied and wool and hemp were purchased to be kept in stock. Preaching at Wiveton church had stopped in 1593, because of an outbreak of plague, and Bacon submitted a request to the bishop of Norwich to allow preaching again. Various hundredal rate assessments were collected by the constables, listing the names of thirty Wiveton contributors. In 1599 Bacon was carrying out a national task, impressing men for the navy: from Wiveton three men including a ship master were listed and in 1602 a list was given of men paid to go to Chatham, including one Wiveton man. The full list gave detailed descriptions of the age, stature, hair colour, and whether the men had beards! This is but one parish of dozens that were in the area of Bacon's responsibility as a justice of the peace. Stiffkey Hall, his main residence, was a national, county, hundredal and parochial centre, with every level of issue being dealt with and decisions of all sorts being made there.

The surviving notebook kept by Robert Doughty, a Norfolk JP after the Restoration in 1662 to 1665, shows how much a rural justice of the peace was required to undertake three generations later.[16] As Rosenheim says of him, he

In 1711 the Corporation of Great Yarmouth successfully petitioned parliament to allow the building of a second church in the town and in 1714 John Price of Richmond was commissioned to design the project. The result was the splendid church of St George in King Street, built on the summit of a low but prominent hillock on the southern edge of the medieval town. One of the finest Baroque churches in England, it was closed and deconsecrated in 1959 and narrowly escaped demolition before being rescued and converted into a theatre and arts centre.

was 'not of a rural aristocrat dispensing roughshod justice on the unfortunates of the surrounding community. Rather he is a conscientious player, but only one of many, in the complicated network of decision making and persuasion of command and compromise that made up the fabric of the administration of seventeenth-century law.' Many of the cases with which he had to deal related to illegitimacy, because of the risk of the bastard child becoming a drain on the poor rates. For example, on 20 October 1665 the overseers of West Beckham complained that Katherine Thurton from St Giles, Norwich, had come to live in West Beckham but was legally settled in St Giles and had borne a male bastard child which was likely to be charged to their parish. They requested that West Beckham be discharged of responsibility for them. On 3 September in the same year Edmund Bell of Thurgarton, labourer, was brought before Doughty, threatening to kill his wife and her children. On 4 September he threatened she should suffer worse, 'whereupon', wrote Doughty, 'I sent him to Bridewell'. In many ways Doughty, and the actions taken towards his troublesome case, foreshadows the cases, and the work, with which the modern range of social services now deals.

The land

The medieval landscape was one of open fields, sub-divided into furlongs (bundles of strips), riverside meadows, heaths and commons. As already explained, one important impact of the Black Death was to quicken the process of taking in or enclosing with hedges and ditches and so 'privatising' land. The tenants still paid quit rents (the remnants of feudal rents) and cash rents for their newly enclosed pieces, but the basis of agricultural activity in the community was fundamentally altered.

The period following the Dissolution also saw the growth of many new estates, such as that of the Hobarts at Blickling, but some older estates decayed as, for example, at Gimingham on the north-east coast.[17] Gimingham Soke was one of the properties of the Duchy of Lancaster, an area of quasi-royal jurisdiction consisting of several manors. By the mid-sixteenth century the park was in the tenancy of Peter Rede, and in 1553 a commission was appointed to examine the state of the Soke. It reported that what must once have been a fine manor house, with a hall, knight's hall, steward's chamber and gatehouse, was now in great decay. The commission estimated that the park was of 123 acres and could support 200 head of deer, a bull, milch cattle and two geldings, but that it was short of feed in winter. A wood of 'ground grown with grett old thornez' had been lately stubbed up by Peter Rede, who had made many other major changes: he had split up the park and divided it into seven enclosures and parts, separated by hedges, ditching and pales, and had felled and cleared the 'stubbed' (uprooted) wood of its oak, ash and old thorn. There was also a great wood called South Wood, of 120 acres with some old oaks, but in the previous five years 117 great oaks were sold and Rede had let in 50 neat cattle, to the great destruction of the springing (or young saplings) of the wood. The Gimingham records also include references to 'sea-fall land' and land already in the sea, showing that coastal erosion was becoming a major problem.

Although the main period of enclosure was after 1750, and is discussed in the following chapter, in some parishes it took place at an earlier date by private agreement between lord and tenants. Thus the Cawston map of *circa* 1600 shows how enclosure was 'biting' into the remnants of the open fields, as the yeomen of the parish established themselves at the expense of the smaller tenants.[18] At Horstead, where Kings College, Cambridge, was lord of the manor, in 1599 the college made an agreement with its tenants to enclose the heaths of the parish over which common rights had existed.[19] A long indenture stated of the tenants that:

> On their behalfe ... the Heaths and Commons within the towns of Stannyngale and Horsted ... belonging to the said Manor should be severed and divided with severall porcions ... to be enjoyed by them, their heires and assigns for ever in severaltie.

The lords of the manor and their farmers, those who rented the tenancy of an estate from a lord and then ran it for their own profit and paid long-term rents to the main landowner, were to receive a proportion of these heaths in recognition of their loss of grazing rights because all rights of pasture, shack and foldage were to be extinguished on all lands in the village. The indenture argued that without any claim or use of common or shack the land might be employed 'to the best improvement of all ... being much more to their profit'. This enclosure, which was much earlier than in many Norfolk manors, was a last stage of a process that had been taking place, sporadically and in an unsystematic fashion, for many decades.

Other changes resulted from the social ambitions of the upwardly mobile to establish themselves on country estates. In the seventeenth century Horstead, like so many villages within striking distance of Norwich, was fair game for the new generation of merchants from the city who were looking for property upon which to spend their new wealth. This process began in 1565 at Heggatt in Horstead, when Richard Warde of Gorleston bought 100 acres there. It was land that had previously been occupied by several small copyhold properties, but it now became part of a growing landed estate: by 1588, having acquired several other holdings and amalgamated them with the Heggatt property, Warde's family held 265 acres. In 1664 a Norwich merchant, Thomas Morse, bought the estate and then in 1675 it went to Thomas Baret, another Norwich merchant. The Barets derived their wealth from conveying goods to Antwerp and New England, and they held land until 1805.

New estates and new farming

Norfolk is famous for Turnip Townshend and Coke of Norfolk (who is discussed in the next chapter). For many decades they have been identified in popular histories as key figures of 'the agricultural revolution'. The implication is that they were contemporaries, working towards the same goals at the same time. That is not, however, the case – they did not even overlap in time. Charles

'Turnip' Townshend (1637–1738) was born well over a century before Thomas Coke, 'Coke of Norfolk' (1754–1842), but the two men have become linked in the story of the county and indeed that of English agricultural history. Clearly the story is more complex, and while both unquestionably made important contributions to the development of farming there was a whole phalanx of lesser-known landowners who were also significant, and below that a class of squires and yeomen who helped to develop the new farming and to transform the agriculture of their county.

As Alan Simpson points out, 'the Townshends had a place in farming annals before they were ever linked with the turnip'.[20] The earlier chapter on wool and sheep showed that the Townshend family had great flocks in the Raynham area even in the early sixteenth century – by 1547 they had 4,200 sheep. This seems impressive but, to put it in perspective, Sir Richard Southwell of Reymerston had over 13,000 sheep on 14 different fold-courses, and when he died in 1557 Sir William Fermour of East Barsham had 17,000 sheep on 25 different grounds. However, in the second half of the seventeenth century Charles Townshend developed this existing farming strength and began to innovate in the management of commercial sheep farming, trying new strategies and experimenting with imaginative approaches to the resources of his estates. Rosenheim stresses that he gave much attention to ditching, hedging, muck and marl: 'protecting the integrity of enclosures and deciding where to take in new ones were chief concerns for Townshend.'[21] Marling was regarded as a capital investment, and manure from the stables was very important – as was the very rich and fertile pigeon dung for special projects. For example, in 1706 Townshend experimented with putting pigeon dung on the meadows in the park. All the major landowners had managers (usually known as bailiffs) to run their estates, and Townshend employed Thomas Warde, a strong character who was willing to oppose sending Townshend's carriage horses to London because he needed them to prepare newly enclosed land for crop growing.

In the 1720s Townshend began to reorganise the geography of his estates to promote greater efficiency, consolidating his holdings in South Creake and Shipdham so that large tenant farms could be created. His scattered holdings were compacted into coherent, ring-fenced units, and he also amalgamated his small tenant farms with new leases: for example, twelve small farm tenancies at South Creake in the 1690s had been replaced by a single tenant in 1701. The leases were lengthened to an average of ten years. The sowing of clover and turnips was made a requirement, but the turnips were not a crop: instead, they were intended as cattle fodder, so that stock could feed on them and at the same time manure the land, or they acted as a break in the corn and grass rotation of seven years, allowing the land to be enriched and replenished. At West Rudham John Money, the tenant, had a lease as follows:

> Item the said John Money covenanted to use the said marled brecks in this manner. The first year of every breck is to be summerly [i.e. fallow]; the second year rye; the third year summerly and marl; the fourth year wheat; the fifth year barley; and the sixth year oats; and at the same time

laid down with clover etc. But if it be found that this method be not
convenient for the said marled brecks, then it is agreed that some method
shall be taken as shall be settled between [Townshend] and John Money.

Item the said John Money agrees to use the 176 acres of marled ground
in the closes after this manner. The first year when the ground is marled
is to be turneps, the second year barley, the third year wheat and the
fourth year barley and then laid down with clover etc.[22]

Thomas Coke (1697–1759; created earl of Leicester in 1744) was the
great-uncle of 'Coke of Norfolk', and was also closely involved in agriculture
and estate management. He was a descendant of Sir Edward Coke, lord chief
justice to Elizabeth I, and inherited the estate which had been built up by his
eminent forebear. It was a vast inheritance – some 60,000 acres in 77 manors,
of which the Holkham estate was but one.[23] A map of the estate, drawn in 1720,
shows that the great East Field was then still unenclosed, but innovation and
improvement were already under way. Two generations later Arthur Young

Holkham is the largest park in Norfolk, centred on the great house which was built between 1734
and 1764 for Thomas Coke, 1st earl of Leicester. The park itself covers over 3,000 acres, while
the farming estate has over 25,000 acres. On this map of 1882 the main elements of the parkland
landscape can be identified. The old village of Holkham was a thriving settlement which in 1267
received a market charter, but by the sixteenth century had gone into decline. When the creation
of the great park began in 1722 the village, which was in the vicinity of the present house, was
systematically dismantled. The last houses were drowned by the creation of the lake in 1770–72.
The old hamlet of Holkham Stathe, beside the main road from Wells to Burnham Market, was
rebuilt as a model village to accommodate the displaced cottagers, and can be seen north of
the hall. The medieval church, always away from the centre of population, is now isolated in
woodland in the north-east corner of the park.

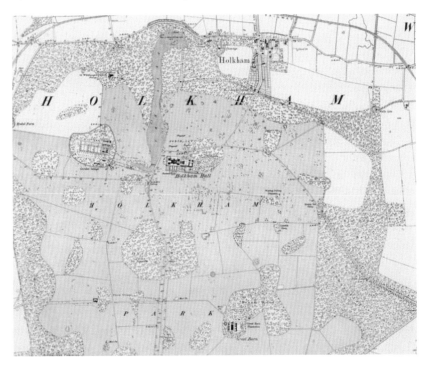

considered that fertilisers were a vital part of Norfolk husbandry, and Coke's work in the second quarter of the eighteenth century demonstrated the great potential of this aspect of farm management. The application of huge loads of marl went hand in hand with enclosing former open fields, breck and heath; the planting of huge lengths of blackthorn hedges (the plants being known as 'layers'); and massive investment in new ditching. For example, in 1726, on Thomas Haylot's tenanted farm at Godwick, 117,250 layers were planted and 1,062 rods of new ditches dug. Hurdles (to be used while hedges grew) were cut from Tittleshall Wood and a layer nursery was established. Animal muck was also a valuable product – the estate paid tenant farmers for the muck that remained in the yards at the end of their tenancies – and there was heavy expenditure on buildings. Thus, a new barn at Weasenham cost the exceptionally large sum of £172 (very much more than a typical house for a smallholder).

The estate records are very good, giving important insights into management but also allowing, for example, the compilation of full lists of tenant farmers and their holdings in the period from 1717 to 1728. Thus, Coke's 807-acre estate at Great Massingham had one main and two other tenants, indicating that very large tenant farms had been created. The property at North Elmham was different from all the others in that its 345 acres was a deer park previously belonging to Norwich Cathedral Priory. In 1717 the park keeper, Andrew Pigg, gave 17 bucks to Thomas Coke's friends and relatives from the herd of 500 deer, because at that date there was no deer park at Holkham. Thomas began to design his new park before he began his house, the future Holkham Hall. The Great Lawn was established on the north side of the house and the Great Wood on the crest of the hill to the south and the park was extended. As the park and woods were laid out the lines of old lanes were replaced by a new road layout. In 1728 the Great Wood was ready for planting and thousands of beech, birch and holly saplings purchased. The ilex, the evergreen holm oak for which Holkham is famous, was introduced a little later.

Thomas Coke the elder's planting and design work at Holkham points to another emerging trend. In addition to changing the farming landscape of Norfolk many landowners had a great interest in improving the aesthetic appeal of their estates through landscaping. One of these was Robert Marsham (1708–97) of Stratton Strawless, five miles north of Norwich and next to the village of Marsham from which his family took its name. He returned from Cambridge in about 1730 to run the estate; as a young country squire he began to keep his 'Indications of Spring' by noting the first appearance of snowdrops and many other plants as well as birds and insects; he included 26 items in his list and he kept the records until his death.[24] Much of his estate was heathland, and he began to give special attention to his plantings. He was especially keen on beech trees, but planted Scots pine and other conifers on the lightest soils, grew Spanish chestnut for fencing, and also hornbeam. Marsham kept records of other species and became famous for his correspondence with the great Hampshire naturalist and diarist Gilbert White, in which they exchanged notes and news on every aspect of their natural history observations. Sadly, apart from a few surviving individual trees, the landscape which Marsham created was virtually obliterated by the construction of an airfield during the First World War.

The Wyndhams or Windhams (originally 'Wymondham', after the town from which they took their name) of Felbrigg became major landowners in Norfolk from the 1450s, after purchasing the estate from the Felbrigg family, an earlier and distinguished landed and military line. Having acquired Felbrigg, John Wymondham went on to buy other extensive estates at Wicklewood and Crownthorpe near Wymondham. This emergence as a new land-owning family stood the family in good stead for, like so many others in their position, they were able to capitalise on the land redistribution that followed the Dissolution: Edmund Wymondham secured the former priory of Beeston. In 1599 Sir John Wyndham divided his lands between his four sons; in 1616 Thomas Windham inherited Felbrigg, and in 1665 it passed in turn to his half-brother William. His beautifully kept Green Book (an estate record book) has survived and provides a fascinating picture of a successfully maintained estate in the period after the Restoration.[25] It reveals the culture and interconnections of the county land-owning families in this period. Thus, William noted that in 1678 he planted trees on the west side of his flower garden, given to him by Mr Earle out of his Cawston nursery. He then refers to his own nursery, which supplied trees to make a copse for his deer, and in 1687 noted that Sir John Hobart of Blickling had given him 1,000 birches towards enlarging the wood. Deer parks and gardens interested him more than farming details – the deer in his park were carefully noted as totalling 236, of which there were 16 bucks, 24 soars, 28 sorrells, 26 pricketts, 10 havers, 90 does and teggs and 30 fawns. He regularly culled seven brace of bucks and six brace of does a year.[26]

The estate was managed in the main by leasing farms out, using carefully drawn up leases which set out a series of obligations upon the tenants. In 1677 William made a lease to Theophilus Waterson of Gresham, referring to the use of a field called Rush Close. Waterson was to pay £8 10s. for the feed of his stock until 1678. Then for seven years he was to plough the field and keep it in crops and to pay 18s. per acre rent and all parish charges. Land ploughed was to be levelled and drained, and muck to be put thereon 'as Mr Windham should appoint'. The corn was to be divided in the field, and Waterson had to take Mr Windham's half to his barn at Felbrigg. Each part brought into tillage was to be fallow for the first year, then to grow wheat, barley and finally oats. For the five last years Waterson was to put it all down to olland – that is, to grass for more than two years. He also had to do the ditching and fencing. Despite this concern for the detail of farming, much of the Windham estate was as yet unimproved: a lot of the tenanted land was still divided into small and perhaps inefficient pieces: for example, Robert Foster of Roughton rented 12¼ acres, but it was divided into ten small parcels of land. Consolidation of such holdings was a developing theme of the eighteenth century.

The yeomen

As we have seen, much of the northern part of the county had large estates with socially elevated landowners, but what of those areas where there were fewer great estates and where established yeomen families had a more important role? Examples include the central part of Norfolk around Dereham on the clay lands, and the good soils of the north-east of the county, both of which had many prosperous yeomen by 1650. Their prosperity in part derived from diversification, since many of the substantial yeomen were engaged in the worsted and woollen industries, with wives and daughters carding and spinning and a son weaving. The additional income that this offered made it possible to enhance lifestyles, and to rebuild and extend houses. The evidence of probate inventories reveals that by the early eighteenth century many Norfolk yeomen had income levels which approached, or even exceeded, those of the minor gentry.

For example, the 1728 inventory of William Warner of North Walsham listing the following rooms in his comfortable and substantial farmhouse: the parlour, parlour chamber, kitchen chamber, dairy chamber, garret, kitchen, brewhouse, backhouse, backhouse chamber, dairy, barn and stable. Warner had a large mixed farm: the inventory includes 18 acres of land sown with wheat (valued at £2 an acre), and in the barn were 35 combs of unthreshed wheat, 50 combs of barley, 16 combs of oats and 16 combs of 'buck'. Threshed grain was stored in the house – 15 combs of wheat, 8 of oats, and some 'maslin' (a mixture of wheat and rye, sown and harvested together). A comb was a measure of four bushels, a measure of volume rather than weight, but it is clear that this represented a sizeable production of different sorts of grain, with a total value of £84 5s. The livestock are also enumerated: eight horses and mares, ten milking cows, eleven young cattle, four Scots cattle and ten calves, as well as six fat bullocks. The total cattle herd was therefore 41, quite large even by modern standards, and the importance of dairying is reflected in the presence of seven cheese vats among the items in the outhouses. The farm also had 112 sheep, reminding us of the local production of woollen textiles, and ten small swine and a boar. The valuation of the inventory was £394 16s., and Warner also had land which brought the overall total to £563 5s.[27]

South of Norwich was the wood-pasture country, on the poorly drained boulder-clay plateau. The river Tas flows off the plateau, through the Forncetts and past Caistor St Edmund, to join the Yare a short distance downstream from Norwich.[28] The parish of Tasburgh is representative of many communities in this part of the county. There in 1666 John Tunolde, yeoman, left goods valued at £71 8s. His house, enlarged by the building of a chamber with a fireplace over the hall, also had a dairy, a feature often found in this pastoral district. The inventory lists, among other items, malt, peas, malt querns (grinding stones), bread-corn, wool cards, a spinning wheel and new and old hemp. These latter suggest a secondary income from textile production. The dairy was well equipped with a cheese press, churns, cheese vats, tubs, milk vessels and four cheeses. Tunolde's farm stock included five milking cows, two year-old

cattle, one yearling, four weaning calves, 35 sheep and a horse with its foal.
He probably farmed about 80 acres and had some common grazing on the Tas meadows.[29] Robert Goose of Tasburgh was a very successful yeoman and linen weaver, and in 1731 left goods to the value of £444.[30] His house included a weaving shop with a chamber over it. In the shop were five looms 'with things belonging', as well as grey yarn, white and grey yarn, and linen cloth on the looms. There is a possibility that Robert employed other weavers, rather than just having his family working there. He, too, had a mixed farm, and since wood-splitting equipment was mentioned he probably owned one of the many small pieces of woodland in the area.

Rather earlier, in 1603, an inventory was made of the goods of John Allgard, a glover.[31] In contrast to Tunolde and Goose, whose inventory values signify very great prosperity and material wealth, Allard's was only valued at £35 11s. 9d. His stock in trade, though, is detailed and demonstrates the sophistication of the glover's trade: he had ten small dogskins, 48 sheepskins, one woolskin, 23 calf skins, four horse hides, two cow hides and eleven more sheepskins. There were eighteen dozen and eight pairs of gloves, 51 bags, 23 purses, sixteen money bags, fifteen small purses and two pairs of hedging gloves. Allgard was also a weaver. He had coarse wool, a spinning wheel, unpulled hemp, 2¾ yards of coarse linen cloth, thirteen pieces of linen yarn, and hemp seed. He also had a Geneva Bible. The valuation seems low, but he may well have owed money to the local curriers and tanners who supplied his skins and hides. Probate inventories give an insight into only a minority of the population, but they are nevertheless a valuable source of evidence about the yeomen and craftsmen of the county in the seventeenth and eighteenth centuries. Warner and Tunolde reflect the prosperous upper end of the yeomen families and help to demonstrate the differences between the more mixed central part of the county and the solidly dairying southern part. Rural craftsmen were widespread: linen was the most important textile being produced in south Norfolk by the early eighteenth century, while animal hides, the raw material of the tanners, glovers and other leather-working trades, were a very valuable and large-scale by-product of stock rearing.

Matters of faith: challenge and dissent

The religious compromise of Elizabeth's reign brought thirty years of comparative harmony and tolerance, but in the 1580s and 1590s this began to crumble, and during the reign of James I (1603–25) tensions came to the surface, not only between Protestants and Catholics but also within the Church of England. Puritans, Baptists and other nonconformist groups began to move away from the mainstream of the Church, and to take steps to separate themselves completely. Robert Browne (1550–1630), from Rutland, was an influential figure in the Congregational movement. He went to Corpus Christi College, Cambridge, and became chaplain to the fourth duke of Norfolk. Under his protection and that of Lord Burleigh, Elizabeth's chief minister, he survived severe criticism directed at his support for a Congregational

meeting in Norwich.[32] Browne and Robert Harrison, master of the Great
Hospital in Norwich, had come to believe that each church should choose its
own pastor and that direct communication was possible between an individual
and God (rather than via the clergy as intermediaries). In 1580 they set up
the first Congregational church in Norwich. Bishop Freke (1575–84) zealously
persecuted this group, and many of its members emigrated to Middleburg in
Zeeland.[33]

During the early seventeenth century Norwich Cathedral became a symbol of
religious division between, on the one hand, the increasingly radical Corporation
and a range of nonconformist groups and, on the other, the bishop, dean and
prebendaries, who stood 'at the apex of the official established church'.[34] The
dean and chapter appointed twenty parish clergy in the city, but the more
zealous Protestants in Norwich saw the cathedral as a 'fountain of superstition'.
The city council funded puritan preachers, lectureships and sermons, to
remarkable effect, and many of the citizens moved towards nonconformity in
the later part of James I's reign and into that of his son, Charles I. By the early
1630s, as popular worship turned away from it, much of the cathedral was in
effect abandoned or had been turned over to other uses: two of its chapels,
for example, became private houses. Nonconformity was therefore rampant in
Norwich by 1635 and this was soon brought to the attention of William Laud,
from 1634 archbishop of Canterbury, who had been charged by King Charles
with the task of purging the Church of England of dissent, and enforcing the
high church forms of liturgy and worship.

In 1635 Mathew Wren, a supporter of Laud, became bishop of Norwich.
He removed numerous nonconformist clergy in 1636, depriving them of their
livings and forcing them out. Many emigrated to Holland or to the new colonies
in North America, to form the nuclei of puritan congregations there.[35] Under
the influence of Laud and Wren the cathedral was restored and beautified,
and its decorations and furnishings greatly enhanced. The hangings in the
choir were upgraded, often by benefactions from individuals, and even the
city corporation provided two massive silver-gilt candlesticks. Music returned
to the choir, having been banished under the influence of puritanism, and
the cathedral became a centre of 'traditional' church services, which were so
popular that attendance was almost too great, despite the addition of galleries.
Yet with the coming of the Civil Wars, and the rapid exertion of parliamentary
and puritan influence, all changed again. During the political and religious
instability of the 1640s the response of the nonconformists in Norwich was
to seize the advantage, taking control of the city magistracy and government
and already by 1640 holding a majority in the assembly chamber. Bishop Hall
(1641–46) was branded 'as a delinquent' and his cathedral was ransacked. He
recalled that:

> It is no other than tragical to relate the carriage of that furious sacrilege,
> whereof our eyes and ears were the sad witness under the presence of
> Linsey, Tofts the Sheriff and Greenwood. Lord what work was here!
> What clattering of glass! What beating down of walls! What tearing up

of monuments! What pulling down of seats! What wresting out of irons and brass from the windows and graves! What defacing of arms! What demolishing of curious stone work, that had not any representation in the world but only of the cost of the founder and skill of the mason.[36]

Sir Thomas Browne recalled that the destructive procession was preceded by some who blew upon organ pipes. In the market place near the market cross: 'with shouting and rejoicing the organ pipes, vestments, the leaden cross from the green yard, the service books and the singing books, all these monuments of idolatry [were] sacrificed to the fire.'

The Civil Wars and Commonwealth

The Civil Wars of the 1640s were the bloodiest conflict ever fought on British soil. Recent estimates suggest that perhaps 100,000 people died in the fighting or as a direct result of warfare, a death rate which is proportionately much greater even than that of the First World War. And this was the first major war in our history when very large numbers of civilians died, as a result of sieges, bombardments and massacres. The war affected all parts of the country, and nobody could escape its impact. Yet it was not evenly spread, and the extent of military action in any particular area depended on many factors – for example, the allegiances of the local landowners, the strategic nature of a place, and the religious complexion of the population as a whole. Norfolk, despite its great wealth and large population, saw comparatively little fighting. Writing about Norwich, Hopper points out that 'familiar features of Civil War history are absent: there was no garrison warfare, no punitive raiding, no widespread plundering nor movements by clubmen. Yet the city was far from peaceful.' As he observes, Norwich and much of Norfolk was deep in parliamentarian territory and defended by the formidable power of the Eastern Association, perhaps the best-equipped and best-organised fighting force in England during the first years of the war, and one which counted Oliver Cromwell among its commanders.[37]

War began in the late summer of 1642, and continued until the main royalist forces conceded defeat in 1645, but this apparent peace was followed by several more years of sporadic fighting, so modern historians tend to refer to 'civil wars' in the plural. In Norfolk itself, real military action was limited to Norwich and Lynn. Elsewhere there was little disruption, at least on the surface. At Thetford, for example, the wars 'scarcely disturbed the proceedings of the Corporation'.[38] The town, and its borough council, were solidly puritan and parliamentarian. Yarmouth was also firmly parliamentarian and even sacrificed its civic plate, melting it down to provide silver for funding the parliamentarian cause. It is even said that in 1648 Cromwell and his counsel met at a Mr Carter's house there and took the fateful decision to put the king on trial for high treason.[39]

Lynn did see a short period of military activity in August 1643, when Sir Hamon le Strange was governor of the town. He was a royalist and had taken over considerable supplies of guns and gunpowder which, together with a hasty strengthening of the fortifications, were made ready to defend the town against a parliamentarian attack. The parliamentary commander, the earl of Manchester, duly arrived with his forces, and set up a cannon on the opposite bank of the Great Ouse in West Lynn. This lobbed shots, somewhat aimlessly, across the river into the town, some landing in the Tuesday Market Place and one cannon ball striking St Margaret's church in the Saturday Market. A compromise was reached: le Strange escaped, Manchester took possession of this important strategic and commercial centre, and for the rest of the war Lynn remained a parliamentary town which was important for bringing in military supplies that could be sent up river into the East Midlands.[40]

The situation in Norwich was much more complex and shifting. The corporation and the cathedral vied for authority. As noted above, the puritan elements which dominated the corporation encouraged action against the Church of England, and in his memoirs written in 1648 Bishop Hall recorded the sad destruction of many of the contents of the cathedral and the burning of the vestments in the market place. He had fled from Norwich in 1646, but the mayor elected in that same year, John Utting, was opposed to further desecration of the churches. This caused political turmoil and popular mayhem. Rumours that Utting was to be removed (for his moderation) and the hardliner Christopher Baret imposed on the city led to a riot in the market place on 18 May 1646. Colonel Fleetwood's parliamentary troops forced their way into the city, and many rioters fled to the Committee House, where gunpowder was stored. Some 98 barrels blew up, causing massive damage to many buildings including the churches of St Peter Mancroft and St Stephen, and leaving about 100 people dead or injured; the event became known as the *Great Blowe*. On 8 November 108 citizens were prosecuted for rioting, seven of them being executed in the castle ditches (a witch was executed at the same time). In 1650 a second major riot led to six more executions, the men being hanged on a gallows between the cross and the well in the Market Place.[41]

The balance between royalists and parliamentarians continued to fluctuate. Some parts of the city, such as Over-the-Water where many strangers lived, were more nonconformist than others, and so were more overtly anti-royalist. Yet in such areas the balance between the various nonconformist groups itself altered constantly. The city was a confusing complex of different allegiances and different degrees of political involvement. From 1649, under the newly formed republic, other tensions emerged. Discontent with taxation became just as marked as in the reign of Charles I twenty years before. In 1634 it had been demanded that Norfolk provide for the navy, as a compulsory levy, a ship of 624 tons with 233 men at a cost of £7,800.[42] This prompted grievances which, with other tax demands faced by other counties, were a significant cause of the discontent that led to war. During the Long Parliament, which sat from 1640 to 1653, the imposition of this Ship Money became highly controversial once more, and already in 1649 Norwich Corporation had complained bitterly and vociferously that taxation was hitting its trade and increasing poverty in the city.

Disillusionment with the parliamentary government soon followed, and the Restoration of May 1660 was greeted with acclaim and much relief in the city and county. At Beeston next Mileham the vicar wrote in the parish register that 'May 29 our gracious Souvereigne Lord King Charles the Second was joyfully received into London after many years most unworthy banishment on his Majesties happy escape from his Cruell Enemies: Ol. Cromwell & his Most wicked Complices, never to be forgotten.' A decade later the vicar of Alburgh wrote excitedly in his register 'That on Wednesday September the 27 1671 King Charles the Second did come through Harlston In his progress to Yarmouth and from thence to Norwich'. The king visited Norwich on 28 September, and a letter written to a friend in London by Thomas Corie, the recorder of the city, described the gathering at the Duke's Palace:

> It is likewise easier to be conceived than set down here, the vast confusion and crowds of people of all sorts which offered to press into the Duke's Palace to see so noble a sight as Norwich never before was honoured with; for indeed I think almost half of all the people in Norfolk and Suffolk were got together within the city ... but [thanks to] the great precaution, care and vigilance of my Lord Howard ... some hundreds of people, all plentifully, nobly and orderly [were] served at supper without the least confusion.[43]

The Commonwealth, not unexpectedly, had seen full toleration of nonconformity and dissent, and persecution of Catholics and some groups of Anglicans. Many dissenters who had gone into exile between 1620 and 1640 returned to England: thus, William Bridge, who had previously been deprived of his Norwich parish, came back from Rotterdam and he and his followers set up 'a separate and independent church' in the city. This, the Old Meeting House in Colegate, was among the first of many: between 1643 and 1660 some 36 Congregational churches were established in Norfolk and Suffolk.[44] In contrast, many mainstream Anglican clergy were now themselves ejected from their livings. One case, the Reverend Nethaniel Gill of Burgh-next-Aylsham, illustrates their experience. His registers, full of Latin and Greek quotations, gave way to forthright English in describing some of his flock ('base borne, the bastard child of the whore Parnell Read', for example). In 1644 Gill was ejected from his church by the earl of Manchester, Oliver Cromwell's military commander in Norfolk, but he kept the parish registers and, while living nearby, continued to baptise and marry his congregation. In 1647 he was accused, with other clergy, of still preaching in his church, and in 1651 he had to retire to Bungay. In 1660, though, on the Restoration of the monarchy, he returned to Burgh and recorded in its register that 'Nethaniel Gill (after 17 years sequestration by traitors, rebels, Anabaptists, Quakers and Presbyterians) was restored to his rectory of Burgh and preached on Christmas Day 1660'. The sympathies of Ketton Cremer, one of Norfolk's best-known essayists, lay with the established church: 'when every allowance has been made, the treatment of the Royalist clergy still remains a cruel and sordid business.'[45] Using diaries and reminiscences of many Anglican clergy he produced a sad picture of the lives of many Norfolk clergy during the Commonwealth.

During the Commonwealth period the bishopric of Norwich was abolished, as was the Church of England itself, and so too were the dean and chapter of the cathedral. The city and county (arguing that the precincts of the cathedral were part of Blofield hundred) and residents of the Close all argued over the spoils. The fifteen-year interlude was less damaging here than in some cathedrals (for example, Lichfield lay in ruins and horses were stabled in its nave). Thomas Searle later wrote that 'the late most heathenish and tyrannical oppression and persecution began here 1641 and ended 8 May 1660. Gloria Deo in Excelsis', but it could have been worse.[46] Indeed, in the 1680s Norwich Cathedral at last became the flourishing diocesan centre that for so long it had failed to be. This was partly because of a series of forceful individuals who had charge of cathedral and diocesan affairs. Foremost among these was Humphrey Prideaux, appointed as a prebendary in 1681 and serving as dean from 1702 to 1724. During his service of almost 45 years he 'dominated Norwich Cathedral ... and tried to steer the cathedral on a middle course through the turbulent and violent waters of Norwich city politics'.[47] As the eighteenth century began the Tories, who represented the high-church Anglicans in Norwich, and the Whigs, an alliance of low-church Anglicans and nonconformists, tried to influence appointments to the cathedral chapter, variously striving to spend the income of the cathedral on the buildings themselves or to enhance the wealth of the members of the chapter. Prideaux sought to compromise in these battles, and meanwhile improved the record-keeping, reorganised the archives, saw to the re-establishment of the cathedral estates, and greatly boosted the income from them.

The Nonconformist churches

Nonconformist churches kept full records of their appointments of ministers and the attendance of their members. This allows us to analyse the support for these new denominations, and to see where their appeal lay. The minutes of Guestwick Congregational Church for the period 1652–95, for instance, give a vivid picture of the care with which they chose their ministers.[48] The pastor throughout this period was Richard Worts, but on his death in 1692:

> The Church being again destitute fell into division occasioned by some who endeavoured to bring in one Mr Hasbourd, the design of which others fore-seeing would prove destructive to the church and interest of Christ amongst them would by no means yield unto that motion which occasioned great heats and divisions, yet the majority of the Church kept up their assemblies spent many hours in prayer to God for one to go in and out before them: and procured what help and assistance they could from other hands to carry on the Lord's Day work amongst them.

Authorities in London were consulted and a Mr Mills was sent up to Norfolk to visit the unsettled congregation at Guestwick, after 'an unanimous and urgent call to come and fix with them and take care and oversight of them'. He agreed to stay, upon condition that there should be changes to the meeting house and that he could have a convenient house nearby to dwell in. This was

agreed. Two members went to see him and accepted the terms, and on 6 June
1695 he arrived, at which point a full list of members of the congregation was
made: there were two deacons, 31 brethren and 60 sisters.

The bickering at Guestwick was far from unusual, for seemingly endless
sub-division was characteristic of this period of nonconformity. As early as
1645–46 a breakaway group of Congregationalists, known as Baptists, formed
at Pulham and Ingham, and Joseph Kinghorn's ministry in Norwich soon
saw a growth in strength. A second, separate, group, the General Baptists,
developed under the wing of Thomas Grantham at the end of the seventeenth
century. The Society of Friends (Quakers) grew in numbers in Norfolk in the
late seventeenth century. In 1672 Henry Fell, a member of a leading Quaker
family, was imprisoned, whipped and expelled from Thetford, where the mayor
described him as 'an idle, vagrant person and a seducer of the people, a very
suspitious Jesuitical deluder, and one who denyeth the oathe of Alleagance and
Supremacy'. He was sent back to Ulverston in Lancashire. Mason suggests
that many Quakers were imprisoned, including more than 200 women, and
that 350 died in prison between 1660 and 1672. In 1688 Quakers benefited
more than any other group from the Glorious Revolution when William III
became king, and from 1696 they were allowed to give an affirmation instead
of the oath.[49] As the map shows, there were two clusters of early nonconformist
chapels. One was in the north-east of the county, the area of worsted spinners
and weavers with direct sea contact with the Low Countries, and the other
in the wood-pasture area in south Norfolk, where linen spinning and weaving

Nonconformity in
Norfolk in the 1670s
(after Ede and Virgoe,
2005).

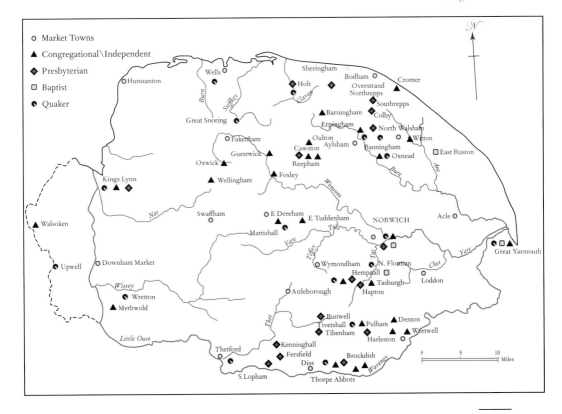

The Old Meeting House, tucked away down a narrow alleyway off Colegate in Norwich (and very difficult to photograph because of parked cars) was opened in 1693 to serve the city's large Congregationalist community, which traced its origins to the 'free churches' set up there following the influx of refugees from the Low Countries in the mid-sixteenth century. After many decades of persecution, fines and the threat of imprisonment, nonconformist dissenters were finally granted toleration in 1690 and four years later the chapel was opened. The architecture, a solid and sensible red-brick box, is Dutch-influenced.

took place. Elsewhere there were more great estates, so landlord influence was much stronger (mainly benefiting the Anglican Church) and there was a smaller proportion of craftsmen and yeomen, the two groups to whom nonconformity seemed particularly to appeal.

The survival of Catholicism

The Catholic population of Norfolk had a very difficult time after the Dissolution. Mary I briefly brought back the Catholic ritual, and the visual aspects of the 'old faith' began to reappear (though in more remote areas they had perhaps never gone). Rood screens were re-erected and masses said; statues of saints were again part of church furnishings; and obsequies for the souls of the dead again formed part of the liturgy. Essential to this process was the replacement of Protestant clergy with Catholics: in 1554, under instructions from the queen, 228 new incumbents were instituted to benefices in the diocese of Norwich following a comprehensive purge of Protestants. But the revival of Catholicism was, like Mary's reign, of short duration. In Elizabeth's reign, from the beginning of 1559, attendance and worship at the services of the Church of England was required by law, allegiance to the Pope became a criminal offence (and the 'papist' liturgy and its symbols were outlawed). By 1583 Catholics were overtly persecuted and many were prosecuted at the assizes, including especially key figures such as Humphrey Bedingfield, who was alleged to have heard mass several times. A group in Colney (just outside Norwich) were also accused of

Oxburgh Hall is perhaps the most beautiful, and certainly the most romantic, of the great Norfolk houses which are open to visitors. The house was completed in 1482 for Sir Henry Bedingfeld, whose family have lived there ever since, and it was one of the first major English houses to be built of brick. This, of course, gives it a particular visual delight – the warm pinkish-red glow of the brickwork reflected in the still waters of the great moat and contrasting with the smooth green turf of the lawns is an unforgettable sight. It was a pioneer house in another way: although built just after the Wars of the Roses, it was never intended for defence and was, from the outset, designed as a comfortable and approachable family home and the centre of a great estate. PHOTOGRAPH SUSAN MADDOCK.

hearing mass; some, including many women, were imprisoned for a month.

In 1585 financial punishments were imposed upon Catholics, and many agreed to pay fines rather than attend the Church of England. For example, Henry Kervile of Wiggenhall St Mary paid £50, a very large sum indeed. James I (1603–25) introduced further penalties for not taking the oath under the Act of 1606 which demanded recognition of the sovereign as lawful and rightful king and the repudiation of the papal claim to depose heretical princes. Charles I appointed 'pursuivants' with powers to confiscate the goods of Catholics from their houses. During the Civil War most Catholics were royalists, in Norfolk as elsewhere in England and Wales, and in consequence they suffered further penalties during the Commonwealth period. Mason comments that during the reign of the Catholic king James II (1685–88) his co-religionists experienced a 'short period of sunshine for Catholics', but in East Anglia the numbers of Catholics continued to dwindle: a return of 1708 listed only 664 in Norwich diocese (and a mere 13 in the diocese of Ely), whereas in the diocese of Chester, where Catholicism remained strongest, some 9,125 were recorded.[50]

There were a number of important Catholic families in Norfolk; the Bedingfields were best known, but among the others were the Lovells of East Harling and the Downes of Great Melton. The Jernegans of Costessey were also leading Catholics. In 1555 Mary granted them the manor in thanks for their support during the weeks when the attempt to place Lady Jane Grey on the throne presented massive challenges to the queen. Sir Henry Jernegan built Costessey Hall in 1564 and changed the family name to Jerningham. In 1559 Elizabeth had ruled that all must attend the Church of England, but Sir Henry built a secret chapel in the roof of the hall. The family were thus dedicated to their Catholic faith, but they were also loyal to the queen, who stayed at the Hall with Henry's widow in 1571 on her East Anglian progress.[51] Their case proves a point often made by historians but less obvious to contemporaries: that most Catholics were devotedly loyal Englishmen and Englishwomen, whose allegiance to the Crown was unwavering and who only wished for the right to follow their faith in private peace.

Schools

The importance attached to charity and giving to Christian good causes did not disappear with the Reformation and Dissolution, though the objectives and the nature of the beneficiaries changed considerably. Benefactors whose forebears had given to the Church or monastic houses now began to leave lands or money with which to endow charities for the poor, or almshouses, or schools for poor children. They also left funds to support poor scholars to go to Oxford and, because of its geographical proximity, especially Cambridge colleges. Most Oxbridge colleges had special connections with particular parts of the country, and in Cambridge it was Corpus Christi and Gonville and Caius which were best supported by Norfolk benefactors.[52]

Ancient schools (that is, those of genuine medieval or early Tudor origins) are less numerous in Norfolk than in many other counties. Some, such as the grammar schools at Aylsham and Diss, disappeared many years ago, but there were simply fewer post-Reformation benefactors than in the fast-growing and industrialising areas of Lancashire and the West Riding of Yorkshire, where almost every town and many large villages had a grammar school. In the seventeenth and eighteenth centuries several schools and able clerical teachers sent students to Cambridge from small places such as Scarning and Hingham, but the picture was patchy.

Thetford Grammar School was founded in 1566 by Sir Richard Fulmerston, a beneficiary of the Dissolution and a servant to the duke of Norfolk, who endowed a grammar school for 30 boys and a hospital for four elderly and deserving poor people. In the 1670s, after a rather turbulent period of decline and recovery, Sir Joseph Williamson gave further endowments to the school which enabled it to flourish. It has survived to the present day and is now an independent grammar school. At North Walsham the founding of a school was one of the last great acts of patronage in the dying days of the once-glorious Paston family. In 1606 William Paston 'purchased two acres of ground in

North Walsham and thereupon hath built and erected a School House where he intends the youth shall be trained up'.[53] Swaffham also benefited from a major benefactor when in 1725 Nicholas Hamond gave the first £500 of a considerable endowment to be used to build a school for 20 youths and to employ 20 poor persons. This foundation survives as Hamond's School. In King's Lynn Thomas Thoresby's will of 1510 was followed in 1534 by the founding of a grammar school in the chancel chapel of St Margaret's church. Six scholarships to Cambridge were provided from Thoresby's very generous donation. This school also had considerable vicissitudes and in 1630, to supplement its provision, the corporation of Lynn founded a Writing School.[54] Yarmouth had a post-Dissolution grammar school, founded in 1551 on part of the site of St Mary's Hospital on the east side of the Market Place. In 1757, as happened with many such schools, it became moribund and lapsed. It was not refounded until 1862.[55]

Already before the Dissolution at least three schools had existed in or around the cathedral in Norwich, so that there was a long tradition of classical and musical education in the city. Norwich School itself was established as a royal foundation of King Edward VI in 1547. Formerly, the bones of the monastic dead had been kept in the undercroft of the carnary chapel attached to the cathedral priory, lit by circular windows allowing viewing of charnel remains. In 1551 the newly established charity bought the chapel, removed the bones, and moved the school there. Archbishop Parker subsequently established scholarships for the school to Corpus Christi College, Cambridge.[56] These schools were all established to provide a classical education, linked with the teachings of the Established Church, and by 1750 some of them had ceased to function as grammar schools. Financial difficulties and educational deterioration were commonplace, and by 1750 some schools, such as those at Aylsham, Feltwell and Great Yarmouth, had ceased to offer a classical syllabus because the masters had been told, or forced, to concentrate on reading, writing and arithmetic.

In 1699 the Society for the Promotion of Christian Knowledge was founded to encourage the establishment of charity schools. The first in Norfolk was opened in Norwich in 1708 and by 1719 there were 12 in the city, at each of which a charge of a penny or twopence per week was made and clothing provided. Four Dissenters' Schools were also opened in Norwich and one in Lynn. But there were still relatively few such schools in 1750. In Norwich spinning was taught for a period but the question of the purpose of these schools – the uncertainty about whether they were for education or for practical instruction – eventually brought this role to an end. There were widespread concerns about how 'unsettling' education might be for the lower orders. In 1755, for example, Bishop Hayter urged teachers in the diocese to be careful 'not to disturb and unsettle that regular subordination of persons one to another'. Pupils were not to be encouraged to aspire to the higher ranks of society.[57] And in 1750 there were still many parishes in Norfolk that had no school of any kind.

The poor

Parallel with the evolving state system of dealing with the poor, founded on the legislation of 1598 and 1601, was the charitable assistance that had been an established practice before the Reformation and continued under the new circumstances of the Church of England. In 1549 Archbishop Cranmer, when forbidding the saying of masses to the souls of the dead, had encouraged charitable provision to help the living. This was usually in the form of small sums left to 'the poor men's box' which was placed in each church. But wealthier benefactors also made direct gifts of lands, buildings or income from their lands for specified purposes. These were usually to help the poor, the sick, the aged or children. For example, at Castle Rising in north-west Norfolk, Henry Howard, earl of Northampton and younger brother of the fourth duke of Norfolk, founded a hospital for the needy, infirm and aged. It was for twelve women, and Howard specified that:

> They must be of honest life and conversation, religious, grave and discreet, able to read, if one such be had, a single woman, her place to be void on marriage, to be 56 years of age at least, no common beggar, harlot, scold, drunkard, haunter of taverns, inns and alehouses.[58]

A beautiful courtyard building of warm, red brick was built between 1609 and 1615 by Howard at a cost of £451, a very considerable sum at the time. It still operates, and on special days the resident pensioners still wear bright red cloaks carrying the Howard arms. The hospital is now governed by the Mercers' Company of London and a board of trustees.

The greatest charity in Norwich was the former St Giles Hospital, known after the Dissolution as the Great Hospital and refounded in 1547. The former religious charity was dissolved and after a long legal struggle the site and buildings were retained by the city. It was endowed with a number of new estates, and St Helen's church was secularised and divided internally, with a men's ward in the nave and one for women in the chancel. This, which still survives, is ornamented by the famous Eagle ceiling, bearing the arms of Queen Anne of Bohemia (wife of Richard II). Fifty-four paupers, many nominated by the Guild of St George or by individual aldermen, occupied the hospital. As Carol Rawcliffe points out, only a tiny fraction of the city's poor could live there, and 'it was as much a showcase for conspicuous altruism on the part of an elite frightened by civic unrest, as St Giles had been a sturdy defence against the imagined fires of purgatory and miasmas of heresy'.[59] Many of the Norwich parishes had their own charities. In 1692, for example, St Peter Parmentergate was endowed by the brothers Cooke with a hospital similar to that at Castle Rising. The ladies chosen as inmates had to have lived in Norwich for at least ten years. Sadly, no buildings survive, and nor does a parish house left by Elizabeth Berney in 1622, on the site of which an infant school was later built. The Great Hospital owned 13 properties in the parish, the rent from which helped to provide its income, and an alderman of Conesford, in which the parish lay, had rights to recommend suitable occupants to that hospital.[60]

Acts of Parliament of 1598 and 1601 required each parish to choose overseers of the poor each year. These officials were answerable to the vestry (the leading parishioners) and to the justices of the peace. The appointment of an overseer had been required in principle since the 1550s, and was reiterated in legislation of 1572, but it only became universal from 1601. At Cawston in central Norfolk, George Sawer, a leading yeoman of the parish (and indeed described as a gentleman in 1614) was both churchwarden and overseer at the time of the 1601 Act. He was very conscientious and, by good fortune, his parish papers have survived in Norfolk Record Office.[61] These reveal that as in most parishes in Norfolk there was an attempt to employ the 'able' poor in weaving and spinning flax, wool or hemp. Alvington Street, on the southern edge of the parish, had many poor spinners and knitters, 'who live by their hand labour with their children to be employed'. John Allen, for example, was listed having seven children between 14 and one year old, the four eldest working as

The almshouses at Castle Rising, formally The Hospital of the Holy and Undivided Trinity, known as Howard's Hospital, were founded by Henry Howard, Earl of Northampton (died 1614) as a memorial to his grandfather Thomas, 3rd Duke of Norfolk, who died in 1554. It provided accommodation for twelve women from the parish, each having a room with a bedstead, chair and table. The rules were strict: each woman was to be 'of an honest life and conversation, religious, grave and discrete, able to read ... a single woman, 56 years of age at least, no common beggar, harlot, scold, drunkard, haunter of taverns'. Four centuries later the almshouses still provide sheltered accommodation. The single-storey red brick ranges are around a central courtyard, though the two-storey 'gatehouse' over the entrance adds a touch of more ambitious design.

The Fulmerston almshouses in Old Bury Road, Thetford were, as the stone tablet indicates, founded in 1610 under the terms of the will of Sir Richard Fulmerston, who had died in 1566. Fulmerston, a protégé of the duke of Norfolk and a minor government official, had become very wealthy in the 1540s by the acquisition of most of the former monastic lands in Thetford. His executors failed to fulfil his wishes and in 1610 Thetford Corporation secured a private Act of Parliament, making themselves trustees and building the almshouse for the accommodation of four elderly and deserving poor from the town. The lower tablet, in white stone, quotes Hebrews 12 verse 14: 'Follow peace and holiness with all men, without the which no man shall see the Lord.'

knitters for him. Many other children living in the same street were listed as spinners, and we may suppose that Sawer was supplying them with their raw materials.[62] This was all in the first flush of activity and enthusiasm following the passing of the 1601 Act, but George gave the firm impression that he was going to keep an eye on the poor in his parish so that they would not become a drain on parish funds.

From 1601, therefore, every community had an obligation at law to organise the relief of the poor, a substantial formal task that was the responsibility of the overseers. However, it was usual for the churchwardens to look after the wide range of small local charities that began to appear after the Dissolution. These were usually much less spectacular than the provision of almshouses – thus at Hempnall several inhabitants made very modest bequests to the poor, tokens of their own charity and awareness of their community. William Sporle, who died in 1616, left £10 to the poor of the parish, to be distributed over four years. The feoffees appointed by the villagers were trustees for various other charities: Robert Row left £10 to provide bread for the poor for the first Sunday in Lent, and in 1691 Henry Bunn gave 3s. 4d. per annum to be distributed to the poor. Individually, these were trivial sums, but collectively with others they made a modestly useful contribution to the well-being of the disadvantaged within the community. At Hempnall the feoffees also owned two cottages that could be leased to the poor, a very early precursor of the idea of social housing,[63] but in many communities a poor house or town house (before long often called the 'workhouse') was established in which at least some of the poor could be placed. Tate notes that the Poor Law imposed the dual duty of supporting those who could not work and of providing work for those who could not find it for themselves.[64] In 1695/96 an Act allowed the building of a workhouse in Bristol and this prompted the building of urban workhouses elsewhere in the country, as at Norwich in 1711 and North Walsham in 1701.

The work of the overseers of the poor occupied a great deal of time and generated extensive local discussion in all rural communities. For North Walsham an excellent set of accounts survives for 1701. The overseers set aside the house for the poor, known as the Town House, and their accounts detail its operation, much of the expenditure being on the provision of clothing for the resident paupers:

Mr Wasey for cloth, fear nothing (a stout coating material) and other things 9s. 11½d.
to making Bacon's coat 2s.
to cloth for two shirts and making 5s. 9d.
to a pair of breeches to Mr Teasdale 3s. 6d.
To Mr Robin for Ann Turner's fluxings [bleeding] £5
to her nurse and subsistence £2 12s.
To a spinning wheel for William Starr's wife 3s.
To 4 yards [and] ¾ of cloth for a coat and waistcoat and breeches 11s. 10½d.
to 2 yards of linen for lining 1s. 8d.
thread and tapes 6d.
to buttons and mohair 1s. 6d.
making all for Tuck's boy 7s. 6d.[65]

By 1740 the town had to rent bigger premises for a workhouse and full accounts survive for repairing the property and equipping it: £88 was spent on the building and £23 7s. in furnishing and equipment. It cost £26 15s. 6¾d.

to feed 24 paupers in the first quarter-year after the workhouse was opened. The poor there earned £3 18s. 8¾d., mainly by spinning yarn and doing some weaving, and the proceeds helped to offset the costs of the workhouse. The main items of food were beef, wheat, beer and cheese, and lesser items included oatmeal, milk and butter. But the costs of the system rose inexorably, and the view emerged in the later eighteenth century that the Poor Law encouraged the poor in habits of indolence and dependency on handouts (an argument by no means unfamiliar 250 years later). A great debate followed, and in 1834, under the Poor Law Amendment Act, the system was reformed radically.

Architecture and buildings

Some of Norfolk's most famous and architecturally most interesting buildings date from this period. New wealth, created in part by the acquisition of former monastic estates or by the lucrative potential of service under the Crown, allowed families such as the Hobarts of Blickling, the Wodehouses of Kimberley Hall, the Sheltons of Shelton Hall and the Windhams of Felbrigg, to extend and modernise older buildings or to build completely new ones. The great houses at Blickling and Felbrigg were both constructed in the 1620s, with rich ornamentation and decoration on which craftsmen of excellence were employed. After a long interlude during the 1640s and 1650s, the time of the Civil Wars and the Commonwealth, a new phase of building began. Immediately after the Restoration of Charles II in 1660 Sir Jacob Astley built his 'Christopher Wren' type house at Melton Constable, while the talented architect Sir Roger Pratt designed and built his own beautiful house, Ryston Hall near Downham Market, in 1669–72. Some of the great houses have gone – Kimberley and

The Augustine Steward House stands opposite Norwich Cathedral, one wing spanning Tombland Alley which remains a public right of way. Although the house is said to date from 1530, research by the late Marion Hardy suggests that in fact it was built in the late fifteenth century and altered or extended subsequently. Augustine Steward was born here in 1491, the son of a leading city mercer and alderman, was himself a wealthy mercer, and became a dominant figure in Norwich society and government during the reigns of Henry VIII, Edward VI, Mary I and Elizabeth, serving as mayor three times and MP for the city twice. The house had a stone undercroft for storage, a shop and workshop at street level, and accommodation for the Steward family on the first floor.

In a county which is so rich in great country houses and stately homes, Blickling Hall is among the best. The house was built in 1616–27 for Sir Robert Hobart, the lord chief justice in the latter part of the reign of James I, on the site of a much older moated house which had been the home of the Boleyn family (Anne Boleyn is said to have been born there). One of the finest of all Jacobean mansions, it cost almost £12,000 (about £1.75 million in today's values) and its magnificent symmetrical façades look out at the south-west front and the south-east side across the 55 acres of formal gardens. These were laid out in the early seventeenth century, with terracing and avenues, but were much altered in the Victorian period when fussy flowerbeds were introduced. In the 1930s they were simplified and sympathetically restored to their present form.

Shelton, for example – and many others have later additions, modifications or remodellings. But the two great houses at Blickling and Felbrigg, set in superb parks and gardens, are some of the finest examples of early seventeenth-century country houses in England, and have been intensively studied, researched and analysed. Both are now National Trust properties, and as such are visited by many thousands of people each year.

Blickling Hall (1619–30) has an unforgettable approach from the Saxthorpe road, facing directly on to the front of the great brick house, which is bounded by its two wings of service buildings and edged by yew hedges. Designed by Robert Lyminge, it was built by Sir Henry Hobart, a lawyer, and continued in the family until it was placed in the hands of the National Trust in 1940. Among the features for the visitor to savour are the long gallery (the library) and its ceiling plasterwork, and the dining room with its great fireplace. As with so many of the great houses of this period Blickling's setting, with the formal gardens east of the house, and the beautifully landscaped park with its sinuous lake to the west, sets it off perfectly.

Almost contemporary with Blickling is Felbrigg Hall, begun in 1621 and completed in 1624 for Thomas Wyndham. It has a front range as memorable as that of Blickling, although smaller in scale. Later, in 1675–78, a west range, designed by William Samuel, was added in high-quality brickwork, providing a highly effective contrast with the earlier range of Tudor brick and Ketton stone. My personal choice of 'favourite room' is the beautiful library, looking out on to the great park to the south.[66]

The Blickling estate covers almost 5,000 acres, including 950 acres of woodland and parkland. The north-west and north-east sides of the house look out across these more informal landscapes, including the lake. The Jacobean house had two deer parks, and around 1720, and again on a grand scale in the 1760s, these were re-landscaped. The 2nd duke of Buckingham, who inherited the estate in 1760, created the lake, almost a mile long (though now reduced in length) and undertook extensive planting. This is a very good example of the later eighteenth-century 'natural' style of landscape design, contrasting with the geometry and formality of the gardens around the house.

In contrast to these celebrated examples, Heydon Hall is not well known, but it has an equally interesting history and very fine buildings. Built between 1581 and 1584 by Henry Dynne, who had made a fortune in government service as an auditor of the exchequer, it stands on the northern edge of a wooded park into which avenues splay out southwards from the house, the park itself being defined within its tree belts by the Holt and Wood Dalling roads. The red brick house is of three storeys, five bays and brick mullions, and the upper windows have pediments. Once there were additional wings, which were later removed, and outbuildings have been added to the original design. The church contains monuments to the Dynne family, the Earles, the Bulwers and Bulwer-Longs. Erasmus Earle, who bought the estate in 1643 and died in 1667, was a leading lawyer during the Commonwealth. His mortal remains lie beneath a massive black slab memorial.

Between 1619 and 1637 Sir Roger Townshend began his house at Raynham, with William Edge as his master mason. Townshend died before the project was completed, and the final stages were finished under the auspices of Horatio Townshend, the first viscount, who moved there in 1656. Having finished the house, he turned his attention to the layout of the splendid park. Pevsner and Wilson term Raynham the 'paramount house of its date in Norfolk … introducing the classicism of Inigo Jones' in the early years of his career.[67] Wolterton Hall was built between 1727 and 1741 for Horatio Walpole, the brother of Sir Robert. The architect was Thomas Ripley, 'who owed his advancement to the patronage of the Walpoles', and had already designed the Admiralty in London. Wolterton has seven bays by three bays and is designed in a form of simplified Palladianism: 'On the whole Wolterton Hall deserves more acknowledgement, Horace Walpole being right when he remarked that it was one of the best houses of the size in England.'[68]

Even more impressive, in its sheer scale of design and estate layout, is Houghton Hall (1722–27). To stand on the grand balcony steps, looking almost to infinity to the limits of the great park with its huge 'unused' lawns, stretching between landscaped parkland, underlines the difference between flamboyant wealth and the ordinary man. Sir Robert Walpole, prime minister to George I and George II, employed Colen Campbell and James Gibbs to produce this Palladian mansion which was built internally of brick but coated in a warm skin of Aislaby sandstone from Yorkshire. Its outstanding internal feature is the stone hall, a perfect cube of 40 by 40 by 40 feet. The stables (1733–35) form a great courtyard for a large number of horses. The original medieval village of Houghton, of which only the church survives, had a manor house north-west of the present house. Badeslade's map of 1720 shows that the old village still survived at that date, but one of the sixteen formal avenues which were part of the grand design was already cutting through it. The old village was gradually removed to allow the site to be absorbed within the ever-expanding park. The area was landscaped and a new model village constructed at the park entrance in 1729. By 1800, when Joseph Hill surveyed the estate, the property covered 17,000 acres. A very great deal of effort and expense went into preparing the setting for the house, with vast numbers of trees being bought. In 1721 Fulke Harold, Walpole's gardener, noted that he had 50 female weeders and 29 men digging gravel to prepare the ground for planting. Now one of the homes of the marquis of Cholmondeley, Houghton, with the house itself, its deer park, great lawns, fine avenues, gardens and magnificent stable block, is well cared for and a major attraction.[69]

Just fitting into the period is perhaps the most famous of all these great houses, Holkham, built by Thomas Coke between 1734 and 1753. Holkham is known both for the building itself, for its setting in the magnificent park and for its continuous ownership by the Coke family. Two important recent studies, one of Thomas Coke, the builder of the hall, by D.P. Mortlock, and a biography of Coke of Norfolk by Susanna Wade Martins provide excellent accounts of its builder and of its later owner.[70] Like the other houses considered in this chapter, it resulted from the considerably increased wealth enjoyed by the family which owned it. The present house replaced an earlier hall built by Sir Edward Coke, whose earlier Tudor house at Godwick has already been mentioned. A century and a half later Thomas Coke, having completed the Grand Tour with William Kent and being in close contact with Lord Burlington and Matthew

Brettingham, probably designed the great Palladian house himself. It was built from local brick with quoins, looking from a distance as if it were built in stone. The great entrance hall contrasts with the stone hall of Houghton. The interior, with its statuary and art collection, is a superb example of the artistic and cultural aspiration and achievement of the aristocracy in the first half of the eighteenth century.

Francis Blomefield (1705–1752)

Our understanding of Norfolk's history has been shaped by the county's historians over many generations. Anyone interested in the history of Norfolk, or its places and people, is likely to refer many times to Francis Blomefield's *Essay towards a Topographical History of the County of Norfolk*, either in the five-volume edition published 1739–75 or the magisterial 11-volume one of 1810. Much later, it was discovered by Walter Rye, himself one of the county's great historians, that much of the material in the earlier version drew on the work of the seventeenth-century antiquarian Peter le Neve. David Stoker, who has written extensively on Blomefield, refers to the 'Little Society of Icenian Antiquaries' (in which he included John Kirkpatrick, Thomas Tanner, Benjamin Mackerell and Thomas Martin) as further important providers of source material.[71] In the case of the 1810 edition, only six volumes are all or largely the work of Blomefield, the Reverend Charles Parkin of Oxborough having completed the rest. Volumes III and IV are perhaps the most outstanding, being devoted to the history of Norwich.

As well as drawing on the work of many earlier antiquarians and topographers Blomefield sent out a questionnaire (with 80 questions in 20 sections) to the clergy of the county, seeking information on topics which began with Roman remains and finished with the valuation of the benefice. This was a daunting list for a busy incumbent to answer. It was too much for Joseph Lane, rector of Saxlingham, who replied with this refusal: 'First of all, that I find nothing in either of my parishes worthy to be communicated to the public [and second] that should there be anything related to the manors or customs thereof, worthy to be taken notice of, I should by no means to presume to do it, not thinking it either civil or grateful, to expose the private properties of a friend, and a gentleman, without his leave to the public observations of mankind.' However, many were much more co-operative. Given that Norfolk had more than 750 parishes the task of collecting and sorting this information, even when shared with Parkin, was monumental. Sadly smallpox caught Blomefield when he was only 47. He died of the disease, but his legacy is remarkable and quite invaluable.

12

Norfolk 1750 to 1830

MID-EIGHTEENTH-CENTURY Norfolk was a county of many great estates, prosperous in their farming income and graced with mansions and grand houses. Compared with most other English counties, these large estates, owned by the aristocracy and higher-ranking gentry, were unusually dominant, both economically and as a component of the landscape. On these estates the bulk of the land – that which was not occupied by the parks or the home farms – was leased by tenant farmers, and thus in the county as whole the proportion occupied by the smaller freeholders (the minor gentry and the yeomen) was significantly less than in much of the rest of England. In terms of arable production, the major crops were wheat in the north-east – south of Cromer and north of Norwich – and barley, with turnips, in the north and north-west, where sheep were also kept in substantial numbers. On the wet boulder clays of central and southern Norfolk there was much more mixed farming, with cattle, some sheep, and a dairying element with butter and cheese production. In mid-century there was still a sizeable area of indigenous woodland on the clay lands, but the large estates were also planting extensive (and costly) new woodlands in and around their parks.

1750s–1770s	early phase of expansion of Methodism in the county
1754–1842	Thomas William Coke of Holkham, the great landowner and agriculturist
late 1750s	beginning of development of the tourist industry in Great Yarmouth
1766	King's map of Norwich
1770–1820	Main period of parliamentary enclosure and turnpike road development in Norfolk
1779	Opening of Bure Navigation
1791	Publication in London of Tom Paine's *The Rights of Man*
1797	Founding of Norwich Union Insurance Company
1797	Faden's map of Norfolk
1805–1837	Bishop Bathurst of Norwich
1810	Wymondham enclosure Act
1811	Publication of the eleven volumes of Blomefield's history of Norfolk
1811	Population of Norwich 37,395 (grows to 68,000 by 1851)
1812	Attleborough enclosure award
1824	Construction of the new city gaol in Norwich
1826	Opening of the North Walsham and Dilham Canal
1827	Improvement of the Little Ouse navigation to Thetford
1830	Millard and Manning's map of Norwich
1832	Parliamentary reform: abolition of the rotten borough of Castle Rising

On the coast Yarmouth was an important fishing centre, fast growing in importance, and King's Lynn, Wells and the Glaven ports including Blakeney and Cley were busy moving barley out and bringing in a wide variety of goods such as timber from Scandinavia and, most important, coal from the Tyne. Norfolk has no coal deposits and as, in the mid-eighteenth century, peat and wood began to decline as a domestic fuel so coal imports from north-east England grew correspondingly. Norwich was at a commercial peak – perhaps its greatest-ever relative importance – with its production of fine Norwich Stuffs and other textiles. Thetford was still declining, but many of the other market towns were becoming important focal points for more local trade and commerce, emphasised by the construction of the turnpikes and by the improvement of navigations for local river and canal traffic. Malting and brewing were emerging as major new industries at, for example, Diss and East Dereham, while agricultural engineering was soon to develop as another local industry which assumed a major role in the economy of some towns. Some traditional industries, though they continued to flourish, were reorganised and reshaped by new patterns of economic activity. Thus tanning, once almost universal, became increasingly focused on a few centres such as Reepham and, especially, Norwich.

In Britain the late eighteenth century was a time of industrialisation. But in Norfolk this extremely important development was having little immediate impact. The county was not developing the more mechanised factory-based production of textiles, which was transforming the old cloth trade of the West Riding of Yorkshire and south Lancashire. There, the changes in that industry were increasingly associated with the rapid expansion of towns and emergence of new urban centres, and the industrial sector was increasingly reliant on coal and new canals and navigations which formed regional and inter-regional networks, unlike the purely local waterways of East Anglia. In areas such as Yorkshire the demand for machinery and the widespread use of the steam engine led to the growth of heavy engineering and stimulated rapid expansion of the iron and steel industry, as at Sheffield. Elsewhere the use of water power had long encouraged industrialisation in the Pennine valleys of Derbyshire, Lancashire and the West Riding.

Norfolk did not, and perhaps could not, share in these trends. The county has no coal, no commercially viable iron ore, and no fast-flowing rivers and streams to provide power for machinery. Industrialisation increasingly bypassed the area and began to undermine the county's long-established production. The population growth seen in the North and the Midlands was also absent, and the population increase in Norfolk was very slow from the mid-eighteenth century onwards. By the end of the century, and especially during the Victorian period, many Norfolk people emigrated to the expanding urban areas elsewhere in Britain, or even went abroad. In parts of the county, the signs of population *decrease* became apparent.

In 1797 the cartographer William Faden published a new county map of Norfolk, surveyed and engraved at a scale of approximately one inch per mile.[1] This provides us with an excellent snapshot of the state of the county at the

The early nineteenth-century windmill at Cley, seen here across the reedy marshes of the silted Glaven estuary, is one of the most celebrated landmarks of tourist Norfolk. The first documentary evidence for the mill is a sale advertisement of June 1819, which refers to it as 'newly erected', and it operated until just before the First World War. In the early 1920s it was converted into a holiday home – a very early instance of such a change of use – and since then has remained in residential and holiday use. It is a five-storey tower mill with a seventy-foot span of sails (which no longer operate) and in the 1870s had three sets of millstones for grinding corn.

Norfolk was a county of windmills, with a notable concentration in the Broads and, to a lesser extent, the Fens where they were used to power drainage pumps. Others ground corn, crushed bones for fertiliser, ground lime for cement, drove cotton mills and mustard mills, and ground bark for the tanning trade. Alison Yardy and Martin Scott have calculated that in 1854 there were some 423 working mills in the county, of which 38 were in the city of Norwich. The last working windmill was at Billingford in 1956. Researchers have worked out that there are the remains, or intact buildings, of about 120 corn windmills in Norfolk. At Weybourne the tower mill that stands by the side of the coast road was built in 1850, and worked until about 1916. The cap and sails are replacements – for many years they were missing, but new ones were made and installed in 1968–69.

end of the century. Many parliamentary enclosures had already taken place but the remaining, and often very extensive, commons, heaths and marshes stand out clearly. Andrew Macnair's modern coloured version brings these features out even more sharply.[2] The differences between the various sub-regions show up well, emphasising the point that Norfolk was then, and to a considerable extent still is, a county of distinct and enduring local differences.

Looking at Faden's beautiful map, rich in detail and packed with topographical interest, we can see how the landscape lay. A great and broad stretch of sandy heathland ran northwards from Norwich as far as Aylsham. Mousehold Heath, north-east of the city, was one of the largest areas of open heath, upon which several manors and parishes still retained, and exercised, the right to graze their flocks intercommunally. Today, only a part of this once-great expanse of heathland and common survives, to provide a major amenity and open space for Norwich. In sharp contrast, north-west of Norwich lay the boulder-clay plateau, with its cold and heavy soils that were poorly drained and very difficult to work before the advent of sub-surface tile-draining in the 1840s. Villages on the plateau, such as Mattishall, Reymerston and Cranworth, still had large areas of common grazing land in the late eighteenth century, and when enclosure finally took place many deep ditches had to be dug and watercourses straightened, to improve drainage and allow more intensive use. Badley Moor, was a large wet tract intercommoned by several villages.

Methwold, Norfolk's largest parish, lay on the Fen edge, extending eastwards across the sandy soils of the breck. Here in 1797 the great warren still survived, as did several thousand acres of open field around the little town. To the west of the heaths lay the marshland of Methwold Common, stretching far into the Fen. The 'Methwold severals' were lands which were already in individual ownership, where new drainage cuts had been dug to make them more usable. Beyond Sam's Cut Drain lay Methwold Fen, a very wet area. But this was not economically useless land – quite the opposite, for the cutting of peat, and rights of fishing, eeling and wild fowling, made all this land valuable. It added greatly to the range and diversity of resources available to the people of Methwold, as it did for all other Fen edge communities. The straight drains, like enclosure roads, reflect the new drainage work that was gradually taming the Fen and making it more productive. Sam's Cut itself dated from as early as 1636, and formed part of Vermuyden's large-scale project to drain the Fens, cutting across the earlier twisting watercourses in order to accelerate run-off.

Randall Burroughs of Wymondham (1761–1817) farmed on the clay lands, and his account of working those wet, difficult lands from 1794 to 1799 provides a valuable comparison with, for example, the estates at Holkham and Raynham.[3] Burroughs went to Emmanuel College, Cambridge, and on to Lincoln's Inn in 1779. His elder brother held land in the Burlingham area as well as in Wymondham. Randall consolidated the Wymondham lands into his estate by agreement with his brother. He then married Ann Denton of Burfield Hall, an estate lying just to the west of Wymondham, thereby acquiring another 202 acres, and in 1795 he moved into the hall. By good fortune and business acumen his estate had become the largest in Wymondham by the time the enclosure award was made in 1810: he already held 1,100 acres and gained a further 273 from the award. He also subsequently bought a number of other small allotments of the former commons.

Burroughs worked a five-course arable system on his land, rather than the traditional four-course system of the great estates with their lighter soils. He planted wheat, barley, turnips and clover, and sometimes oats instead of the first barley crop and peas in place of wheat. Livestock provided additional income, were a source of traction, and gave rich manure to maintain the fertility of the land. Manure was best produced by keeping cattle in yards, so that it could be collected and applied systematically (rather than relying only on the random manuring of grazing animals). Burroughs usually kept about a dozen to a yard and fed them on turnips. They were kept in yards at night and, whenever possible, on grass by day near to the farm, even in winter. Stock was sold to a local butcher on Norwich market or, as a last resort, at Smithfield. He bred some of his bullocks but also bought in Scottish and Irish stock at the great fairs held at Horsham St Faith, Hempton Fair near Fakenham, or Harleston, the last being close to the Waveney Marshes where large numbers were reared.

Perhaps surprisingly, he also kept a flock of over 100 sheep, some being fed on the turnips and the younger sheep being allowed to feed on the stubble after harvest. Until enclosure took place, Burroughs had many common rights, and his sheep seem to have been the traditional Norfolk breed. As well as developing the cultivation of crops and maintaining the livestock, Burroughs placed great importance on the physical management of the land – the hedging and draining, and the upkeep of the farm buildings. In 1804 Arthur Young described how, in the area between Attleborough and Hingham close to where Burroughs farmed, 'draining is well established and much done'.[4] Burroughs was removing small closes, thereby eliminating uneconomically small plots of

The Row at Weeting, in the south-western corner of Norfolk just north of Brandon, is claimed, surely correctly, to be the longest thatched building in Britain – it is a terrace of ten cottages. Research by Tim Bridge and Weeting History Group suggests that The Row was perhaps built in the middle of the eighteenth century and that it may well have been a development of cottages for workers on the estate of Charles Henry Coote, 9th Earl of Mountrath, an eccentric Irish peer who bought extensive estates in the area in the 1750s. It has been carefully restored after the middle cottages were badly damaged by fire in April 2011.

land, improving hedgerows and digging up pollards. He used little marl but great amounts of yard, town and ditch muck, especially before he sowed turnips. Straw was kept in the barn until needed in the yard. His was perhaps a typical large eighteenth-century Norfolk farm, representative of many others. It had a brick barn and cattle yard, cart house, riding stables, granary and wagon lodge. The farm servants were hired by the year at 9 to 10 guineas, but most of his field workers were day labourers, and he usually employed between ten and fifteen men. Burroughs was farming on a large scale and was a man of considerable significance in the Wymondham area. He was undoubtedly better educated than most of the tenant farmers on the great Holkham estate, but the scale of his farming was comparable to theirs.

Parliamentary enclosure

A crucial change in the second half of the eighteenth century was enclosure, the process whereby the commons and open fields, communally managed and under manorial control, were divided into regularly planned hedged fields and became private freehold properties. Nationally, the great majority of parliamentary Enclosure Acts were passed in two great phases, between 1750 and 1780 and again between 1790 and the 1830s. In Norfolk there were over 300 Acts affecting a total of about 40,000 acres.[5] The Acts laid down the framework for the process of enclosure and appointed commissioners to make and carry out the awards. The procedure was, by the 1790s, very standardised: the boundaries of the parish were confirmed, statements of claims to land ownership and tenancies were submitted, and the layout of new roads, field boundaries and the allocation of allotments of land were stated. The majority of commons, heaths and wastes were enclosed (especially in the second period), and as part of this process lords of the manors gained as of right one-sixteenth part of such lands in lieu of their lost rights of soil and grazing. Enclosure maps summarised the awards, giving a vivid cartographic picture of new landscapes which are often instantly recognisable today, more than two centuries later. An example of the phrasing of an Enclosure Act is given below:

> An Act of 1812
> for inclosing land in the Parish of Attleborough in the County of Norfolk
> whereas there are within the Parish of Attleborough ... several open fields, half-year lands, shack lands, fens, commons and waste grounds ... and whereas ... Sir William Smyth, Sir Thomas Beevor and Fairfax Francklin, clerk, are, or claim to be, entitled to the soil of the said commons and waste grounds in the said Parish of Attleborough and whereas the said Sir William Smyth is patron of the Rectory and parish church major part, with Attleborough minor part annexed, and the said Fairfax Francklin is Rector of the said Rectory ... And whereas the said commons and waste grounds, in their present state and condition, yield very little profit to the several persons interested therein; and the said

Open Fields, Half-year Lands, Shack Lands and Fen, are inconveniently situated for their respective owners … it would be greatly advantageous to the said persons interested in the premises, if the rights of sheepwalk and common in, over and upon the said half-year lands [etc.] were extinguished and the said open fields [etc.] were divided, and specific parts and shares thereof allotted to the several persons interested therein according to their respective shares, estates, rights and interests in over or upon the same.

The process of parliamentary enclosure in Norfolk started with an Act for Stokesby in 1720 and ended in 1863 with that for Saxlingham. Within the county two peak periods can be identified, not exactly coincident with the overall national pattern because they are more concentrated in a shorter space of time: first, the 1760s and 1770s, and second, the emergency period during the French Wars from 1790 to 1815. Of the more than 300 Acts for Norfolk some affected more than one parish, so that in total about half the communities in the county were affected to a greater or lesser extent.[6] Some Acts were aimed at 'tidying up', so that exchanges of land could allow the creation of more coherent properties, while others were concerned only with small or residual areas of commons that had not been enclosed earlier. But some, such as those at Ashill and Wymondham, were far more ambitious and dealt with large swathes of a parish. It was generally accepted by landowners that the creation of larger land units, made possible by enclosure, allowed easier cultivation by plough teams and the opportunities for hedging and ditching made stock management easier. There was also a view that 'commons encourage idleness',[7] the argument being that prior to enclosure, to eke out a living, the poor only needed to put a cow on the common and had to do little extra work. After enclosure, they had to work hard, for someone else and for a wage, because there was no longer anywhere for them to put a cow!

Changes in the road pattern were another important consequence of enclosure. New straight roads, as on the former commons of Wymondham, linked allotments which replaced the erstwhile open grazing lands. Old roads which were no longer needed, and which were often narrow and winding, were closed: they were irrelevant to, and would have obstructed the laying out of, the new geometric landscapes and new patterns of ownership. The opportunity might be taken to close roads and tracks which ran close to mansions, manor houses and rectories, thereby increasing the privacy and seclusion of the elite residents. Thus, a contemporary sale catalogue for North Elmham Hall stated that 'the mansion is most conveniently situated – a few minutes walk from the village – although quite shut off from it'. Road diversions, approved by the JPs who all knew one another and were often the instigators of enclosure, were laid out so that important houses were set away from the new roads. Elsewhere, as for example at Watton and East Dereham, the commons which edged the town were subdivided into many small plots which were allocated to those who held ancient tenancies in the town. In many cases these units were too expensive for their new owners to fence and drain, and were quickly bought up and consolidated by larger landowners. However, at Toftwood, south of

Enclosure roads near Carleton Rode and Ketteringham, resulting from the replanning of the landscape which took place in the late eighteenth century as a result of parliamentary enclosure. The road from Upgate Street, near Carleton Rode, via Spooner Row to Wymondham is a classic example, with its long straight alignments, edged by hawthorn hedges and with occasional sharp bends. It crosses the former commons of Carleton and Besthorpe, the former being labelled on Faden's map of 1797 as 'Lately Inclos'd'.

The enclosure road at Ketteringham shows the characteristic great width: the modern carriageway is about 25 feet wide, but the curtilage of the enclosure road extends from the trees on the left to the trees, hedge and ditch on the right, a width of 60 feet.

Dereham, an entirely new settlement grew up as cottages were built on these recently created smallholdings.

The rising price of corn during the Napoleonic wars made it possible not only to cover the cost of enclosure but also to receive a quick return on the investment. Overall, large estates got larger as they also received allotments in lieu of their loss of manorial rights on the commons. The sometimes overdrawn picture in which large numbers of peasants were made landless by the enclosure awards is to some extent balanced by the new holdings created as a result of the sub-division of common land into allotments. But a smallholder allotted perhaps five acres in three pieces would be faced with large and perhaps unaffordable fencing and drainage bills and it was this that enabled the 'larger men', such as Randall Burroughs, to eat up the 'smaller men' by buying up their allotments. Yeomen farmers with perhaps 50 to 100 acres probably gained land, but many smaller tenants quickly sold their allotments and just kept their cottages. Planting new hedges, ditching, and constructing new roads all demanded labour but those who lived in properties that were recently 'enclosed' on the edge of commons, and which were not recognised as 'ancient' holdings with common rights, did lose out.

We can see how it all worked in practice by taking the example of the Enclosure Act for the parish of Ashill, two miles north-west of Watton, which was passed in 1785. The award was made in the following year,[8] which was remarkably rapid progress, perhaps because there were only three major landowners and so the allocation of properties was less complex than in parishes where the claims of many individuals had to be considered. As the enclosure map shows, about one-third of the parish with 'whole year enclosures' (land over which designated stock could graze at all times) was unaffected by the award. In the remainder, grazing rights were abolished, four open arable fields were enclosed, and the two commons – Low with 131 acres and High with 802 acres – were also divided. Lord Petre, the dominant lord of the manor, acquired allotments totalling 599 acres, underlining the point that those who already had most also gained most. Reid commented that by 1813 the names of half a dozen of the smallest landowners had disappeared from the local records, implying that they had sold their holdings and departed, but the lords of the three manors in the parish, received much the greatest share.

Compared with the experience of Wymondham, the enclosure of Ashill was fairly straightforward. Wymondham was a huge parish of 11,000 acres, with the ancient market town at the centre but with several sizeable outlying hamlets.[9] As in so many other Norfolk parishes, the greater part of the commonland in

During the second half of the eighteenth century, and into the early nineteenth, parliamentary enclosure transformed the landscape of much of Norfolk, with the disappearance of commons, greens and roadside waste and the division of such areas into regular geometric fields, mostly put down to arable use. Relatively few of the lowland commons of the county emerged unscathed, but one particularly good example is at Fritton, near Long Stratton, where the triangular common, almost ¾ mile long and ½ mile wide at its broadest, and covering 67 acres, is a reminder of how the edges of many Norfolk villages once looked, although it is no longer regularly grazed. Because of the absence of herbicides wild flowers flourish and there are over twenty species of grasses.

Wymondham lay towards the edge of the parish – there were more than 3,000 acres of heath and common grazing on the fringes, while nearer to the town was a complex of common fields where much land has been enclosed piecemeal long before the parliamentary award was made in 1810. In the remaining open fields, however, the strip system survived relatively unchanged until that time, as the example of Northfield demonstrates. Several different manors held lands in this field. In the same part of the parish two deer parks, the Great Park and Gristle Wood, had survived into the sixteenth century, when they were disparked and subdivided, although their long curving boundaries still show up clearly when seen from the air. As already noted, a pattern of straight and wide enclosure roads, the base-lines of a grid of new rectangular fields, was superimposed on the ancient landscape, dramatically changing the appearance of the parish of Wymondham. Here, as in some other parishes, a few smaller commons survived and, as will be shown later, these now have great ecological importance.

Pressure for enclosure came from landowners and leading stock farmers, those who as we have seen were main beneficiaries in terms of land allocations. But the motive for the change was economic, driven by a desire for greater efficiency of management, and the requirements of a changing pattern of agriculture. In Norfolk the stock farmers argued strongly for enclosure because, following developments in selective breeding, the improved strains of sheep and cattle needed secure enclosures to ensure pedigree stock. To have these prize animals intermingling with inferior beasts, and thereby losing their pure lineage, would have been disastrous.

The remarkable changes in stock in Norfolk formed a major part of the broader 'agricultural revolution'. Arthur Young, in his report on the agriculture of the county published in 1804, quotes many examples of local farmers carrying out careful comparisons between breeds, to try to upgrade their herds and flocks. Young paid special attention to those who specialised in sheep. For example, Money Hill of Waterden, a tenant on the Holkham estate, sold a fine flock of Norfolks in 1798 and the next day bought 1,000 Southdowns.[10] He argued that the fleeces of the latter were of much better quality, and that their breeding rate was superior. His 700 Southdown ewes produced 660 lambs. In March 1790 a Mr Overman carried out a careful comparison of 24 two-year-old 'traditional' Norfolk wethers and ten Southdowns of the same age: the Southdowns produced a return per sheep which was 3s. 11d. greater than that of the Norfolks. Thomas William Coke of Holkham was by far the best-known Norfolk farmer. He brought in the New Leicester breed and Southdowns to his estate, and when Young was writing the merits of both were being carefully assessed. Coke was immensely proud of his agricultural achievements, and of his sheep: Thomas Weaver's famous picture shows him with his Southdowns in 1807. The smaller Norfolks gradually lost ground and they have only been saved, or recreated, by rare-breed enthusiasts and by the Gressenhall Rural Life Museum on its farm.

The indigenous Norfolk cattle, blood-red with a white mottled face, received a poor press: 'they do not offer much that is interesting,' commented Young.

More important by the late eighteenth century were the Scottish cattle which were driven down to fairs such as that at Horsham St Faith, a key event of the Norfolk farming year. A century before Arthur Young, in the late 1690s, Celia Fiennes had commented on the importance of the Waveney Valley marshes for the fattening of beef cattle, and this tradition was still practised into the nineteenth century. An offshoot of the stock-fattening and -rearing industry was the production of leather, a vital source of raw materials for the Norwich shoe industry which supplanted the textile trade from the middle of the nineteenth century. Yet though Young showed little interest in the local cattle they were in fact a crucial part of the mixed farming system of north-east Norfolk. As already noted, they were fed on turnips in the yards in winter, and their dung was carefully collected, stored and then spread on the fields to help to maintain soil fertility. Although Thomas Coke is much better known for his famous sheep, he also built up a herd of Devon cattle and in 1837 won a prize for a fat Devon at Smithfield.[11] In 1784 his estate still employed twelve oxen in harness for carting, and oxen were still being used for haulage on some Norfolk farms in the early years of the nineteenth century.

Parliamentary enclosure 'tidied up' the landscape of a great deal of Norfolk, regularising boundaries, straightening roads, and eliminating the wild, rough or unkempt places. The large areas of heath, marsh and fen depicted by Faden in 1797 very largely disappeared as they were fenced, drained and sub-divided into a rectangular landscape. Neat uniform hawthorn hedges edged the many miles of new wide roads that ran ruler-straight across the former commons, and smart red-brick farm buildings were erected outside the villages, out in the fields. In some villages, where poor families lived on the edge of commons,

New Buckenham Common is one of the best surviving examples of the typical 'grazing common' which was once so characteristic of Norfolk. Still grazed by cattle in the traditional fashion, and with a varied mixture of scrub, grassland and rich flora (including rare orchids) and a scatter of intermittent shallow pools and damp areas, it is now a Site of Special Scientific Interest. The common and the tiny town of New Buckenham together constitute the parish that was carved out of 'Old' Buckenham in the twelfth century when the town was founded.

enclosure may well have contributed to the first stage of the protracted decline in the rural population, although this did not show up strongly until after the 1851 census. But what is certain is that parliamentary enclosure in Norfolk produced some of the most far-reaching changes to have affected the county's society, economy and landscape in the past five centuries.

Church and chapel

The affairs of the diocese of Norwich were relatively tranquil during the eighteenth and early nineteenth centuries. Indeed, under Bishop Bathurst (1805–37) it was known to some as the 'Dead See'. Throughout the diocese the clergy – almost exclusively educated at Oxford or, especially, Cambridge – were often the younger sons of gentry families and they enjoyed the attitudes, privileges and lifestyles of the squires and country gentlemen to whom they were so closely related. Many livings, such as those of Mattishall and Hethersett, were in the gift of Cambridge colleges – both of those were held by Gonville and Caius, which also had several other Norfolk parishes. It was usual for college men to be appointed to college-owned livings. Weston Longville, Parson Woodforde's parish, was in the gift of New College, Oxford, his college, of which he was a fellow.

Our Father, which art in Heaven, Hallowed be thy Name. Thy Kingdom come. Thy will be done in Earth, as it is in Heaven. Give us this day our daily bread. And forgive us our trespasses, As we forgive them that trespass against us. And lead us not into temptation; But deliver us from evil; For thine is the Kingdom, And the Power, And the Glory, For ever and ever. Amen.

I Believe in God the Father Almighty, Maker of Heaven and Earth: And in Jesus Christ his only Son our Lord, who was conceived by the Holy Ghost, born of the Virgin Mary, suffered under Pontius Pilate, was crucified, dead, and buried, He descended into hell; The third day he rose again from the dead; He ascended into Heaven, and sitteth on the right hand of God, the Father Almighty; From thence he shall come to Judge the quick and the dead. I believe in the Holy Ghost; The holy Catholick Church; The Communion of Saints; The Forgiveness of Sins; The Resurrection of the Body, And the Life everlasting. Amen.

JOHN MANN and LUKE VERNON, CHURCH-WARDENS 1772.

The prayer board at St Margaret's, Cley, was painted and put in place in 1772. This was a time of major problems for the Church of England, with the rapid growth of Methodism providing a more appealing alternative to Anglican worship. It was also a period of fast-increasing literacy, even in remote rural Norfolk. Prayer boards such as this, simply painted in large black letters, were a powerful visual aid in a time before prayer books and service sheets. Here the Lord's Prayer and the Creed were writ large for the congregation to follow.

Particularly if they had a curate who could undertake the more tedious or onerous everyday duties, many of the clergy threw themselves into the study of the history, archaeology and natural history of the county. For example, the historian Francis Blomefield (1705–52), who we met in the previous chapter, was rector of Fersfield in south Norfolk, and it was while he was the incumbent there that he worked on his monumental *Essay towards a Topographical History of the County of Norfolk*. It was through the distribution of questionnaires to his fellow clergy that Blomefield collected much of his information.

James Woodforde (1740–1803) was rector of Weston Longville from 1776 until his death. While Woodforde, through his celebrated diaries, has charmed and delighted many, ecclesiastical historians have not always been so enthusiastic. Ronald Blythe wrote, in a comment that may well not appeal to the loyalist members of the Parson Woodforde Society, that 'Woodforde is the spiritually comatose base of the Church of England still unawakened by Wesley and by the sacramentalists of the Oxford Movement'.[12] But Beresford's edition of *The Diary of a Country Parson*, in six volumes, provides a wonderful picture of clerical and gentry life in late eighteenth-century Norfolk, while Blythe himself, in a beautifully illustrated selection, gives many extracts that summarise Woodforde's life and circumstances. For example, on 3 December 1776 Woodforde held his 'Tithe Frolic' when the farmers of the parish paid him a total of £262 2s. for their tithes and for the rent of the glebe. The party broke up at 10 p.m., after having consumed beef, mutton and plum puddings 'in plenty'. Those present drank six bottles of wine, one and a half gallons of rum, and much ale. Three weeks later, on Christmas Day, Woodforde records that he fed seven poor people before they all went to church, and gave old Richard Bates an old black coat and waistcoat.

Woodforde had a fish pond which was emptied every so often, as the easiest way in which to catch the fish, and on one occasion he killed nearly 100 toads at one time; he fished at Lenwade Mill where he had his malt made for his own brewing; and he harvested his glebe with the help of his servants. He regularly visited the local gentry such as the Honourable Charles Townshend at Honingham and the Custances at Weston Longville. On major occasions he visited Norwich, attending the quarter sessions and especially the assizes, when the county JPs and the visiting judges met to deal with many cases. They were socially important events; the name Gentlemen's Walk in Norwich market place is an echo of these occasions. On 24 March 1783 he went to see the great procession to celebrate both the peace with France and Bishop Blaise's feast day; Blaise was the patron saint of the Norwich wool trade. Five months later, on 4 September 1783, he dined with the bishop of Norwich and had one of those huge meals for which his diaries are so famous. Woodforde at Weston Longville, and Smith at Mattishall collected both great and small tithes on behalf of their colleges and Smith's assiduous collection of every possible tithe, and his pain-staking keeping of tithe accounts, have already been mentioned. Tithe became an increasingly contentious subject, as new crops such as turnips and rape were added to the basic hay and cereals of the medieval system and to the tithe calves, lambs, ducks and chickens which were more usually paid for in cash. Perhaps revealingly, there are few references to church services in Woodforde's diaries and, though he was a socially aware rector with his tithe suppers, feeding the poor and giving pennies to poor travellers, his church duties seemed to have sat fairly lightly on him.

The differences of opinion between dissenters and Anglican clergy were developing particularly fast by the 1830s. The tithe system, enshrined in law and a fundamental element in the financing of the Church of England, was a major source of dispute. Nonconformists, in particular, saw no reason to pay their tithes towards the maintenance of a church which they neither supported nor attended. This produced acrimonious quarrels within communities, setting farmers against clergy and dividing the parish. For example, the Reverend Charles Hyde Wollaston of East Dereham had a number of dissenters as members of his vestry and he urged more Anglicans to attend meetings when issues of expenditure were discussed, in the hope of outvoting the nonconformist contingent. In 1834 he despaired of the actions of the dissenters on the vestry, and on 22 January he wrote a stern letter to his parishioners:

> I feel that I have a personal claim upon your attendance, and unless you wish your poor to be oppressed, your church to be degraded, its officers to be insulted, and your pews to be occupied by Dissenters, you must attend the vestries; you must choose a majority at least of parish officers from the members of the Church, and you must support your Minister and Church Wardens in what they know to be essential for the preservation of your rights and privileges.

This was a reflection of the clashes that could develop over the spending of church rates and tithe income because of the hostile attitude of nonconformists. The tithe issue was eventually resolved – not to the liking of the Church of England – by the Tithes Commutation Act of 1836, which converted all tithe payments to fixed monetary sums and thereby ensured that their values would dwindle away over time.

Cyril Jolly in *The Spreading Flame* (an historical account of the growth of Methodism in Norfolk) provides the following, albeit somewhat biased, picture of English society in the eighteenth century. It emphasises the importance of Methodism in the changing nature of religion in this country, and this county, in the years after the 1740s:

> Before Methodism arose in the early eighteenth century, the life of England presented a sombre picture of spiritual destitution. Wickedness openly flaunted itself throughout the land and among all classes. The court was vulgar and society coarse. Most prominent statesmen were unbelievers, noted for the immorality and grossness of their lives; Sir Robert Walpole, the prime minister, was no exception, setting an example of brazen licentiousness. Much of literature was foul and the church was ineffectual. The organised church fell into two main groups: Anglicans and Dissenters, neither was making any impact on the people.

Norwich has the largest close of any English cathedral, its 85 acres constituting a miniature city within a city, with almost eighty residential buildings. Hooks Walk, now one of the most delightful parts of the Close, was once the main pathway which ran from the Lower Green (behind the cloister on the south side of the cathedral) to the Gooseberry or Great Chequer Garden. This area was one of the 'ends', or peripheral housing areas of the Close, separated from the central area by a gate. Here lived many of the servants of the medieval cathedral priory, and this lower status is still evident in the tightly packed housing. In this view of Hooks Lane the vernacular architecture of flint, dating from the late medieval period and the sixteenth century, contrasts with Georgian red-brick refacing.

John Wesley, expressing his concerns about the state of the Established Church, commented on 'indolent clergymen, pleasure taking clergymen, money liking clergymen, praise loving clergymen, preferment seeking clergymen – these are the wretches that cause the order [the Church of England] in general to be contemned.'[13] Three evangelists, John and Charles Wesley and George Whitefield, came to Norfolk in the 1750s, often preaching in the open air. The Wesleys focused on Norwich, King's Lynn and Great Yarmouth, but the most influential local preacher in Norfolk was James Wheatley. Admitted as a preacher by John Wesley in 1742, Wheatley was subsequently ejected from the Methodists but in 1751 was allowed to return and preach in Norwich under the trees in Tombland.[14] Wesley said of him that 'his preaching was an unconnected rhapsody of unnecessary words', but Wheatley received such a response that a 'tabernacle' was built on Timber Hill in Norwich.

Serious unrest in Norwich in 1752 led to a new tabernacle being built in the parish of St Martin at Palace, for which Thomas Ivory (better known for designing the Assembly House) was the architect. Before long George Whitefield was able to comment that 'God has caused us to triumph even in Norwich'. John Wesley's last visit to Norwich was in 1790, when he observed: 'how wonderfully the tide is turned! I am become an humble man at Norwich. God has at length made our enemies to be at peace with us.' He noted that

The Lower Green of the cathedral close, originally edged by monastic buildings and the houses of cathedral functionaries in the medieval period, became one of the most fashionable parts of the city in the eighteenth century. Here and on the adjacent Upper Green were the prestigious residences of wealthy citizens. Today, this is still an eminently desirable place to live, although a number of the fine seventeenth- and eighteenth-century houses are now used as offices by legal and financial firms.

the only sermons being preached in Norwich churches on 17 October were at the cathedral and St Peter Mancroft,[15] revealing evidence for the failure of the Anglican clergy to engage and guide their congregations with lively addresses.

In contrast to the city, the experience of Stokesby in Flegg is typical of the way in which a Methodist community might be established. A house in the village was hired for worship in 1801, but when a second house, used for meetings, changed hands it was feared that the new landlord, a Stokesby farmer, would not want worship to continue. However, he was revealed to be a supporter, and even brought his family to the meetings. In 1811 the group built a chapel with a school room and chaise-house. The farmer, Norton, gave them a ten-year loan which he waived in his will in 1829. This was additional to loans, which were also waived, to fund Methodist premises at Martham, Caister, Ludham and Filby.[16] This reveals how the generosity of individual adherents could greatly alter the circumstances of Methodist activity – in this case in the Broadland area – and shows a pattern which in some senses parallels the medieval benefactions made to the parish churches some 500 years before.

Social issues and rural discontent

'Ghosts from the early nineteenth century haunt modern-day East Anglia: ragged clothed and sullen ghosts of dispossessed and desperate farm labourers and their families. Their way of life is now gone, their flimsy cottages long since collapsed, their horse ploughs and threshing sticks exhibits in rural museums, the men themselves remaining to us only as entries in parish registers.'[17] This quotation, from Leeder's *Fire over East Anglia*, paints a very different picture from that which has emerged for the previous centuries, because the archival sources used in this present study have been largely those of the *owners* of

The bridewell at Wymondham, like that at Walsingham, was built in the 1780s by the county magistrates as part of their reforms to the county's custodial system. It replaced an earlier prison building on the same site – there are records of a prison here as early as 1609. The building is square in plan and includes a house at the front for the governor, and 22 cells (most of them 12 feet by 7 feet and housing two or three prisoners per cell at peak times). In reality, it was rarely used to capacity. In the late 1830s and early 1840s an average of nineteen prisoners were held there, and from the early 1850s until its closure in 1878 it mainly housed women prisoners. It later became a police station and courthouse and is now the Wymondham Heritage Museum.

The bridewell or house of correction at Walsingham was built in 1787, one of several built in Norfolk in this period as the county magistrates sought to increase the available prison space and to make short-term prison accommodation available in the different parts of the county. The prison was designed on the model devised by the prison reformer John Howard. It had eight cells (including a 'dark cell' used for those being punished for disciplinary offences in the prison), a chapel and a day room. It was greatly enlarged in 1822–23, when sixteen more cells and five treadmills were added. The prison closed in 1861 and an unsuccessful attempt was made to convert it to a steam-powered cornmill (hence the tall chimney on the right of the picture).

large estates such as Felbrigg and Holkham. These obviously provide an 'estate' perspective, while the records of churches and preachers, though they look at society from a different viewpoint, also reflect the views and attitudes of the higher ranks of local society. While some of the radical historians of nineteenth- and early twentieth-century East Anglia perhaps overdraw the picture in the other direction, exaggerating the problems for ordinary folk, there is no doubt that many villagers, especially after the end of the Napoleonic wars, lived much as the quotation above suggests. Furthermore, though between 1840 and 1870 farming in Norfolk was relatively prosperous, the example of housing in Sporle, which is discussed in the next chapter, shows that this prosperity did not necessarily extend down the social ladder as far as the labourers.

There were two major periods of discontent in rural Norfolk in the early nineteenth century: the first in 1822, and the second in 1830.[18] Leeder argues that not only the collapse of corn prices (which was responsible for a wave of unrest nationally) but also the decline of handloom weaving and spinning, especially of linen, led to serious poverty among many families in south Norfolk. The second or supplementary income earned by women and children disappeared, and the poor returns associated with low corn prices meant that tenant farmers could not pay their tithes, rents or labourers' wages. Because of the reduced wealth of the community as a whole, the poor rate could not produce enough to help the new poor by providing relief. The labourers focused their anger on the farmers and, in particular, on their new machinery. In 1822 six Shimpling men, together with four from Wymondham, six from New Buckenham and eight from Long Stratton were imprisoned for between two and six months each for breaking machinery. On Thursday 28 March a major incident took place at Winfarthing, when a large gathering from surrounding parishes threatened the peace; the yeomanry cavalry were mustered, and urgent requests were sent for regular cavalry. Leeder, tracing the history of his forebears, showed how George Fortis (his ancestor) and Noah Peake were executed for their part in a major disturbance at Bressingham on 25 February 1822, when stacks were fired. Both men had fought at Waterloo and earned their blue and red Waterloo medals, but that was not enough to save them from the gallows.

The area between Diss, Wymondham, Long Stratton and New Buckenham was the focus of major outbreaks of machine breaking and stack firing. The Reverend Wright of Kilverstone, writing to the home secretary Robert Peel, suggested that there was an absence of major gentry in the district and that it was an area of small farmers, many of whom could not afford the extra burden of the Poor Law payments to the destitute unemployed labourers.[19] Eventually a combination of more severe punishments, including the hanging of Fortis and Peake, and more rapid use of the military quietened these outbursts, but in 1830 there were renewed waves of discontent. The *Norfolk Chronicle* of 11 December 1830 reported on an outbreak at Attleborough:

> The family of the Reverend F. Franklin, were disturbed by an assemblage of riotous persons about 10 o'clock on Saturday evening; they continued their yells and execration till about 3 o'clock on Sunday morning when

they insisted on Mr Franklin's coming down and showing them where a hand chaff engine was kept which they threatened immediately to destroy.

On the following day a parish meeting discussed and agreed proposals to increase the wages of labourers and to reduce tithe payments. These measures proved insufficient and the situation became more serious. A mob destroyed the chaff engine and two others nearby, the magistrate went to Wymondham for military help, and an officer with twelve men arrived and read the Riot Act. The threat of opening fire on the rioters was sufficient to make them return to their homes.[20]

In her map of the riots of 1830 Wade Martins shows that they were most noticeable on the boulder-clay lands and the good soil area around North Walsham. As in 1822 the west Norfolk area, with its large estates, and Broadland were not seriously affected, and nor was the south-east of the county. There seem to have been three elements in the unrest of 1830, a period when 150 parishes received 'Swing' letters, sent by a mythical Captain Swing and threatening the owners of threshing machines. First, there was opposition to mechanisation and raids were made to smash the machines or set fire to stacks. Second, wage riots flared around Diss. And third, there were tithe riots in which labourers demanding better wages joined forces with tenant farmers who wanted a reduction in tithes.[21] The gradual improvement in economic conditions which took place after 1830 was followed by the abolition of the Corn Laws in 1846, allowing prices to fall. Wade Martins argues that despite these varied problems, in the 1820s and 1830s, 'Norfolk farming was still a model for the rest of the country to follow'. It was not until 1870 that the influx of massive quantities of cheap corn from the prairies of North America began to affect the arable farming of eastern England, a matter discussed in the next chapter.

Rivers and roads

The crucial importance of the Great Ouse river system to the growth of Lynn in the medieval period and the sixteenth and seventeenth centuries, and of the Wensum and Yare system to Norwich and Yarmouth, has already been discussed. Further major improvement of the rivers, including their partial canalisation, took place in the second half of the eighteenth and the early nineteenth centuries. In principle Norfolk, with its slow-flowing rivers and modest altitude, ought to have been promising territory for the development of navigations and canals, but the nature of the county meant that there was comparatively little economic impetus for such projects. Many schemes failed to come to fruition, and others were purely local in character.

In the west of the county the potential for river traffic was significantly greater because of the connectivity of the huge river system of the Great Ouse and its many tributaries. Lynn depended on this trade, its location enhancing its competitiveness, whereas its older rivals – places such as Castle Rising, Wells and the Glaven ports – had no inland waterways to feed them. In the case of the former the port dwindled completely, while at Wells, Blakeney and other

River navigations and canals in eighteenth century Norfolk

north-coast ports the trade remained primarily local. The Ouse was navigable from Huntingdon via Ely to Lynn, *en route* picking up trade from Bury St Edmunds, Thetford and Cambridge. The three west-flowing tributaries from Norfolk – the Little Ouse, the Wissey and the Nar – were each navigable along their lower courses, as far up as Thetford, Stoke Ferry and Narborough respectively, with the help of staunches and locks. West of the Great Ouse the ancient Well Creek provided a waterway from Lynn to Wisbech, and the old Bedford River a link with Earith.

Nevertheless, several proposals to provide the apparently obvious, and technically very straightforward, waterway connection from Thetford, along the upper Little Ouse to the Waveney (the two rivers rise in the same fen, between Lopham and Redgrave) and thence to Diss, Bungay and Lowestoft all came to nothing. Likewise, a serious suggestion in 1753 that a canal could be built from the Nar, via Swaffham and Dereham, to the Wensum and thence to Norwich was also abortive. Although the centre of the county was comparatively low-lying (certainly compared with the North and East Midlands, where extensive canal networks did emerge) it is doubtful if water supplies were sufficient for the substantial numbers of locks that would have been required. Perhaps more pertinently, it is unclear how much commercial traffic might ever have used such a waterway.[22]

The waterway network of the Broads, suitable mainly for small vessels with a shallow draught, was based largely on natural rivers and the short cuts and creeks linking to the Broads themselves. However, two modest schemes for canalisation were implemented. The river Bure was made navigable downstream from Aylsham as far as Coltishall between 1733 and 1779, and the little River Ant from Antingham via North Walsham to Dilham by an Act of 1826. Short stretches of new straight channels were dug and narrow locks installed where water mills had long existed (as at Briggate on the Ant and Buxton on the Bure). The narrow boats, known as wherries, were especially suited to moving fertilisers and coal upstream and grain from this productive corner of the county downstream for export. Enough trade was generated for the small outlying hamlet of Millgate to develop at the head of navigation in Aylsham, where malting and milling took place. Relatively remote from competing railways until the 1870s, these two canals maintained a limited local traffic until 1912 when the legendary Great Flood burst the locks of both streams.

A third area of early river traffic focused on the Yare, Wensum and Waveney, to which Great Yarmouth was the key. The Wensum was navigable for keels, and later for wherries, as far as New Mills on the western side of Norwich, provided that goods were transhipped from sea-going vessels at the South Quay in Yarmouth. Norwich itself remained a thriving river port until well into the twentieth century, and other minor ports on the Yare network included

Norfolk's rivers are slow-flowing and sluggish, but the larger ones provided plenty of water-power to drive large mills grinding corn or engaged in other industrial processes such as paper-making. Buxton Mill spans the river Bure, halfway between Aylsham and Coltishall. The four-storey mill, built of white-painted brick and weatherboard, was constructed in 1754 by William Pepper, although there had been one on the site as far back as the eleventh century. It had two wheels, harnessing a fall of 7 feet, and was served by the Aylsham Navigation (opened 1779), which bypassed it by a lock on the north side of the river. The mill closed in 1970 and was badly damaged by fire in 1991, after which it became a hotel and is now used as holiday apartments.

Loddon (on its tributary, the Chet) and Reedham. The Waveney was navigable downstream from Bungay, via Beccles, to Yarmouth and, using the cut linking with Oulton Broad, to Lowestoft. In 1833 the New Cut, a broad and straight three-mile canal, was opened from the Yare at Reedham to the Waveney at St Olaves, allowing steam ships travelling to and from Norwich to bypass the shallows of Breydon Water and thus to use the port of Lowestoft rather than Yarmouth. It flourished briefly until the 1860s, when railway competition took away most of its traffic. Ultimately, therefore, the Norfolk waterways were never linked across the county, and three largely self-contained systems functioned – the Great Ouse, the Broadland network, and the Yare, Wensum and Waveney. Each has more recently undergone a renaissance, with the growth of pleasure and leisure boating. The surviving Broadland waterways are probably busier than at any time in their history.

By the High Middle Ages, around 1300, the road system of Norfolk already focussed on Norwich and Lynn, but there was no coherent county-wide network and many physical problems remained. In the Fens, the Broads and the marshland area west of Yarmouth roads were almost entirely absent, while in the heavy clay areas they existed but were often impassable. Even today the village of Welney in the Fens often has its main route cut by floods during the winter. Nonetheless, some roads were of crucial national significance, most conspicuously the great highway which linked London with Norwich via Newmarket. From 1554 onwards individual parishes had statutory responsibility for the upkeep of roads within their boundaries, levying a highway rate to pay for this and making use of statute labour, whereby all able-bodied men had by law either to undertake work on the roads or to pay a monetary sum to avoid having to do so.

We have seen how hundreds of miles of new byroads were laid out during the period of parliamentary enclosure, but the improvement of the main

The turnpike network in Norfolk was centred on Norwich (from which nine roads radiated) and King's Lynn, the focus of a complex of local routes extending into the Fens. Despite the dramatic changes produced by road improvements since 1945, many of the attractive milestones erected by the turnpike trusts survive. Here we see (left) the milestone east of Barford on the Norwich and Watton turnpike (1770) and (right) that at Tacolneston on the New Buckenham turnpike (1772). The latter rather optimistically signs London, although the turnpike never extended further than New Buckenham town.

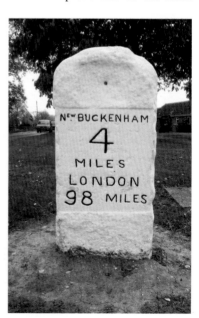

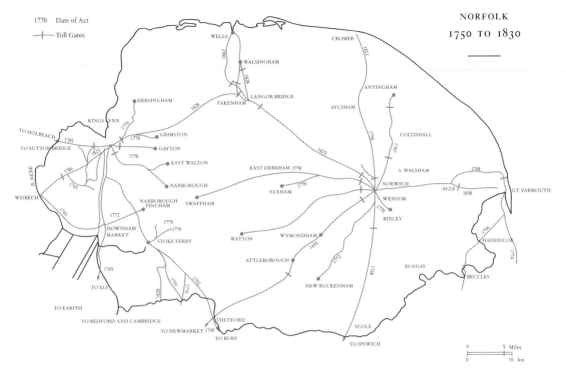

1770   Date of Act

—┼— Toll Gates

WELLS

CROMER

WALSINGHAM

ANTINGHAM

DERSINGHAM

LANGOR BRIDGE

FAKENHAM

AYLSHAM

KINGS LYNN

GRIMSTON

COLTISHALL

TO HOLBEACH

GAYTON

TO SUTTON BRIDGE

EAST WALTON

EAST DEREHAM 1770

S. WALSHAM

R. NENE

NARBOROUGH

YAXHAM

NORWICH

ACLE

GT YARMOUTH

WISBECH

NARBOROUGH FINCHAM

SWAFFHAM

WENSUM

DOWNHAM MARKET

STOKE FERRY

WATTON

WYMONDHAM

BIXLEY

ATTLEBOROUGH

BUNGAY

HADDISCO

TO ELY

NEW BUCKENHAM

BECCLES

TO EARITH

TO BEDFORD AND CAMBRIDGE

THETFORD

SCOLE

TO NEWMARKET 1768

TO BURY

TO IPSWICH

0   5 Miles

0   10 km

inter-urban roads of Norfolk resulted from the development of turnpikes. The turnpike principle was simple: groups of promoters, empowered by Act of Parliament, undertook to improve a road in return for receiving income from fixed interest bonds and from charging tolls. The roads which were turnpiked passed out of parish control, though all non-turnpiked roads remained a parochial responsibility. The first Norfolk Turnpike Act was passed in 1695, covering the Wymondham to Attleborough section of the London–Norwich highway. This was only the fourth such Act in Great Britain, but despite this early promise very little more was done in the next seventy years. Only from 1770 onwards was a more concerted effort made to improve the county's main highways, though there was never any attempt to provide a coordinated approach, and each turnpike was separately planned, developed and managed. A network of sorts thus arose by accident rather than design. It confirmed the existing road pattern and the centrality of Norwich and, to a lesser extent, Lynn. Sections of these ancient roads were straightened, widened, drained and surfaced, and some short stretches of new road were constructed, but the only substantial completely new route was that from Norwich to Yarmouth (with the famous or notorious Acle Straight) which was laid out in 1830. As with the waterway improvements, groups of landowners and Norwich merchants invested in these roads so that the flow of goods from their estates into the towns could be improved. The much-improved main-road system certainly generated a great deal of extra traffic, so much so that in the vicinity of Norwich all of the narrow medieval gates into the city were demolished in the 1780s – a major improvement for traffic flow, but in retrospect a tragic loss to architectural heritage.[23]

The turnpike roads of Norfolk

The detailed evidence for the operation of one turnpike illustrates the way in which the system worked. The new turnpike from Norwich to Aylsham was completed in 1796, on the alignment of the existing road,[24] and was extended to Cromer under a second Act of 1809. The trustees included a group of Norwich bankers, among them the Kerrisons and Gurneys, and textile manufacturers such as the Harveys. The county support came from the landed gentry thought whose land the turnpike passed or closely adjoined. These included the Harbords of Gunton, Bulwer of Heydon, Chad of Thursford and the earl of Orford. Among the professional men – the local clergy, lawyers and doctors – we also find Nathaniel Kent and William Repton, both influential landscape surveyors. The costs of the scheme included the building of turnpike cottages; the setting of gates; straightening some stretches of road, as at Ingworth; a new road across Roughton Heath; and new culverts and bridges. The tollgates and their cottages were soon let to the highest bidders, who then had the task of collecting (or 'farming') the tolls. Three of these cottages were built north of Aylsham, at Ingworth, Hanworth and Northrepps, and others existed at Marsham and Hellesdon between Aylsham and Norwich.

A remarkably full set of accounts has survived from 1794 to 1870. The total income in that period was £79,077 (therefore, an average of only just over £1,000 a year) and the total expenses £50,297 with a balance of £25,882. This was a notably modest sum with which to recompense the investing trustees. The best year was, perhaps surprisingly, as late as 1858, with receipts of £2,492; the worst was 1801, with a mere £113. In 1877 the railway from Norwich to Cromer was finally completed, and immediately the turnpike lost most of its toll-paying traffic. The last meeting of the trustees was in the same year and, after selling all the cottages, the trustees wound the business up with a balance of £254 10s. 6d., which was divided between the parishes through which the road ran and which now resumed responsibility for the upkeep of the road.

As the map shows, the main roads from Norwich to Lynn (via Fakenham), Swaffham, Thetford, Scole, Yarmouth, North Walsham, Cromer and Wells were turnpiked, but the only proper network of *inter-connecting* roads was in the west of the county, between Lynn, Thetford and across the Fens. Several of the schemes which were completed, such as the roads to Watton, Bixley, New Buckenham and Yaxham, were clearly 'unfinished'. Thus Trowse Hill (at Bixley) was turnpiked in 1770, but the logical extension to Beccles and/or Bungay was never implemented.

Changing towns

The later eighteenth and early nineteenth centuries saw extensive changes in the towns of Norfolk, with developments built in new architectural styles, considerable urban expansion, commercial growth and economic change, and the disappearance of familiar landmarks. These produced elegant Georgian buildings, new streets and often impressive public buildings, and our understanding of the processes of change is informed not only by the surviving physical evidence but also by the growing number of maps, plans and engravings of town and street scenes.

Norwich had been the subject of extensive mapping before 1750, with the plans surveyed and drawn by Thomas Cleer in 1686, James Corbridge in 1727 and Francis Blomefield in 1746. Samuel King produced a fine new map in 1766, and an even more detailed survey was undertaken by Hochstetter in 1789. Millard and Manning were contracted by the city council in 1830 to produce a map which recorded the rapid growth that was taking place, and Muskett followed with yet another map in 1849.

King's map of 1766 is enlivened by attractive little drawings of the smart brick buildings which were beginning to replace the earlier medieval and Tudor structures of timber and wattle and daub. He showed the new Octagon Chapel, designed by Thomas Ivory in 1754–56, the (now much added to) Assembly House of 1754–55, and the new theatre built in about 1750 and subsequently very greatly altered. These three buildings show how the religious and cultural life of the city was expanding, and reinforces the impression that this was one of the greatest periods of intellectual growth in the history of Norwich. Between 1770 and 1775 William Ivory, the son of Thomas, built the Norfolk and Norwich Hospital on virgin land outside St Stephen's gates. The Norwich Union fire office was built in Surrey Street in 1764, with additions by Soane in the same year, and the now-demolished cavalry barracks was also constructed in this period. All these developments emphasise the central place that Norwich occupied in Norfolk life, as the county town, administrative centre, commercial and economic focus, and largest town by far. They also highlight the fact that within England this was still a leading, and flourishing, provincial capital.

The 'garden city' or 'city in a garden', as Norwich had been known, was beginning to grow into the open ground in and behind All Saints Green and northwards along Magdalen Street, Botolph Street and St Augustine's. In many areas lanes developed behind main street frontages as new workshops spread – for example, between Colegate and Oak Street and down to the river Wensum. As we have seen, the city gates were demolished in the 1770s and 1780s as traffic increased, and substantial sections of the defensive wall also disappeared. The medieval city had been bursting at the seams, and it now seemed that, with the breaching of the tight cordon of gates and walls, a flood of development spread outwards. Millard and Manning's map shows that by 1830 there was significant building extending a considerable distance beyond the ancient walls.[25]

The population of Norwich was increasing in the middle of the eighteenth century, when the city was probably the second largest in England after London itself (vying with Bristol for that title). Armstrong suggests that the population in 1695 was about 29,000, and that by 1786 this had grown to about 40,000. Thereafter the rate of growth slackened and the population even fell slightly in the 1790s. The 1801 census produced a figure of about 38,500, and by that year the city had slipped rapidly down the national league table: it was the tenth largest in England, overtaken not only by places such as Manchester and Birmingham but also by Plymouth, Leeds and Newcastle.

In the years after 1811 growth resumed and the expansion of the city between then and 1831 was unprecedented. The population grew from 39,000

The Octagon Chapel in Colegate, Norwich, was completed in 1756 to the designs of Thomas Ivory, the highly talented local architect also responsible for the city's Assembly House. It was originally a Presbyterian chapel and in its plan it closely resembles the egalitarian designs of eighteenth-century kirks in Scottish towns such as Kelso. However, it became Unitarian in the early nineteenth century, a denomination which 'welcomes people of all religious faiths and none [with] no dogma or creed, and takes inspiration from all religious teachings, as well as from science and the arts'. The octagonal form, both in Scotland and in Norwich, reflects a desire to provide equality among the congregation.

The Assembly House in Norwich is generally regarded as being among the finest Georgian public buildings in England. It was built in 1754 to the designs of the outstanding local architect Thomas Ivory, and was intended by the Corporation as place for holding assemblies, balls and other entertainments. In 1876 it became a girls' school but in 1950 it was carefully restored and returned to its original use, as a meeting place and venue for arts and cultural events. Further restored after a major fire in 1995, it remains one of the city's most popular arts and social centres.

Surrey House, the headquarters of Norwich Union in Surrey Street, Norwich, is one of the best-known works by the celebrated Norwich architect George Skipper (1858–1948). It was built in 1900–12 and perfectly summarised the dignified and slightly ponderous style known as 'Edwardian Baroque', with lavish and opulent use of fine materials for the interior – marble, gilding, mahogany and crystal – and a powerful display of wealth and solidity externally. The company was just over a century old when the new headquarters was constructed. It, and the building, weathered the many changes of the remainder of the twentieth century, including the devastation of the 1942 blitz which destroyed so much of this part of the city centre, but in 1997, its bicentenary year, the company demutualised and was floated on the Stock Exchange, which swiftly led to mergers, renaming and in 2009 the disappearance of the name Norwich Union. Such is said to be progress.

to almost 63,000 in just twenty years, though the newer industrialising cities grew even more rapidly. By 1851 the population had reached 68,000.[26] This was impressive, but comparative figures tell a rather different story. For Norwich the intercensal growth rate in 1831–1841 was only 2 per cent whereas nationally it was 14.5 per cent, and even in 1841–1851, when Norwich expanded by 9.5 per cent, this was still markedly lower than the national figure of 12.7 per cent.[27] Most of this rapid new growth took place in what are now the inner suburbs but were then open fields on the edge of the medieval city – districts such as Heigham, New Sprowston, New Catton and the Unthank Road area. In the inner-city parishes growth was slowing and, indeed, some began to experience population decline. The new industries such as brewing, foundries and shoemaking were beginning to replace crowded yards, as in St Paul's parish, and the expansion of the retailing and commercial centre gradually began to displace residents from crowded central streets.

Edwards pointed out that in the years immediately after 1800 the production of textiles in Norwich actually benefited from the expanding cotton industry in north-west England. Local manufacturers bought in cottons from Lancashire and also silks from Macclesfield to produce worsted camletts and silk worsted shawls. For a time these relatively specialist items were a major Norwich trade – in each year from 1800 to 1815, for example, the East India Company ordered between 16,000 and 24,000 worsted camletts from Norwich merchants and in 1802 one Norwich manufacturer had an order for 60,000 silk and worsted shawls.[28] However, the textile industry began to decline after the end of the Napoleonic wars, and it succumbed inexorably to competition from northern England. The 1851 census revealed that textiles in that year still employed 5,500 people in the city, but by that time the growth in shoemaking had created an industry of equal and growing importance, with 5,000 workers.

Banking and insurance, now a vital component in the economy of modern Norwich, began to develop from 1756 when Charles Weston, a brewer, opened the first bank in the city. In 1804 Thomas Bignold opened his Union Bank to handle premiums for the fast-growing Norwich Union Fire Insurance Society, which had been founded in 1797. Banking families intermarried with one another and also into merchant families, creating a powerful set of interwoven dynasties which controlled an ever-greater proportion of the

No. 18 Colegate, Norwich, is a fine example of a merchant's house built in the early eighteenth century, when this ancient street, north of the Wensum, had become one of the most fashionable in the city for wealthy members of the business community. Built of red brick and with a fine symmetrical seven-bay front, and an imposing doorway opening directly on to the pavement, it originally had a substantial garden at the rear (now reduced in size by recent building) stretching down to the river.

commercial, political and social life of the city. A lengthy series of new banks, banking failures and bank mergers followed, many of these businesses having strong Quaker links. Several were established by yarn merchants, worsted makers, wool combers and wool factors. In the case of Harvey and Hudson's Crown Bank, agricultural wealth led to them acquiring the receivership, or administration, of the Land Tax, adding to their solid commercial base.[29] The long line of banking families and firms from Weston onwards included, by 1836, Kerrison, Gurney & Co., Hudson & Hadfield, Harvey & Hudson, Tompson & Barclay, and Ives. Norwich was one of the most important banking and financial centres outside London, and these alliances of bankers, merchants and traders were powerful and influential.

The extract from Millard and Manning's map of 1830 shows the new area of Peafield, where a series of terraces was constructed in about 1820. The windmill, which was then still in open country, was built in 1824. The area lay beyond the city wall, and was developed on or adjacent to a series of brickfields, reminding us that Norwich had valuable deposits of brickearth to supply the new building boom. Outside the gate of St Giles the new city gaol, completed in 1824, adjoined open land and stood close to a lime kiln. This is now the site of St John's Roman Catholic cathedral, beneath which lie the great caverns of the disused chalk workings which supplied the kilns (and which occasionally cause major subsidence problems in the Earlham Road area).

In Yarmouth the herring fishery remained the major industry, but the potential of the town as a resort began to be exploited in the second quarter of the eighteenth century. In 1759 sea baths – that is, baths filled with sea water – were opened at the Bath House, now the Bath Hotel. A Georgian holiday guide, having extolled the merits of Yarmouth, noted that there was 'not a beggar to be seen, so admirably is the police conducted, and the miseries of the lower order of people so humanely attended to'.[30] Fast coach services to Norwich, known as 'flying machines', were established by 1768, and in 1813 a steam packet from Norwich greatly accelerated the journey by river.[31] In 1830 the new Acle Straight was driven across the marshes from Acle to Yarmouth. All these transport developments – together with coastal steamers which also landed visitors – greatly assisted the growth of the holiday trade, turning Yarmouth into a popular resort by the beginning of the 1840s. The new focus on the holiday industry led to expansion east of the walls on to the Denes where terraced housing and parks were laid out. The older trades – its port activities, its fishing and its maritime tradition – remained essential to the town's prosperity, and the St Nicholas Naval Hospital, built outside the walls on the Denes in 1800, reflected Yarmouth's naval importance.

In 1757 King's Lynn had 400 sailors, 250 of whom were in the Royal Navy. The population of the town then was about 10,000, but the economy was in the doldrums and commercial and demographic growth was absent. This was a period of depression and decay for Lynn, whose population had only risen to 10,096 by 1801. Thereafter there was a revival, albeit slow at first, and in 1851 the population had reached 20,000. But economic distress and very widespread poverty were apparent: in 1801 about 10 per cent of the population

The Old Vicarage, in Church Plain, Great Yarmouth, is a remarkable survivor, emerging relatively unscathed when the church of St Nicholas, two hundred yards away, was almost destroyed by bombing in the air raids of 1942. It now faces a pleasant green, but sadly beyond that is the busy dual carriageway which sliced through the northern part of the ancient town in the 1970s. The Old Vicarage was built in 1718 and was extended in 1781. Its three-storey red brick façade of the early eighteenth century blends well with a remarkably sensitive late nineteenth-century extension (left), and the whole composition reveals the wealth and sophistication of the borough, and the very wealthy ecclesiastical living of St Nicholas, in the early years of the reign of George I.

The Old Gaol House at King's Lynn was built in 1784, adjacent to the medieval Guildhall, and was designed by William Tuck, a carpenter. The prison yard is to the rear, with four of the original cells of the 1780s, and a brick cell block erected in 1937.

could be classified as 'pauper', and out-migration began to gather pace. A trickle became a flood: in 1836 alone some 800 emigrants went overseas from the Lynn area, and in 1837 no fewer than 1,500 people sailed from Lynn (and 600 from Yarmouth) to Canada. Further emigrant ships left in 1839.[32] Many of these people were country dwellers from the rural hinterland, but it is clear that the economy of west Norfolk was stagnant and that emigration was an attractive prospect for many. Lynn was also unhealthy: in 1832 there were 35 deaths from typhus, typhoid and cholera, and in 1852 William Lee, reporting for the Board of Health, noted that the Purfleet was being used for the town's rubbish and had become an open sewer.

Lynn shared in the enthusiasm for Methodism, and other nonconformist denominations, which was so widely apparent in eighteenth-century Norfolk. The growth of Methodism was such that in 1813 no fewer than thirty preachers were based in the new Wesleyan Methodist Church, where the leading members were from the humbler classes – mainly traders and craftsmen. The Baptists, in contrast, had a more obviously middle-class congregation in their new chapel opened in 1808, whereas Primitive Methodism was attracting the labouring poor, such as the porters, sailors and fishermen, to their chapel of 1820. The Congregationalists and Unitarians also built chapels.

Thetford benefited from the improvements to the Little Ouse, which was sporadically navigable from the medieval period onwards. In 1675–77 Henry, Earl of Arlington, took over the management of the navigation tolls from the borough and then improved the channel, building eight staunches (one-way sluices, which carried boats downstream but required them to be hauled by horses through what was in effect a weir when they were travelling upstream). This improved the commercial potential of the river, and the corporation took back the navigation under its own control in 1696 and in 1750 rebuilt the staunches. Another revival took place in 1827 after which the bulk of the corporation's income came from the navigation tolls. The improvements to the Great Ouse system as a whole made it possible for coal and timber imports to reach Thetford and for the grain and malt being processed there to be sent down river to Lynn for export. Several significant local industries emerged in Thetford in the later eighteenth century. Agricultural engineering became very important under the Burrell family, which later specialised in the manufacture of steam traction engines – by the mid-nineteenth century Thetford was one of the largest producers of such machinery in Britain. Cornelius Fison, a Thetford businessman and leading nonconformist, began to import cattle cake and oil seeds, and these processes eventually led to the growth of a fertiliser business on the riverside, bearing the name which became world-famous. Another of the riverside mills became important for paper making.

The size and plan of Thetford changed markedly after about 1750. The completion of the Norwich to Newmarket turnpike in 1766, together with the improvements in the river, led to the establishment of these new industries, reviving the almost moribund commercial life of the town and creating an industrial zone along the banks of the Little Ouse. The population rose sharply, almost doubling from 2,240 in 1801 to 3,934 in 1841. The market place shifted from south of the castle to the west of it and a new shopping area developed around it. There was an attempt to develop a spa around a chalybeate spring, and a bath house was built in 1818 though, as Crosby remarks, 'the prospect of drinking iron water in a damp meadow in a remote corner of Norfolk was not enough to establish a flourishing resort'; by 1838 it had closed.[33]

Some of the smaller market towns were also developing in this period. Swaffham was mapped by Faden in 1797, his plan showing the north–south market place at the junction of the London, Norwich and Lynn roads which were turnpiked in 1770. Castle Acre Street ran due north, heading for the much decayed town of that name. But though to a traveller Swaffham might have presented a modern and bustling appearance, this was to some extent deceptive. Even in 1797 the town was still only one building deep around the market place and its approach roads, and everywhere had a country aspect behind the urban façades. The butchers' shambles lay north of the assembly rooms,

The Baptist church at Diss is prominent in this view, standing out on the skyline above the wooded slopes that edge the mere. Built of the distinctive yellowish-grey brick that is widely found in villages and towns along the Norfolk–Suffolk border, the church was opened in 1860, though the Baptist congregation in the town dates back to 1788 and was the base from which Baptists evangelised the wide rural areas down towards Eye and across south Norfolk. The architecture of the church, with its twin square towers, reminds us that by the mid-Victorian period the nonconformist denominations were far less reticent about making a visual statement when they built their places of worship.

The market place was the centre of every medieval town, both geographically and in terms of its economy and society. But market places were not necessarily fixed, for the reorientation of a town (either deliberately or by a longer-term historical process) and the shifting of its centre of gravity could leave a market place badly placed. At Thetford the market in the post-Conquest period lay in the outer part of the castle bailey close to the ancient fording point over the Little Ouse that was in use by the Icknield Way two thousand years before. But in the later medieval period the focus of the town began to shift westward, towards the line of the main London to Norwich road. In 1782 the inhabitants petitioned for the removal of the market to a better site beside the guildhall and St Cuthbert's church. This area was already used extensively for informal trading and in 1786 the move was formally agreed. The old market became a tranquil and peaceful backwater.

The attractive ornamental walks along the Little Ouse at Thetford were laid out in the 1820s. On the right bank is Spring Walk, which was designed as a gravelled public promenade giving access to a pump room built over a chalybeate spring in the waterside meadow between the Little Ouse and the Thet. The spa was opened in 1818 and for a time was a great success, helped by a notably effusive guide to the 'city of Thetford' and the 'healing virtues inestimable yet suffered so long to remain neglected and unknown' of the iron-rich waters. However, the promised miracle cures did not materialise and in 1838 the pump room closed.

The Old Gaol in Thetford is possibly the most complete and unchanged example of a small borough prison anywhere in England. It stands at the western end of the medieval market place, and on the site there was a market house and gaol at least as early as 1290. The gaol was rebuilt in 1796 and enlarged in 1816, when the decorative panels showing shackles were placed over the doors – a neat image of early nineteenth-century punishment – with the commemorative plaque embellished with the arms of the borough. A visitor in the late 1820s described how 17 people were incarcerated in a room 18 feet 9 inches by 9 feet, and how the gaoler ran away after opening the door because the stench was so terrible. In 1857 the county took over the running of the gaol and it became the borough's police station, though still in occasional use as a prison until its final closure in 1891.

THIS GAOL was Enlarged in the Year 1816.

and the Free School (Hamonds School) was east of London Street and south of the parish church. The population in 1801 was 2,200 and by 1841 this had grown to 3,358. The assembly rooms (1776–78) and the market cross erected for the Earl of Orford in 1781–83 underlined the social role of Swaffham in west Norfolk, and in the middle of the eighteenth century a racecourse was laid out, further emphasising this distinctive character. As the town was the western centre of the county's legal system its bridewell was enlarged in 1844; in 1839 its shirehall was built as the centre for elections and the venue for meetings of the quarter sessions in that part of the county; and in 1834 the new Poor Law Union workhouse was built. Reflecting the town's prosperity in this period, the market place is edged by many handsome Georgian brick buildings.

The Guildhall in Thetford stands on a site used for civic purposes since the Middle Ages, The medieval guildhall, a black flint building, was largely rebuilt in 1799–1800, with a new council chamber, courthouse (until 1833 the Lent assizes for Norfolk were held here), cupola and clock tower. In 1901 it was discovered that the eighteenth-century rebuild was a bodged job, so a major reconstruction and restoration of this attractive building had to be undertaken. The Guildhall symbolises well the long and proud tradition of municipal independence of this small borough, which since 1974 has been subsumed within Breckland District Council.

Among the greatest, though one of the most controversial, sons of Norfolk was Tom Paine, author of *The Rights of Man* (1791) and other incendiary political tracts, active in both the American and French revolutions, a powerful influence upon global political theory for two centuries, and therefore a man vilified and admired in equal measure. He was born in Thetford in 1737 and it is likely that his passion for freedom, individual rights and liberty was stirred in no small measure by observing the 'exclusive, indolent, venal and undemocratic' corporation in his home town. In 1964 the proposal of American benefactors to erect a statue of Paine in Thetford divided the town from top to bottom, many arguing that he was a traitor to his homeland who should have been hanged. Fortunately, the statue was erected and now has a special place on the Tom Paine trail.

Reepham, a very much smaller town and one little known to visitors to the county, lies tucked away in the centre of Norfolk. Two parish churches, for Whitwell and Reepham, and the ruin of that of Hackford all stand in one churchyard at the east end of what was earlier known as Hackford Market Place. As at Swaffham, buildings stood only one deep around the market place but, unlike Swaffham, Reepham had two industries that remained of crucial importance until the 1870s: tanning and brewing. The two tanneries used the stream in Whitwell that ran along the edge of the common, while the surrounding wet clay plateau not only had cattle grazings but also the woodland which supplied the oak bark, essential in the process of steeping and tanning the hides. The Hackford tannery, which was run by the Bircham family, was a considerable business: the goods in the inventory of Samuel Bircham, who died in 1779, were valued at a total of £1,462 14s. (comparable in value to the assets of many members of the minor county gentry) and included 199 sole hides, 177 other hides, 15 horse hides and 84 sheepskins. The Bircham family later switched to brewing, and deeds of 1807 refer to a mansion, stables, brewery and malting office.[34] Their mansion remains on the north side of the market place.

Aylsham, on the rich loams of north-east Norfolk, has a long history. As at Swaffham and Reepham, a ring of brick buildings, many of which were formerly timbered, surrounds the market place which lies just south of the splendid

The Assembly Rooms in the market place at Swaffham were built in 1776–78, and the south front (seen here) was added in 1817. There have been several subsequent alterations, but it remains an excellent example of a type of building found in almost all late Georgian market towns in Norfolk and elsewhere. They were used for assemblies (social gatherings, with dancing and a buffet supper) of the sort described by Jane Austen, and could be used for theatrical performances, exhibitions, meeting places for the local gentry and yeoman farmers, and music and concerts. Swaffham is particularly fortunate that its Assembly Rooms continue to fulfil the same role for the town after a continuous history of almost 250 years.

1 Market Place, Wymondham, is ostensibly a gracious late eighteenth-century town house, of three storeys and five bays, and with a particularly elegant doorway framed in Doric columns. However, as is so often the case in the market towns of Norfolk, a symmetrical and regular red brick façade of the reign of George III conceals an older structure behind. At the rear of the building is a timber-framed cross wing datable to the early seventeenth century.

During the late eighteenth and early nineteenth centuries the agricultural transformation of Norfolk gathered pace, and in most towns (especially after the repeal of the Corn Laws in 1846) a corn exchange was built as a venue for the selling and buying of grain and other agricultural commodities and as a social centre, meeting place and focus for community activities. At Diss the 'handsome and commodious' Corn Hall was built in 1854, in a prominent location in St Nicholas Street and at the top of Market Hill. Its elegant classical frontage is very sharp contrast to the more vernacular domestic-scale architecture of the rest of the street. It included facilities for the magistrates' courts (with a holding cell), and a library and reading room, an excellent demonstration of the dual commercial and community role. Remarkably, the Corn Hall continued as a place for agricultural trading until the 1990s – perhaps the last instance in England of such a building fulfilling its original purpose.

parish church. The building of nearby Blickling Hall has already been noted, and it had a major influence upon the town, generating business and greatly increasing prosperity in the seventeenth and eighteenth centuries. Aylsham mill lies north-east of the town on the river Bure, on a very ancient site. In 1524 the income from the mill was left by Robert Jannys to provide a headmaster for the grammar school. In 1773 the mill became the terminus of the new scheme to make the river Bure navigable from Coltishall to Aylsham: an Act of Parliament authorised the construction of five locks, and new channels were cut to shorten and bypass the bends of the river. In 1779 the Bure Navigation was opened, and local landowners took out shares to finance it. Wherries of 16

Aylsham market place is adjacent to the churchyard, and the old north–south road through the town runs along its eastern edge. The market at Aylsham was chartered in 1296, and documentary evidence shows that originally the market place was a roughly square space, fronted by timber-framed buildings, some with open lower storeys. As this was a successful market, land was valuable and permanent buildings gradually began to encroach, producing the rather more irregular layout seen today. Many of the surrounding buildings were later rebuilt but some still have their medieval timber-framed structures concealed behind Georgian and Victorian brick façades. The cream-coloured Black Boys Inn (built 1710–20) dominates the south-west corner, its large central doorway having been an open-arched entrance for carriages until the 1930s.

tons burden and drawing 3½ feet of water would take barley, pollards, beans, osiers, marl, manure, wheat, flour and malt downstream to Yarmouth, while timber deals, coal, billets, fish and salt, maize, seeds, cinders and oilseed cake came upstream to Aylsham.

In the eighteenth century the Parmeter family became the major shareholders in the navigation and a vivid picture of their activities is given in the will of William Parmeter (1793):

> I give and devise all that my messuage and dwelling house wherein I now dwell together with the malthouses, granaries, houses, out houses, yards, gardens, orchards, lands and grounds … being in Mill gate Street in Aylsham … to Robert Parmeter my brother. Also … I give all that my estate and interest and terms of years to come and unexpired … in all that staithe, yard, grounds and bank with the warehouses, houses and buildings erected in part of the same situate standing, lying and being next to Aylsham navigation and also all my subscriptions or shares of £220 lent and advanced on the credit on the tolls of the said navigation, by the said Robert Parmeter my father deceased and all interest to my brother Robert.[35]

The period from 1750 to 1840 therefore saw major and far-reaching changes in the political, social and economic history of the county. The four boroughs – Norwich, Lynn, Yarmouth and Thetford – were expanding fast. The movement of goods within the county was improved and facilitated by waterway and turnpike networks based on Norwich and Lynn, but these developments also stimulated changes in smaller market towns, notably Downham Market and Aylsham. The appearance of towns and villages changed as orange and reddish brick replaced many of the older timber or flint buildings. In towns such as Swaffham, Aylsham and Hingham the market places were framed by the fashionable Georgian façades of houses and shops, though quite a few were simply refacings of older timber-framed buildings. Social provision of new schools, chapels and workhouses was changing the face of many communities and also affecting the operation of their social structures. Discontent over the use of new machinery on the land, and the loss of common rights, led to many minor and some major riots in the 1830s, but for decades the great landowners had been improving and enhancing the large estates with parks and model farms. Parliamentary enclosure led to a redrawing of much of the landscape, henceforth characterised by long neat hawthorn hedges, ruler-straight roads with broad verges, and geometric patterns of large, square or rectangular fields.

Stoke Holy Cross mill spans the little river Tas five miles south of Norwich. There has been a watermill on this site since at least the fifteenth century but the present building dates mainly from 1747, after its predecessor had been destroyed by fire. The mill was used for papermaking and corn-milling (in the early nineteenth century there were seven pairs of millstones, making this among the largest mills in East Anglia). In 1814 Jeremiah Colman, a Norwich flour miller, took the lease of the mill from Edward Ames, who manufactured mustard there. Colman, who in 1823 went into partnership at Stoke Holy Cross with his brother James, decided to continue the mustard business at the mill and the rest, as we know, is history. The mill itself closed in the 1940s, and it is now a restaurant.

The view of the broads from the top of St Helen's church, Ranworth, reveals the characteristic interplay of water, woodland, farmland and the reedbeds which is so crucial to the ecology and vegetational succession of the area. In the middle of the picture is the eastern arm of Ranworth Broad, with Ranworth Marshes and the Bure Marshes beyond, with the low hills of the erstwhile island of Flegg on the horizon.

13

The Broads

F OR MANY VISITORS the Broads are probably the major attraction which
   draws them to Norfolk – indeed, for plenty of outsiders 'the Broads'
are synonymous with the county itself, no matter how false that impression
might be. For well over a century this has been one of the most significant
areas of East Anglia in terms of conservation, landscape protection, and the
challenges of reconciling commercial pressures with the need to protect fragile
and vulnerable habitats. The quiet twisting waterways, the small but beautiful
broads themselves, the wide variety of wildlife and the many villages edging
the shallow valleys, their flint churches standing high, combine to produce
memorable images. In the late Victorian and Edwardian period the growth of
pleasure boating opened up these often secret and hidden places to the wider
world.

   The tidal estuaries of the rivers Ant, Thurne, Bure, Yare, Chet and
Waveney weave and wind among the fertile soils of east Norfolk and the boulder
clays of south Norfolk and north Suffolk. The complex sequence of changes
in land and sea levels over many centuries has meant that the estuaries, which
developed as a result of sea-level rise after the last glaciation, have steadily

c.1200	Start of large-scale peat-cutting by Norwich Cathedral Priory and St Benet's Abbey
c.1400	Flooding of peat workings begins, leading to creation of the Broads
fifteenth–sixteenth centuries	Reed and thatch cutting, fishing, duck shooting and wildfowling develop as local trades
1670	Yarmouth Pier and Haven Commissioners formed (control river up to Hardley Cross)
1790s	Increased pumping using windmills to drain wetland areas
1795	34 keels and 118 wherries registered for use on Broadland waterways
1844	Railway line from Norwich to Yarmouth opened
1851	Steam drainage begins in the Halvergate Marshes
1861	Sea Breach Commissioners permanently established to maintain sea defences
1865	Railway line from Norwich to Cromer via Wroxham opened
1880s onwards	Many waterways silting and increased coastal retreat as erosion accelerates
1880 and 1895	Wild Birds Protection Acts, aimed particularly at Norfolk Broads
1912	Major flooding on Broadland rivers: end of navigation on the Ant and Bure
1926	Norfolk Wildlife Trust formed: by 1988 owns 11,551 acres on eleven sites
1938	Serious flooding in the Broads
1950 onwards	Severe pollution from agricultural run-off
1953	Catastrophic flooding in coastal areas of Broadland (the North Sea floods)
1988	The Broads Authority established and the area becomes a national park
2000	Whitlingham Country Park opened on river Yare east of Norwich

filled with silts brought in by the sea and carried down from the interior by the rivers, and also with organic material – and especially peat – that grew in the lime-rich marshes of the upper valleys. The characteristic natural vegetation which emerged in these areas was based on salt marshes nearer the sea and thick woodland, of the damp and waterlogged fen-carr type, further upstream. The constant battle of land and sea, so familiar in our own time, has carried on for untold centuries. In the Roman period, two millennia ago, the coastline was at least two miles east of the present one (that is, farther out in the North Sea), and it may well be that some Roman settlements have been lost as sea level has risen and erosion has chewed away at the soft coastal cliffs. Two thousand years ago Flegg, historically divided into the hundreds of East and West Flegg, was an island with tidal openings to the north and south. The Great Estuary, the mouth of the Yare and its many tributaries, then lay open between Caister by Yarmouth and Burgh Castle and rivers were navigable, at least for barges, as far as Caistor St Edmund and perhaps there was a port for sea-going shipping at Reedham. Yet that was destined to change, for the Great Yarmouth peninsula, a large sandspit extending southwards from Flegg across the once-wide mouth of the Yare estuary, was by the time of the Norman Conquest sufficiently firm and solid to support settlement.

The fact that the Broads were man-made, the result of the flooding of vast peat workings, is now well attested.[1] Painstaking documentary research and landscape fieldwork in the 1950s and 1960s revealed that the creation of these steep-banked open water lakes took place in the early medieval period, when incursions of water formed the Broads more or less as now know them. The cutting of accessible peat seems in part to have been driven by the need for fuel to supply the voracious demands of Norwich Cathedral Priory and St Benet's Abbey, both of which had extensive landed estates in the area. Norwich Cathedral Priory held the advowson of four Ormesby churches and owned a small estate in the area. An account of peat output for the Ormesby turbaries listed the production of 'lasts' of turves (a 'last' being a measure of 10,000 peats, each 2 to 3 feet long and 3½ inches square). In 1336–37, for example, 10½ lasts were dug, the 105,000 turves being enough to fill a peat barn, and in 1338 two lasts were used on the manor, five lasts were sold for profit, and three lasts were sent up to the priory in Norwich by water – eight men carted the peat to Yarmouth, whence it was sent by boat up river.[2] In just two and a half years, therefore, almost a quarter of a million turves were dug. The scale of the enterprise is hugely impressive – and this was just one of several large landowners who were exploiting this precious resource. As air photographs and tithe maps show, the effects of medieval peat cutting can be seen in the geometric straight-edged sections of some of the Broads, such as Hickling, and in the long narrow peninsulas, formerly the baulks between the various cuttings, which project into the open water. None of the Broads is more than about six feet deep, which is one reason why vegetation can so easily begin to infill the surviving lakes and waterways.

The area had many other valuable assets: the Ashby and Thurne manors of St Benet's Abbey sent wheat, malt, 20 pigs, 100 geese and 600 eels to the abbey in 1341. Originally there were also saltings, where salt was evaporated from seawater, but by the fourteenth century Runham was the only manor in Flegg that still had salt workings. The people of the Broadland settlements also dug their own peat as well as cutting reed and sedge and taking fish, eels and birds from the marshland. The cleared upper marshes and the ancient salt marshes, which with embanking became freshwater marshes, were valuable for grazing cattle and sheep, and the tidal creeks were important for salt production. The grazing marshes were particularly valuable and many upland and inland parishes included distant detached portions in the Broads, upon which their stock could graze.[3] The land ownership and land use were extremely complex and heavily fragmented. Hickling parish, for example, shows intricate interlocking patterns of marshland and upland. East Field, West Field and Stubbs Close were all high-quality arable land and, as one example among many, in 1646 Robert Cock bequeathed four small estates, one to his wife and three to his daughters, and described his lands as freehold and copyhold, consisting of closes, crofts and marshes. This suggests that he owned or had specific rights to marshland as well as arable, underlining how the economy of a typical Broadland parish was an interplay between the 'upland' and the 'lowland'.[4]

The open water of the Broads themselves occupies a comparatively small area within the much wider and more extensive expanses of marshes and fens in the drowned valleys. The navigable river courses permitted trade by water to places far inland, such as Stalham, Ludham, Loddon and of course Norwich. The keel and the wherry were the two main types of craft used on these rivers. The keel was the earlier form, although its origins are uncertain. It had a central mast, a square sail, a rounded bottom, and its cabin was in the bows. The larger wherry had a bigger mast farther forward, a big gaff sail, an externally attached keel which could be removed in very shallow water, and a cabin in the stern.[5] In 1795 a register of inland waterway craft was drawn up by the town clerk of Yarmouth. It listed 34 keels and 118 wherries, confirming that the keels were in decline by this date.[6] The surviving keels were used for the roughest work, such as carrying heavy timber. Lighters for moving reed bundles were also much used, and on the small watercourses and backwaters punts were the ubiquitous local craft.

The impact of man in Broadland

It is always dangerous to give impressions of unchanging landscapes, for change is ever present. Today the Broads echo to the noise of motor boats, large river launches with loudspeakers, combine-harvesters cutting the corn, and everywhere cars and more cars. In the winter the distinctive smell of Cantley's sugar-beet processing is carried on the easterly winds. The scene is entirely different from what we would have seen a century ago, although the framework of the landscape is relatively little altered. To see and understand the character of 'traditional' Broadland we must turn to Emerson's classic photographs, the notes compiled by Arthur Patterson and Richard Lubbock on the fauna of Norfolk, and more recently Bob Malster's careful recording of the life and character of 'old Broadland'. These give us a picture of the Broads as they once were, and provide us with what is, to a considerable extent, a folk memory of the past.

The Broads themselves, and the fen, fen-carr and grazing marshes with which they were surrounded, provided a living, or the substantial part of a living, for thousands of people. This was never a deserted landscape, and there was always a sizeable local population – indeed, in the period after the Norman Conquest it was among the most densely populated parts of England. The villagers exploited the many assets of the region, in addition to peat. That resource was itself cut on a much smaller scale, for purely local use, after the early fourteenth century, because of the effects of a deteriorating climate: coastal inundation as a result of increased storminess, and a significant rise in sea level, flooded the older and larger peat cuttings. But throughout Broadland reed (*phragmites communis*) was cut for thatching and its regular and frequent harvesting ensured that the fen-carr did not recolonise the fringes of the lakes. Similarly, the beds of saw sedge (*cladium mariscus*) could be maintained by regular harvesting: it is pliable and was, and still is, used for ridging the roofs thatched with Norfolk reed. Both products had markets outside the Broads, especially in Norwich, where until the early sixteenth century thatched roofs were very widespread. From that time onwards the city authorities actively sought to promote rebuilding with tile or stone roofs, following problems with fires. Rushes (*juncus var.*) were cut for cattle fodder, making a sort of hay, and were also used for flooring and for rushlights. There was therefore a continuing and extensive exploitation of the 'undergrowth' of the lake and marsh fringes.

Some of the work in the Broadland fens and marshland was seasonal, and arable land away from the flat wet valley floors provided farmwork in the intervals. The building of keels, wherries, canoes, reed lighters and punts was an activity in every village. In 1851, for example, Ludham had a population of 981, of whom six were described in the census returns as marshmen, three boatmen, two boatbuilders and two thatchers. There were staithes at Womack Water, Ludham Bridge and How Hill from which local produce was moved even after the arrival of the railway at Potter Heigham.[7]

Given the watery world in which the inhabitants of Broadland lived, it is no surprise that fishing was a vital local trade. A wide range of fish was caught, including roach (the most widespread), tench, carp (especially on Fritton Lake), common bream, and eels, a local speciality.[8] In the summer of 1905 Patterson noted an eel catastrophe, when thousands of eels died throughout the Broads – though no fish died.[9] The catching of eels was well organised along the river Yare, and in the mid-eighteenth century Blomefield noted that there were 19 licensed eel setts downstream from Norwich. Birds' eggs were also collected in large numbers: it was recorded in 1821 that a single egger of Potter Heigham took 160 dozen peewits' (green lapwing) eggs from the nearby marshes, a matter of great concern to the Reverend Richard Lubbock. Like so many of the nineteenth-century clergy he was an excellent naturalist, and wrote widely on the natural history of the Broads, though as well as deploring the destruction of Broadland wildlife he was not beyond shooting many birds:

'in a duck shooting expedition in 1819 he killed 11 bitterns without searching particularly for them'.[10] There was a good market for the duck that were shot by the wildfowlers who plied the backwaters in punts, and for those birds caught in the decoys. Duck decoys were established as early as the seventeenth century. The ducks were driven into them, led by tame ducks and by dogs running along the side, and they could then be caught and killed at the narrow end. Decoys were made at Acle in 1620, Buckenham 1636 and Fritton 1670. They declined in the period after 1850, but that at Fritton remained in use until the 1950s.[11] Malster wrote of 2,400 ducks being killed at the Fritton Decoy in 1879/80. These were mainly mallard but also some teal and widgeon.

Although the divisions between watercourses, open water, fen-carr and grazing marshes still exist, that is primarily due to careful conservation work over the past sixty years. The natural processes of silting and vegetation growth would inevitably mean that the broads themselves would disappear in the fullness of time, and the marshes and fens would gradually dry out. Already by 1900 many former small broads had been gradually choked by fen vegetation, so that only small navigation channels were left and the open water had disappeared. The Nature Conservancy's diagram from its 1965 *Report on Broadland* shows that although the deeper peat cuttings were still open many of the shallow ones had disappeared completely. Several new chemical components, especially nitrogen and phosphorus, were added to the river waters from 1850 onwards. Parliamentary enclosure over the previous hundred years had facilitated the wholesale reorganisation and reorientation of agriculture, so that run-off from large new areas of arable land was added to the rivers supplying the Broads. The population growth of Norwich, as the city expanded, created major changes, for large quantities of sewage were released into the Yare

The duck decoy at Ranworth, now within the protection of the Norfolk Wildlife Trust in its nature reserve, made use of an arm of the broad. The principle on which this, and the many other Norfolk examples (now mostly gone) was based, was that the arm narrowed and tall reed fences were placed along both sides as a barrier. The ducks could be driven along the water, into the narrow end where they became trapped in nets and captured. This example was certainly in use in the early nineteenth century. It appears as an illustration in Lubbock's *Observations on the Fauna of Norfolk* (1845), but is probably considerably older than that.

and the Wensum via the sewer outfalls as modern sanitation systems were built in the mid-nineteenth century. The smaller towns, as they grew, also added to this damaging pollution. In the twentieth century, and especially after 1950, the massive use of nitro-fertilisers meant a major new source of pollution, while the expansion of tourism in Broadland, and the rapid increase in the use of motor boats and holiday cruising produced further problems.

Early tourism

Water, boats, wildlife and, initially at least, the perception that these were areas with tranquil isolation were strong factors in encouraging prosperous middle-class visitors to holiday on the Broads. In 1882 Jarrolds of Norwich published Christopher Davis's *Handbook to the Rivers and Broads of Norfolk and Suffolk,* which ran to no fewer than fifty editions and prompted the writing of many other guidebooks and descriptive volumes. In 1903, for example, D.A. Dutt published his influential descriptive guide, *The Norfolk Broads,* and from that time onwards a steady and continuous flow of publications popularised and promoted the area.

Christopher Davis's boat was 'a four ton centre board una-rigged yacht adapted for single handed sailing'. As the tourist industry developed, small sailing boats of this type were in growing demand, and boatyards such as Loynes at Wroxham developed for boat building and hiring. Loynes began as a boatbuilder in Norwich, moved to Wroxham in 1878, and then began to hire boats out. At the 1883 International Fisheries Exhibition in London the firm

The twin communities of Wroxham and Hoveton have emerged as the capital of the Broads, developing as a small town of about 5,000 people centred on the high-arched and originally medieval bridge which carries the main road from Norwich over the Bure. This has been a centre for boating since the late nineteenth century, but a more remarkable phenomenon has been the extraordinary growth of Roy's of Wroxham. Alfred and Arnold Roy ran a village store at Coltishall in the 1890s, and in 1899 opened a store at Wroxham to cater for visiting boat-based holidaymakers. In the 1920s and 1930s it expanded fast, marketed under the catchy (and still used) slogan 'The World's Largest Village Store'. Today the firm, still an independent family business, dominates Hoveton (Roy's of Hoveton doesn't sound as euphonious!) and it has become a tourist destination in its own right.

Everywhere along the Broadland waterway network has felt commercial and development pressures resulting from a massive growth in pleasure-boating since the Second World War, and a major challenge facing planners since the 1960s has been to ensure that this does not further damage the fragile and often deteriorating ecosystems of the area. An obvious strategy has been to designate certain places where substantial development can take place and to balance that with strict controls elsewhere. The capital of the Broads, Wroxham and Hoveton, has therefore seen very extensive new development of riverside housing and retailing and marina construction. This view shows the new 80-berth marina on the Wroxham side.

advertised 'cabin yachts from three to fifteen tons fitted with every convenience for cooking and sleeping'.[12] In 1893 Press Brothers of North Walsham, millers and maltsters, had fitted out five of their wherries, properly equipped for hiring parties. This was a sign of the times: boats formerly intended purely for commercial use were being converted to serve the new Broadland economy as pleasure wherries. By 1891 Davis's *Handbook* listed 37 boatbuilders and owners with boats for hire.

The railway companies began to publicise the area as a holiday destination, supplementing their earlier promotion of the coastal resorts such as Cromer and Sheringham. In 1893 the Great Eastern Railway published its *Summer Holidays in the Land of the Broads*. The opening of the Norwich and Yarmouth line in 1844 had seriously damaged the wherry river trade, and as the network expanded it competed directly with the other commercial traffic on the waterways of Broadland. In 1865 work began on the Norwich to North Walsham line via Wroxham, and by 1877 a line linked Cromer with the Broads. In 1883 an alternative to the Norwich–Reedham–Yarmouth line had been built via Acle, opening up a new area to the holiday trade. Meanwhile, in 1877 the Great Yarmouth and Stalham Light Railway linked those two towns via Martham and Stalham and in 1893 this became part of the Midland and Great Northern Joint Railway which linked the Broads to Leicester and the Midlands. This greatly increased the accessibility of the heart of Broadland, and the links to more distant places had a dramatic effect on tourist business.

That accessibility, and the increased tourist trade, are reflected in the statistics for the numbers of vessels on the Broadland waterways. By the 1880s the first steam launches were working, and the first internal combustion engine boats followed in the 1890s. In 1931 the Blakes' list of available boats totalled 495, of which 100 were motor cruisers. By 1995 there were 2,445 hire craft registered on the Broads, roughly half being motor cruisers, and there were also 10,040 private craft of which 3,500 were motor cruisers. The holiday year, once confined to the summer months, has extended inexorably, so that today, for example, many boats are hired out for Christmas. The result of this huge increase in tourism has been growth in holiday accommodation and the development of Wroxham and Stalham as the centres of this new tourist industry.

The grazing marshes and coastal protection

But as well as tourism and all that went with it, the marshlands, fens and riverside flats of east Norfolk continued to have an important agricultural role. As with the Fenlands of west Norfolk, the marshes had to be drained if they were to provide good grazing. Mosby's diagram shows the layout of a typical drainage pattern.[13] A multitude of drainage windmills, as shown on the 1890 map in Williamson's *The Norfolk Broads*, lifted the surplus water from the marshes to the rivers. However, in contrast to the situation in the Fens, there was no wholesale shift to the use of steam mills, probably because the east Norfolk marshes, being composed largely of silt, did not sink and shrink when they were drained. That was a major problem in the Fenland, but in Broadland it was not a serious challenge and so only a much smaller lift was needed. Nevertheless, in the mid-nineteenth century some steam pumping was introduced. The first steam engine was built in 1853 as part of an ambitious plan to drain the Halvergate triangle and the lower parts of the flood plains.

Far more challenging than draining the marshes was the task of protecting the coastline. The sea coast of the Broads is composed either of low cliffs of very soft glacial debris, or of sand dunes. Both are particularly vulnerable to erosion, and sea flooding has been a frequent problem for many centuries. This frequent flooding led to the establishment in 1861 of the permanent Sea Breach Commissioners, whose task was to construct and maintain coastal defences along the shore from Cromer to Yarmouth. Erosion rates were among the fastest in the British Isles – only in the Holderness area of east Yorkshire was there a comparable challenge – and it was estimated that between 1904 and 1946 the coast between Cromer and Caister receded by as much as 300 feet, with an alarming retreat of about 450 feet south of Winterton. In some places, in just the two years 1945–46, as much as 200 feet disappeared. These figures may at first glance seem comparatively modest, though the average loss was about six feet per year in the first half of the twentieth century, but extrapolated over the period since the beginning of the eighteenth century, when the first really detailed evidence appears, this means that at least a quarter of a mile has gone and in some stretches of the coast more than half a mile. The destruction of property is very apparent: not least in the tumbled remains of churches and houses, including the remnants of the church that now lie on the beach at Eccles.

There was a further problem. As well as the loss of land which it represented, rapid coastal erosion was wearing away the slightly higher ground that protected the very low-lying flat lands behind from inundation by the sea. As it proceeded, the risk of major flooding grew. In 1938 the barrier was breached and particularly severe floods swept through the dunes into the Broads. During the 1940s and the beginning of the 1950s erosion accelerated: in 1952 at Walcott, for example, sixty feet of dunes and cliff went almost at one time. Worse was yet to come: the tremendous North Sea storm of 1953, one of the most severe in historical times, caused massive damage and heavy loss of life all along the coasts of the Low Countries, Denmark, north Germany and eastern England. Because of the storm surge, the sea on the Norfolk coast rose to more than twelve feet above normal high-tide mark, combined with ferocious battering of the shore by huge waves. The dune belt was broken at Horsey, and immense quantities of saltwater rushed inland, flooding in to the Broads, drowning over 100 people and inundating many square miles of farmland. The fragile and precarious inter-relationship between the coast and its hinterland was all too obvious.[14]

Windmills were extensively used for drainage purposes in the Broads from the seventeenth century to the twentieth, and quite a few survive today. The five-storey windpump at Horsey (here minus sails because repair work was in progress) was the very last to be built (in 1912, on the site of an eighteenth-century predecessor). It raised water from the fen beside the Hundred Stream to the level of the dyke (in the foreground) which fed the water into Horsey Mere. The area is only just above sea level and a mile and a half from the shore, and the land around has been flooded many times – most notably during the devastating North Sea floods of 1953.

Conservation and management

'Navigation was the first use of Broadland that demanded organisation':[15] in 1670 the Yarmouth Pier and Haven Commissioners were created with the power to levy tolls on vessels using the river. Their authority extended inland as far as Hardley Cross, where it met that of the city corporation of Norwich, and it included the tributary rivers. In 1866 a new Act set up sub-committees for the Yare, Bure and Waveney, allowing them to set separate tolls for each section. The commission took over the task of managing and regulating the use of the river in a wider sense, a matter of major importance as the growing use of motor boats began to threaten erosion of the banks and other detrimental consequences. The commissioners tried to resist pressure to control and reduce the numbers of boats, but they did enforce regulations which limited the speed of vessels in an attempt to minimise erosion. In 1988 responsibility for navigation was handed to the new Broads Authority, which is discussed in more detail below.

The exceptional range of wildlife habitats, and the rarity of much of the Broadland flora and fauna, meant that from the mid-nineteenth century onwards various attempts were made to protect and conserve parts of the area. Indeed, Broadland was a sort of laboratory for many key aspects of the early conservation movement, as it developed from the 1860s onwards. In the 1880s the first Wild Birds Protection Acts were passed, particularly to protect Breydon Water, and in 1895 amendments to these Acts gave special protection to Hickling Broad and the Trinity Broads. Further cover came with the Protection of Bird Acts of 1954 and 1967. The Royal Society for the Protection of Birds acquired Strumpshaw Marsh in 1975 and grazing marshes near Berney Arms Mill in 1985/86. Earlier than this, the need to acquire land to protect the wildlife on it, by preventing inappropriate development and conserving special habitats and landscapes, led to the creation in 1926 of the body which is now the Norfolk Wildlife Trust. This pioneering and innovative organisation owns

Hickling Staithe was originally the landing place closest to Hickling village for commercial vessels, and particularly wherries, which plied the Broads waterways, transporting coal, peat and grain. It was also a centre for basket-making, the baskets being used in the fishing trade. The railways reached the area in the 1870s and the waterborne trade dwindled rapidly, to be replaced by boating for leisure and pleasure. In the 1880s the inn at the staithe was renamed The Pleasure Boat, and since the late Victorian period this has been one of the most popular destinations for holidaymakers on boats.

Hickling Broad is the largest of the broads of Norfolk and Suffolk, with an area of just over a square mile. Like all the broads it is very shallow, the main navigation channel being only 5 feet deep. It connects with Heigham Sound and then via a tidal channel with the river Thurne. Hickling Broad was originally considerably larger, and it is edged by extensive areas of reedbeds (the largest in England) and wetland, with several small ponds and small broads. The broad is of major importance for its ecology, is a national nature reserve, and has been managed by the Norfolk Wildlife Trust since 1945. Birds include common crane, bittern and marsh harrier, and it is the most important British location for the spectacular swallowtail butterfly.

sites at Hickling Broad, Barton Broad, Ranworth and Cockshoot Broads and Surlingham, all acquired between 1945 and 1952 at a time when pressures on habitats and environments were becoming considerably more acute. By 1986 the Trust had purchased some 1,155 hectares in total, spread between eleven sites in Broadland. A parallel research-orientated body, the Nature Conservancy Council (now Natural England), was established in 1949 and a hierarchy of national nature reserves and sites of scientific interest developed. The nature reserves and SSSIs in Norfolk are shown on the Nature Conservancy map of 1985.

The problem of 'who looks after what' had always been a difficulty in the organisation and management of the Broads. After the Second World War the Town and Country Planning Act 1947 established a basic regulatory framework for development and house building, here as elsewhere, while the Water Act of 1973 handed all responsibility for drainage to the Anglian Water Authority, which in turn became the privatised Anglian Water in 1984. The National River Authority merged the various river boards and eventually became the

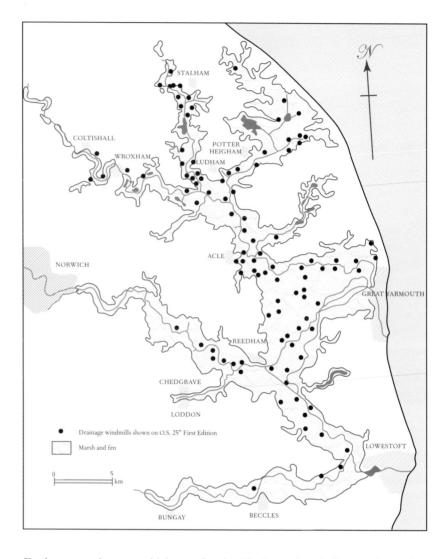

Windmills in the
Broads in the 1890s
(after Williamson,
1997).

Environment Agency, which was faced with the major challenge of restoring
and upgrading the quality of water in the rivers and in the Broads themselves.
During the 1970s and early 1980s there was a lengthy and sometimes heated
debate about the future of the Broads in planning terms, involving not only
government agencies but also Norfolk and Suffolk county councils (which were
the main planning authorities for the area), the six district councils, as well
as many private and commercial interests. The outcome was radical. Rather
than tinker with the confused and to some extent *ad hoc* system already in
place, a new structure was created. The existing commissioners, agencies
and authorities were either abolished or compelled to cede some or all of
their planning powers to a newly created body, the Broads Authority, and the
Broads were designated as, in effect, a national park (at that time the only one
in lowland Britain). The two county councils and six district councils have
representation on the Broads Authority and, despite much initial apprehension,
the organisation seems to work effectively.

Commerce and tourism

As late as 1971 there was still commercial traffic on the Yare, much of it associated with the Cantley sugar-beet factory. In 1936 there had been 753 journeys, moving 375,000 tons, mainly of coal, grain, timber, petrol and oil cake. By 1971 this had fallen to 176 journeys and 70,400 tons and by 1988 only seven journeys with under 3,000 tons.[16] After this commercial river traffic ceased. Although there had been various proposals, over many decades, to establish a fully fledged river port in Norwich for commercial shipping, using the stretch of the river close to the Carrow Road football ground, none had come to fruition. The narrowness of the river meant that the small size of ships that could reach Norwich was an insuperable limitation, while coal, the most significant traffic to the city, ceased to be used for gas and electricity production as North Sea oil and natural gas came on stream. The corn mills, already closed, stood on land that in the 1980s and 1990s became so valuable that large blocks of residential flats, rather than commercial or industrial properties, replaced them. The river in Norwich has therefore become a visual asset to be overlooked by wide-glazed living rooms and balconies, not the location for business premises, commerce or industry. The same process has taken place at Loddon, at the head of navigation on the little river Chet.

The use of the rivers for tourism has taken an opposite direction. The ever-increasing potential of the tourist trade ensured that the development of other riverside communities was geared ever further towards pleasure boating. By 1891 there were 37 boat hirers on the Broadland waterways, with Thorpe, Brundall, Wroxham and Horning already well established. Almost sixty years later, in 1949, there were 547 boats for hire, 301 of them motor boats. In 1979 there were 2,257, of which only 107 were sailing boats: the transformation of the river economy was almost complete.[17] There is little likelihood that commercial traffic will ever be re-established, but the dynamism of the tourist sector is continuing, with all the pressures of pollution, congestion, riverside development and potential threats to conservation and ecological protection that it brings in its wake. The Nature Conservancy Council's map of 1965 gives a clear picture of the pressures of the boat-hire industry on the waterways: since that date development has continued apace.

Despite the creation of the Broads Authority, the development pressures and the planning conflicts remain. For example, the *Eastern Daily Press* for 14 August 2009 carried the heading 'Disneyworld would wreck Broads'. This revealed how plans for further leisure areas, with a huge pleasure centre between Norwich and Wroxham, could create fresh problems, exacerbating tensions between, on the one hand, the desire to maintain the 'natural' (though, as we have seen actually man-made) Broadland landscape and, on the other hand, the economic and commercial imperative to ensure the future of the Broads as a major tourist destination. Individual projects might sometimes be rejected, but for the foreseeable future there will always be schemes and development proposals which, while possibly bringing economic benefits and employment, also risk damaging the fragile environment of the area.

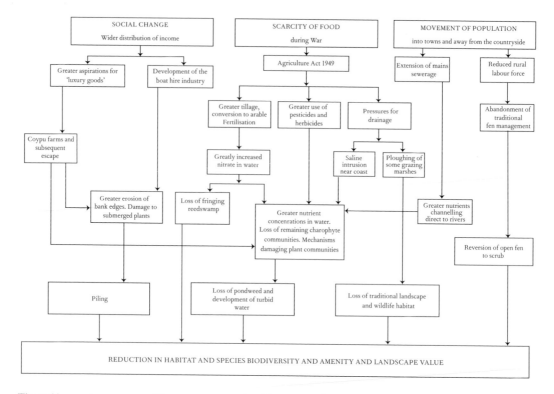

The problems and
challenges: habitat
reduction and
landscape change
in the Broads since
the early twentieth
century (after Moss,
2001).

We can sum up. A wide range of ecological processes have interacted with human activities to create the unique and precious character and landscape of the region. This special identity is under continuous and serious threat, and the problems have been superbly summarised in Moss's diagram above. He concludes that there are still three conflicting issues:

1. Preserving and enhancing the natural beauty of the Broads
2. Promoting the enjoyment of the Broads
3. Navigation rights and rules.

In the future, whatever the short-term and specific circumstances, these sometimes conflicting and always challenging factors will continue to shape the destiny of this remarkable part of the county.

14

Vernacular architecture in Norfolk

M ANY of Norfolk's major houses and churches have already been discussed in previous chapters, but the variety and survival of more modest buildings in the county – the wealth of vernacular architecture – is one of its greatest delights and a priceless historical asset. Depending on the balance of building materials used, especially as a result of local variations in geology and resources, most Norfolk towns and villages have a range of buildings using flint, timber and brick. Flint was used in especially north and north-west Norfolk; brick is most common in east Norfolk; and timber is found particularly in the central and southern parts of the county. These are of course generalisations, not rigid divisions, but the differing character of buildings and towns and villages is apparent from any drive across the county. Indeed, it is part of the rich variety of landscape and townscape which contributes so much to our visual appreciation of Norfolk.

The earliest surviving buildings, those which were constructed in the medieval period, are normally of flint. Very few are truly vernacular, for almost all buildings in Norfolk dating from before 1500 are of high status – churches, castles, and monastic remains. The use of flint was followed by the increasing use of timber, with sophisticated architectural styles and advanced carpentry techniques. A wealth of timber buildings survives from the period between the beginning of the fifteenth century and the early decades of the eighteenth. Historically, the use of timber gradually gave way to brick, which was initially used for refronting and then for entire buildings from 1650 to 1750. Clearly, therefore, the different traditions overlapped – flint was paralleled by the use of timber, then timber with brick – and much depended on the status of the builder or owner, the local materials available, and whether the building was located in town or country.

Norfolk lacks a satisfactory building stone, apart from carstone (a lower cretaceous sandstone) which is found in a belt running from the north-west coast near Hunstanton southwards towards Stoke Ferry and Hockwold. This means that for vernacular buildings – those which did not use expensive imported materials – there was no really suitable material apart from flint, which occurs in indefinite layers in the chalk. Though of necessity it became the major material used over much of the county, it has no bedding planes or vertical joints from which ashlar (dressed stone) can be formed. To make a wall with flint therefore needs a great deal of mortar, which is used to glue the flint nodules or shaped flints together. Mortar was produced by burning chalk, and the 'raft' of chalk under Norfolk provides, at key accessible points,

Date	Timber	Flint	Building stone	Brick
pre-Roman	General use in Bronze Age and Iron Age for huts; also religious buildings such as Seahenge and Arminghall Henge	Mainly used for weapons rather than building (Grimes Graves)		
Roman	Huts at Caistor St Edmund	Walls of Roman towns and forts (Caistor St Edmund, Caister by Sea, Burgh Castle)		
AD 700 >	Round and rectangular huts in the Anglo-Saxon period	Particularly important for the characteristic round towers on parish churches		
1000 >	Original wooden structures at Norwich and Thetford castles	Very extensively used for church building	Caen stone for major projects (Norwich Castle and Cathedral, Castle Rising)	
1100 >	In general use for small dwellings	Used in castles (Norwich, Castle Rising, Castle Acre)		
1200 >	Open halls; becoming the standard material for the frames of houses in the south-east of the county, and in mid-Norfolk	Weeting Castle	West Walton Church (Barnack Stone)	
1300 >		Norwich city walls	Terrington St Clement church (Barnack Stone)	First use of brick: Cow Tower, Norwich; some parts of Norwich city walls
1400 >		Baconsthorpe Castle; Norwich and King's Lynn Guildhalls	Cawston Church tower (1480s)	Prestige buildings; Hales Barn; Oxborough Hall (1480s)
1500 >	Floors inserted into open halls; jettied houses; Elm Hill fire, Norwich (1507)	Extensively used for lesser buildings	Ketton stone (from Rutland) used for large prestige houses	Used for chimney stacks in timber halls of lesser (yeoman) houses
1600 >	Fires at North Walsham (1600) and Wymondham (1615) discourage use of timber			Brick facings used for timber-framed walls; employed on a grand scale at Blickling and Felbrigg
1700 >	Rarely used for major buildings by this time, though still widespread for small houses	Holt fire: flint much used in the rebuilding of the town	Major houses including Wolterton; use of artificial Portland stone	Thomas Ivory uses brick for major projects in Norwich (Assembly House)
1800 >	Internal construction only	Cottages in North Norfolk and Breckland	Mainly used for decorative elements and quoins of brick buildings; some vernacular use in the carstone area of West Norfolk	Standard use for most residential, commercial and industrial buildings throughout the county, though different types of brick employed in the nineteenth century
1900 >		Rarely used until the vernacular revival and conservation work 1970s onwards		
2000 >	Contemporary domestic and commercial	Contemporary domestic and decorative		

The plan and form of Blakeney, the thriving medieval port which in the eighteenth century began to decline as the creek silted, was typical of many north Norfolk villages. A close-packed network of narrow streets and path-like lanes, lined with little cottages. In this view, of High Street, the variety of architectural styles and building materials is immediately apparent: the humble vernacular of flint and plaster walling contrasts with the more formal and showy red brick (with the impressive columned doorway). But closer examination reveals that many of the houses and cottages in High Street have later façades which conceal older timber-framed structures, where modernisation in the eighteenth and nineteenth centuries was largely 'skin deep'.

a plentiful supply of lime as well as of the flint itself. In the west of the county the lowest layers of chalk are in a harder form, that could be worked as 'clunch', a material which has been used as a cut building stone even though it is inferior to sandstones and limestones. It can be widely seen in buildings at, for example, Shouldham and Flitcham. Above the chalk the various glacial deposits towards the surface include boulder clays, from which clay lump could be obtained. It can be used as cut blocks or shaped between shutters (moulds), but in order to survive the elements it needs to be protected by, for example, thick and constantly renewed layers of whitewash. Very fine-grained earths of glacial origin provide easily worked brickearths, and the local supplies were used to make many of the orange-red bricks of east Norfolk and the Norwich area.

Archaeological, and some architectural, evidence indicates that timber was initially the main building material. Spectacular and famous examples include the Bronze Age 'wood henge' at Arminghall and Sea Henge at Holme-next-the-Sea, although these can hardly be considered as 'vernacular' architecture. The glacial deposits supported dense deciduous woodland, especially on the boulder clays, so in the period before the Middle Ages timber supplies were readily available across much of the county. In the Breckland, however, the

The village of Hunstanton is now Old Hunstanton, with its medieval church, manor house and park. In 1862 the railway from Lynn was opened, and the Le Strange family immediately began to develop a seaside resort on the perhaps slightly unpromising shores of The Wash. A pier was built in 1870, and public buildings, hotels and the usual amenities followed, with the green as the focal point on the sloping ground above the low cliffs. Hunstanton is unique among Norfolk resorts in being largely stone-built, and it has a great deal of very attractive late Victorian and Edwardian architecture. The rich gingery-brown colour of the carstone is evident in this view of a row of five-storey boarding houses in Cliff Parade.

Carstone is an iron-stained sandstone, or puddingstone, a ferruginous conglomerate, which extends in a narrow band from Hunstanton to Denver. Within that restricted area it was extensively used for buildings as varied as grand churches and humble barns. Here, at Denver, are late nineteenth-century terraced cottages in which the dark brown carstone is used as the main building stone, the contrasting decorative details being provided by the use of the pale yellow-grey brick which is found widely in Victorian buildings across south-west Norfolk.

New Buckenham was once a market town, but by the late nineteenth century, far from railways and distant from major centres, it had sunk quietly to the status of little more than a large village. As a result there was little incentive for new development, so that today it retains a wealth of vernacular architecture. Recent research by the Norfolk Historic Buildings Group has shown that many of the houses in the town have medieval timber-framed structures, often concealed behind later façades. In this view of the southern end of Chapel Street can be seen no.1, the yellow-painted house at the end with its jettied upper story projecting above the street. Its recorded history probably goes back to the 1540s.

sandy soils quickly deteriorated because of the intensity of early agriculture, so that native oak forest soon gave way to heath and birch scrub and by the time man was looking for a building material timber resources in that area were more limited.

Evidence of early timber-framed buildings is widespread from archaeological sites in the county. During the Anglo-Saxon period timber construction was sophisticated, and many excavated sites from this period have revealed the remains of timber-framed halls at the top end of the social scale (as at North Elmham) through to small rectangular and round houses at the lower end. Timbers were placed vertically in their post holes, but this almost inevitably led to rotting and deterioration of the structure. Later the laying of a horizontal ground sill, placed on a bed of stone or clay, allowed the vertical timbers to be slotted into it, helping to reduce the risk of rapid decay. David Yaxley's reconstruction of the North Elmham hall illustrates a Saxon example of these large buildings.

The best survey of Norfolk buildings prior to the remarkable and pioneering recent studies of New Buckenham and Tacolneston was that by David Yaxley, who researched the buildings in North Elmham which were dated to between 1588 and 1728.[1] He analysed fourteen probate inventories for the period 1584 to

Wymondham has a wealth of vernacular architecture from the early seventeenth century onwards, much of the town having been destroyed in a great fire in 1615. Many fine buildings survive in the very centre of the town, which is so often where commercial pressures and redevelopment have destroyed older structures. Here we see the gentle curve of Bridewell Street, with in the foreground the southern end of the Queen's Head Hotel (1616, though altered in the nineteenth century), then the very fine Old Manor House, built in 1616 for Richard Lyncolne and with its prominent jettied upper storey, and nos 6–8, which likewise date from approximately 1616. All were rebuilt after the street was destroyed in the fire. The Old Manor House has an internal beam which bears a moralising inscription of 1616: 'Live well and die never, die well and live ever.'

The Green Dragon public house in Church Street, Wymondham, is a building of particular interest. It escaped the great fire of 1615, and seems to have been built in the mid-fifteenth century as a shop. In plan it resembled a typical town house of the period: there is a hall range parallel with the street, with a jettied upper floor, and at the rear, not visible in the picture, a cross-wing extends back at right angles along the yard. However, its origins are betrayed by the ground floor at the front, which still has the lovely decorated wooden arches which originally formed an arcaded open shop front.

1614 and eighteen made between 1666 and 1728, dividing the buildings to which they related into two main groups: there were six small houses with ground floors of one to three rooms, and eight medium-sized houses with between four and seven ground-floor rooms. It was assumed that most of these buildings were timber-framed, and Yaxley sought to reconstruct their plans from the inventory evidence. Two examples are given here. The first is the house of Thomas Smith, vicar of North Elmham from 1580 to 1631. It was a three-cell building with a wing at right angles. Smith had a kitchen and parlour either side of the central chimney stack, while a buttery and dairy were at the other end of the kitchen and a brewhouse stood at right angles to it. His study was over the kitchen, as was the kitchen chamber; a chamber over the parlour was the main bedroom with a roofspace above it as a store room; and there was a corn chamber above the buttery and two small chambers above the brewhouse. A much smaller house was occupied by Francis Gillingwater, who died in 1635. The inventory implies that his parlour and the fire-house (the main 'hall') were open to the roof. Gillingwater had a small farm, with perhaps 12 acres of corn land, and he owned a mare, a nag, three foals, three cows, twelve bullocks and three pigs.

Houses of this type appear on many of the contemporary maps, for example, at South Walsham and Flitcham. The house of Thomas Rudd of Elmham, whose inventory is dated 1611, was of one and a half storeys, with a triangular upper space lit 'by small ankle high windows under the eaves or by 12 inch square openings in the gable'.[2] Yaxley quotes the interesting evidence of licences, written out in the Elmham manor court books, which allowed five oaks on the great heath to be cut down to repair houses, while in 1633 an elm was felled for the same purpose. Tenants had to maintain their properties, and much hedge wood was used. He suggests that many cottages were built of poor-quality wood, with timber-framed walls infilled with wattle and daub and with roofs thatched with corn straw. Some of the houses may in fact have been constructed of clay lump. The main reason that so few Tudor cottages survive today is that they were built of inferior materials, boughs and branches or possibly clay lump, and so simply fell down in the course of time. What seem to us to be small, quaint and vernacular cottages, common in many Norfolk villages, were probably rather superior residences at the time they were built.

Yaxley worked on the evidence of inventories for North Elmham where most of the buildings described have long gone, but in New Buckenham Paul Rutledge used a valuable documentary source, a manorial survey, to provide a base for the study of the surviving buildings which was subsequently carried out by the Norfolk Historic Buildings Group. The investigators were able to match some of the surviving buildings to the descriptions which Rutledge studied.[3] Those studying timber buildings here and elsewhere in Norfolk have gradually built up a catalogue of stylistic changes – for example, the types of joints and the size of timbers – and have exploited the potential of dendrochronology (tree-ring dating) which helps to confirm and give greater exactness to the dates of some buildings. The use of dendrochronology in dating the timbers in buildings has produced a valuable timescale of the major timbered buildings in Norfolk, or of timbers used in later buildings.

A dendrochronological table

Building	Dates	Status
Burrage House, New Buckenham	1694–1729	house
Felbrigg House, Felbrigg	1685	manorial
Abbey Farm Barn, Thetford (east gable and roof)	1628	monastic
Pinchpot, New Buckenham	1624	house
Marriott's Warehouse, King's Lynn	1583–84	merchant
Gunter's Farmhouse, Garvestone	1579–98	house
Paston Barn, Paston	1574–85	manorial
The Old Swan, New Buckenham	1573	house
Marriott's Warehouse, King's Lynn	1569–70	merchant
Abbey Farm Barn, Thetford (east end)	1533–36	monastic
Marriott's Warehouse, King's Lynn	1498–99	merchant
Oak Cottage and Yellow Cottage, New Buckenham	1473	house
Old Vicarage, New Buckenham	1451–52	civic
Great Hospital, Norwich (cloister roof)	1447–63	monastic
Dragon Hall, Norwich	1427	display hall
St George's Guildhall, King's Lynn	1417–57	civic
Abbey Farm Barn, Thetford (west end)	1414–39	monastic
Abbey Farm Cottage, Thetford	1405–30	monastic
The Great Hospital, Norwich	1403	monastic
Grange Barn Farm, Ingham	1380–81	manorial
The Great Hospital, Norwich (ward roof)	1378–99	monastic
Prior's Lodgings, Castle Acre	1396–1419	monastic
Prior's Lodgings, Castle Acre	1366–90	monastic
Prior's Lodgings, Castle Acre	1356–92	monastic
Lodge Farm, Denton	1355–1360	manorial
At George's Guildhall, King's Lynn	1347–1430	civic

Paston Great Barn was built in 1581 and, as an inscription on it proudly states, 'THE BILDING OF THIS BEARNE IS BI SIR W PASTON KNIGHTE'. This is among the largest thatched barns in Britain, a superb example of carpentry and vernacular architecture but also a powerful demonstration of the wealth which farming might generate when estates were carefully managed by confident and progressive landowners. It is not only an ancient monument but also a site of special scientific interest because of its remarkable assemblage of resident bat species.

The beautiful doorway at the southern end of Dragon Hall was built in late 1420s and is decorated with a very fashionable ogee arch, set within a more traditional 'Gothic' archway, and embellished with heraldry. Despite the exceptional quality of the building and its architecture, Dragon Hall , which served as the main trading hall and warehouse for Robert Toppes and his commercial empire, had a relatively short heyday. After Toppes died in 1467 the hall was sold, converted to residential use and divided up. Between the two World Wars (when it was part of a warren of squalid properties crammed on to yards and backlands by the river), it was almost demolished in a slum-clearance programme.

As the table on page 310 shows, a run of dates from 1347 to 1729 has now been constructed for Norfolk.[4] The civic buildings of King's Lynn and of four monastic sites provide some of the best results because they are major structures that have survived with a high degree of completeness, and in many cases had massive timber frames and floors. Because they are of great historic and archaeological interest the money has been found to date them. There are still many small manor houses, farms and barns that would merit similar examination. Where intensive research projects have been carried out on villages with known 'early buildings', as at New Buckenham and Tacolneston, many more examples have come to light.[5] This suggests that future research will greatly increase the available evidence and further develop our understanding of this key aspect of the county's vernacular building stock. The complex architectural history even of relatively modest buildings is highlighted by intensive investigations such as these. The Old Vicarage in New Buckenham, for example, is one of the earliest 'domestic' buildings dated so far. Its timbers were felled in the winter of 1451–52, and it is thought that it began as an open-hall guildhall, which was later floored with an upper storey, and had a chimney built at the west end during alterations in about 1612. Like so many timber-framed buildings in Norfolk, it was subsequently given a brick front (in this case as late as 1867). Some 12 feet at its eastern end were demolished in 1949.[6]

Flint can be seen in nearly all the churches of the county and in the cellars and ground floors of buildings such as Dragon Hall in Norwich. Later it was used in such major buildings as Baconsthorpe Castle and Mannington Hall, and this gives a common characteristic – a family resemblance – to many of Norfolk's great buildings. Flint can be worked in a variety of ways. Knapping, the shaping of the nodules to produce a flat face, often created a blacker appearance than that of unknapped flint. This could be used to decorative effect, allowing patterning. Elsewhere, as at Aylsham and Loddon churches, flint may give a lighter, greyer appearance. The medieval walls of Norwich and Yarmouth and the guildhalls of Norwich and Lynn further emphasise the importance of flint for prestige civic and community building projects in the medieval period, while its historic status as the architectural symbol of Norfolk has meant that it continues to be used for major new buildings such as the Forum in Norwich, where it is employed in decorative panels, and in the new walls around the Norwich Castle gardens.

Many Norfolk churches were built using flint, and it is a fascinating exercise to study the different forms and uses of what might seem to be an unpromising material. Here at Happisburgh church we see (to the left – the east wall of the south aisle) halved flint nodules, mostly oval; then rough and irregular flint rubble randomly placed, with recent repair work (below the window) in uncut nodules in very approximate rows; and decorative work of square knapped flints in the panels of the buttress.

Extravagant use of flint in cottages at Blakeney: here the quoins, which give strength to the corners of the house and the main garden wall, are made of brick, which is common in eighteenth- and nineteenth-century vernacular buildings in this area which has no stone. The infill is made of many thousands of small uncut flint pebbles, set in mortar. The front garden wall is made of flint rubble in coarse mortar, with a surface layer of similar small pebbles to match the house.

Aylsham church (St Michael and All Angels) is an outstanding example of flint construction, showing how the medium was as well suited to complex architectural forms as it was to the simple shapes of the Anglo-Saxon and Norman periods. The nave and aisles date from the thirteenth century, the tower from the early fourteenth, and the transepts were completed in 1377. The church was described in the eighteenth century by Blomefield as 'a noble pile' and he suggested that it was built by John of Gaunt – certainly, the powerful role of the Duchy of Lancaster, whose Norfolk estates centred on Aylsham, may have contributed to its very high quality and architectural sophistication.

Flint is widely used for decorative work but because it cannot be carved this is invariably in the form of patterns of flat-cut or knapped faces, usually geometrically arranged, set flush with the supporting stonework and therefore called flushwork. Quite widely in East Anglia this method was used to create emblems, such as monograms, crowns, quatrefoils and crosses. At the grand church of St Nicholas, New Buckenham, the buttresses of the west tower display, unusually, heraldic shields and other devices picked out in flint.

313

In towns such as Thetford vernacular architecture of the fifteenth and sixteenth centuries was often disguised behind later façades, especially those of red or (in Thetford) yellowish-grey brick which were erected in the eighteenth century to present a more fashionable appearance. However, recent restoration and conservation work have frequently revealed good surviving examples of much older structures hidden beneath later work. This pair of cottages in Old Market Street, Thetford, complete with twenty-first-century artistic adornments, was formerly the 'Good Woman' public house but was converted into cottages in 1910. It dates from the early sixteenth century and has a timber frame, jettied on the first floor, above a brick infill lower storey.

Nether Row in Thetford was in a block of four roughly parallel streets which filled the gap between the market place laid out in about 1200 and the Anglo-Saxon town to the west. This seems to have been a planned medieval suburb, probably dating from the thirteenth century. Today it is the only survivor, the other three streets having fallen victim to redevelopment in the 1960s. The decorative use of white-painted brick and flint gives these eighteenth century cottages a particularly charming character.

Although Norfolk lacks much stone suitable for ashlar, two important sources of Jurassic oolitic limestone have had great significance in the county. The Normans worked the limestone of Caen, on the coast of Normandy, and brought astonishing amounts into central and east Norfolk: the two outstanding examples of its use are for the cathedral and the castle in Norwich. But many parish churches also have quoins (the corner stones of right-angled walls) of this stone, indicating that it was not only employed in royal or aristocratic building projects. Closer at hand, but still requiring a lengthy journey by water and road transport into Norfolk, were the extensive quarries at Barnack in the Soke of Peterborough, which were owned by the abbey of Peterborough. The Fenland waterway system allowed large quantities of this beautiful golden-yellow stone to be moved westwards, and some even reached Norwich Cathedral. Barnack stone has a more shelly, rougher texture compared with that from Caen. It was used especially in the churches of west Norfolk, such as those at Terrington St Clement and West Walton. The only other local building stone, the carstone, is an orange iron-stained sandstone which lies below the chalk. This produces the highly distinctive appearance of vernacular buildings in a line from Hunstanton to the southern edge of the county at Hockwold.

The Golden Lion, at the top of the green in the centre of Hunstanton, is an attractive example of the conscious use of the vernacular tradition in a town which is in fact a late Victorian development. The railway came to Hunstanton in 1862 and a new town was planned close to the station and south of the old village. Buildings such as the Golden Lion were an attempt (and a successful one) to suggest that the town was not a brash upstart but was rooted in antiquity – its traditional design and materials imply that it had been there for centuries. The unique colour of the local carstone, a remarkable shade of gingery-orange, is well shown in this attractive building.

Brick was initially produced in clamps, open-air sites where the unfired bricks were covered over and baked and burned. The highly uncertain and variable temperatures meant that the bricks were almost inevitably of different textures and qualities, with a high percentage of misfires, but later purpose-built kilns produced bricks of a more consistent colour and size. The different 'systems' of laying bricks, the 'courses', give rise to distinctive patterns for brick walling. The earliest brick coursing was of English bond, with alternate courses of headers and stretchers, but by the beginning of the eighteenth century the Flemish bond, of alternate headers and stretchers on the same course, became standard. Valuable dating evidence can be found where buildings carry a date, such as that of 1666 on a barn at Colton. From the late sixteenth century brick gables were often stepped, and a more ornamental Dutch type began to appear on the grander houses of the yeomen and gentry. Blickling was one of the earliest major houses where brick was employed, and it has its beautiful brick barn and courtyard buildings. At nearby Aylsham there are some important examples of early brick buildings in the town, including the Old Hall, built in 1686 with Flemish bond and described by Pevsner and Wilson as 'a perfect specimen of an early classical house'.

The covering of timber frames with a brick skin was a major feature of many buildings after 1700. Robin Lucas made a detailed and extensive study of the Norfolk brick industry and the use of brick in buildings across the county, concluding that by the end of the eighteenth century – and prior to the arrival of the railways – brick making was surprisingly widespread, with 114 documented

Bayfield House (1 White Hart Street) Aylsham is a superb example of the fine eighteenth-century houses, often built by and for professional men such as lawyers and physicians, which can be found in most Norfolk market towns. It was built in the 1740s and is carefully placed so that it fills the view along Red Lion Street, then the main road from Norwich to the north coast.

brickyards in Norfolk. There were very few in the Broads, north-west Norfolk and the group of small parishes just to the south of Norwich, but other places, such as Swaffham and Holt, were visually 'brick' towns, and they had four or five brickyards each, even though their surface soils were sandy.[7]

Stylistic changes

Norfolk has numerous surviving houses of the lesser gentry and yeoman that were built in the century after 1550. Many of these were originally built as modified versions of the traditional 'hall houses'. In their medieval form these had a main hall which was open to the rafters and with one end separated by a screen from the body of the hall. The entrance into the house led into the resultant 'screens passage'. In the modified form a chimney stack was added externally on the long side or inserted into the hall, and a floor was added to create an upper storey. In the 1960s, when it began serious research on vernacular architecture, the Royal Commission for Historic Monuments developed a classification (using its study of Cambridgeshire as a model) in which distinctions were drawn between 12 classes of vernacular building. Classes A to D were medieval and sub-medieval, evolving from open-hall houses; H to L were broadly of the seventeenth century; and T to U of the eighteenth century.[8] In his work in Norfolk during the past twenty years Adam Longcroft has applied this broad classification to the vernacular architecture of the county. A typical plan of category J, which occurs frequently in Norfolk, is illustrated by Willow Farm, Morley St Botolph. Many houses were built or rebuilt following this pattern, reflecting greater prosperity for farmers, and perhaps especially those with secondary incomes from textiles. As shown by Longcroft,[9] the baffle entry from the front entrance was on one side of the central stack, and the staircase continued to be wrapped round the far side. With the introduction of first-floor rooms the stack may have had to carry three or four flues to allow each room to have a hearth. A different arrangement is that of Longcroft's type-T buildings, where the stacks were in the gable ends. Dairy Farm, Tacolneston, is a good example (dating from about 1640), and Longcroft points out how these houses were usually of a somewhat higher social status.

Rather than farmhouses being constructed or developed as long houses, with residential accommodation and farm buildings such as barns and shippons in a single row – as so many were in the north of England – in Norfolk a wing was normally built at right angles to the house but connected to it if expansion were needed to accommodate growing families or living-in labourers. This additional wing might have contained a kitchen, buttery and brewhouse with a chamber over, as at River Farm in Honing. The former kitchen, in the older part of the house, then became the parlour, and all the sleeping accommodation was moved upstairs. Alternatives or additions to that model included examples with single-floor 'outshots', which might also be used for kitchens or for storage: these extensions had the so-called 'cat slide' roofs. They were usually tiled, continuing the roof from the main ridge: tiles may have been more practical than thatch for the shallower pitch of this type of structure.

In lesser gentry houses staircases wrapped around the mid- or end chimney stacks gradually became less popular. Sometimes a stair turret was added at the rear of the house, as at Hall Farm, Ketteringham. If a house was being 'upgraded', the middle bay might be used for a full stairwell, which was more spacious and also gave a greater sense of design and thus status. Wacton Hall and Woodhall in Hethersett are good examples of this sign of upward social mobility. The practicalities of expanding an existing house often led to the building of a second parallel range, as can be seen at Waxham Hall. This allowed a significantly more generous ground-floor space than the 16- to 18-foot width of the basic timber frame. The next stage, which really marked the end of the vernacular, was to build square-plan houses, attempting to avoid the difficult problem of having a roof 'valley'. This was impossible if there were parallel ranges – a feature which is frequently still troublesome for modern owners.

Estate maps

Norfolk has a particularly fine heritage of manorial and estate maps, from the mid-sixteenth century onwards, and the buildings shown on these help us to reconstruct the appearance of settlements in the early modern period. Excellent examples include the maps of Cawston, Binham and South Walsham. The last-named, drawn in 1775, depicts cottages, almost certainly of sixteenth-century date, which are shown with single chimneys or, much less frequently, two. Small clusters of farm buildings are also shown. The parish of Cawston is superbly mapped from the years around 1600 onwards, and some of the smaller maps of the area are highly informative. The Binham map of 1655 shows a group of the smaller domestic buildings similar to that owned by Thomas Rudd of North Elmham, discussed earlier in this chapter. Many were of flint and brick. Two of the buildings on the 1655 map have two chimneys and two are shown with three, one of them being the manor house at the east end of the market place. The small terrace in the market place, which still survives, is shown very clearly.

Farm buildings

As the maps of Flitcham and South Walsham show, farm buildings were becoming more specialised by the early seventeenth century. The main building outside the farmhouse was the barn, in which corn would be stored after the harvest and before threshing. A threshing floor, open on both sides of the barn, allowed winter threshing of the corn and provided a through-route for unloading. Threshing the corn produced loose grain, which had to be put in a separate corn store, or granary, usually built clear of the ground on pillars or stands in order to prevent infestation by rats or other vermin. Alternatively, grain might be stored in the house, where the chances of infestation were much reduced: many farm inventories from 1550 onwards record the various grains in store, often on the first floor of the farmhouse or in the vance roof or loft space.

The barns themselves varied widely both in size and in the materials used for their construction. Those in central and south Norfolk often have a full timber frame and a structure very similar to that of the open-hall houses which were being divided or being rebuilt by the 1550s. Some were very obviously built as showpieces: Sir James Hobart's magnificent barn at Hales, built in about 1485, is probably the earliest brick barn in the county to survive. Its queen-post roof and great braced tie beams are on a massive scale. The building was 184 feet long and 30 feet wide, and its north end had stabling and accommodation for a stockman who lived over the animals. A regularly spaced pattern of ventilation slots prevented an excessive rise in the temperature of the corn which was stored before threshing. This superb building was originally thatched, and it has recently been re-thatched to return it to its original appearance. Near the coast are two flint barns of impressive scale. Waxham Barn has recently been restored by Norfolk County Council and, as the photograph below shows, it has a massive storage area: as at Hales, the roof is of alternating hammer-beams, huge tie beams and queen-posts. It is of 19 bays, and the building is 185 feet long and 35 feet wide. It was built by the Wodehouse family in about 1570 – they had acquired the estates of Bromholm and Hickling priories at the Dissolution, and much of the ashlar used in the buttresses of the barn is of such high quality that it might well have come from the monastic buildings. A little farther to the

The great barn at Waxham was built in the last quarter of the sixteenth century and is therefore exactly contemporary with the perhaps better known example at Paston. In the 1990s, when it was a state of great decay, and the roof had been wrecked in the great hurricane of October 1987, it was acquired by Norfolk County Council and restored, together with the two wings on either end which housed cattle sheds. Much of the magnificent roof, of alternating hammerbeam and queen post trusses, was replaced during the restoration programme.

north is the famous Paston barn, built in 1581 by Sir William Paston. It survives even though the adjacent hall has disappeared. The barn is 164 feet long and 59 feet high, built of coursed flint with brick and ashlar dressings, and with a roof of alternating tie beams and hammer-beams with arched braces and wall posts. Pevsner and Wilson argue that the hammer-beams are for show rather than function, so this barn, like some of the other exceptional examples, was built with architectural grace as much as practicality in mind.[10]

The brick barn built in 1666 at Colton shows that by the Restoration period brick was being used more widely on the larger estates in the county. It would be fascinating to know what the construction of these barns cost their owners. No accounts survive for the examples mentioned above, but a set of accounts giving a picture of the building of a brick barn has survived from 1710. It concerns the barn in the Great Park at Wymondham, a property belonging to the Hobart family.

The charges of building a new brick barne at the
Great Park Farm in Wymondham, 1710. [NRO NRS 16013]

	£	s.	d.
Robert Thompson and his men for making and burning 70 thousand one hundred brick for the barn at 5s. per 1,000	19	10	6
Daniel Stebbing for felling and binding 2,400 faggots at 2s. 6d. per 100	3	0	0
Stebbing for 14 days work in digging the ground to sink a brick kill	0	14	0
Small 2,900 faggots at 3s. per hundred	4	7	0
Day 1,760 faggots at 3s. per hundred	2	12	6
Day 21 days digging at kill and digging sand	1	1	0
Cushion 1,200 thorn faggots at 2s. 6d. per 100	1	0	0
Cushion 900 thorn faggots at 3s. per 100	1	7	0
Kemp 1,200 faggots at 2s. 6d. per 100	1	10	0
Edward King a mason in Wymondham for building the kill	3	19	0
Thomas Randall for brick for the kill	2	2	0
Edward King for building barne 4 hundred and 26 yards at 8d. per yard	14	4	0
Lime at 8s. 3d. a chaldron – 27 chaldron	11	2	9
Richard Kemp of Ashwellthorpe – hurdles (3 dozen)	15	0	0
Kemp for 300 table brick	0	12	0
Mr Sharper at the Common Staithe Norwich for 24 fathoms of reeds 10d. a fathom	1	0	0
[illeg.] –	0	12	0
Sand from Wymondham Common	0	12	0
Pittsand from Ketteringham	0	18	0
For fetching 60 fathom of reeds from Langley	0	8	0
approx.	120		
To the carpenter's work in felling timber – 16 oaks, 14 ashes	1	10	0
Dimensions spars 21ft in length, roof 72ft long			

There was a large wood within the park and also (as there still is) a massive hedge bounding it. The kiln was presumably sited on a good clay deposit, which is not costed. Nor do the sixteen oaks and fourteen ash trees needed to roof the barn appear in the accounts, so the bottom-line figure understates the overall cost significantly. At 72 feet in length and 21 feet in width this barn was small in comparison with the three already mentioned, but the detailed evidence for the building of the kiln and fuelling is very valuable. The barn was built of brick even though historically the area had sufficient timber – the town of Wymondham was rebuilt in wood after the great fire of 1615. Perhaps by the early eighteenth century timber was less readily available or perhaps the influence of the Hobarts, with their tradition of brick building at Blickling, was significant. The Hobarts owned reed beds along the river Yare and they held the lands of the erstwhile Langley Abbey, so they had access to reed and thatch, even though by this time these materials had been banned in Norwich because of the fire risk that they posed.

The towns

So far, this chapter has concentrated on rural buildings, but what of the architecture and form of the towns? Were they simply an amalgam of cottages and of larger two- and three-hearth houses – in other words, an organic development from large village to small urban community – or did the nature and functions of a town create changes in layout, with an element of planning? In the case of Binham the map of the market place suggests the former: that an existing rural village acquired market functions and thus in principle one of the key attributes of a town, but that after the dissolution of the priory the market, and the town itself, failed and sank back to village status. There was no evidence either of formal planning or extensive new building. A comparable example was Cawston, although there the reasons for eventual decline were more complex. At Aylsham a rental of about 1624 gives a more complicated picture.[11] In the 1620s not only was nearby Blickling Hall being rebuilt by the Hobarts, who were also lords of the manor of Aylsham, but much new building took place in the town itself. A number of these Jacobean buildings survive intact, while others remain but in a modified form. The brick façades of many

Even in Norwich a substantial number of timber-framed buildings of the late medieval period and the sixteenth and seventeenth centuries survive. In the commercial centre of the city all have gone, but on the outer fringes of the centre – the narrow lanes and small streets in areas such as Hungate, St Gregory's and St Giles – missed by large-scale redevelopment in the period since 1750 much remains. In Elm Hill the slum-clearance scheme of the mid-1920s would have destroyed two entire streets of buildings dating from the decades around 1500, but the rescue and rehabilitation of the area in the 1930s saved this wealth of vernacular architecture for posterity.

houses in the market place conceal earlier timber-framed buildings, often with cellars and aligned at right angles to the street frontage. For example, 18 Red Lion Street presents a Georgian façade of two shops with end chimneys, but the front of The Old Tea Room is in fact an end-on timber-framed building dating from about 1550, with a massive central stack almost certainly on the line of an earlier hall.[12]

A reconstruction of the centre of Aylsham shows how shops and other messuages were grouped around the market place with a secondary cluster near the mill.[13] This was a much more focused layout than that of smaller failed market towns. As the town developed and continued to prosper commercially, further building and rebuilding took place. Gradually a continuous façade replaced the more broken pattern of narrow end-on plots. The 1607 will of Thomas Halifax referred to his 'new mansion house' containing a shop and a chamber on the market place, providing accurate documentary evidence that this was a period of rebuilding and addition to properties. Furthermore, in Aylsham, as in other successful trading towns, the market place itself changed shape, and the plots fronting it became more intensively used. In the more dynamic towns such as this, as the land facing onto the market place became fully occupied by buildings, further alterations in layout took place. The range facing the street might contain a shop and perhaps some form of craft activity, as revealed by the North Walsham examples, with living accommodation either above the shop or in a range behind the working premises. Swan Yard in King Street, Norwich, is one of the few medieval yards to survive and shows a form of this layout. Access to and from the market place was crucial, but encroachment by buildings often made the approaches narrow, dark and inconvenient. To avoid the need to pass along these constricted streets – and especially on market days when there was so much congestion – back lanes which ran behind the houses and yards became crucial as a supply route, in effect the tradesman's entrance. Good examples include Paradise Lane and Vicarage Street in Downham Market and Back Lane in Wymondham.

Nelson Street in King's Lynn was described by David Lloyd as 'narrow, slightly writhing ... perhaps the most attractive street in the town'. It has many plastered timber-framed houses, some of them jettied with the upper floor boldly overhanging the street below, while the charming Georgian brick frontages conceal much older timber structures behind. On the right of the picture is the pink painted exterior of Hampton Court, built in the late fifteenth century as a row of shops.

This section of the six-inch map of 1882 reveals the quite extraordinary, and unique, street pattern of the ancient heart of Great Yarmouth, with the sinuous curves of King Street, Howard Street, Middlegate Street and South Quay outlining the shape of the sandspit which gradually extended south in the eleventh and twelfth centuries, deflecting the mouth of the Yare to provide a sheltered haven and creating potential building land. The most likely explanation of the hundreds of tiny narrow rows which run east-to-west across the axis of the sandspit is that, as the shore slowly shifted south, new lines of huts and sheds were built at the high-water mark at the tip of the spit, only to be left high and dry in due course as the spit grew further. Another row of buildings then grew up, and the older ones became narrow passageways. The difference in the patterns of development within and without the line of the medieval walls is remarkable.

In King's Lynn, and to a lesser extent along King Street in Norwich, commercial properties gradually expanded towards the riverside. In Lynn the channel of the Great Ouse slowly shifted westwards by natural processes, probably assisted by the extensive dumping of urban waste on the water's edge, and new warehouses were built on this infill. In Norwich there is little evidence of the river Wensum having changed its course in this way, but in King Street larger properties gradually grew into this space towards the river. In St Peter Southgate parish, at the south end of King Street, a number of properties had tanks in their plots for holding live fish until they were ready for market. In Yarmouth the unique physical geography led to a different layout,

South Quay in Great Yarmouth has a great variety of different architectural styles and periods from the sixteenth century to the early twentieth. At the north end is the great red-brick Town Hall, opened in 1882, and in the centre of the view is the Port and Haven commissioners' office of 1907, but the other buildings are mainly of the seventeenth and eighteenth centuries. These were prestigious addresses and the impressive Georgian architecture is a reminder of the prosperity of the town's merchants during its commercial heyday as an international port.

Holt was the oldest and most important market town in north Norfolk, its market being recorded in the Domesday survey of 1086. The original market place was a huge rectangle with a funnel-shaped entrance at each corner giving access from the ancient roads to Cley, Norwich, Baconsthorpe and Cromer. Over the centuries much of the market place was infilled by complex pattern of buildings and very narrow lanes. In 1708 most of the town was destroyed by fire, but it was rebuilt on the same property boundaries. In this view of part of the north side of the present market place some of the medieval infill blocks can be seen, with the lanes between.

with the merchant houses edging the south quay and their yards backing on to Tollhouse and Middlegate Streets. The celebrated Yarmouth Rows, with lanes only as wide as a handcart, ran east to west, densely built up with tiny one-up one-down properties.

The map of Dereham made in about 1757 shows the market place of one of Norfolk's larger market towns, which had developed under the auspices of the great monastery of Ely which had extensive estates in the hundreds of Launditch and Mitford, for which Dereham was the central place.[14] The map gives considerable fine detail about features such as chimney stacks, the alignment of properties, and the inn signs of the town. The compact built-up area, with its infilling round the market place, is very clear, and the shambles are prominently shown. This layout was paralleled in North Walsham (a manor of the bishops of Norwich), Swaffham and Holt, the north side of the latter having a particularly good pattern of narrow lanes and irregular blocks resulting from piecemeal infill.

Three case studies

The Mere makes Diss unique among Norfolk market towns – indeed, there is nowhere else in England with a comparable position. The lake is 5½ acres in area, with a maximum depth of 20 feet; the underlying rock is porous chalk, which allows the water table to fluctuate. By AD 1000 Diss had replaced Scole as the focus of this section of the Waveney Valley. Clusters of timber-framed buildings survive to remind us that the town lies in the wood-pasture area of the county. They line Mere Street, Market Street, St Nicholas Street, Church Street, Mount Street and Denmark Street; another group edges Fair Green to the south of the main road by the bridge. The town is wrapped around the north of the Mere, its splendid parish church providing a key focal point north-east of the lake and Market Street running down the east side of it. The most striking surviving buildings are the King's Head in the Market Place and Dolphin House, a former public house, which carries a date of 1520. At the junction of the Market Place and St Nicholas Street is a late fifteenth-century timber building with an angle post which has carvings of the Annunciation and the Nativity. The problems of the maintenance of timber-framed buildings are well illustrated by the history of the now demolished Guildhall. In 1755 the trustees gave John Barnard permission to repair a new floor, to redaub the walls and construct a new ceiling in order to provide a safe and warm room.[15]

Swaffham, like so many of the other market towns, lay around its church. Faden's map of 1797 shows the town as little more than one building deep, enclosing the broad market place. By that time it had the appearance of a Georgian, brick-faced town and today it remains one of the least altered in

The mere at Diss gives the town a unique topography and provides an attractive amenity in conjunction with the adjacent park. The medieval town developed around the north and eastern sides of the mere, extending down the western side in the eighteenth and nineteenth centuries.

The attractive sloping market place at Diss is dominated by the parish church of St Mary with its gothic framework supporting a weathervane (built in 1906 but a copy of an earlier structure). The market place, like those in some other Norfolk towns, was once considerably larger having been reduced in area and made more irregular by the gradual encroachment of frontages into the street.

the county. In the later eighteenth century it became a social centre for west Norfolk, with many resident gentry. Nicholas Hamond had endowed the town in 1725 with a new grammar school and with lands to cover its costs, while the market cross was erected for the earl of Orford in 1781–83, reflecting close links with the Houghton estate. A racecourse was established for the local gentry, and the town had emerged as a centre for the legal system. A bridewell was built in 1599, replaced by a House of Correction in 1787, and the shirehall was built as a centre for elections in the west of the county and as a venue for meetings of the quarter sessions.

The third example is Holt, which lies on the back of the Cromer Ridge, the great moraine of glacial debris left behind after the retreat of the ice sheet and now the highest and hilliest part of Norfolk, one of the most attractive areas of the county. The deep valley of the river Glaven lies to the west: the stream rises east of the town and flows south off the ridge, but at Hunworth makes a sharp turn northwards to reach the sea at Cley. Spout Common, at the west end of the town, and the gravel pits to the north, provided plenty of the flints with which Holt was built. As late as 1840 the flint and brick town was still just the frame around the large irregular Market Place, the only exception being a new suburb to the south of Albert Street, which included New Street, and a short extension along the Norwich Road. As the photographs show, an interesting mixture of buildings survived the great fire of 1708. A recent discovery at Norfolk Record Office gives the name of those who experienced losses in the fire, listing 57 owners of property and 16 owners of butchers' stalls. Mr Blyford, for example, the owner of a house in the Market Place, suffered losses of £520 for that and other houses. The Maid's Head, owned by Mr Dewing, sustained £300-worth of damage.[16] The church of St Andrew was much rebuilt in 1727,

The market place at Swaffham is perhaps the best in Norfolk, a great triangular open space which originally opened out from the main Norwich–Lynn road at its head. The town received its market charter in 1214 and it then grew, albeit quite slowly, until the seventeenth century: in 1620 it had 133 market stalls and fourteen shops. The market place is lined with late Georgian houses, many of them rebuilt after a fire in 1775 which devastated the southern part and the upper end of London Street. The graceful and classical market cross or butter cross was built in 1781–83 as a gift to the town by its patron, George Walpole, 3rd Earl of Orford, of nearby Houghton Hall.

with a 'feeble' restoration, and then in 1862–64 and 1866–74 was extensively altered by Butterfield who (according to Pevsner and Wilson) 'over restored it'. As the tithe map shows, the area of market stalls between Bull Street and the market proper was, like that in North Walsham, still in a medieval form in 1840 but by 1888 the stalls had become small shops, built mainly in flint.

Conclusion

Norfolk has a wide and fascinating variety of building materials and styles in its hundreds of settlements. The core of any village is usually, though not invariably, the church which, with few exceptions, is built of flint. Around the church might be some timber-framed buildings surviving from the fifteenth to the seventeenth centuries. Beyond the core are Tudor and Georgian former farm houses or small cottages. In north Norfolk many are built of flint, while those in the south of the county, as in Diss and Wymondham, use timber. Outside this core area of inns, forges and craft premises would be a scatter of larger groups of farm buildings with brick barns and one or two gentry houses dating from *circa* 1550 onwards, the latter perhaps within moated enclosures and set in their own enclosed and landscaped parks or gardens. In virtually every village there is also at least one Primitive Methodist chapel and probably also a Wesleyan Methodist and Baptist chapel, and occasionally Quaker or Unitarian meeting houses. Attached to many of these are schoolrooms and meeting rooms providing social focal points secondary to those of the church. The fascination of these many settlements is that no two, from the church outwards, ever have quite the same blend of materials, periods or functions of their buildings.

The 14.30 from Dereham to Wymondham approaches the overbridge at Danemoor Green on Sunday 1 June 2014, headed by ex-LMS 46115 'Scots Guardsman' running tender first. The line from Wymondham to Dereham was opened in 1847 and the extensions to Lynn in the following year and to Fakenham in 1849. Passenger services between Lynn and Dereham ended in 1968 and on the Dereham–Wymondham section in 1969, although freight traffic as far as Ryburgh continued until 1981. The line was reopened to Dereham by a preservation trust in 1997, and the aim is to extend it eventually to Fakenham.

15

1830 to 1914

T o those familiar with the work of the landscape painters of the Norwich School, who were active from the end of the eighteenth to the middle of the nineteenth centuries, the timeless images of quiet rivers – often with cattle on their banks – of river craft with large sails, and of rich woodlands in the surrounding countryside, stay in the memory. Their pictures of Norwich, perhaps showing the boom towers and boatyards, portray buildings surviving from the earlier days of the city such as those of the New Mills. Like Constable's paintings of the Stour valley, they have stamped our minds with memorable images and have captured a place and period for posterity. These artists did not want to paint small, run-down cottages with poor families around the doors, and preferred to depict a thriving and prosperous county, with beautiful rural landscapes and a lively and flourishing city at its heart. Despite this, however, to other observers the growing signs of stagnation and decline were all too obvious. By 1851 the population of much of rural Norfolk had reached its peak. Thereafter, many villagers left to move to the fast-growing industrial towns or, full of optimism, to take advantage of the apparently unlimited opportunities in North America and Australia. Government-sponsored schemes encouraged the unemployed to start new lives in the fast-expanding farmlands of the Mid-West and the grain lands of south-east Australia.

The establishment of a centralised system for tackling poverty, under the 1834 Poor Law Amendment Act, defined the way in which government legislation would affect people's lives. A generation later the introduction of compulsory school attendance was another step in this direction. The Factory Acts of the 1830s and 1840s laid down minimum conditions of employment and the Parliamentary Reform Acts of 1832, 1867 and 1885 shaped the modern electoral system. The rapidly expanding world trade in corn and meat was reorientating the English farming system, hand-in-hand with new patterns of urban growth at home. The first exodus of population to Canada in the 1830s was followed by a haemorrhage of people from rural Norfolk to the United States, Australia and New Zealand. Land values dropped as rents fell, and many estates in the county were put up for sale. The development of a rail network came late to Norfolk, but by 1882 all the main market towns had a station: some, such as Aylsham and North Walsham, had two, and Norwich had three. Against this broad picture of national and world trends, the often-troubled experience of Norfolk and its people can be considered in more detail.

1834	New Poor Law: sixteen new union workhouses built in the county by 1855
late 1830s	Large-scale emigration from Norfolk, especially to Canada
1844	First railway in Norfolk; network expands for next sixty years
1840s–1850s	expansion of brewing and malting; development of insurance industry in Norwich
1846	Repeal of the Corn Laws means cheap imported grain floods home market
1849–1852	The period of the 'explosion' of Methodism in Norfolk
late 1840s/early 1850s	decline of Norwich textile industry and development of boot and shoe manufacturing
1850–1870	The period of 'High Farming' in Norfolk
1850–1870	Colman's of Norwich undergoes large-scale expansion
1851–1861	Peak decade for population in rural Norfolk: thereafter, steady decline to 1970s
1850s–1880s	Restoration of parish churches and building of many new village schools
1850s–1880s	Rapid growth of holiday industry in Great Yarmouth, with two new piers
1850–1888	Reverend Benjamin Armstrong, diarist, is vicar of East Dereham
1857–1893	Bishop Pelham of Norwich revives Church of England in East Anglia
1866–1899	Dean Goulburn of Norwich further galvanises Anglican faith in county
1870s–1880s	Sandringham House and its estate bought and developed by the Prince of Wales
1877–1900	Major development of 'Poppyland' after railway reaches Cromer and Sheringham
1880s to mid-1890s	Wave of emigration from Norfolk to Australia
1880s–1890s	Major period of country-house building in Norwich fringes for wealthy businessmen
1884–1910	Building of St John's Roman Catholic church (now cathedral) in Norwich
1893	Royal Commission on Agriculture publishes report, with extensive Norfolk evidence
1890s–1900s	Poverty and declining congregations of many rural parishes
1913	Peak year for the Great Yarmouth herring fisheries

Churches, chapels and schools

The previous chapter showed how, during the eighteenth century, there was considerable religious upheaval in Norfolk, against the background of a Church of England which was beset with problems. Within the higher levels of the diocese of Norwich there were long periods of torpor and inactivity, and not until the middle decades of the nineteenth century was this lethargy ended. Of Bishop Pelham's long episcopacy, stretching from 1857 to 1893, Mason said that, 'there has undoubtedly been a greater development of church work and church extension than in any former period of that time'.[1] Pelham's primary visitation, his first grand tour of the great diocese of Norwich, was in 1858, and was followed by others in 1865 and 1872. It was noted that in the seven years between 1858 and 1865 some eighty parsonages and 247 churches were repaired, 130 new schools established, and a diocesan inspector of education appointed. The first diocesan conference was held in 1879. Clearly, the previously somnolent and stagnant diocese had been galvanised into action, and rapid change was in progress. In 1866 Edmund Meyricke Goulburn was appointed dean of Norwich, a post he held until 1889. Like his predecessor Dean Prideaux, he kept highly informative diaries – fourteen volumes survive, so that much more is known of him than of other nineteenth-century deans.[2] He had been headmaster of Rugby School, following a brilliant Oxford career, and was assisted by four quite exceptional residentiary canons: Adam Sedgwick, Woodwardian Professor of Geology at Cambridge; George Archdall, former Master of Emmanuel College;

James Heaviside, Professor of Mathematics at Imperial Services College; and Charles Robinson, Master of St Catherine's College. This amazingly erudite quartet supported their traditionalist dean, who expressed the view that 'cathedrals should be devoted to the cultivation of worship in its highest form; they should lead the way for other churches in the perfection of music and song and they should be places of meditation and deep study.'

Goulburn was in favour of the status quo and clearly took great care in all his appointments. He improved the cathedral in many ways, beginning with its heating system! He was a fine preacher and very much in demand socially. The deanery became an 'open house'. Goulburn and his wife Julia had half a dozen servants but no secretary and personally carried out a great deal of hand-written correspondence. More widely, he arranged for better endowments in order to pay improved stipends to the cathedral staff and, like Prideaux, saw the cathedral as giving a clear lead in religious matters in the diocese.

Many Anglican churches underwent restoration of some kind during this period. Thus, Cromer and Hethersett parish churches had their ruined chancels rebuilt and at Booton, near Reepham, the Reverend Whitwell Elwin dramatically rebuilt the church, removing the old west tower and substituting a pair of towers instead and filling the vast empty nave with light from wonderful stained glass. Lutyens described the result as 'very naughty but in the right spirit'.[3] As Norwich expanded a number of new parish churches were built, such as St Philip, Heigham, built in 1871 and now demolished, and St Mark, Lakenham (1844). In many of these parishes a new type of incumbent was to be found. A good example is William Wayte Andrew, vicar of Ketteringham from 1840 to 1889. When Andrew was appointed vicar, Ketteringham was a small, closed parish south of the main Norwich to Wymondham road. Having been appointed, Andrew acquired a new patron and squire, Sir John Boileau, who

The elaborate crenellated brick wall dividing the churchyard from the grounds of the hall at Ketteringham is highly symbolic because it divides the secular from the sacred, the church from its patron. In the mid-nineteenth century the irascible squire, Sir John Boileau, engaged in a bitter and vitriolic thirty-year feud with the vain and humourless vicar, William Andrew. The latter was a low church and almost Calvinist figure who vehemently opposed the squire's plan to place a memorial window to his dead wife Catherine, incorporating an image of St Catherine, for the saint would smack of popery and Andrew feared that the parishioners might think she was the Virgin Mary. It was, in miniature, a reflection of the battles that were raging in the Church of England itself.

saw himself as a medieval lord of the manor with the 'good' of his villagers as one of his main aims. Andrew, though, regarded the 'good' of his parishioners as his main responsibility. In his fascinating study *Victorian Miniature*, Owen Chadwick used their respective diaries to show how they clashed on many issues, such as the management of the church school that had been built by the squire. He noted that 'Andrew was an enthusiast in the best and worst senses of that term. He had no reading but the Bible, or books directed to the understanding of the Bible. ... If he went out for an afternoon's walk he took a bundle of tracts in his pocket and distributed them to travellers along the Norwich to Wymondham road.'[4] He was very popular with his parishioners, and many outsiders came long distances to hear him preach. His lifestyle was in every way different from that of the more famous Parson Woodforde. Andrew did not approve of dancing at Ketteringham Hall and was without question a very serious, though well-liked, cleric. His patron did not share his attitudes and therein lay conflict.

Diaries can provide us with evidence of the real feelings and perceptions of their writers. Those of the Reverend Benjamin Armstrong, vicar of East Dereham, give a vivid picture of the trials and challenges of running a large parish between 1850 and 1888. He arrived in Dereham and in his diary gave his first thoughts on his neighbouring clergy:

> With the exception of one earnest-minded evangelical and a young Anglo-catholic priest, I cannot say much for the numerous neighbouring clergy. Indifferentism is the prevailing feeling among them, and the farm, the Petty Sessions, or the Union Board are their occupations. They live like educated and well disposed country gentlemen, and seem to have no taste for the 'work of the ministry'.
>
> The lay people, however, are well disposed towards the Church, which is the more praiseworthy in a period of great religious excitement.[5]

Like Andrew, Armstrong was one of the new type of devoted and dedicated clergy. He was much concerned with the physical appearance of his church and persuaded the rector to pay for the repairs and improvements to the fine chancel:

> How complete is the difference between the former and present appearance of the chancel of Dereham Church. When I first came it was considered a sort of out house to the church! The pavement was broken, the furniture worn out and the place never used. Now it is beautifully painted and restored, and daily filled with the devout and attentive congregation. With candles lighted, the instrument playing and the departing daylight still coming in through the painted glass the effect is really fine.

Here we see clearly the influence of the Oxford Movement, harking back to the medieval period as a reaction to the views of the 'low churchmen' who regarded the appearance of a building as less important than the sacraments. In the high-church approach the use of candles, painted glass and colourful decoration was stressed as a reminder of the medieval past.

But the story was not uniformly optimistic and positive. In her analysis of the North Walsham deanery for the period 1898 to 1920 Susan Yaxley gives us a picture of the life of rural parishes at the end of the century.[6] Poverty and decline are prominent themes. For example, at Dilham church on 20 October 1901 there were just six communicants and an offertory of 5s. 9d. The comment was made that since there were 220 people in the parish, 'the average attendance at the Lord's Supper which last year was seven and this year as yet eight is sadly deficient'. On 16 August 1898 Bishop John Sheepshanks visited Edingthorpe

The little Primitive Methodist chapel at Binham, now closed and converted into a house, was opened in 1868. A simple, plain and neat building, with a classical style, it seated 100 people. It was in marked contrast to the very large urban chapels (or 'temples') which Primitive Methodists were building in major towns. This reflects the small rural community which it served – for in the mid-Victorian period Primitive Methodism was particularly strong among the agricultural labourers and other farmworkers of the remote Norfolk countryside.

Harriet Martineau was born in Norwich in 1802, daughter of a wealthy Unitarian cloth manufacturer. In her twenties she became an active campaigner on a wide range of social issues, with a special emphasis on women's rights, female education and anti-slavery, and became a prominent and widely read political philosopher. Her brother James (1805–1900) was perhaps Britain's leading religious philosopher and Unitarian theologian of the second half of the nineteenth century. As children they attended services at the Octagon Chapel in Colegate, and in 1907 a large Sunday School and Hall were built adjacent to the chapel, paid for by public subscription as a memorial to James. In the Norwich of their youth there was a powerful and nationally important culture of nonconformist intellectual debate and reform, including figures such as Elizabeth Fry (née Gurney).

church and his verdict was that 'it looks very poor'. The rector listed the very large number of costs falling on the parish: for example, he had to pay the poor rate of £35 3s. 8d. as well as many other items for repairs. His comment was that 'the parishioners will easily understand that very little is left for the comely adorning of the church'. An open-air service in the Roughton valley in June 1901 did attract a good attendance, but in Paston and Edingthorpe parishes, where the school was closed for 38 days in one year by order of the medical officer of health, 93 children were on the register but the average attendance was only 68 and this lost the school some of its government grant. In 1899 Tunstead school was closed for eight weeks in the spring because of illness, and it was commented by the school visitor that the writing of the catechism, a key element in a 'proper' religious education, needed much attention.

The major nonconformist development of the nineteenth century was the rapid growth of Methodism. This was prone to explosive tensions, as the movement underwent internal fission and reorganisation.[7] Between 1849 and 1852 these tensions affected both the rural county areas and the city of Norwich, as Methodist congregations went their separate ways, in many cases depending on the preferences of local preachers. A key factor was the authority (or lack of it) of the Conference, Wesleyan Methodism's ruling body, over the separatist elements and individual local activists such as W.H. Cozens-Hardy. By 1857 the Wesleyan Reformers had merged with other groups to form the United Methodist Free Churches, but in 1851, when the religious census was taken, the Primitive Methodists, originating in 1810, had become the main nonconformist group in the county.

Virgoe and Williamson, in their maps based on the 1851 religious census, demonstrate this dominance.[8] In Norfolk after 1810 the appeal of the Primitive Methodists had swept across the county, and in many villages a chapel was founded during this period. This denomination was closely linked to the craft trades and especially, and not surprisingly in Norfolk, to the developing agricultural trade unions. Major union figures such as George Edwards and George Ricks were adherents. However, this link was not always the rule, and in many places chapels voted against allowing their premises to be used as union meeting places.[9] Howkins quotes George Edwards regarding the tension between chapel and union: 'I will admit at once that the Nonconformists have not moved along these few years as fast as some of the more ardent spirits amongst us could have wished, and they have far too much ignored the fact that Christ came to redress social wrongs as much as to prepare the way for a higher life.'

Meanwhile, the Catholic faith, never wholly eradicated, maintained a tenuous existence in the eighteenth century but, as in the rest of the country, was reborn and reinvigorated from the 1790s as penal and restrictive legislation was lifted or no longer enforced. Public worship was permitted from 1791, but in Norfolk the small numbers of adherents meant that the building of new churches was long delayed. Having had a small chapel in Willow Lane, the Catholics of Norwich eventually benefited from the generous gift of the 15th duke of Norfolk, Henry Fitzalan Howard, who paid for the lavish and

The Roman Catholic cathedral of St John, Norwich, is (after Westminster) the largest in Great Britain. It was built in 1882–1910 as a mere parish church, to the designs of George Gilbert Scott junior, and entirely paid for by Henry Fitzalan-Howard, 15th duke of Norfolk. Scott, who like the duke clearly envisaged that this might one day become a cathedral, designed a monumental structure in the Early English style, which was then regarded as the purest expression of medieval architecture. The location, at the summit of the hill on Earlham Road, helps to give it a truly dramatic appearance, with its towering cliffs of masonry. In 1976 it became the cathedral church of the newly created diocese of East Anglia, giving Norwich two cathedrals, each a masterpiece.

The interior of the Roman Catholic cathedral is sensational and awe-inspiring, demonstrating George Gilbert Scott's mastery of the shapes and concepts of medieval architecture, and with particularly dramatic use of light and shade in the otherwise almost gloomy cavern of the great nave. Here the south aisle shows the attention to detail – marble columns, ornately decorated capitals – and the perfection of the Gothic architecture. As in any late Victorian medieval-style church, the architecture is indeed more perfect than would ever be found in a genuinely medieval building.

magnificent parish church of St John, built (to commemorate his marriage) between 1884 and 1910 on the site of the former Norwich gaol just outside the western wall of the city. Designed by George Gilbert Scott junior and John Oldrid, it marked the last flourish of the Howards in Norfolk and was on a scale befitting a medieval benefactor – seventy years after its completion it deservedly became the cathedral for the newly created diocese of East Anglia. Elsewhere in the county pockets of traditional élite Catholicism remained, such as the Jerninghams at Costessey and the Bedingfelds at Oxburgh.

The New Poor Law

The nineteenth century saw the beginning of a more centralised administrative fabric and the gradual creation of a system of local government which affected rural areas as well as towns and cities. The New Poor Law of 1834 was a sign of the future, with its rational and coherent structure and highly developed bureaucracy. The cost of looking after the poor rose sharply after the Napoleonic wars, prompting public debate about the financial burden of the poor law system and the logic and wisdom of the assistance given to paupers. There was a strongly expressed argument that the system encouraged people to rely on poor relief and discouraged them from working or supporting themselves. The new law adopted a more rigorous approach, creating a deterrent (in the form of the union workhouse) in the hope that this would reduce the expectation that the State would provide. Throughout England and Wales parishes were grouped into poor law unions, each centred on a market town, and each union was obliged to build a centrally located union workhouse. But in Norfolk the experience was somewhat different, because here there were already a significant number of older unions, the result of locally inspired moves in the eighteenth century to rationalise the Old Poor Law. The guardians appointed to run the unions exercised very wide authority, from choosing a suitable site for the workhouse and selecting the architect, to appointing its staff and overseeing its running. However, after 1834, in common with the unions in rest of the country, they were minutely scrutinised and controlled by the Poor Law Commissioners in London, who exercised a powerful influence upon the operation of the new system.

Under the 1834 Poor Law some sixteen new workhouses were built in Norfolk, in addition to the 12 earlier incorporations which already had workhouses and which were modified between 1834 and 1859. The best known of the latter was the Gressenhall House of Industry (opened in 1777) which

The Docking Union Workhouse stands amid fields about half a mile west of the village of Docking, beside the road to Heacham. It was built in 1835–36, immediately after the implementation of the Poor Law Amendment Act, 1834. The Docking Union covered a huge rural area, with 36 constituent parishes. The workhouse was built to what became a classic design, the architect being the county surveyor, John Brown, who was responsible for seven other workhouses in East Anglia. It had two cruciform wings, each linking with a tall central block. Today the north and south arms of both wings have been demolished, leaving two long ranges and the central block. In 1881 the 86 residents were in the care or custody of a staff of five. Of the residents 40 were aged 60 or more, and 16 were ten or under, indicating that the workhouse had become primarily a home for the impoverished elderly and pauper children.

The disused chapel at the Depwade Union Workhouse stands in splendid isolation beside the roaring traffic of the A140 a mile north-west of Pulham Market. The workhouse was built in 1836 and was designed by William Thorold to accommodate 400 inmates, on a model cruciform plan advocated by the Poor Law Commissioners. After 1930 the workhouse became first a public assistance institution, then a hospital and residential care home, before becoming a hotel and, now, converted into apartments.

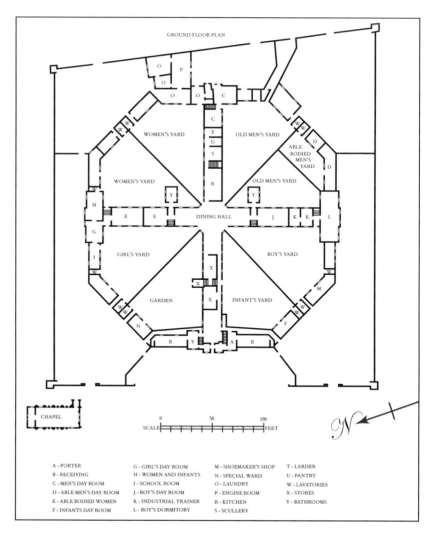

GROUND FLOOR PLAN

WOMEN'S YARD

OLD MEN'S YARD

ABLE BODIED MEN'S YARD

WOMEN'S YARD

OLD MEN'S YARD

DINING HALL

GIRL'S YARD

BOY'S YARD

GARDEN

INFANT'S YARD

CHAPEL

SCALE 0 50 100 FEET

A - PORTER
B - RECEIVING
C - MEN'S DAY ROOM
D - ABLE MEN'S DAY ROOM
E - ABLE BODIED WOMEN
F - INFANTS DAY ROOM

G - GIRL'S DAY ROOM
H - WOMEN AND INFANTS
I - SCHOOL ROOM
J - BOY'S DAY ROOM
K - INDUSTRIAL TRAINER
L - BOY'S DORMITORY

M - SHOEMAKER'S SHOP
N - SPECIAL WARD
O - LAUNDRY
P - ENGINE ROOM
R - KITCHEN
S - SCULLERY

T - LARDER
U - PANTRY
W - LAVATORIES
X - STORES
Y - BATHROOMS

The plan of the Depwade Union workhouse at Pulham Market, built in 1836 served the hundreds of Mitford and Launditch. Now a historically important group of listed buildings, it has become the home of Norfolk Rural Life Museum and the headquarters of the County Landscape Archaeology team. It had 60 acres of land and its own farm (which is still functioning as part of the Rural Life Museum). Wicklewood workhouse, just outside Wymondham, was also built in 1777 as the workhouse for Wymondham and Forehoe Hundred. It also had 60 acres of farmland upon which the occupants could work and provide fresh food. The building was paid for by the establishment of a tontine of 110 shares, each of £100, which meant that, unlike Gressenhall, there was no loan to be paid off. The Norwich architect Thomas Ivory and his son William, both well known for their buildings in the city, designed the Wicklewood workhouse. Elsewhere, the plans of the post-1834 Depwade and Downham Market workhouses show that great care was taken with their design, including the segregation of the inmates (male from female, young from old) and the provision of spartan facilities for working, living and sleeping.

It is never easy to reconstruct, as a historical or heritage exercise, the living conditions of the poor. Conditions were initially harsh, and rigorous discipline was imposed, but before long the system was modified and attitudes changed. The severity of workhouse life was ameliorated, and indeed some felt that for

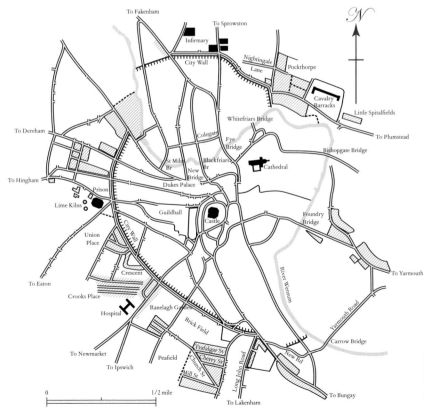

Norwich in 1830 showing (shaded) the earliest areas of development outside the line of the medieval walls.

the inmates life was actually better. The workhouses had to publicise their menus and it is this that helped to create the image of the 'pauper palace', the diet being better than it was in many of the poorest homes in the community. With architects such as Ivory and Donthorne designing these new and major buildings, some of which are now listed, and with their surrounding gardens and farms, the workhouses made a significant impact on the landscape of the period, in some ways similar to that of the new generation of country mansions. Over the doorway of the Rollesby House of Industry (1775) was inscribed a succinct summary of the aims of such establishments:

> For the instruction of youth
> The encouragement of industry
> The relief of want
> The support of old age
> And the comfort of
> Infirmity and pain.

This is a picture of social idealism that still has plenty of echoes in the twenty-first century.[10]

Social change

The population of England and Wales grew by 350 per cent between 1801 and 1901, but neither Norfolk as a county nor Norwich as a city achieved anywhere near this rate of growth. At best, population grew slowly, and in many parts of the county there was actually a dramatic decline in population in the decades after 1851, a decline which continued into the 1920s and 1930s. The experience of some sample parishes in Wayland Hundred, in the south-west of the county, can be used to illustrate this:

	1801	Post-1801 peak		Post-1801 low point	
Ashill	482	1861	721	1931	494
Breccles	139	1841	160	1921	91
Merton	134	1861	194	1911	133
Scoulton	246	1851	365	1921	224
Watton	693	1911	1,436	1921	1,331

Even Watton, the market town of the hundred, showed a decline by the end of the century. It was clear that outward migration, driven by desperate rural poverty, was a crucial factor in this demographic decline, a fact of which contemporaries were well aware: to the 1871 census returns for the hundred of Mitford a note was added, commenting that 'the migration of young people to towns and to the mining districts is stated to be the principal cause of the decrease of population in the Mattishall sub-district'.

The records of many Norfolk parishes show that the overseers of the poor considered it preferable to spend money to help families leave rather than run the risk of them becoming a long-term financial liability to the parish. The scheme promoted by Lord Durham in the 1830s to speed up English settlement in Canada is illustrated by the parish records of Shropham, which show that help was given to the James and Bilhouse families.[11]

Emigrants from Shropham, 24 June 1836.

The under-mentioned emigrants belonging to the Parish of Shropham sailed from the Haven Mouth, Yarmouth, on board the *Indemnity* of Sunderland for Port St Francis, Canada ... which is about 90 miles beyond Quebec.

		Age
William James } man and wife		42
Charlot James }		39
William		23
John		21
Charles		17
Sarah Ann		14
Benjamin		12
James		10
Charlot		8
Frederick		6
Rebecca		3
Harriet		1

Mary Ann 19 not to be found.

The Bilhouse family, with another six children, were included in this group. The town agreed to borrow £80 from the Poor Rate to pay for the two families to emigrate. The removal of 16 young people from the village affected its age structure in the future, and the population decline was notably rapid in this remote and purely rural community: Shropham had 411 people in 1801, and the figure had risen to 513 in 1851, but had almost halved, to only 279, by 1931.

In the 1880s further emigration was encouraged, this time to Queensland in Australia. Free and assisted passages were offered to 'certain classes': on 5 January 1884, for example, the journal *Daylight* advertised 'Free passages to single women and domestic servants who are in great demand and receive high wages and to agricultural labourers (single men) of 17 to 35 years of age'. Assisted passages were available to approved females such as nurses and seamstresses and to labourers such as ploughmen, gardeners, miners, navvies and their families. However, on 27 July 1889 *Daylight* published an article making it clear that all was not perfect and that among those who had arrived in Australia there were a 'number of men who were out of employ'. The Queensland Emigration Commission and their local agent visited many of the county's railway stations at fixed times to meet interested people. The officials came to Beighton, Long Stratton and Brockdish and 'stirring, convincing addresses being delivered, many more converts were made'. On 4 March 1889 it was stated that a large party drawn mainly from north Norfolk would be leaving to 'embark two days later for the Colony on SS *Lucetta*, which takes the new Governor, Sir H. Norman, also to the Colony'.[12]

Something of the complexities of the movement of population can be seen in a remarkable piece of analysis that has been carried out by John Peake.[13] The computerisation of census returns has made it possible to show both the places of origin of immigrants to a parish and that of emigrants, so Peake could map the numbers of people leaving the Glaven Ports and their destinations, as well as noting inward migration. He found that a large number had left Norfolk by 1881 to settle in Westoe and South Shields in County Durham. The men, perhaps not surprisingly given their Norfolk place of residence, were from shipping backgrounds and moved into related work in the North East. In County Durham in 1881 we find that there were 1,196 migrants from the Norfolk coastal towns, including 135 from Yarmouth, 135 from Blakeney, 50 from King's Lynn, 41 from Wells, 41 from Salthouse, 49 from Cley and 8 from Wiveton. The decline of the smaller flows of coastal shipping, the arrival of the railway, and the lack of work on the land, all contributed to this outward movement. Peake points out that Cley and Blakeney, though scarcely urban, also had some incomers from other, even more rural, Norfolk parishes in 1851 and 1881. Some 36 per cent of those enumerated in 1881 were born outside the three parishes but elsewhere in Norfolk. In 1881 94 per cent of Blakeney's population was born in Norfolk, but the total still fell despite this influx. The three Glaven Ports all declined between 1851 and 1881: Blakeney shrank from 1,107 people to 804, Wiveton from 245 to 184 and Cley from 980 to 720.

The increasing use of investigative royal commissions became a feature of Victorian government. In 1893 the important and very revealing report on *The State of the Agricultural Labourer* was published, against the background of a prolonged and miserable agricultural depression which had been damaging to landowners and workers alike. Commissioner Fox chose the Swaffham Poor Law Union as his case study to illustrate the condition of rural housing, and examined in detail the parish of Sporle, just east of Swaffham town. There, for example, he investigated the case of Frederick Bocking, who lived in a brick and tile cottage which was in a fair state of repair. Frederick shared the house with his wife and nine children, who ranged in age from 18 years down to a small baby. There was one main room 12 feet by 13 feet, a back kitchen 9 feet by 8 feet where the four boys slept, and upstairs there were two bedrooms.

Terraced housing in Melton Street, Melton Constable, was built by the Midland and Great Northern Railway Company for its employees. This street was begun in 1881, only a year after the railway arrived in the parish, and was laid out on a greenfield site, and was followed by four others on a very roughly planned layout, together with more straggling speculative housing down the hill and along Briston Road. The houses were, by contemporary standards, of excellent quality, and the use of patterned brickwork and varied alignment means that they do not resemble working-class housing in industrial centres – instead, the model is more like Crewe or Swindon, albeit on a miniature scale, including larger dwellings at corners and ends, intended for foremen in the works.

The former village school at Melton Constable was built in 1896, as is proudly proclaimed on the datestone, and enlarged in 1900 and 1906 to cope with the growth of this extraordinary industrial village. It was paid for partly by the local landowner, Lord Hastings, and partly by the railway company. In the courtyard at the front stands the roll of honour, since this was the most prominent public space in the community. The monument and tablet were designed by the engineering department of the Midland and Great Northern Railway.

The 1886 six-inch map shows the extraordinary circumstances of Melton Constable, until a few years before a completely obscure and very small village in mid-Norfolk with a population of just over 100. In 1880 the Lynn and Fakenham Railway was authorised to build an extension to Norwich via Melton Constable. It was opened in 1882, followed in swift succession by lines from Melton to North Walsham (1883) and Cromer (1884). This unexpected emergence as a major railway junction meant that the railway company chose the parish for a new locomotive works (opened in 1883), mainly for repair work, and a carriage works. The workforce grew rapidly, and a tiny industrial 'town' sprang up amid the fields. The map shows its first terraced housing (Melton Street). By 1911 the population was almost 1,200. The Midland and Great Northern Railway Company (which ran the four lines from 1896) provided a wide range of social and community facilities, so this was truly a company town. The works closed in 1936 and by 1964 all the railways had gone too. The population is now roughly half what it was in 1911.

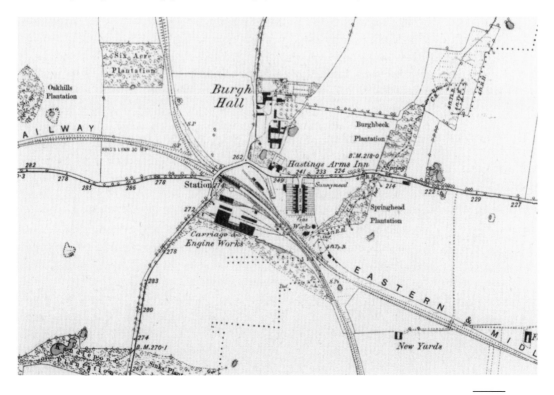

The family had a garden of about one tenth of an acre, a shed, a well 100 yards away, and a closet. For this, they paid £4 a year in rent. A note was added that the rural sanitary authority, a new form of local government established under the Public Health Act of 1875, had ordered the property to be closed because it was unfit for human habitation. Elsewhere in Sporle, the investigation recorded how an old man named Bullam, his three daughters and three grandchildren, 'all work in the fields'. This was a remarkably detailed survey, and such reports did much to challenge and demolish visions of the pastoral rural idyll.

By the 1880s, therefore, social and economic conditions in rural Norfolk were deteriorating rapidly. A letter from the tenant farmers on the Hare estate at Stow Bardolph, written in January 1882, makes clear the hardship faced by the labourers. The tenants requested a reduction of 20 per cent in their rents. In meeting a deputation of his workers Mr Hare explained his own perspective. He emphasised the loss and extra expenditure which he and other landowners had been suffering during the previous seven years, because of extraordinarily bad seasons and thus poor harvests, fierce foreign competition, increased taxation, and the rise in the price of labour.[14]

The sentimental view of rural England in the mid-nineteenth century, an image of happy rustics and a traditional lifestyle as yet untroubled by mechanisation and social instability, is one way of portraying life in a county such as Norfolk in the 1850s. The reality, as we have seen, was very different. In this alternative vision the undervaluing of labour as against produce must be stressed, together with the prosperity of the farmer/landowner: with labour so plentiful and so very cheap, it was possible for the owners of farming property to do well, at least until the twenty-year depression which began in the mid-1870s. The illusion of fair shares for all can also be refuted. The use of child labour, the ferocious treatment of poachers, and the final fate of the poor, driven to the union workhouses, must all be highlighted. Emigration to Canada, the answer for the younger and more determined men and their families, was a solution for some. Others were less fortunate.

For a minority the picture was less bleak. Some of the major Norfolk landowners, as at Holkham and Houghton, were providing new properties for their tenants, and their example was followed by some of the lesser estates. In parts of Norfolk the picture was one of slow improvement in the living and working conditions of the agricultural labourers. But the evidence provided by the survey of Sporle was dark indeed, and was the typical experience of many thousands of people across the county, but it was not invariably the case that conditions were that bad. Only patient research in local-history sources will eventually build up a more complete picture of the rural districts of Norfolk in the late nineteenth century.

The towns

In 1934, in his *English Journey*, J.B. Priestley wrote that 'Norwich is really a capital, the capital of East Anglia', and implied that it was a flourishing, resilient and buoyant place. A hundred years earlier Bayne, writing in 1833, had a diametrically opposite perception: he argued that 'the city was never in a worse state'.[15] Handloom weaving, for long a mainstay of the Norwich economy, was faced with intense and unremitting competition from the northern machine looms, became uneconomic and therefore underwent rapid decline. Attempts were made to provide improved transport systems to compete with the canal networks and nascent railway systems of the coalfields and industrial areas of the North and the Midlands. One instance was the construction of the new cut across the Yare marshes in 1833, intended to provide a fast route from Norwich to Lowestoft. Impressive in its scale and engineering skill, the canal was a financial disaster: by 1844 it was bankrupt. That, perhaps, is a metaphor for the industries of Norwich and the economy of its region.

Nonetheless, while the manufacturing trades of the city could not compete with the more dynamic and better-placed rivals which had emerged in other parts of Britain, some sectors of the local economy grew and thrived. The great market at Norwich, one of the largest in the kingdom, was praised even by the often-disparaging William Cobbett, while Bayne noted that the grain and malt trades were flourishing and that the livestock market was particularly successful. Norwich began to specialise in what we now call the tertiary sector of service trades, and in manufacturing which used the products of the agriculture of Norfolk. By the middle of the nineteenth century four great firms – Pattesons, Bullards, Morgans, and Young & Co. – dominated the important brewing industry, while the Norwich Union Fire and Life Insurance Societies, and the city's banking sector, became increasingly important.

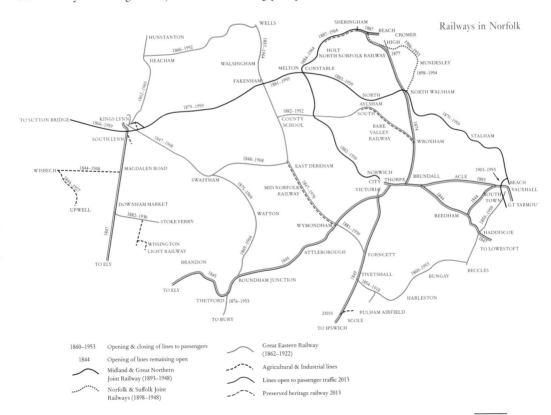

Railways in Norfolk

1860–1953	Opening & closing of lines to passengers	
1844	Opening of lines remaining open	
	Midland & Great Northern Joint Railway (1893–1948)	
	Norfolk & Suffolk Joint Railways (1898–1948)	
	Great Eastern Railway (1862–1922)	
	Agricultural & Industrial lines	
	Lines open to passenger traffic 2013	
	Preserved heritage railway 2013	

Norwich was the focus of the county's turnpike system, with long-distance road links to London and other major provincial towns as well as roads of lesser importance. Inevitably the city also then became the centre of the new railway system, developed between 1844 and 1880. The first line in the county, that from Cambridge and Ely via Thetford (1845), terminated originally at Trowse Station. Subsequently, the Yarmouth line came into Thorpe Station, the Ipswich line to Victoria and the last to be opened, the Midland and Great Northern route from the Midlands, ended at City Station. In many ways this last location was the most accessible for the business centre of the city but it came much later than the others and always seemed rather an afterthought. Eventually the London and Cambridge lines were linked with the Yarmouth line by the short connection at Trowse, crossing the river at the swing bridge, and this guaranteed that Thorpe Station (with its ample space for associated freight yards and carriage sidings) become the most important: Victoria finally closed for passengers before the First World War, while Trowse became a minor halt and has been closed for many years. The Trowse site, though, remained important for goods traffic: it was ideally situated to serve Colmans' new mustard factory, while gasworks and later an electricity generating station depended initially on the coal coming up the river but latterly on their rail

The City of Norwich Technical Institute, opened in 1899, is a fine example of late Victorian municipal enterprise. Its purpose, as stated on a commemorative tablet affixed to the building, was to provide 'a school of science and art and for technical instruction applicable to trades and manufactures'. The industrial base of the city had been eroded by competition (especially in the textile trades, by then almost vanished), and there was very serious concern that Norwich was, to use a modern term, deindustrialising. The institute was intended to provide a focus for innovation in design and technology which would reinvigorate the commercial strength of the city. Today the impressive building on the bank of the Wensum is the St George's Building of the Norwich University of the Arts, which traces its ancestry back to the pioneering Norwich School of Design, established in 1845.

connections. What had been a floodplain of grazing marshes until 1844 rapidly became a part of newly re-industrialising Norwich.

Other industries came and grew apace, replacing the old textile trades. Much the most significant was footwear, for which Norwich became one of the main centres in England by the end of the nineteenth century. Between 1841 and 1861 the boot and shoe industry developed with remarkable speed, the number of employees rising from 1,740 to 6,000 over this period. Many domestic textile workers moved from their garrets and took new jobs in the footwear factories, where they were trained to use sewing machines and other mechanised production methods.

The agricultural nature of much of Norwich business is well illustrated by the growth of Colmans. By 1852, on their new Carrow site, they were producing mustards, flour and cornflour, starches and blues (for laundries). They set a high standard in the working conditions for their employees and by 1864 had built a new school on Carrow Hill; provided a works kitchen and a dispensary; and employed a trained nurse, the first in any factory in England. The company introduced a far-sighted and pioneering staff pension scheme in 1899. Back in 1878 it had bought the Lakenham cricket ground for the benefit of the staff, and their wages were the highest in Norwich.[16]

Chocolate-making by Caleys, printing by Jarrolds, and made-up clothing also became significant trades. Later in the nineteenth century Boulton and Paul began to make iron and steel structures, including frameworks for buildings such as lighthouses, while Laurence Scott, the leading engineering firm in the city, was notably innovative in the years around 1900 when it began to produce electric motors and other modern products. Yet overall, and despite these dramatic developments, Norwich remained a low-wage city, its industrial concerns employing a high percentage of women and with a very low level of trade-union membership. The picture is therefore complex: although the older industries had gone, the crisis of the 1820s and 1830s had been overcome. But the new trades did not necessarily bring prosperity to the workforce.

This period is marked by further growth of the city, extending well beyond the line of the ancient walls. The Town Close estate, a wedge of property between the Norwich and Ipswich roads reaching to Cringleford, was the most distinctive development, with properties in large gardens on lease from the Town Close, a major city charity, for rateable values of £20 per annum upwards. This is still a highly desirable residential area. Muthesius suggests that after 1860 Norwich houses tended to be rather larger than those in towns such as Leicester and Derby. The emergence of large new suburbs was made possible as major landowners such as the Unthank family sold land off to developers and, in turn, to builders. The scale of this release of land, and the sale of sizeable coherent blocks, allowed a degree of town planning, rather than the incoherent piecemeal building so characteristic of other urban centres. Clement Unthank kept a meticulous record of each of these properties sold, and to whom, and in the area of Unthank Road the result was a large sequence of streets of terraced houses, with small front gardens and the distinctive tunnel entrance at intervals, giving access to several back gardens and yards. Some of these

George Skipper (1858–1948) was one of the leading Norfolk architects of the late nineteenth and early twentieth centuries, although his work is very little known outside the county. An outstanding work is the elegant and beautifully decorated London and Provincial Bank at the bottom of London Street, Norwich (1906–08). A classic of Edwardian Baroque, it fits cleverly into an awkward narrow space, impressive without being over-dominant. The rich decoration of the façade includes not only the chubby putti shown here, but also lavish swags of fruit and flowers which drape the sides of the round windows close to the roofline.

During the second half of the nineteenth century Norwich began to expand rapidly, spreading outwards beyond the line of the medieval walls along the axes provided by the main roads radiating from the old city. The attitudes of landowners helped to shape the direction and character of this growth. In the south-east sector Unthank Road became the key route, and on both sides a densely populated new residential area developed with streets of terraced houses. On this map of 1882 the parallel streets, newly built, have filled in the area between Unthank Road and the Norfolk & Norwich Hospital off Newmarket Road. The street pattern reflects the shapes of the former fields, as individual landowners collaborated with builders to develop their own properties and did not seek to coordinate with neighbouring owners to produce a logical layout – the very awkward angles and dead ends in the area immediately west of the hospital betray the way in which ancient property boundaries dictated the shape of the late Victorian suburb.

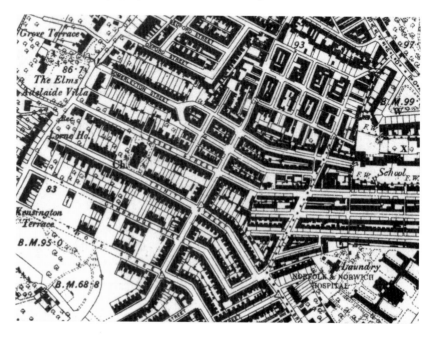

The railway reached Norwich on 1 May 1844 when the line from Yarmouth opened, quickly to be followed by the line from Cambridge (opened to Trowse in July 1845 and to Norwich Thorpe station in December that year). The city eventually had three stations, with Victoria (1849–1916) and City (1882–1959) long since closed. The present Thorpe station, as it is often called even though since 1959 it has been the only one, was built in 1886 to the design of John Wilson, in a style which clearly draws inspiration from the great European stations of the period – in particular, the great 76-foot dome and the port-cochère are reminiscent of French railway architecture. The ironwork and glazing of the concourse have recently been restored and the station now handles over 4 million passengers per year.

In 1913 Norwich Corporation opened a new purpose-built wholesale fishmarket in Mountergate, close to the Wensum, and the railway station at Thorpe. It replaced the old fishmarket in St Peter Street, which was at the top of the market place in the city centre. The site is now disused and the latest planning policies prepared by the City Council suggest that this may be the site for a new multi-storey car park.

areas of mid- to late-Victorian housing have now been demolished but others, such as the Arlington area, have been upgraded and improved and remain as attractive and successful examples of nineteenth-century development.

West of the medieval walls lay the Pottergate area, a district of tightly packed artisan terraces within which the new parish church of St Philip, now demolished, was built in 1870 as the focus for a newly created parish. To the north of St Augustine's Gates and Magdalen Street Gates a major area of development spread over the Wensum into New Catton, with new schools built after 1870, and a series of mission halls and new churches including St Mary Magdalen (1903) and St Luke (1914). As the families working in the new shoe factories and other industries moved out of the squalid and over-crowded yards in the inner city, improved transport became necessary and a system of electric tramways was laid out from 1900 along key routes such as Magdalen Street, Earlham Road, Dereham Road and Thorpe Road.[17]

In Yarmouth the herring industry reached its peak just before the First World War. In 1913 some 1,163 boats were fishing from the port, catching that year approximately 125,000 tons of fish. The herring curing and smokehouses were vital parts of Yarmouth's economy. Russia, Poland and Germany were the main markets, but the two world wars changed this pattern of trade for ever. In its heyday the herring trade was symbolic of the town's economy and generated

Norwich grew rapidly in the second half of the eighteenth century and into the mid-nineteenth, though the pace of its expansion lagged well behind the meteoric growth of northern and midland industrial cities. As the city grew, the area along the riverside, from Trowse upstream to Pockthorpe and Colegate, emerged as a zone of industrial development and working-class housing, albeit broken by the cathedral precincts and varied by the steep slopes on the left bank of the river. The Bishop Bridge gasworks at Gas Hill (no sentiment in that street name!) included four fine cast-iron gasholders of *circa* 1880, one of which can be seen across the rooftops in this view from the castle.

In the later nineteenth century there was extensive redevelopment of the area between the city centre and Thorpe railway station in Norwich, along the axis of Prince of Wales Road, which had been built in 1860 to provide a direct link to the station. Prince of Wales has become Norwich's notoriously noisy entertainment location, packed with raucous crowds on Friday and Saturday nights, and the solemnly substantial buildings at the top of the street have also changed. The headquarters of Anglia Television was built in 1882 as the Norfolk and Norwich Agricultural Hall, the foundation stone being laid by the earl of Leicester whose ancestor, Thomas Coke, had been one of the great agricultural improvers of the mid-eighteenth century. The classical building beyond is also part of the television complex, but was built in 1866 as the head office of the Crown Bank, and from 1875–1969 was the city's head post office.

The main area of middle-class and superior suburban development in nineteenth-century Norwich was along the Newmarket and Ipswich roads, where the trustees of the Town Close estate only released building land for quality development, protected by strict covenants and with an emphasis on social exclusivity. The development nearest the city centre, and one of the earliest to be built, was The Crescent, next to Chapelfield and just along from the site of St Stephen's Gate which was demolished at the end of the eighteenth century. Here the eighteen houses, consisting of two terraces linked by a central block, have small rear gardens but longer front ones, with a delightful tree-filled communal garden in the centre of the development. They were built in the early 1820s and remain charming, despite the incessant noise of traffic on the inner ring road a few yards away.

The terraced housing in Rupert Street, off Unthank Road in Norwich, is typical of much
of that built in the city towards the end of the nineteenth century and in the years before
the First World War. The characteristic Norwich plan for terraced housing involved shared
tunnel-passageways which gave access to the back yards or back gardens of a group of four
properties, the residents in the outer two having rights of way across the land of the inner
two. In this street, close to the city centre, there was extensive bomb damage in 1942 (the four
houses on the left had substantial repairs to roofs and windows in the late 1940s). In the 1970s
the area was the subject of an urban improvement scheme, with small-scale sensitive infill,
pedestrianisation of some short sections of street and the removal of through traffic.

powerful and distinctive social patterns – notably the armies of fishwomen
who came to Yarmouth seasonally from Scotland and north-east England to
gut and prepare the catch on the quaysides. This pattern of working survived
long enough, and the women sufficiently fascinating to early cameramen, to be
recorded not only in numerous photographs but also on some of the earliest
moving film to be shot in this country.

Yarmouth's second economy, based on the holiday industry, has already been
mentioned. In the later nineteenth century the building of hotels, guesthouses
and cheaper accommodation for visitors extended the urban area onto the
Denes, east of the walls. The mixture of buildings was described forcefully by
Hedges as 'a hotchpotch of conflicting styles guaranteed to instil a slight feeling
of nausea into the aesthetically inclined'.[18] After the arrival of the railway in
1844, and in particular the Midland and Great Northern in 1879, this industry
prospered and the town became a favoured resort for the working classes of
cities such as Leicester, Birmingham and Nottingham. The Wellington Pier was
built in 1853 and the Britannia Pier in 1858. In 1889, on August Bank Holiday
Monday, a correspondent for the *Daily Telegraph* reported that 'There never
were such sands or such songs as I heard on holiday time down at Yarmouth'.[19]
A description in 1900 stated that

Yarmouth stands near the top of the list of the most popular resorts of this country, very few towns having a larger aggregate of pleasure and health seekers ... gradually the good people have come to recognise the substantial advantages to be derived from the summer visitor. It is safe to say that no town is so solicitous for the comfort of its guests – no expense is spared by the municipal authorities to make the town healthy and attractive and their efforts are fully appreciated by the large numbers who are drawn hither increasing year by year.[20]

As many as 60,000 visitors stayed during the season and a further 20,000 on single days. The population rose from 45,000 in 1881 to 51,000 in 1901. The new Town Hall was built in 1880, the Winter Gardens were moved to Yarmouth from Torquay, and happy trippers caught their trains back to the Midlands by midnight!

Given its key situation King's Lynn did not grow as fast as might have been expected. Indeed, it lost population between 1851 and 1861, but it was reported in *Harrod's Directory* in 1868 to be a thriving port and market town. In 1854 the building of the Corn Exchange in the Tuesday Market emphasised its continuing agricultural importance, as a commercial centre for much of west

The Great Yarmouth Port and Haven Commissioners offices on South Quay were opened in 1909. Built of Cornish granite but with very good flintwork (notably the chequer patterned gable) this fine building was a proud statement of the importance of what was then still one of the world's greatest fishing ports. The carved relief on the gable top depicts a steamship. During the 1920s the fishing industry went into rapid decline, but the Port and Haven Commissioners oversaw a reorientation of the maritime trade and the modernisation of port facilities, culminating in the deeply troubled and highly controversial outer harbour project at the end of the twentieth century.

The *Lydia Eva* (YH89) now moored on the Yare at South Quay in Great Yarmouth, is the world's last steam-powered herring drifter. Once there were hundreds: in 1914 there were 1,006 vessels registered at Yarmouth, almost all of them in the herring trade. *Lydia Eva* was built in 1930 at King's Lynn but was based in Yarmouth and worked the fishing trade for eight years, but business was bad and in 1938 she was sold, before being transferred to military ownership. In 1971 she was bought for preservation, as the last example of her type, and in 2010 she finally came home to Yarmouth.

Norfolk with a hinterland that extended from the clay plateau in the east, via the chalk uplands, to the flat peaty fens in the west. In 1847 Lynn was linked by rail to Ely and London and also to Norwich and Yarmouth. In 1862 a new line to the Midlands was completed and also one to the north to Hunstanton. Ironically, though, rail development elsewhere meant that Lynn's important coal and river trade declined. To counter these problems, in 1865 the Alexandra Dock was opened, followed by the Bentinck Dock in 1883. These did increase traffic through the port (though the river trade never recovered), but overall the economy of the town did not expand to any great extent. The population grew little in this period and there was considerable emigration from the area.

Lynn did develop some new industries. As the port for an arable farming area it shipped malting barley and grain, while the demand for fertilisers for the same arable farms led to the establishment of a fertiliser plant. Three engineering firms developed: in 1851 Savages moved from Dereham to Lynn to make the 'Juggernaut traction engines'; from 1875 Dodman specialised in boilers; and from 1874 Coopers, the only survivors to the present day, began to make mechanical diggers. The town grew along the London and Railway roads; in 1893 a technical school was established; and in 1905 a Carnegie library was

The Hall Quay and South Quay at Great Yarmouth, from the Haven Bridge, which is the fourth on this site. The earliest bridge was erected in 1427, replacing a ferry (though a foot ferry continued to operate until the late Victorian period); the present bridge was opened in 1930. The town hall was opened in 1882, designed by John Bond Pearce, a Norwich architect who was also responsible for, among other buildings, the Agricultural Hall in Norwich. Pearce specialised in large, dominating and bulky red-brick buildings in a rather heavy Gothic style, qualities exemplified by Yarmouth town hall. Beyond is South Quay, with its very varied sequence of buildings from the sixteenth century, via elegant Georgian, to 1950s blocks of flats.

Victoria Arcade in Great Yarmouth occupies the site of Row 74, which until the 1880s was an exceptionally narrow passageway between King Street and Howard Street. The building of the arcade reflects the commercial pressures to expand the shopping centre of the town in the later nineteenth century.

The Purfleet in King's Lynn was used for small vessels from the medieval period, and a stone quay is recorded here in the 1540s. Warehouses were built along the quay and some remain today. The long low premises to the left were the headquarters and drill hall of the Army Service Corps Norfolk and Suffolk Brigade, as displayed on the large painted sign on the side wall of the adjacent building. The latter was built in the early seventeenth century and extensively altered in the mid-nineteenth. It has three vaulted undercrofts and was used for warehousing: it was formerly used for dry storage by the firm of P. Cortlandt, whose name and the words 'DRY STORAGE' can faintly be made out on the elaborate sign above the main door. The building was used as a wine store until the end of the 1970s.

The cast-iron sign over the archway of 19 King Street, King's Lynn, reads: JOHN AICKMAN'S FOUNDERY MDCCCXXVII. The foundry was in the yard behind, and Aickman (who died in 1843) also ran a blacksmithing business on the same premises. The firm carried on until 1877. The yard behind was originally used for warehousing, but its development as an industrial site was characteristic of the small-scale industrialisation which affected many Norfolk towns in the later eighteenth and early nineteenth centuries. Although it is often said that the county was bypassed by the industrial revolution, many small industrial sites did emerge in this period. Aickman's foundry, for example, supplied structural ironwork such as ties, beams and joists, to mills and domestic properties widely across west Norfolk and the Fenland.

built. Despite its doldrums in the mid-century, by 1900 Lynn was assuming the character of a regional centre, not only for north-west Norfolk but also for a considerable area of the eastern Fens.[21]

In the mid-nineteenth century the arrival of the railway destroyed much of the road and river traffic to Thetford but the rise of Burrells 'to the status of the largest traction engine manufacturers in the world'[22] changed the town. Charles Burrell, who lived from 1817 to 1900, developed the manufacture of steam engines for both static threshing and bailing and for mobile ploughing and drilling, and after 1848 focused especially on traction engines. By 1875 an even greater variety of fairground and steam roundabout engines were being produced. It was the major employer in the town but after the First World War, with the diminishing importance of steam power in agriculture, and the transformation of farming methods and technology, the works finally closed. The older Thetford industries – tanning, malting and brewing – continued

The corn exchange at King's Lynn, on the Tuesday Market, was built in 1854, the heyday of the Norfolk corn business and a crucial time as it followed the repeal of the Corn Laws (1846) which exposed British farmers to international competition and opened up the grain trade. The design is exuberant, confident and lively (Pevsner in 1962 thought it 'jolly and vulgar'), with four giant Ionic columns and a statue of Ceres, the goddess of agriculture, standing on the top of the pediment as though wondering whether to jump.

Thetford stagnated during the first half of the nineteenth century, scarcely growing beyond its medieval boundaries, but after the 1860s there was a modest revival in its commercial fortunes and some population growth. A few areas of new housing were added, including Castle Street, where in the late Victorian period a couple of rows of small terraced properties were built in the very distinctive local brick, with its characteristic yellow-fawn colour known (a little perversely) as 'Thetford Greys'.

and even expanded close by the railway. The watermill, which became a paper-making mill, developed into a plant producing moulded paper and has survived. Fisons fertiliser plant was nearby. As noted earlier, Cornelius Fison, founder of the firm, was a leading Thetford figure, and depended on river transport. The nineteenth-century recovery of Thetford was not to last, and after Burrells collapsed in 1928 the town was in decline until after the Second World War.

Other Norfolk market towns developed rural industries during this period, and East Dereham, centrally situated, is one example. Its population, contrasting with that of the surrounding villages which generally declined, grew from 4,385 in 1851 to 5,545 in 1901. Despite many proposals, the building of a direct east–west rail route from Norwich via Dereham to Lynn was never completed and the influence of the railway, though important, did not last. As the map opposite shows, Dereham in the later nineteenth century had many public houses, two breweries and a number of other agricultural industries. The map of the sale of Tuthill's Brewery in 1828 underlines the importance of such a business in the relationship of a market town to its surrounding area: nearly every Norfolk market town had similar links. The breweries had their own maltings, but the arrival of the railway led to new and larger maltings being built in Dereham to serve national breweries such as Whitbreads. The role of the town as a centre for a wide agricultural area resulted in the establishment of an iron works to serve local farming needs, while the carriage works reflected its position on a major east–west main road.

The charming cast-iron bridge of 1829, over the Little Ouse at Thetford, replaced a wooden structure known as the Christopher Bridge (the St Christopher Inn stood beside it) recorded as early as 1610. Given the importance of this crossing, on the London–Norwich road, there must have been an earlier structure. The bridge marked the head of navigation on the Little Ouse and just below it there were wharves where goods for the town were unloaded or were trans-shipped to carts for distribution to the rural area around.

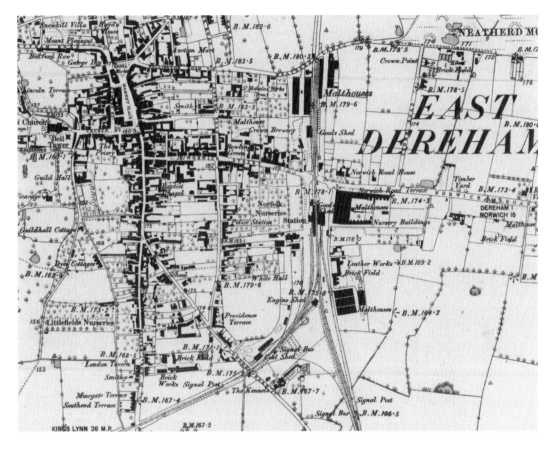

East Dereham (or Dereham as it is now known) was and remains the largest town in mid-Norfolk. It was a property of the fabulously wealthy abbey of Ely, and the administrative centre of their extensive Norfolk estates. This, together with its geographical centrality and situation on the main east–west highway from Norwich to Lynn, help to explain its considerable prosperity, in the medieval period and through to the present day. This extract from the 1st edition six-inch map of 1882 shows the parish church of St Nicholas (left hand side) and the great rectangular market place with three large blocks of infill buildings. In the eighteenth century the town emerged as a major centre of the brewing industry and the arrival of the railway (1847) gave this a further boost, as the great malthouse complexes and breweries clearly indicate – and there were at least 27 pubs and beerhouses in the area portrayed!

Similar patterns of development can be seen in a number of other towns in the county, with brewing and malting common to most of them. Diss, on the southern edge of the county, was the centre of a linen-spinning and -weaving industry which was in decline by 1800, but brewing remained important into the middle of the nineteenth century. It had three breweries in 1800 and four in 1845. In 1800 John Dyson bought one of the breweries from W.W. Simpson together with 23 public houses and a further sixteen which had agreements to take Diss beer. The county boundary had no significance in the service area which this brewery supplied. Harleston too had a brewery sale in 1828, when Kerrich's Brewery was sold with its 47 attendant public houses and it too overlapped the county boundary. Harleston's population increased from 1,662 in 1841 to 2,907 in 1901.

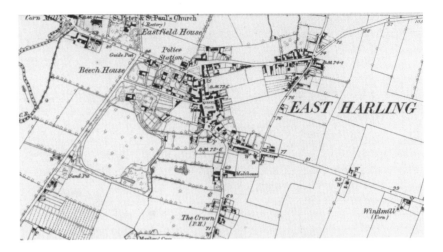

East Harling was one of the smaller of Norfolk's numerous market towns. It received its market
charter in 1475, obtained by Sir Robert Wyngfeld, controller of the royal household, from his
boss King Edward IV. Away from main routes and on the edge of the sandy wastes of Breckland,
this was not at first sight an especially auspicious location for market trading, but the huge
sheep and cattle flocks gave considerable wealth, reflected in the fine parish church and the great
twice-yearly fairs, and the market flourished into the late nineteenth century. The 1854 directory
records a wide range of crafts and trades in the parish (which had 1,200 people) and the 1882
map, shown here, portrays a local centre of some importance. With the exception of the church
the architecture of the town is unassuming, and the square market place of the late Middle Ages
survives intact.

Bidwell's Brewery and Maltings was the last
survivor of an industry which flourished in
Thetford between the fifteenth and early
twentieth centuries. The business was
family-run for generations and the Bidwells
became not only the wealthiest family in
the town but also (using their abundant
money) the leading political dynasty on the
corrupt and oligarchic corporation from the
beginning of the eighteenth century until
its reform in 1835. The brewery buildings
in the old market place, shown here, were
erected at the beginning of the nineteenth
century and closed in 1924 when the firm
was taken over by Bullards.

At Swaffham the Corn Exchange was built in 1858, its purpose proudly displayed by the roundle on the gable at the front, which shows a large sheaf of corn. The architects were the brothers John and Matthias Goggs, who practised in Swaffham but worked on public buildings in many places across mid-Norfolk (for example, the corn exchange at Dereham). Writing at the beginning of the 1960s Nikolaus Pevsner described the building as 'a depressing round-arched structure of red and yellow brick like a Methodist church', but tastes have changed and most people now consider its giant arches, patterned brickwork and decorative windows to make an attractive and idiosyncratic building of considerable historical interest.

Aylsham town hall, in the market place and occupying the site of older encroachments, was built in 1856–57, in a rather old-fashioned 'Georgian' style, quite unlike the contemporary Gothic designs so popular in larger towns and cities. It served as the headquarters of the Aylsham Rural Sanitary Authority (1872–94) and Rural District Council (1895–1935), a demonstration of the important role of such market towns as local centres for their immediate hinterland. Since 1974 Aylsham has been part of Broadland district, based at Thorpe St Andrew.

Pegs Yard, which runs off Red Lion Street in Aylsham, is a good example of a form of urban plan very characteristic of Norfolk market towns. Historically, at right angles to the main street were building plots for single properties – the house faced onto the street and behind it lay gardens, yards, outbuildings and workshops. Eventually, in the more flourishing towns, some of these backlands were used for small cottage properties, accessed by arched entrances or passageways from the main street. Where these survive they are now cherished as attractive townscape, but in the 1850s – in Aylsham as elsewhere – the congested cottages of the yards and courts were notoriously congested, squalid and unhealthy.

The map of Swaffham in 1882 encapsulates the successful Norfolk market town. With its good road connections and location near the middle of the county, but far from any competitor, Swaffham served as an important local centre. The railway station, gasworks, waterworks and cottage hospital remind us that the impact of Victorian progress and municipal improvement could readily be felt even in such comparatively remote places. The great market place shows the infilling which had taken place over the previous 300 years, with the Assembly Rooms, Corn Exchange and other public buildings occupying parts of the central area. Yet, as with almost all such towns, the countryside was only a few yards away, and there were still farms and smallholdings close to the market place.

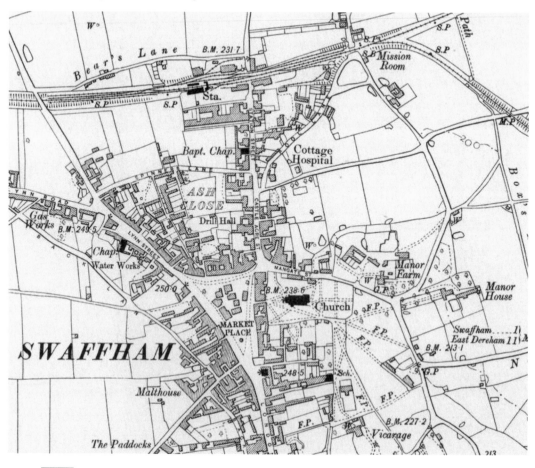

'Poppyland' and the Railway Coast

The arrival of the railways from Norwich to Cromer in 1877 and from Peterborough to Sheringham and Cromer in 1887 led to a rapid growth of the two coastal resorts. It also encouraged a lesser growth at Mundesley, with the building of the Hotel Continental in 1892, the Manor Hotel in 1900, and in 1898–99 the first big tuberculosis hospital to be built in England. In 1886 Clement Scott, a *Daily Telegraph* journalist, wrote his 'Poppyland Papers' and these, written at the time of the arrival of the railways, did much to popularise the area. He sang the praises of Overstrand and Sidestrand in particular, but his image of 'Poppyland' caught on as the marketing label for the whole of this stretch of coast.

Cromer and Sheringham offered holiday environments that contrasted sharply with the raucous working-class liveliness of the Yarmouth area. Cromer was regarded as the more 'popular' of the two but both offered the superb north coast of Norfolk together with the attractive inland countryside of Poppyland, as well as golf which emerged as a major attraction for visitors of superior social status in the second half of the nineteenth century. Cromer's development as part of the respectable holiday industry had begun as early as the 1780s with the building of a number of hotels, and as a result of its choice by Norwich banking families, the Gurneys, Hoares and Barclays, as a place for summer residence. In the 1850s the Bellevue Hotel and the Westcliffe Hotel were built. There were bathing machines on the beach, and the great medieval church was restored and its chancel rebuilt. Cromer lay within the estate of the Bond Capell family, who bought Cromer Hall in 1852. They owned most of the town and promoted and guided its development in many ways, including the provision of amenities

The name 'Poppyland' was coined in the early 1880s by the (not very good) poet and theatre critic Clement Scott, who visited Overstrand and Sidestrand in 1883 and wrote a somewhat sentimental poem entitled 'The Garden of Sleep', containing the immortal lines: 'On the grass of the cliff, at the edge of the steep / God planted a garden – a garden of sleep! / 'Neath the blue of sky, in the green of the corn, / It is there that the regal red poppies are born! / Brief days of desire, and long dreams of delight, / They are mine when Poppy-Land cometh in sight.' The name was soon adopted by railway companies and other promoters of tourism to refer to the stretch of north Norfolk from Sheringham to Cromer and Mundesley.

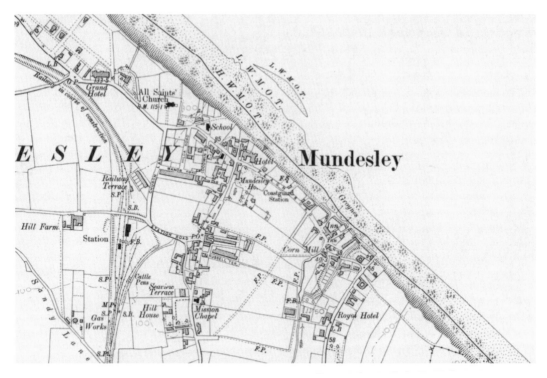

In 1898 the Norfolk and Suffolk Joint Railway was opened from North Walsham to the small but growing coastal village of Mundesley. The line was extended via Overstrand to Cromer in 1906 and can be seen under construction on this map of 1905. The main intention of the promoters was to stimulate the development of two major new coastal resorts, at Mundesley and Overstrand. An 1899 guidebook reported that 'Already Mundesley is "laying itself out" to meet the demand that will soon be made upon it as a popular holiday resort. New houses stand out in a contrast ... with the quaint dwellings in the old village ... and notice-boards call attention to "desirable building plots".' During the Edwardian period three hotels were built, together with a gasworks and other amenities, and the population grew from 411 in 1891 to 1,161 in 1921.

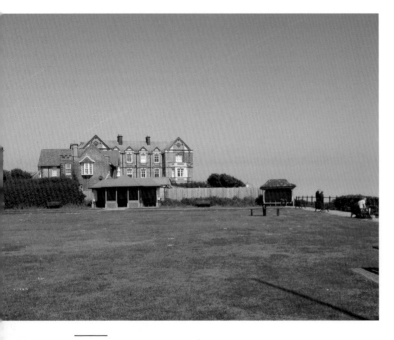

The Manor Hotel, Mundesley, was opened in 1900, a classic example of late Victorian red-brick seaside architecture. At this point the development of a resort was in full swing, and to give an air of antiquity to a brand-new building the name 'Ye Olde Manor Hotel' is picked out in white brickwork on the gable above the main entrance. The growth of the resort was faltering and Mundesley is now a curious place – not quite a village, not quite a town, with large Edwardian buildings and terraces of seaside villas scattered among older cottages along the narrow roads of the original village.

Cromer Pier was completed in 1899, near the dawn of the Edwardian Age which saw the town as one of the most fashionable resorts on the East Coast. Together with the creation of the esplanade and promenade at the foot of the cliffs, this marked the transformation of the old fishing community into a tourist destination of considerable importance. The last cargo of coal from Hartlepool was landed on Cromer Beach in 1887, and by then the fishing trade was virtually defunct, these workaday activities being superseded by the more genteel pleasures of the social élite: no less a celebrity than the Empress Elisabeth of Austria had lived in the town for several months in 1887.

The Cliftonville Hotel at Cromer, built in 1894 and extended in 1898, is the last survivor of three giant hotels which were built in the late nineteenth century on the clifftop west of the old town: the others were the Grand Hotel (1891), the site of which is now occupied by the blocks of flats to the left, and the Marlborough House Hotel (1885), whose fate was even more ignominious – the site is now a Morrison's petrol station. The building of these hotels, and other grand establishments in the town, was a response to the major increase in socially superior tourist traffic coming to north Norfolk following the expansion of the rail network in the previous three decades. The railway arrived belatedly in 1877 and soon, as a guidebook of 1900 expressed it, there were 'hotels of a size and magnificence that make the little town on the cliff seem humble in comparison [and] adorn the unpretentious seafront like jewels on the dress of a simple village maid'.

The links at Sheringham extend westwards from the town along the bracingly breezy cliffs towards Weybourne. Golf emerged as a major attraction when this part of the coast developed as a popular tourist area from the 1870s onwards. The light sandy soils were particularly suited to laying out greens and bunkers and the scenery and fresh air fitted the healthy seaside image. The ladies could stroll on the esplanade or promenade; the children could play on the beach under the watchful eye of nanny or nurse; and the men of the family could escape to the links and the nineteenth hole. The Sheringham Golf Club was opened in 1891.

such as the cottage hospital. Trains ran directly to London, stopping only at North Walsham, and the tourist boost led to the building of the esplanade and pier in 1894. Cromer's new status as an urban district from 1888 was marked by the building of a town hall in 1890.

Sheringham consisted of two settlements, Upper and Lower. The ancient parish church of All Saints, with an early fourteenth-century tower, lies in the upper village, while Lower Sheringham had long been an important fishing settlement and small port with a jetty which proved very difficult to maintain in the face of constant damage by heavy seas. Like Cromer it was largely in the hands of one family – in this case, the Upchers of Sheringham Hall, who held the manor from 1812. Sheringham Hall was built between 1812 and 1818 to the design of John Adey Repton and set in grounds landscaped by his father, Humphrey Repton (for which one of his famous Red Books survives). The National Trust acquired the house and the beautiful wooded park in 1987.

The clifftop shelter and pool at the western end of The Esplanade at Sheringham date from the mid-1920s. The Esplanade is an unfinished seaside development – it was started in the 1890s as part of an exclusive planned extension to the old fishing village, with the huge red-brick Grand Hotel (now demolished and replaced by nondescript flats) as its focus. The broad esplanade, edged on the cliff side by ornamental gardens laid out in the mid-1920s, stops abruptly at the edge of the golf course, but was clearly intended to continue further (aerial photographs of 1920 show a grassed-over section extending another hundred yards, and large empty plots of land where anticipated development had failed to materialise).

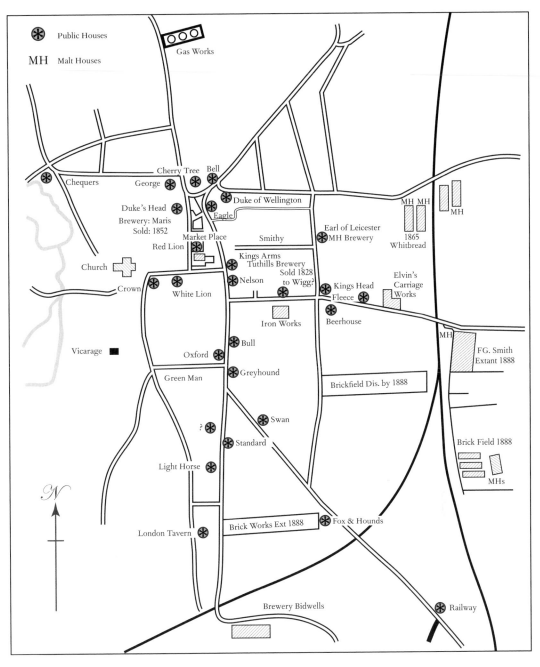

Industries and public houses in East Dereham in the later nineteenth century.

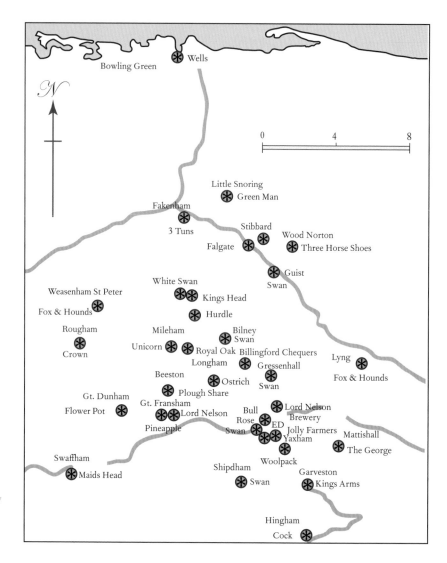

The Dereham Brewery
and its tied houses in
1828. ED marks East
Dereham.

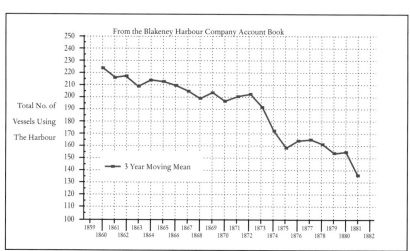

The decline of small
ports: vessels using
Blakeney Harbour
1859–1882 (after
Hooton, 1996).

Like that of the Bond Capells in Cromer the Upcher influence in Sheringham was considerable: thus, White's Directory of 1845 noted they had contributed a chapel-of-ease in Lower Sheringham and a school and reading room.

After the arrival of the railway the estate sold off 94 plots in 1893, and so began the real development of Sheringham as a resort. New roads were laid out by the estate and a good deal spent on improved sea defences, very necessary in view of severe storms in 1840, 1854, 1877 and 1912. The town spread eastwards along Cliff Road and a planned layout was developed westwards, behind the new Grand Hotel which was built in 1898 and demolished in 1974. On the seaward slope of the Cromer Ridge to the south of the railway a new development emerged on Hooks Hill. To serve this growth in population, which rose from 1,381 in 1881 to 3,768 in 1911, St Peter's church was built in 1895–97 and St Joseph's Roman Catholic church in 1908–09. A golf course, Gurneys' Bank and urban council offices underlined the growing sophistication of the town.

Sheringham's fishing economy still survived: a directory of 1875 refers to 200 boats fishing for cod, skate, whiting, crab and lobster; there were five rope-spinning yards, five whelk coppers and three boatbuilders. As late as 1903 there were still 80 fishing boats and 300 fishermen. The great change in the atmosphere of Sheringham is seen by comparing the observation given by the Craskes in the 1870s – that it contained 'fair specimens of probably every filthy smell in the county. The coast is dangerous and drowning the commonest shape in which death visits the village' – with that of *The Lady* on 31 August 1893 which sang its praises: 'not only does Sheringham boast of those quiet seaside attractions but when tired the holiday-keeper can wander inland and roam deep in the lovely beech woods at the back. Here in the springtime can be found quantities of primroses, delicate wood sorrel and banks blue with wild hyacinths.' Sheringham retained a rather more peaceful atmosphere than its larger neighbour.[23]

Cley, Blakeney and Wiveton, at the mouth of the river Glaven, were collectively known as the Port of Blakeney, which continued to flourish for much of the nineteenth century. The railway never reached the area, and the small ports retained their trade serving the agricultural hinterland. Hooton's study of *The Glaven Ports* contains much detailed analysis of this trade.[24] Business fell away sharply in the 1880s, but until then passengers were still sailing from the Glaven to Newcastle and even London; the imports were chiefly coal, timber and oilcake and the exports were grain and flour. As the shipping declined, some local traders turned to oyster, crab and mussel catching and used the railway from Holt to get the produce to the markets quickly, but by 1900 Kelly's Directory reported that 'very few vessels are now employed in oyster fishing'.

Further west lies Wells-next-the-Sea, with a better protected harbour compared with the open coast of Cromer and Sheringham. It too lies virtually within the bounds of one estate, that of the Cokes of Holkham, and this has always been a limiting factor in expansion to the west. The harbour is the outlet for only a very small stream, but it is protected by a wide stretch of salt marsh and a series of dunes beyond this. It has, however, had many problems of silting and awkward access: there were major reports on its possible improvement, by

Mylne in 1781 and by Smeaton in 1782, and Acts of Parliament were passed in 1663, 1769, 1839 and 1844 in order to improve the position. At first the natural creek between the church and a seaward spur of upland provided a well-sheltered site, but this was cut off by an embankment built in 1760 by Sir Charles Turner of Warham. He also constructed the first bank to the north of the quay to improve the outlet and this was later extended by the earl of Leicester along its present alignment.[25] In 1845 White's Directory listed seventeen master mariners of whom three owned boats, seven pilots, four rope makers and one boatbuilder, and there were 67 vessels registered at Wells. The main imports were rape, linseed cake, coal and timber and the main exports were corn and oysters. The oyster and mussel beds were very productive.

The town has a grid-like plan; Pevsner and Wilson suggest that it may date from a charter of 1202 which allowed Ramsey Abbey to expand the town and use it for grain exports. The church, rebuilt after a fire of 1879, lies well back from the present town in relation to the earlier creek. Another suggestion is that the south–north lines of the streets may have been needed to move sheep from the arable upland to summer grazings on the marshes. The quay is the focus of the town, and the Buttlands perhaps the most attractive part architecturally. The arrival of the railway from Dereham in 1857 and from King's Lynn in 1866 did not lead to any rapid growth – indeed the population dropped from 3,657 in 1851 to 3,450 by 1861. This phenomenon was, as we have seen, not unusual for Norfolk villages but was exceptional for one of the small towns. There was no sudden development of hotels or boarding houses, and Wells was, like Thetford, under-provided with modern drainage. An Act of 1844 was passed to improve the quality of its roads and in 1891 a report on its deplorable sanitary conditions was produced. Within a few years change was under way. By 1905 the first guide to the town and its surrounding area had been published and Wells was beginning to be discovered by tourists.

In north-west Norfolk, Old Hunstanton was another estate village, owned by the long-established le Strange family. In 1845 Henry le Strange decided to build a carefully planned, socially select new town in his parish. He wrote that it was to be built 'with the view to meeting the express desires of many families in Norfolk and neighbouring counties to have the opportunity of enjoying the advantage of sea air and prospects'. The young William Butterfield was appointed as architect in 1845, and le Strange reported that he was 'delighted with the idea of having a place to build *de Novo*, we propose to have it all in the Old English style'. The original plan of detached cottages around a village green was unbalanced by the arrival of the railway in 1862, and several terraces took their place. A sizeable town eventually developed, and New Hunstanton, as it was christened, became a popular place for family seaside holidays. Carstone was much used in building the town and this, together with its carefully planned origins, gave an attractive unity to the new buildings.[26]

The great estates

By the middle of the nineteenth century farming in Norfolk had recovered from the depression which followed the Napoleonic wars. J.J. Mechi, in his *How to Farm Profitably*, published in 1864, commented that 'the more meat you produce the more manure you make and consequently the more corn you will grow on the arable portion', a philosophy willingly espoused by Norfolk farmers and landowners. Holderness argued that the high yields of barley in east Norfolk, on good soils, preceded the classic 'high-farming' period between 1850 and 1870 because the good management of bullocks for their dung had been long established: 'East Norfolk husbandry deserves its reputation as the cradle of high farming in Britain.'[27] The barley straw provided forage and litter, but the lynch-pin of the system of intensive fattening was the turnip, which, with the barley straw, had fattened Norfolk bullocks from as early as the 1680s, a pattern which lasted into the mid-nineteenth century. Turnips fed sheep in west Norfolk, and bullocks but not dairy cows in east Norfolk (where a diet of turnips was found to taint the milk and render it unpalatable).

The keeping of large numbers of bullocks led to the cover, or housing, of stock in large farmyard complexes with central turnip houses. By 1850 bullock sheds, often very expensively built, had become the rule, and the sophisticated 'winged' stock yard began to appear. John Hudson, a Holkham tenant at Castle Acre, has already been noted as a high farmer *par excellence*. In this period he was using oil cake, linseed and rape oil and buying 150 to 200 tons of feed a year for his 1,500 acre estate, on which he wintered between 100 and 140 steers; this cost him between £2,500 and £3,000 per annum. The significance of new agricultural machinery must also be noted. When Hudson died in 1869, his farm sale included 30 ploughs and harrows, scarifiers, cultivators and rollers, a reaping machine, and a threshing drum powered by a steam engine.[28] This emphasises that the steam engine had arrived, but that it was still only suitable for large farms. The rapid growth of Burrells in Thetford shows how the agricultural engineering industry was developing quickly by this date.

Farm leases were important contributions to the new meat-producing farming in what was still primarily an arable area. Stipulations as to cropping patterns varied from six-course shifts to the Norfolk four-course system, but Wade Martins and Williamson argue that leases were there to be altered. As these changed, tenant farmers could begin to switch emphasis and to reorientate their farming practices. Marling was an important element of many leases, one of the foundation stones of the Agricultural Revolution. Crop yields increased in the eighteenth century, a trend to which field drainage improvements and the use of artificial fertilisers contributed greatly. In 1842 Lawes patented a method of making superphosphates for fertilisers, and guano was imported from South America after the 1850s. These products came at a hefty price, so they were used on cereals but not on turnips.

The influence of the large estates has been highlighted as a major theme in Norfolk history, and this importance continued into the twentieth century. Some of the long-established estates, such as Holkham, Houghton, Blickling and Hunstanton, continued to maintain a prominent role. Holkham was perhaps the outstanding instance, but in other cases new wealth took over and funded development. Sandringham is, of course, best known as the royal family's Norfolk home. In 1862 the Prince of Wales, the future Edward VII, bought the estate from Charles Cowper for £220,000. The original house, built in 1771, was replaced in 1870 by what Pevsner and Wilson describe as a mansion in 'frenetic Jacobean' style. After a fire in 1891 had damaged the upper parts of the house a second storey was added. The house is of brick with Ketton stone dressings, and the estate walls are of carstone with brick dressings. A proposal in 1960 to demolish the house and rebuild it in a contemporary style was resisted. The gardens were laid out in 1860 and the two lakes dug in the 1870s. Intensive and extensive planting of what was formerly an open heath with many rhododendrons and pine trees has produced a new wooded landscape, across an estate of more than 7,000 acres which includes Wolferton, Babingley, West Newton and parts of Appleton and Dersingham.

The 7,000-acre Sandringham estate was purchased in 1862 by the Prince of Wales (later Edward VII) and the existing unremarkable house was demolished. It was replaced between 1870 and 1883 by a vast Victorian mansion in Jacobean style which, in the words of Miranda Carter, was 'the height of modern British aristocratic comfort … with thirty flushing lavatories ordered from Thomas Crapper & Co.'. The remodelling of the great estate continued apace, with huge plantation woodlands (essential for game cover), pheasantries, a completely rebuilt village of model cottages at West Newton, and vast lawns, lakes and shrubberies. It quickly became a dominant element in the landscape and social structure of north-west Norfolk, providing a great deal of employment (in 1901, for example, there were 13 gardeners and 12 domestic grooms living in accommodation in the stable yard) and today making a major contribution to the local economy as a leading tourist attraction.

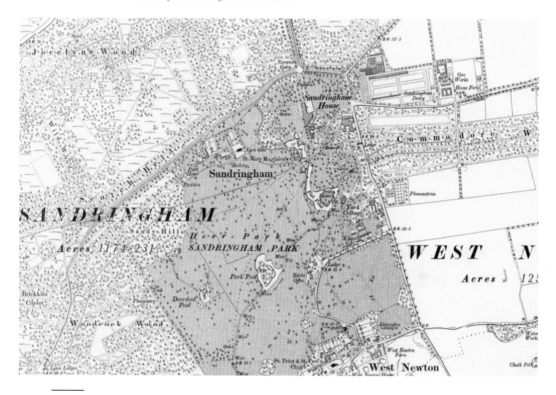

At Haveringland a remarkably well documented house was built rather earlier, between 1839 and 1842, for Edward Fellowes. It was designed by Edward Blore, the architect of Buckingham Palace.[29] Fellowes was a wealthy man with a large estate at Ramsey Abbey in Huntingdonshire, where Blore had already built another large house for the family between 1837 and 1839. The extraordinary dominance of landed estates is Norfolk is revealed by the fact that although in 1873 Fellowes had 4,083 acres in the county, he was ranked only 50th in the league table of Norfolk landowners! Haveringland was built in the 'Italianate' style, with its south-west and east faces in Bath stone. This had to be moved, at vast expense, to Yarmouth and Norwich by boat and then along the Cromer turnpike to Haveringland. The rest of the large complex was constructed of locally kilned brick and the well-wooded estate provided a quarter of the timber. As the estate map shows, much of the sandy heath to the east of the parish had already been planted by this time but more followed. Mackley showed that 86 men were at work at the peak stage of building and that 249 in total had worked on it. The cost, carefully controlled by Blore and minutely recorded in the accounts, was £38,595 18s. 8½d., and over 60 years a further £45,000 was spent on it. Furniture was brought in by road from London, not Norwich. The rental of the Norfolk estate was insufficient for all this extravagant spending, and it could only be funded with extra income from the Ramsey estate. A project such as this was of great benefit to the nearby community while it was under construction, because it needed a huge labour force, and afterwards employment in the gardens, woodlands, farmlands and the house itself was a major factor in the local economy; a gasworks sufficient to fuel 100 lights used further labour. But the prodigious cost of maintaining this house took its toll. It was a 'white elephant', and after a period of wartime occupation was demolished in 1952. By then the estate had lost much of its ornate woodland to an airfield, and turkey sheds now cover areas of former runways.

The prosperity of Norwich, in the heyday of the worsted trade, allowed many merchants and newly wealthy bankers to acquire country property and build new houses around the fringes of the city. A ring of such estates appeared. Some owners, such as the Harveys, who were brewers and bankers, bought old manor houses and replaced them with new halls. Catton Park was built by the Ives and then taken over by the Harveys. The park was laid out by Humphrey Repton as his first commission and it is now listed, providing a valuable green space close to Norwich. Others built anew. In 1865 Crown Point Hall was built south of the city by Sir Robert John Harvey, a banker. Described by Pevsner and Wilson as being in an 'unexciting Elizabethan style in red brick [with] a profusion of moulded stacks', it is on a fine site overlooking the Yare Valley and set in a new park, and cost £20,000 to build. The estate was bought by J.J. Colman, founder of the mustard firm, in 1872: he added a splendid conservatory to the building. At Taverham the Micklethwaite family built their 'neo-Jacobean' hall in 1859, designed by David Brandon and replacing an earlier hall.[30] It has been a private school since 1920, and the park and estate, together with the road diversions around it, still survive. The Gurneys occupied a number of

Norwich became a
significant industrial
centre in the eighteenth
century. The 1845
directory lists a huge
range of trades,
from agricultural
machinery makers,
boatbuilders and brass
and tinplate workers,
via ironfounders
and limeburners, to
soap manufacturers,
trussmakers and
worsted spinners. The
heavier trades and
industries tended to
be concentrated along
the riverside below
Foundry Bridge and
when the railway came
in 1845 this reinforced
the trend towards
industrial development.
Both sides of the
Wensum became lined
with warehouses,
coalyards, factories
and workshops.
Most have now been
swept away as part
of the comprehensive
redevelopment of the
area, but just upstream
from Carrow Bridge
some survive. There
is a strong likelihood
that most of these will
disappear in the next
few years.

buildings on the Norwich margins. Earlham Hall, now the Law School of the University of East Anglia and famous as the birthplace of Elizabeth Fry, was extended by the Gurneys who employed Edward Boardman to add a library in 1908. The family had land in many of the villages on the fringe of Norwich. They built a new hall at Thickthorn in Hethersett in 1812, and John Gurney rebuilt Sprowston Hall in 1872–76 in the popular Elizabethan style. North-east of Norwich the Stracey family accumulated an estate of nearly 5,000 acres at Rackheath. Their fortunes were founded in the law and government service in India, from which they gained a baronetcy. Their 'large square mansion … not fully Victorian in character'[31] dates from 1852–54 and is now the centre of a residential development.

Breckland, with its poor, sandy soils, was attractive to nineteenth-century would-be estate owners, and considerable tracts were bought primarily as shooting estates. A number of these have been devoured by the Battle Area and others were badly damaged when the whole region became a military training area. One village which is outside the Battle Area, although it suffered from military development in the Second World War, is Weeting, on the north bank of the Little Ouse opposite Brandon.[32] There changes first took place when the earl of Montrath established a sporting estate in about 1770. He transformed the layout of Weeting from a small village surrounded by sheep walks to a grand landscaped estate, planting woods and hedgerows, diverting roads, building a new hall, and landscaping its garden including a ha-ha. In 1805 the Angersteins, Russian merchants who also founded the National Gallery, bought the estate; they rebuilt the hall and the church and planted another 1,000 acres of woodland. The parish became a gentleman's estate with all the usual features. After 1870, when land values fell, it was sold several times and after its use by the army in the Second World War the hall was demolished in 1952. Much of its site is now covered by new housing, but the impact of the landscaping of the estate still remains.

The nineteenth century in Norfolk: a summary

Faden's map of 1797 provided us with a picture of a largely unenclosed landscape in which the extensive medieval survivals of heath, common and waste remained. By 1850 parliamentary enclosure had removed most of these. The landscapes of straight roads, hawthorn hedges and new farms had been laid out across the face of the county, with many road diversions around country estates, leaving them isolated in their newly wooded parks and edged by large new lakes to provide a suitable setting for the houses. For some, at least, the century was a time of prosperity and lavish spending.

For others, though, the rapid growth of population until 1851 produced a disturbing and distressing increase in rural poverty. The official perspectives focused increasingly on deterrence, and the provision of safety-net care for the less fortunate. The New Poor Law of 1834 saw the more formal pattern

The Burston Strike School building stands on the green in this otherwise pleasant but unremarkable south Norfolk village. In 1914 the teachers at the village school, Annie and Tom Higdon, were sacked by the managers after a long-running dispute in which they were apparently victimised. All but six of the school's 72 pupils then went on strike in support of the Higdons, who carried on teaching in temporary premises while gathering funds for a new building. The 'Strike School', shown in this view, was opened in 1917, by which time the strike itself had become nationally famous, though causing deep social divisions in Burston itself. Technically, it continued until the death of Tom Higdon in August 1939. The strike was much publicised by the trade unions, the Labour Party and other organisations because of its significance for workers' rights and the solidarity of the movement. It also reflects the important element of grassroots radicalism in rural Norfolk a century ago, a characteristic which has long since faded away.

The new school building at Burston was funded by voluntary contributions from individuals and organisations across the British Isles, all of them eager to support this worthy cause. In this view a selection of the engraved stone plaques, recording donations, may be seen. Benefactors include branches of the National Union of Railwaymen; rural trade unionists from Wiltshire; individuals from Cleator in Cumberland, Ogmore Vale and Pontycymmer in Glamorganshire and even that hotbed of radicalism, Chalfont in Buckinghamshire; and Windle Labour Club in Lancashire. The remarkable geographical range indicates the way in which the school strike became a *cause célèbre* for the labour movement.

of union workhouses established, but many parishes found it cheaper to pay for poor families to emigrate, to Canada in the 1830s, and to North America and Australia later in the century. After 1851 rural populations began to fall, and by 1880 corn prices also fell as the new colonial lands were opened up to agriculture and imports of cheap grain undermined the domestic market. From 1844 onwards the arrival of the railways increased access to the larger towns and to some of the smaller, while the new docks at King's Lynn improved the trade of that town. A major impact of the railways was along the coast, where the Midland and Great Northern served growing resorts from Hunstanton to Yarmouth. 'Poppyland' became the new marketing brand for the north Norfolk coast. Yarmouth added tourism to its major role as a fishing centre, and the Broads emerged as a new tourist attraction.

After 1830 Norwich burst its medieval seams and spread beyond the walls. Its growth of new, mainly working-class, housing spread around its northern and western margins. The great days of its worsted industry faded and by the 1860s the shoe trade replaced it. The turnpikes and railways confirmed Norwich as the capital of Norfolk and north-east Suffolk, and its role as a financial and commercial centre increased as its banking and insurance functions grew. But, fundamentally, Norwich had long since lost its place as the second city of England, and it was now eclipsed by new industrial cities such as Leeds, Sheffield, Birmingham, Nottingham and Manchester.

16

Norfolk from 1914 to 1945

THE significance and importance of Norfolk's geographical position, projecting into what used to be called the German Ocean, is a theme that has run through the history described in this book. The accessibility of the county first to a succession of prehistoric peoples, then to the Romans, Saxons, Danes and Flemings, has been instrumental in creating the Norfolk we know today. Economic and commercial prosperity, the result of thousands of years of trade, and an enriching of the culture of the county in matters as diverse as dialect and architecture, have come from this proximity to Europe. Each of the Norfolk ports developed a specialism in trade with northern Europe, though the patterns differed very markedly between, for example, King's Lynn, Norwich and Yarmouth.

But there was another side to the coin, for at times of war the danger of attack from the sea was a major issue, and in many ways Norfolk, like other coastal counties of southern and eastern England, was potentially in the front line. In 1539 the Crown took over responsibility for coastal defences, and a full coastal survey was made for the first time. Later in the sixteenth century defence works were built along the coast between Lynn and Yarmouth. In 1587, at the time when the Spanish threat was reaching its height, and a year before the Armada, an enquiry was made into the state of the vulnerable Norfolk coast with a view to putting it in a condition of secure defence. A strong bulwark was erected at Crotch, one mile from Lynn, and from there to Weybourne Hope the coastline was to be fortified. Sheringham Old Hythe was considered to need defence and Mundesley, Bromholme and Winterton Rode were all seen as places where 'a great fleet might well ride'. Two other bulwarks, at Lowestoft and at the mouth of Yarmouth Haven, were also regarded as essential.

These defences were revived in 1778 at the beginning of the revolutionary wars with France and her allies – at that point the infant United States of America, as well as the French. In 1797, during the Napoleonic wars when invasion by France was a real and terrifying prospect, the defences of Norfolk consisted merely of a battery on the heights at Gorleston, four batteries on Yarmouth shore, batteries at Lowestoft and Cromer, and a fort at Lynn. Major Bryce, sent from London to survey the coast, apparently did not regard Weybourne beach as a weak point and thought the enemy would not consider attacking the coast of north Norfolk (perhaps because the larger warships of the late eighteenth century could not land there readily), but he suggested that troupes of four guns should be placed at Cley and Wells. By 1805 a chain of Martello towers had been built from the Thames northwards, but the

1914	Yarmouth and Lowestoft bombarded by German Navy
1914–16	Airfields hastily built for Royal Flying Corps and RNAS; provision of coastal batteries
1915	First air raid in British history (Zeppelins bomb Yarmouth, Sheringham and Lynn)
1916	Huge losses suffered by Norfolk Regiment on the Somme
1916–18	War Agricultural Committee controls farming, with drive to improve food output
1916–18	Rapid expansion of aircraft building (Mann Egerton, Shorts, Boulton and Paul)
1919	Council housing begins on a large scale: Norwich builds Mile Cross Estate in the 1920s
1920	Unemployed labour used to build parks and gardens in Norwich
1924	Sugar-beet factory opened at Cantley
1928	Closure of Burrells works at Thetford (the town's largest employer)
1929	New Barclays Bank building on Bank Plain, Norwich
1930–39	Concerted effort to build council housing: 4,727 constructed in Norwich alone
1935–39	Major programme of slum clearance in Norwich and other towns
1938	Completion of City Hall in Norwich
1938–43	18 new airfields for RAF and 12 for USAF transform parts of Norfolk
1939	Outbreak of Second World War and defining of five defence lines to resist invasion
1939–45	extensive ploughing of grassland in Norfolk, to grow food (potatoes, sugar beet) and flax
1940	Building of coastal defences (batteries, pillboxes, beach obstructions)
1940–43	43 air raids on Norwich, and major attacks on Great Yarmouth and Lowestoft
1942	Baedeker raids on Norwich (27–29 April) cause massive destruction and 231 deaths
1941–42	Rachel Dhonau's Mass Observation diary charts the local impact of war and air raids
1945	End of Second World War

construction programme did not reach Norfolk – that at Aldeburgh in Suffolk was the furthest north.[1]

In the twentieth century the two world wars dramatically highlighted the uncomfortable fact that Norfolk was vulnerable to attack and invasion, and in both wars the defensive strategy involved turning the county into a huge aircraft carrier. Using planes based at the many airfields that were built on the flatter lands, shipping could be protected and enemy territory across the sea could be attacked. But enemy planes could, and did, reach Norfolk.

The First World War

Almost a century without serious threat of invasion from Europe followed the end of the Napoleonic wars in 1815, and Norfolk's coastal defences were in effect abandoned. By the end of the nineteenth century they had either crumbled away, been dismantled, or were completely obsolete. In the Edwardian period the growing fear of German militarism prompted the War Office to look once more at coastal and other defences in southern and eastern England, but nothing was accomplished in Norfolk, and Kent observes that 'when the First World War broke out in 1914 there were no effective defences in the whole of Norfolk'. On 3 November 1914 the vulnerability of the county was demonstrated dramatically when German warships crossed the North Sea at speed, quite unhindered, and bombarded Great Yarmouth, though causing little damage and no casualties. The raid was a prelude to the much more destructive attack on Scarborough, Whitby and Hartlepool a month later. In April 1916 a

German battlecruiser squadron bombarded Lowestoft and Yarmouth during a naval battle, killing four civilians on shore. By this time coastal batteries had been established, as at Weybourne, where there were six heavy field guns, and pill boxes were erected at many coastal sites. A second line of defences was constructed on the east bank of the river Ant.

The county was also vulnerable to air attack. On 19 January 1915 the first ever air raids on Britain took place when zeppelins bombed Yarmouth, Sheringham and Lynn, and although damage was limited and casualties few, the attacks prompted a new programme of defence works, including anti-aircraft batteries. Norfolk's topography, with extensive areas of relatively flat and thinly populated farmland, and its highly suitable geographical location, made it a natural choice for the construction of airfields as the Royal Flying Corps was being developed. During the war, from 1914 to 1918, a total of thirty airfields were built in the county, divided between the Royal Naval Air Service and the Royal Flying Corps: Pulham had an airship station, and Hickling Broad was a seaplane calm-water diversion site.[2]

The war memorials in every town and village in Norfolk remind us of the thousands of men who were lost in battles and campaigns in France and elsewhere. Many villages have memorial halls and memorial playing fields as additional reminders of this terrible period, and hardly a church is without a memorial tablet or a shining brass plate commemorating the lost young lives of the squire's sons. The First World War placed exceptional demands on the army, and recruitment was an overwhelming preoccupation from the outset. The Norfolk Regiment was recruited from across the county and when Kitchener's army lost 60,000 men on the Somme in the first two hours of the attack on 1 July 1916, the new service battalions of the Norfolk Regiment were among the victims: the 7th Battalion lost 489 men; the 9th 448; and the 8th 105. The latter lost a further 662 men in the following week. By the end of July all three battalions had, in effect, ceased to exist as effective formations.[3] They had to be rebuilt, and in October 1916 the 9th Battalion was used again, this time supported by tanks, and lost another 239 men. From Norfolk as a whole, though the county's losses were not exceptional by national standards, there were 12,000 killed and many more wounded, from a total of 100,000 men who served and a county population of 500,000. On its roll of honour the City of Norwich recorded 3,544 killed.

Ironically, perhaps, the best known of all Norfolk's wartime casualties was none of these. Nurse Edith Cavell was born at Swardeston in 1865, the daughter of the Reverend Frederick Cavell, and in 1915 was executed by the Germans in Belgium for helping Allied prisoners to escape. The best-known female casualty of the First World War, and a national heroine, she is buried in the grounds of Norwich Cathedral.

This was the first major war in which airships, aircraft and submarines were used, and the new technologies of warfare stimulated the defence manufacturing industries, in Norfolk as elsewhere. Three local firms – Mann Egerton and Boulton Paul of Norwich, and Savages of King's Lynn – diversified into aircraft production, and Short's seaplanes, vital in U-boat defence, were made by Mann

Egerton from 1915. The process was scarcely planned: pressures of time and the limitations of technology meant that the production of aircraft was hasty and standards rudimentary: 'It is no exaggeration to say that aircraft design was still at the stage when calculations were made on the back of old envelopes.' Sample aircraft were supplied to contractors to 'copy'.[4] The German U-boat campaign was very successful, and the submarines operated virtually with impunity until February 1917. Seaplanes were based at Yarmouth but they operated from the open sea, making taking off and landing hazardous. However, from the start of 1917 the Curtis flying boats, with wireless communication, improved the area of coverage and meant that submarines could no longer cruise on the surface. From September 1916 the celebrated 'blimps', or airships, which were based at Pulham St Mary patrolled the Norfolk coastal waters.

In very marked contrast to the experience in the Second World War, food rationing did not come until late in the first war, and was not fully implemented until 1918. Here, too, the efficiency and standardisation of the system were very limited and decisions seemed arbitrary: details of the cost of food, contained in the records of the guardians of the poor, show for example that the guardians of the Wayland Poor Law Union and those of Aylsham debated about to whether to cut butter from the diet of inmates and replace it with margarine. At Wayland this was agreed but in Aylsham it was not.[5] Meat supplies lasted reasonably well until 1918, but then a shortage was recorded and an *Eastern Daily Press* headline proclaimed: 'Local Meat Supply: how a shortage is being met. Ensuring the Sunday Joint.' Even after three and a half years of warfare the Sunday joint was still a standard item of consumption – but in April 1918 meat rationing was introduced.

The separation of husbands from their wives and families caused much unhappiness. Meeres quotes several cases where the NSPCC inspectors criticised the separation allowances paid to women, allowing them to drink too much and not care for their children. In the cases quoted mothers were sentenced to prison, with hard labour, and children to stay in the local workhouses 'until their fathers returned from the war'.[6] The war left 200,000 war widows in Britain and 350,000 children without their fathers.[7]

The county between the wars

With the return of peace in November 1918 thought could be given to the future, in a troubled world. Norfolk, in the medieval period perhaps the richest county in England, was now among the poorest. Its economy and employment were still heavily dependent upon agriculture, a sector that was experiencing major problems, and the county's infrastructure was inadequate and underdeveloped. Unemployment was rising, population decline in the more remote rural areas was gathering pace, and average incomes were among the lowest in England.

The problems of rural housing highlight the challenges facing local authorities and the private sector alike. The legacy of housing in country districts was, as already shown in chapter 13, seriously deficient. The worthy desire to provide decent housing for ex-soldiers and to raise the quality of rural housing in general was underlined by the provisions of the 1919 Housing and Town Planning Act which, building on the foundation of two earlier pieces of legislation, the Housing Acts of 1890 and 1909, empowered local authorities to condemn cottages and to acquire land upon which to build new houses. The aim was fine in principle, but a host of practical and financial problems, and conflicting government decisions, in fact meant that little of benefit could be achieved.

In Walsingham Rural District, for example, all these problems were apparent. In 1919, under pressure from the government to develop a sizeable housing programme, the council decided it needed 367 houses. The land was priced at £35 an acre and government approval was sought – but no decision was made except that the council was told to prioritise housing for railway workers at Melton Constable, the depot of the Midland and Great Northern Railway. Agricultural workers, the great majority of those on the waiting lists, would not benefit, and even the housing at Melton Constable was to be built without a piped water supply, so that the proposed baths and WCs were disallowed. Much of rural Norfolk had no piped water until after the Second World War, partly because of government economies in the 1920s. In September 1919 a survey and report identified 497 unfit houses in the Walsingham area, all of which should in theory have been demolished, with replacement housing being built, but shortages of building materials limited new construction. Some houses were finally built using wood or concrete blocks and with thatched roofs. Rents were another problem, for only ex-service tradesmen could afford the recommended rents, which were far beyond the means of agricultural labourers. When some homes were finally built 'they were despite rather than because of central bureaucracy'.[8]

In the Breckland a different, and very dramatic, influence was at work. The shortage of timber during the war, for pit props in particular, prompted the government to establish the Forestry Commission in 1922.[9] The new body looked round for areas of poor land which could be acquired at bargain prices and planted with fast-growing coniferous species to secure timber supplies. Among the areas selected was Breckland, where the sandy soils and poorly developed agriculture were a winning combination. By 1934 some 25,000 acres of former breck had been planted. Scots and Corsican pine were the main species, but along the roads there were 'fire screens' of Spanish chestnuts and copper beech. A new village, Santon Downham, was laid out for Forestry Commission staff and smallholdings for 200 forest workers were established for those who worked part-time (for about 150 days a year) for the Commission. Several of the private former shooting estates in the area were also planted with conifers, such as the Kilverstone estate on the eastern edge of Thetford. Since the Second World War the now huge forest of Thetford Chase has become a major amenity, especially for the fast growing town of Thetford, and it gives the town a setting which is unique in England, approached along the A11, A134 and B1107 through seemingly endless miles of dark forest.

As already shown, farming was in deep depression from 1870 to 1914, but

The building of the Anglican shrine of Our Lady of Walsingham began in 1931 with the erection of a replica of the Holy House, inside a small pilgrimage church. The project was the inspiration of Father Alfred Hope Patten, who had been vicar of Walsingham since 1921. In 1922 he had set up a statue of Our Lady, based on the image on the medieval priory seal, and this immediately began to attract the devout from the Anglo-Catholic wing of the Church of England. Walsingham is now the most important pilgrimage destination in England, with a Roman Catholic shrine at the Slipper Chapel a mile south at Houghton St Giles, and an Orthodox shrine. The Anglican shrine has been greatly extended to form a large complex of residential and conference buildings set around peaceful gardens.

Pilgrimage has become a small industry in Walsingham, with a proliferation of buildings associated with the shrines to Our Lady, accommodation for visitors, and several shops which sell icons, devotional gifts, statuary, vestments, incense, communion wafers, candles, altar cloths, and church plate. It would all have been very familiar 600 years ago.

Norfolk is a dry county, with substantial areas that have relatively little surface water, and a topography and geology which militate against the building of reservoirs. Most rural communities did not obtain piped water until the 1930s or even later, and were completely reliant on wells. Even when water supplies did extend into the countryside, the lack of hills and reservoirs meant that the use of natural gravity feed, so standard in the north and west of England, was impossible. Water therefore had to be pumped into huge, tall water towers located on the tops of low hills and ridges, from which it could then be supplied by gravity. These giants of the rural scene, often painted in brilliant and eye-catching white or in monumental polychrome brickwork, began to appear in large numbers during the late Victorian period and the most recent was constructed only in 1980. There are over fifty of them and 25 are listed buildings. This is the water tower at Walcott, just inland from Happisburgh.

the advent of war radically changed this gloomy picture. The desperate need to provide more home-produced food and to reduce imports had an immediate effect on the arable sector, as the acreage under wheat was expanded rapidly. There was much argument about the wisdom of ploughing up poor land in order to grow crops, but wartime urgency usually made this inevitable.[10] The livestock sector was also affected: there were many reports that 'cattle were being prematurely sold for slaughter on Norwich Market in 1915'. As with other key sectors of the economy, agriculture was soon brought under state, or quasi-state, control: in 1916 War Agricultural Committees, known colloquially as War Ags, were established – there were 20 such bodies in Norfolk. Farmers were instructed to improve their standard of farming, and the War Ags undertook detailed surveys to identify land that could be put to better use: thus, pieces of land in the Broads and South Norfolk were noted as uncultivated, while 'farms at Reedham and Loddon were "not properly cultivated", and a strong letter was sent to the farmer at Earsham Hall requiring him to cultivate his land'.[11] Some farms were taken over – for example, in 1917 Formby's Farm in Long Stratton. Machinery, especially tractors, could be hired. By the end of 1917, 1,700 more acres of cereals were being grown in Norfolk and 3,000 acres of pasture had been ploughed.[12] But more intensive growing of cereals meant declining fertility, since rotation cycles were broken, fewer stock were kept, pig and sheep numbers fell, and the amount of animal dung for fertiliser was reduced. But with guaranteed sales and controlled prices, farm incomes rose

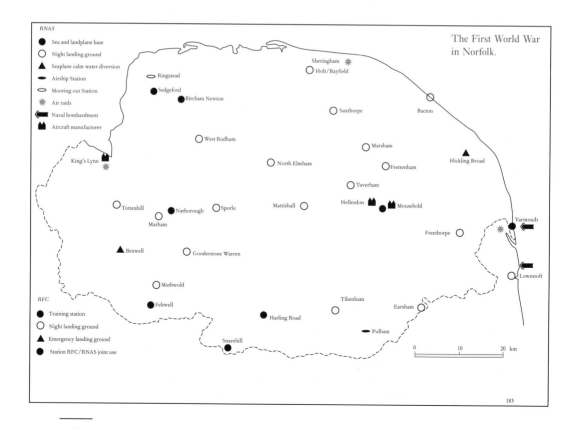

The First World War in Norfolk.

183

during the war: for example, on the Everingtons' farm at Castle Acre returns rose to £12,001 in 1919/20 from £6,500 in 1913/14.[13]

After the war agriculture continued to develop, and traditional patterns of farming began to disappear as new crops and new techniques were introduced. Sugar beet had been grown experimentally in Suffolk from 1868, and as production increased the beet was shipped to Holland for processing. This was clearly a manufacturing process that could be undertaken in England, and in 1912 the Anglo Netherlands Sugar Corporation built an experimental factory at Cantley. After a hesitant start, and with some government help, by 1924 the Cantley plant was firmly established and, indeed, was overtaken by fast-growing demand. It was estimated that to supply a sugar-beet factory some 500 acres had to be cropped and in 1927 a second Norfolk factory was built at King's Lynn. The development of sugar beet as a major new crop coincided with extensive remodelling of farms in some parts of the county. By 1945 the East Anglian Real Property Company had bought 5,000 acres in east Norfolk, where it laid out new field boundaries and very large fields, and built groups of new farm buildings. The rotation of sugar beet, potatoes, wheat and barley was established, the beet tops either being ploughed in when still green or used as a valuable feed for livestock.[14]

In this period, too, piggeries were added to many farms. Local processing plants, as at North Elmham, served this expanded business. But it was in dairying that the biggest change occurred. Whereas only a few decades before a dairy herd of 60 milking cows was regarded as large, in the mid-1930s many Norfolk herds had 300 or more animals, and 'by 1935 dairying was regarded as the most stable aspect of farming practice in the region'. Landlords such as Captain Meade at Earsham built new dairies for their tenants, and in 1938 model cowsheds were provided for three farms on the Worstead estate.[15] The economies of large-scale farming were becoming apparent, and Norfolk, as elsewhere in East Anglia, could potentially benefit from factors such as good rail links to London. By the mid-1930s James Keith of Castle Acre was farming no less an area than 14,000 acres, including several stretches of heathland which he reclaimed and brought into cultivation. His business approach emphasised dairying (including the supply of fresh milk for the massive London market) rather than fattening bullocks. Proximity to beet factories and improving transport links became key features influencing the growth of specialised crops and vegetables, especially in the Fens.

Norwich and the towns

The 1919 Housing Act compelled councils to 'build homes fit for heroes', and the first great wave of municipal house building began – only to be slowed down abruptly two years later for political and financial reasons. Norwich City Council was an enthusiastic and imaginative exponent of top-quality council housing, and the Mile Cross Estate, between the river Wensum and Aylsham Road, was designed by Professor Adshead of Liverpool University Department of Architecture to a remarkably high standard. It is now a conservation area

Between the wars Norwich Corporation developed an enviable reputation for progressive and enlightened social policies, including education and housing. Before the First World War it had been planning to build council housing and had bought extensive areas of farmland on the periphery for this purpose, and for allotments. The building of the Mile Cross estate began in 1920 and by the end of 1932 almost 1,500 council houses had been built there, some 40 per cent of the city's total. The estate was designed on garden city principles and the distinctive pattern of geometric and curving roads and closes, lined with semi-detached houses each with a garden, is very clear on this extract from a map of 1937. The plans also included schools, shops, parks, pubs and churches, trying to create a 'real' community, and the houses were designed in a variety of styles including many with a 'cottage' feel. In 1979 almost the whole estate was designated a conservation area.

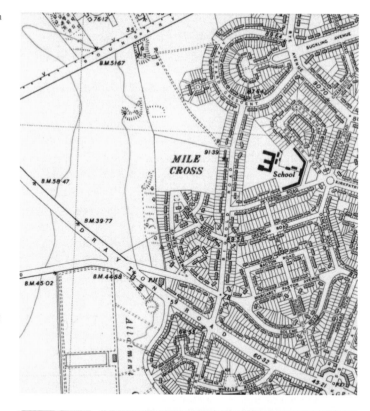

The saving of Elm Hill in Norwich was one of England's earliest and most important conservation victories. This street of late medieval and sixteenth-century buildings had once been a prestigious part of the city, but by the nineteenth century had decayed to become slum housing, notoriously insanitary and desperately poor. In 1926–27 the city council proposed a comprehensive slum-clearance scheme but the Norwich Society, founded four years earlier, undertook a comprehensive survey which identified not only the wealth of buildings of architectural and historical interest but also ways in which the street could be restored and revived. The restoration work began at the end of the 1920s and was immediately recognised as a triumph. Today Elm Hill is one of the most treasured elements in the superb townscapes of central Norwich, and a much-visited tourist attraction.

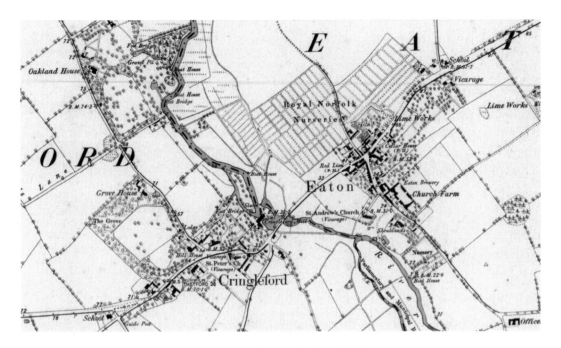

In 1911 Norwich had a population of 121,000, a quarter of the total for Norfolk. It had grown very rapidly since the 1840s, attracting migrants from rural Norfolk but not further afield (in 1911 86 per cent of the city's inhabitants were Norfolk-born). At this time places such as Catton, Costessey and Eaton were quite separate villages well beyond the built-up area. Today the population of Greater Norwich is about 300,000 and a tide of bricks and mortar, concrete and tarmac has flooded across the villages and fields around the old borough. This map of 1882 shows how it was a century and a half ago, when Eaton and Cringleford were small rural communities, twins on either side of the river Yare. During the 1920s suburban growth reached the edge of Eaton, and now, since it lies within the line of the southern bypass, Cringleford is part of the greater Norwich built-up area even though administratively it is governed not from City Hall but from South Norfolk District Council's offices at Long Stratton.

and is generally considered to be one of the finest and most successful of all inter-war housing schemes. As well as building new homes, councils were also instructed to develop slum-clearance programmes to remove the legacy of poor housing inherited from previous generations. This policy was given top priority from 1930 onwards, and the definition of unfit housing was substantially extended. By the mid-1930s, therefore, many of the ancient but squalid courtyards within the city had been classified as slums and cleared. Thus, much of historic King Street, by the river, was demolished in 1935, while Elm Hill, now regarded as one of the most attractive and architecturally precious streets in any major English city, only narrowly avoided the same fate.

Accelerated slum clearance needed much-increased rates of new building, so large estates were built (much more cheaply than at Mile Cross) on Mousehold and in a fringe along the western and south-western edges of the city. By 1935 Norwich had built 4,727 new houses on six estates and had used up almost all the land it had bought for housing. Over a thousand private houses had also been built, but these tended to be as part of 'ribbon' development, for example those along the Plumstead Road east of the city.[16]

Among the greatest of all inter-war civic building projects was the construction of City Hall, Norwich, started in 1936 and opened by the King George VI and Queen Elizabeth in 1938. Although controversial in that it required the clearance of a substantial area of the medieval city and numerous houses which even then were recognised as being of historical significance, the city gained a building which is among the masterpieces of English inter-war architecture, a magnificent counterpart to the Norman castle which faces it across the market place. It formed part of a wider scheme for a civic centre which included the remodelling of the market, the widening of several nearby streets, and the moving of the cenotaph (1924) to face city hall.

The design of City Hall in Norwich, by Charles James and Stephen Pierce (winners of a competition with 143 entrants), was strongly influenced by contemporary Scandinavian architecture (and especially City Hall in Stockholm, built 1911–23), with clean sweeping lines of great simplicity and, like its Swedish inspiration, a tall clock tower with a copper-sheathed belfry. The superb Art Deco detailing has survived almost intact: (left) one of the pair of stylised bronze lions (reflecting the two lions on the city's coat of arms), sculpted by Alfred Hardiman, which flank the great flight of steps to the main entrance and (right) the Bethel Street façade with the city arms flanked by iconic Art Deco angels holding swords (by Eric Aumonier).

Within the old city there were other changes. Planning for the future was increasingly characteristic of towns and cities in the 1920s and 1930s, and schemes for redevelopment and 'improvements' were put forward in Norwich as elsewhere. The first suggestions that an inner ring road was needed appeared in the late 1920s, but the greatest project was the construction of City Hall, the major building in inter-war Norwich and one which 'must go down in history as the foremost English public building of between the wars',[17] as Pevsner and

Wilson excitedly wrote. Occupying a whole block, from which many sixteenth-, seventeenth- and eighteenth-century buildings were cleared, City Hall fills the west side of the market place, the steep slope meaning that it presides monumentally over the area. The tall square tower, a landmark visible for many miles, and the magnificent central colonnade guarded by two fine civic lions and with bronze doors portraying city crafts and industries, are key features of a masterly architectural composition that owes much to Dutch and Scandinavian influences, consciously or unconsciously echoing the city's time-honoured links across the North Sea. Another major building from the period between the wars is that the former Barclays Bank on Bank Plain, designed by Edward Boardman, the Norwich architect, and built in 1929–31. It is a sign of changing times that this massive building, with its entrance hall built to impress users with the might and power of the firm, is no longer used as a bank.

The problem of unemployment in Norwich after the First World War led to four major projects for the creation of city parks, at Eaton, Waterloo, Heigham and Wensum. In 1921 some 10,000 men were unemployed in the city, and the council appointed a war veteran, Captain Sandys-Winch, a trained horticulturist, as its first superintendent of parks and gardens, overseeing the landscaping of 600 acres and the planting of 20,000 trees. He employed 130 men for three years on laying out Eaton Park, which had a band pavilion, two large boating pools and a wide variety of sports pitches. With their landscape now mature, and delightful, these classic examples of 1920s landscape design make an invaluable contribution as open spaces for the population in the areas which surround them. They have been so successful that in the 1990s they were awarded a Heritage Lottery Fund grant towards restoration and updating. These parks were showpieces, though they were not the first: back in 1899 the City Council had bought 11 acres at Catton, where the park was opened in 1904, and in 1906 it had acquired land on the south-western edge of the city. The Norwich Playing Fields Open Spaces Society was a driving force in these purchases.

In post-war Yarmouth, as in so many other towns, unemployment was a severe problem. The collapse of the Russian herring market, which previously had taken 90 per cent of Yarmouth's production, threw 800 of the 1,300 fisherman out of work. Public-works schemes were provided for the unemployed – the building of the roads and sewers on the Barrack Estate and the construction of a new sea wall from Sandown Road to Beaconsfield Road were two examples. The influenza pandemic of 1918 to 1919 hit Yarmouth badly. However, Mears comments that 'the period between the wars saw considerable improvements in the living conditions of most people, especially in housing'. Council houses were built on the North Denes, Southdown and Gorleston followed by further developments, and by 1928 the town's own electricity generating station supplied two-thirds of the population and also some of the neighbouring villages. In 1930 the new Haven Bridge was opened by the Prince of Wales, allowing further growth in Southdown.[18]

After the Great War unemployment was the biggest issue in Lynn. Here, too, public works were an important strategy for creating jobs, and the borough council built some housing in South Lynn and a new swimming bath.

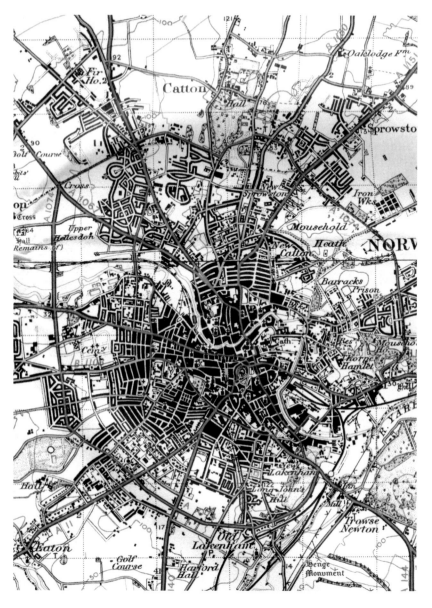

In 1945 Norwich had about 120,000 people and ranked 32nd by population in a list of English
towns and cities (in 1801 it had been 8th). This map shows how the close-packed medieval
city had sprawled outwards in the previous hundred years, first with the development of the
'terraced suburbs' in areas such as Thorpe Hamlet, Unthank Road and New Catton, and the
more exclusive lower density growth along Newmarket Road, and then by the building of the
large peripheral council estates at Mile Cross, Earlham and elsewhere, immediately identifiable
by their geometric street patterns and accommodating over 30,000 people moved out from the
centre under slum-clearance programmes. The outer ring road had been strung together by
combining existing roads and new construction (most prominently on the western stretch from
Unthank Road to Aylsham Road), but remained (and of course remains) incomplete in the
problematic area around Thorpe.

Conditions in many of the old yards within the town remained desperately poor (the local medical officer condemned as unhygienic the keeping of rabbits and poultry in these yards), and expenditure on education, at £10 per child per year, was 'one of the lowest of all local authorities in England'. In the 1920s very few Lynn children progressed to secondary education, although by 1933 the Lynn Municipal Technical Institute had been opened for the teaching of commerce and engineering.[19] Inter-war Lynn was in the doldrums economically and socially: it had lost the commercial dynamism hitherto provided by shipping and maritime activities, and had not found either a replacement for these, or a way of revitalising that business.

Lynn might have suffered, but Thetford was even worse off. The collapse of Burrells' agricultural engineering works which had specialised in the production of steam traction engines, was a profound blow. After a successful wartime phase the company failed to adapt its production to modern methods or modern requirements – steam machinery was not where the future lay – and it closed down in 1928. It had been Thetford's largest employer. Already by 1920 the town was in decline: 'it appeared as if the stagnation of the early medieval and early modern period was to be repeated, since the chances of reversing these trends were negligible in a small, isolated town with outdated amenities and no obvious geographical advantages.' In 1921 the corporation, itself impoverished and under-resourced because of the very low rateable value of the town, started a number of small public works such as clearing the river of debris, laying kerbs and pavements, renovating the Nuns Bridges bathing place, and tidying up Castle Meadow. The depression was such that these projects were still in action in the 1930s, by which time the town had become a 'severely depressed area'.[20]

The Second World War

Throughout Norfolk it is possible to see the squat, stark concrete pillboxes which were built at the beginning of the Second World War to guard important river crossings and key road junctions. The authorities were acutely aware that the Norfolk coast was open to possible attack and, as Kent comments, 'all those places recommended for fortification during the Armada were fortified in 1940'.[21] This is a comment which highlights the influence of geography, not a lack of imagination! With its sandy beaches, low cliffs and smooth profile the coast was potentially the location for a German invasion, and it was virtually lined with pillboxes, many of which have since been washed into the sea by incessant coastal erosion. Between Lynn and Yarmouth fourteen coastal batteries were installed, with 28 heavy guns, while onshore minefields, strings of huge concrete blocks, and steel scaffolding, lined the beaches. Weybourne was regarded as a particularly vulnerable spot, just as it had been four centuries earlier. A second line of defences ran along the Ant valley followed by five further lines inland, the last along the Little Ouse in the south-west of the county. After the war much of this was quickly cleared, but minefields on fast-eroding cliff lines remained a serious danger for decades.

The remains of a Second World War pillbox on the top of the low cliff at Weybourne Hope are a reminder that between 1939 and 1945 the coast between the Wash and the Solent was the most heavily defended part of Britain. The sandy Norfolk coast presented few natural obstacles to a German invasion, and so every effort was made to protect it. An almost continuous line of pillboxes and trenches extended from Cley to Happisburgh, supported by thousands of concrete blocks and anti-tank mines on the beaches and tangled festoons of barbed wire and scaffolding. A peak was reached in 1943, but the removal of the defences was well under way by the middle of 1944 when the threat of invasion had receded. By the end of 1946 almost everything was gone apart from pillboxes, some concrete blocks, and gun emplacements. Since then coastal erosion and cliff falls have destroyed many of the sites. The one shown will, before long, tumble to the beach.

The Second World War in Norfolk.

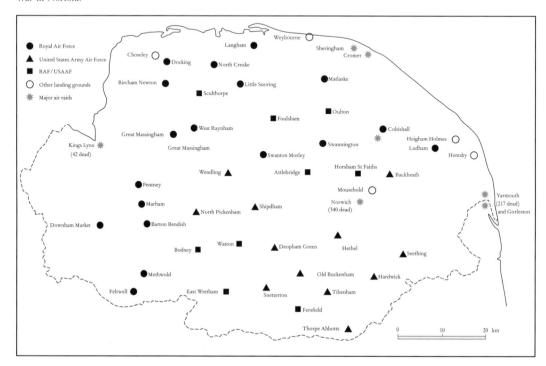

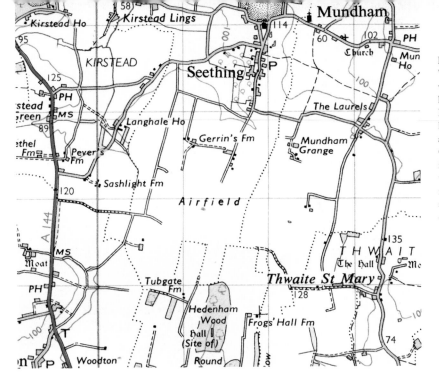

During the Second
World War there
were 45 airfields and
landing grounds in
Norfolk. The flat or
low-lying countryside
and proximity to
Germany made that
inevitable. Farmland
was requisitioned,
roads were closed,
and runways laid
out with the greatest
possible speed. After
1942 many were built
for, or taken over by,
the United States
Air Force. This was
the case at Seething,
built in 1942–43 with
a 6,000-foot long
main runway and two
4,200-foot secondary
runways. It was used by
the 448th Bomb Group,
a part of the 2nd Air
Division of the 8th
American Air Force,
as a base for Liberator
bombers. The map
(published in 1954)
shows the impact of
airfield construction in
terms of road closures:
today, the roads from
Seething village to
Hedenham and from
Thwaite St Mary to the
A144 (now B1332) have
been rebuilt, but minor
lanes and tracks have
never been replaced.

To a much greater extent than in 1914–18, the flat topography of the county made it the location for airfields. Huge tracts of farmland were commandeered, and airfields hastily laid out, a process that began just before the war in 1938, and continued until 1943. Eighteen new airfields were built for the RAF and twelve for the United States Air Force, while a further nine were shared, giving a total of 39 in the county. As Fairhead points out, these were virtually self-contained townships, adding to the local population and leaving a visual impact of runways, hangars and residential quarters.[22] At some places, such as Swanton Morley and Sculthorpe, a new community emerged substantially larger than the neighbouring village. Wartime exigencies meant that roads were closed because they were severed by runways, and in some cases new roads were later built to avoid the airfields, but often the truncated stubs of closed roads remain or, as at Deopham, the modern road actually follows the line of the abandoned runway. Elsewhere, short new railway branches were built to bring in fuel supplies. These air bases had a further impact on the landscape, in that massive gravel workings for runway materials were dug along the valley floors leaving many lakes as, for example, at Pensthorpe and Lenwade.

After the war the majority of the airfields were closed, and by the late 1970s fewer than a dozen remained in regular use. The fate of the remains varied: in some cases, as at Seething, most of the land was returned to agriculture, but at Haveringland the medieval parish church, against the walls of which Mosquitos were parked during the war, stands among empty concrete runways in a bleak landscape that was once part of the landscaped park with wooded avenues running out to and beyond the church. At the beginning of the twenty-first century one of the two survivors, Coltishall, was wound down and decommissioned, a move which had a serious impact on the local economy and leaves many questions about the future use of the immense site. Only RAF

Marham, east of King's Lynn, survives (2013) as an active flying base, although by far the most successful airbase of Second World War vintage is Horsham St Faith, which now prospers as Norwich International Airport. Its daily flights to Amsterdam remind us of that age-old link with the Low Countries which has been so important in the city's history.

During the First World War, Norfolk had experienced the first direct attacks by enemy forces which England had seen for several centuries. Thirty years later the county was again in the front line, and the experience was infinitely more traumatic. In her carefully researched record of the impact of the blitz on Norwich, Joan Banger listed 43 air raids on the city between 9 July 1940 and 6 June 1943. Initially the raids were small and random, involving single aircraft, although the aircraft factory of Boulton and Paul and the nearby Colman's works were badly damaged in more targeted raids. By August 1941 there had been 27 raids, and 81 citizens had been killed. After that came quiet, and eight months passed with no raid. However, on the nights of 27 and 29 April 1942 the city experienced a terrifying and concentrated blitz, which killed a total of 231 people and caused massive devastation in the city centre and the suburbs alike. Many familiar landmarks were destroyed, most of St Stephen's Street, Orford Place and Chapel Field gutted, and swathes of terraced houses in areas such as Rupert Street were razed. This was one of the so-called Baedeker raids, in which the Luftwaffe singled out historic cities – York, Canterbury, Exeter and Bath were also badly damaged at the same time.

On 22 June there was a major raid in which incendiary bombs were dropped. Fires raged through other parts of the city centre, and the roofs of the cathedral transepts were set ablaze, the building being saved by the prompt action of firewatchers and members of the public. There were further

The coasts of Norfolk were a front line in wartime and also a potential danger to ships and shipping in the unpredictable North Sea, so defences and warnings were required. Here at Happisburgh the 85-foot high lighthouse, erected in 1791, stands above a Second World War pillbox. The lighthouse was originally one of a pair, but the other was demolished in 1883, not long before the site was washed away. The present lighthouse was converted to electricity in 1947 and in 1987 was declared redundant by Trinity House. After protests, in 1990 by special Act of Parliament it was transferred to a local trust and is the only independently run lighthouse in Great Britain.

Despite the heavy losses suffered during the air raids on Great Yarmouth in the Second World War, substantial areas of rows survive in parts of the town, including those running off the Market Place and Howard Street. There is an inherent problem about finding uses for the properties on the rows, because of lack of vehicular access and, in the case of shops, the fact that they are tucked away out of view. In some cases the rows are scarcely used and are becoming gap-toothed and derelict, or serve simply as alleyways between properties. It is no longer possible to imagine them crowded with tiny houses and teeming with residents.

Each of the Yarmouth rows had an official number – the only way to identify individual addresses in this extraordinarily intricate pattern. Most, though, also had names, with varying degrees of formality and recognition: Row 60 was Austin Row, because the Augustinian Friars of Gorleston had a small cell or town house here. Today one side of the row has completely gone and is now, as in so much of the back areas of the town, a large car park.

major raids on 2 and 13 August.[23] In total, 340 people in Norwich were killed during air raids in 1940–43, and over 100 injured, while the scale of physical destruction is revealed by the statistics that almost 14 per cent of the housing stock was either destroyed or severely damaged, and only 15 per cent emerged completely unscathed.

Not surprisingly, given its location and the importance of its harbour and maritime facilities, Yarmouth (like nearby Lowestoft) was a major target for air raids. Between 1940 and 1943, a total of 217 civilians were killed. Because of its vulnerability many local people had been evacuated from the town, which probably helped to reduce the number of casualties, but nonetheless, the loss of life was proportionately much greater than in Norwich. Here, too, the physical destruction was traumatic. During the three heaviest raids, on 7 April and 9 July 1941 and 25 July 1942, large parts of the town's unique and historic rows were destroyed, while in the last the great parish church of St Nicholas, one of the largest in England, was badly damaged. There were also service losses; in March 1943, a raid killed 34 servicewomen were worked as maintenance crews for the motor torpedo boats, motor gunboats and mine layers based at the port.[24] Other towns were raided, including Cromer and Sheringham, and on 12 June 1942 the most serious individual incident of the war in Norfolk occurred, when

Sheringham has recently developed a lively and entertaining specialism in art and sculpture trails, including annual 'themed' trails and others which are permanent, as well as decorative murals to brighten up the concrete walls of the promenade and seafront. In 2008 local sculptor Mitchell House was commissioned to produce three cold cast bronze plaques, one commemorating rescues by the local lifeboats, another the local lobster fishermen, and the third, shown here, being a remembrance of Sheringham during the Second World War, showing families on the beach behind the coiled barbed wire of the Front Line defences along the Norfolk coast.

the crowded Eagle public house in King's Lynn was destroyed by a single bomb, killing 42 people. Even rural Norfolk did not escape: one dramatic incident, for example, occurred at Bawdeswell in November 1944 when an RAF Mosquito, returning from a bombing raid over Germany, crashed on the parish church, which was destroyed in the ensuing blaze.

Rachel Dhonau, an official recorder for the Mass Observation organisation, kept a detailed diary through 1941 and 1942 when she worked first in the Food Office in Sheringham and then taught at City of Norwich School though still living in Sheringham. Her observations on wartime life give a vivid picture of the period. On 29 April 1942, for example, having returned to her hostel in Norwich, she woke to the sound of bombs: 'The raid was short but very intense in our area. There were some big fires started and the college to which the hostel belonged was burnt down.' She commented on the plentiful fresh fish in Sheringham and, living near so many airfields, regularly recorded the waves of allied planes passing over the coast to bomb Germany – a policy to which she, with a German father, was increasingly opposed.[25] In an epilogue to her main diary in 1943 she was asked to comment on the food situation in her area. She replied that it was worse than at any time since the war began, and 'I think women grumble and argue more to make sure they have "their rights" … [and pass] remarks such as "it's no use to taking your basket down the town, you won't find anything to put in it".'

17

After the Two Wars

ONLY two decades after the end of the First World War, the 'war to end all wars', a still traumatised population – which had also experienced the Great Depression – was plunged into the Second World War. For Norfolk, as we have seen, the physical impact of the second war was infinitely greater than the first. When peace came, in the summer of 1945, great swathes of Norwich and Yarmouth lay in ruins; familiar buildings were burnt-out shells or were now marked only by weed-choked patches of rubble, and across the county many square miles of land had been gobbled up by the construction of airfields and defence installations. The coastline was festooned with barbed wire and littered with concrete blocks and barriers. But, overall, the human losses were less: village war memorials carry far fewer names from the Second World War than from the First. And in 1945 a great question hung over Norfolk, as over any other part of the country: what would the future bring, and how would the huge physical, social and economic disruption of the previous six years be eased and smoothed? In Norfolk, which had been marked out for the previous century by its rural poverty and population decline, the prospects for the countryside seemed particularly uncertain.

There were, however, wider considerations in a world where planning and broad economic and social strategies had become a mainstay of national and local government. Norfolk was inexorably drawn into national plans and regional projects, increasingly influenced by external factors and decisions made in distant places. In Norfolk, as in all of East Anglia, the period after the war saw the county subject in many ways to the growing strength and widening impact of London. This meant that Norfolk was increasingly seen by planners in Whitehall ministries as part of a region which extended for a hundred miles and more around the capital, so changes in the county had to be seen as part of much broader changes across south-east England as a whole. By the 1970s, as transport links improved and accessibility grew, Norfolk also began to experience the power of the private sector – population decline was stemmed, long static small towns began to grow, new economic activity migrated towards the county, and a palpable sense of dynamism replaced the slow pace of Norfolk life.

These processes and trends began very swiftly after the end of the war. The wartime devastation of London and the need for a massive rehousing drive, linked with an interventionist planning philosophy which was given statutory force by the Town and Country Planning Act of 1947, produced ambitious proposals for change. Fundamental to the legislation were the introduction

1945	end of Second World War
1945–70	heyday of Great Yarmouth as a holiday resort; holiday camps at Hemsby, Caister
1947	Town and County Planning Act
1950	Norwich city boundary extended to include area of Heartsease Estate
1951	population of Norfolk 550,000
1958	pioneering urban improvement project for Magdalen Street, Norwich
1960–70	extensive closure of rural railway lines in Norfolk
1962–75	expansion of King's Lynn from 28,000 to over 35,000 people (now 43,000)
1963	opening of University of East Anglia in Norwich
late 1960s	development of Bowthorpe on western edge of Norwich
1967	pedestrianisation of London Street, Norwich (first such scheme in Britain)
1967	opening of Norwich Airport on former Horsham St Faith's airbase
1968	opening of County Hall
1970	completion of Norwich inner ring road (apart from south-east sector)
1974	local government reorganisation: seven district councils (including Norwich)
1976	creation of Roman Catholic diocese of East Anglia; cathedral St John's, Norwich
1988	establishment of the Broads Authority
1989	centenary of Norfolk County Council
1990	some 183 primary schools had been closed in Norfolk since 1947
1992	completion of Norwich Southern Bypass
1994	destruction of Norwich Library by fire; replaced by The Forum
2004	study shows almost 30 per cent of Thetford's population are of Portuguese descent
2011	population of Norfolk approximately 880,000; Greater Norwich about 210,000
2012	plans for dualling of final sections of A11
early 21st century	planning challenges: population growth, Norwich northern bypass, urban sprawl

of green belts (and especially that which girdled London to prevent further outward growth of the metropolis) and the principle of decentralisation of population by means of overspill. This, in turn, was associated with the push for slum clearance on a grand scale, redeveloping the inner boroughs of London and displacing population in very large numbers. The twin mechanisms by which overspill was to be achieved were the building of new towns (starting at the beginning of the 1950s with places such as Harlow and Stevenage) and the expansion of existing towns away from London, where the urban community was to be greatly enlarged on a planned basis by the reception of population from the capital.

No new town was designated in Norfolk, although various possibilities were occasionally aired. Instead, two of the largest of all the expanded town schemes were located in the county, at Thetford and King's Lynn, both of which were rapidly enlarged and transformed by the process. With hindsight the absence of a formal new town was perhaps a mistake, for it could have been not only the core which absorbed short-term overspill but also the base for further private-sector growth. But in the 1950s it was scarcely imagined that intensive development pressures and housing demand would affect Norfolk. The county was still generally regarded as relatively remote place, and to many people it was a backward area far beyond the reach of London's influence. Half a century later, the picture is fundamentally changed. The expansion of Thetford and King's Lynn took place with the enthusiastic support of their borough councils, convinced that only deliberate action of this sort – and the large-scale investment in housing, urban amenities and employment opportunities which it brought – could turn round the ailing economic and social conditions of their towns.

In the aftermath of the Second World War, the other urgent need locally was for replacement housing at Norwich and Yarmouth, both of which had lost thousands of homes through the bombing of tightly packed central areas. Both councils engaged in major new council-housing projects, such as the great estate at Lakenham on the southern edge of Norwich. Elsewhere new building remained very limited, except of course in Thetford and Lynn. Most market towns saw a modest amount of new council housing, and in a few places nearer to Norwich some commuter housing was built – notably in the Drayton and Taverham area in the 1960s and 1970s – but the really impressive change has come since the end of the 1980s, all across the county. In a lot of the smaller towns there has been a clear phasing of development, once the housing pressure had begun to build up thirty years ago: first would come a bypass, curving round the perimeter of a country market town, then there would follow a variety of infill schemes, building over the spare and vacant land between the old boundary of the built-up area and the new bypass (a simple and straightforward process); and now, in some cases, phase three is seen in growing pressure to build beyond the bypass, in the wedges between radial roads (a much more challenging and controversial stage). These patterns can readily be seen at, for example, North Walsham, Loddon, Aylsham, Holt, Dereham, Fakenham, Swaffham and Downham Market.

Movement

As a rural county with several hundred small villages Norfolk has an extremely complex and exceptionally lengthy road network, with thousands of miles of narrow 'byways'. Drivers are only too aware of the twisting nature of its roads, many of which follow the lines of medieval furlongs. When the cow parsley is in full flower the lanes are lined with white clouds of blossom and little else seems visible. Each market town (and, revealingly, each *former* market town) is at the centre of a web of small roads and Norwich is the focal point of the main threads, a radial sequence of great highways which include the A11, for many centuries one of the key roads of England.

Despite its complexity, the railway network did not fulfil its promise, nor realise its potential. There was never a satisfactory east–west route across the county, and the tangled rural network in the north of Norfolk was circuitous, slow and somewhat inconvenient. The thinly populated character of rural Norfolk, and the rather ramshackle nature of the services offered, meant that traffic was always limited. Without significant heavy industries, no natural resources such as coal and iron, and only one really large urban centre, the county was not encouraging ground for efficient and profitable railway operation, and the holiday and fish trades, for example, could not compensate

Fishing was the mainstay of the numerous small ports and larger harbours of north and east Norfolk from the earliest times until the twentieth century. The trade expanded in the later medieval period with the opening up of the northern waters between Scotland, Norway and Iceland, and the heyday of the herring trade was in the fifty years to 1914. But coastal or inshore fishing was also important, and the crab and lobster fisheries in particular became synonymous with places such as Sheringham and Cromer, and small boats such as these at Sheringham (top) and beached on the shore at Weybourne (bottom) continue the trade. Locally caught seafood now has a special cachet, and 'finest Cromer crab' attracts a gourmet market.

for this. Therefore, the loss of rural railways began early, with the withdrawal
of passenger services on the country branch line from Stoke Ferry to Downham
Market in 1930 and the closure of the line from Wymondham to Forncett in
1939. In 1952 the line from Heacham to Wells closed, followed a year later by
the Waveney Valley line through Harleston and Bungay to Beccles. Much more
extensive was the ruthless chopping back of the Midland and Great Northern
routes across the county, with the wholesale closure of the lines linking Lynn
with Yarmouth via Fakenham, the branch to Norwich City station, and the
coastal route through Mundesley. The Beeching cuts of 1964–68 were the
inevitable culmination of this process: Wells lost its line to East Dereham in
1964, and in the same year the line from Swaffham to Watton and Thetford. In
1968 the route from King's Lynn to Dereham went, followed shortly afterwards
by the line from Dereham to Wymondham, and in 1969 the Lynn–Hunstanton
line was also closed. As a result of these cuts most Norfolk market towns lost
their rail facilities, the only proper rural branch line which survives being that
from Norwich to Cromer and Sheringham (and the fate of that was in the
balance for some years).

Nevertheless, Norwich is still the focus of five lines – those to London,
Cambridge and Peterborough, Cromer, Yarmouth and Lowestoft – and these
have all experienced a remarkable renaissance since the dark days of the 1960s.
In retrospect, the most serious and regrettable closures were the line from
Lynn to Wymondham via Dereham, and that from Lynn to Hunstanton, both
of which would now be well used and have much development potential. The
loss of many of the others was probably unavoidable – and indeed, hard-nosed
economics suggests that at least some should never have been built in the
first place. In the 1980s and 1990s the two main lines, from London to
Norwich *via* Ipswich and from London to Lynn *via* Cambridge, were both
completely transformed by electrification. This not only meant a greatly
improved rail service, but also placed both Norwich and Lynn within the
outer-commuter zone of London. The two key market towns *en route* – Diss
and Downham Market – have been revitalised and have shown remarkable
population growth, and that in turn has affected villages within easy reach
of those stations.

The rest of the surviving network has also experienced revival. The line
from Norwich to Cambridge and the Midlands has been rejuvenated, and
traffic levels are growing fast on the axis linking Thetford, Attleborough and
Wymondham. Remarkably, business on the Cromer and Sheringham branch
is among the fastest-growing in the country, as commuter traffic develops
because of road congestion. Recent ambitious proposals to make Norwich the
eastern hub of a new east–west cross-country route to Bedford, Milton Keynes,
Oxford and Bristol may soon come to fruition. It is a far cry from the slow
and meandering country trains of the 1930s and 1950s, and today and in the
future the railways will be one of the factors which help to shape the growth
patterns of Norfolk and its burgeoning population.

Just as the railway network ossified in the inter-war and immediate post-war
periods, the road network remained unimproved. After the Second World

War, as Ayton points out, the central government view was that Norfolk was a low priority for new road building, and that remained true for two decades.[1] However, in the late 1970s and early 1980s the county's road network at last saw investment. The A47 from Norwich to Lynn was improved by bypasses at East Dereham and Swaffham, and the A11 saw major upgrading, albeit in frustratingly piecemeal fashion, with the building of bypasses at Wymondham, Attleborough and Thetford, and the dualling of the stretches in between. The final stretch of dual carriageway between London and Norwich south-west of Thetford, opened in 2016. But much of the A47 to the Midlands and, notoriously, the A17 to Newark and the A140 to Ipswich remain single-carriageway, albeit with bypasses around most significant communities. This means that Great Yarmouth's new harbour has no continuous dual-carriageway link with the Midlands.

Despite the problems of the road network, there was a great deal of new construction in the period from 1960 to 2005, and most market towns are now bypassed and long stretches of new inter-urban 'A' road have been constructed. Much the most important single project, however, was the building of the Norwich Southern Bypass, completed in 1992, which takes all long-distance east–west traffic away from the city. Its logical extension to the north of the city, and passing the airport is now (2017) under construction. As already shown, the building of bypasses has stimulated development – the 'spare' land between older built-up area and bypass is always ripe for residential and commercial building – while the major interchanges on the trunk roads are nodal points for potential growth. This can be seen very clearly at the south end of King's Lynn on the A10, at Wymondham and Attleborough on the A11, and at Thickthorn and Trowse on the A47.

Norwich, by far the largest urban area in the county and the centre of its road and public transport network, has especially difficult problems. There have been three successive attempts to alleviate chronic traffic congestion. The construction of an inner ring road around the outside of the medieval city walls was completed in the 1970s, following its inclusion in the 1945 Norwich Plan. An outer ring road, completed in the 1960s around roughly three-quarters of the city, served the needs of the traffic moving between suburbs and, to a disturbing extent, carried long-distance traffic through residential areas. The 'missing' section from Thorpe round to Lakenham meant that heavy inter-urban and intra-urban traffic was forced on to the inadequate road system round Thorpe station and long-suffering Bracondale. The need for the southern bypass, finished in 1992, reflects the spread of its post-war housing estates and the movement of industry out on to greenfield sites created by the outer ring road.

In terms of the relationship between planning strategies and major axes of communication, three lines of movement seem currently to be most favoured by long-term thinking. These are the electrified railway and greatly improved A10 route to King's Lynn; the A11 and the railway line to Ely and Cambridge; and the A140 and the electrified main line to London via Ipswich. Downham Market, Diss, Thetford, Attleborough and Wymondham would seem to be the obvious growth points on these routes, and the rapid population increase and expanding built-up area in all of these emphasise the vital importance of excellent communications for physical growth and commercial development.

Social provision

Norfolk is a very large county which, despite major population growth since the 1970s, still has a relatively small population in relation to its geographical extent: currently there are about 880,000 people, compared with approximately 600,000 thirty years ago and half a million in the early 1950s. The county has a large mileage of small roads, and many smaller communities are remote from an urban area and not easy to access. It is noticeable that the East Anglian Air Ambulance has made a major contribution to Norfolk's medical services, because it is particularly suitable for serving a scattered population.

Inward migration has been a crucial factor in the county's population increase. Initially much of this was made up either of resettled overspill from

The problem of a high level of second home ownership in the attractive villages and small towns is now a topic of major concern to local people and planning authorities alike: in the north Norfolk coastal belt over 40 per cent of properties are now second homes. The area first became a popular tourist destination in the mid-nineteenth century, but until the 1950s there were few second homes because transport links to the coastal districts were relatively poor. Car ownership transformed the picture, and even in the early 1950s the growing number of holiday homes (and the resultant increase in prices and unbalancing of the housing market) were attracting comment. The Blakeney Neighbourhood Housing Society was founded in 1946 by Norah Clogstoun, a regular visitor who moved to the village in 1938. Her initial concern was to rectify the often squalid and insanitary nature of the picturesque cottages, by buying them up and converting them, but more recently the focus has been on providing social housing for local people, so that they can afford to remain in the area.

Greater London, geographically concentrated in Thetford and Lynn, or of voluntary movement by older people who wanted to retire to the country. The latter movement was directed especially to the Norfolk coast, affecting towns and villages in the area from Wells, through Sheringham, Cromer and Mundesley, to the holiday resorts north of Yarmouth. Today, more than 20 per cent of the population in the coastal belt is aged 65 or over, a percentage which rises sharply in the favoured retirement areas such as Cromer.

In the past 50 years population decline has slowed down and many parishes are now increasing for the first time since 1851, especially those in the hinterlands of Norwich, Lynn, Thetford and Yarmouth. These locations benefit from easy access to large urban areas (which, given the almost total loss of traditional village services and shops, is increasingly regarded as essential) and they also have good or even excellent communications with London and other cities. In contrast, some parts of the county are still too remote to attract commuters, and the gradual loss of local employment in agriculture and services has meant continuing population decline. Thus, the triangle between Hunstanton and Sheringham inland to Fakenham is, except for coastal communities, still experiencing a slow decline, as is a smaller area in Norfolk's southern fenland.[2] Perhaps the most impressive reversal of fortunes has been in the small market towns. Some of these were dying on their feet in the 1960s, and others were only just managing to sustain growth. But the increases in recent decades have been spectacular: East Dereham more than doubled in population between 1951 and 2001, from 6,642 to 15,659 (most of the increase being since 1981), North Walsham's population almost tripled, from 4,733 to 11,998 during the same period, and Wymondham expanded from 5,665 to 12,539. Even Fakenham, for long one of Norfolk's smallest and most isolated towns, is now ringed by new roads, industrial estates and a tide of recent housing.

However, all this growth, reversing the image and the reality of generations, was planted on a county which was in some key senses ill prepared to deal with it. The county council and district councils were not accustomed to spontaneous growth, or private-sector development pressure, except in a few favoured locations. Much of the planning in the 1950s and 1960s was based on an expectation of continued stagnation and poverty, and on the assumption that, as with the railway network, social and cultural facilities would have to be 'downsized'. In a hard-hitting account of Norfolk's education system up to 1989, Nigel Wright noted that in 1968, even though education was the largest item in the Norfolk County Council budget, it still spent less per head on education than any other county. The county's record was definitely poor: in 1984 government inspectors criticised the lack of text books, the shabby schools and the over-stretched system.[3]

Thus, the question of how far children should travel to their first schools, and what forms of transport should be provided, has long been a problem for Norfolk. In the 1930s the Education Committee agreed to help children having to travel three miles or more to their schools. They decided cycling was the only practical option: those travelling 'a considerable distance' were provided with a bicycle, a waterproof cape and leggings! By 1937 180 bicycles and 116 cycle allowances had been granted.[4] But in the post-war educational climate the concentration of resources on larger units, in the interests of efficiency and the provision of a broad-based, properly taught curriculum, became an imperative. Norfolk, like other large rural counties such as Devon, the North Riding of Yorkshire and Lincolnshire, had a multitude of very small village schools, with only one or two teachers and rudimentary facilities. Between 1947 and 2000 some 183 primary schools were closed and this, with the parallel closing of village shops, pubs and churches and the withdrawal of rural bus services, has been seen by many commentators as marking the death knell of the traditional village community. The perception that the process needed to be slowed, and preferably arrested, has meant that in the past decade there has been a perceptible change of attitude: as Nigel Wright comments, in the foreseeable future support for small communities seems likely to continue and school closure will be very much a last resort.

Changing agriculture

After 1939 the farmers of Norfolk, working heroically to meet the challenge of the desperate wartime demand for food, further extended the area under the plough and produced a major increase in production (despite the loss of so much land to the needs of airfield construction). This momentum was sustained after the war, and agricultural subsidies kept farming prosperous well into the 1970s. In this primarily arable county, with its easy topography, mechanisation offered many opportunities and there was a dramatic increase in its use during the 1950s. Just as rapidly, the number of agricultural labourers fell. Mechanisation achieved maximum benefits in large areas of uninterrupted space for huge ploughs and harvesters, so hundreds of miles of hedges disappeared between 1950 and 1980; fields and whole farms were amalgamated, and the landscape was transformed. The countryside east of Bury St Edmunds in Suffolk became known as a grain prairie, and in parts of south and mid-Norfolk a comparable landscape began to emerge. Closely linked with this was the extensive and intensive use of artificial fertilisers, which saw yields of wheat, barley and sugar beet rise greatly and the numbers of sheep and cattle fall commensurately. Norfolk maintained its status as a leading agricultural county but, as Douet comments, 'farmers no longer needed livestock, nor did they need to follow a strict rotation to maintain fertility'. Comparing 1912 with 1972, he showed how barley had become the dominant cereal crop in all areas apart from the silt fens. He noted that cattle densities had increased only on the boulder-clay land and had fallen in the Fens, while the density of sheep dropped dramatically across the county, even in the Breckland. Sugar beet had replaced fodder crops, and cereals increased to over half of the total acreage. The human cost was high: the number of workers per hundred acres virtually halved in all of Norfolk except the silt fens between 1912 and 1972.[5]

Some farmers moved in another direction, capitalising on technology and following the path of intensive rearing – a system for which Norfolk, with its

Since 1945 agriculture in Norfolk has been transformed, in large parts of the county almost beyond recognition, by fundamental changes in patterns of landownership and the financial circumstances of farming, technological revolutions, and the evolving international context within which British farming operates. This has had a profound effect upon the landscape, ranging from the amalgamation of farming units and the grubbing up of hundreds of miles of hedgerows, to the introduction of new crops. The most visible of the latter is the intense primrose-yellow of oilseed rape, thousands of acres of which fill views of the county in April, the blankly yellow rectangular fields standing out glaringly from the background of more traditional greens and browns. This view is from the tower of St Helen's church, Ranworth.

large flat fields, was especially suited. Helped by wartime official encouragement of pig rearing, the development of huge pig farms was a significant trend in the period from 1950 onwards. In the 1920s and 1930s poultry rearing had grown in importance across East Anglia as a whole, partly because 'back to the land' pioneers found this to be one of the few agricultural tasks that was within their capacity. During the 1950s and 1960s the emergence of mass markets for poultry meat, a development inextricably linked with the improved technology of freezing and the retailing revolution brought about by supermarkets, galvanised what had previously been a minor element of the farming system. The processing of poultry, especially turkeys, was very important in Norfolk, with the famous Bernard Matthews and his commercial empire making at least one Norfolk-accented word, 'bootiful', familiar across the kingdom. There were other ways of diversifying: farm shops provide an ever-widening range of home produce, while farmers experimented with new crops, or with specialisms such as organic farming, or with the introduction of new stock. For example, llamas, alpaca and ostriches are now to be seen on some Norfolk farms. Others developed visitor centres and tourist attractions, such as the display of rare breeds at Hindolveston, and the large zoo at Banham (known to some, from its smaller origins, as 'Banham monkey house'). The conversion of farm buildings and their cattle yards and barns to holiday accommodation has provided additional income for many farms, especially near the coast.

The stock markets of Norfolk have largely gone, vanishing along with the animals upon which they depended. The Castle Hill cattle market in Norwich is now a shopping mall; others such as Aylsham and Acle have closed. However, the central point of the farming year in Norfolk, the county agricultural show at Easton, continues to flourish: the great range of agricultural machinery is an attraction to most small boys, but the stock categories and horse show are still well supported. Climatic change is already reflected in the establishment of vineyards in Forncett St Peter and Ashwellthorpe, a development likely to be

Livestock farming declined sharply in Norfolk during the nineteenth century, as grain growing and other arable agriculture such as market gardening began to dominate over much of the county. During the 1930s, when agriculture was in depression, rural incomes were very low, and yet many unemployed town dwellers sought to move to the countryside to try to eke a living; the raising of poultry and pigs experienced a significant increase. Since the 1970s large-scale pig farming has become a major element in the farming economy of Norfolk, and a very obvious visual element in the landscape. The upper picture, taken from the ramparts of the Norman castle at Castle Acre, shows the distant prospect of a pig farm between Newton and West Lexham, while the lower picture is from the road between Methwold Warren and Feltwell, close to the edge of the fens.

Leeder's animal feed mills at Long Stratton is a modern successor to an ancient industry, and its family origins are shown by the Victorian directories and censuses from the 1870s onwards which record members of the Leeder family as farmers and millers of Stratton St Michael. A late eighteenth-century brick tower mill can be seen in the picture, forming the centrepiece of a large complex of industrial buildings of the nineteenth and twentieth centuries – steam power was introduced in 1914. Rural industry was of course widespread in the county, with trades such as milling, paper-making, village foundries, and sawmills, but little now remains – though the great sugar beet factories at Wissington and Cantley, for example, continue to process agricultural products.

as successful as the long-established vineyard at Bruisyard in Suffolk. Perhaps the most successful 'farm shop' is that on the royal estate at Sandringham, but nearby at Heacham another form of alternative farming, the colourful and fragrant lavender fields, has been around so long that it can be marketed as 'traditional'. Thus, the pattern of farming in the period from 1950 to 1980 – an ever greater focus on large units, intensive cereal production, and mechanisation – has been varied by a multitude of other enterprises, smaller and more specialised units which concentrate on niche markets and high-value products. Despite all this, it is impossible to imagine that farming of any sort will ever again be a major employer in a county which was for so many centuries dominated by agriculture.

Building conservation

As we have seen, Norfolk has a great wealth of market towns and historic villages, many of them full of listed buildings and sprinkled with ancient monuments and glorious historic churches. In 1947 legislation created the system of listing buildings and designating ancient monuments, and twenty years later the idea of statutory protection was extended to include designation of whole areas of towns and villages: the conservation area has been an outstandingly successful device, instrumental in the protection of historic and attractive places. There are now over 270 designated conservation areas in Norfolk, seventeen of them in Norwich, and they range from intimate medieval townscapes and small unchanged rural hamlets, to inter-war council estates and the grand set-pieces of civic architecture. The first Norfolk designations were at Heydon and New Buckenham, both places of outstanding architectural interest, distinctive layouts and with interesting histories.[6] Heydon is a classic estate village and New Buckenham a medieval new town little altered by later development and with its surviving medieval common. Some areas of distinctive landscape quality have also been listed, of which the largest is the Glaven valley to the west of Holt, and a second that of the Bure valley to the north of Aylsham.

Listed buildings are defined as those which are of 'special architectural and historical interest', the list being compiled by English Heritage for the Secretary of State. The statistics for Norfolk are an impressive reflection of the remarkable length of its recorded history and the rich variety of its architecture. The county has over 10,000 listed buildings and more are being added on a regular basis, especially as those built in the last hundred years are assessed for possible protection. The current figures reveal 539 Grade 1 buildings, 722 classed as Grade 2*, and 8,740 with Grade 2 status. Not surprisingly, those accorded Grade 1 status are outstandingly important and of national or even international significance – great country houses such as Holkham and Blickling, incomparable churches including Salle and Cley, vernacular buildings such as the great barn at Hales Hall, and public buildings from the medieval Guildhall at Lynn to the City Hall of the 1930s in Norwich. The Grade 2* lists include most of the more modest medieval and later churches, lesser monastic ruins and smaller country houses, while Grade 2 – numerically much the most important category – ranges from farmhouses, barns and Georgian and Victorian townhouses, railway stations and early industrial architecture, to some curios such as the dog kennels in Costessey Park. One-third of the listed buildings are in the market towns, and a line from Blakeney through Dereham to Thetford is an approximate boundary: to the west there are far fewer listed buildings than there are east of the line.[7]

But listed buildings and conservation areas are only part of the story. Norfolk has an exceptional wealth of archaeological heritage, now inventoried and recorded on databases and maps. These indicate at least 17,500 known archaeological sites, together with more than 22,000 recorded find spots and scatters, in excess of 200 maritime and inter-tidal sites of archaeological importance, and over 400 scheduled monuments. The latter include internationally celebrated sites such as Grimes Graves, the Roman town at Venta Icenorum, and Norwich Castle, as well as places less familiar to the wider world, for example Baconsthorpe Castle and Bromholm Priory ruins, and small or vernacular features including mills and milestones, earthworks and prehistoric burial mounds.[8]

The Grade 2* listed buildings include many churches, and many of these still serve as the focal point for their parishes. At Reepham, for example, there were three churches in the town centre, of which two remain. They exemplify

By the middle of the twentieth century King Street in Norwich had become one of the most run-down and deteriorating parts of the city, with a legacy of squalid housing, industrial decay and severe social deprivation. The city council had cleared a good deal of slum housing in the area during its ambitious rehousing programme of the 1930s, and other renewal schemes were formulated. Extensive redevelopment was undertaken at the southern end, around the junction with Rouen Road, but policy changes in the mid-1970s led to an increasing emphasis on restoration, rehabilitation and sensitive infill. In the course of this work medieval and sixteenth-century buildings were discovered beneath later semi-derelict façades, and today much of the street has been attractively restored and brought back to life.

the problem of the Church today, for only St Mary, the parish church of Reepham itself, is still used, whereas St Michael, the parish church of Whitwell, is redundant. However, at least here there is an alternative, since as the two parishes are interlocked St Michael's is now available for community and social use. Many isolated churches are still in use, but quite a few others, such as Godwick and Egmere, are simply ruins. But the maintenance and upkeep of those that are still open, many of them wonderful buildings of national significance, is a huge strain on small communities: for example Ketteringham and Great Melton churches, among scores of other very small parishes.

The listing of farmhouses, barns, manor houses and some town houses has protected many from extreme conversion or even demolition, as in the cases of the Wymondham farmhouse and the Hingham barn. At what point in its deterioration and decay a listed building must be deemed beyond salvation is often difficult to determine. Conservation is also about context: in the centre of Norwich, for example, small former weavers' cottages, themselves in good repair, sit unhappily and uncomfortably amid twentieth-century commercial buildings. Barns and groups of farm buildings range from Grade 1 as at Holkham, Hales or Waxham, the last beautifully restored by Norfolk County Council, to the more ordinary buildings which, while themselves not remarkable, complete a grouping where the main house is 2* listed. Once a building is 'saved', there arises the problem of its future use, and the strong possibility of planning battles over alterations and adaptations which might be needed to ensure survival but which might offend the purist. Nowhere is this challenge more apparent than in farm buildings that are no longer required for agriculture – many hundreds of seventeenth- to nineteenth-century barns in Norfolk are now 'desirable' conversions, attractive residences for those who can afford them.

The development to be allowed in villages that do not have conservation-area status poses further questions. Before 1974 Loddon Rural District Council employed a team of architects, Tayler & Green, to build their new generation of council houses. Those in Loddon, for example, with careful use of materials and pleasing grouping, were acclaimed by Pevsner and Wilson, who noted that their treatment of the development 'was an instrumental force behind the philosophy of the *Essex Design Guide* of 1973 and that of the Bowthorpe Villages'. In many other villages it was easier for linear development to dominate, allowing council houses to spread out along one or two roads, separating them from the inner village layout: this can be seen in Little Walsingham, for example, or in Bawburgh where private housing with much better grouping has been developed nearer to the village core.

Windmills and watermills were spread widely across the county – in the Domesday Book a watermill is recorded for almost every manor. Later windmills were often paired with watermills, while in the eighteenth and nineteenth centuries many others were built as drainage mills. The Norfolk Windmills Trust has saved a number of these fine buildings, such as Stubbs Mill in Hickling, and private owners have managed to save others, as at Denver

Wymondham Abbey is unusual among Norfolk churches in having a range of excellent twentieth-century furnishings. Ninian Comper's reredos was constructed in the 1920s, his finest work, and in 1962 the beautiful font cover, designed by the architect Cecil Upcher, was presented to the church as a memorial to Canon Frederick Jarvis, vicar of Wymondham 1932–53. The font itself dates from 1440 and is in a characteristic Norfolk style, with an octagonal bowl decorated with deeply carved angels and symbols of the Evangelists, and a stem carved (as at New Buckenham) with lions and wild men. The font cover deliberately recreates the towering late medieval font covers of churches such as Salle and Cawston, though brightly painted as they doubtless once were.

and East Dereham. Mills tell of earlier economies and provide key points in often flat landscapes. Many watermills survive after conversion to other uses. At Buxton, Bawburgh, Lenwade, Loddon and Itteringham, for example, they have been transformed into dwellings, but at least their form and siting have survived as a result. But the only working watermill in the county, providing much-prized flour, is at Letheringsett on the Glaven west of Holt.

Nature conservation

Parliamentary enclosure eliminated most of the commons which were once so ubiquitous in Norfolk outside the Fens and the Broads. A few managed to survive and several of these have become important conservation areas or Sites of Special Scientific Interest (SSSIs). *Nature in Norfolk*, published in 1976, listed 48 reserves with a total area of about 11,500 acres and since then many further reserves have been added. There are now 21 National Nature Reserves in the county, and no fewer than 164 SSSIs. The majority of the reserves are

From the low headland at Weybourne Hope the crumbling slipping cliffs, chewed by the sea in every gale, give way to the long line of Blakeney Point, stretching into the distance. The shingle bank was created by, and is now maintained by, the westward-moving longshore drift which brings an endless supply of material from the eroding cliffs between Overstrand and Weybourne. Over the centuries the spit has extended across the mouth of the wide shallow bay on which stood the small ports of Salthouse, Cley, Blakeney and Morston, and behind it saltmarshes have formed. This geomorphological process is entirely dependent upon the continued erosion of the cliffs, and interruption to that would in turn set in motion the attrition and erosion of Blakeney Point and the flooding of the saltmarshes. The destruction of one part of the coast means the extension of its near neighbour.

managed by the Norfolk Wildlife Trust, with a half a dozen in the care of the National Trust, three important sites by the RSPB, and the Welney Washes by the Wildfowl Trust. Not all of these reserves are open to the public every day. They can be divided into several categories according to their natural ecology and topography. Perhaps the best known are those at Snettisham, Titchwell, Cley, Blakeney Point and Scolt Head, which together form a semi-continuous belt of sand and shingle spits and saltmarshes along the north coast. Hunstanton cliffs provide a home for kittiwakes, and the coast of the Broads has another reserve at Winterton Dunes. They attract huge numbers of sea birds, both permanent residents and temporary visitors which come with the seasons, and include a unique series of plant habitats which, together with seal colonies, provide further variety. In all of these reserves the landscape itself is a great attraction for a wide range of holidaymakers – in particular birdwatchers and those who like messing about in boats – and the ecological richness adds much to the character of the area.

Inland there are two broad categories of land that survived enclosure – the heathlands and the small wet commons. Those heathlands that lie on glacial sands and gravels have low agricultural value, or were once exploited for agriculture but have since reverted to heath or woodland. Some of them are now managed by conservation bodies, which endeavour to maintain and enhance their landscape and ecology. For example, East Wretham heath with its two meres is a major survivor, and other heaths such as Roydon Common are gradually being cleared of conifers in order to extend the important heathland habitat, home of birds such as the stone curlew and many specialised plants. Inland from the north coast are important areas of heathland at Salthouse and Kelling. Sites such as these also have important archaeological remains which survive because agriculture has barely touched them. Grimes Graves, the area of Neolithic flint mines three miles north of Thetford, is perhaps the most important of these sites. Little ancient woodland survives in Norfolk because of the long agricultural history of the county, with intensive use over the millennia. Three surviving examples are Wayland Wood to the south of Watton, Ashwellthorpe Wood south of Wymondham and Foxley Wood near Reepham. These woods are all accessible and are being managed as they once would have been in their medieval heyday.

Some small wet commons escaped enclosure and their valuable plant and animal habitats are increasingly being taken into protection or management by a range of bodies. A beautiful small one is at Flordon (where permission must be obtained for access) while the commons at Booton and Whitwell near Reepham are good accessible examples. The excavation of valley gravels for the construction of airfields during the Second World War has left a number of sites that have gradually become flooded or waterlogged, creating fen and lake landscapes, as at Lenwade and especially at Pensthorpe where the wildlife possibilities of this relatively new feature are being cleverly exploited. The Broad created at the University of East Anglia was also the result of the quarrying for gravels. In a few other places, unique habitats have been protected, such as the chalk grassland on Ringstead Downs.

The people of Blakeney, like the inhabitants of every other community on the Norfolk coast, have always been acutely conscious of the power of the elements. Coastal erosion caused by fierce waves, breaches in sea defences of shingle or concrete, and the risk of flooding at high tides and surges remain a major threat – indeed, with seal level rise and climate instability the danger is probably growing. In many places there are flood markers. The one shown here at Blakeney indicates the dates 1887 and 1978: on the latter occasion the water was 4.9 metres or 16 feet above normal sea level, but in December 2013 the flooding was over six feet deep on the quay itself.

Since the end of the Second World War the question of access to the countryside has been raised many times and has been the subject of national legislation. Norfolk's very extensive areas of arable land do not lend themselves to access by footpath, and in some parts of the county (such as the area south of Wells towards Fakenham) the density of footpaths is exceptionally low by national standards. The intricate networks of paths and trackways that formerly criss-crossed the area were extinguished upon enclosure in the eighteenth century. However, several long-distance walks have been or are being created. The Peddars Way from Thetford to the north coast at Thornham was the first; it follows the Roman road along the crest of the so-called East Anglian heights. A new coast walk, the Peter Scott Way, follows the seabank from Sutton Bridge to King's Lynn, while the Weavers Way runs diagonally across the east of the county from Yarmouth to Cromer, and Marriotts Way makes use of the former Midland and Great Northern railway line leading north-west out of Norwich.

The towns

The post-war planning legislation centred on the Town and Country Planning Act of 1947. In advance of this Norwich, like many other towns and cities, was already considering the future shape of the urban area, and produced its first comprehensive plan in 1945.[9] This envisaged extensive decentralisation of population, partly because of major war damage to the housing stock, and partly in the expectation that continued slum clearance would displace large numbers of inner-city residents. New housing was quickly built on greenfield sites beyond the outer ring road on the west, north and east of the city. The municipal boundary was very tightly drawn, and to this day, areas such as Hellesdon and Sprowston, which are physically integral with the Norwich built-up area, lie outside the city boundary. This meant that land for new housing within the city was swiftly exhausted, and therefore two extensions were obtained: these allowed the Heartsease Estate to be developed on the

north-east side from 1950 and the Bowthorpe Estate on the west side from
1968. The latter was planned to accommodate 13,500 people in three distinct
'villages', each with its own services and next to a new industrial zone along
the A47. In many ways Bowthorpe was Norwich's premier development of city
housing; it has expanded fast and is now generally regarded as a successful
piece of urban planning.

Devastation as a result of the 1942 air raids on 'Norwich over the Water',
north of the Wensum, created cleared spaces on which there was initially new
factory building and, subsequently, the development of the Anglia Square
precinct, to give the area its own focus and to serve as the home of Her
Majesty's Stationery Office – which was housed in a notably ugly building.
With the closure of HMSO the area entered a period of decline and plans are
in progress to revive it, and to demolish and replace some of the insensitive
1950s and 1960s building. Elsewhere in the area, new housing replaced Bullards'
Brewery on the river; the scheme was done quite sensitively, and the banks of
the river Wensum have now become a linear feature of amenity value. This is
in great part due to the work of the Norwich Society, the first civic society in
England. Perhaps its best known achievement was in 1927, when it saved from
demolition Elm Hill and its many Tudor buildings. In 1958 the society carried

Anglia Square was the great hope of the Norwich planners in the late 1960s and early 1970s – a
brand new commercial and retailing focus which would reinvigorate Magdalen Street, which had
become something of a backwater, and would link in with the new inner ring road which crossed
the street by a huge concrete flyover. With its upper level car parks, shops at ground level, and
four tall office blocks it would be the modern image of an ancient city. Brutally set down in an
intricate townscape, it was soon regarded with abhorrence and was, in commercial terms, far less
successful than its designers had anticipated. While the shops are thriving the office blocks are
empty and the upper level is a windswept wasteland. In the spring of 2014 outline plans were
announced for a comprehensive redevelopment of the site.

The 1942 blitz devastated a large swathe of the tightly packed residential area around Vauxhall Street, south-west of central Norwich. In the late 1960s plans were drawn up for the comprehensive redevelopment of the district, including not only the bombed sites but also the surviving properties that had been earmarked for slum clearance. The scheme included a new neighbourhood shopping centre in Vauxhall Street, a tall block of flats, semi-detached and terraced housing, and smaller blocks of flats and maisonettes. A key feature was the creation of a pedestrian route which linked with the city centre via an underpass beneath the inner ring road at Chapelfield Gardens. Almost half a century later the area looks a little tired and in need of a facelift, but the principles on which it was based have worked well.

out a project to revive Magdalen Street as an important shopping axis for the northern half of the city, a scheme which attracted international attention. It highlighted the value and wisdom of restoration rather than reconstruction, and in 1967 Norwich pioneered the pedestrianisation of London Street, the first such scheme in any English city and a vitally important step in late twentieth-century urban design.

A great deal of thought was given to development schemes within the medieval city, and there was a strongly held view that major shopping centres on the fringes of the city should be avoided, to prevent the emptying of the city centre. After a protracted controversy and considerable heated debate, and following massive archaeological excavations in the castle bailey, the new Castle Mall shopping centre with its deep underground car parking space was opened in 1998.[10] This was followed by the construction of the Chapelfield Shopping Centre, within the medieval walls and on the site of the former chocolate factory. Finally, the extensive tracts of derelict and deteriorating industrial land and railway sidings south of Thorpe Station were redeveloped between 1990 and 2000. The Riverside area has major leisure, recreation and shopping facilities and residential flats. Yet despite these efforts to keep retailing within the medieval city and its immediate surroundings, a necklace of large new retail parks has developed beyond the outer ring road during the last twenty years. On the northern edge of the city the pressures for peripheral development have been particularly intense. One factor behind this was the purchase in 1967 of the former RAF air base at Horsham St Faith by the city and county councils, for use as a civil airport. From small beginnings of 36,000 passengers in 1971/72 it now has half a million a year and is aiming to double this. The airport has become the focus of large-scale commercial and warehousing development.

The employment figures for 1951 and 1998 show how, over that period of almost half a century, the shoe industry, once so important to the well-being of Norwich, declined almost to vanishing point. In contrast, the hotel and restaurant trade has risen sharply in importance, while the financial services represented by Norwich Union, now Aviva, and other insurance businesses quadrupled their employment. But the biggest increases in employment came in the education and healthcare sectors. The development of the University of East Anglia since 1963 has led to a huge increase not only in those engaged in tertiary education itself, but also in the many activities which service the sprawling university complex, and in the closely related field of scientific research. UEA is linked to the Science Research Park, which is focused on plant and food research and has been described as 'the largest concentration of plant science expertise in Western Europe'.[11] The Norwich School of Art and Norwich City College have also expanded greatly. By 1998 over 7,000 people in Norwich were employed in education. The University Hospital, on its new campus near UEA, and the private Spire Hospital have encouraged new schools of medical studies to develop at the university. More than 11,000 people are now employed in healthcare.

Norwich, like many of England's cathedral cities, has to deal with the problem of how far to preserve the face of its historic past and how far to adapt its fabric to suit the needs of a successful city of the twenty-first century. It has its castle, the cathedral with its precinct, some thirty remaining churches (about half of the total that existed in the Middle Ages), the Guildhall, and many other buildings dating from the fifteenth to the eighteenth centuries. Norwich is the cultural centre of Norfolk and north-east Suffolk, with its museums, theatres and concert venues. The Norfolk and Norwich Festival is one of the oldest and most highly regarded in the country. The city is also, of course, the religious centre of a large Church of England diocese (although it lost Suffolk to the new diocese of St Edmundsbury in 1914), and the cathedral is the focus of a wide range of religious and cultural activities, exemplified by the opening of its striking refectory and, most recently, its new Hostry. The Roman Catholic Cathedral of St John, centre of the diocese of East Anglia,

The construction of an inner ring road in Norwich was a key feature of the plan for the city which was drawn up in 1945, after the extensive devastation caused by the 1942 blitz. In the mid-1960s work began on the dual carriageway. North of the Wensum the recently reinvigorated Magdalen Street was cut in two by a notorious flyover, and south-west of the centre the road ran close beside the best remaining stretch of the city wall (there were proposals, only just rejected, to demolish the latter). The scheme was never completed, and a combination of cost, public opposition and environmental considerations led to the abandonment of proposed sections from the top of Bracondale over to Thorpe and along the riverside to Pockthorpe.

During the 1960s and 1970s the massive growth in the insurance industry meant that Norwich Union, founded in the city in 1797, rapidly outgrew its older premises. The result, unfortunately from the point of view of the townscape of the south-west side of the city centre, was the building of a series of huge new concrete office blocks stretching along Surrey Street and Westlegate.

The Castle Mall shopping centre in Norwich was conceived at the end of the 1970s as a strategy for expanding the city's retail area without intruding too obviously into the historic streetscapes. Comprehensive redevelopment, of the sort undertaken in the bombed areas during the 1950s, was not feasible. Work on the mall, which is partly underground, began in the late 1980s and was completed in 1993 at a total cost (including car parks, road building and landscaping) of £140 million. It occupies parts of the castle grounds and the old cattle market and links in with Timberhill, one of the oldest surviving streets in the city centre. The gardens on top, which are integrated with the castle ditch and other earlier features, have become a very popular city centre park.

has recently added a narthex to its facilities. The Castle Museum, with its nationally important art gallery housing an incomparable collection of English landscape watercolours, dominates the city physically and is a cultural beacon of national importance. Many other major buildings, such as the Assembly House and Blackfriars Hall, add to the richness not only of the architectural heritage but to the city's social and cultural life.

A major regional city merits an appropriate civic centre. Fifteenth-century Norwich already had a dramatic and impressive one, in the form of the great sloping market place, bounded by St Peter Mancroft church and the Guildhall, and in the 1930s the towering grandeur of the new City Hall added greatly to the sense of civic dignity. All are overlooked by the castle keep, while the eastern boundary, the broad Gentleman's Walk, though architecturally less impressive, reinforces the sense of space. The Norwich plan of 1945 went further with proposals for the centre, involving extensive demolition to build law courts, a library and assembly halls as well as local government offices. Much of this did not materialise, although the new central library, opened in 1964 and destroyed by fire thirty years later, was a prominent exception, creating a new public space facing St Peter Mancroft. The library has now been replaced by the Forum, which includes a replacement library and a wide range of other facilities. The new Law Courts have replaced a derelict area between the cathedral and the river, while the Theatre Royal has occupied its present site for 250 years and the market is still on its Norman site, though recently sensibly updated.

An outer zone of Greater Norwich has a ring of high schools with their playing fields, not to mention several rugby grounds, Norwich City Football Club training ground, a ski slope and Whitlingham Country Park with its

In the late 1950s Norwich Corporation cleared a substantial area of property between Bethel Street and Theatre Street and there built the new central library, opened in 1963. It also accommodated the Norfolk Record Office. On 1 August 1994 an electrical fault sparked a catastrophic fire which destroyed the building, and with it over 155,000 books, including most of the county local history collection, and almost 150,000 other items. Fortunately the priceless and irreplaceable archives were saved by the heroic efforts of record office staff. On the site of the library rose its replacement, The Forum, opened in 2001 and costing £65 million. This dramatic addition to the city's townscape takes its place as a new chapter in an architectural sequence – from its steps one can see the Norman keep, the great medieval church of St Peter Mancroft, the magnificent 1938 City Hall, the Georgian Assembly House and the 1950s redevelopment of bomb-ravaged Rampant Horse Street.

In the 1970s and 1980s the industrial area along the left bank of the river Wensum, south of
Norwich station and close to Carrow Road stadium, was steadily abandoned as factories and
firms closed. The planning opportunity that this represented was grasped by the development
of residential apartments, entertainment venues, restaurants and leisure amenities, together
with supermarkets and large retail units and a new road network. Whether the result is an
aesthetic triumph is perhaps debatable, but there is no doubting the liveliness of the area and the
commercial success of the project. In this view, looking downstream, the redevelopment of the
left bank contrasts with the run-down nineteenth-century warehousing opposite.

sailing and fishing on the northern edge of the Colman estate. The former
Earlham Park with its University Broad and walkway along the river Yare
provides a western boundary to the city. Debates are continually taking place
as to where and in what form new housing and commercial developments are to
be allowed. A static city loses ground to its neighbours, and Norwich, despite
its great history and with its historic core, has continued to expand.

Two themes have dominated the story of Yarmouth since the Second World
War.[12] The first and the more significant is that of the river Yare, its outfall
to the sea and its management to secure the best conditions for the survival
of a major port. The second is that of the tourist industry which replaced the
herring fishery as the town's major employer after 1970. Engineering problems
at the outlet of the river and along all the quays have occupied the borough
council ever since the war, when much damage was done and there was very
little maintenance. Yarmouth initially recovered from the loss of the herring
trade by becoming an oil depot and building a large oil-fired power station.
Then the discovery of North Sea oil and gas provided the basis for a rapid
growth in business, first in the building of the platforms and rigs and then in
supplying them. By the 1970s most of the quays were involved in servicing the
North Sea industry, but the steady decline in production in the southern North

Much of the Great Yarmouth was devastated by bombing during the Second World War, including many of the famous rows. After the war the reconstruction programme took scant account of the historic street pattern and the usual litany of demolition in the 1950s and 1960s took further toll, creating the gappy and forlorn townscape which lies behind South Quay and the market place. As part of the rebuilding long three- and four-storey blocks of flats were built in the middle of the town, as here on South Quay, helping to keep a sizeable resident population in the central area.

In 2012 the port of Great Yarmouth handled 889,000 tons, of which 238,000 tons were agricultural products and 157,000 was oil and other fuels. Most of the remainder is recorded in the government statistics as 'general cargo'. This means that the port is roughly as busy as Boston, but handles less than half the traffic of, for example, Ipswich. The main trading countries were France, North Africa [Tunisia, Morocco and Mauritania], the Netherlands, Spain and Norway. Vessels still tie up along the South Quay, as they have done for almost a thousand years, but the glory days of Yarmouth as a port, when its waters were crowded with fishing vessels, are now over a century in the past.

Sea after 1985 soon affected the levels of trade. Locally, wind power began to challenge North Sea oil and gas: windfarms were set up at West Somerton, and from 2003 an offshore wind farm of 30 turbines was constructed on Scroby Sands. A second aspect of the development of the port was the ambitious project for the construction of an outer harbour, to allow larger shipping to link Yarmouth more firmly to Europe. Its construction was funded by a consortium of local authorities and the European Union, and it is now owned by Eastport UK, the trading name of the Port Company Ltd. The history of the harbour has been troubled, but it is now emerging as a main supply base for the North Sea energy industries.

The holiday industry has provided a second theme to the story of Yarmouth after the two world wars, both in the town itself and in some of the adjacent coastal villages. As fishing declined the provision of accommodation and seaside amenities increased. Facilities were typical of resorts in the inter-war period and through the 1950s: 'gardens, promenades, boating lakes, model yacht ponds, bowling greens, a swimming pool, tennis courts, piers and a pleasure beach alternate along its five miles of fascinating sea front ... as the central beach gathers the majority who love the company of their fellows

Until the 1870s Hemsby was a small and obscure fishing and farming community on the shore north of Yarmouth. In 1878 the Midland and Great Northern Railway opened its line from North Walsham to Yarmouth, with a station at Hemsby, and the first visitors soon came to stay, including holidaymakers from the East Midlands. Between the wars holiday camps were opened all along the stretch of coast between Hemsby and Lowestoft, focusing on the existing resort of Yarmouth, and over the years a sprawl of holiday chalets, bungalows, caravan sites, amusement and entertainment facilities, cafes and shops has developed. Today, with its miles of golden sand, Hemsby is still a popular resort, a byword for deafening noise and visual garishness, its atmosphere redolent of fried onions, candy floss and diesel fumes, quite eclipsing the salty tang of the sea.

The colourful line of beach huts at Sheringham is a reminder that seaside holidays retain their appeal for many, despite the alternative attractions of the Costas or the Caribbean. Tourism remains vital to Norfolk's economy – an estimated 15 per cent of the county's workforce are employed in the tourist industry, a far higher proportion than in agriculture, energy or manufacturing – and improved road and rail access, the trend towards letting holiday cottages, and diversification into eco-tourism and other new leisure activities, have all helped to ensure the resilience of the sector.

Norfolk's resorts have faced many challenges in the period since the Second World War, as traditional 'bucket and spade' holidays have declined, competition from package tours and Mediterranean temptations has grown apace, and Victorian and Edwardian amenities no longer attracted visitors in huge numbers. At Hunstanton (right) the remedy has been to provide new facilities along the promenade which, while not in keeping with the traditional image of the resort, do manage to attract visitors in large numbers – as this photograph, taken on a chilly grey Bank Holiday in 2014, testifies.

to the north and to the south are large tracts of sand and marram grass … ideal for family picnics and bathing parties.'[13] In the period 1945 to 1974 on summer weekends an astonishing 750 coaches arrived at Beach Station every day. By 1960 it was necessary for high-quality popular entertainment to be provided and in the 1967 season, for example, Morecambe and Wise headed a prestigious list. A greyhound stadium was opened in 1946 and supplemented an existing racecourse. Yarmouth had all that a popular seaside resort needed. The Sealife Centre and Time and Tide museum have been two relatively recent additions. Nearby neighbouring villages have grown fast and Hopton, Caister and Hemsby all acquired holiday camps. Fritton Country Park on the Suffolk border has added another asset to the area. After the damage of the Second World War and the demand for improved housing, Yarmouth grew to the west of the river into Bradwell and Belton and, to a lesser extent, north to Caister and south into Gorleston. But its economic fortunes have been precarious, and the decline of the traditional seaside holiday in the 1970s and 1980s further challenged its well-being.

Lynn expanded fast between 1962 and 1975 after the agreement with the GLC to take London overspill. The population increased from 28,000 to 35,000, with new housing focused on the north of the town in the new estates at Gaywood and the Woottons. The expansion of this richly historic medieval trading town was not invariably a happy experience: 'Half of the [town centre] was demolished to accommodate the supermarkets and car parks required to service the new suburban population [and] it is sad to report how much of Lynn's Victorian heritage has been bulldozed, including important historical sites.'[14] Paul Richards, a major force behind Lynn's more recent conservation programme, comments that 'if the full town expansion plan had been implemented this redevelopment would have been even more drastic'. The other side of the picture has been the work of the King's Lynn Preservation Trust; the restoration of St George's Guildhall, now in the hands of the National Trust, became a focal point for the Lynn festivals. The Greenland Fishery, Hampton Court and the Hanseatic Warehouses have all been restored and are key elements of surviving medieval Lynn. The Greyfriars, the Redmount

Hampton Court, in Nelson Street, King's Lynn (below), is a quadrangular building with a very complex history. The south wing (left) is a fourteenth-century merchant's hall house, incorporating stonework from an even earlier building and with a contemporary steeply pitched timber roof. On the right, the north wing was built in the late sixteenth century, probably replacing earlier buildings, while the west wing (centre) was originally a warehouse, built in the later fifteenth century alongside the river. By the early seventeenth century the river had long since receded and the warehouse range was converted to residential use. The east range (off picture) on Nelson Street was designed as a row of shops. The name is derived from John Hampton, a master baker who became a freeman in 1645. By the 1950s the whole complex was deteriorating rapidly, but in 1959–62 the King's Lynn Preservation Trust and Mrs E.A. Lane undertook the complete restoration of the whole building and its division into 15 dwellings.

King's Lynn,
True's Yard.

The Hanseatic warehouse on St Margaret's Lane in King's Lynn was built between 1475 and 1480, for the merchants of the Hanseatic League after the 1474 Treaty of Utrecht had confirmed the privilege of the League to open trading bases in selected English ports. The League, a North Sea trading collective of over 170 towns, cities and associated places, had been trading with Lynn since the thirteenth century (mainly with merchants from Hamburg, Lübeck, Bremen and Danzig), dealing in furs, wax, fish, cereals, pitch, cloth and timber imported from Europe, and exporting corn, wool, leather, salt and lead. The Lynn warehouses are only remaining Hanseatic buildings in Great Britain. In 1751, after the riverside warehouse had been left high and dry by the westward shift of the quays, it was sold to a local merchant.

The quays at Lynn were developed on land which was reclaimed from the Great Ouse as the shore was gradually shifted westward during the medieval period. It has been suggested that this may have been due to a combination of natural silting and artificial reclamation involving the tipping of rubbish. The lands so created could eventually be used for housing, streets, warehousing and the quays themselves. The port of Lynn remains busy, but in the late nineteenth and early twentieth centuries the commercial heart of the port began to shift northward, a process encouraged by the opening of the Alexandra Dock (1869) and the Bentinck Dock (1883). Today many of the quayside buildings have been restored and new development has generally been in keeping with the scale and the traditional architectural styles.

The five-storey brick tower of Clifton House, King's Lynn, was built in about 1570 by George Walden, a wealthy merchant of the port. The architectural evidence indicates that it was probably used for business purposes, serving as a watchtower but with four floors of very comfortable and lavishly decorated rooms which could be used to entertain business clients. The house itself is much older, with a twelfth century window, fourteenth century undercrofts, and complete medieval tiled floors, as well as outstanding interiors of the early eighteenth century.

The long vista of King's Lynn from West Lynn, across the Great Ouse, is perhaps reminiscent of a waterside town in the Netherlands, which would be appropriate given the very close trading links between Lynn and the Low Countries over so many centuries. In this view the towers of St Margaret's church are the dominant feature, with the fascinating variety of old, restored and (mostly acceptable) new building lining the quay.

The north end of the riverside at King's Lynn remains a busy industrial area, centred on the two enclosed docks of 1869 and 1883. The port handles a wide range of commodities including cereals and pulses, animal feed, fertilisers, timber, bulk liquid products and steel. The town's industries are many and varied, ranging from the production of specialist medical devices such as inhalers, via the manufacturing of paper for newspapers, to commercial refrigeration equipment.

Chapel and the Clifton Tower are the latest buildings to have been renovated, as has True's Yard, a series of fishing cottages which have been turned into a successful heritage centre.

The port of Lynn has experienced disturbing fluctuations in trade and thus in prosperity, but still serves a key role in the export of malting barley. The rather poor road links with the Midlands, and the absence of a direct westward rail route, restrict imports, which are confined to petroleum, steel, animal feeds and fertilisers. However, industrial development has continued and Lynn has recently seen the opening of the largest paper mill in the United Kingdom, an important boost to its economy. The bypassing of Lynn by a new section of the A47 led to a reduction of traffic congestion in the town, while the improvement of the A10 and the electrification of the railway line to Cambridge and London have helped to reduce the sense of isolation in a town which is the largest centre for many miles in each direction.

Amazingly, even after the Second World War Thetford lacked 'any form of modern sanitation, with no sewerage system and only a partial network of surface drains ... only 23% of houses had flush toilets and they drained

In the late 1960s Thetford was chosen as the place to film the iconic television series *Dad's Army*, and under the guise of Warmington-on-Sea it appears in many episodes. The reason for this seemingly odd choice, for a town thirty miles from the coast, was that its ambience as a faded small borough, little changed by the twentieth century, perfectly replicated the image of the slightly down-at-heel resort of the fictional series. Now, almost half a century later, 'Dad's Army' is itself history, and Thetford has a new heritage to celebrate. There is a 'Dad's Army' museum, a 'Dad's Army' heritage trail and down by the river just above the Town Bridge sits the figure of a man on a bench – the actor Arthur Lowe playing the fictional Captain Mainwaring, in a pseudo-historical TV series that looks back to fictionalised real events of the Second World War.

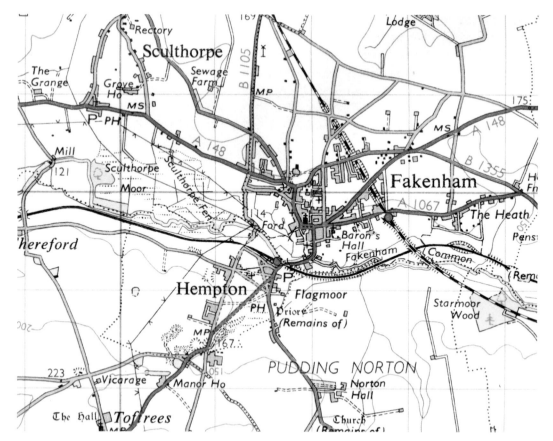

In the early 1950s most market towns in Norfolk seemed to be dying. Their populations were
either static or falling, commercial life was ebbing away, employment opportunities were limited,
and average incomes were way below the national average. On this map of 1954 Fakenham still
has two railway lines but both were destined to disappear within a few years, and the town
consists of little more than its medieval core and a few small suburban streets. It had just under
3,000 people. Today, thanks to car-based commuting and the rapid expansion of Norfolk's
economy and population, Fakenham has undergone a transformation, and it has tripled in size
to almost 9,000 people. Surrounding by sprawling housing estates, it is reinvigorated though, as
planning reports observe, the expansion of the retailing sector has not kept pace with population
growth.

into cesspools or the river, 45% had pail closets and 32% (414 houses) had
privy middens relying on ground absorption.'[15] The town had stagnated
economically for decades, losing employment as its traditional industries
declined, and with a virtually static population. It was the most depressed
and least dynamic of Norfolk's larger urban communities. In 1949–52 a full
sewerage scheme was finally installed, but as Thetford lost even the temporary
benefits of war work its economy was in an even worse state. The only answer
seemed to be to take drastic action, and in May 1957 the borough council
signed an agreement with London County Council to construct 1,500 houses
on 283 acres of land, to accommodate 5,000 overspill Londoners. The first
tenants moved from London in April 1959, and a 40-acre industrial estate
was planned along the A11. This and the new housing were south-east of the

town, spreading over the area of the ancient Saxon borough of pre-Conquest
days which had not been settled since.

There were even more ambitious proposals that Thetford should be allowed
to grow to a town of 75,000, but by the 1970s 'town expansion and overspill
schemes had begun to lose their attraction'.[16] Various other planning policies
came and went, and the aim was eventually modified to a more modest town
of 22,000. By 1986 the population was 21,000, which was five times the level
of half a century before. The cheapness of land and other incentives certainly
helped to attract new employment – between 1959 and 1968 fifty companies
moved into Thetford, many of them from Greater London, and 9,000 new jobs
were created. New shopping centres were built along the north bank of the
Little Ouse and between Tanner Street and King Street, and landscaping has
been carried out along the river. But there was too little regard for the attractive
historic townscape, and, as Crosby concludes, 'Thetford has in the last 40 years
lost too much of its historical and architectural heritage and it cannot afford to
lose any more'. The parallel with Lynn is close.

In 1958 Thetford was designated as an 'expanded town' to receive overspill population from
Greater London and between 1965 and 1975 the town centre was extensively redeveloped to
provide new shopping areas, car parking and service areas. The results were dire, as this view
of the rear of the King Street shops illustrates all too well. The crudity and sheer ugliness were
in tragic contrast to the many unremarkable but pleasant eighteenth- and nineteenth-century
buildings that were swept away (though it could have been worse – the original plans included
overhead roads threading the small and fragile town centre at rooftop level). Between 1961
and 1981 Thetford's population grew from 5,399 to 19,591, and it now stands at approximately
25,000, making it the fourth largest town in Norfolk. About 12 per cent of the population were
born in Portugal.

Conclusion

Changes in the long-term planning system, and in the local government system, have for some years been creating confusion about the future of Norfolk. In 1974 Norwich, which since the fifteenth century had been a county in its own right, was reduced in status to a district within Norfolk. Since that time the city council has sought every opportunity to regain autonomy, and in 2009–10 it seemed likely that this would happen, when the government moved towards legislation which would make the city a unitary authority. Immediately after the 2010 general election the coalition government cancelled those plans. The city has also sought to extend its boundaries in order to take in areas of new development and to allow a co-ordinated approach to the future development of Greater Norwich (currently split between the city itself, and Broadland and South Norfolk districts). There is particular concern over the expanding science park area linked to the University of East Anglia and the Norfolk and Norwich University Hospital, which is seen as its next zone of industrial and commercial development. The building of a new northern bypass to the city is related to plans for an eco-town to the north-east, in the Rackheath area between Norwich and Wroxham.

The electrified railway lines from Norwich to London and King's Lynn to Cambridge, roughly paralleled by the A140 and A10 respectively, are seen as

A dramatic change in the demography and society of parts of East Anglia began to develop in the mid-1970s, when Britain joined the European Union, and rapidly accelerated in the first decade of the present century. The influx of migrants from countries such as Portugal, Poland, Slovakia and the Baltic republics has had a powerful local impact. In the Fenland parts of the county East European migrants have emerged as a major and controversial element, fundamentally changing the statistical profiles of ethnicity and employment and becoming an important political issue. Here, at the entrance to the sugar factory at Wissington, the signs are clear.

During the inter-war period, when British agriculture was in the doldrums and there was
a widespread concern about its long-term future, successive governments investigated and
encouraged the development of alternative crops. The traditional patterns of Norfolk agriculture
were no longer viable, and the fodder crops that had been popular since the seventeenth century
– turnips, mangolds and swedes – were increasingly uneconomic. In the Edwardian period
Dutch interests had invested in sugar beet and had built the first factory, at Cantley on the side
of the Yare below Norwich, in 1912. After 1918 this crop was greatly expanded and in 1925 the
sugar refinery at Wissington, near Downham Market, was opened (above). Today this is the
largest in Europe, and is fed by 3 million tons of sugar beet brought from a 50-mile radius. The
washings produced 5,000 tons of aggregate a year, the waste pulp makes 140,000 tons of animal
feed per annum, and the annual output of sugar is 420,000 tons.

key axes for future growth, while the line from Norwich to Cambridge, and the
parallel A11, are also considered as the twin threads that run through another
axis for growth via Thetford, Attleborough and Wymondham. The scenic and
protected coast and the Broads, now in effect a national park, face the challenges
of coping with increasing numbers of tourists and retirement residents, and
the need to protect and preserve areas of crucial significance for conservation.
Breckland, a distinctive region of the county, remains largely in the hands of the
army, which is likely to continue. The bulk of the county remains agricultural
in its land use, and primarily arable. Wheat and barley are its key crops, but
an increasing number of small specialist agricultural enterprises break up the
largely arable landscape of the county. But the agricultural labour force is a
fraction of what it was half a century ago, a minute proportion of the numbers
a hundred years ago. Whatever happens in the future, much of traditional
Norfolk has already vanished.

In the 1960s the economy of the United Kingdom was transformed by the remarkable
development of North Sea oil and gas resources. For Norfolk there were opportunities for new
employment, though the highly advanced technology meant that these were far more limited
than had perhaps been imagined. In 2013 roughly 500 people were employed in the oil and gas
industry in the county, or only 0.1% of the workforce, although many working in engineering
and related trades serviced the energy industry. A site at Bacton, on the coast between
Mundesley and Happisburgh, was chosen in the mid-1960s as one of the three great terminals
for onshore delivery of North Sea gas. Opened in 1968, the Bacton terminal, almost a mile
across, provides a surreal contrast to the rural and coastal landscape around.

18

Conclusion

T HIS BOOK has given an overview of the story of Norfolk and its people, a journey which started almost a million years ago on the foreshore at Happisburgh. It finishes in the early twenty-first century with many changes looming on the horizon. Norfolk is certain to see further large population growth over the next few decades, and where to put these people and how they will move around remain issues that generate heated discussion. Norwich, the hub of the county and by far its largest urban area, has to face more of these pressures than elsewhere. Today the population of Greater Norwich is just over 200,000, but this seems certain to increase significantly in the coming years. The northern distributor road, though not completing the full circle of an outer ring road, will generate massive pressure for residential and commercial development along its route. In rural Norfolk, which might have had caravans all along its coast and ribbon development along many of its country roads, planning legislation has helped to prevent much unsightly and inappropriate development, but that too may change if the most drastic proposals for the relaxation of planning laws come to pass.

Natural gas, oil and now wind power, both inland and offshore, have had huge impacts on some stretches of the coast especially at Great Yarmouth and now perhaps at Wells. At Bacton the energy which superseded that of our nineteenth-century coalfields comes ashore, but how long will North Sea gas reserves be sustained? The threat and growing reality of rising sea level are emphasising the problem of erosion along the Norfolk coast and raising the question of how much of it can be protected. The noise of military aircraft is rapidly decreasing: RAF Coltishall has gone, and the future of RAF Marham is under discussion. The USAF at Lakenheath and British helicopters at Wattisham still fly over the county and their activities focus on the enlarged Breckland Battle Area. But the noise of traffic on the A11 grows as that vital artery becomes ever busier.

The Norfolk landscape is not dramatic. There are no mountains or high hills, no waterfalls or rocky crags, but it is nevertheless tremendously diverse, with a superb coastline, the endless flatness of the Fens, the intricate wetlands of the Broads, the woodlands and lanes of south Norfolk and the gravelly ridges of the north. Key landscape themes recur in this study, most of them relating to the physical background of gentle valleys, wide marshes, tidal estuaries, crumbling cliffs and sand dunes, broads and fens. Against this physical background are the villages which reflect earlier environments – the timber buildings in the south of the county, flint in the north, and everywhere the textures and style of the bricks used for vernacular housing from the sixteenth century onwards. It is a county still of great houses, of sweeping parks and large estates, but there are many smaller and no less attractive manor houses and Georgian rectories, often circled by moats or set in intimate parklands of their own. It is a county of a small, twisting roads, of lost railways and of reedy waterways plied by pleasure boats.

Norfolk has several hundred small villages set amid a scatter of often beautiful and always historically rich market towns. At the centre is Norwich, one of the great historic cities of Europe, with a remarkable heritage of medieval churches, monastic buildings, cathedrals, a great castle, and a glorious assemblage of domestic and commercial architecture. But Norwich is not a museum piece. Though it was once the second city of England, it is now a thriving and vibrant commercial centre, an artistic and cultural focus, and a proud and independent regional capital.

This is a county with a past stretching back into the dimmest mists of time, across whose soil some of our most celebrated national figures have walked – from Boudica, to Mary Tudor and Elizabeth, Nelson and Turnip Townshend, Elizabeth Fry and Edith Cavell. Everywhere bears the imprint of that past. Parts of Norfolk are less changed than almost any other area in England. Every chapter in its history is fascinating. The next ones will be no less interesting.

Appendix

Agricultural terms used in Norfolk

assart   a medieval term for a piece of land taken in from waste or wood (also a verb: to assart, assarting)

breck   a piece of heathland cropped sporadically

close   an area of land, hedged or ditched (that is, enclosed) in the ownership of one person

common   land over which specified properties had rights of grazing particular numbers and kinds of stock

extent   a written survey of an area of land, usually a manor

foldcourse   an area of land, which could be arable or waste, or both, restricted to the use of a particular flock of sheep

furlong (wong and went)   a sub-division of an open field, usually 220 yards long

headland   land at the end of a number of strips in a furlong when the plough turned

heath   land covered in heather, bracken or scrub

meadow   grassland managed for hay production

messuage   a plot of land with a house on it

open field   the major arable units of a parish; in Norfolk there were usually more than three

precinct   a part of a parish or estate chosen in a survey for its convenience e.g. between two roads

shack   the right to put stock on arable land after the harvest

shift   an area of the field system devoted to a particular cycle of cropping

strip   an individual holding within a furlong of an open field, sometimes known as a piece or a land

tenement   a land-holding (from the Latin *tenere*, to hold)

terrier   a list of lands with their abuttals (that is, a verbal description of the pieces of land to which each adjoined)

toft   a plot of land with a house on it, but often applied to a *former* house site

References

Chapter 1: The early settlement of Norfolk

1 Personal communication from Dr Peter Robins.

2 B. McWilliams, *Fossil vertebrates of the Cromer Forest Bed in Norwich Castle Museum* (Norwich Castle Museum, 1967).

3 J. Davies, *The Land of Boudica* (Heritage Marketing and Publications Limited/Norfolk Museums and Archaeology Service, 2009) 26. This valuable recent study has been used in several places to update news of discoveries up to and including the Roman period.

4 J. Wymer, 'Norfolk and the History of Palaeolithic Archaeology in Britain', in *A Festival of Norfolk Archaeology* (Norfolk and Norwich Archaeological Society, 1996).

5 R. Jacobi, 'The Mesolithic of Northern East Anglia and Contemporary Territories', in C. Barringer (ed.), *Aspects of East Anglian Prehistory* (Geo Books, 1985).

6 Davies, *The Land of Boudica*, p. 39.

7 Davies, *The Land of Boudica*, p. 42.

8 F. Healy, 'Farming and Field Monuments: the Neolithic in Norfolk', in C. Barringer (ed.), *Aspects of East Anglian Prehistory*, p. 77 and fig. 5.1.

9 Davies, *The Land of Boudica*, p. 59.

10 J. G. Clark, 'The Timber Monument at Arminghall and its affinities', *Proceedings of the Prehistoric Society* new ser.2 (1936) pp. 1–51.

11 R. R. Clarke, *East Anglia* (Thames Hudson, 1960; reprinted SR Publications, 1971) p. 67.

12 Healy, 'Farming and Field Monuments', fig. 5.7.

13 G. Larwood and B. Funnell (eds), *The Geology of Norfolk* (Paramoudra Club, 1970).

14 H. Bamford, *Beaker Domestic Sites in the Fen Edge and East Anglia* (East Anglian Archaeology no.16, 1982).

15 Ibid., pp. 30, 54.

16 T. Ashwin, 'Norfolk's First Farmers', in T. Ashwin and A. Davison (eds), *An Historical Atlas of Norfolk* (3rd edition, Phillimore, 2005) (hereafter *Historical Atlas of Norfolk*) pt 8.

Chapter 2: The Bronze Age and Iron Age in Norfolk

1 R. R. Clarke, *East Anglia*, p. 89.

2 Ibid., photograph 16

3 A. Lawson, 'The Bronze Age in East Anglia', in C. Barringer (ed.), *Aspects of East Anglian Prehistory*.

4 Davies, *The Land of Boudica*, p. 71.

5 A. Lawson, *The Barrows of East Anglia* (East Anglian Archaeology no. 12, 1986).

6 Norfolk Archaeological Unit Annual Review, 1998–99, pp. 8–9.

7 B. Cunliffe, *Iron Age Communities of Britain* (Routledge and Kegan Paul, 1978 edition) p. 30.

8 Davies, *The Land of Boudica*, p. 92.

9 Clarke, *East Anglia*.

10 T. Ashwin and S. Bates, *Excavations on the Norwich Southern Bypass, 1989–91, Part 1* (East Anglian Archaeology no.91, 2000).

11 A. Rogerson, 'Arable and Pasture in Two Norfolk Parishes', ch. 5 in J. Davis and T. Williamson (eds), *Land of the Iceni: the Iron Age in Northern East Anglia* (University of East Anglia Centre for East Anglian Studies: Studies in East Anglian History 4, 1999).

12 P. E. J. Wiltshire and P. Murphy, 'Current knowledge of the Iron Age Environment and Agrarian Economy of Norfolk and Adjacent Areas', ch. 6 in Davis and Williamson, *Land of the Iceni*.

13 T. Ashwin, 'Excavations of an Iron Age Site at Silfield, Wymondham, Norfolk, 1992–93', *Norfolk Archaeology* vol. 43 (1996) pp. 241–82.

14 B. Robinson and T. Gregory, *Celtic Fire and Roman Rule* (Poppyland, 2003) pp. 15–18.

15 R. R. Clarke, 'A Hoard of Silver Coins of the Iceni from Honingham, Norfolk', *British Numismatic Journal*, vol. 28 (1956) pp. 1–10.

16 Davies, *The Land of Boudica*, p. 36.

17 Peter Salway, *Roman Britain* (Clarendon, 1981) pp. 14–15.

Chapter 3: Roman Norfolk

1 Davies, *The Land of Boudica*, p. 120.
2 Ibid., pp. 160–1.
3 Ibid., pp. 181–2, 184–5.
4 Ibid., 205.
5 C. Green, 'Leylands Farm, Hockwold cum Wilton', in *Settlement, religion and industry on the Fen-edge: three Romano-British sites in Norfolk* (East Anglian Archaeology no. 31, 1986) p. 65, fig. 41.
6 B. Ayers, *Norwich: a Fine City* (Tempus, 2003), pp. 20–2.
7 Salway, *Roman Britain*, p. 655.
8 T. Lane and E. Morris (eds), *A Millennium of Saltmaking: pre-Historic and Romano-British Salt Production in the Fenland* (Lincolnshire Archaeological and Heritage Reports: series 4, 2001) pp. 162–249.
9 D. Atkinson, 'A Roman Villa at Gaytonthorpe', *Norfolk Archaeology* vol. 23 (1929) pp. 166–209.
10 E. Greenfield, 'The Romano-British Villa and Bath House at Little Oulsham Drove, Feltwell, excavated 1962–64', in *Settlement, religion and industry on the Fen-edge: three Romano-British sites in Norfolk* (East Anglian Archaeology no. 31, 1986).
11 W. Bowden and D. Bescoby, 'Recent Research at Caistor Roman Town', *The Annual 19* (2010); D. Edwards and Peter Wade-Martins, *Norfolk from the Air* (Norfolk Museums Service, 1987).
12 Clarke, *East Anglia*, p. 117.
13 D. Gurney, 'A Romano-Celtic temple site at Caistor St Edmund', in *Excavations at Thornham, Warham, Wighton and Caistor, Norfolk* (East Anglian Archaeology no. 30, 1986).
14 W. Bowden, 'Architectural innovation in the land of the Iceni: a new complex near Venta Icenorum, Norfolk', *Journal of Roman Archaeology* no. 24 (2011).
15 *Burgh Castle: Excavations by Charles Green, 1951 to 1961* (East Anglian Archaeology no. 20, 1982).
16 Davies, *The Land of Boudica*, pp. 211–13.
17 Ibid., p. 224.
18 Ibid., pp. 228–9.

Chapter 4: Norfolk under the Anglo-Saxons and Vikings

1 *The Anglo-Saxon Chronicles* (trans. Anne Savage: Heinemann, 1983) p. 29.
2 K. Penn, 'Early Saxon Settlements', *Historical Atlas of Norfolk*, pt 14.
3 C. Hills and K. Penn, *The Anglo-Saxon cemetery at Spong Hill, North Elmham Pt.2* (East Anglian Archaeology no. 11, 1981)
4 B. Green and A. Lawson, *The Anglo-Saxon Cemetery at Bergh Apton, Norfolk: Catalogue* (East Anglian Archaeology no. 7, 1978).
5 E. Crowfoot, 'Section VI, The Textiles', in B. Green and A. Rogerson, *The Anglo-Saxon Cemetery at Bergh Apton, Norfolk* (East Anglian Archaeology no.7, 1978) pp. 98, 99.
6 P. Rogers, *Cloth and Clothing in Early Anglo Saxon England* (CBA Research Report 145, 2007) pp. 28, 29, figs 2, 21.
7 C. Hills, *The Anglo-Saxon cemetery at Spong Hill, North Elmham Pt. 1* (East Anglian Archaeology no.6, 1977) p. 31.
8 Peter Wade-Martins, *Excavations in North Elmham Park, 1967 to 1972* (East Anglian Archaeology no.9, vols 1 and 2, 1980).
9 J. Hall *et al.* 'Excavation at Attlebridge, 1989', *Norfolk Archaeology* vol.42 (1996)
10 A. Rogerson, 'Middle Saxon Norfolk (*c.*AD 650–850)', *Historical Atlas of Norfolk*, pt.15
11 T. Pestell, 'The After Life of Productive Sites in East Anglia', in T. Pestell and K. Ulmschneider, *Markets in Early Medieval Europe* (Windgather, 2003), p. 123
12 S. Jennings, *Eighteen Centuries of Pottery from Norwich* (East Anglian Archaeology no. 13, 1981).
13 E. O. Blake (ed.), *The Book of Ely* (Royal Historical Society, 1962) p. xvi.
14 A. Davison, 'Medieval Settlement Desertion', *Historical Atlas of Norfolk*, pt 43.
15 H. Hallam, 'Eastern England', in H. Hallam (ed.), *The Agrarian History of England and Wales vol. 2, 1042–1350* (CUP, 1988).
16 O. Beazley, *Excavations in St Martin-at-Palace Church, 1987* (East Anglian Archaeology no. 96, 2001) p. 5.
17 Frank Stenton, *Anglo-Saxon England* (Oxford University Press, 1968) pp. 319–20.
18 *The Anglo-Saxon Chronicles*, trans. Savage, p. 149.
19 K. Skipper and T. Williamson, 'Late Saxon Social Structure', *Historical Atlas of Norfolk*, pt 19.
20 K. Penn, 'Medieval Unplanned Towns', *Historical Atlas of Norfolk*, pt 35.
21 T. Pestell, 'The After Life of Productive Sites in East Anglia', in Pestell and Ulmschneider, *Markets in Early Medieval Europe*, p.124.
22 D. Dymond, 'Medieval and Later Markets', *Historical Atlas of Norfolk*, pt 37.
23 B. Ayers, *Norwich*, p.23.
24 Ibid., quoting the *Liber Eliensis*.
25 B. Ayers, unpublished lecture given at Dragon Hall, Norwich, 11 March 2008.
26 K. Penn, 'The Origins of Thetford', *Historical Atlas of Norfolk*, pt 21.
27 A. Crosby, *A History of Thetford* (Phillimore, 1986), p. 18.

Chapter 5: The Norman Conquest and its aftermath

1   J. Coad, *Castle Acre: Castle and Priory* (English Heritage, 1998).
2   As given in volume 2 of P. Brown's edited edition of Domesday Book for Norfolk (Phillimore, 1984).
3   *Victoria County History of Norfolk*, vol. 2 (1906).
4   G. Munford, *An Analysis of the Domesday Book of the County of Norfolk* (London, 1848).
5   M. Morris, *The Bigod Earls of Norfolk in the Thirteenth Century* (Boydell, 2005).
6   P. Brown (ed.), *Domesday Book: Norfolk*, pts 1 and 2, 8.21; pt 2, 15.4.
7   B. Cornford, *Medieval Flegg* (Larks Press, 2002).
8   S. Heslop, *Norwich Castle Keep: Romanesque Architecture and Social Context*, Centre of East Anglian Studies, 1994, p. 11.
9   Ibid., p. 66.
10 F. Meeres, *A History of Great Yarmouth* (Phillimore, 2007), p. 22.
11 P. Richards, *King's Lynn* (Phillimore, 1990).
12 D. Owen (ed.), *The Making of King's Lynn* (British Academy, 1984).
13 C. S. Dence, *Portrait of a Village: Castle Rising* (privately published, 1980).
14 N. Pevsner and B. Wilson, *Buildings of England: Norfolk vol. 2* (Yale University Press, 1999) p. 253.
15 *Victoria History of the County of Norfolk*, vol. 2, between pp. 314 and 315.
16 Pevsner and Wilson, *Norfolk* 2, p. 593.
17 G. Munford, *Domesday Book*, p. 88 (there were 250 churches recorded in Norfolk, 26 in Norwich, with 28 chapels in Norwich and 13 in Thetford).
18 Pevsner and Wilson, *Norfolk* 2, p. 726.
19 Ibid., p. 763.
20 Ibid., pp. 663–4.

Chapter 6: Early medieval Norfolk

1   B. Cushion and A. Davison, *Earthworks of Norfolk* (East Anglian Archaeology no. 104, 2003) pp. 59–61.
2   B. Cushion *et al.*, *Some Deserted Village Sites in Norfolk* (East Anglian Archaeology no. 14, 1982) pp. 42–8.
3   A. Rogerson, 'Moated Sites', *Historical Atlas of Norfolk*, pt 33.
4   F. Davenport, *The Economic Development of a Norfolk Manor, 1086–1565* (Cass, 1967), chapter 2, 'The Demesne', pp. 20–48.
5   H. Hallam, 'Eastern England', p. 157.
6   B. M. S. Campbell, 'The Extent and Layout of Common Fields in Eastern Norfolk', *Norfolk Archaeology* vol. 38 pt 1 (1981). This section draws on the above article.
7   M. Bailey, *A Marginal Economy?* (Cambridge University Press, 1989). This is the main source for this section and the two maps.
8   Ibid., p. 129.
9   A. E. B. Owen, *The Records of a Commission of Sewers for Wiggenhall, 1319–1324* (Norfolk Record Society vol. 48, 1981).
10 H. C. Darby, *Medieval Fenland* (David & Charles, 1974), quoting Mary Bateson, 'The register of Crabhouse Nunnery', *Norfolk Archaeology* vol. 9 (1892) pp. 1–71.
11 Norfolk Record Office (NRO): Richard Cooper of Terrington St John, 1584 NCC 315 Bate and Inv NCC 2 11.
12 Cornford, *Medieval Flegg*, p. 58, quoting NRO DCN 61/39,40,41 (Ormesby accounts).
13 Cornford, *Medieval Flegg*.
14 J. Jennings, *The Origin of the Broads* (Royal Geographical Society [RGS], 1952); J. Lambert *et al.*, *The Making of the Broads* (RGS, 1960).
15 O. Rackham, 'Medieval Woodland', *Historical Atlas of Norfolk*, pt 26.
16 H. C. Darby, *The Domesday Geography of Eastern England* (Cambridge University Press, 1952).
17 E. Miller (ed.), *The Agrarian History of England and Wales*, vol. III, 1348–1500 (Cambridge University Press, 1991) p. 7.
18 P. Pobst (ed.), *The Register of William Bateman, Bishop of Norwich, 1344 to 1355 vols I and II* (Canterbury and York Society vols 30 and 31, 1996).
19 Ibid., p. 119, nos 828 and 825.
20 M. Ormrod and P. Lindley, *The Black Death in England* (Paul Watkins, 1996), p. 63.
21 A. Davison, *Deserted Villages in Norfolk* (Poppyland, 1996).
22 Ibid., p. 79.
23 W. Hudson and J. C. Tingey, *The Records of the City of Norwich vol. 1* (1906) no. XLI; and Ayers, *Norwich*, p. 87.
24 C. Harper Bill and C. Rawcliffe, 'The Religious Houses' in Rawcliffe and Wilson (eds), *Medieval Norwich* (Hambledon, 2004) pp. 101–15. This is an excellent short history of the four orders of friars in Norwich.
25 Ibid., p. 102.
26 B. Ayers, *Norwich* (English Heritage, 1994) pp. 66–8.
27 E. Rutledge, 'Economic Life', in Rawcliffe and Wilson, *Medieval Norwich*.
28 P. Richards, *King's Lynn*.

29 F. Meeres, *Great Yarmouth*; this section draws on Meeres and also on J. McBride, *A Diary of Great Yarmouth* (author, 1998).

30 R. A. C. Hedges, *Yarmouth is an Ancient Town* (Great Yarmouth, 1959), p. 23.

31 A. Crosby, *Thetford*, pp. 30–55.

32 Ibid., p. 41.

33 J. Hooton, *The Glaven Ports* (Blakeney History Group, 1996).

34 Ibid., pp. 33–4.

Chapter 7: Wool, sheep and textiles

1 This section draws on Ann Sutton, 'The Early Linen and Worsted Industry of Norfolk', *Norfolk Archaeology* vol. 40 pt 3 (1989) pp. 201–25.

2 U. Priestley, *The Great Market* (University of East Anglia Centre for East Anglian Studies, 1987).

3 W. Hudson and J. C. Tingey, *The Records of the City of Norwich*, vol. 2 (1910), p. 243, and vol. 1 (1906), pp. 74–5.

4 M. Bailey, 'Sheep Accounts of Norwich Cathedral Priory, 1484–1534', in *Poverty and Wealth* (Norfolk Record Society, vol. 71, 2007) pp. 82–3.

5 P. Rutledge (ed.), *Skayman's Book, 1516–1518* (Norfolk Record Society vol. 61, 1987), p. 109 [modernised text].

6 Ibid., p. 97.

7 J. Gairdner (ed.), *The Paston Letters, 1422–1590, vol. 2* (AMS Press Inc., New York, 1965), pp. 197 and 232.

8 T. Williamson, *The Transformation of Rural England: farming and the landscape, 1700–1870* (University of Exeter Press, 2002) pp. 53–82, 'The Light Land Revolution'.

9 The National Archives: E122 194/9 (Yarmouth Port Book and Customs Account 26 Henry VI, 1447–8: account of Simon Burton and John Bale, collectors).

10 Hudson and Tingey, *Records vol. 2*, p. 180 and no. 333 (court held Saturday 30 May 1562).

11 Iris Coe, mss notes kindly loaned to the author.

12 J. Venn, *Biographical History of Caius College* (Cambridge University Press, 1896)

13 K. Allison, 'The wool supply and the Worsted cloth industry in Norfolk in the 16th and 17th centuries', unpublished Ph.D. thesis, University of Leeds, 1956.

14 H. Mason, *History of Norfolk* (London, 1884), p. 156 quoting Chapter House Record Office, County Bag, Norfolk, 10.

15 F. Blomefield, *An essay towards a topographical history of Norfolk*, vol. 1 (1739), p. 72.

16 A. Simpson, *The Wealth of the Gentry, 1540–1660* (Cambridge University Press, 1963) p. 195.

17 This section draws on Richard Wilson's chapter, 'The Textile Industry', in Rawcliffe and Wilson (eds), *Norwich Since 1550* (Hambledon, 2004), pp. 219–41.

18 A. D. Bayne, *A Comprehensive History of Norwich* (1869), pp. 580 and 594; and Wilson, 'The Textile Industry', p. 241.

19 U. Priestley (ed.) *Letters of Philip Stannard, Norwich Textile Manufacturer, 1751–1763* (Norfolk Record Society, vol. 57 (1994), pp. 9 and 11.

20 P. Clabburn, *The Norwich Shawl* (Norfolk Museum Service, 1995).

21 Bayne, *Comprehensive History*, p. 580.

22 Ibid., p. 594.

Chapter 8: Churches and parishes

1 N. Batcock, 'Medieval Churches in use and in ruins', *Historical Atlas of Norfolk*, pt 28.

2 A. Davison, *Six Deserted Villages in Norfolk* (East Anglian Archaeology no. 44, 1988).

3 Pevsner and Wilson, *Norfolk 2*, p. 771.

4 Pevsner and Wilson, *Norfolk 1*, p. 698.

5 P. Cattermole and S. Cotton, 'Medieval Parish Church Building in Norfolk', *Norfolk Archaeology* vol. 33 pt 3 (1983).

6 Ibid., p. 268.

7 Pevsner and Wilson, *Norfolk 1*, p. 247.

8 D. King, *The Medieval Stained Glass of St Peter Mancroft, Norwich* (British Academy, 2006) Appendix 2, 145–54.

9 D. Mortlock and C. V. Roberts, *The Popular Guide to Norfolk Churches* (2 vols, Acorn Editions, 1981).

10 NRO ANW 15/1: Saxlingham glebe terrier, 1614.

11 NRO PD 295/35: faculty for a new rectory at Redenhall

12 *Towards a History of Mattishall* (Mattishall Society, 1977) p. 35 quoting *The Tithe Book of the Rev John Smith, Vicar of Mattishall, 1781–1801* (Gonville and Caius archives VIII, 32).

Chapter 9: Norfolk from 1350 to 1550

1 B. Cornford, *Medieval Flegg*, pp. 142–3.

2 F. Davenport, *Economic development of a Norfolk manor*, pp. 74–5.

3 M. Hicks, *Late Medieval England, 1272 to 1485* (Stackpole Books, 2001). pp. 141–2.

4 B. Cornford, *Medieval Flegg*, p. 46.

5 C. Hoare, *The History of an East Anglian Soke* (Bedfordshire Times, 1918).

6 Ibid., quoting patent roll 5, Richard II, Pt 2, 312, membrane 12d.

7 L. Redstone, *The Cellarer's Accounts for Bromholm Priory, Norfolk, 1415–16* (Norfolk Record Society vol. 17, 1944).

8 Ibid., p. 77.

9 *Victoria County History of Norfolk, vol. 2,* pp. 359–363.

10 C. Hoare, *East Anglian Soke,* pp. 178–80.

11 R. Virgoe (ed.), *Illustrated Letters of the Paston Family* (Macmillan, 1989); Norman Davis (ed.), *The Paston Letters and Papers of the 15th Century* (Clarendon Press, 1976).

12 C. Dallas and D. Sherlock, *Baconsthorpe Castle, Excavations and Finds, 1951 to 1972* (East Anglian Archaeology no. 102, 2002).

13 Virgoe, *Paston Family,* p. 94.

14 I. Friel, *The Good Ship* (British Museum Press, 1995), frontispiece.

15 D. Dymond, *The Register of Thetford Priory, Part 2* (Norfolk Record Society vol. 60, 1995–6) p. 744.

16 These are listed in full and fascinating detail in the online 'Medieval markets and fairs gazetteer to 1516' (http://www.history.ac.uk/cmh/gaz/norf.html)

17 P. Clark and P. Slack, *English Towns in Transition 1500 to 1700* (Oxford University Press, 1976) p. 128.

18 K. Farnhill, *Guilds and the Parish Community in Late Medieval East Anglia, 1470 to 1550* (York Medieval Press, 2001).

19 Ibid., pp. 104–26.

20 D. Owen, *Making of King's Lynn,* p. 61.

21 A. Crosby, *Thetford,* p. 38.

22 C. Harper Bill (ed.), *The Register of John Morton, vol. 3, 1486–1500* (Canterbury and York Society, vol. 89, 2000).

23 *Victoria County History of Norfolk,* vol. 2, p. 255.

24 C. Arnold-Baker, *The Companion to British History* (Routledge, 2001), pp. 893–4.

25 S. Land, *Kett's Rebellion* (Boydell, 1977), pp. 40–1.

26 Ibid., p. 49.

27 Ibid., pp. 71–2.

Chapter 10: The Fens

1 NRO. Hare 643/5 118X2, 'Correspondence with reference to setting up Butter Market'.

2 A. Young, *General View of the Agriculture of the County of Norfolk 1804* (reprint David & Charles, 1969), pp. 447 and 450.

3 A. Young, *General View of the Agriculture of the County of Lincolnshire 1813* (reprint David and Charles, 1970), pp. 345–6.

4 H. Godwin, *Fenland: Ancient Past and Uncertain Future* (Cambridge University Press, 1978), p. 140.

5 J. Mosby, *Land of Britain 70: Norfolk* (London School of Economics, 1936) p. 237.

6 S. Wade Martins, 'Building for Smallholdings: a Norfolk Case Study', *Journal of Norfolk Historic Buildings Group no. 3* (2007), pp. 76–84.

7 R. Kemp, 'Horticulture', in *Norwich and its Region* (British Association for the Advancement of Science, 1961).

Chapter 11: Norfolk from 1550 to 1750

1 Over the past twenty-five years these papers have been magnificently researched and edited in a project begun by A. Hassell Smith: *vol. 1 1556–1577* ed. A. Hassell Smith, Gillian M. Baker and R. W. Kenny (Norfolk Record Society vol. 46, 1978 and 1979); *vol. 2 1578–1585* ed. A. Hassell Smith and G. M. Baker (NRS vol. 49, 1982 and 1983); *vol. 3 1586–1595* ed. A. Hassell Smith and G. M. Baker (NRS vol. 53, 1987 and 1988); *vol. 4 1596–1602* ed. V. Morgan, J. Key and B. Taylor (NRS vol. 64, 2000); *vol. 5 1603–1607* ed. V. Morgan, E. Rutledge and B. Taylor (NRS vol. 74, 2010).

2 H. Castor, *She-Wolves: the women who ruled England before Elizabeth* (Faber & Faber 2010) p. 414.

3 F. Blomefield, *Topographical history of Norfolk,* vol. 4 (1806), p. 274.

4 Z. Dovey, *An Elizabethan Progress* (Alan Sutton, 1996): this section draws on Dovey's account.

5 J. Pound, *The Norwich Census of the Poor 1570* (Norfolk Record Society, vol. 40, 1971).

6 Ibid., p. 9.

7 F. Blomefield, *Topographical history of Norfolk,* vol. 7 (1807) p. 94.

8 C. Morris (ed.), *The Journeys of Celia Fiennes* (Cresset Press, 1947) p. 148.

9 G. D. H. Cole (ed.), *Daniel Defoe: a tour through England and Wales* (2 vols Everyman, 1959).

10 A. Metters, *King's Lynn Port Books, 1610 to 1614* (Norfolk Record Society, vol. 73, 2009).

11 D. Higgins, *The Ingenius Mr Henry Bell* (Phoenix, 2002).

12 A. Hassell Smith, *County and Court: government and politics in Norfolk, 1558 to 1603* (Clarendon Press, 1974): I have drawn on this volume for much background.

13 Ibid., p. 27.

14 Ibid.

15 V. Morgan, J. Key and B. Taylor (eds), *The Papers of Nathaniel Bacon of Stiffkey, vol. 4, 1596 to 1602* (Norfolk Record Society vol. 64, 2000).

16 J. Rosenheim (ed.), *The Notebook of Robert Doughty,*

1662 to 1665 (Norfolk Record Society vol. 54, 1989) p. 19.

17 C. Hoare, *An East Anglian Soke*, pp. 318–19.

18 C. Barringer, 'Cawston', in *Exploring the Norfolk Village* (Poppyland, 2005), p.109.

19 P. Millican, *A History of Horstead and Stanninghall, Norfolk* (Norwich, 1937): this section draws on Millican's study.

20 Simpson, *The Wealth of the Gentry, 1540 to 1660*.

21 J. Rosenheim, *The Townshends of Rainham* (Wesleyan University Press, 1989).

22 Ibid., pp. 151–2.

23 D. P. Mortlock, *Aristocratic Splendour, Money and the World of Thomas Coke, Earl of Leicester* (Sutton, 2007).

24 R. W. Ketton Cremer, 'Robert Marsham', in *A Norfolk Gallery* (Faber & Faber, 1948) pp. 149–61.

25 E. Griffiths (ed.), *William Windham's Green Book, 1673 to 1685* (Norfolk Record society vol.66, 2002) p.66.

26 Ibid., pp. 60–1.

27 NRO: William Warner of North Walsham 1728 Inventory ANF/11/3/131.

28 A series of inventories transcribed by Sylvia Addington of Tasburgh illustrates the nature of this area.

29 NRO: J. Tunolde NCC Inv 21/96 1606.

30 NRO: R. Goose NCC Inv 731–2.

31 NRO: J. Allgard NCC Inv 19/208 1603.

32 J. Browne, *The History of Congregationalism in Norfolk and Suffolk* (Jarrold, 1877).

33 Mason, *History of Norfolk*, p. 579.

34 I. Atherton and V. Morgan, *Norwich Cathedral: church, city and diocese, 1096-1996* (Hambledon, 1996), ch. 27, p. 541.

35 J. Evans, *Seventeenth-Century Norwich* (Clarendon, 1979), p. 88.

36 Atherton and Morgan, quoting the works of Joseph Hall (12 vols, Oxford, 1857), vol. 1, p. 55.

37 A. Hopper, 'The Civil Wars', in Rawcliffe and Wilson, *Norwich since 1550*, p. 89.

38 Crosby, *Thetford*, p. 64.

39 Meeres, *Great Yarmouth*, p. 25.

40 Richards, *King's Lynn*, pp. 125–7.

41 Blomefield, *Topographical history of Norfolk*, vol. 3 (1806), pp. 394–401.

42 Mason, *History of Norfolk*, p. 268.

43 Ibid., p. 345.

44 Ibid., p. 581.

45 Ketton Cremer, *Norfolk Gallery*, pp. 95–124.

46 Atherton and Morgan, *Norwich Cathedral*, p. 557.

47 Ibid., pp.563–75.

48 NRO: FC11/1 records of Guestwick Congregational Church.

49 Mason, *History of Norfolk*, p. 587.

50 Ibid., pp. 569–77.

51 E. Gage, *Costessey Hall* (Costessey, 1991).

52 B. Garrard, *Wymondham Grammar School* (Wymondham Heritage Society, 2010).

53 C. Forder, *History of the Paston School* (North Walsham, 1981), p. 23.

54 Richards, *King's Lynn*, p. 114.

55 Hedges, *Yarmouth is an antient town*, p. 88.

56 R. Harries *et al.*, *A History of Norwich School* (Norwich, 1991).

57 M. F. Lloyd Prichard, 'The Education of the Poor in Norfolk, 1700 to 1850', *Norfolk Archaeology*, vol. 33, pt 3 (1964), pp. 321–31.

58 Dence, *Castle Rising*, p. 25.

59 C. Rawcliffe, *Medicine for the Soul* (Sutton, 1999), p. 239.

60 M. Rodgers (ed.), *The Ecclesiastical History of St Peter Parmentergate* (King Street Publications, Norwich, 2009).

61 C. Barringer, 'George Sawer of Cawston' (*The Annual*, no. 12, 2003).

62 NRO: Sawer papers M148/15, 624 x 8.

63 M. C. Cubitt, *Book of Hempnall* (Halsgrove, 2008), p.41.

64 W. Tate, *The Parish Chest* (Phillimore, 1983), p. 226.

65 C. Barringer (ed.), *North Walsham in the Eighteenth Century* (North Walsham WEA, 1983).

66 J. Maddison, *Felbrigg Hall* (National Trust, 2003): an excellent guide and history.

67 Pevsner and Wilson, *Norfolk 2*, pp. 600–9.

68 Pevsner and Wilson, *Norfolk 1*, pp. 730–2.

69 Pevsner and Wilson, *Norfolk 2*, gives a very full account of the building, pp. 428–36; D. Yaxley (ed.), *Survey of the Houghton Hall Estate by Joseph Hill, 1800* (Norfolk Record Society vol. 50, 1984).

70 Mortlock, *Aristocratic Splendour*; S. Wade Martins, *Coke of Norfolk, 1754 to 1842: a biography* (Boydell, 2009); Pevsner and Wilson, *Norfolk 2*, p. 413.

71 D. Stoker, 'Francis Blomefield as a Historian of Norfolk', *Norfolk Archaeology* vol. 44, pt 2 (2003), pp.181–201, 'Francis Blomefield as a Historian of Norwich', *Norfolk Archaeology* vol. 44, pt 3 (2004), pp. 387–405, and *The Correspondence of the Reverend Francis Blomefield* (Norfolk Record Society vol. 55, 1990–92).

Chapter 12: Norfolk 1750 to 1830

1 C. Barringer, 'Introduction', *Faden's Map of Norfolk, 1779* (Lark's Press, 1989).

2 A. Macnair, *Faden's Map of Norfolk digitally redrawn* (2005).

3 S. Wade Martins and T. Williamson (eds), *The Farming Journal of Randall Burroughs, 1794 to 1799* (Norfolk Record Society, vol. 58, 1993–95): this section draws on that text, pp. 1–38.

4 Young, *Agriculture of Norfolk*, p. 392.

5 M. Turner, 'Parliamentary Enclosure', *Historical Atlas of Norfolk*, pt 63.

6 Ibid.

7 A. Macnair, 'Foulsham and North Elmham', *Norfolk Archaeology*, vol. 44, pt 2 (2003), pp. 269–92.

8 A. Reid, 'The Process of Parliamentary Enclosure in Ashill', *Norfolk Archaeology*, vol. 38, pt 2 (1979), pp. 169–77.

9 J. Ayton, 'Parliamentary Enclosure at Wymondham, Pt 1', *The Annual*, no. 16 (2007), pp. 36–52.

10 Young, *Agriculture of Norfolk*, p. 451.

11 Wade Martins, *Coke of Norfolk*, p. 114.

12 R. Blythe, in his introduction to *A Country Parson* (Oxford University Press, 1985), p. 9.

13 John Wesley, *Sermons on Several Occasions*.

14 J. Browne, *Congregationalism in Norfolk and Suffolk*, p. 189.

15 C. Jolly, *The Spreading Flame, the Coming of Methodism to Norfolk, 1751 to 1811* (no date or publisher).

16 Ibid., pp. 58 and 73.

17 M. Leeder, *Fire over East Anglia* (Mouse Press, 1999) p. 1.

18 S. Wade Martins, 'The Riots of 1830', *Historical Atlas of Norfolk*, pt 65.

19 Mason, *History of Norfolk*, p. 496.

20 C. Barringer, 'Attleborough', in *Exploring Norfolk Market Towns* (Poppyland, 2011).

21 S. Wade Martins, 'The Riots of 1830', and 'Agriculture in the mid 19th Century', *Historical Atlas of Norfolk* pt 66.

22 A. Davison, 'Inland Waterways', *Historical Atlas of Norfolk*, pt 75.

23 A. Davison and R. Joby, 'Early Roads and Turnpikes', *Historical Atlas of Norfolk*, pt 74.

24 V. Belton, *The Norwich to Cromer Turnpike* (author, 1998).

25 C. Barringer, 'The Changing Face of Norwich', in Rawcliffe and Wilson, *Norwich since 1550*.

26 A. Armstrong, 'Population 1700 to 1950', Rawcliffe and Wilson, *Norwich since 1550*.

27 Ibid., p. 261.

28 J. K. Edwards, 'Industrial Development of the City 1800 to 1900', in C. Barringer (ed.), *Norwich in the Nineteenth Century* (Gliddon Books, Norwich, 1984) p. 140.

29 R. Ryan, 'Insurance and Banking', Rawcliffe and Wilson, *Norwich since 1550*, p. 363.

30 G. Nobbs, 'A Georgian Holiday Guide', in *Bygone Yarmouth: an illustrated history of a seaside resort* (Macklow Publications, 1971) p. 9.

31 Meeres, *Great Yarmouth*, p. 57.

32 Richards, *King's Lynn*, pp. 75 and 78.

33 Crosby, *Thetford*, p. 80 and chapter 5.

34 NRO: deeds of Bircham Brewery 1640 to 1927: BRA 1164/6 760X3.

35 NRO: William Parmeter of Aylsham, flour merchant 1793 NCC 86 Stills.

Chapter 13: The Broads

1 Lambert *et al*, *The Making of the Broads*.

2 Cornford, *Medieval Flegg*, pp. 58 and 61.

3 T. Williamson, *The Norfolk Broads* (Manchester University Press, 1997) p. 45.

4 C. Barringer, 'Hickling', in *Exploring the Norfolk Village*; NRO NRS 1986/11/B1.

5 R. Malster, *The Norfolk and Suffolk Broads* (Phillimore, 2003) ch. 8, 'Keel and Wherry': this volume is a detailed study of Broadland life and culture.

6 NRO: Y/C38/3.

7 J. Snelling, *Ludham* (Mumby, 1999) p. 78.

8 E.A. Ellis *The Broads* (New Naturalist Series, Collins, 1965).

9 A. H. Patterson, *Wildlife on a Norfolk Estuary* (Methuen, 1907) p. 312.

10 Malster, *Norfolk and Suffolk Broads*, p. 130.

11 Williamson, *Norfolk Broads*, p. 90.

12 Malster, *The Broads* (Phillimore, 1993) and *The Norfolk and Suffolk Broads*, 2003.

13 J. Mosby, *The Land of Britain 70: Norfolk*, p. 196.

14 A. Crosby, 'Changing the face of Norfolk', in C. Wilkins Jones (ed.), *Centenary: 100 Years of County Government in Norfolk* (Norfolk County Council, 1989) pp. 44–9.

15 B. Moss, *The Broads* (Harper Collins 2001), p. 263.

16 M. George, *The Land Use, Ecology and Conservation of Broadland*, Packard, Fig. 11b, p. 359.

17 Moss, *The Broads*, p. 177.

Chapter 14: Vernacular architecture in Norfolk

1 D. Yaxley, 'Buildings in North Elmham', in P. Wade-Martins (ed.), *Excavations in North Elmham Park, 1967–72* (East Anglian Archaeology no. 9, 1980).

2 Ibid., p. 167.

3 P. Rutledge, *New Buckenham: a planned town at*

work, 1530 to 1780 (Norfolk Archaeological and Historical Research Group, 2000).

4 A. Longcroft (ed.), *The Historic Buildings of New Buckenham* (Journal of the Norfolk Historic Buildings Group, no. 2, 2005), fig. 45.

5 A. Longcroft (ed.), *The Tacolneston Project* (Journal of the Norfolk Historic Buildings Group, no. 4, 2009)

6 Longcroft, *Historic Buildings of New Buckenham.*

7 R. Lucas, 'Brickmaking', *Historical Atlas of Norfolk*, pt 78.

8 P. Eden, 'Post Medieval Houses in Early England', in Lionel Munby (ed.), *East Anglian Studies* (Heffer, 1968).

9 Longcroft, *Tacolneston*, fig. 5, 73.

10 Pevsner and Wilson, *Norfolk* 1, p. 638.

11 F. Macdonald (ed.), *Aylsham in the Seventeenth Century* (Aylsham Local History Society and Poppyland, 1988).

12 Charlotte Barringer, report to Norfolk historic Buildings Group 2005.

13 C. Barringer, map in *Aylsham in the Seventeenth Century.*

14 N. Boston and E. Puddy, *Dereham: the biography of a country town* (G. A. Coleby, 1952) frontispiece.

15 NRO: PD 100/263.

16 NRO: Executors of Cozens-Hardy, 11.2.76, Holt Box.

Chapter 15: 1830 to 1914

1 Mason, *History of Norfolk*, p. 562.

2 N. Henderson (ed.), *The Goulburn Norwich Diaries* (Canterbury Press, 1996).

3 Pevsner and Wilson, *Norfolk* 1, p. 409.

4 O. Chadwick, *Victorian Miniature* (Cambridge University Press, 1960) p. 90.

5 H. B. Armstrong (ed.), *A Norfolk Diary: the Diary of the Rev Benjamin John Armstrong* (Harrap, 1949).

6 S. Yaxley (ed.), *The Rector will be glad* (Larks Press, 1992).

7 C. Binfield, 'Church and Chapel', in Rawcliffe and Wilson (eds), *Norwich since 1550*, p. 416.

8 N. Virgoe and T. Williamson (eds), *Religious Dissent in East Anglia* (University of East Anglia, Centre of East Anglian Studies, 1993).

9 A. Howkins, 'Politics or quietism: the social history of Nonconformity', in Virgoe and Williamson, *Religious dissent*, pp. 73–91, esp. 86–8.

10 A. Digby, *Pauper Palaces* (Routledge and Kegan Paul, 1978) p. 74.

11 NRO Shropham parish records BD20/325 1836.

12 'Emigration to Queensland', *Daylight*, 2 March 1889 (Norfolk Heritage Centre).

13 J. Peake, 'They seek them here, they seek them here', *Glaven Historian no. 7* (2004).

14 NRO: Hare 5271.

15 Bayne, *History of Norwich*, p. 393.

16 C. Clark, 'Work and Employment', in Rawcliffe and Wilson (eds), *Norwich since 1550*

17 S. Muthesius, 'Norwich Housing', in Barringer (ed.), *Norwich in the Nineteenth Century*, pp. 100–10.

18 A. Hedges, *Yarmouth is an antient town*, p. 60.

19 Ibid., p. 61.

20 NRO: SO 141/1.

21 Richards, *King's Lynn.*

22 Crosby, *Thetford*, p. 113.

23 Pevsner and Wilson, *Norfolk* 1, pp. 660–4, A. Reid (ed.), *Cromer and Sheringham* (University of East Anglia Centre for East Anglian Studies, 1986), and S. and R. Craske, *Sheringham, a century of change* (Poppyland, 1985) have all been used in this section.

24 J. Hooton, *The Glaven Ports*, p. 222 and figs 47 and 48.

25 K. Bennison, mss in the author's collection.

26 C. Barringer, 'Hunstanton', in *Exploring the Norfolk Village*, pp. 25–6.

27 B. Holderness, 'The Origins of High Farming', in B. Holderness and M. Turner (eds), *Land, Labour and Agriculture 1700 to 1920* (Hambledon, 1991) pp. 157.

28 S. Wade-Martins and T. Williamson, *Roots of Change* (British Agricultural History Society, 1999) p. 137.

29 Pevsner and Wilson, *Norfolk* 2, p. 628 and A. Mackley, 'Haveringland Hall', *Norfolk Archaeology* vol. 43, pt 1 (1998).

30 Pevsner and Wilson, *Norfolk* 1, p. 688.

31 Ibid., p. 642.

32 C. Barringer 'The Brecks: Weeting', in *Exploring the Norfolk Village*, Poppyland 2005, pp. 36–43.

Chapter 16: Norfolk from 1914 to 1945

1 J. Barney, *The Defence of Norfolk, 1793 to 1815* (Mintaka Books, 2000), pp. 22–5.

2 F. Meeres, *Norfolk in the First World War* (Phillimore, 2004), pp. 103–5, 113–18.

3 N. Mansfield, 'Volunteers and Recruiting', in G. Gliddon (ed.), *Norfolk and Suffolk in the Great War* (Gliddon, 1988), p. 27.

4 N. Forder, 'The New Technology', in Gliddon, *The Great War*, pp. 42–26.

5 Meeres, *Norfolk in the First World War*, pp. 114–15.
6 Meeres, quoting *Eastern Daily Press*, 6 January 1915.
7 Meeres, *Norfolk in the First World War*, p. 177.
8 A. Martin, '"Shattered Hopes and Unfulfilled Dreams": Council Housing in Rural Norfolk in the Early 1920s', *The Local Historian*, vol. 35 no. 2 (May 2005), pp. 107–19.
9 J. Mosby, *Land of Britain 70: Norfolk*, pp. 176–9.
10 S. Wade Martins and T. Williamson, *The Countryside of East Anglia, 1870 to 1950* (Boydell, 2008) p. 23.
11 Ibid., p. 24.
12 A. Douet, 'Agriculture in the Twentieth Century', *Historical Atlas of Norfolk*, pt 86.
13 Wade Martins and Williamson, *Countryside of East Anglia*, Boydell 2008, p. 26.
14 Ibid., pp. 30–1.
15 Ibid., p. 32.
16 Meeres, *A History of Norwich* (Phillimore, 1998), p. 190.
17 Pevsner and Wilson, *Norfolk* 1, p. 262.
18 Meeres, *Great Yarmouth*, pp. 108–10.
19 Richards, *King's Lynn*, pp. 147–9.
20 Crosby, *Thetford*, pp. 114–16.
21 P. Kent, 'First and Second World War Coastal Defences', *Historical Atlas of Norfolk*, pt 87.
22 H. Fairhead, 'Airfields of the Second World War', *Historical Atlas of Norfolk*, pt 89.
23 J. Banger, *Norwich at War* (3rd edition, Poppyland, 2003).
24 Meeres, *Great Yarmouth*, pp. 113–18.
25 R. Malcolmson and P. Searby (eds), *Wartime Norfolk: the diary of Rachel Dhonau, 1941 to 1942* (Norfolk Record Society vol. 68, 2004).

Chapter 17: After the Two Wars

1 J. Ayton, 'The Pattern of Roads in the Twentieth Century', *Historical Atlas of Norfolk*, pt 85.
2 J. Wright, 'Late Twentieth-Century Demography and Services', *Historical Atlas of Norfolk*, pt 91.
3 N. Wright, 'Education, Health and Welfare', in Wilkins Jones (ed.), *Centenary*.
4 Ibid., p. 72.
5 Douet, 'Agriculture in the 20th Century', *Historical Atlas of Norfolk*, pt 86.
6 P. Rutledge, *New Buckenham* and A. Longcroft, *The Historic Buildings of New Buckenham*.
7 C. Davison and P. Tolhurst, 'Conservation Areas and Listed Buildings', *Historical Atlas of Norfolk*, pt 92.
8 Norfolk Landscape Archaeology, *Annual Review*, 2009.
9 City of Norwich Plan, 1945.
10 B. Ayers (ed.), *Norwich Castle: Excavations and Historical Surveys, 1987 to 1998, pts 1 and 2* (East Anglian Archaeology no. 132, 2010).
11 P. Townroe, Chapter 19, Norwich since 1945 in Rawcliffe and Wilson (eds), *Norwich since 1550* (Hambledon and London, 2004), p. 481.
12 A. Hedges, M. Boon and F. Meeres, *Yarmouth is an Antient Town* (Blackall Books, 2001); Meeres, *Great Yarmouth*.
13 Meeres, quoting NRO SO 141/3 (no date); this section draws on Meeres, pp. 118–19.
14 Richards, *King's Lynn*, pp. 137, 139.
15 Crosby, *Thetford*, p. 117. This section draws on pp. 117–23.
16 Ibid., p. 121.

Index

Acle 293, 295, 407
Acle Straight 271, 277
Aickman, John 356
Albini, William d' (I and II) 70, 87, 89, 93, 96, 99, 108, 215
Albon, William 171
Alburgh 233
Aldeby 186
Allen, John 241–242
Allgard, John 229
Ames, Edward 287
Andrew, William Wayte 331–332
Angerstein family 374
Anglia Television 351
Anmer 40
Antingham 149, 269
Ant, river 2, 4, 269, 289, 379, 391
Appleton 372
Appleyard family 210
Archdall, George 330
Arminghall Henge 7, 11, 18, 23, 26, 304–305
Armstrong, Rev Benjamin 330, 332
Ashby 169, 290
Ashill 36, 255–257, 340
Astley, Sir Jacob 244
Ashwellthorpe 118, 171, 211, 407, 413
Athulf, Bishop 58
Attleborough 104, 145, 152, 172, 249, 253–255, 266–267, 271, 401–402, 431
Attlebridge 55
Aylsham 6, 66, 68, 74, 134, 137, 169, 173, 206, 214, 216, 238–239, 252, 269, 272, 284–287, 312–313, 316, 321–322, 329, 361–362, 380, 399, 407, 409

Babingley 89, 372
Bacon family 8
Bacon, Henry 217
Bacon, Nathaniel 205–208, 219, 221
Bacon, Sir Nicholas 211
Baconsthorpe 137, 155, 174–175, 304, 312, 324, 409
Bacton 40, 99, 170–171, 432
Badley Moor 252
Baldewyn family 138–139

Banham 16, 407
Barclay family 277, 363
Baret, Christopher 232
Baret, Thomas 223
Barford 270
Barnard, John 325
Barningham Winter 147
Barton Bendish 30–31, 176
Barton Broad 299
Bateman, Bishop William 119
Bates, Richard 261
Bathurst, Bishop 249, 260
Battle Area 374
Bawburgh 411–412
Bawdeswell 396
Bawsey 56
Beachamwell 148
Bedford Levels/River 192, 194, 204, 268
Bedingfield, Sir Henry 237
Bedingfield, Sir Humphrey 210, 236
Beeston next Mileham 233
Beeston Priory 227
Beeston St Lawrence 110
Beighton 341
Bell, Edmund 222
Bell, Henry 126, 218, 220
Belton 423
Bergh Apton 53
Berney Arms 298
Berney, Elizabeth 215, 240
Berney, Richard 215
Besthorpe 256
Bickerston 60
Bignold, Thomas 276
Bigod, Hugh 108
Bigod, Roger 70, 73
Bilhouse family 341
Billingford 40, 46–47, 53, 132, 251
Binham 99, 145, 151–152, 158, 169, 186, 318, 321, 333
Bircham, Samuel 284
Bitcham Ditch 31
Bixley 272
Blackdyke 200
Blackwater River 53
Blakeman, Syware 111
Blakeney 5, 131, 146, 167, 172, 175, 177, 183, 250, 267, 305,

312, 342, 368–369, 403, 409, 412, 414
Blakeney Point 3, 5, 412–413
Blickling Hall/Estate 107, 205–206, 211, 222, 227, 244–246, 285, 304, 316, 321, 371, 409
Blomefield, Francis 106, 151, 206, 248–249, 261, 273, 292, 313
Boardman, Edward 374, 389
Bocking, Frederick 342, 344
Boileau, Sir John 331–332
Boleyn family 159–160
Boleyn, Sir William 211
Booton 145, 161, 331, 413
Boudica, queen 7, 35, 37
Boughton 210
Bowthorpe 398, 411, 414–415
Bracon Ash 210
Bradenham 59
Bradwell 423
Brampton 35, 39–40, 46
Brancaster 35, 47, 49
Brandon (Sfk) 85, 253
Brandon, David 373
Breccles 64, 340
Breckland 1, 3–4, 18, 31, 105, 111–114, 130, 139, 305, 374, 381, 405
Bressingham 139–140, 266
Breydon Water 46, 48, 116, 270
Bridge, William 233
Brigg family 159
Briggate 269
Broads, Broadland 2, 3–4, 13, 56, 105, 107, 116–117, 135, 251, 268–270, 289–302
Broads Authority 289, 300
Brockdish 341
Bromholm [Priory] 99, 101, 170–172, 186, 319, 377, 409
Broome Heath 17
Broomhill 177
Browne, Robert 229–230
Browne, Sir Thomas 231
Brown, John 337
Brundall 40, 123, 301
Buckenham 293
Bullam family 344
Bulwer family 272

Bungay (Sfk) 172, 220, 233, 268, 270, 272, 401
Bunn, Henry 243
Bure, river 2, 4, 39, 152, 249, 268–269, 285–286, 289, 294, 298, 409
Burfield Hall 252
Burgh Castle 7, 35, 46–49, 55, 61, 290, 304
Burgh next Aylsham 145, 152, 233
Burlingham 252
Burnham Market 225
Burnham Thorpe 60, 103
Burn, river 5, 103
Burrell, Charles 356
Burrell family 279, 3788
Burroughs, Randal 252–254, 256
Burston 374–375
Buxton 269, 412

Caister [on Sea/by Yarmouth] 35, 40, 46–48, 55, 75–76, 86, 66, 173–174, 264, 290, 296, 304, 398, 423
Caistor St Edmund [by Norwich] 7, 11, 30, 34–36, 40, 43–46, 55, 66, 228, 290, 304, 409
Calthorpe family 216
Cantley 291, 301, 378, 385, 408, 431
Carleton Forehoe 162
Carleton Rode 256
Carman, Thomas 210
Castle Acre 7, 66, 70–71, 74, 94–96, 156, 304, 371, 385, 407
priory 7, 94, 96, 99–100, 170, 185–186, 310
Castle Rising 7, 87, 89–94, 172, 178, 240–241, 249, 267, 304
Catfield 116
Catton 275, 350, 373, 387, 390
Cavell, Edith 379
Cawston 74–76, 105, 137, 145, 153–154, 156–159, 165, 208, 223, 241–242, 304, 318, 321, 411
Charles II, king 233
Chet, river 50, 56, 270, 289, 301
Christmas, Nicholas 168
Cleer, Thomas 273
Clere, Sir Edward 211
Cley [next the Sea] 5, 96–97, 131, 146, 163, 167, 175, 250–251, 260, 324, 326, 342, 369, 377, 392, 409, 412–413
Cnobheresburg 47, 61
Cnut, King 59, 64–65, 68, 74
Cockshoot Broad 299

Coke family 2, 8, 96, 247, 369
Coke, Sir Edward 162, 247
Coke, Thomas [the elder] 206, 225–226, 247
Coke, Thomas [the younger] 134, 224, 247, 249, 258–259
Colman, Jeremiah 287, 373
Colman, Thomas 207
Colney 145, 236
Coltishall 269, 285, 294, 393
Colton 316, 320
Comper, Sir Ninian 99, 411
Cooper, Elizabeth 210
Cooper, Richard 115–116
Coote, Charles Henry (Mountrath) 253, 374
Corbridge, James 273
Corie, Thomas 233
Costessey 238, 336, 387, 409
Cowper, Charles 372
Coxford 186
Cozens-Hardy, W.H. 334
Crabhouse Nunnery 115, 119
Cranworth 252
Crashfield, Richard 210
Creake Abbey 103
Cringleford 347, 387
Cromer 8, 131–132, 170, 184, 248, 272, 289, 295–296, 324, 331, 343, 363–366, 369, 377, 395, 400–401, 404, 414
Cromer Ridge 3, 5, 13, 326
Crowe, Priscilla 142
Crown Point 373
Crownthorpe 45, 227
Custance family 261
Cut-off Channel, the 42, 199–200, 204

Danemoor Green 328
Davis, Christopher 294
de Gray, Robert 210
de la Pole family 156, 158, 175
de Vaux family 163
Defoe, Daniel 206, 218
Denton 310
Denton, Ann 252
Denver 40, 42, 46, 104, 192, 194–195, 199–200, 204, 306, 411
Deopham 50, 393
Depwade Hundred/Union 60, 109, 338–339
Dereham [East] 8, 56, 69–70, 96, 131, 151, 215, 228, 250, 262, 268, 324, 328, 330, 332, 354, 358–359, 367–368, 370, 399, 401–402, 404, 409, 412
Dersingham 372
Deye, Isabel 171

Dhonau, Rachel 378, 396
Dilham 133, 249, 269, 333
Diss 31, 40, 46, 60, 172, 238, 250, 266–268, 280, 325–327, 359, 401–402
Docking 40, 337
Doughty, Robert 206, 219, 221–222
Downes family 238
Downes, John 210
Downham Market 2, 42, 104, 162, 192, 195, 200, 244, 287, 322, 339, 399, 401–402, 431
Drayton 173, 399
Drury, John 210
Dudley, John 189
Dudley, Robert 210
Dunham, Great 66
Dunning, Michael 209–210
Dunston 40
Dunwich (Sfk) 51, 58, 61
Dussindale 189
Dynne, Henry 246
Dyson, John 259

Earle, Erasmus 246
Earlham 211, 374, 390, 420
Earsham 172, 219, 384–385
East Barsham 224
East Harling 176, 238, 360
Easton 60
East Raynham 136
East Wretham 413
Eaton 25, 387
Eau Brink Cut 192, 201
Eccles 40, 147, 297
Edge, William 246
Edingthorpe 333–334
Edward I, king 99
Edward II, king 101, 170
Edward III, king 134
Edward IV, king 166
Edward VI, king 239
Edward VII, king 330, 372
Edwards, George 334
Edward the Elder, king 67–68
Egmere 410
Elisabeth, Empress of Austria 365
Elizabeth I, queen 206, 210–211, 216, 238
Elsing, Richard 133
Elwin, Rev Whitwell 331
Ely Abbey 51, 66, 70, 72–73, 75, 96, 112, 131, 151, 324, 359
Erpingham Hundreds 59, 75, 77
Erpingham, Sir Thomas 165
Etheldreda, Saint 51
Eynsford Hundred 60

Faden, William   192, 249–250, 252, 256, 259, 280, 325
Fakenham   56, 96, 151, 162, 188, 216, 272, 328, 399, 401, 404, 414, 428
Fastolf, Sir John   2, 136, 166, 174–175
Fiennes, Celia   206, 216
Felbrigg [Estate]   145, 205–206, 227, 244–245, 266, 304, 310
Felbrigg, Sir Simon   2
Felix, Saint   58, 61
Fell, Henry   206, 235
Fellowes, Edward   373
Felmingham   110
Feltwell   39, 42, 192, 194, 200, 239, 407
Fen Causeway   40–42, 46
Fenn family   176
Fens, Fenland   2, 3–4, 16, 20, 24–25, 40–41, 53, 56–57, 70, 77, 89, 105, 114–116, 138–139, 146, 155, 191–204, 251–252, 296, 405
Fermor family   106, 134, 138, 205, 216
Fermor, Sir Henry   188
Fermor, Sir William   206, 224
Fersfield   261
Filby   264
Fincham   40
Fison, Cornelius   279, 358
Fitzalan family   108
Fitzroy, Henry (duke of Richmond)   130
Fleg, Simon de   119
Flegg(s)   25, 60, 65, 75, 78, 135, 169, 264, 288, 290–291
Flitcham   3, 305, 309
Flordon   413
Flowerdew, John   188
Forehoe Hundred   60, 339
Forncett(s)   105, 107, 109–110, 168, 172, 228, 401
Forncett St Peter   64, 407
Fortis, George   266
Foster, Robert   227
Foulsham   117
Foxley   25
Foxley Wood   117–118, 171, 413
Franklin, Reverend F.   266–267
Fransham   30–31, 56
Freebridge Hundred   57
Freke, Bishop   206, 230
Fritton   257
Fritton Lake   292–293
Fry, Elizabeth   374
Fulmerston, Sir Richard   238, 242
Fundenhall   63, 104

Fursey, Saint   61

Garvestone   310
Gaytonthorpe   41–42
Gaywood   424
Gaywood River   88
Gerven, Robert   111
Gill, Nethaniel   233
Gillingwater, Francis   309
Gimingham   159, 172, 222
Glandford   132
Glanville, William de   101
Glaven, river   131–132, 163, 251, 326, 369, 409, 412
Gnatingdon   136
Godwick   162, 210, 226, 247, 410
Goggs, John and Matthias   361
Goose, Robert   229
Gorleston   86, 377, 389, 395, 423
Goulburn, Dean Edmund   330–331
Gramborough Hill   50
Great Dunham   145
Great Ellingham   145, 152
'Great Estuary'   41, 290
Great Massingham   10, 226
Great Melton   16, 176, 238, 410
Great Ouse, river   2, 3, 42, 88, 163, 191–192, 194–195, 200–201, 204, 267–268, 279, 323
Greenhoe Hundred(s)   60, 172, 219
Green, John   188
Greenaway, Ralph   221
Gresham   173, 227
Gressenhall   258, 337, 339
Grey, Lady Jane   207–208, 238
Grimes Graves   11, 18–19, 21, 23, 304, 409, 413
Grimshoe Hundred   60
Grimston   65
Grys, John   119
Guestwick   60, 234–235
Guiltcross Hundred   60, 172, 220
Guist   136
Gunton   272
Gurney family   143, 272, 277, 363, 373–374
Gyrth [Godwinson]   70, 74

Hackford   97, 149, 284
Haddiscoe   102
Hainford   17
Hales   7, 62–63, 102, 145, 156, 319, 410
Halifax, Thomas   322
Hall, Bishop   206, 230–232
Halvergate Marshes   289, 296
Hamond, Nicholas   239, 326
Hanworth   272
Happing Hundred   59

Happisburgh   3, 4, 6, 11–13, 40, 59, 147, 312, 383, 392, 394, 432
Harbord family   272
Hardley Cross   289, 298
Hare family   205, 216, 344
Hare, Sarah   162
Hare, Sir Thomas   195
Harford Bridge   211
Harford Farm (Caistor)   30, 34
Harleston   96–97, 172, 233, 253, 359, 401
Harold II, king   70, 74
Harold, Fulke   247
Harpley   17
Harpley Common   22
Harrison, Robert   230
Harvey family   272, 277, 373
Haveringland   373, 393
Hay Green   56
Haylot, Thomas   226
Heacham   401
Heaviside, James   331
Heckingham   62–63, 102, 145
Hedenham   393
Heggatt (Horstead)   223
Heigham   275, 331
Heigham Sound   299
Helhoughton   136
Hellesdon   272, 414
Hempnall   243
Hempstead   107
Hempton   96, 253
Hemsby   398, 422–423
Henry I, king   70, 83, 89
Henry III, king   99, 126, 170
Henry IV, king   178
Henstead Hundred   72
Herfast, Bishop   51, 58
Hethersett   41, 97, 188, 260, 318, 331, 374
Heydon   173, 246, 272, 409
Heydon family   134, 137–138, 165–166, 173–175, 2–5
Hickling   116, 119, 170, 291, 319, 411
Hickling Broad   116, 290, 298–299, 379
High Lodge (Sfk)   13
Higdon, Annie and Tom   375
Hilborough   114
Hill, Joseph   247
Hill, Money   258
Hindolveston   135, 407
Hindringham   66, 135
Hingham   188, 238, 253, 287, 410
Hoare family   363
Hobart family   106, 206, 213, 215–216, 222, 244, 320–321
Hobart, Sir Henry   245

Hobart, Sir James 156, 319
Hobart, Sir John 227
Hockham 31
Hockwold 11, 20, 37, 39, 303, 315
Holkham [Hall/Estate] 8, 41, 205, 225–226, 247–249, 252, 258, 266, 344, 371, 409–410
Holkham Stathe 225
Holme next the Sea 5, 26, 40, 305
Holt 60, 66, 96–97, 246, 317, 324, 326–327, 369, 399, 409, 412
Honing 110, 317
Honingham 33, 261
Honingham Thorpe 60
Hopton 423
Hopton, Bishop John 209–210
Horning 110, 170, 172, 301
Horsey 60, 29
Horsham St Faith 170, 186, 253, 259, 394, 398, 416
Horstead 206, 223
Houghton 247, 326, 344, 371
Houghton St Giles 382
House, Mitchell 396
Hoveton 64, 110, 294–295
Howard family 2, 8, 73, 94, 134, 168, 172–173, 186, 190, 206, 212, 216, 219, 220
Howard, Henry 240–241
Howard, Thomas 3rd duke 186, 220, 240–241
How Hill 292
Howys, Sir Thomas 136
Hoxne (Sfk) 11, 13, 58
Hudson family 277
Hudson, John 371
Hudson, Thomas 210
Humbleyard Hundred 60
Hundred Foot Drain 192, 194, 204
Hunstanton 3, 6, 8, 40, 104, 166, 205, 303, 306, 315, 370, 372, 401, 404, 413, 423
Hunworth 326

Iceni, the 26, 28, 33–37, 43–47
Icknield Way 33, 40, 42, 68, 281
Ingham 235, 310
Ingworth 272
Islington 163
Itteringham 412
Ivory, Thomas 263, 273–274, 304, 339

James family 341
Jannys, Robert 214, 285
Jarvis, Rev Frederick 411
Jernegan/Jerningham family 238, 336
John of Gaunt 169, 313

Joskyns, James 186–187
Jurnet family 85

Katherine of Aragon, queen 99
Keith, James 385
Kelling 50
Kelling Head 5
Kelling Heath 16
Kempstone 40
Kenninghall 94, 172, 208, 210, 220
Kent, Nathaniel 272
Kerdeston 106–107, 149
Kerdiston family 160
Kerrison family 272, 277
Kervile, Henry 237
Keswick 11, 13, 60
Ketteringham 256, 318, 410
Kett, Robert / rebellion 139, 187–189, 206, 208
Ketton Cremer, Robert 205, 233
Kilverstone 105, 266, 381
Kimberley 216
Kinghorn, Joseph 235
[King's/Bishop's] Lynn 1, 2, 8, 56, 68, 85, 87–88, 99, 105, 117, 125–127, 151, 162, 175, 177–178, 184, 191–192, 199, 201, 205, 218, 231–232, 239, 250, 263, 267–268, 270, 272, 277–278, 287, 310, 323, 328, 342, 353–358, 370, 376–379, 385, 389, 391, 395–396, 398–399, 401–402, 404, 414, 424–426
  Clifton House 425
  Corn Exchange 353, 357
  Customs House 218, 220
  docks 354, 376, 425–426
  Greyfriars 125
  Hampton Court 127, 322, 424
  Hanseatic Warehouses 424–425
  King Street 87, 356
  Millfleet 87–88
  Nelson Street 322, 424
  Newland 87
  Old Gaol House 278
  Purfleet 87–88, 279, 356
  Queen Street 127
  St George's Guildhall 127, 166, 311–312, 424
  St Margaret 87, 176, 232, 239, 426
  St Nicholas 87, 176, 211
  Saturday Market Place 87, 182, 232
  South Gate 125, 166
  Thoresby College 126–127
  Trinity Guildhall 127, 181–182, 409
  True's Yard 424, 427

Tuesday Market Place 87, 232, 353, 357
King, Samuel 273
Kirby Cane 60, 145
Knettishall 40
Knyvett, Joan 176
Knyvett, Sir Thomas 211

Laade, William 182
Lakenham 331, 347, 399, 402
Lane, Joseph 248
Langham 59
Langley 150, 321
Launditch hundred 172, 219, 324, 339
Leeder family 408
Lenwade 261, 393, 412–413
Le Strange family 8, 134, 137, 166, 216, 306, 370
Le Strange, Hamon 231–232
Letheringsett 412
Litcham 66
Littister, John 168
Little Cressingham 18
Little Ouse, river 2, 33, 45, 68, 85, 111, 114, 129–130, 200, 249, 268, 279, 281, 358, 391
Little Snoring 148
Loddon 56, 62, 145, 155–156, 270, 291, 301, 384, 399, 411–412
Long Stratton 40, 257, 266, 341, 384, 387, 408
Lopham 220, 268
Losinga, Bishop Herbert de 51, 54–55, 58, 70, 78–79, 82, 86, 151
Lovell family 238
Lovell, Margaret 176
Lowestoft 269–270, 345, 377–379
Loynes of Wroxham 294–295
Lubbock, Richard 292–293
Ludham 110, 264, 291–292
Lynford 14, 19
Lyminge, Robert 245
Lyng 16

Mannington 107, 120, 166, 312
Margaret of Anjou, queen 99
Marham 394
Marriotts Way 414
Marsham 226–227, 272
Marsham, Robert 206, 226
Marshland Cut 195
Marshland Fen 201
Martham 75, 111, 167–169, 264, 295
Martineau, Harriet 333
Mary I, queen 8, 207–210, 238
Matthews, Bernard 406

Matlaske   147
Mattishall   37, 97, 134, 138–139,
   161–162, 252, 260–261, 340
Mattishall Burgh   139
Mautby, Margaret   166
Melton Constable   244, 342–343,
   381
Mendham   96
Merton   145, 152, 210, 340
Methwold   24, 112, 169, 203, 252,
   407
Micklethwaite family   373
Middle Level Drain   192, 199, 201
Middleton   2, 41
Mileham   108
Miller, Simon   210
Millgate   269
Mitford Hundred   59–60, 96, 324,
   339–340
Molycourt Priory   186
Money, John   224–225
Morley St Botolph   188, 317
Morley family   160
Morningthorpe   144
Morse family   143
Morse, Thomas   223
Morston   5, 167, 412
Morton, Archbishop John   182
Motte family   147
Mousehold [Heath]   84, 117, 188–
   189, 212, 252, 387
Mountjoy Priory   119
Muckleborough Hill   50
Mulbarton   60, 142
Mundesley   8, 9, 170, 363–364, 377,
   401, 404, 432
Mundford   4, 132

Narborough   31, 268
Narford, Robert de   103
Nar, river   2, 13, 31, 39, 41, 88, 94,
   111, 191, 268
Neatishead   110
Nene, river   3, 39, 191–192, 196,
   201
New Buckenham   89, 92–94, 146,
   178, 207, 259, 266, 270, 272,
   307, 309–311, 313, 409
Newton by Castle Acre   63, 407
Norfolk, dukes of   73–74, 94, 140,
   172–173, 186–187, 210, 218–
   220, 334–335
Norfolk Estuary Company   201
Nordelph   42, 192, 195, 201
Norman, William   177
North Creake   103
North Elmham   51, 53–55, 58, 85,
   226, 255, 307, 309, 318, 385
Northrepps   272

North Walsham   56, 59, 64, 69–70,
   96, 110, 115, 133, 149, 168,
   215–216, 228, 238–239, 243–
   244, 249, 267, 269, 272, 295,
   304, 322, 324, 329, 343, 364,
   399, 404, 422
Norton Subcourse   59
Norwich   2, 8, 24, 40, 44, 46, 51,
   56, 58, 60, 65–69, 77–85, 117,
   120–125, 134–135, 137–138,
   141–143, 145, 151–152, 168,
   172–173, 175, 177–182, 186,
   205–206, 209–217, 222–223,
   230–233, 239, 250, 261, 263,
   267, 269–277, 287, 291, 301,
   333–335, 344–352, 373–374,
   376–377, 379, 385–390,
   304–396, 399, 401–402, 407,
   414–416
 Airport   394, 398, 416
 All Saints Green   273
 Anglia Square   415
 Arlington   350
 Assembly House   122, 263,
   273–274, 304, 419
 Augustine Steward House   244
 Bacon House   217
 Bank Plain   378, 389
 Ber Street   66
 Bishop Bridge   78, 123, 125, 189
 Blackfriars   121, 124, 212, 419
 Botolph Street   273
 Bowthorpe   398, 411, 414–415
 Bracondale   402
 Carnary College/Chapel   216,
   239
 Carrow Abbey   70, 82, 119, 169,
   212
 Carrow (Colmans)   346–347
 Carrow Road   11, 15–16, 301,
   420
 castle   7, 70–71, 77–78, 80,
   82–84, 304, 315, 417
 Castle Gardens   312, 418
 Castle Mall   416, 418
 cathedral/diocese   55, 58, 70, 74,
   78–82, 97, 116, 133, 135–136,
   145, 152, 167, 209, 212, 226,
   230, 233–234, 263–264, 289–
   290, 304, 315, 321–322, 417
 Catholic cathedral   277, 330,
   334–336, 398, 417, 419
 Chapelfield   121, 394, 416
 churches   62, 152–156, 213–215,
   417
 City Hall   179, 388–389, 409,
   419
 city walls   105, 120–121, 304
 Close, The   263–264

 Colegate   233, 236, 273–274,
   276, 350
 College in the Fields   212
 Conesford   212, 240
 Cow Tower   120, 123, 304
 Dereham Road   350
 Dragon Hall   137, 311–312
 Earlham Road   277, 335, 350
 Elm Hill   173, 304, 321, 386–387,
   415
 Erpingham Gate   79, 164–165,
   216
 Ethelbert Gate   180
 Fishergate   66
 fish market   349
 Forum, The   312, 398, 419
 Foundry Bridge   81, 123, 374
 Fye Bridge   67
 gasworks   350
 Great Hospital   105, 121, 123–
   124, 213, 230, 244, 310
 Greyfriars   212
 Guildhall   134, 166, 179, 214,
   218, 304, 312, 418
 Heartsease Estate   398, 414–415
 Holm Street   40
 Hook Lane   263
 King Street   84–85, 137, 143,
   173, 214, 322–323, 387, 410
 London Street   348, 398, 416
 Magdalen Street   273, 350, 398,
   415–416
 market place   83, 142, 232
 Martineau Memorial Hall   333
 Mile Cross estate   378, 385–387,
   390
 Mousehold [Heath]   84, 117,
   188–189, 212, 252, 387
 Newmarket Road   348, 351, 390
 New Mills   269, 329
 Norfolk & Norwich
   Hospital   273, 348
 Norwich School   216, 239
 Norwich School of Design
   [Art]   346, 417
 Norwich Union   249, 273, 275,
   417–418
 Oak Street   273
 Octagon Chapel   273–274, 333
 Old Meeting House   233, 236
 Over-the-Water   67, 120, 212,
   232, 415
 Palace Plain   79, 82, 145
 parks   389
 Peafield   277
 Pockthorpe   350
 Pottergate   350
 Prince of Wales Road   351
 Pull's Ferry   79, 81

railway stations 346, 349
ring roads 388, 390, 398, 402
Rose Lane 84
Rupert Street 352, 394
St Andrew's 172, 215
St Andrew's Hall 121, 124
St Augustine's 273
St Clement 62
St Etheldreda 84, 214
St Faith's Lane 79
St George Colegate 214, 217
St George Tombland 213
St Giles 145, 152, 277
St Gregory's Alley 84
St Helen 123–124, 240
St Julian 85, 214
St Lawrence 40, 62
St Leonard's Priory 70, 82, 186,
    212
St Mark 145
St Martin at Palace [Plain] 64,
    189, 263
St Mary in the Field 105,
    121–122
St Michael at Thorne 85
St Paul's 275
St Peter Hungate 213
St Peter Mancroft 85, 134, 145,
    152, 154–156, 179, 214, 232,
    264, 419
St Peter Parmentergate 85, 214,
    240
St Stephen 85, 145, 152, 214,
    232, 394
Science Research Park 417, 430
southern bypass 18, 30, 33, 387,
    398, 402
Surrey House 210, 275
Surrey Street 273, 275, 418
The Crescent 351
Thorpe Hamlet 390
Thorpe Road 350
Timberhill 263, 418
Tombland 40, 67, 78–79, 180,
    244, 263
Town Close 347, 351
University of East Anglia 374,
    413, 417, 420, 430
Unthank Road 24, 275, 347–348,
    352, 390
Vauxhall Street 416
Wensum Lodge 84–85
Westwick [Street] 66, 122

Odo, Bishop 89
Old Buckenham 89, 93–94, 186,
    259
Ormesby(s) 290
Ormesby Broad 116

Ormesby St Peter 60
Ormes, Cecily 210
Oulton Broad 270
Outwell 192, 197–198
Overstrand 363–364, 412
Oxburgh 107, 175, 237, 304, 336
Oxnead 162
Oxwick 60

Paine, Thomas 249, 283
Pakefield (Sfk) 11–13
Parco, prior Richard de 151
Parker, Matthew 189
Parker, Sir Henry 188
Parmeter family 286
Parr, William 189
Paston 110, 211, 310, 320, 334
Paston family 2, 134, 145, 162,
    165–166, 170–171, 173–175,
    205, 216
Paston, Sir William 211, 238–239,
    310, 320
Pateson family 143
Paxton, Thomas 186–187
Peake, Noah 266
Pearce, John Bond 355
Peddars Way 1, 3, 19, 22, 37,
    39–40, 42, 95, 414
Pelham, Bishop 330
Pensthorpe 120, 393, 413
Peter Scott Way 414
Pigg, Andrew 226
Plais, Hugh de 108
Pole, Michael de la 156
Pollet, Thomas 177
Popham, Sir John 221
Poppyland 330, 363, 376
Potter Heigham 110, 116, 292
Pounder, Edmund 172
Prasutagus, king 7, 35, 37
Pratt, Sir Roger 244
Press Brothers 295
Prideaux, Dean Humphrey 206,
    234, 330
Pudding Norton 106
Pulham(s) 72, 235, 338, 379–389
Pye Road 37, 40

Quidenham 210

Raedwald, king 58, 61
Ranworth 150, 288, 293, 299, 406
Raynham 8, 206, 224, 246–247, 252
Read, Parnell 233
Rede, Peter 222
Redenhall 96–97, 154, 161
Reedham 50, 270, 290, 295, 384
Reepham 97, 148–149, 161, 250,
    284, 409–410, 413

Repton, Humphrey 366, 373
Repton, William 272
Reymerston 224, 252
Richeldis of Faverches 99, 102
Ricks, George 334
Ringmere 68
Ringstead Downs 413
Roberdes, Thomas 177
Robinson, Charles 331
Rollesby 340
Rose family 159
Rougham 105, 107
Roughton 17, 60, 227, 272, 334
Row, Robert 243
Roydon Common 413
Roy's of Wroxham 294
Rudd, Thomas 318
Rudham 170
Runham 291
Ryburgh 328
Rye, Walter 248
Ryston Hall 244

Saham Toney 36–37
St Benet's Abbey [at Holm] 51,
    59, 64–65, 70, 73–74, 96–97,
    110–111, 118, 151, 169, 186,
    216, 289–290
St John's Eau 195
St Olaves 270
Salle 133, 145, 159–160, 409, 411
Salle, Sir Robert 168
Salmon, Bishop 216
Salter's Lode 194
Salthouse 18, 50, 342, 412
Samuel, William 245
Sam's [Cut] Drain 92, 194, 252
Sandringham 330, 372
Santon Downham 114, 381
Sawer, George 241
Saxlingham(s) 159–160, 248, 255
Scarning 238
Scole 37, 40, 46, 272, 325
Scolt Head 413
Scott, Clement 363
Scoulton 340
Sculthorpe 393
Seahenge 23, 26, 40, 304–305
Seaman, William 210
Searle, Thomas 234
Sedgeford 55, 132, 135–136
Sedgwick, Adam 330
Seething 393
Segrym, Ralph 176
Sheepshanks, Bishop John 333–334
Shelfanger 140
Shelton 211, 244
Shelton, Sir John 186
Shelton, Sir Raphe 211

Sheringham   5, 8, 295, 363, 365–366, 369, 377–379, 395–396, 400–401, 404, 423
Shimpling   266
Shipden   131–132
Shipdham   224
Shouldham   305
Shropham   28, 341
Sidestrand   363
Silfield   33
Skaynham, John   136
Skipper, George   348
Skrope, Lady Ann   183
Smallburgh   110
Smeeth, The   115–116, 139, 182, 197, 201
Smith, Rev John   161–162, 261
Smith, Thomas   309
Smythe, Anthony and Elizabeth   212
Snettisham   30, 33, 39, 89, 145, 413
Somerton   60
Sotherton, Nicholas   188
South Acre   13
South Creake   24, 32, 224
South Elmham (Sfk)   58
Southery   203
South Lopham   63, 104, 145
South Walsham   309, 318
Southwell family   205
Southwell, Richard   136, 186, 224
Southwell, Robert   171
Sowell, Robert   186–187
Spelman, Henry   49
Spencer, Bishop Henry le   168
Spenser, Joan   183
Spong Hill   51, 53
Spooner Row   256
Sporle   342, 344
Sporle, William   243
Sprowston   275, 374, 414
Stalham   110, 291, 295296
Stanfield Hall   210
Stannard, Philip   142–143
Steward, Augustine   244
Stibbard   136
Stiffkey   50, 131, 140, 205, 221
Stiffkey, river   5, 31
Stigand, Archbishop   89
Stoke Ferry   268, 303 401
Stoke Holy Cross   287
Stokesby   255, 264
Stow Bardolph   162, 202, 216, 344
Stow Bedon   31
Stracey family   374
Strange, Robert   184
Stratton Strawless   40, 226
Strumpshaw   298
Suckling, Robert   215

Sudbury, Christopher   207
Sutton   60
Sutton Bridge   191, 196, 201, 414
Swaffham   4, 66, 115, 131, 136, 151, 180–181, 192, 197, 239, 268, 272, 280, 282, 284, 287, 317, 324–327, 342, 361–362, 399, 401–402
Swafield   59, 171
Swanton Abbot   59, 64
Swanton Morley   393
Swardeston   379
Swein, king   65, 68

Tacolneston   270, 307, 311, 317
Tasburgh   228–229
Tas, river   4, 18–19, 30, 44, 109, 228
Tatterford   132
Taverham   373, 399
Ten Mile River   200
Terrington(s)   115, 192
Terrington St Clement   56, 145, 154–156, 163, 182, 200, 202–203, 304, 315
Terrington St John   115, 138
Thetford   4, 7, 8, 18, 29, 36, 40, 51, 56, 65, 66, 68–69, 85, 101, 105, 130, 132, 134, 165, 177–178, 182, 186, 189, 209, 231, 235, 242, 249, 268, 272, 279–283, 287, 310, 314, 346, 356–358, 360, 381, 391, 398–399, 401–402, 404, 409, 414, 427–429, 431
Bell Inn   128
Bidwell's Brewery   360
castle   70–71, 85, 281, 304
Castle Street   357
cathedral/diocese   55, 58, 68–69, 73–74, 85
Chapel of Blessed Virgin Mary   182
Dad's Army   427
Fulmerston almshouses   242
Gallows Hill   11, 45, 68
Grammar School   238
Guildhall   281, 283
Holy Sepulchre   119, 130
King Street   187, 189
market places   280–281, 314
Nether Row   314
Nuns' Bridges   129, 391
Old Gaol   282
priory   70, 73, 99, 113, 130, 135, 177, 186
St George nunnery   186
Spring Walk   281
Warren Lodge   112–113

Thetford Chase   381
Thet, river   33, 68, 111, 129
Thickthorn   374, 402
Thoresby, Thomas   126, 239
Thornham   1, 131, 414
Thornton, Katherine   222
Thorold, William   338
Thorpe [St Andrew]   301, 361, 402
Thurgarton   169, 222
Thurne   169, 290
Thurne, river   289, 299
Thursford   272
Thwaite St Mary   393
Tiffey, river   186
Tilney All Saints   163, 183, 201
Titchwell   16, 413
Tittleshall   226
Toftwood   255–256
Tong's Drain   195
Topclyffe, Richard   211
Toppes, Robert   137–138, 175–176, 311
Townsend, Thomas   210
Townshend, Charles 'Turnip'   223–224, 261
Townshend family   2, 138, 206, 224
Townshend, Horatio   246
Townshend, Roger   136, 140, 246
Trewe, Robert   184
Trinity Broads   298
Trowse   30, 272, 346, 350, 402
Tuck, William   278
Tuddenham, Sir Thomas   136, 175
Tunolde, John   228–229
Tunstead   169, 334
Turbe, Bishop   87
Turner, Sir Charles   370
Turner, Sir John   220

Upcher family   366
Upwell   42, 153, 197–198, 201
Utting, John   232

Vallibus, John de   97
Valognes, Pierre de   151
Venta Icenorum   7, 34, 43–46, 50, 66, 409
Vermuyden, Cornelius   192–195, 199, 252

Wacton   109, 318
Walcott   297, 383
Walden, George   425
Walpole family   2
Walpole, George   326–327
Walpole, Horatio   247
Walpole, Sir Robert   206, 247, 262
Walsingham   37, 264, 381–382, 411

Walsingham Priory 99, 102, 119, 127, 217
Walsoken 201
Warborough Hill 50
Warde, Richard 223
Warde, Thomas 224
Warenne, William de 70–71, 74–75, 94, 100, 108
Warham 370
Warham Camp 3, 11, 31–32
Warner, William 228
Wash, The 3, 6, 41, 200, 202, 306
Washes, The 192, 194
Waterden 25, 258
Waterson, Theophilus 227
Wattlefield 118
Watton 4, 255, 270, 272, 340, 401, 413
Waveney, river 4, 17, 40, 50, 116, 259, 268–270, 289, 298
Waxham 110, 318–319, 410
Wayland hundred/union 340, 380
Wayland Wood 413
Weasenham All Saints 18
Weavers Way 414
Weeting 108, 253, 304, 374
Welbourne 138
Welland, river 191
Well Creek/Channel 192, 197–198, 204, 268
Wells [next the Sea] 131, 175, 177, 225, 250, 267, 272, 342, 369–370, 377, 401, 414
Welney 270
Wensum, river 2, 4, 13, 19, 40, 46, 64, 66, 81, 83, 86, 120, 123, 137, 267, 269–270, 294, 420
Wereham 200
Wesley, John and Charles 263
Westacre 99, 119
West Beckham 222
West Dereham 104
West Downham 41
West Harling 11, 29–30, 33, 112–113
West Lexham 07
West Lynn 201, 232, 426
West Newton 372
Weston, Charles 276
Weston Longville 24, 33, 60, 159, 260–261
West Raynham 135

West Rudham 17, 224–225
West Runton 2
West Walton 66, 75–77, 138, 145, 152–153, 163, 201, 304, 315
Westwick 59
Weybourne 5, 251, 365, 377, 379, 391–392, 400, 412
Wheatley, James 263
Whimpwell 147
Whitefield, George 263
Whitlingham 19, 289, 419–420
Whitwell 149, 284, 410, 413
Wicklewood 227, 339
Wiggenhall(s) 114–115, 192, 199, 201
Wiggenhall St Mary 197, 201, 237
Wiggenhall St Peter 163
Wilby 188
William I, king 70–73, 77–79, 89
William II, king 83
Williamson, Sir Joseph 238
Wimbotsham 195, 216
Winfarthing 168, 266
Winterton 45, 60, 296, 377, 413
Wisbech & Upwell Tramway 198
Wissey, river 2, 13–14, 111, 192, 200, 268
Wissington 408, 430–431
Witton 24, 64, 110
Wiveton 5, 131, 163 175, 221, 342, 369
Wodehouse family 216, 244, 319
Wolferton 372
Wollaston, Charles Hyde 262
Wolterton 247, 304
Wood Dalling 56, 246
Woodforde, James 159, 260–262
Wood Norton 56
Wood, Robert 211
Wootton(s) 424
Wormegay 66, 119
Worstead 59, 110, 133, 137, 165, 385
Worts, Richard 234
Wortwell 161
Wren, Bishop Matthew 206, 230
Wroxham 289, 294–296, 301
Wymondham 33, 45, 50, 96, 98–99, 106, 118, 130–131, 162, 180–181, 188, 215–216, 219, 249, 252, 255, 257–258, 266–267, 271, 285, 304, 309, 327, 339,

398, 401–402, 404, 410, 413, 431
Abbey 89, 101, 103, 131, 186, 215, 411
Bridewell 265
[Great] Park Farm 106, 320–321
Wymondham, Edward 227
Wymondham, John 227
Wyndham/Windham family 206, 227, 244–245
Wynford 183
Wyngfeld, Sir Robert 360

Yare, river 2, 4, 13, 18–19, 25, 30, 44, 50, 83, 218, 228, 267, 269–270, 289–290, 294, 298, 301, 420
Yarmouth [Great] 1, 6, 8, 47, 66, 68, 70, 6–87, 99, 116, 127–130, 141, 151, 169–170, 175, 177–178, 186, 205–206, 218, 231, 233, 239, 249–250, 263, 267, 269–272, 277–278, 287, 290, 295–296, 330, 342, 350, 352–355, 376–379, 389, 395, 399, 401, 404, 414, 420–423
Austin Row 395
Bath Hotel 277
Denes, The 277, 352, 389
Grammar School 239
Market Row 128
Naval Hospital 277
Old Vicarage 278
Outer Harbour 422
piers 352
Rows, The 128, 323–324, 355, 395
St George 221
St Nicholas 86–87, 278, 395
South Quay 323–324, 353–355, 421
Southtown 389
Tolhouse 126, 129
Town Hall 324, 353, 355
town walls 87, 105, 126
Victoria Arcade 355
Yarmouth Pier & Haven Commissioners 289, 298, 324, 353
Yaxham 272
Young, Arthur 192, 197–199, 225–226, 253, 258–259